Encyclopaedia of FERNS

An Introduction to Ferns, their Structure, Biology, Economic Importance, Cultivation and Propagation

DAVID L. JONES
B.Ag.Sc., Dip.Hort.

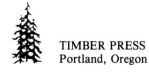

TIMBER PRESS
Portland, Oregon

TIMBER PRESS
Portland, Oregon

First published in Australia by
LOTHIAN PUBLISHING COMPANY
PTY. LTD., MELBOURNE

Published in 1987 in North America by
TIMBER PRESS
9999 S.W. Wilshire
PORTLAND, OR 97225
Reprinted 1988

ISBN 0 88192 054 1

Frontispiece
Tropical Fern House, Royal Botanic Garden, Kew
Photo W. R. Elliot

Designed by Arthur Stokes
Typeset by Acton Graphic Arts Pty Ltd,
Hawthorn Victoria 3122 Australia

Printed in Hong Kong

To my wife Barbara
who introduced me to ferns

[redacted]

Contents

Part Two: The Cultural Requirements of Ferns

Part Three: Pests, Diseases and other Ailments of Ferns

Part Four: Propagation and Hybridization of Ferns

Foreword

The foundation of fern growing was substantially laid almost 200 years ago when John Lindsay, then a surgeon in Jamaica, reported to Sir Joseph Banks of his success in growing a number of different fern plants from spores. At Banks' suggestion the news was communicated to the scientific and horticultural world through the Transactions of the Linnaean Society of London. Whilst nurserymen developed the technique, the increasing number of customers who established 'Stove-houses' to grow sub-tropical and tropical plants demanded more and different plants, the majority of which reached our shores in an unhappy state on the exposed decks of the maritime fleet. Almost by chance, another doctor, Nathaniel Ward, of Whitechapel, East London, hit on the idea of a closed glass case which protected the plants from the rigours of diverse climates. He was encouraged to develop the idea by an expert nurseryman, George Loddiges, who conducted an experiment by sending a variety of plants, ferns among them, by sea to Australia. In November, 1834 the consignment arrived safely in Hobart having crossed several climatic boundaries.

Today the movement of living plants still presents problems. Although the speed of aircraft has advantages over sea-going ships, the cost of freight and the risk of introducing plant diseases is high. However, fern spores are more ideally suited to the logistics and economics of transporting by air-mail and thanks to the increasing number of spore banks and distribution schemes, the enthusiastic grower can find an ever-widening range of species suitable for his or her own specific needs. And, unlike the early nineteenth century, keen growers of ferns are found in every country in the world.

Gardening is a personal occupation: there is an intimacy that exists between the gardener and the plants that are tended. Plants and ferns are no exception, although they do not speak, they have behaviour patterns which must be understood in order to give them the conditions they require for a successful – and happy – life, bringing, in turn, enjoyment to us, the grower. We are concerned with what might go wrong, with diseases, pests and disorders, we need to learn of the cultural requirements and how to encourage that vital aspect, the procreation of the species – the production of more spores to find their way into our spore bank. And above all we want to realize the vast potential of what there is in the fern world to bring into our gardens, shade houses, conservatories and living rooms.

This book, so rightly called an *Encyclopaedia*, tells us so much of the hows, whys and wherefores of fern growing. David Jones has extensive personal knowledge of so many species of plants from a wide variety of habitats – one of the many advantages of living in Australia. Here he shares his knowledge of ferns and allied plants in an explicit, tactful way. (In the field, David never discusses the ecological preference of plants in their hearing!) The author is widely travelled and has experience of many species in the field. He has already written books on Australian native ferns and on exotics in cultivation there. This book is not only a synthesis but much more extensive, telling us wherever we may live, what we can grow for the best effect and enjoyment, and how to do it well.

The fern cult, of which this book is a part – and a milestone – is a good example of those fashionable fads which are constantly buffeting biologists and distracting their attention, tempting them to develop research interests that might otherwise have been ignored. As David Elliston Allen puts it, when writing of the Victorian Fern Craze, 'without the great popular interest in ferns, due to motives more aesthetic than truly scientific, the stimulus in academic circles to study their structure, classification and reproductive systems would almost certainly have been much weaker . . . 'I believe this popular interest is reviving fast and that "taste, pure and simple" is again flaunting this "productive" subject under scientists' noses'.

This book is aimed at the amateur and professional grower and will, I believe, help establish a fashion, however pure and simple or, relying on aesthetics alone, will continue to flaunt a challenging subject under the scientists' noses.

A. CLIVE JERMY
Head of Fern Section
British Museum (Natural History)
London.

Preface

Ferns are once again becoming popular with the general gardening public. This upsurge in popularity is not so much a craze, as was the fern boom of the Victorian era, but rather a position of strength with the unique ornamental aspects of ferns being recognized and catered for. Ferns are again an important sector of the nursery industry and are commonly available in garden centres, florists and even on supermarket shelves. Fern fanciers have created an enthusiastic demand and spore exchanges run by fern societies in many countries now offer a wide range of species and cultivars for selection. This interest is paralleled in botanical circles where serious studies on different groups of ferns are in progress.

There are many books on the botanical and horticultural aspects of ferns written for specific countries or conditions, but few are comprehensive and deal with a range of climatic regions, soil types etc. This book brings together a lot of information in the one place and should appeal to the professional student and the fern enthusiast, as well as plant lovers with a casual interest. It is hoped that it will be the first of a few volumes, the succeeding ones to deal in more detail with groups of ferns and species worthy of cultivation.

In compiling this book I have made every effort to keep up-to-date with fern nomenclature, although this is a difficult task. As with any group of plants, name changes in ferns must be expected following botanical research. Some of the names used in this book may have changed by the time it is published. There is also the problem of disagreement among botanists and alternate sets of valid names being available for some groups of ferns. Commonly known or recent synonyms and alternative names have been catered for by a cross-indexing system.

This book is designed to stimulate interest in ferns both as an intriguing group of plants and as appealing ornamental subjects. The use of botanical terms has been kept to a minimum and they have been explained where they are first used. A detailed glossary is included, not only as an aid to this book, but also to help interested people interpret botanical papers, floras etc. Appendices provide detailed lists not included in the text. Only well known common names are included.

The book is illustrated by 250 colour plates and more than 150 black and white photographs. The majority of the colour photographs were taken by me but a number were taken by other people and these are credited on the plate. Line drawings (prepared by the author) are also included to explain important structural features of ferns as well as to illustrate a number of species included in the book. A complete illustrated coverage of ferns, although highly desirable, is beyond the scope of this book.

It is important to realize that variations in frond dimensions occur because of soil, climatic and genetic factors and any such information provided in this book can only be a guide. Cultural advice is based on experience but cannot be taken as binding and should be interpreted in the light of prevailing local conditions.

Acknowledgements

I gratefully acknowledge the assistance of many people who gave their information and time willingly. I am particularly grateful to Clive Jermy of the British Museum, for his encouragement, constructive criticism of the manuscript and for writing the foreword. Chris Goudey was a very enthusiastic helper providing information, specimens and organizing many of the black and white photographs. Len Lawler was of inestimable help in locating pertinent papers (often from obscure journals) dealing with various aspects of fern nomenclature and biology.

I am particularly grateful to my wife Barbara for once again efficiently converting my scrawled manuscript to a readable form.

Charlie and Joan Haden were unstinting in their help, providing hospitality, innumerable specimens and giving me free access to their wonderful collection of ferns.

I thank Allan Balhorn, the former Editor and John Clasper, Photographer of *Your Garden* magazine for allowing me access to the range of black and white photographs in the *Your Garden* library, and for taking specific shots at my request.

I thank Reginald Kaye for allowing me to use the extract on fern cultivar classification from his excellent book *Hardy Ferns*.

Professor R. E. Holttum provided welcome information on some puzzling groups of ferns. Barbara Parris from the Royal Botanic Gardens, Kew, helped with the identification of some ferns. Jim Croft was very helpful with aspects of New Guinea ferns.

Jim Hutchinson, David Beardsell and Dennis Hearne provided scientific information particularly on tissue culture. John Bolger patiently read the manuscript and allowed me to photograph his ferns. Others who gave me access to their collections include Peter and Lois Olson and Anne Horsfall.

I sincerely thank Rodger Elliot for taking many excellent colour photographs on my behalf and for allowing me to use a couple of diagrams from *An Encyclopaedia of Australian Plants Suitable for Cultivation*.

Ted Rotherham took close-ups of fern material which I provided. Photomicrographs of fern spores were kindly provided by Dr T. C. Chambers, Professor of Botany, Melbourne University. Others who helped with photographs were Trevor Blake and Bruce Gray.

I thank John McPhee of the Australian National Gallery for permission to use photos of the fern-work chest of drawers.

Acknowledgements

Finally I would like to thank Louis Lothian for his patience and encouragement of the project from the start.

Photographic Credits

Black and white and colour photographs are credited under the plate. *Your Garden* magazine has been particularly generous in permitting the use of photographs. Most black and white photographs have been taken by *Your Garden* or Chris Goudey. Those black and white photographs for which no credits are given, have been provided by *Your Garden*.

Arrangement of Text

For convenience the text has been divided into seven parts.

1 Introduction, structure and botany of ferns. This part provides an introduction to ferns and fern allies, their economic importance to mankind as well as considerable details of their structure, botany and life cycle. A major aim of this part is to unravel some of the complexities of ferns and present botanical and biological aspects in an easily understood form. Other interesting details in Part One include the numbers of ferns and fern allies, their distribution and preferred habitats, horticultural aspects of colourful and aromatic fronds and the origin and classification of fern cultivars.

2 The cultural requirements of ferns include the major factors which ferns like and dislike in an environment, and in soils. Fern nutrition is covered in detail including information on fertilizers, manures and lime.

3 Pests, diseases and other ailments includes details of the various maladies which afflict ferns together with suggestions for their control.

4 Propagation and hybridization includes detailed methods of the propagation of ferns by vegetative techniques and from spores. A separate chapter deals with the techniques of fern hybridization.

5 Specialized culture, repotting and housing. This extensive section deals with ferns as indoor plants and for outdoor containers, the techniques of potting and repotting (including suitable potting mixes) and specialized cultivation in baskets, terrariums, bottle gardens, walls etc. Housing in greenhouses (heated and unheated) and shadehouses is dealt with in a separate chapter.

6 Some 700 species of ferns and common cultivars are covered briefly. A standardized layout is used and is explained at the start of Part Six.

7 Lists of ferns for specific conditions and purposes.

Abbreviations

aff.	affinity
alt.	altitude or alternative botanical name
cm	centimetre
cv.	cultivar
diam.	diameter
Epi.	epiphyte
ft	foot, feet
fl. oz	fluid ounce
g	gram
gal	gallon
kg	kilogram
L	litre
m	metre
m^2	square metre
μ	micron
mL	millilitre
mm	millimetre
oz	ounce
ppm	parts per million
sp.	species (singular)
spp.	species (plural)
S.Trop.	subtropical
Temp.	temperate
Terr.	terrestrial
Trop.	tropical
yd	yard

Conversion Charts

one inch=25 mm or 2.5 cm
one foot=30 cm
one yard=90 cm
one metre=39.6 inches=100 cm
one micron=1/1000 mm
one mile=1.6 kilometres
one ounce=30 g
one pound=450 g=0.45 kg
one kilogram=1000 g
one fluid ounce=30 mL
one pint=600 mL
one gallon=4.5 L
one litre=1000 mL

Part One

Introduction, Structure and Botany of Ferns

1 Introduction to ferns and fern allies

Ferns and their allies are a natural group of plants in a major division of the plant kingdom called the Pteridophyta. They do not produce flowers and, because their method of reproduction is not obvious, they are included with other plants which have similar reproductive characteristics. They are all termed cryptogams (literally translated this means 'hidden marriage'). Such plants include algae, mosses and liverworts. Ferns and their allies have many features similar to mosses and algae but are usually differentiated from these simpler plants as *vascular* cryptogams, because only they (in this group of plants) possess the important internal vascular structures associated with water, nutrient and hormone transport within the plant.

Pteridophytes have been a prominent part of the Earth's vegetation for millions of years. In fact, in eons past, relatives of the present day ferns and fern allies dominated the vegetation and were the major living form of plant. In the extensive forests that covered the Earth in the Carboniferous period, tree-like Clubmosses and precursors of the Horsetails attained heights of well over 30 m. This stature is difficult to imagine when compared with the small plants of these groups which exist today. The origin of ferns and their allies is uncertain but it is believed that they have close relationships with algae rather than mosses and may have originated from them.

The division Pteridophyta can be subdivided into three or four classes according to morphology, structure and details of the reproduction method. One class, the Filicopsida (in some older books known as the Filicales), comprises the true ferns, while the other classes are known as the fern allies (Psilotopsida, Lycopsida and Equisetopsida). The easiest way to distinguish between these two important groups of pteridophytes is by their leaves. The fern allies (except *Isoetes*) have small scale-like structures known as microphylls and ferns have large leaves (the familiar fern fronds) known as megaphylls.

The classes of ferns and fern allies can be further subdivided into subclasses, orders and families. These classifications are governed by features of the reproductive system such as the shape and wall ornaments of the spores and sporangia (the structures in which the spores are borne), and how these are arranged. Below the level of family the plants are grouped into genera and species.

(unknown)

Cladophlebis roylei

Fern Fossils — Photos C. G. Goudey

The fern allies consist of two or three classes of plants which are natural groups. Their botanical features are dealt with in more detail in Chapter 3 but they can be introduced here as the Fork Ferns, the Clubmosses and the Horsetails.

The Fork Ferns have traditionally been regarded as a fern ally; however, recent work challenges this view, and the modern treatment of Tryon in their book of 1982 includes them as a very primitive group of the true ferns.

NUMBER OF SPECIES

Estimates of the number of species of pteridophytes are in the range of 10–12,000 in 230–50 genera. This includes 7–8 genera and about 1600 species of fern

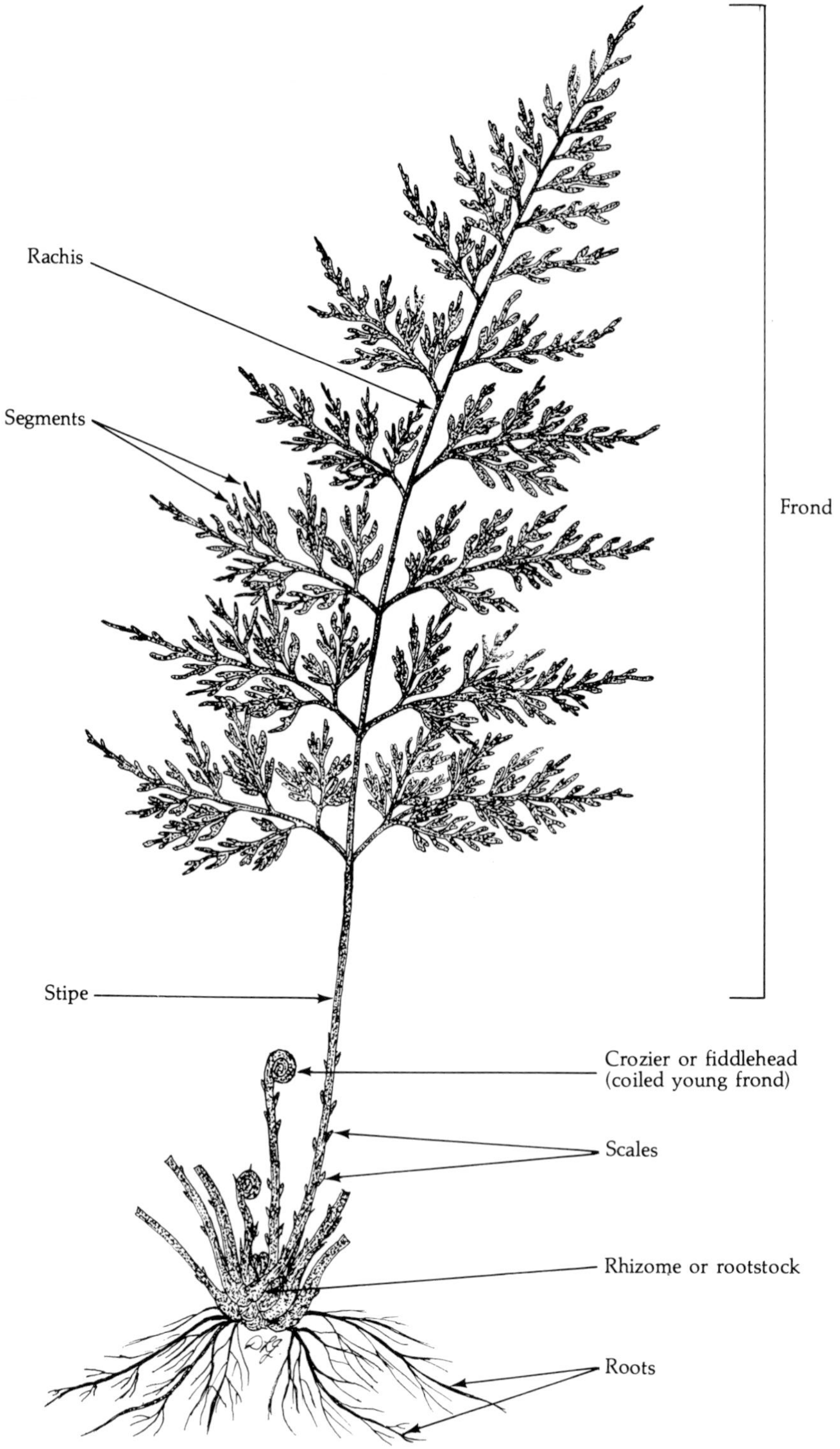

Basic structures of a fern plant

allies and 240 genera and about 10,400 species of true ferns. More species await discovery and description by botanists. Variation in the tallies arises because of disagreement among botanists and researchers about the delimitations of species and genera. With about 12,000 species, the pteridophytes are indeed a very significant group of the world's flora.

GROWTH FEATURES

Ferns and fern allies are basically woody plants, which grow on the ground (terrestrials), on rocks (lithophytes), or on trees (epiphytes). A few are climbers with slender stems produced at intervals from a terrestrial rhizome.

The fern allies have much-reduced and rather insignificant leaves which may be all alike or of two different types (sterile or fertile). They may have a much-reduced stem and grow in discrete clumps or have widely creeping and freely branching stems. The stems may be buried, or are visible on the surface of the soil or support. Fertile cones (strobili) which contain sporangia are sometimes a conspicuous feature of the fern allies.

The ferns have a distinctive set of fronds which may radiate to form a crown. These fronds vary in size

Scales on crozier of *Cyathea cooperi*
Photo E. R. Rotherham

Dicksonia fibrosa — *Hypolepis tenuifolia*

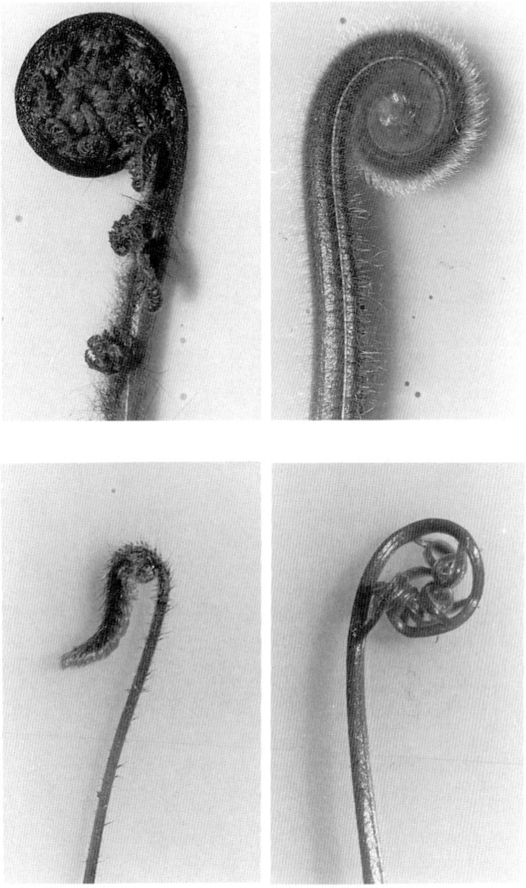

Pellaea falcata (non-circinate vernation) — *Stenochlaena palustris*

Fern Croziers or Fiddleheads — Photos C. G. Goudey

from tiny structures one cell in thickness to massive fronds over 4 m (160 in) long and of complex division. Young fronds of all ferns (except those in the family Ophioglossaceae) are coiled characteristically (a condition known as circinate vernation) or hooked like a shepherd's crook (known as non-circinate vernation). This is an excellent guide to identifying ferns but it is not infallible, as members of the insectivorous flowering plant genus *Drosera*, for example, also have coiled young leaves. In species of *Ophioglossum* (a fern genus) the young fronds are not coiled but simply lengthen from the base.

Fern rhizomes vary from short and thick to long creeping and wiry. In some species they are erect and in the tree ferns they form a characteristic woody trunk. The young parts of the rhizome are protected by hairs, bristles or flattened papery structures known as scales.

Ferns do not flower; they reproduce by tiny spores

which are carried in sporangia which are usually clustered in a group known as a sorus (plural sori). Sori are most commonly found on the underside of the fronds but in some species they occur on frond margins or on specialized sections of fronds. Sori may be naked, or protected when young by a thin, often membranous, flat structure known as an indusium. Many ferns bear spores on fronds which are of similar shape to the sterile ones. These ferns are termed monomorphic. A number of ferns have specialized spore-bearing fronds that are quite different in size and shape to the sterile fronds and these ferns are termed dimorphic.

Further details on fern structure can be found in Chapter 3.

HABITAT

Ferns and fern allies are most common in wet climates. More species, by far, are found in rainforests than any other vegetation type. These rainforest habitats range from lowland jungles through intermediate altitudes to the unique forests of high altitudes. In rainforests some ferns are found on the forest floor but most species occur as epiphytes on the trunks and branches of the trees which make up the canopy. Here they have access to light, air movement and some humidity from the forest floor, and their roots can roam over the bark, absorbing nutrients and moisture from the surface (but not as parasites). Climbing ferns may also be frequent in rainforests. Some of these may have their roots anchored in the soil of the forest floor, while their uppermost fronds mingle with the outer foliage of the forest canopy.

Pteridophytes are not restricted to rainforests, as many types of vegetation provide conditions conducive to their growth. No other vegetation type, however, supports such variety (and a predominance of epiphytes) as that of the rainforest. In woodlands and open forests the ferns grow mainly as terrestrials, and their distribution and abundance is closely related to water supply. In high-rainfall areas the ferns may be widely distributed through the forest, whereas in drier climates they will be found in wet areas such as around soaks, marshes, swamps or the margins of permanent streams, lakes and lagoons.

Very hardy ferns that grow in semi-arid and arid climates overcome the worst of the dry times by water conserving strategies. Their fronds are generally small and are covered with scales or hairs to reduce water-loss. The fronds may curl in dry periods so conserving water further, or in severe dry spells they may die back completely to a drought resistant subterranean rhizome. In arid climates ferns usually avoid extreme conditions by growing in the shade of boulders, or where their roots can grow in the cool soil under a rock. They are also frequently in positions (such as crevices) where the run-off from rainfall, although limited, is concentrated.

A unique group of Resurrection Ferns and fern allies is found in some of the drier countries such as Australia and Mexico, and in parts of Africa. During dry times the fronds of these ferns lose their colour, dry off and look as if they are dead. At this stage these fronds are quite brittle and can be crushed to powder in the hands. Some of the fronds, however, may be still alive and in a state of dormancy. A few days after heavy rains these apparently dead fronds can re-freshen, the segments expand and re-green, and the life processes restart. Such resurrection plants are found in the genera *Cheilanthes*, *Paraceterach*, *Doryopteris* and *Selaginella*.

A few ferns have adapted to other specialized habitats where they can compete successfully for survival. The Mangrove Fern (*Acrostichum speciosum*) is common in the mud of brackish inlets, estuaries and large tidal rivers of the tropics. A unique group of Aspleniums grows close to the sea, well within the influence of salt spray, e.g. *A. marinum*, *A. obtusatum*. A few ferns are true aquatics and have adapted their whole life-cycle to the presence of permanent fresh water, e.g. *Ceratopteris thalictroides*. Many ferns favour limestone areas and some grow exclusively on the resulting calcareous soils, e.g. *Adiantum capillus-veneris*, *Pellaea dolomiticola*. Some hardy ferns of the alps and northern latitudes tolerate annual covering by snow and long periods of freezing without apparent detriment, e.g. *Grammitis poeppigiana*, *Polystichum cystostegia*.

DISTRIBUTION

Pteridophytes are widely distributed in the well watered zones of the world but are much less common in, or are even absent from, the very dry or severely cold regions. Though they are well developed and frequently quite common in the temperate zones, they really proliferate in the tropics. Not only do the vast majority of species occur within these zones but they can also be the dominant component of the vegetation. In temperate and tropical regions, ferns can be found from the seashore to well inland, and extending from the lowlands to mountains and tablelands over 3500 m (11,500 feet) altitude (e.g. Andes of Peru, mountains of New Guinea, the Himalayas). The highest altitude in which ferns are recorded seems to be about 4200–4400 m (13,800–14,500 feet), e.g. *Cyathea fulva*, *C. caracasana* and *Cheilanthes pruinata*, all from the Andes.

Because they reproduce by spores which can be carried on air currents over long distances, the ferns and fern allies include many species which are very widespread and occupy similar ecological niches in different countries. As a result of geographical isolation and local prevailing conditions, the individuals adapt and change genetically. Thus the widespread species consist of a series of local populations linked by subtle changes. These are, in effect, species in the course of evolution. If populations were sampled at the extreme range of separation, then the plants would probably look quite different. Those from adjacent areas, however, would be much more alike. This is a difficult situation for a botanist to sort out (impossible for a grower), and is one of a number of reasons why groups (such as *Dryopteris*) contain so many perplexing forms.

In a particular climatic regime the pteridophytes of different countries tend to have more similarities than differences (however differences will still be present at the species level). Thus the distribution of groups of ferns is somewhat predictable. This does not mean that endemism is not a strong trait of ferns. Most countries have their unique species, and in areas where climatic conditions are favourable, there is frequently a local specialization of development indicating the ability of ferns to evolve and make use of specific niches in the environment. This can be seen in large continents as well as on isolated oceanic islands.

VEGETATIVE REPRODUCTION

In nature many species of ferns reproduce vegetatively. This means that no sexual process is involved and the resultant progeny are identical in all ways to the parent plant. Vegetative reproduction can be very significant as an adjunct to sporing and may be the sole means of propagation in some wild populations. Some forms of *Bolbitis*, for example, are known to be sterile and yet they populate large areas and spread entirely by vegetative processes. A similar situation exists in some naturally occurring *Asplenium* hybrids which are sterile. Colonies of *Nephrolepis* are often started by a single spore germinating and then local spread is vegetative by the prolific production of stolons. Some species of epiphytic *Lycopodium* may produce numerous tiny vegetative buds (gemmae) in their leaf axils.

Vegetative reproduction occurs by a variety of techniques including simple division followed by death of the connecting tissue; from vegetative buds; by the production of stolons, offsets or tubers; or by processes on the fronds such as bulbils, plantlets and proliferous tips which root and form a separate plant. Apogamy and apospory are also involved (see page 39). The processes of vegetative reproduction are of interest to the botanist, to whom aspects of fern biology are important, and the fern fancier, who can make use of them as techniques of propagation (see Chapter 16).

Dimorphic sterile and fertile fronds of a *Blechnum*

PTERIDOPHYTE CLASSIFICATION

People like to group and categorize the plants and animals around them and the pteridophytes are no exception. Those plants with a common set of characteristics which set them apart from another group of closely related plants are known as species, while a whole group of closely related species comprises a genus. Related genera are grouped into families.

Ferns are a very complex group of plants with numerous variations in important features such as venation, frond architecture, scale morphology, sporangia, sori and spores. This makes them particularly difficult to classify. No less than six classification systems have been proposed since 1938 and the situation is still in a state of flux as no system has been adopted universally. One system is presented in Table 5 on page 56. Some of the systems proposed appear to be quite artificial and have caused more confusion than clarification. As well, there is considerable disagreement among researchers about how to recognize differences, some opting for the concept of a broad, all-encompassing genus while others split groups into a number of smaller, homogenous genera. While these variations on a theme stimulate scientific discussion and fuel the egos of scientists, they cause nothing but confusion for the enthusiasts who like to collect and grow these plants.

HORTICULTURAL APPEAL

Ferns have a tremendous aesthetic appeal and are popular subjects for cultivation in many countries. They are grown in public and private gardens and are widely promoted for indoor decoration. They are popular in tropical and subtropical regions but seem to have attracted an exceptional following in temperate zones where the hardy species are grown outside and the tender ones coddled in heated greenhouses.

Ferns are an integral part of the nursery industry, with many nurseries specializing in their production. A range of proven, reliable, easily propagated ferns are regularly produced and stocked by nurseries, and new species are constantly being introduced by fern enthusiasts. Hybrids and cultivars also play a significant role in nursery production. As these new introductions and hybrids prove themselves under various conditions, they may be taken up by the nursery trade and produced in quantity. With over 10,000 ferns to choose from there is remarkable scope for new ones to be introduced into the horticultural scene.

The variegated leaves of *Pteris argyraea* are natural

COLOUR IN FERNS

People associate ferns with various shades of green and it is pleasantly surprising to discover that other colours are to be found within this group of plants.

New Fronds

The new fronds of many species of ferns are often a different colour to the mature fronds, usually shades of pink, red or purple. This feature is particularly frequent in rainforest ferns, perhaps because the colouration allows more efficient use of the limited radiation which reaches the forest floor.

Prominent among such ferns are many species of *Blechnum* which commonly have bright pink or red new fronds (e.g. *B. articulatum* and *B. falciforme*). Species of *Adiantum* (e.g. *A. cunninghamii*, *A. macrophyllum* and *A. pedatum*), *Doodia* (e.g. *D. aspera*), *Lygodium* (e.g. *L. trifurcatum*) and *Stenochlaena* (e.g. *S. palustris*) also have similar bright colourations on their new growth. Those of *Pteridoblechnum neglectum* are a startling purplish-black and are a most interesting feature. The new fronds of *Dryopteris erythrosora* are in delightful coppery tones, and the unrolling flush of Cinnamon Fern (*Osmunda cinnamomea*) is an attractive cinnamon brown. Species of *Woodwardia* are often in tawny or orange tones. The Japanese Painted Fern (*Athyrium niponicum* var. *pictum*) is well named, for its new fronds are a soft metallic grey with reddish and bluish tints in a most pleasing combination.

This *Adiantum raddianum* cultivar has been selected for its variegated leaflets

Colourful Waxy Deposits

A number of ferns which grow in sunny situations have colourful waxy deposits on the new fronds and on the underside of mature fronds. These secretions make the fronds appear as if they have been dusted with flour. They are thus termed farinose and the secretions are called farina.

The secretions are produced by specialized glands on the fronds and they act as a moisture conserving mechanism. They are white or silvery, yellow or deep gold, or roseate pink. Different colours may be produced within a single species and, occasionally, plants are known with silver wax on some fronds and gold on others.

Secretions of this type are particularly prominent on various species of *Pityrogramma*, and they give rise to such common names as Gold Fern or Silver Fern. They are also commonly found in some species of

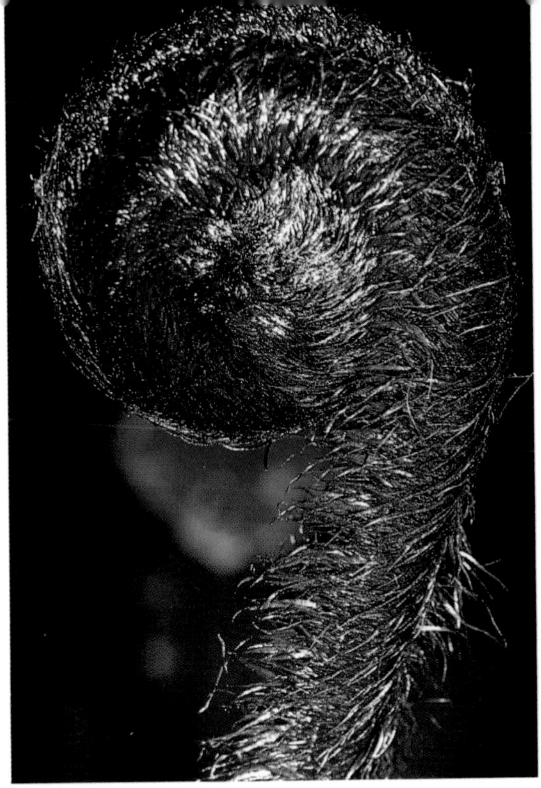

Scaly crozier of *Cyathea cooperi* Photo D. L. Jones

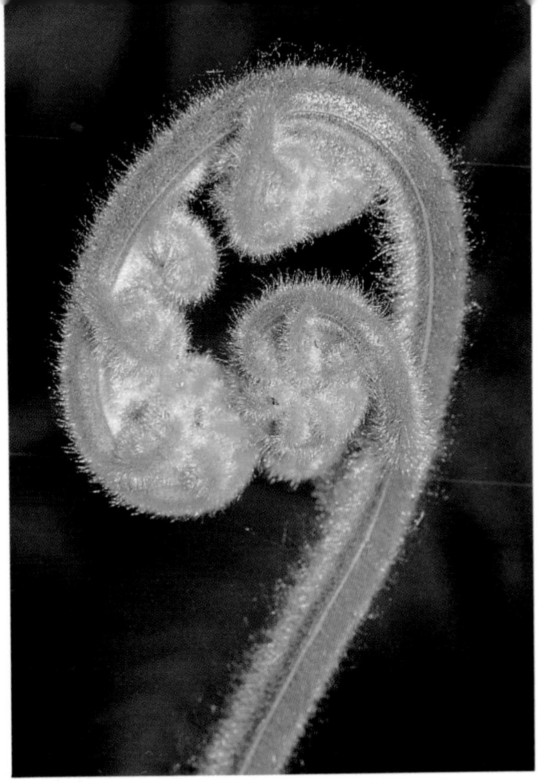

Hairy crozier of *Culcita dubia* Photo D. L. Jones

Naked crozier of *Microlepia platyphylla* Photo D. L. Jones

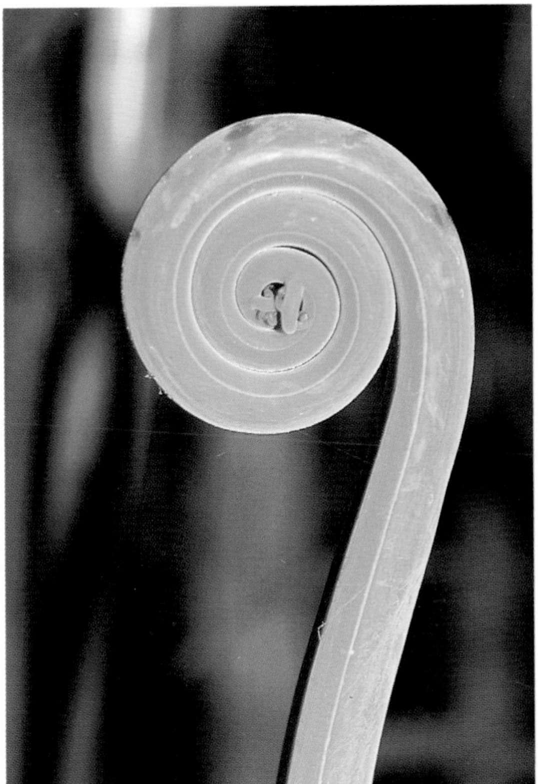

Crozier of *Cyathea robusta* showing coiled pinnae Photo D. L. Jones

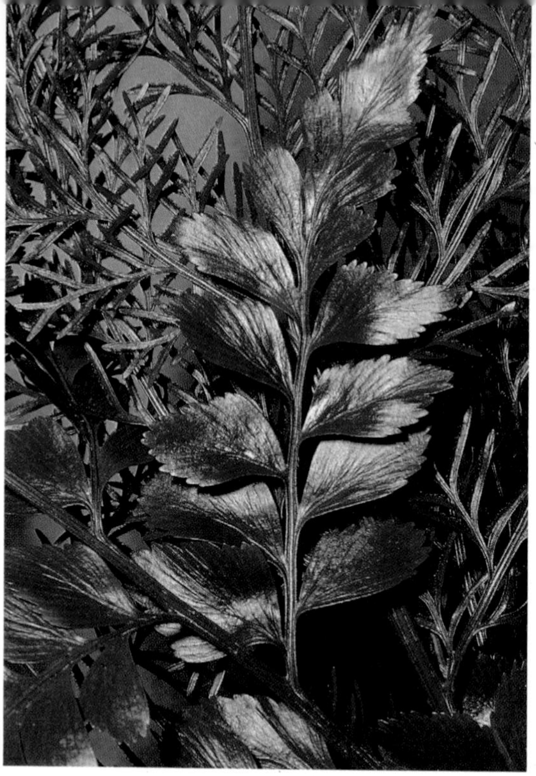

Variation in segment shape of *Asplenium dimorphum*
Photo E. R. Rotherham

Cheilanthes (*C. argentea*, *C. belensis*, *C. farinosa* and *C. papuana*) and *Notholaena* (*N. candida*, *N. incana* and *N. sulphurea*). Other ferns with prominent waxy secretions are *Adiantum poirettii* var. *sulphureum* (yellow), *Negripteris scioana* (white), *Onychium siliculosum* (yellow), *Pterozonium brevifrons* (yellow) and *Sinopteris albofusca* (white).

Waxy secretions of a different and more permanent nature cause the prominent glaucousness of the underside of the fronds of such ferns as *Adiantum novoguineense*, *Angiopteris crinita*, *Cyathea dealbata* and *Cibotium glaucum*.

Variegation

Variegated ferns are not prominent in nature, probably because the reduced chlorophyll levels weaken their competitiveness. *Pteris argyraea* from India and Sri Lanka is perhaps the most striking example of a variegated fern, with a prominent white stripe down the centre of each segment. Another similar, but distinct, variegated *Pteris* is known to occur naturally in Thailand and Indonesia, where it is reported to be quite common.

In ferns, variegated sports tend to be selected and propagated by enthusiasts. These variations may occur naturally or appear spontaneously in cultivated populations. Some, such as cultivars of *P. cretica* and *P. ensiformis*, are propagated in large numbers by nurseries and are now a familiar sight. Variegated selections of *Adiantum raddianum* have also been propagated but they are still mainly found in enthusiasts' collections. A form of *Selaginella martensii*, which produces sporadic clumps of leaves totally devoid of chlorophyll, has been grown in various countries for well over fifty years.

Iridescence

The leaves of some pteridophytes have a striking sheen which has iridescent qualities. This feature alone has made some species of *Selaginella* well known favourites for tropical gardens. The most striking example is the Electric Fern (*S. wildenovii*), with leaves of a startling electric blue colouration. *S. uncinata* has similar properties but is less striking. The New Guinea fern, *Cyclopeltis novoguineensis*, also has unusual iridescent fronds.

AROMATIC FRONDS

Some ferns have attractively aromatic fronds (the smells are actually released from specialized hairs) and add the feature of smell to a collection. The smells are subtle, but noticeable when the plants are brushed against or handled. In Australia, *Microsorum scandens* is known as the Fragrant Fern because of the faint

Waxy gold powder on underside of *Pityrogramma argentea* fronds
Photo E. R. Rotherham

Waxy silver powder on underside of *Pityrogramma calomelanos* fronds Photo E. R. Rotherham

aroma which pervades the bush around it. In New Zealand, colonies of *Paesia scaberula* have a distinctive scent which is most obvious on warm days. Some plants of *Microlepia strigosa* give off a pleasant aroma when handled, while species of *Pityrogramma* have a fragrance that is difficult to define, some people describing it as a 'warm' smell. The fronds of the African Fern, *Mohria caffrorum*, are also scented and are smoked by the indigenous people to relieve head colds. *Asplenium auritum*, from South America, has pleasantly fragrant fronds.

Different species of ferns can have similar scents. The fronds of the South American species, *Anetium citrifolium*, and some species of *Elaphoglossum* (also South American) have a citrus scent. At least three species of ferns have a smell like newly mown hay; the Hay Scented Fern (*Dennstaedtia punctiloba*) from North America, the Hay Scented Buckler Fern (*Dryopteris aemula*) from Europe, and *Dryopteris crispifolia* from the Azores.

Not all of the odours emitted by ferns are pleasant. *Christella dentata, Davallodes hirsutum, Lindsaea odorata* and *Macrothelypteris torresiana* have a musky, acrid odour, and *Hymenophyllum sanguinolentum* has a smell like blood. The leaflet glands on *Phanerophlebia macrosora* exude a faint scent reminiscent of skunk. Possibly the worst is *Adiantum pentadactylon* 'Sanctae Catherinae' which has an odour resembling tom-cats' urine. Many species of *Pteris* emit a similar unusual smell, e.g. *Pteris tremula*.

2 The economic importance of ferns

Ferns and fern allies are of minor economic significance to mankind today, however, the great benefits from past eons when ferns and their allies dominated the world's vegetation and contributed much to the world's coal reserves will always be important. Their contribution has been of inestimable value and is highly significant today in an energy-conscious world. Although there are many uses for ferns and products which can be produced from them, these are mostly of minor importance and local significance.

EDIBLE FRONDS

The fronds of many ferns are edible while they are at the young, tender stage of unrolling, when they are usually known as croziers or fiddleheads. They may contain cancer-producing substances (especially in Bracken) and should be consumed in moderation. The Japanese, who consume large amounts of Bracken shoots, also have the highest incidence of stomach cancer in the world.

Fern croziers may be collected and eaten raw in a salad but are more frequently cooked. When eaten raw the croziers are crisp but with a mucilaginous texture. Preparation for cooking simply consists of washing and the removal of all scales or hairs. The croziers may be cooked whole or sliced up like beans. Cooking consists of boiling in salty water for 30–60 minutes, until they are soft enough for eating, or steaming until soft. The flavour is similar to that of asparagus. In the USA, some fern fiddleheads are regarded as a great delicacy and are sold in cans.

The croziers of the common Bracken Fern (various species of *Pteridium*) are regarded as a great delicacy in many countries (but the tissue may have carcinogenic properties). They are particularly prized in Japan, the Philippines and the USA; they are eaten in various countries of Europe and were important to the New Zealand Maoris. In the USA the large fronds of the Ostrich Fern (*Matteuccia struthiopteris*), which unroll in a spectacular spring flush, are highly regarded as a delicacy and are exploited commercially.

Other ferns which are used for food in the USA are *Osmunda cinnamomea* and *Onoclea sensibilis*. In Norway, the fronds of *Dryopteris filix-mas* are eaten and considered to be a delicacy. The young fronds of *Equisetum arvense* are reported to taste like asparagus when cooked.

In Asia and the Pacific region, the fronds of many ferns are used as vegetables or included in salads (see Table 1). Some are of local interest only, but the most widespread and important are undoubtedly *Stenochlaena palustris*, *Helminthostachys zeylanica*, *Diplazium esculentum* and *Ceratopteris thalictroides* (Water Fern).

TABLE 1
Fern Fronds Eaten in Asia and the Pacific Region

Species	*Eaten*	*Country*
Acrostichum aureum	cooked	Many countries
Angiopteris evecta	cooked	Society Islands
Asplenium affine	cooked	New Guinea
Blechnum orientale	cooked	Many countries
Botrychium spp.	cooked	New Zealand, Himalayas
Callipteris prolifera	cooked	Many countries
Ceratopteris thalictroides	raw or cooked	Many countries
Coniogramme fraxinea	cooked	Fiji
Cyathea contaminans	cooked	Malaysia, India
Cyathea junghuniana	cooked	Indonesia
Cyathea lunulata	cooked	Fiji
Diplazium cordifolium	cooked	New Guinea
Diplazium esculentum	raw or cooked	Philippines
Drynaria rigidula	raw	Celebes
Dryopteris arbuscula	cooked	New Guinea
Dryopteris sparsa	cooked	New Guinea
Helminthostachys zeylanica	raw or cooked	Many countries
Litobrochia sinuata	cooked	Fiji
Lomagramma sinuata	cooked	New Guinea
Lygodium circinnatum	cooked	New Guinea
Lygodium microphyllum	cooked	Malaysia
Microlepia speluncae	cooked	New Guinea
Microsorum commutatum	cooked	New Guinea
Microsorum linguiforme	cooked	New Guinea
Microsorum punctatum	cooked	New Guinea
Nephrolepis biserrata	cooked	New Guinea
Pneumatopteris sogerensis	cooked	New Guinea
Pteris ensiformis	cooked	Philippines
Selaginella opaca	cooked	New Guinea
Stenochlaena palustris	raw or cooked	Many countries
Tectaria degeneri	cooked	Fiji
Tectaria latifolia	cooked	Fiji

EDIBLE STARCH

The central parts of the rhizomes or trunks of many species of ferns contain a starchy material which acts as a storage reserve of carbohydrate for the plant. It can also be exploited by man as a source of food.

The tree ferns, because of their bulky trunks, are an obvious choice and have been used in various parts of the world. Those recorded include: *Cyathea spinulosa* (India), *C. dealbata* and *C. medullaris* (New Zealand), *C. canaliculata* (Madagascar), *C. contaminans* (New Guinea and the Philippines), *C. australis* (Australia), *C. viellardii* (New Caledonia), *Cibotium chamissoi* (Hawaii) and *Dicksonia antarctica* (Australia). Many other species are used in the mountains of New Guinea but specific details are lacking. In most cases the pith in the soft upper part of the trunk is collected, and baked or roasted before eating.

The large fleshy stems of various species of *Marattia* and *Angiopteris* are rich in starch and must have attracted the attention of many people. The New Zealand Maoris thought so highly of *Marattia salicina* that they cultivated plants around their villages for the large starchy stem which they roasted prior to eating. Stems of *Angiopteris evecta* were eaten in a similar manner in various islands of the Pacific and in India.

The rhizomes of smaller ferns were also collected. *Blechnum indicum* is a widespread and locally common tropical fern growing in swampy situations. Its rhizomes were probably collected and eaten in many countries. They certainly were in Australia for they were regarded as an important part of the diet of the Aborigines of southern Queensland, who roasted them before eating. In North America, the rhizomes of *Dryopteris austriaca* were collected and cooked by the Indians, and in Alaska the Eskimos cooked the rhizomes of *D. carthusiana*. The rhizomes of Bracken Fern (various species of *Pteridium*) are also starchy and have been collected and eaten in various parts of the world. They were particularly favoured by the New Zealand Maoris, who soaked and pounded them to obtain a starchy material resembling arrowroot. In some countries the rhizomes of Bracken Fern are eaten after roasting or baked into a poor-quality bread.

The rhizomes of a few other ferns such as *Dicranopteris linearis*, *Diplazium esculentum*, *Drynaria quercifolia*, *Blechnum orientale*, *Lygodium microphyllum* and *Polypodium vulgare* are also recorded as being edible, although those of *Drynaria* are collected only in times of food shortage. A very widespread and weedy fern of the tropics, *Nephrolepis cordifolia*, frequently bears fleshy tubers on its rhizomes, which resemble small scaly potatoes. These look quite tasty but the only record of their use as food seems to be from Nepal where they are eaten after roasting.

A unique form of starch was available to the Australian Aborigines in the form of the fruiting bodies (sporocarps) of the Nardoo (*Marsilea drummondii*). This fern thrives in seasons of abundant rains, and, as the seasonal water-holes dry up it leaves an abundance of hard, woody sporocarps. These are rich in starch and were collected by the Aborigines and ground into a yellowish flour which was made into cakes, roasted and eaten. Although the Aborigines considered it was good fare, Nardoo starch does not seem to have provided much nourishment for those white men who were forced to live on it.

BEVERAGES

The fronds of a few species of ferns can be used fresh or dried, and made into a substitute for tea. In Europe, *Dryopteris fragrans* is used and in California, USA, *Pellaea ornithopus* provides an aromatic alternative when the tea runs out. *Pellaea mucronata* and *Blechnum spicant* fronds can be used in a similar way. One widespread fern which is frequently used as a substitute for tea in many countries is *Adiantum capillus-veneris*. Its fronds are also reputed to have medicinal properties, so the drink may do more than just quench the thirst. An intoxicating drink is made in India by fermenting the starchy material from the trunks of *Angiopteris* species.

Bracken Fern may be used as a substitute for hops in the making of beer and it is claimed that it imparts a distinctive flavour to the final product.

FERNS IN MEDICINE

Ferns have been used by herbalists and purveyors of folk medicine for centuries. Many of these uses have been discredited but some have stood the test of time, and they probably work because of chemicals in the fern's composition or perhaps for psychological reasons. Solutions of the fern are usually taken internally as an infusion (made by pouring boiling water on fresh or dried material), a decoction (made by boiling the fern material in water for 15–20 minutes) or applied externally as a paste or poultice.

TABLE 2
Ferns Useful Against Worms

Species	*Country*	*Part Used*
Acrostichum aureum	China	rhizome
Asplenium adiantum-nigrum	South Africa	fronds
Asplenium furcatum	Africa	rhizome
Asplenium ruta-muraria	USA	rhizome
Blechnum orientale	India	rhizome
Cyathea mannjana	South Africa	fronds
Drynaria quercifolia	India	rhizome
Dryopteris anthelmentica	South Africa	fronds
Dryopteris barbigera	India	rhizome
Dryopteris blandfordii	India	rhizome
Dryopteris carthusiana	Europe	rhizome
Dryopteris cristata	USA	fronds
Dryopteris filix-mas	Europe	rhizome
Dryopteris parallelogramma	Canada	rhizome
Dryopteris schimperiana	India	rhizome
Lycopodium selago	Europe	spores
Pellaea atropurpurea	USA	all parts
Pteridium aquilinum	Europe	rhizome

Parasitic Worms

Various ferns have proved to be effective expellants for stomach and intestinal worms, possibly because of their astringent properties. Preparations are most commonly made from the rhizomes but the fronds of some species are used.

Chest Complaints and Rheumatism

Infusions and decoctions of a number of ferns have been used to cure chest complaints such as asthma (*Adiantum aethiopicum, A. caudatum, A. capillus-veneris, A. pedatum, Asplenium adiantum-nigrum, Dicranopteris linearis* and *Nephrolepis cordifolia*); and rheumatism (*Angiopteris evecta* and *Lycopodium cernuum*).

Bowel Disorders

Many ferns have been shown to have diuretic properties. They include *Adiantum philippense, Asplenium adiantum-nigrum, A. macrophyllum, Blechnum orientale, Lecanopteris carnosa, Lycopodium clavatum, Microsorum punctatum* and *Selaginella lepidophylla*. Dysentery is reputedly cured by *Lygodium microphyllum, Onychium siliculosum* and *Pteris ensiformis*, and *Asplenium trichomanes* and *Psilotum nudum* have laxative properties.

Bruises, Burns, Sprains and Ulcers

External applications in poultices or emollients to wounds, bruises, burns and sprains have reputedly proved to be effective when containing such diverse species as *Acrostichum aureum, Asplenium marinum, Dicranopteris linearis, Dryopteris crassirhizoma, Lygodium microphyllum* and *Osmunda regalis*. Pain is reported to have been relieved by chewing the fronds of *Pityrogramma triangularis* and *Polypodium furfuraceum*. Ulcers have been treated by preparations made from the fronds of *Acrostichum aureum* and *Equisetum xylochaetum* or the stems of *Cibotium barometz*.

Reduction of Bleeding

Coagulation of haemorrhages has been aided by liberal applications of the silky hairs of various *Cibotium* and *Dicksonia* species or the scales of *Cyathea*. A decoction of the leaves of *Adiantum pedatum* or *Lygodium microphyllum* is also supposed to reduce bleeding.

Bites and Stings

The irritation or poisoning of various bites may be relieved by applying the chewed stipes of *Lygodium circinnatum*, or by imbibing a decoction of the stipes of *Oleandra neriformis* or the fronds of *Adiantum capillus-veneris*. The rhizomes of *Oleandra colubrina* and *Pellaea involuta* are also apparently effective. The juice from the young croziers of *Pteridium esculentum* is very effective in relieving the pain of various insect bites when applied direct.

Floral arrangement of dried fern fronds
Photo C. G. Goudey

Miscellaneous

In a relatively modern use various medicinal pills may be coated with the spores of Clubmosses as a waterproofing.

ORNAMENTAL USES

The fronds of many ferns keep well in water and they can be added to floral arrangements as backing material. Those frequently used for this purpose include species and cultivars of *Adiantum, Nephrolepis* and *Pteris*, and species of *Davallia, Dicranopteris, Dryopteris* and *Gleichenia*. In the USA thousands of fronds of *Polystichum acrostichoides* are harvested each year and are sold on the Christmas market, earning the apt vernacular name of Christmas Fern.

The fronds of many ferns can also be used in dried arrangements, and the relatively modern innovation of spray painting with gold or silver adds colour to them. In some countries, fern fronds are collected commercially and freeze-dried and painted before being exported. Those with a hard or wiry texture such as species of *Dicranopteris, Dryopteris, Gleichenia* and *Polystichum* are eminently suitable for this purpose.

In Mexico and some states of the USA, two species of *Selaginella* (*S. lepidophylla* and *S. pilifera*) are sold as novelty items. When dry, plants of these species curl into a tight, round, brown ball but when placed in water the fronds open, re-green and have an attractive appearance. The fronds are also very sensitive to fluctuations in humidity and act as an hygrometer. They are commonly collected and sold when dry. *S. lepidophylla* is known as the Rose of Jericho because of its open appearance.

The inner tissue of a tree-fern trunk is made of tough, resistant material and in many species this presents an attractive appearance. In some countries it is cut, and carved into ornamental shapes or used for vases, cups etc. Some are carved into fancy furniture.

Potted ferns are widely used for indoor and outdoor decoration in many countries.

FERNS AS FERTILIZER

The aquatic free-floating fern genus *Azolla* contains a blue-green alga (*Anabaena azolla*) within its specialized floating chambers. This alga is able to fix nitrogen from the atmosphere and the fern can make use of the nitrogen for its growth. Also, the blue-green alga has access to carbohydrates produced by the fern. Thus the relationship between the alga and the fern is a true two-way symbiosis.

Rice growers in Asia tolerate and even encourage the growth of *Azolla* species on the water of the paddy-fields. They use the nitrogen fixing symbiosis and between crops of rice the *Azolla* is turned in as a green manure to help fertilize the next crop.

EROSION CONTROL

Some ferns have excellent potential for aiding in soil erosion control, especially those species which are weedy or which colonize disturbed earth. Those which combine a weedy habit with a vigorous, spreading root system are ideal. In this group the various species of *Equisetum* are excellent, provided there is sufficient soil moisture. In the tropics, widespread species in the genera *Dicranopteris*, *Diplopterygium* and *Gleichenia* are ideal for stabilizing earth banks. Others with potential are colonizing species in the genera *Cyathea*, *Christella*, *Dipteris* and *Thelypteris*. In New Zealand, *Dicksonia squarrosa* is used to stabilize roadside cuttings. Bracken has been introduced to advantage in some coastal areas of Australia which have been sand mined.

Vase made from inner trunk of *Cyathea*

Photo C. G. Goudey

MISCELLANEOUS USES

The very extensive and fibrous root systems of various species of *Osmunda* have long been prized by orchid enthusiasts as the ideal growing medium for their favourite species and hybrids. The springy, tough fibres are well aerated, yet hold sufficient moisture for root growth, and are quite long-lasting. The fibres surrounding the trunks of *Todea barbara* are similarly useful, as are (to a lesser extent) those of various species of *Cibotium*, *Cyathea* and *Dicksonia*. Rather than being used in the fibrous state these are usually cut into slabs, totems or baskets and are ideal for the growth of epiphytic orchids, gesneriads, bromeliads and ferns. These large ferns have been over-exploited for this purpose but they are now protected in many countries.

The pliant stems or rachises of some climbing ferns may be employed for weaving or plaiting. Those of *Dicranopteris linearis* and *D. curranii* are widely used in Asia for ropes, baskets, seats and house partitions. They may be used whole or split to extract the black, central conductive tissue which is particularly supple and strong (popular for hats). It has been found that the rachises of these ferns are quite resistant to salt water and they are therefore widely used in the construction of fish traps. The long stems of various species of *Lygodium* may also be twisted to form crude cords or woven or plaited into ornaments and bracelets. The rhizomes of *Stenochlaena palustris* may be used for ropes and are important for tying fish traps since they too are resistant to sea-water. The slender conductive tissue can be split from the rachises of the fronds of *Nephrolepis hirsutula* and used to weave hats, mats and baskets.

The scales or hairs of Tree Ferns (*Cyathea* and *Cibotium*) can be used to stuff pillows and cushions. It is claimed that such pillows are very cool on warm nights and are therefore well suited to use in the tropics.

Tree-fern trunks have been used in the construction of dwellings and outbuildings. They can also be used as fences. In New Zealand the Maoris and later the white settlers frequently transplanted Tree Ferns to form a living fence around their habitations. The natives of New Guinea use inverted Tree-fern trunks as supporting struts for their houses and grow epiphytic orchids and ferns on the fibrous trunks. They also use the trunks to construct fences.

The various species of *Equisetum* may be called scouring rushes because of a prominence of silica granules in their structure. Handfuls of their stems have been used for generations to scour pots, pans and other utensils and for scrubbing floors, tables etc. In Japan, the spores of *Lycopodium clavatum* are used to polish wood.

The individual leathery fronds of *Acrostichum aureum* are collected, dried and then used as a thatch for dwellings in Asia. This is a somewhat laborious thatch, since the fronds are relatively small, but the end product is claimed to be excellent. The fronds of

Antique Chest of Drawers decorated with Ferns C 1890, pine (unidentified) stencilled in black ink 80.0 x 95.5 x 45.0 cm.
Photos Australian National Gallery

Bracken Fern (*Pteridium* spp.) can also be used as a rough thatch. Fern fronds also make a comfortable, soft mattress.

POISONOUS FERNS

A few species of ferns and fern allies are known to be poisonous to livestock and to cause stock losses when animals feed on them.

Bracken Ferns of the genus *Pteridium* are found in virtually every continent. Cases of Bracken Fern poisoning of livestock are very common in many countries. The incidence of poisoning is highest when animals eat large quantities of fronds, which can happen easily in times of feed scarcity. Both green and dry fronds can induce poisoning. More significantly, bracken tissue has carcinogenic properties and its consumption by humans should be discouraged for this reason.

Various species of *Equisetum* may be poisonous to livestock. Instances of death are known where hay contaminated with stems of *E. arvense* was fed to horses.

In Australia, the Mulga Fern (*Cheilanthes sieberi*) is regarded as highly toxic to sheep and cattle. Most deaths occur in areas where the fern is abundant, and they are most frequent in poor seasons when little other feed is available. It is quite remarkable that the nearly identical Rock Fern (*Cheilanthes austrotenuifolia*), which often grows with Mulga Fern, has been shown to be non-toxic to livestock. In California, USA, *Notholaena sinuata* var. *cochisensis* has caused the death of sheep.

Other ferns are probably poisonous and their effects will be revealed by research. It should be noted that the fronds of species of *Davallia* and *Lindsaea*, and *Asplenium flabellifolium* have been shown to contain poisonous cyanogenic glucosides, the latter species in significant concentrations.

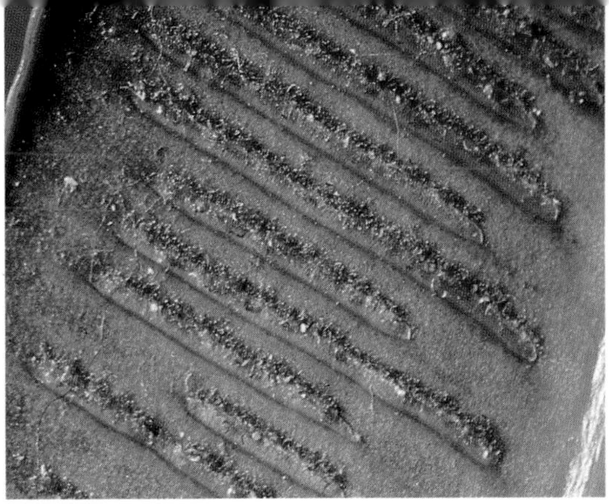

Sori of *Asplenium simplicifrons* (Aspleniaceae)
Photo E. R. Rotherham

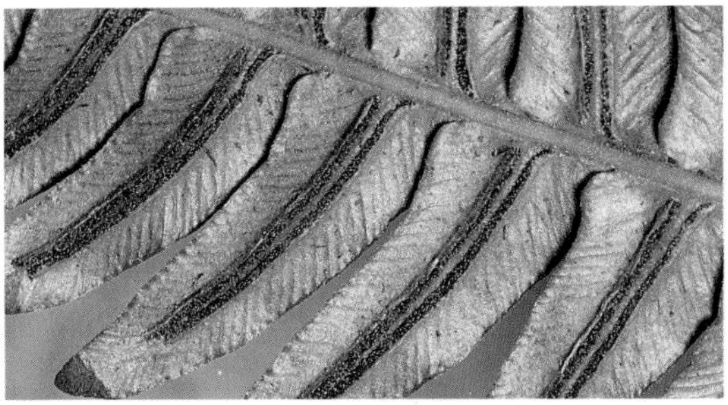

Sori of *Blechnum occidentale* (Blechnaceae)
Photo E. R. Rotherham

Sori of *Amphineuron opulentum* (Thelypteridaceae)
Photo E. R. Rotherham

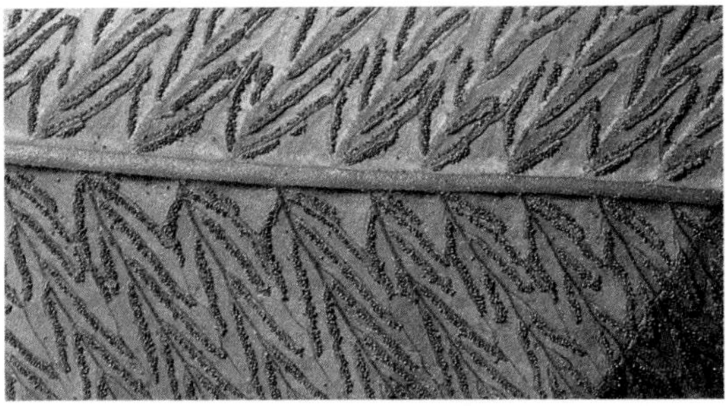

Sori of *Callipteris prolifera* (Athyriaceae)
Photo E. R. Rotherham

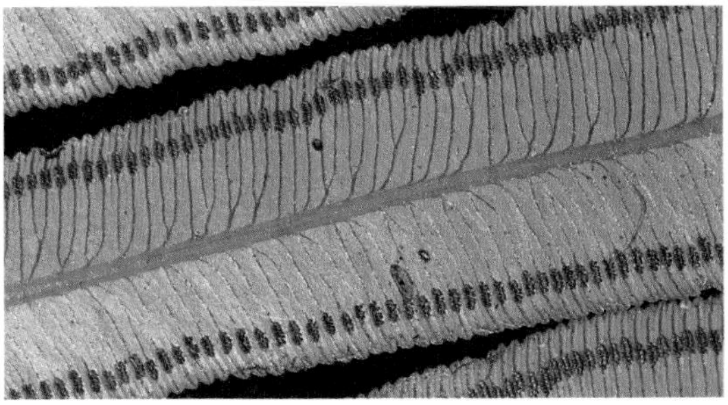

Sori of *Angiopteris evecta* (Marattiaceae)
Photo E. R. Rotherham

Sori of *Cibotium regale* (Dicksoniaceae); top pinna is immature; central pinna is mature and shedding spore; bottom pinna is overmature Photo E. R. Rotherham

Specialized fertile frond apices of *Belvisia mucronata* (Polypodiaceae) Photo E. R. Rotherham

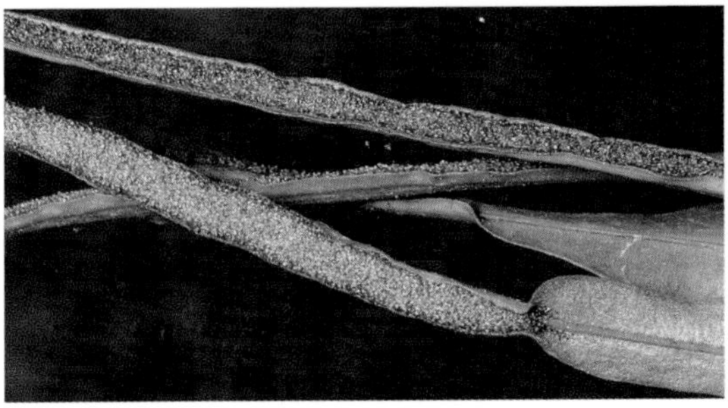

Sori of *Colysis pothifolia* (Polypodiaceae) some Fern Scale insects are also present Photo E. R. Rotherham

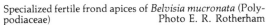

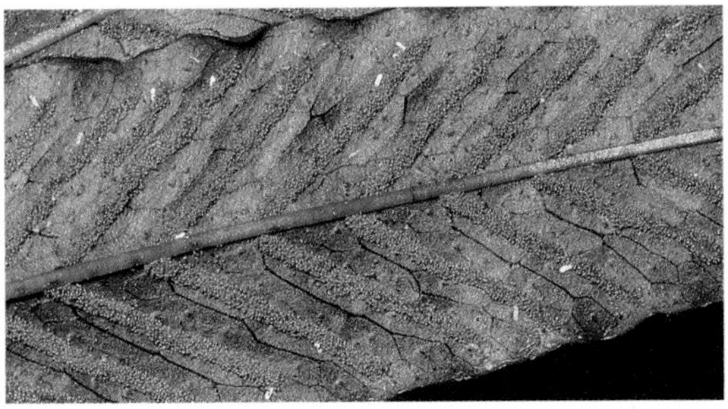

Sori of *Cyathea dealbata* (Cyatheaceae)
Photo E. R. Rotherham

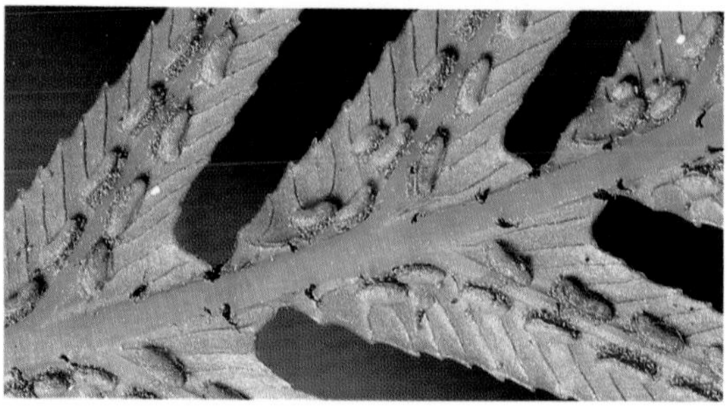

Sori of *Doodia maxima* (Blechnaceae)
Photo E. R. Rotherham

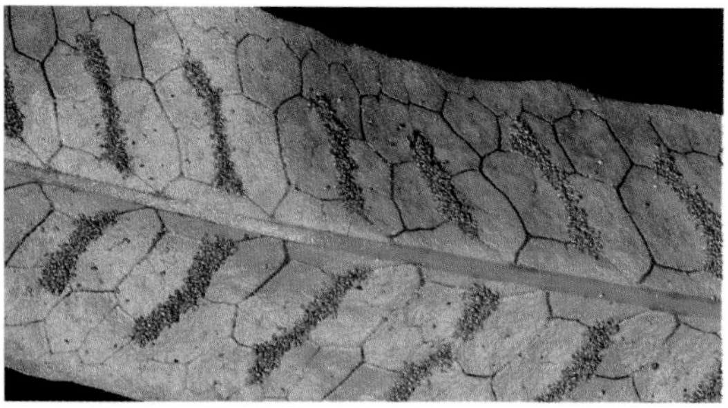

Sori of *Colysis sayeri* (Polypodiaceae) – note anastomosing venation
Photo E. R. Rotherham

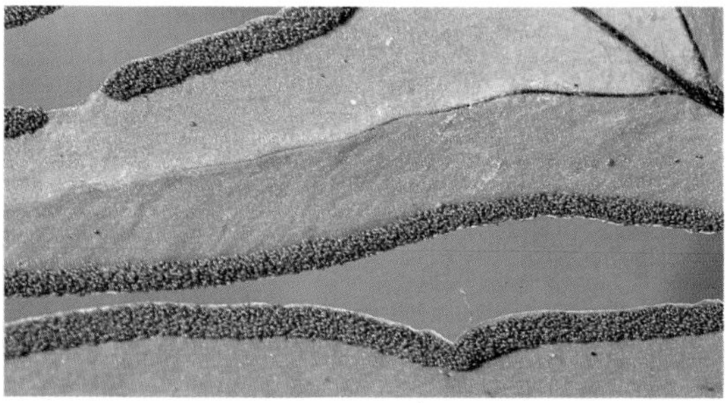

Sori of *Doryopteris pedata* (Sinopteridaceae)
Photo E. R. Rotherham

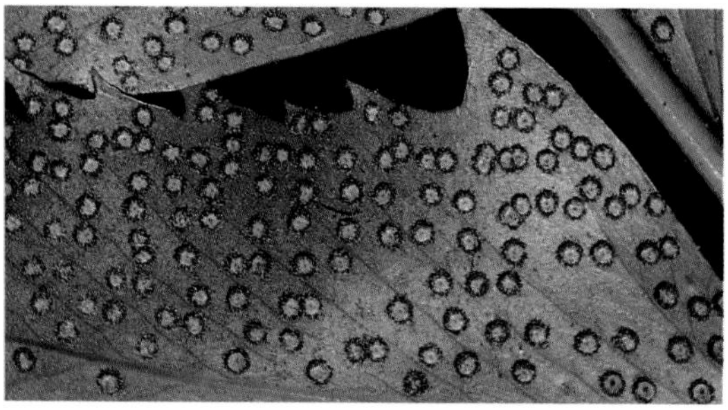

Sori of *Cyrtomium falcatum* (Aspidiaceae)
Photo E. R. Rotherham

Sori of *Lastreopsis decomposita* (Aspidiaceae)
Photo E. R. Rotherham

Sori of *Davallia embolostegia* (Davalliaceae)
Photo E. R. Rotherham

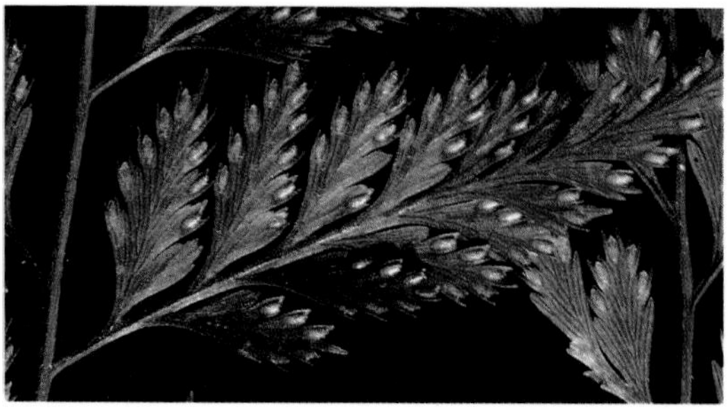

Sori of *Leucostegia pallida* (Davalliaceae)
Photo E. R. Rotherham

Sori of *Lunathyrium japonicum* (Athyriaceae)
Photo E. R. Rotherham

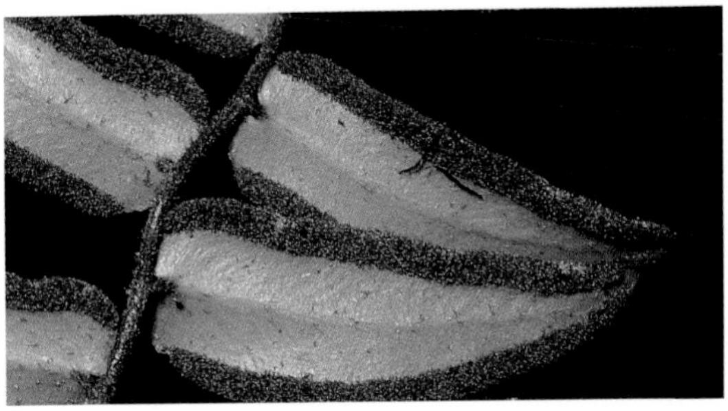

Sori of *Pellaea falcata* (Sinopteridaceae)
Photo E. R. Rotherham

Sori of *Marattia salicina* (Marattiaceae)
Photo E. R. Rotherham

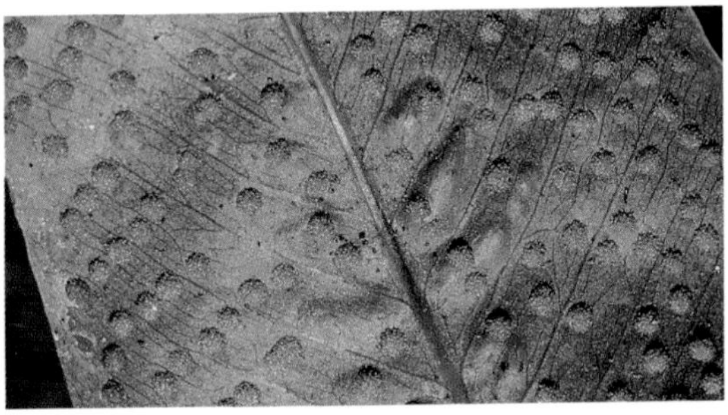

Sori of *Phlebodium decumanum* (Polypodiaceae)
Photo E. R. Rotherham

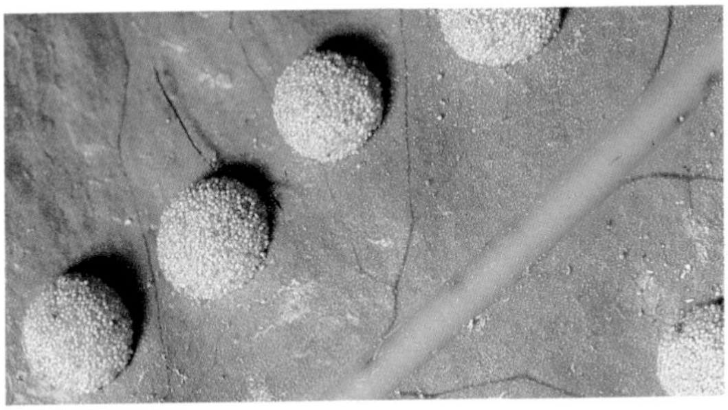

Sori of *Microsorum pappei* (Polypodiaceae)
Photo E. R. Rotherham

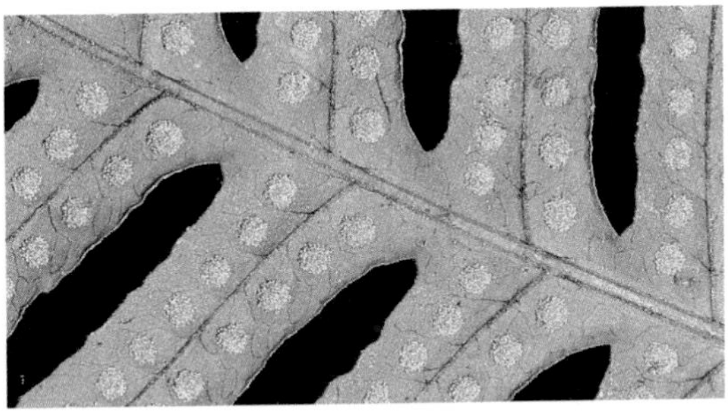

Sori of *Polypodium formosanum* (Polypodiaceae)
Photo E. R. Rotherham

Sori of *Oenotrichia tripinnata* (Dennstaedtiaceae)
Photo E. R. Rotherham

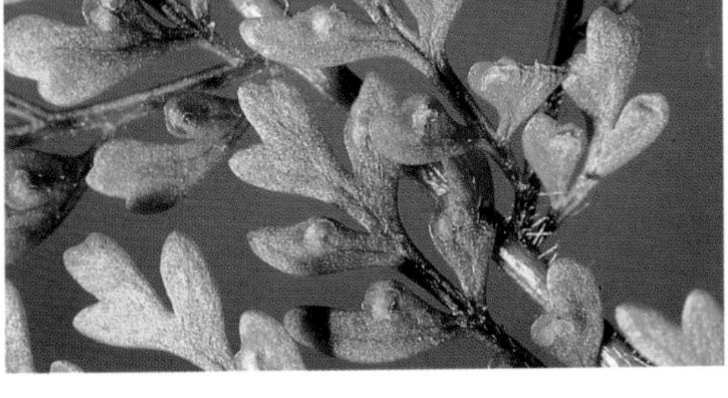

Sori of *Polystichum lentum* (Aspidiaceae)
Photo E. R. Rotherham

Sori of *Polystichum retroso-paleaceum* (Aspidiaceae)
Photo E. R. Rotherham

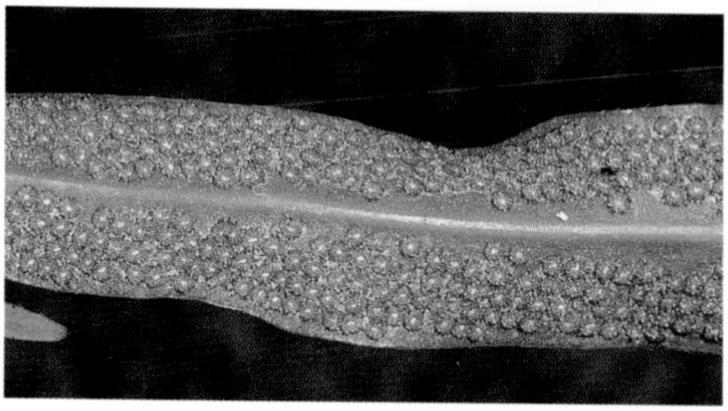

Sori of *Pyrrosia varia* (Polypodiaceae)
Photo E. R. Rotherham

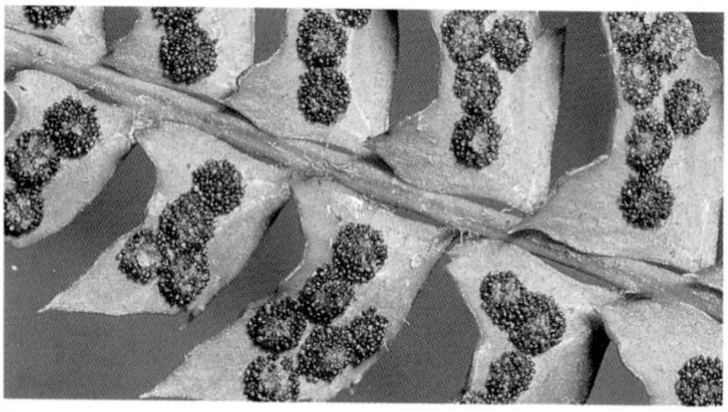

Sori of *Polystichum triangulum* (Aspidiaceae)
Photo E. R. Rotherham

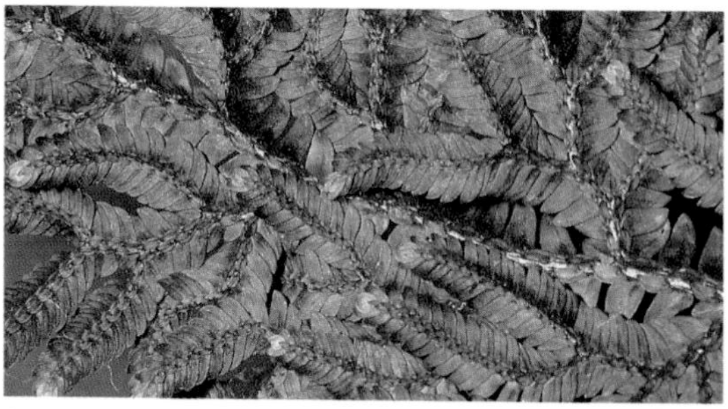

Stems of *Selaginella uncinata* with two types of leaves
Photo E. R. Rotherham

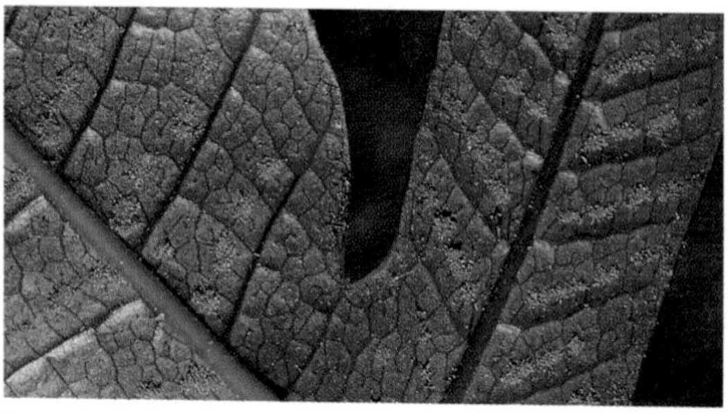

Sori and venation of *Pseudodrynaria coronans* (Polypodiaceae)
Photo E. R. Rotherham

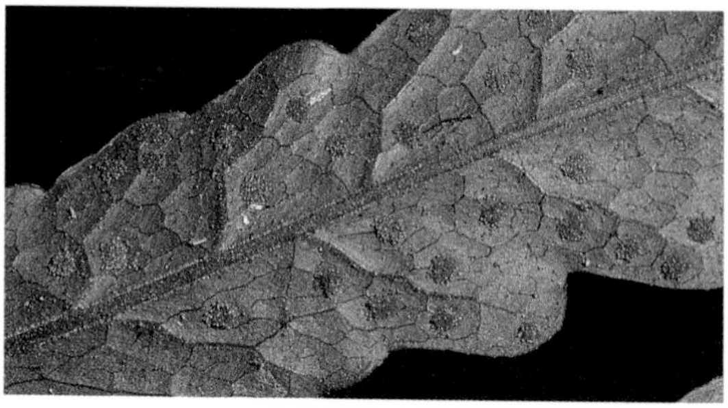

Sori of *Tectaria muelleri* (Aspidiaceae)
Photo E. R. Rotherham

Sori of *Pteris biaurita* (Pteridaceae)
Photo E. R. Rotherham

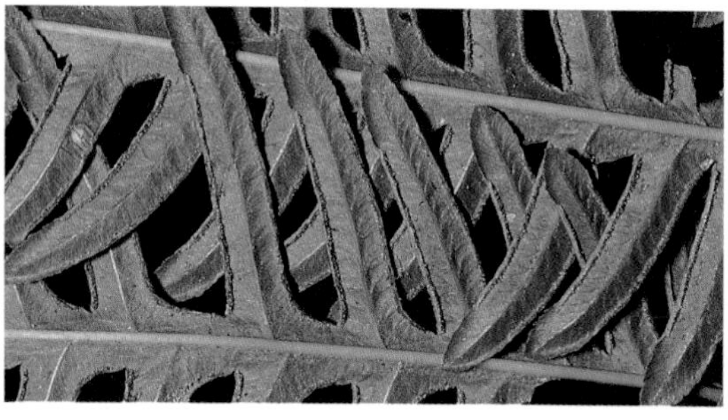

Sori of *Woodwardia orientalis* (Blechnaceae)
Photo E. R. Rotherham

3 The structure of ferns

Ferns are woody, vascular plants, usually with a very distinctive appearance. They are basically similar to other plants but they have specialized spore-producing organs, and their leaves and stems are modified in a manner which may obscure their relationships to other plants. As well, fern botanists tend to use specialized terms for some fern structures. For these reasons, this chapter is necessary to aid in the understanding of the plant group. Further specialized terms not referred to here may be found in the Glossary.

ROOTS

The primary root of a fern arises directly from the embryo soon after fertilization. Its purposes are for the initial anchorage, and for the uptake of water and nutrients for the young fern. Since it does not grow very long and has no ability to increase in thickness, its role is minor and it is quickly replaced by adventitious roots which are produced in succession as the stem grows. They may arise endogenously from the stem or, in some species, from the leaf bases.

The secondary adventitious roots are of major importance to the fern and are produced continually throughout its life as the stem grows. They perform the essential functions of anchorage and the uptake of nutrients and water. Fern roots are capable of branching and each root can develop into a long-lived system but they lack a cambium layer and hence secondary thickening is not possible. The apex of each root is protected by a root cap. Ferns are shallow-rooted plants, so most of the root system occurs in the upper layers of soil.

The development of root systems varies between groups of ferns and may have diagnostic significance. In Cheilanthoid ferns, for example, the lateral roots

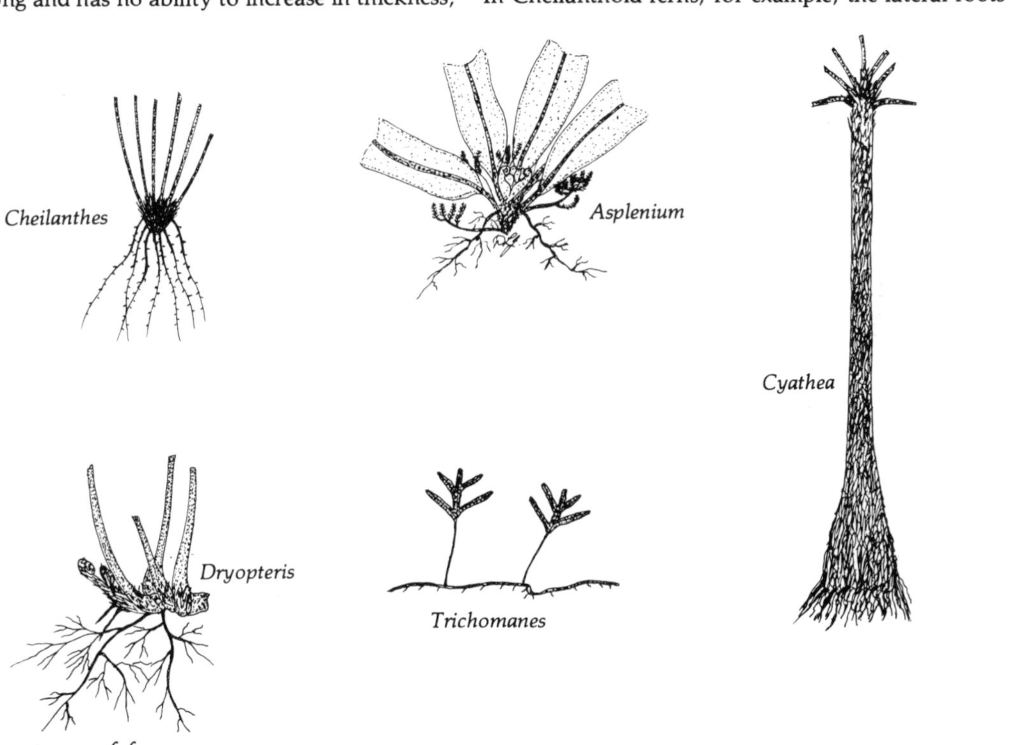

Root systems of ferns

develop only as short stubs and give a characteristic appearance to the root system. Some of the roots of epiphytic Aspleniums appear to be able to grow upwards and form an encirclement around the leaves, or even grow through the leaves into the crown. These roots are very richly endowed with root-hairs and are probably specifically adapted to grow into the litter accumulated by the rosette of leaves. In trunk-forming ferns the roots grow downwards and adhere closely to the trunk until they reach the ground. In tree ferns these roots may form a massive, dense fibrous sheath, while in *Todea* the roots may be wiry and loosely tangled.

Some ferns and their relatives completely lack roots, and their function is taken over by hair-like structures which may be termed root-hairs. Although tiny, these structures have a large (relative) surface area and a tremendous capacity for absorption. They are found on the rhizomes of some filmy ferns and in the fern allies, *Tmesipteris* and *Psilotum*.

STEMS

The stems of various ferns differ in their shape, size and mode of growth. Fern stems are usually called rhizomes; however, some botanists restrict the use of this term to those stems which are long and creeping or climbing, calling any short, compact stem a rootstock. For the purposes of this book, all fern stems, with the exception of trunks, will be called rhizomes. Rhizomes are of major significance because they contain the growing point or meristem of the fern.

Rhizomes are an important feature for fern identification. They may be short-creeping, medium-creeping or long-creeping, in which cases the growing point will be situated at one end; or they may be erect and tufted, in which case the growing point will be situated in the centre of the stem at the apex. Some botanists term a small erect tufted rhizome a caudex. If it is massive and grows erect (as in tree ferns), it is called a trunk but the terms caudex and trunk may be loosely applied to any erect, growing rhizome. In climbing ferns it is important to notice whether it is the rhizome (bearing roots) which is climbing or an elongated rachis (which is rootless).

Rhizomes may be thin and wiry or thick, with a range of variations in between. A thick rhizome may be woody or fleshy. Rhizomes may branch freely or rarely, if at all. They can branch by a simple division (forking) of the apex (known as dichotomous branching) or, more frequently, by lateral branching, when buds arise in association with the bases of leaf stalks.

The disposition and arrangement of leaves and roots on a rhizome can be a useful diagnostic characteristic. If the leaves are borne on the upper surface and the roots on the lower surface, the rhizome is dorsiventral in construction. If the leaves and roots are borne on all sides of the rhizome, even though the leaves grow upwards and the roots downwards the rhizome is termed radial in construction. A short rhizome bearing crowded leaves is usually radial and a long-creeping rhizome is usually dorsiventral. However, exceptions do occur.

Knobby structures or woody protuberances are

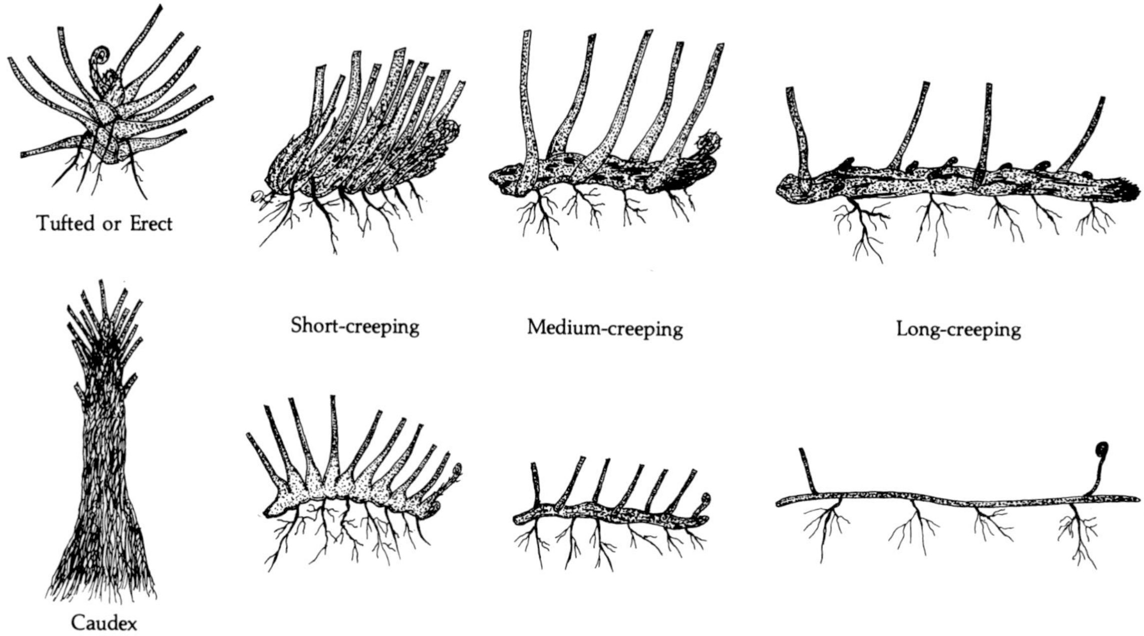

Rhizomes of ferns

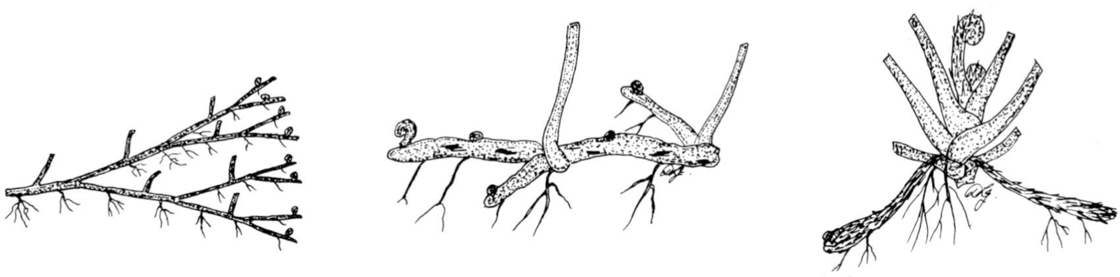

Dichotomous or Forking (*Gleichenia*)

Lateral Branching (*Lastreopsis*)

Stolons (*Blechnum*)

Branching of rhizomes

common on the rhizomes of some ferns and are known as circinate buds. Little seems to be understood about their function, if any.

As ferns are vascular plants, the evolution of tissue for their water, nutrient and hormone conduction is important in their successful survival and proliferation. The height to which some tree ferns grow is proof of the efficiency of their vascular system. The vascular system of a stem is called a stele, and vascular strands pass from it into the leaves and roots. The vascular arrangement can be of some diagnostic value. For example, slicing across the stipe of a fern frond will show the vascular bundles as prominent spots. A simple means of separating two easily confused genera of ferns, viz. *Dryopteris* and *Athyrium*, is by the number of vascular bundles. Species of *Athyrium* have two and those of *Dryopteris* have three, four or five bundles.

The arrangement of the vascular system in fern rhizomes shows great variation, and three main types of steles are found. In primitive ferns, the vascular system forms a solid core and the stele is known as a protostele, e.g. *Gleichenia*. In some ferns with a long-creeping rhizome the stele is tubular and hollow, and is called a siphonostele (occasionally a solenostele). In these ferns the siphonostele is interrupted by leaf gaps where the vascular trace to a leaf is attached, e.g. *Adiantum*, *Microlepia* and *Pellaea*. In ferns with crowded fronds the stele is much dissected by leaf gaps and is termed a dictyostele, e.g. *Cyathea*, *Dicksonia* and *Polypodium*.

Close-up of scales on a crozier of *Cyathea cooperi*
Photo E. R. Rotherham

The naked rhizome of *Polypodium formosanum* (left). The scaly rhizome of *Davallia bullata* (right).

Scales, Bristles and Hairs

The young parts of the stem and coiled fronds of ferns are protected by dry structures which may be scales, bristles or hairs. The shape, size and colour of these structures may be useful or even important diagnostic features.

Scales are papery in texture and are one cell thick. They consist of an arrangement of flat cells, and are attached to the fern by a point on their edge (such as the base) or by some point on their flat surface (when they are known as peltate). If the cell walls of the scales are thickened to form a lattice-work pattern on the surface, they are termed clathrate. The edges of the scales may be entire, lacerate, toothed or ciliate, and such descriptions are of taxonomic significance.

Hairs are elongated structures which consist of one drawn-out cell or a single row of cells. Their length, colour, thickness, rigidity and abundance may be useful diagnostically. For example, *Adiantum pubescens* can be distinguished from *A. hispidulum* by its thin, sub-rigid hairs on the underside of the fronds. Those of *A. hispidulum* are short, stout and quite rigid. *A. diaphanum* bears a few stiff black hairs on its fronds, while *A. hispidulum* has more numerous white hairs. Hairs on the fronds and stipes of some species of *Hypolepis* are glandular-tipped i.e. with a small globule of liquid at the apex.

A bristle is similar to a hair but tends to be very rigid and has an expanded base which is more than one cell thick. Bristles may be characteristic of a genus, e.g. *Dipteris*.

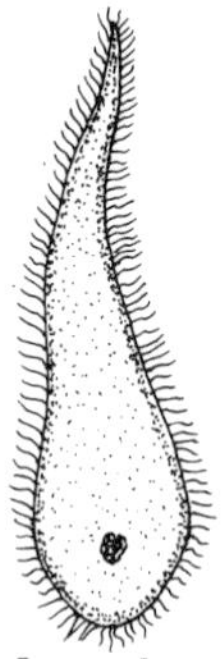

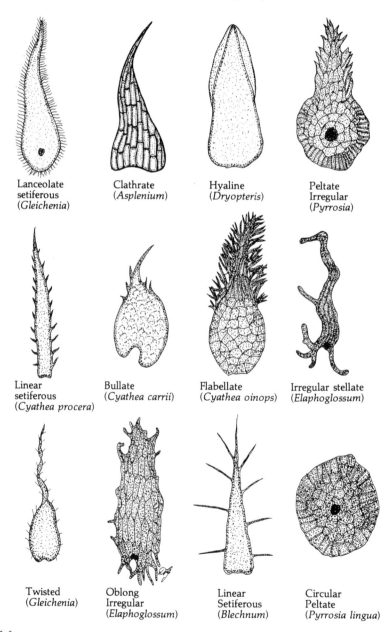

Lanceolate
setiferous
(*Gleichenia*)

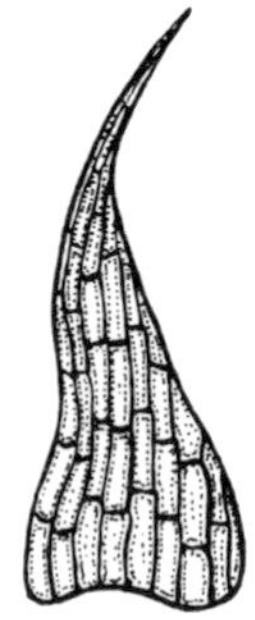

Clathrate
(*Asplenium*)

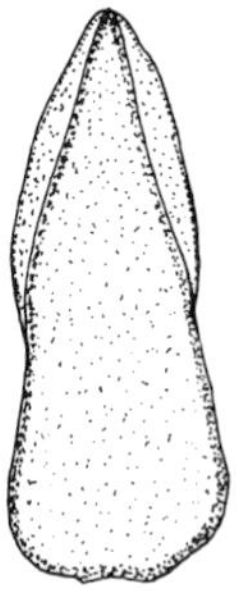

Hyaline
(*Dryopteris*)

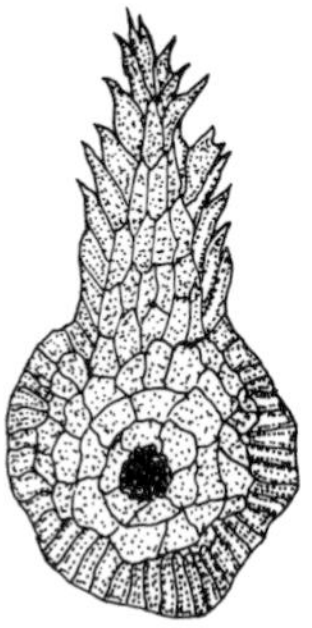

Peltate
Irregular
(*Pyrrosia*)

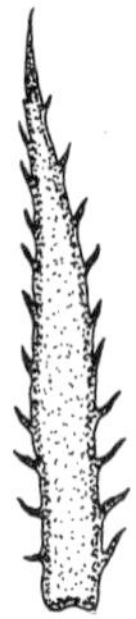

Linear
setiferous
(*Cyathea procera*)

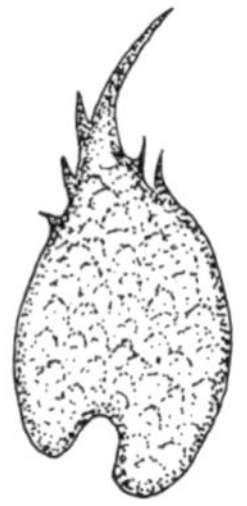

Bullate
(*Cyathea carrii*)

Flabellate
(*Cyathea oinops*)

Irregular stellate
(*Elaphoglossum*)

Twisted
(*Gleichenia*)

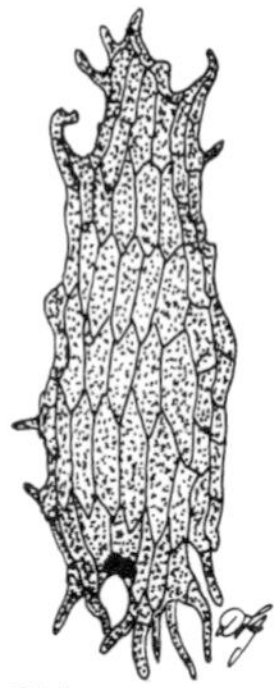

Oblong
Irregular
(*Elaphoglossum*)

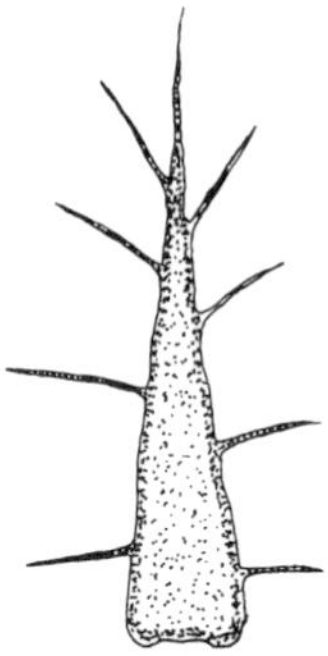

Linear
Setiferous
(*Blechnum*)

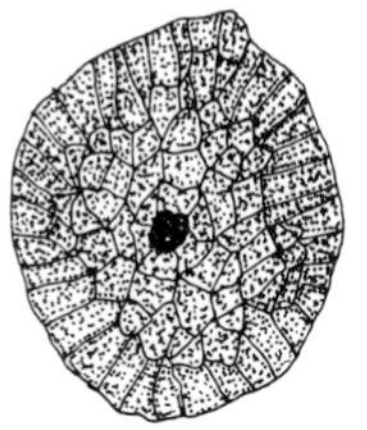

Circular
Peltate
(*Pyrrosia lingua*)

Scales of ferns

Scales on stipe base of *Cyathea brownii*
Photo C. G. Goudey

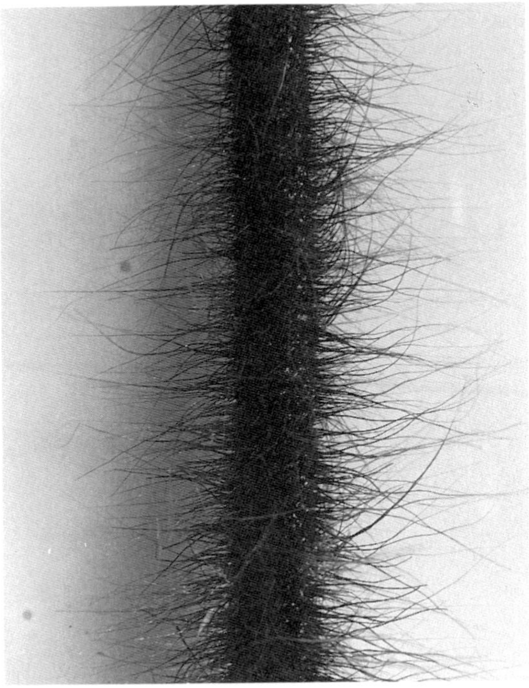

Hairs on stipe of *Dicksonia squarrosa*
Photo C. G. Goudey

LEAVES

Fern leaves are usually called fronds. In most ferns the fronds are crowded or scattered along the rhizome but in ferns with an upright growth habit they are arranged in a spreading or arching crown. Young fern fronds are coiled and are termed croziers. This coiling is termed circinate vernation. In a number of ferns the young fronds are bent like a shepherd's crook instead of being coiled, e.g. *Pellaea* spp. This is known as non-circinate vernation.

Stipes

The basal woody structure of a fern frond, which extends from the stem to the first leaflet or segment, is analogous to the petiole of a leaf and is known as the stipe. It may be entire and rounded in section or grooved on the upper surface. The surface is smooth or roughened, or bears distinct thorns or spines.

Most stipes bear scales or hairs. These are usually smaller than those on the rhizome but are identical in all other respects. Most stipes bear scales on the basal part but in some species the stipes are scaly for their whole length. In some species the scales may be confined to the groove in the stipe. In a few cases, where the rhizome bears only scales, the stipe may carry a mixture of scales and hairs. Hairs on stipes may be glandular. The shape, colour and adornment of the scales and hairs on the stipes can be important diagnostic features.

The stipe may arise directly from the rhizome or be jointed (or articulated) at its point of attachment. In some species the stipe is articulated to a small outgrowth of the rhizome called a phyllopodium, e.g. *Davallia* and *Elaphoglossum*. After the death of the frond, the stipe may be persistent or break off at the articulation, or shed completely, leaving a scar (the coin-spotting on the trunks of some Tree-fern species is an example of the latter type).

In some ferns, small elongated slits near reduced leaflets are termed aerophores. The internal tissue adjacent to them is thin-walled and has numerous air spaces. A pale line running along each side of a stipe is also indicative of this tissue. In a few ferns slime glands in the stipes secrete a mucilaginous material which covers and protects the young fronds.

Lamina

The most prominent portion of the fern frond is the lamina or blade. This is the distal part of the frond and bears the green tissue where photosynthesis takes place. The main stalk or the midrib of the frond is termed the rachis or primary rachis. Secondary, tertiary and higher rachises may be present on divided fronds. The lamina shape and its division are major diagnostic features.

Each species of fern has a characteristic frond shape, and the various mature fronds on a fern do not depart greatly from that shape. The small juvenile fronds which arise on a young fern are usually very different in shape to the mature ones. Frequently, a gradation exists, with each one forming a link in the development. Mature fronds are either sterile or fertile and these may be of similar shape or very dissimilar. If they are of markedly dissimilar shape, the fern is described as being dimorphic for it has two distinct types of frond. Usually the sterile fronds have broad segments and tend to have a lax growth habit, whereas the fertile fronds have narrow segments and are held

Thorns or prickles on stipe bases on *Cnemidaria horrida*
Photo D. L. Jones

erect to aid spore dispersal (Figure p.38). Ferns in which the sterile and fertile fronds are of similar shape are known as monomorphic.

Some climbing ferns are regarded as polymorphic for they have at least three different types of fronds, e.g. *Teratophyllum* spp.. Those fronds on the lower part of the fern (scrambling over rocks and the forest floor) are of a different size and shape to the mature sterile fronds found on the tree trunk and these in turn are very different from the fertile fronds. The basal fronds are called bathyphylls and those mature types found on the trunk are known as acrophylls (Figure p.28).

Frond Division

Fern fronds occur in a wide range of shapes and may be divided in various ways into segments or lobes. The frond shape and type of division are useful diagnostic features.

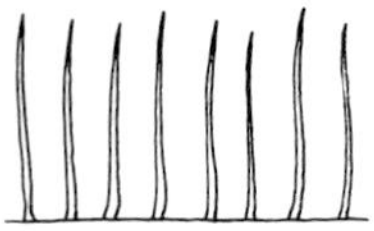

Simple and Spreading Hairs

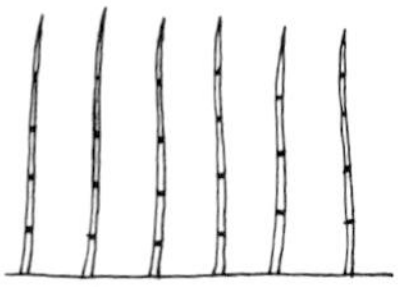

Septate hairs

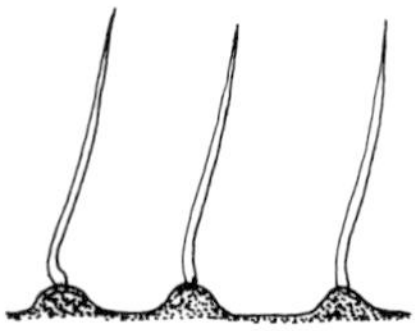

Hairs on Raised Protuberances

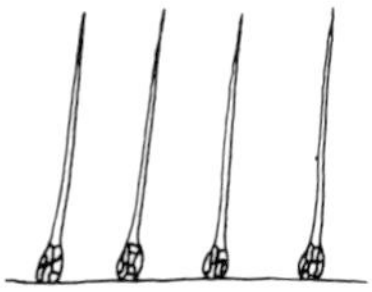

Bristles

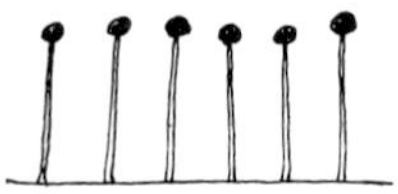

Glandular Hairs

Tangled Hairs

Appressed Hairs

Hooked Hairs

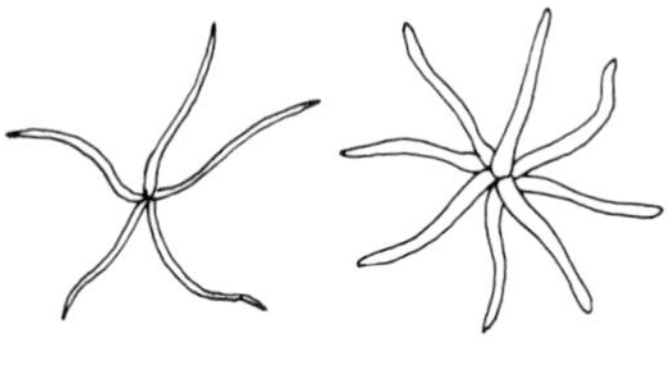

Stellate Hairs

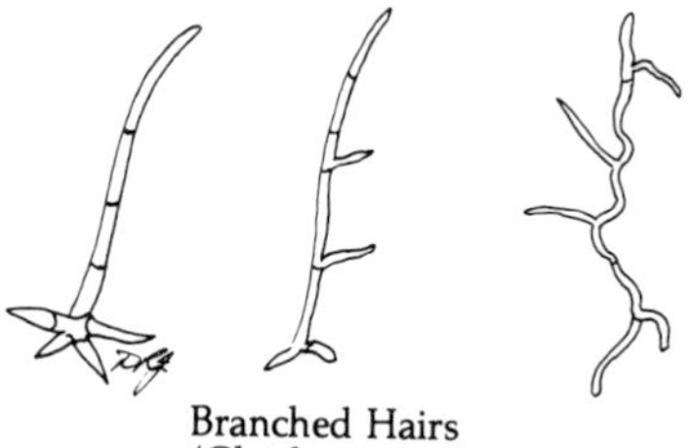

Branched Hairs
(Gleicheniaceae)

Bristles and hairs

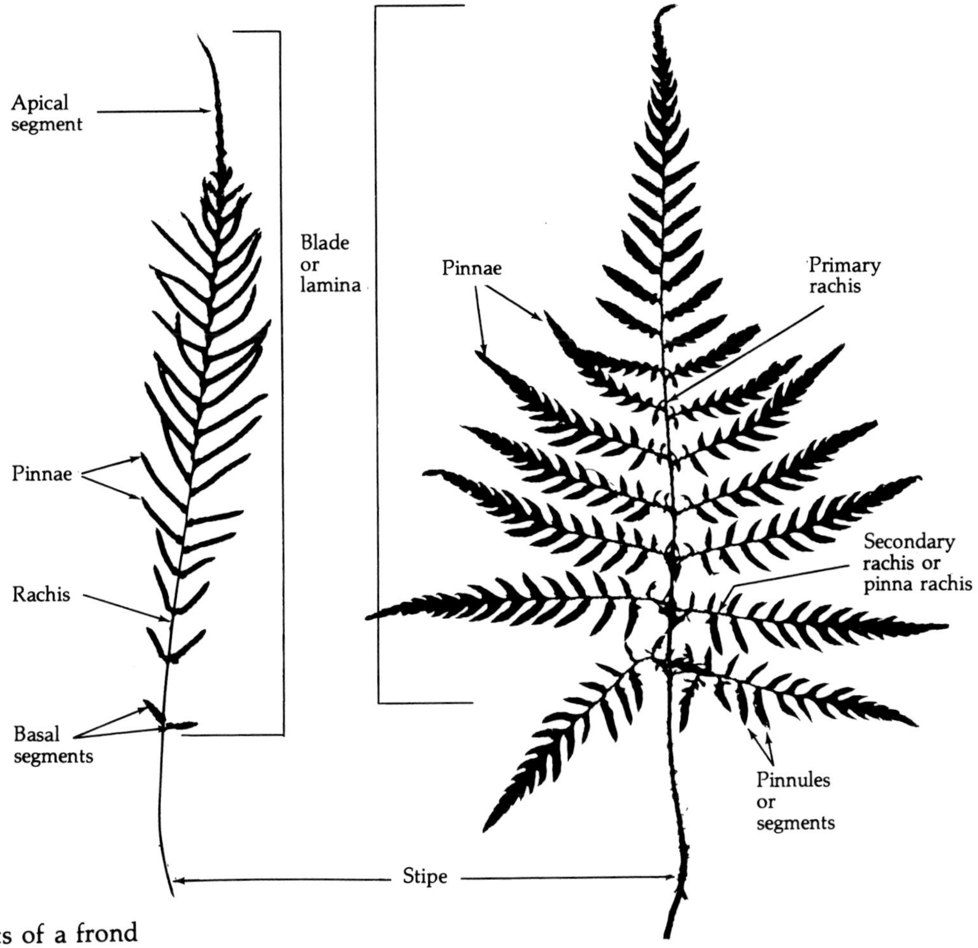

Parts of a frond

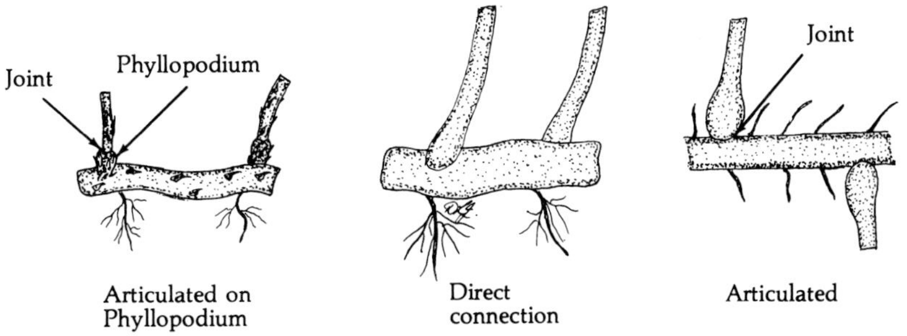

Stipe junctions

The types of fronds most easily recognized are those which are simple and entire. These have a uniform lamina with no divisions or lobes whatsoever. Simple fronds which are divided but with the divisions not reaching to the rachis can be arranged into three groups. In each group the individual segments are called lobes.

The groups are:

1. pinnatifid — with the divisions extending about one quarter to half way to the rachis.
2. pinnatipartite — with the divisions extending half to two thirds of the way to the rachis.
3. pinnatisect — with the divisions reaching more than three quarters of the way to the rachis.

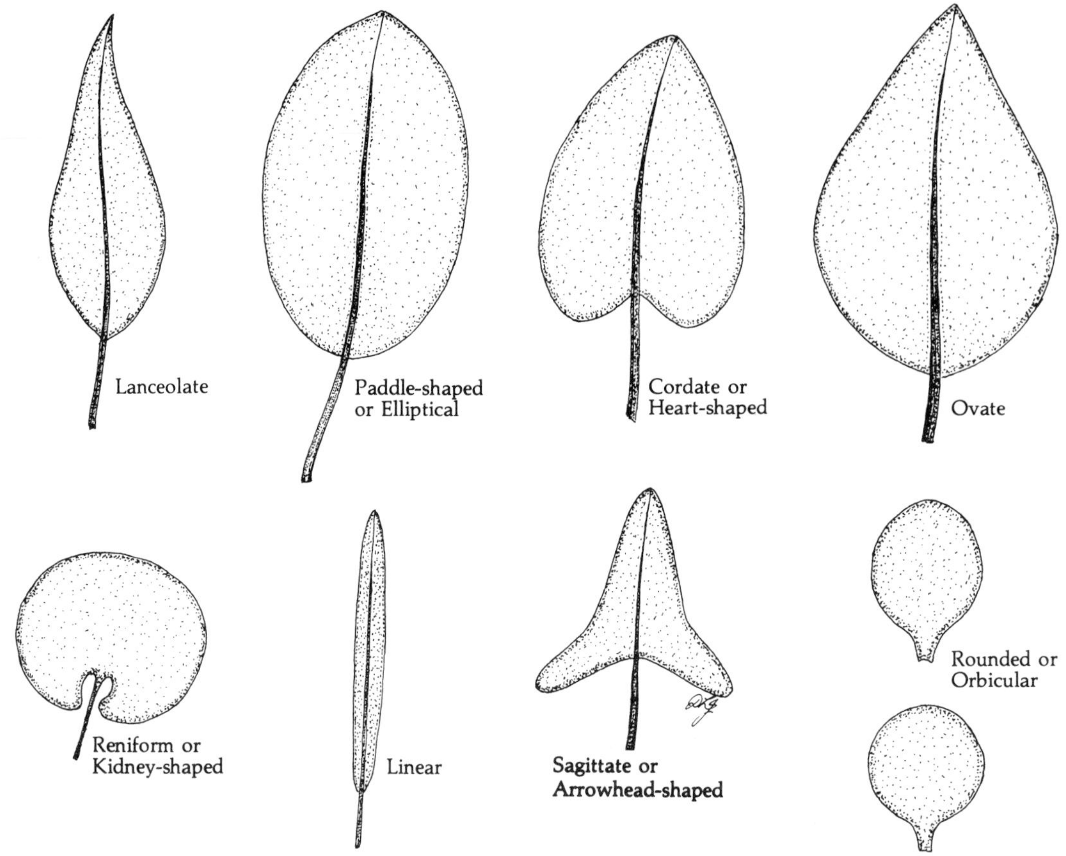

Shape of simple fronds (can also apply to pinnae, pinnules, etc)

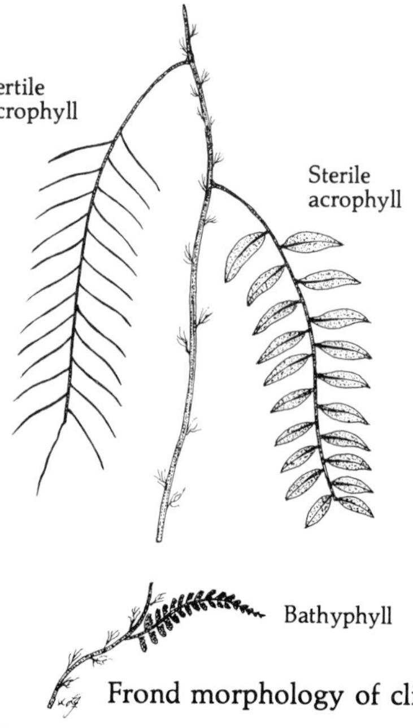

Frond morphology of climbing ferns

These divisions are somewhat arbitrary and the degree of division commonly varies on a single frond. For this reason some botanists prefer to regard any lobed frond, where the divisions do not reach the rachis, as being pinnatifid.

If a frond is divided once, with the divisions extending to the midrib, the frond is said to be pinnate and the lobes are called pinnae (Figure p.29). If the pinnae are lobed but the lobes do not reach the secondary rachis, the frond is bipinnatifid (or bipinnatisect depending on the depth of the division). If the pinnae are divided all the way to the secondary rachis, the frond is twice pinnate or bipinnate, and the segments are called pinnules. Divisions of this nature can increase up to four or five-times pinnate.

When fronds are branched, the arrangement of the pinnae and pinnules can be of significance (see Figure p.29). The main divisions of such fronds are called pinnae and, depending on the number of divisions, these may be primary, secondary or tertiary. The final divisions are the pinnules, which are sometimes called the ultimate segments. The upper surface of the pinna or pinnule is known as the adaxial surface and the lower is the abaxial. The edge of the pinnule which faces the apex of the frond or of the pinna is called

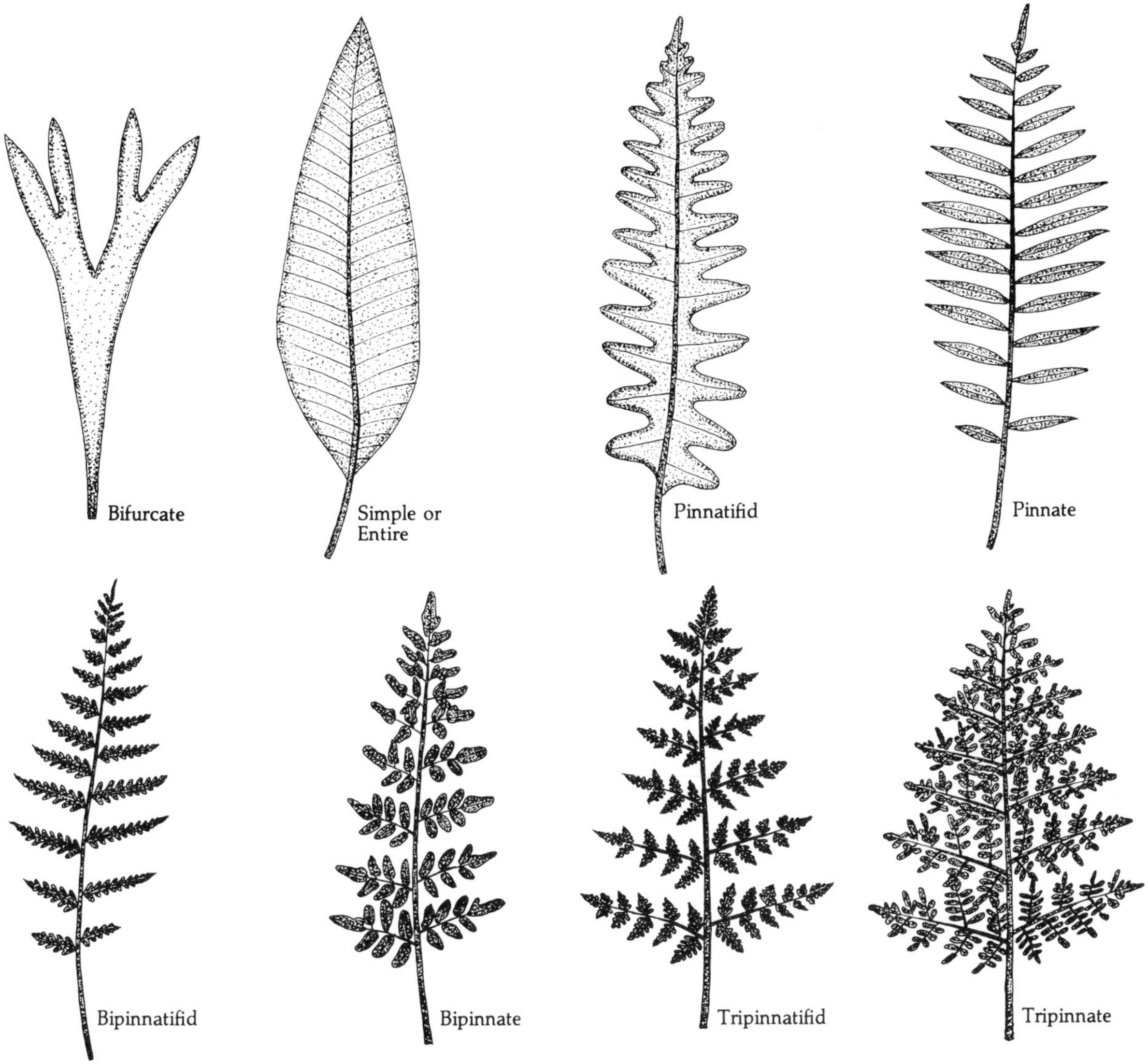

Frond division

acroscopic and that which faces the base is called basiscopic. It is important to note whether the first branch on a primary pinna is produced on the side facing the apex (anadramous) or the base (catadramous) of a divided frond.

Pinna or pinnule shape can be a useful diagnostic feature, as can lobes, teeth and other marginal adornments. The pinnae or pinnules of some species are joined to the rachis by a stalk; others are sessile. In some cases the basiscopic margin is confluent with the rachis and may even run down the rachis for a short distance (decurrent), or up the rachis (surcurrent).

Some fronds are lobed to resemble the shape of a hand and are described as being palmate. If the divisions extend about half way to the rachis the frond is palmatifid, and if they extend closer to the rachis it is palmatisect. A pedate frond is palmately divided but has long basal lobes which arise on a secondary rachis, e.g. *Doryopteris pedata* var. *palmata* (Figure p.31). Some ferns, such as species of *Sticherus*, have flabellate fronds which are basically fan-shaped. Fronds of the genus *Dipteris* are divided into two equal fan-shaped parts resembling butterfly wings (didymous).

The fronds of some ferns are dichotomously divided (or forked) into equal parts, e.g. *Schizaea dichotoma*. In the family Gleicheniaceae the branching is described as pseudodichotomous. The divisions appear as if they are dichotomous but they are actually two equal lateral branches with a dormant terminal bud between

Leaf or leaflet margins

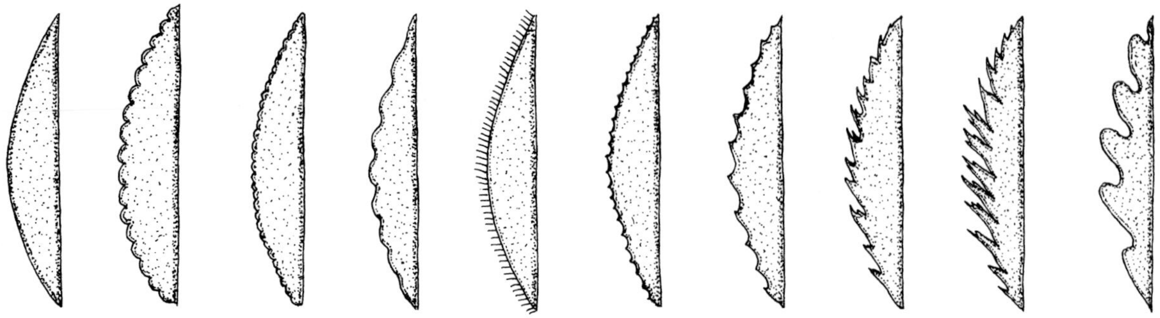

Leaf or leaflet apices

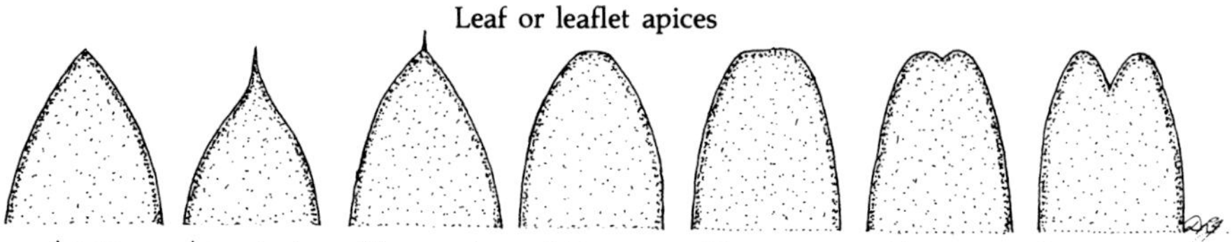

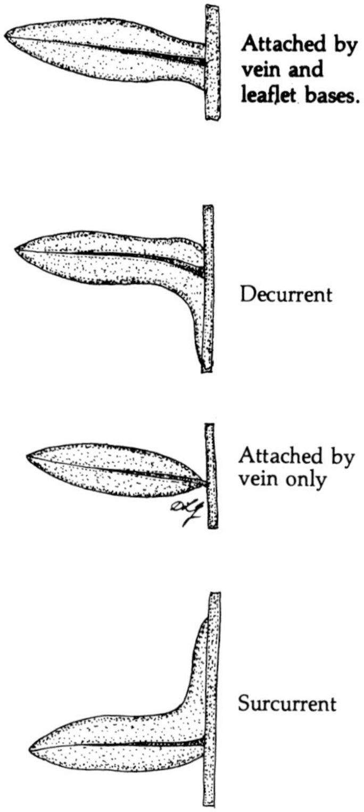

Pinna attachment

them. This bud can grow to form another layer of fronds above the first and in some species many such layers are formed. Fronds of this type are sometimes described as being tiered.

Rachises

The colour of the rachises and the presence of scales or hairs can be useful for separating species. In a number of ferns the rachis may produce vegetative buds and be proliferous (see page 126). The grooving of the rachis is of major importance, particularly the arrangement of grooves at rachis junctions (i.e. whether the grooves are continuous or interrupted) and how they join on to the midribs of leaflets.

Venation

A vein is actually the trace of a vascular bundle and is usually quite prominent on the surface of a frond. In species with fleshy fronds the veins may be hidden, and transmitted light may be necessary to show their pattern. The pattern made by veins is known as the venation and this arrangement is an important taxonomic feature. The venation may be simple, when the veins fork one or more times but the branches do not join up again. The veins commonly end at the edge of the lamina, frequently in a lobe or marginal sorus. All of these veins are free. In some ferns the grouping of free veins may be pinnate and resembles that of a fish's backbone. The main vein of a leaflet is termed a midrib or costa and the smaller side veins are known as costules.

In many ferns the veins rejoin after branching, or join on to neighbouring veins. This results in a reticulated network and this type of venation is called anastomosing. The small areas of tissue enclosed by each network of veins is known as an areole. Various combinations are possible, from a single series of areoles to a complex network. Sometimes free veins may be enclosed within an areole.

False veins are a piece of tissue which resembles a vein but with no underlying vascular tissue. They are believed to be vestigial remnants of pinnae or pinnules which have coalesced during evolution.

Some veins end in hydathodes which are a water-secreting organ. Their function is uncertain but their presence is often revealed by a surrounding accretion of salts left by evaporation. These show up as white spots on the frond and may be conspicuous in species of *Nephrolepis*. They are often termed lime dots.

FERTILE PARTS

Ferns reproduce by spores which are tiny, unicellular structures lacking an embryo. The spores are produced in specialized structures known as sporangia (they are commonly called spore cases). In those ferns grouped in the orders *Ophioglossales* and *Marattiales* the sporangia are large, in small clusters and open by slits or pores. In the majority of ferns the sporangia are smaller, clustered in distinct groups called sori (singular sorus) and open by a different method.

Sori

The sori of ferns are produced on the underside of the fronds. They may be in discrete groups, and round

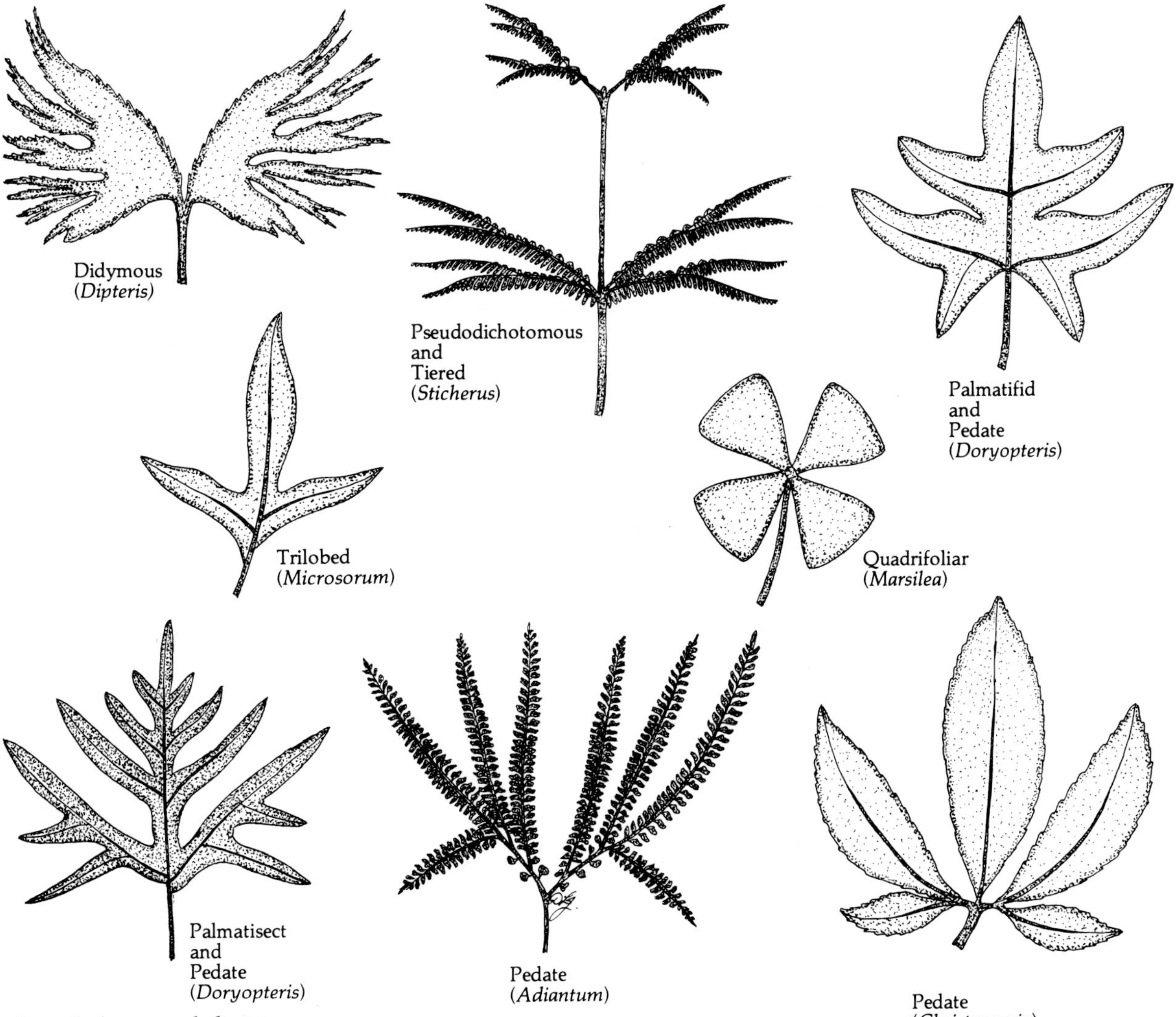

Frond shape and division

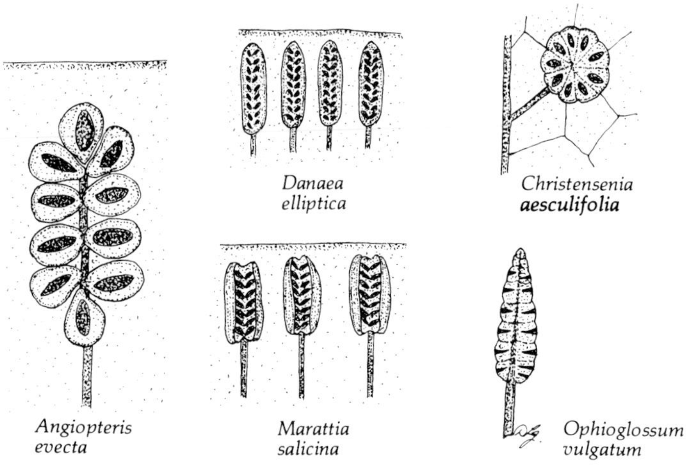

Specialized sporangia of Marattiaceae and Ophioglossaceae

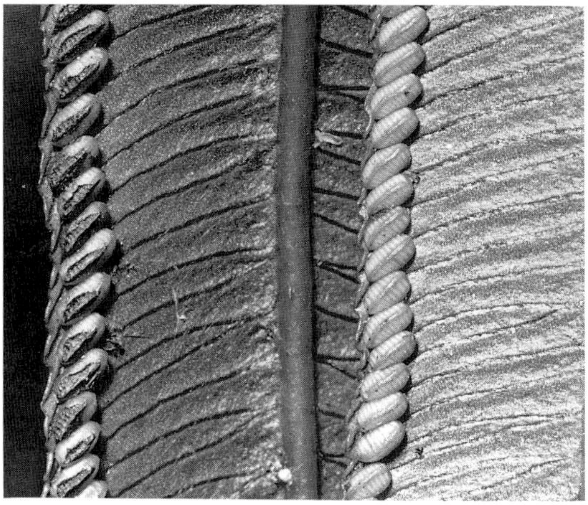

Arrangement of the sporangia of *Marattia salicina*
Photo E. R. Rotherham

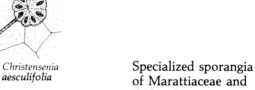

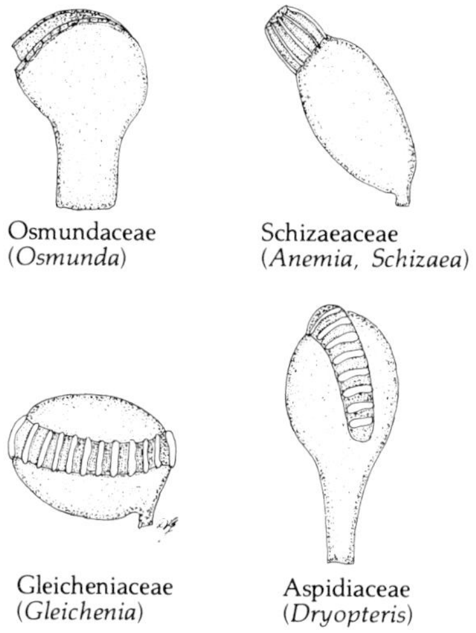

Types of sporangia

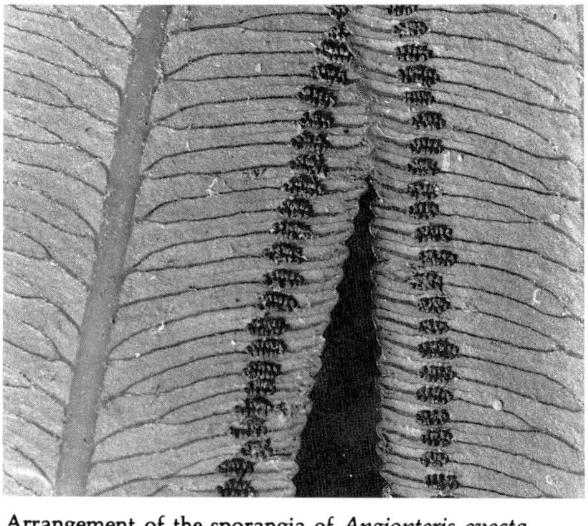

Arrangement of the sporangia of *Angiopteris evecta*
Photo E. R. Rotherham

or elongate in shape, or spread along the veins. Some ferns have elongated marginal sori formed by the overlapping of adjacent sori. These are termed fusion-sori or coensori. Rounded sori are usually situated at the end of a free vein, at a point on its length or at the junction of veins, whereas an elongated sorus (which is not a fusion-sorus) spreads along a vein. Where sori spread along all the veins of a fertile frond, covering the whole lower surface, the arrangement is known as acrostichoid.

Sporangia

Ferns produce large numbers of sporangia. Each sporangium is attached to the frond by a short stalk. Spores are released from a sporangium following contraction of a specialized ring of cells known as an

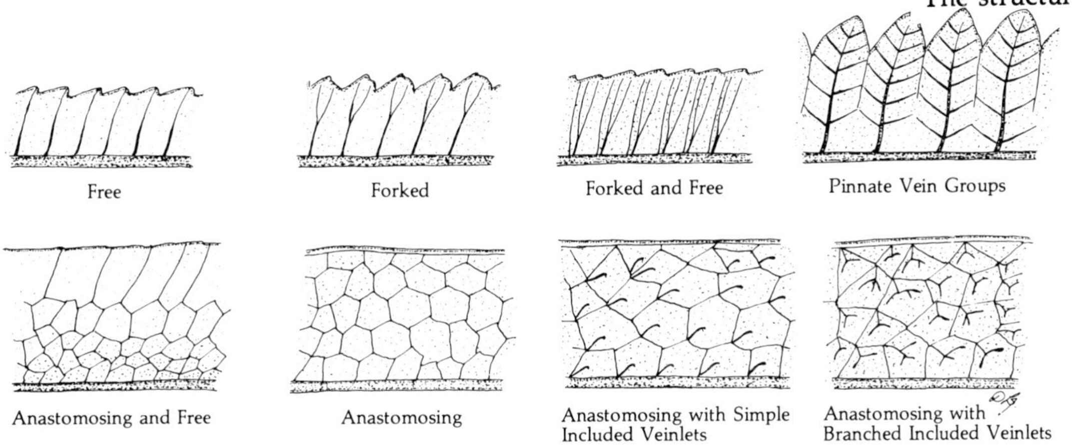

Fern venation

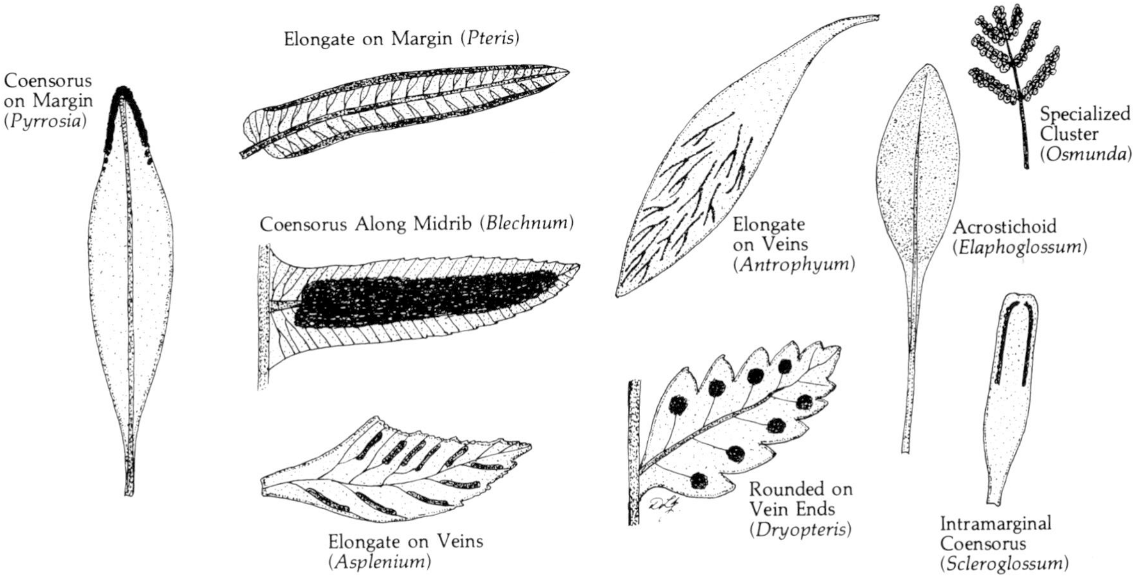

Soral arrangement

annulus. Rupture occurs at a predetermined place known as the stomium.

The shedding of fern spores is an interesting process. Cells of the annulus have thick inner walls and thin outer walls. They are dead and filled with water. As the sporangium matures the water evaporates from the cells, and the annulus begins to straighten, rupturing at the stomium. This bursts the thin walls of the sporangial cells. When the water is all evaporated the cohesive pull of the annular cells becomes stronger than the straightening effect caused by the drying, and the sporangium rapidly returns to its original position, dispersing the spores at the same time. This process may be observed under a microscope or hand lens, and can be stimulated by the heat from an incandescent light.

Indusia

The sori may be naked (exindusiate), when the sporangia are readily visible, or they may be protected by a thin, usually membranous outgrowth from the frond known as an indusium. An indusium may be variously shaped, but its shape is usually characteristic of the species or perhaps even of the genus. Indusia shapes include rounded or circular, elongate, kidney-shaped (reniform), cup-shaped, pocket-shaped and trumpet-shaped. In some genera the sori may be covered by specialized reflexed margins of the frond and these are called false indusia, e.g. *Adiantum* and *Pteris*. Not all genera with marginal sori have a false indusium. *Lindsaea*, for example, has a true indusium, and *Pteridium* has both false and true. In some ferns

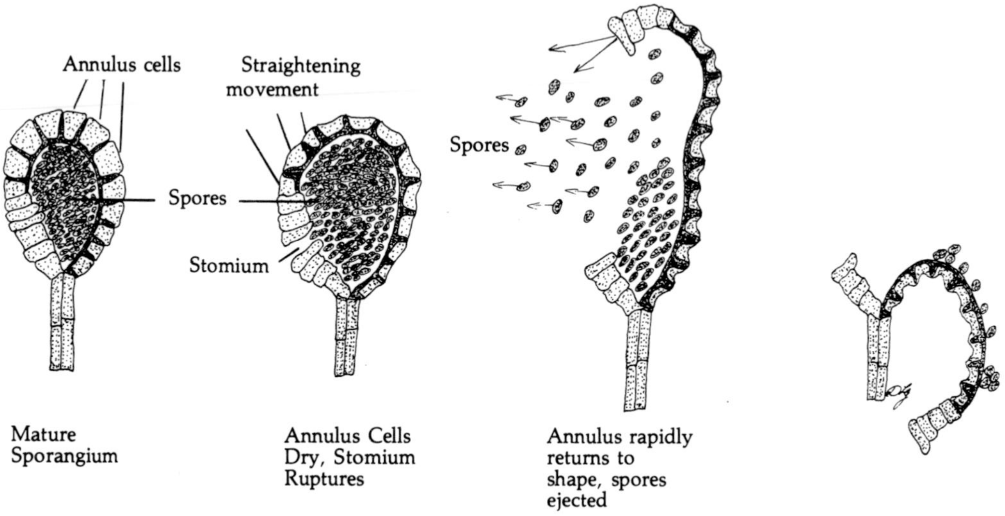

The process of spore shedding

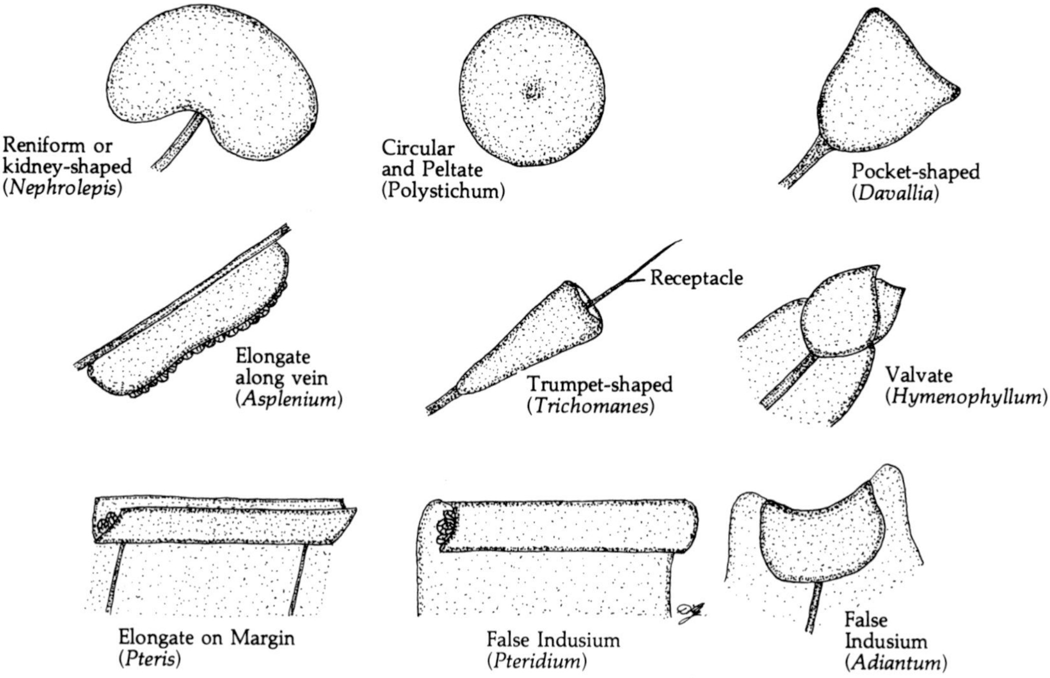

Shapes of fern indusia

A. reniforme

A. hispidulum

A. raddianum

A. capillus-veneris

Variation in the arrangement and shape of the false indusia of *Adiantum* species — Photos C. G. Goudey

with exindusiate sori, hairs or scales are borne among the sporangia. They are known as paraphyses and they act as a protective covering to the young sporangia. Their abundance and shape can be useful diagnostic features.

Spores

Spores are produced in groups of four (tetrads) within each sporangium. Each tetrad is the result of two meiotic divisions of a spore mother cell. The study of spores requires access to high magnification equipment such as a scanning electron microscope. Spore features are of tremendous importance to researchers

Shape of paraphyses

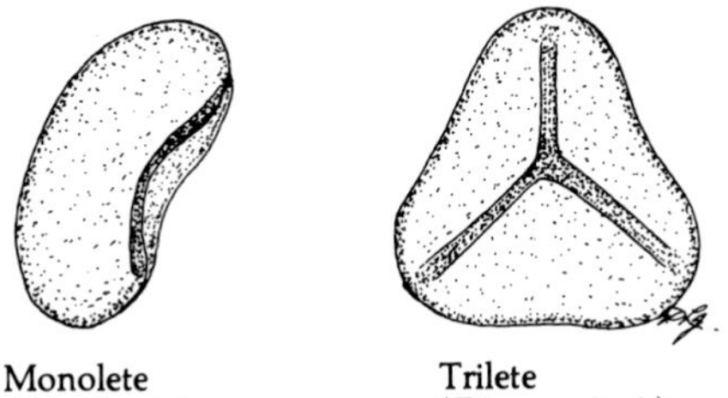

Basic spore shape

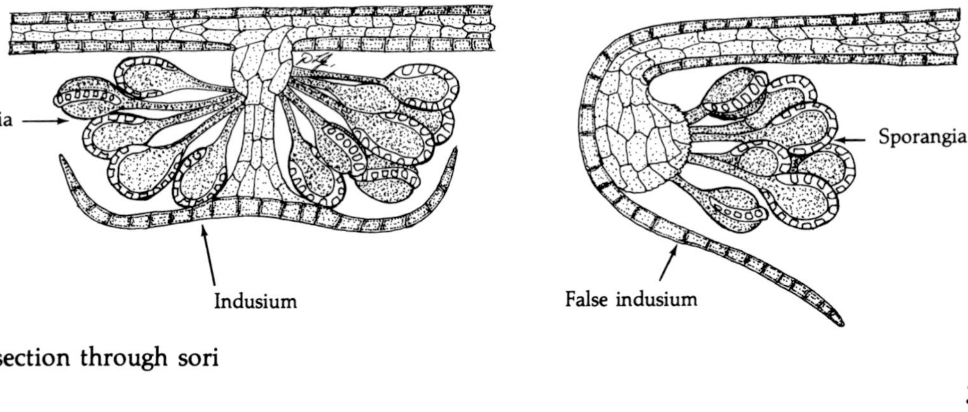

Cross-section through sori

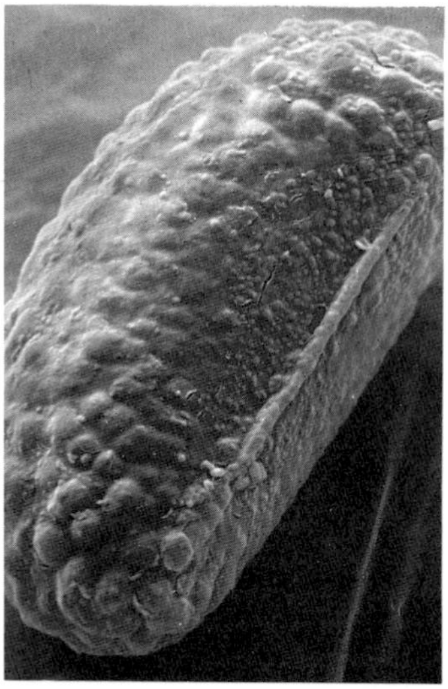

Monolete spore of *Microsorum diversifolium*, x 2760.

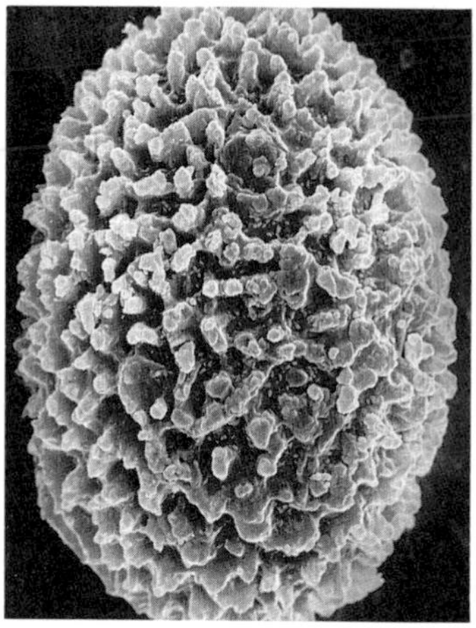

Monolete spore of *Blechnum diversifolium*, x 3070.

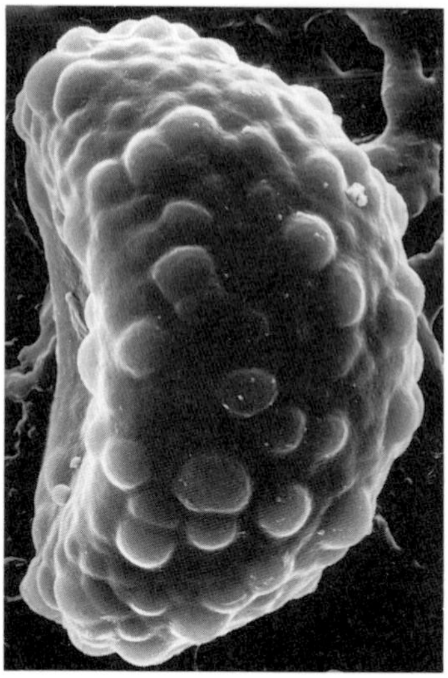

Monolete spore of *Scyphularia pentaphylla*, x 2480

Trilete spore of *Anemia mexicana*, x 1620

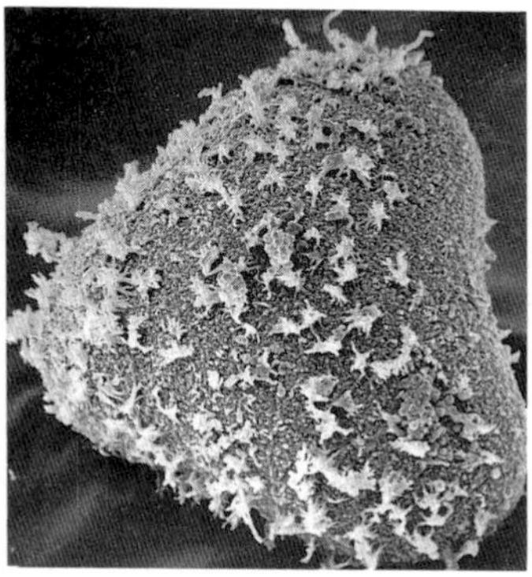

Trilete spore of *Cheilanthes contigua*, x 1590

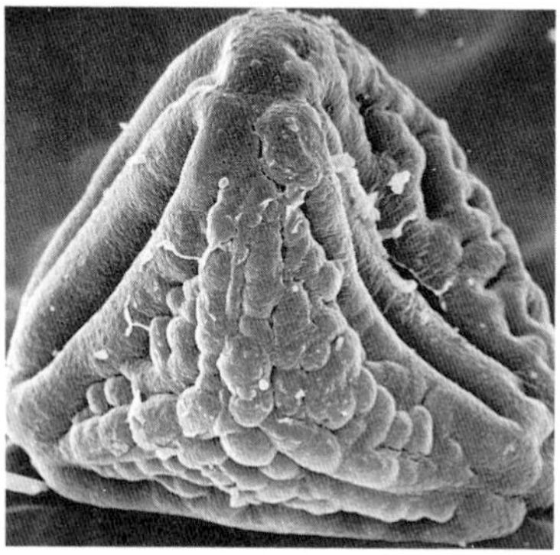

Trilete spore of *Cheilanthes catanensis*, x 1690

Photomicrographs of fern spores showing shapes and wall ornamentation.

Photos Prof. T. C. Chambers

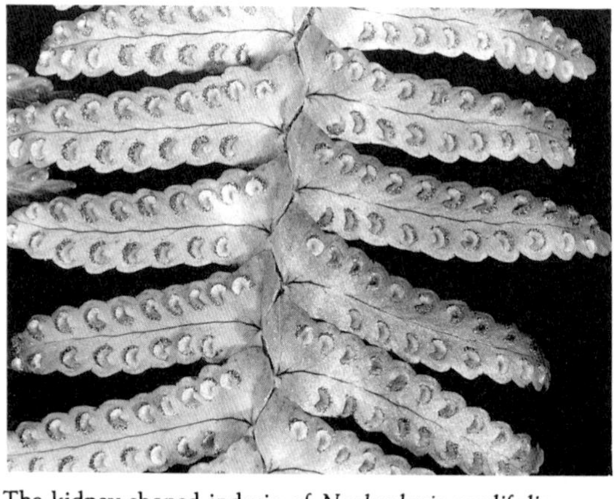

The kidney-shaped indusia of *Nephrolepis cordifolia*

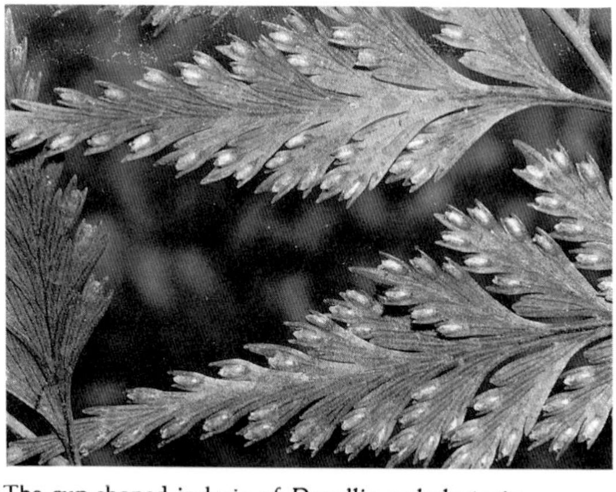

The cup-shaped indusia of *Davallia embolostegia*

Photo E. R. Rotherham

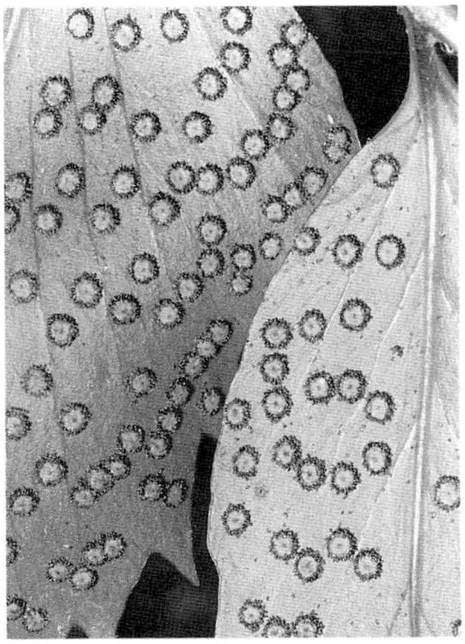

The circular indusia of *Cyrtomium falcatum*
Photo E. R. Rotherham

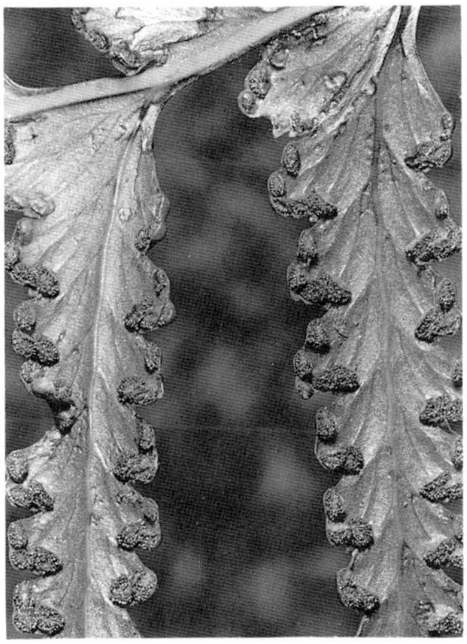

The sporangia of *Microlepia platyphylla* are enclosed in small cups
Photo E. R. Rotherham

The elongated sori of *Diplazium werckliamum*
Photo E. R. Rotherham

The chain-like soral arrangement of *Woodwardia orientalis*
Photo C. G. Goudey

The tiny sori of *Cystopteris fragilis*
Photo C. G. Goudey

Marginal sori of *Pteris kingiana*
Photo C. G. Goudey

because they shed light on evolution and the relationships between various groups of ferns. Spore details, however, are of limited value to the enthusiast and field botanist. They are helpful in the understanding and appreciation of modern fern manuals which are magnificently illustrated with photographs of spores taken at high magnification.

Fern spores are of two basic shapes: monolete or trilete. Monolete spores are roughly the shape of a bean seed and are angled along one edge where they have been pressed together in the tetrad. Trilete spores have three faces and are roughly triangular in cross-section. Some spores have a plain surface and in others the surface is sculptured into ridges or rounded bumps. Some have an external covering known as a perispore and this may be spiny or folded into flat plates or wings.

When shed, the spores appear as a fine dust. Some spores contain chlorophyll and are green, e.g. *Osmunda* and *Todea*. Other species may be grey, brown, black or yellow.

The circular, peltate indusia of *Rumohra adiantiformis*
Photo C. G. Goudey

The naked sori of *Cyathea medullaris*
Photo C. G. Goudey

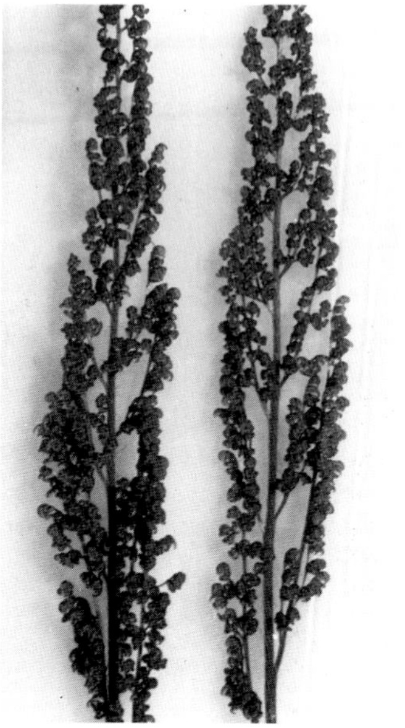

The specialized sporangial clusters of *Onoclea sensibilis*
Photo C. G. Goudey

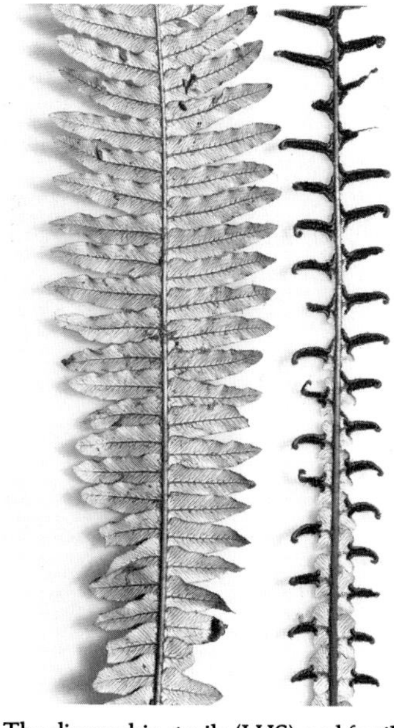

The dimorphic sterile (LHS) and fertile frond of *Blechnum discolor*
Photo C. G. Goudey

The elongated sorus of *Blechnum brasiliense* is close to the midrib
Photo C. G. Goudey

Dicksonia antarctica showing prominent false indusia

4 The reproduction of ferns and fern allies

The pteridophyte structure which is familiar as a plant, has at least two sets of chromosomes, a state that is termed diploid. Pteridophytes may also be triploid (with three sets), tetraploid (with four sets) and even much higher (known as polyploids). This stage of the fern life cycle is known as the sporophyte. Pteridophytes also have a stage in their life cycle known as the gametophyte. This stage contains half the number of chromosomes of the sporophyte, the reduction arising from the process known as meiosis. If the gametophyte contains one set of chromosomes it is termed haploid.

All pteridophytes pass from the sporophyte stage to the gametophyte stage in their development, and this process is known as an alternation of generations. The major steps in the life cycle of a pteridophyte are shown in the accompanying diagram, although the details may vary somewhat with the particular group. Variations in the life cycle of specific groups are considered in the next two chapters.

GENERAL LIFE CYCLE

The spore contains half the number of chromosomes of the sporophyte. It germinates and develops into a variously shaped structure known as a prothallus (or prothallium). This contains the same number of chromosomes as the spore.

The prothallus may contain chlorophyll and be photosynthetic or it may be colourless and rely for its nutrition on a symbiotic relationship with mycorrhizal fungi. Symbiotic prothalli may be buried in soil whereas green prothalli are on the surface where light can reach them. The prothallus lacks true roots and is attached to the soil by hair-like root growths or rhizoids. All the tissues so far mentioned represent the gametophyte generation.

The prothallus continues development and produces sex cells, which develop in specialized organs on its surface. The female sex organs, known as archegonia, contain the female eggs (one per archegonium). The male organs (antheridia) produce the male sex cells which are termed sperm or spermatozoids. These are minute coiled cells, motile by means of sets of long flagella. They swim to the archegonium in a film of water present on the surface of the prothallus, and fertilize the egg. The sperm are attracted to the egg by chemicals released from cells on the walls of the archegonium (malic acid in true ferns, citric acid in species of *Selaginella* and *Lycopodium*).

At fertilization two cells, each containing half a set of chromosomes, unite to form a zygote with a complete set. This is the beginning of the sporophyte generation. This zygote grows and develops into the familiar fern or fern ally structure known as the sporophyte. When mature this produces its own spores to start the process over again.

HETEROSPOROUS LIFE CYCLE

The above may be regarded as a generalized life cycle for a pteridophyte which produces a single type of spore. Some ferns (those in the families Marsiliaceae and Salviniaceae) and fern allies (species of *Selaginella* and *Isoetes*) produce two types of spore and are said to be heterosporous. The smaller spores (termed microspores) germinate into a small prothallus which develops antheridia only. The larger spores (megaspores) bear only archegonia and thus the two types of spore must fall in proximity for fertilization to occur. If they are close together the sperm can swim to the archegonia in a film of water. Fertilization is achieved in the same way as that described for the general life cycle.

ABNORMALITIES IN THE LIFE CYCLE

The life cycles discussed above are outlines of the processes which normally occur when ferns and fern allies reproduce. Departures from the normal, however, are to be expected and a couple of abnormal processes have been shown to be widespread over a whole range of ferns and are particularly common in some groups.

Apogamy

In a number of ferns an interesting form of reproduction occurs whereby the sexual fusion of cells is by-passed and the sporophyte arises directly from vegetative buds formed on the cushion of the prothallus. This is, in effect, a form of vegetative reproduction. Although the fern produces apparently normal spores these in fact contain the same number of chromosomes as the sporophyte (not half the

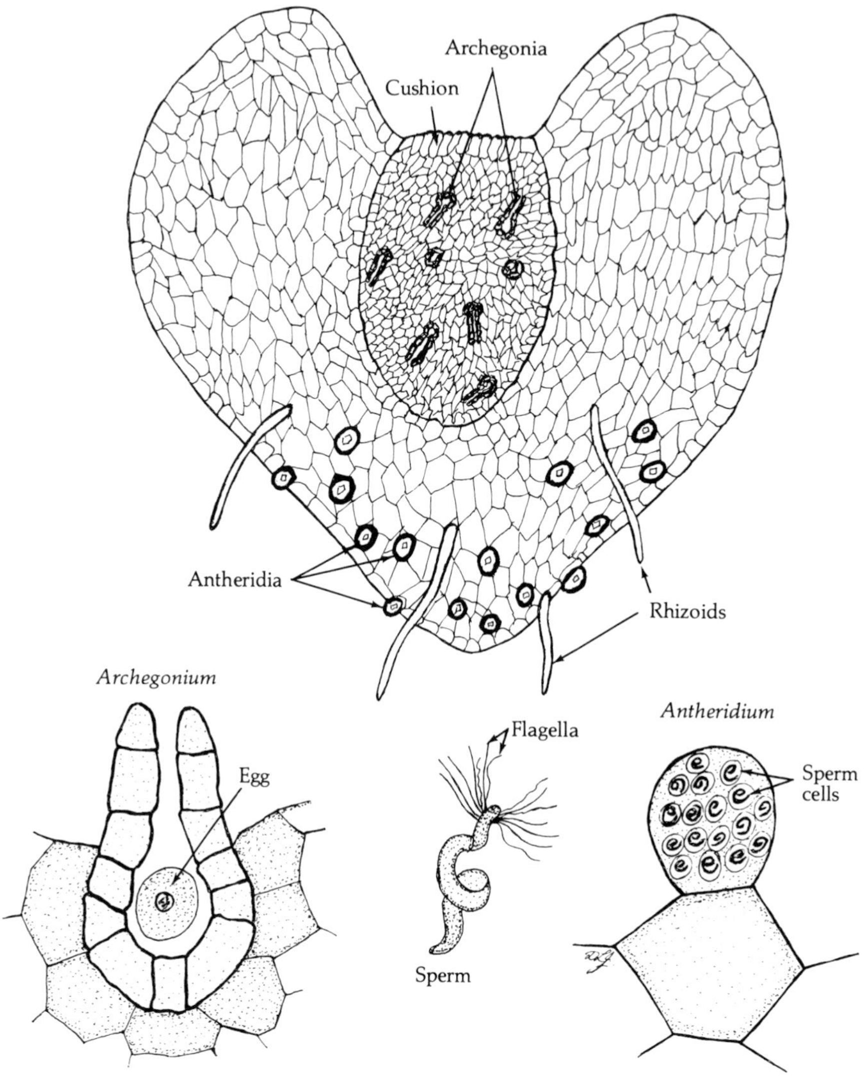

Fern prothallus and sex organs

number as in a normal species which undergoes the process of meiosis). Thus the prothallus itself gives rise to the sporophyte by simple budding.

The process of apogamy is now known to be very widespread among ferns and is common in many genera. Cultivated species which frequently reproduce by this method include *Cyrtomium falcatum* and *Pteris cretica* and cultivars of *Athyrium filix femina, Phyllitis scolopendrium* and *Polystichum setiferum*.

Apogamy has been shown to be common in many ferns which grow in dry habitats such as species of *Cheilanthes* and *Notholaena*. By this technique of reproduction they bypass the need for free water during fertilization and are therefore better adapted to the arid environment.

Apogamy is of great importance to the fern botanist because it can result in the proliferation of forms which have unusual chromosome numbers, e.g. haploids, or even sterile hybrids, e.g. triploids. Thus it is a technique by which unusual forms of a fern can regenerate and become established in the wild. By studying variations in natural populations, germinating spore samples and relating these to chromosome counts, the botanist can determine if apogamy is involved in variation within any species. For example, the accidental doubling of chromosomes may be perpetuated by apogamy and the resultant plants will have a different appearance to the original. Triploids are plants with three times the normal complement of chromosomes and usually arise from hybridization.

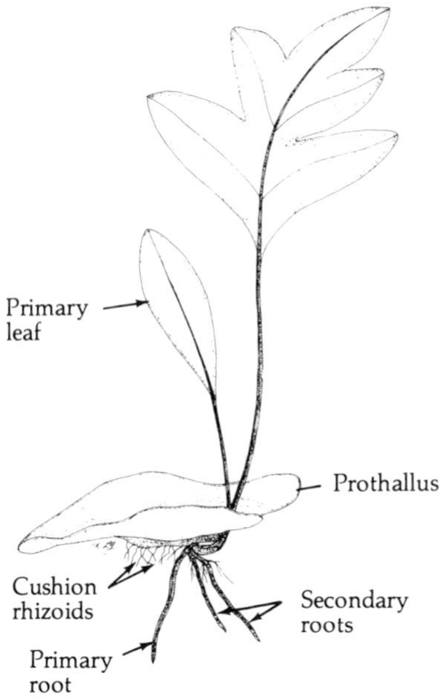

Fern sporeling

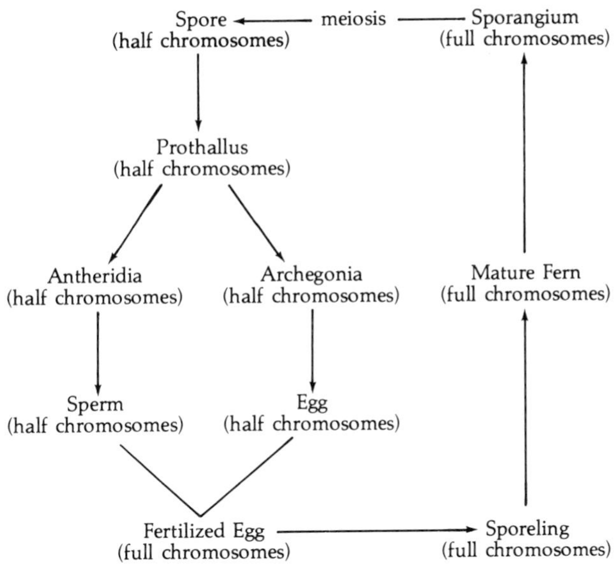

Scheme of Life-cycle of a Fern

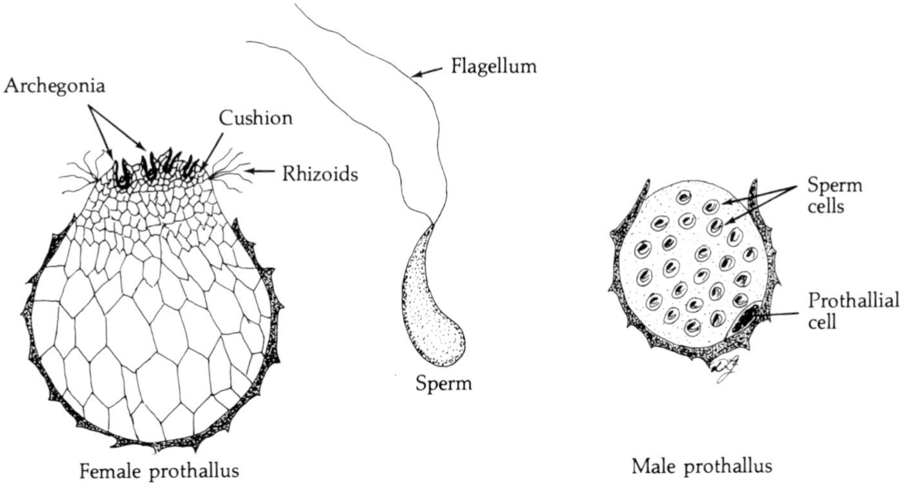

Prothalli of *Selaginella*

Such plants are sterile but if an apogamous system of reproduction occurs a whole population of triploids may become established in an area.

Apospory

This is a form of vegetative reproduction whereby spores are eliminated entirely from the reproductive process. It occurs when a prothallus grows directly from a frond of the sporophyte. In most cases the prothallus replaces sporangia and arises directly from the sorus but examples are known where the prothallus can grow as a continuation of the tip of the frond. These aposporous prothalli can give rise to antheridia and archegonia in the normal fashion although in some instances apogamy can occur, further complicating an unusual situation.

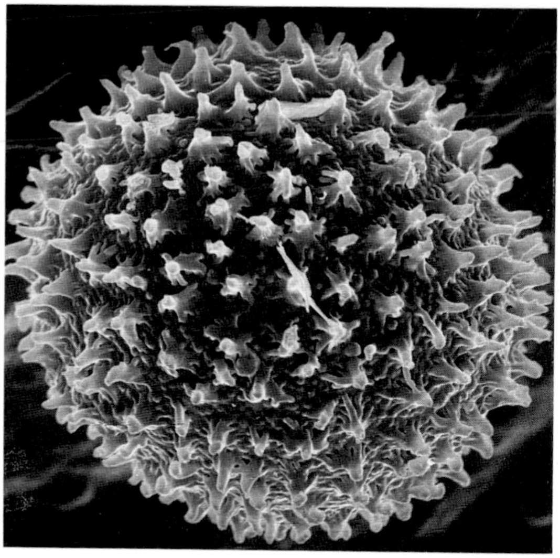

Cheilanthes distans, × 1670

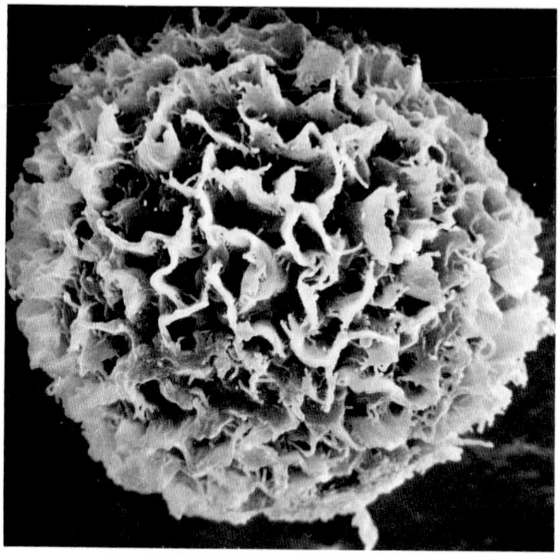

Cheilanthes austrotenuifolia, × 7245

Spores produced as the result of apogamy – note the general round shape

Photos Prof. T. C. Chambers

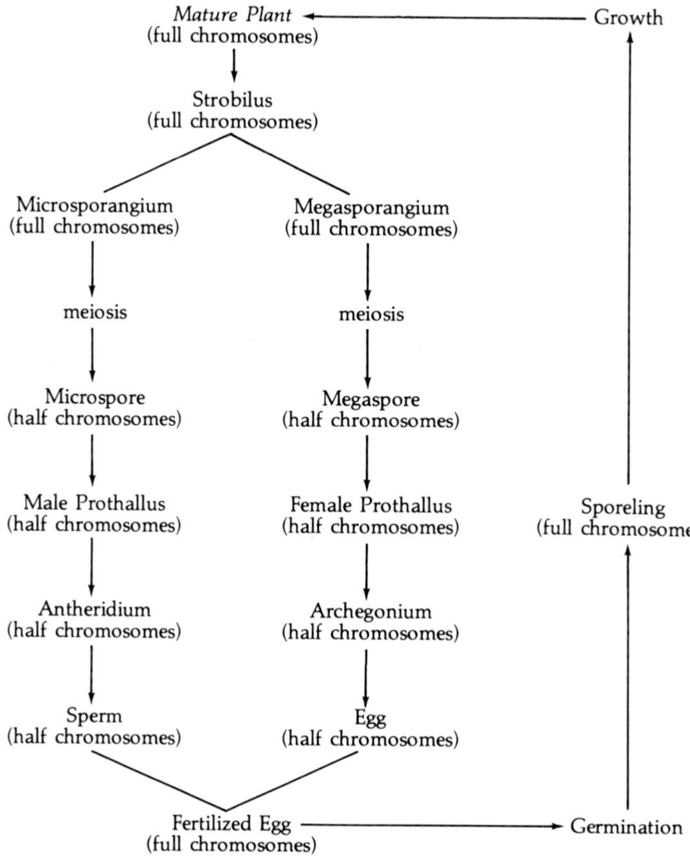

Scheme of Life-cycle of *Selaginella*

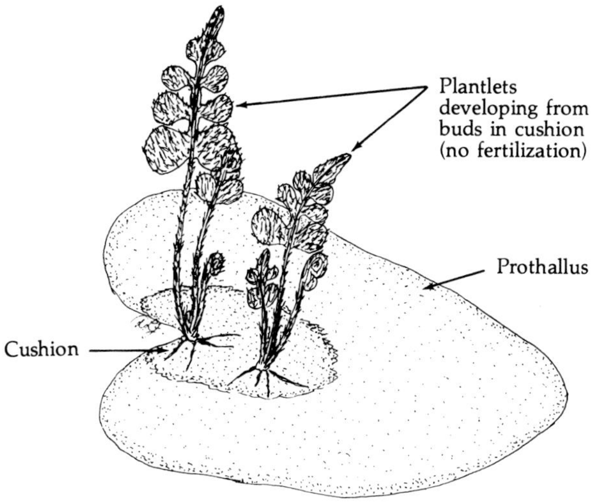
Plantlets
developing from
buds in cushion
(no fertilization)
Prothallus
Cushion

Apogamy

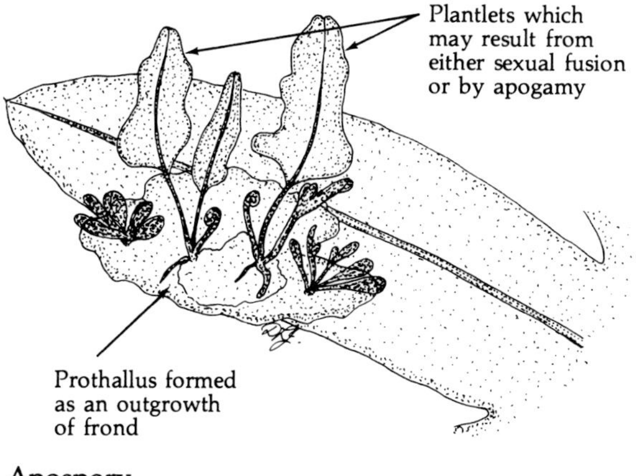
Plantlets which
may result from
either sexual fusion
or by apogamy
Prothallus formed
as an outgrowth
of frond

Apospory

5 The fern allies: their classification, structure and life cycle

The fern allies are a polymorphic group of plants with obvious relationships to the true ferns but with important structural differences. They do not possess a distinctive frond but their leaves are small (microphylls) or linear (*Isoetes*), with a single vein and are arranged along simple or branched stems. The fern allies reproduce by spores which are produced from sporangia, however the sporangia are borne in the axils or on the apices of specialized sporophylls, not on the lower surface of leaves as in the ferns. The sporophylls of fern allies may be scattered along apparently unspecialized stems or crowded into specialized cones termed strobili. Spores may be of one type (homosporous) or of two types (heterosporous), the spores being termed megaspores and microspores. In *Psilotum* and *Tmesipteris* the spores are borne in specialized structures formed by the fusion of two or more sporangia (termed syngania).

Classification

A classification of the surviving fern allies is shown in Table 3. Features of the fern allies are summarized in Table 4.

Structure and Life Cycle

The following text provides some details of the various orders of the fern allies together with the structure and life cycle of relevant examples.

ORDER PSILOTALES

This order comprises two genera (*Psilotum* and *Tmesipteris*) in the solitary family Psilotaceae. They have traditionally been regarded as a very primitive group of fern allies, however, recent work challenges

TABLE 3
Classification of the Fern Allies

Class	*Order*	*Family*	*Genus*	*Common name*
Psilotopsida	Psilotales	Psilotaceae	*Psilotum*	Fork-ferns
Psilotopsida	Psilotales	Tmesipteridaceae	*Tmesipteris*	Fork-ferns
Lycopsida	Lycopodiales	Lycopodiaceae	*Lycopodium, Phylloglossum*	Clubmosses and Tassel Ferns
Lycopsida	Selaginellales	Selaginellaceae	*Selaginella*	Clubmosses or Spikemosses
Lycopsida	Isoetales	Isoetaceae	*Isoetes, Stylites*	Quillworts
Equisetopsida	Equisetales	Equisetaceae	*Equisetum*	Horsetails or Whisk Ferns

TABLE 4
Significant Features of the Fern Allies

Feature	*Psilotum*	*Tmesipteris*	*Lycopodium*	*Phylloglossum*	*Selaginella*	*Isoetes*	*Equisetum*
Leaf Type	scale-leaf or absent	cladode or phyllode	microphyll	linear	microphyll plus ligule	linear phyllode plus ligule	scale leaf
Leaf Arrangement	scattered	spiral	spiral or rows	spiral	spiral or rows	compressed spiral	whorls
Sporangial Arrangement	synganium	synganium	strobilus or scattered	strobilus	strobilus or scattered	in swollen leaf base	strobilus
Heterosporous	no	no	no	no	yes	yes	no
Homosporous	yes	yes	yes	yes	no	no	yes

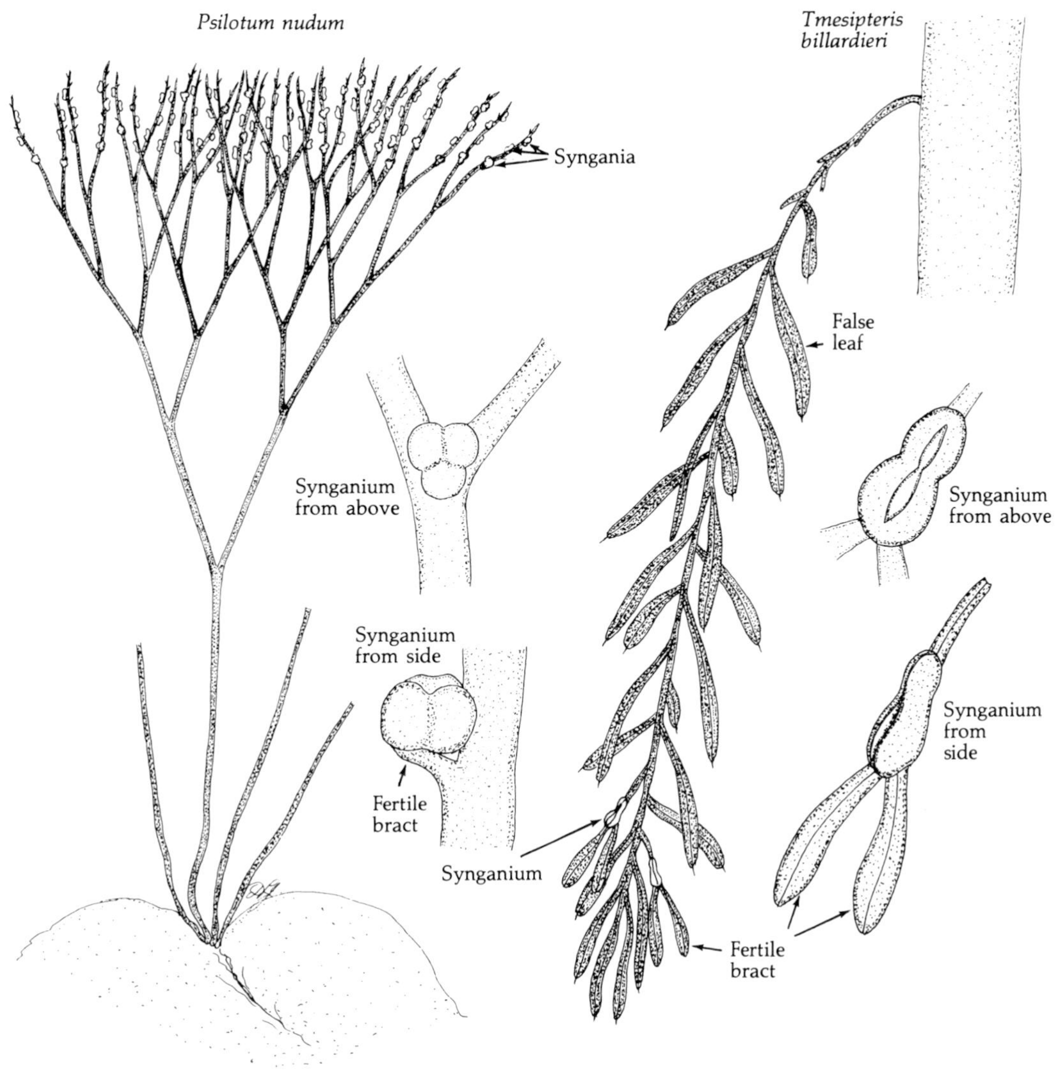

Plant structures of *Psilotaceae*

this view. Studies of their leaf development, gametophytes, chemistry and aspects of their reproduction have revealed many similarities with true ferns. The approach of some modern workers is to include the Psilotaceae in a primitive subclass with the true ferns (e.g. Tryon 1982).

Plant Structure

Whatever their classification, they are nevertheless interesting plants. All species lack roots and rely entirely for water and nutrient uptake on a simple buried stem covered with rhizoids. The aerial stems arise directly from the buried stem with little differentiation of internal organs, but with considerable structural modifications. A comparison of the structure of the two genera will show how closely related they are and also how they differ.

In *Psilotum*, the buried stem is crowded and much-branched but in *Tmesipteris* the stem is fleshy and creeps through the substrate supporting it. Thus, the aerial stems of *Psilotum* are clustered while those of *Tmesipteris* are borne at intervals. In *Psilotum* the stems are flattened or angular, are photosynthetic, and the leaves are reduced to scale-like structures or are completely absent. In *Tmesipteris* the angular or rounded stems are not photosynthetic and the leaves are replaced by flattened, leaf-like processes which are photosynthetic. These are disposed along the stems in a spiral manner. The aerial stems of *Psilotum* fork repeatedly but the stems of *Tmesipteris* are simple and fork rarely. The sporophylls or fertile bracts are bifurcated and in *Psilotum* are reduced and scale-like: in *Tmesipteris* they resemble the leaf processes. In both genera the sporangia are united into a specialized structure known as a synganium. In *Psilotum* this is usually trilocular and the loculi are rounded: in *Tmesipteris* most are bilocular and the compartments are elongated.

Life Cycle

The spores of both genera germinate in the dark, i.e. when buried in soil or in the fibres of a tree-fern trunk etc. The prothallus becomes infected with an endophytic fungus (mycorrhizal symbiotic association) at about the three-cell stage of development. The prothallus develops to become a tubular, colourless structure with numerous rhizoids all over its surface. Antheridia and archegonia develop over the whole surface of the prothallus. Motile multiflagellate sperms produced by the antheridia swim to the archegonia and effect fertilization. The sporophyte which develops is a colourless, leafless, rootless structure which is tubular and has numerous rhizoids growing from all over its surface. This structure grows to the surface of the soil or trunk and produces a small, weak shoot which is photosynthetic. Eventually, new shoots are

A clump of the primitive fern ally *Tmesipteris tannensis*, Lord Howe Island Photo D. L. Jones

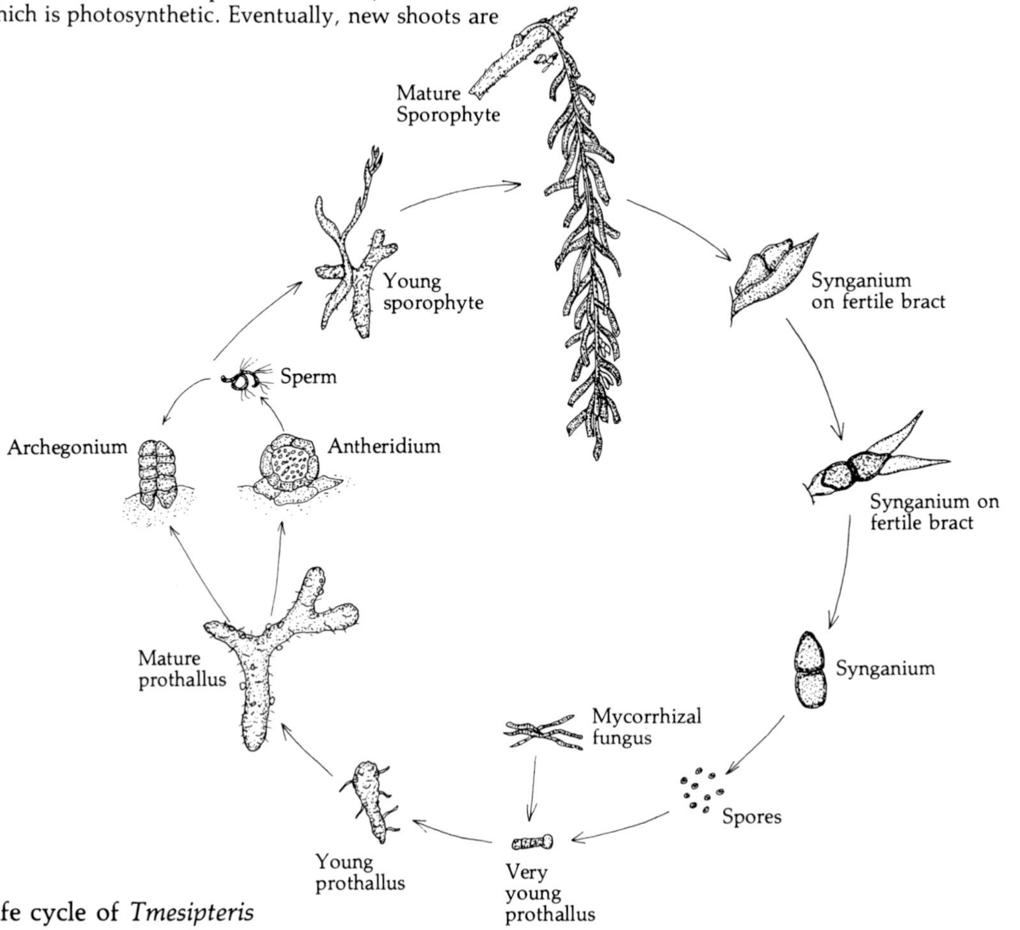

Life cycle of *Tmesipteris*

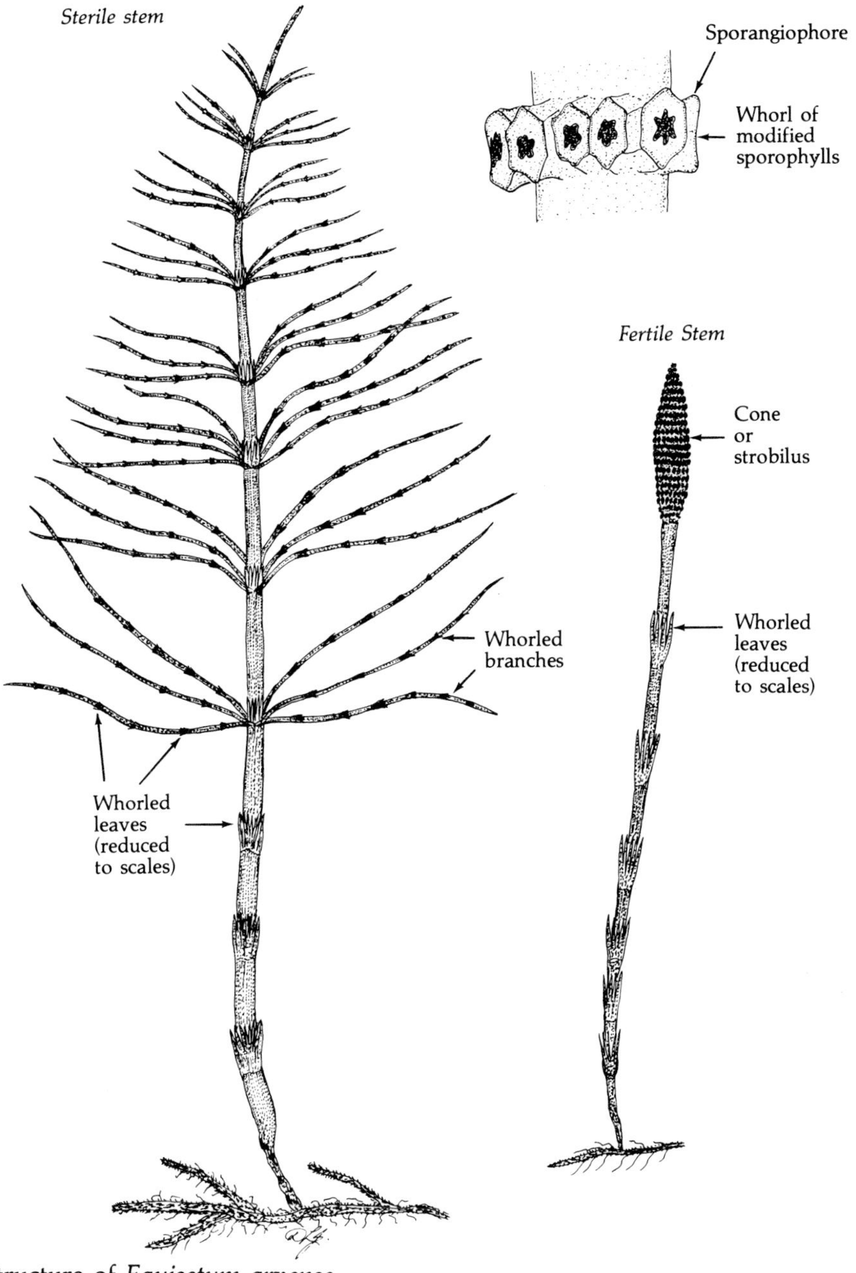

Plant structure of *Equisetum arvense*

produced and the sporophyte becomes established. This process is sexual. In its young stages the sporophyte can also produce small bulbils and gemmae which are a form of vegetative reproduction.

ORDER EQUISETALES

This order comprises the single genus *Equisetum* (the Horsetails or Whisk Ferns) in the family Equisetaceae. Today, although they are a common component of some vegetation types in various parts of the world, the Horsetails are a mere fraction of the numbers that existed in eons past. They were particularly well developed in the Carboniferous period, and together with their relatives contributed substantially to the coal reserves laid down during that time.

Introduction Structure and Botany

Plant Structure

The structure of a Horsetail plant is quite interesting. It has an underground rhizome which branches freely and bears numerous, wiry roots along its length. In some species, specialized lateral roots thicken into tuber-like structures which develop, break off from the parent and have the ability to grow as separate plants (e.g. *E. arvense*). The rhizome sends up aerial shoots at intervals along its length. These grow vertically and increase in length by the division of a single apical cell. These aerial stems are tubular and hollow except for a partition at each node. Thus they consist of nodes and internodes in a series of elongated joints. Small scale-like leaves, each with a single vein, are borne in whorls which sheath the stem. These protrude at the end of each whorl as small teeth. Slender lateral branches radiate in whorls from each node and give the plant a characteristic appearance. They do not arise in the leaf axils but alternate with them. The stems and branches are green and capable of photosynthesis. Usually the stems are hard and covered with siliceous deposits.

The aerial stems may be sterile or fertile. In some species specialized fertile stems may be of a different structure and arise at different times of the year to the sterile stems. Spores are produced in specially modified sporophylls which are massed together in a cylindrical cone or strobilus. These cones terminate the main aerial stem and in some species the lateral stems as well. Each sporophyll (known as a sporangiophore) consists of a short stalk carried at right angles to the axis, ending in the centre of a flat, plate-like structure. On the lower surface of this flat structure, each sporangiophore bears 5–10 sporangia. The spores produced are all of one type and are green. They have an interesting modification in that each spore has four strap-like arms or elaters attached. These elaters are hygroscopic and move with variations in humidity and if wet, for example, by rain. These movements serve to tangle the elaters of adjacent spores so that when dispersed, they are shed in groups.

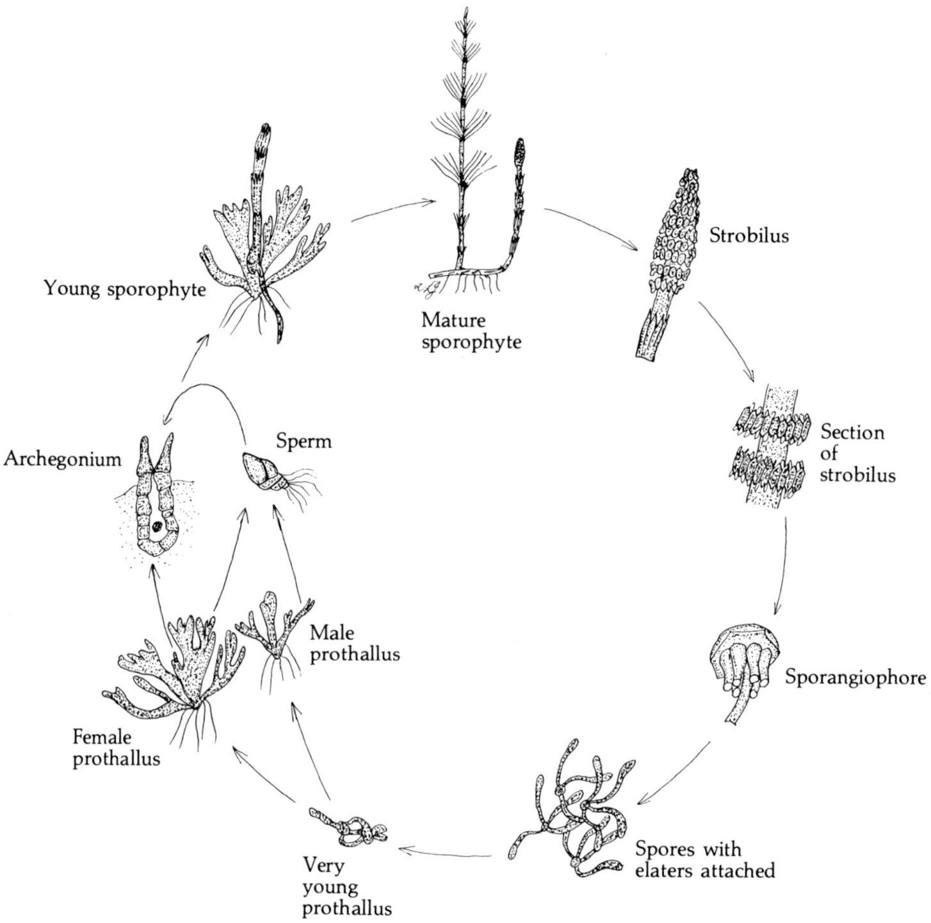

Life cycle of *Equisetum*

Psilotum nudum growing in a rock crevice
Photo D. L. Jones

Life Cycle

The spores of *Equisetum* contain chlorophyll and germinate in the presence of light on the surface of the soil. When the spores germinate they form an irregular, strap-shaped prothallus which is attached to the ground by rhizoids. Each prothallus is green, photosynthetic, and may develop lobes or branches. In some species the prothalli are bisexual, but in many others they are unisexual. Bisexual prothalli bear the archegonia on the thick central portions; the antheridia are confined to the lobes. In unisexual prothalli, the females are large with many lobes and the males tend to be smaller and with few lobes. Motile multiflagellate sperm produced by the antheridia swim to the archegonia and effect fertilization. The sporophyte develops as a single small green shoot. This is succeeded by an accessory shoot which develops from the base of the first shoot and grows bigger than it. The plant develops through a succession of such shoots until it attains maturity.

ORDER LYCOPODIALES

This order comprises two genera (*Lycopodium* and *Phylloglossum*) in the family Lycopodiaceae. *Lycopodium* consists of about 250 species but *Phylloglossum* is monotypic. Some workers split *Lycopodium* into many genera. Although *Lycopodium* is well represented today, there is evidence to suggest that the genus was of greater prominence in times past.

Plant Structure

Most species of *Lycopodium* grow as terrestrials in the ground, however, a significant number occur as epiphytes on trees or rocks; these are popularly known as Tassel Ferns. All species have wiry roots which may be attached directly to aerial stems or arise from specialized subterranean stems. Aerial stems may be erect, pendulous or climbing, and entire or branched. Branching may be by simple forking at the tips or by lateral shoots.

Lycopodiums as a group have simple leaves, termed microphylls, which may be borne in whorls or in a spiral pattern on the stem. The sporangia are greatly modified and consist of a simple kidney-shaped sac which contains the spores, all of which are a single type. Each sporangium is borne singly and is subtended by a special leaf termed a sporophyll. The sporophylls may be borne on non-specialized parts of a stem or grouped in cones or tassels termed strobili. These cones may be simple or dichotomously branched.

Lycopodiums are variable in some features of their morphology and structure and have been grouped into three subgenera (viz. *Cernuistachys*, *Lycopodium* and *Selago*). These groupings are based on such factors as the point of origin of the roots, the morphology of the sterile leaves in relation to the fertile leaves, the branching habit, and the shape and thickness of the cells in the wall of the sporangium. *Lycopodium* is a complex genus with a variety of features which seem to defy orderly grouping. The origin of the roots can be of interest. In most species they emerge directly from the stems, however, in all Tassel Ferns and in a few other terrestrial species of the subgenus *Selago* they descend through the cortex of the stem for some distance before emerging. The spores of *Lycopodium* are released from the sporangia by a central slit.

Phylloglossum drummondii is a tiny terrestrial with a basal group of linear leaves arranged in a spiral, and a short stalk bearing a terminal strobilus. A single type of spore is produced.

Life Cycle

The place of germination of the spores of *Lycopodium* varies. Spores of species in the subgenus *Cernuistachys* are short-lived and germinate on the surface of the soil in light, but for those in other subgenera, spores will only germinate in the dark. For these groups the spores are quite long-lived and lie without germinating until buried in the soil or litter. Prothallial and sporophytic development may be in one of three ways.

1. Subgenus *Cernuistachys* and *Phylloglossum drummondii*

In this group the spores germinate on the soil surface to form a prothallus which is partially green and partially infected by mycorrhizal fungi. The upper part of the prothallus is green (and thus photosynthetic) and develops leaf-like lobes. The lower part of the prothallus is conical, colourless and is buried in the

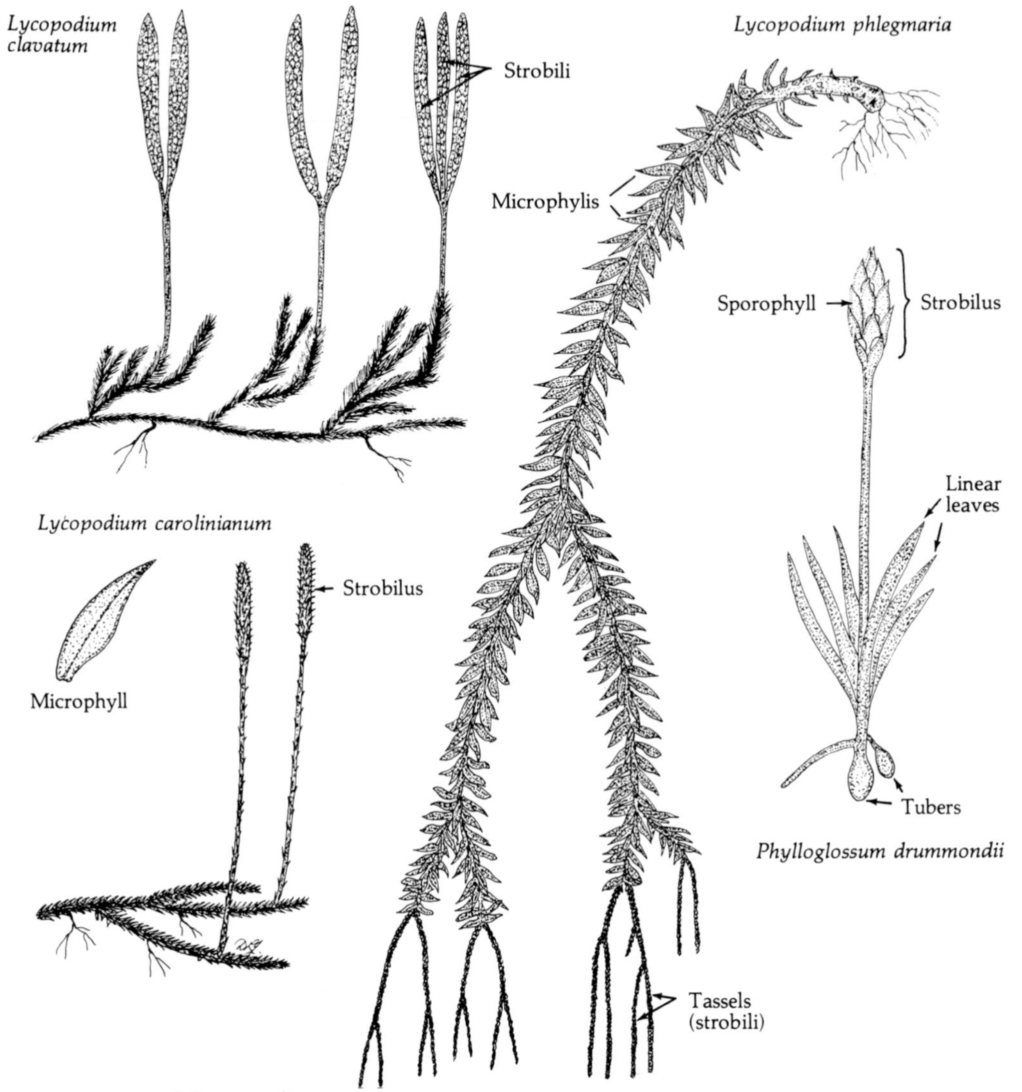

Plant structures of Lycopodiaceae

soil. This is the site for infection by mycorrhizal fungi. Antheridia and archegonia develop on, and between, the lobes on the surface part of the prothallus. Motile sperm swim from the antheridia to the archegonia and effect fertilization. The sporophyte initially develops as a small green shoot. Development in this group of Lycopodiums is rapid with the sporophyte emerging within twelve months of the spore germinating.

2. Subgenus *Lycopodium*

In this group the spores only germinate in the absence of light and they live in a dormant state until buried. They then germinate to form a massive, subterranean prothallus which is colourless and becomes infected by mycorrhizal fungi. They can be erect in the soil and have no leaf-like lobes. The formation of sexual organs may take a long time (10–15 years) and in the meantime the prothallus continues development with the aid of the mycorrhizal fungi. When fertilization is finally completed, the sporophyte may form a haustorial-like structure and be parasitical on the prothallus until it becomes self-sufficient. Some species such as *L. laterale* form small swollen bodies near the soil surface and these are both photosynthetic and mycorrhizic. They continue a separate existence until leaves, stems and roots are sufficiently developed.

3. Subgenus *Selago* (including epiphytic tassel ferns)

In this group the spores will only germinate in the dark and they lie dormant until they are washed into a crevice or buried by litter and humus. They germinate to form an attenuated, repeatedly-branched prothallus which is colourless and relies on mycorrhizal infection for nourishment. This prothallus is attached by numerous root hairs. As the prothallus grows forward and branches it also decays behind so that eventually the branches may become separate prothalli. The prothalli may also propagate by the formation of numerous gemmae. These are small pear-shaped bodies which arise from the surface cells of the prothallus. They separate readily and may germinate to form their own prothallus. In adverse conditions, thick-walled gemmae may be produced as survival structures. Archegonia and antheridia are borne on the upper side of enlarged branches of the prothallus. After fertilization, the sporophyte develops roots and a small green shoot bearing a couple of small leaves. Development continues until the plant is independent.

ORDER SELAGINELLALES

This order comprises the solitary genus *Selaginella* in the family Selaginellaceae. *Selaginella* is a world-wide genus of approximately 700 species. It has relatives in previous geological eras and has probably been a dominant plant family for millions of years.

Plant Structure

Selaginellas are generally small plants with a creeping or clumping growth habit. Most species are terrestrials but a few grow as epiphytes. The stems may be simple or branched and the roots usually arise at the point of branching. Branching is mainly lateral but in some species is by forking of the growth apex. Some species produce rhizophore-like structures which grow through the air for some distance before taking root. It has been established that these structures are in fact true roots and not rhizophores.

Selaginellas have simple, single-veined leaves termed microphylls. These may be borne spirally around the stem but are more usually borne in four ranks. Each leaf bears a small structure called a ligule, on the upper surface at its base. The sporangia are modified and consist of a simple, rounded sac. Two types of sporangia are borne – megasporangia and microsporangia. A megasporangium produces four large whitish spores known as megaspores; the microsporangium produces many small dust-like spores known as microspores. Each sporangium is borne separately and is subtended by a special leaf termed a sporophyll (i.e. megasporophyll and microsporophyll). The sporophylls are borne in a specialized cone termed a strobilus. The sporangia are arranged in each strobilus so that the microsporangia are borne in the upper part and the megasporangia in the lower part.

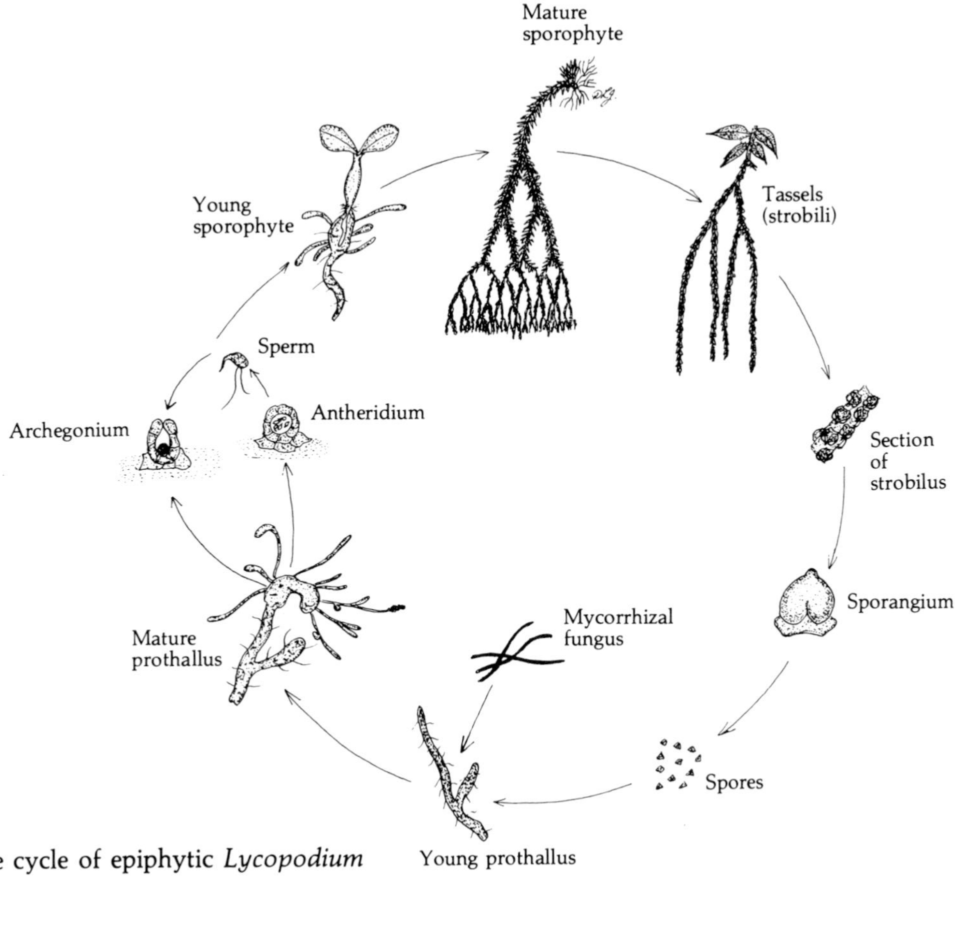

Life cycle of epiphytic *Lycopodium*

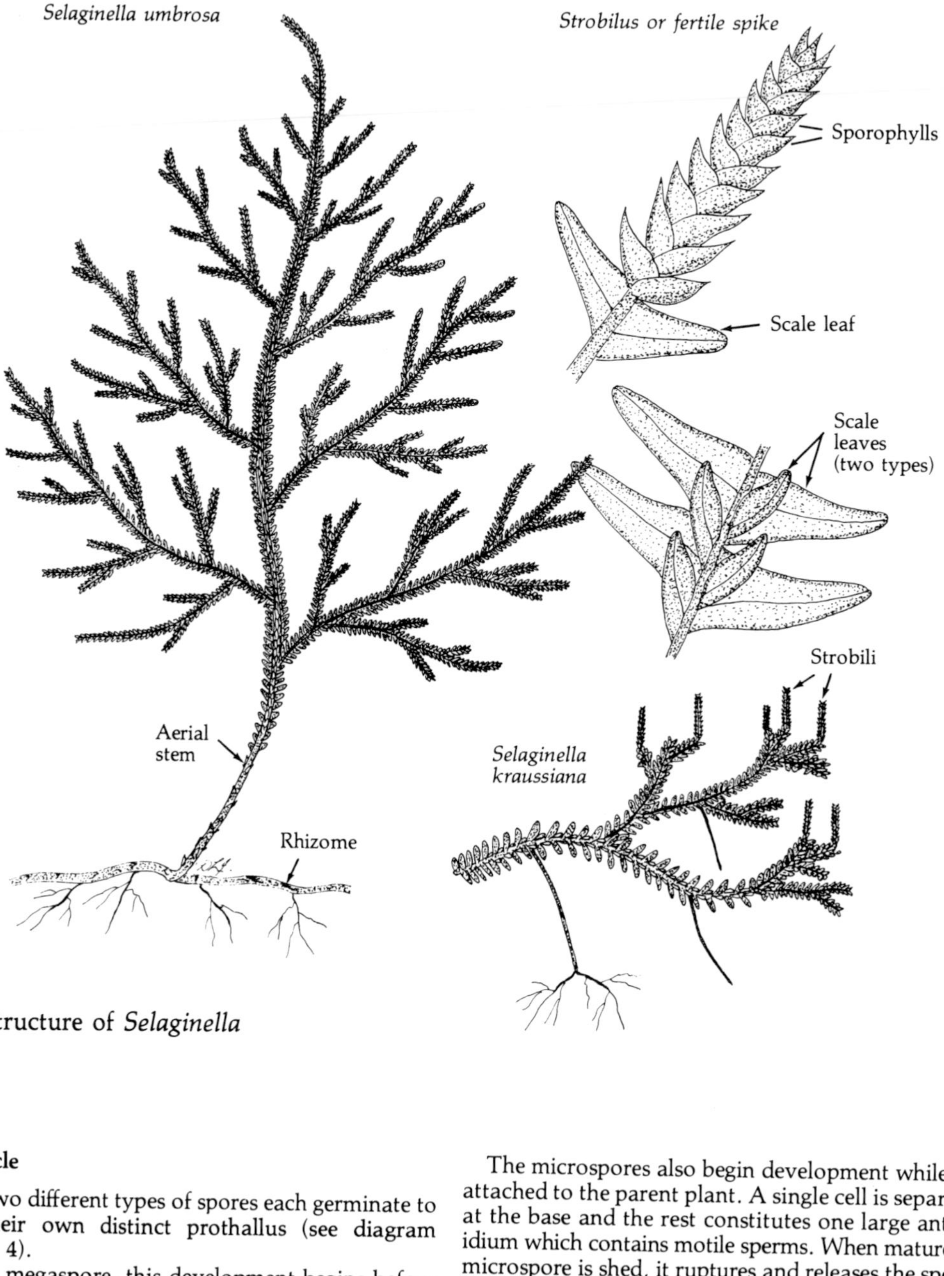

Plant structure of *Selaginella*

Life Cycle

The two different types of spores each germinate to form their own distinct prothallus (see diagram Chapter 4).

In the megaspore, this development begins before it is shed from the plant. Cell division occurs within the spore and nutrient reserves are accumulated in the lower portion. When the megaspore is shed onto the soil it splits at the apex because of the pressure induced by cell division and expansion. This split reveals a small, green prothallus developed in the surface tissue, and contains the female archegonia. At this stage of development, the prothallus is supported mainly by the storage products from the sporophyte which are stored in the basal cells.

The microspores also begin development while still attached to the parent plant. A single cell is separated at the base and the rest constitutes one large antheridium which contains motile sperms. When mature the microspore is shed, it ruptures and releases the sperms which swim to the archegonia (which are on the megaspore) and effect fertilization. The sporophyte develops as a tiny, slender plant bearing a few leaves.

ORDER ISOETALES

This order comprises the single genus *Isoetes* (Quillworts) in the family Isoetaceae (some workers also separate the genus *Stylites*). *Isoetes* consists of about 150 species scattered around the world. There are fossil

Schizaea bifida showing sorophores Photo D. L. Jones

Sterile and fertile fronds of *Helminthostachys zeylanica* Photo D. L. Jones

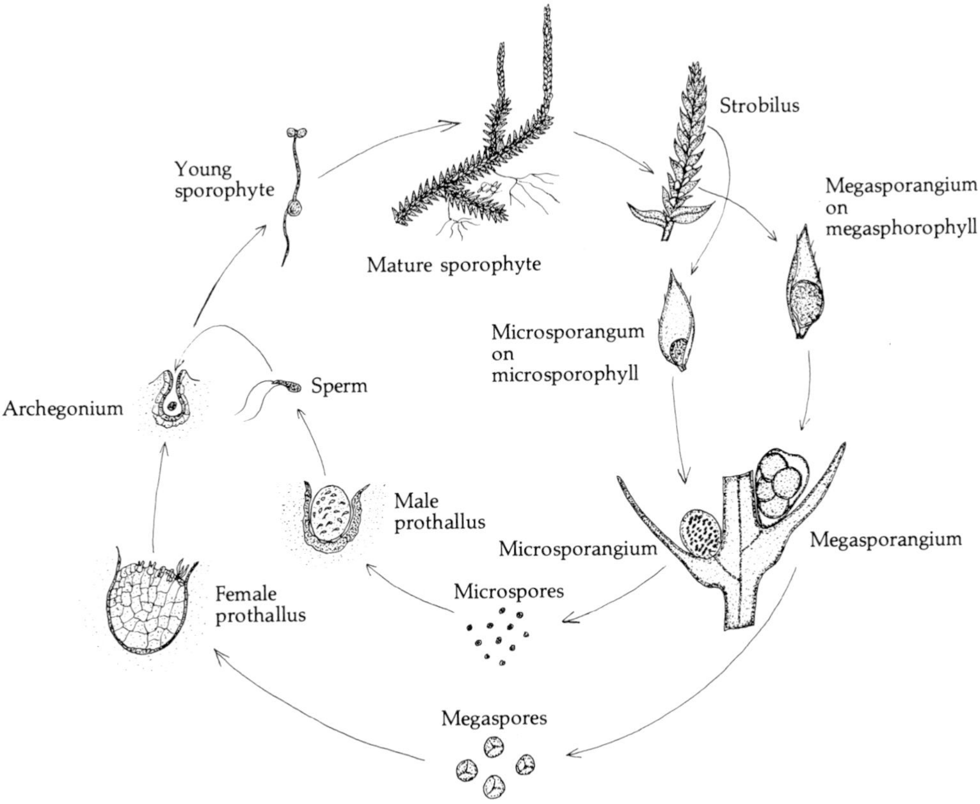

Life cycle of *Selaginella*

records of *Isoetes* or their relatives extending back to the Triassic period.

Plant Structure

Species of *Isoetes* are grass-like herbs which may be annuals or perennials. They commonly grow around the margins of swamps and lakes, or in low lying areas subject to periodic inundation. A few species are aquatics.

The stem of Quillworts is reduced to an expanded fleshy structure (known as a corm) which increases in thickness as the plants grow. The roots of Quillworts

The herbaceous *Ophioglossum nudicaule* showing sterile and fertile fronds Photo D. L. Jones

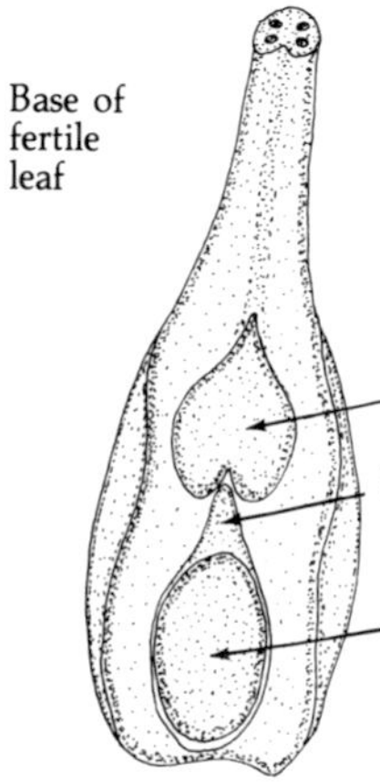

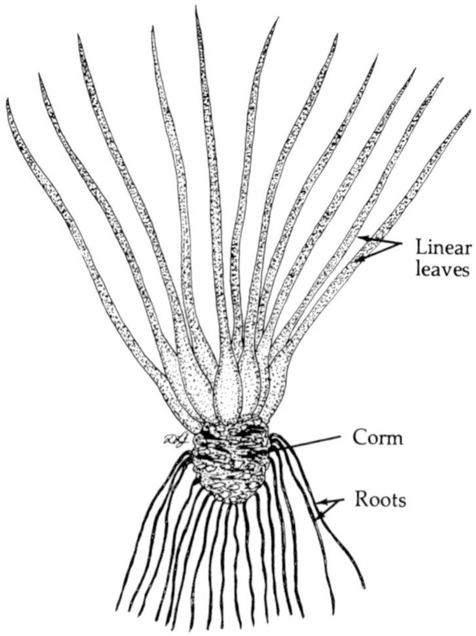

Plant structure of *Isoetes*

A colony of *Grammitis diminuta*, Lord Howe Island Photo D. L. Jones

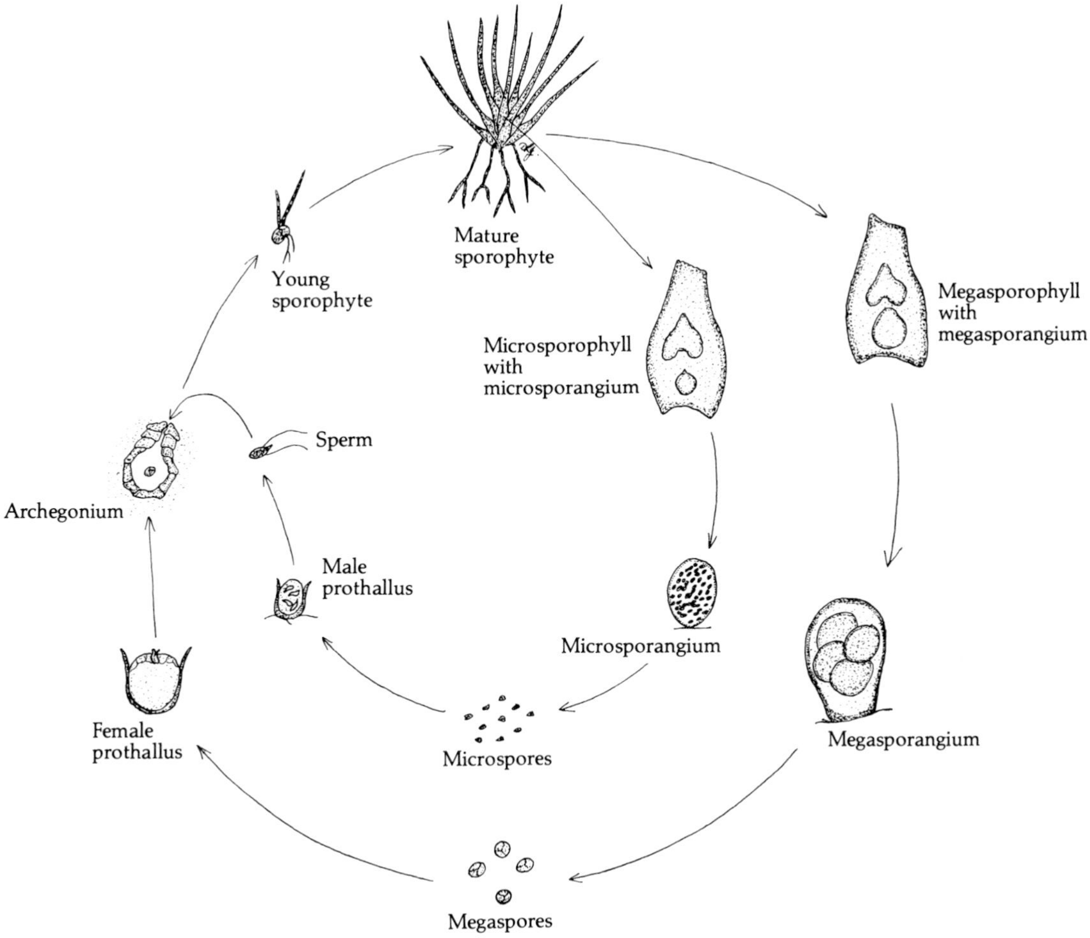

Life cycle of *Isoetes*

branch freely in a dichotomous manner. Leaves are simple and filiform (or quill-like). In most species they are arranged spirally on the stem with each leaf expanding at the base and bearing a small ligule above a sunken pit (the fovea). The fovea is the site where sporangia are borne. The inner leaves of each plant are normally sterile and the central ones bear microsporangia at the base. Each of the outer leaves usually bears a megasporangium at its base. This arrangement is variable depending on the species and may also change with seasonal growing conditions.

Life Cycle

The megaspore develops while still attached to the plant, takes in nutrients and undergoes limited cell division. It is shed after limited development and ruptures to expose a small prothallus bearing one to a few archegonia. The microspore also undergoes some development while on the plant and when it ruptures it exposes a very small prothallus containing a single antheridium which released four flagellate, motile sperm. These swim to the megaspore and effect fertilization. The sporophyte initially expands as a small leaf-like structure which eventually develops leaves and roots.

6 The ferns: their classification, structure and life cycle

The ferns are a very large, complex group of plants which number more than 10,000 individual species. They can be separated from the fern allies by the development of complex leaves (fronds), which contain a much-branched vascular system (veins). Reproduction is by spores produced in sporangia. For the majority of the ferns the sporangia are produced on the underside of the fronds, however, in the order Ophioglossales and family Schizaeceae, the fronds may bear a separate fertile section. In most species of ferns there is some organization in the arrangement of sporangia such as grouping into sori. Spores are mostly of one type but the water ferns of the families Marsiliaceae and Salviniaceae are heterosporous producing microspores and megaspores. In the primitive family Marattiaceae the spores may be produced in solitary sporangia or from fused structures known as syngania.

Classification

There is considerable controversy about the classification of the ferns and no less than fourteen different classifications have been proposed over the last 100 years. One classification system is presented in Table 5.

The ferns make up the class Filicopsida, and most workers agree that this class can be further subdivided into three orders (Ophioglossales, Marattiales and Filicales [or Polypodiales]). The first two orders are quite small and contain primitive ferns, whereas the Filicales contains the vast majority of species which are a very complex array of form and structure. The classification within the Filicales is also subject to much discussion and variation by researchers.

An old but useful classification of the Filicales is to divide them into two subclasses depending on the origin and structure of the sporangia. The two groups are Eusporangiatae and Leptosporangiatae, or as they are more commonly referred to, the eusporangiate and the leptosporangiate ferns. The eusporangiate ferns have a multi-layer of cells in the sporangial wall and these are derived from more than one leaf cell. The leptosporangiate ferns, on the other hand, have a single layer of cells in the sporangial wall and arise from a single cell in the leaf epidermis. These contain a fixed number of spores. Although useful, this division of the true ferns corresponds closely with the above classification since the orders Ophioglossales and Marattiales comprise the subclass Eusporangiatae, while the Leptosporangiatae consists of the Filicales (see Table 5).

TABLE 5
A Classification of the Ferns (class Filicopsida)

Order	*Family*	*Example of Genera Included*
Ophioglossales	Ophioglossaceae	*Ophioglossum, Botrychium, Helminthostachys*
Marattiales	Marattiaceae	*Marattia, Angiopteris, Danaea*
Osmundales	Osmundaceae	*Osmunda, Todea, Leptopteris*
Plagiogyrales	Plagiogyriaceae	*Plagiogyria*
Stromatopteridales	Stromatopteridaceae	*Stromatopteris*
Gleicheniales	Gleicheniaceae	*Gleichenia, Sticherus, Dicranopteris*

Order	Family	Genera
Polypodiales	Grammitidaceae	*Grammitis, Ctenopteris*
	Polypodiaceae	*Polypodium, Platycerium, Microsorum*
	Cheiropleuriaceae	*Cheiropleuria*
	Dipteridaceae	*Dipteris*
Matoniales	Matoniaceae	*Matonia, Phanerosorus*
Schizaeales	Schizaeaceae	*Schizaea, Anemia, Lygodium*
Pteridales	Negripteridaceae	*Negripteris*
	Sinopteridaceae	*Cheilanthes, Doryopteris, Pellaea*
	Cryptogrammataceae	*Cryptogramma, Llavea, Onychium*
	Pteridaceae	*Pteris, Acrostichum*
	Adiantaceae	*Adiantum*
	Hemionitidaceae	*Hemionitis, Conigramme, Pityrogramma*
	Vittariaceae	*Vittaria, Antrophyum*
	Parkeriaceae	*Ceratopteris*
Platyzomatales	Platyzomataceae	*Platyzoma*
Marsiliales	Marsileaceae	*Marsilea, Pilularia, Regnellidium*
Hymenophyllales	Hymenophyllaceae	*Hymenophyllum, Trichomanes*
Hymenophyllopsidales	Hymenophyllopsidaceae	*Hymenophyllopsis*
Loxsomales	Loxsomaceae	*Loxsoma*
Dicksoniales	Thyrsopteridaceae	*Thyrsopteris*
	Dicksoniaceae	*Dicksonia, Culcita*
	Cyatheaceae	*Cyathea*
Dennstaedtiales	Dennstaedtiaceae	*Dennstaedtia, Hypolepis, Histiopteris*
	Lindsaeaceae	*Lindsaea, Odontoloma*
	Thelypteridaceae	*Thelypteris, Cyclosorus, Goniopteris*
Aspidiales	Aspleniaceae	*Asplenium, Pleurosorus*
	Dryopteridaceae	*Dryopteris, Polystichum, Lastreopsis*
	Lomariopsidaceae	*Lomariopsis, Bolbitis, Elaphoglossum*
	Oleandraceae	*Oleandra, Arthropteris, Nephrolepis*
	Davalliaceae	*Davallia, Humata, Davallodes*
Blechnales	Blechnaceae	*Blechnum, Doodia, Woodwardia*
Salviniales	Azollaceae	*Azolla*
	Salviniaceae	*Salvinia*

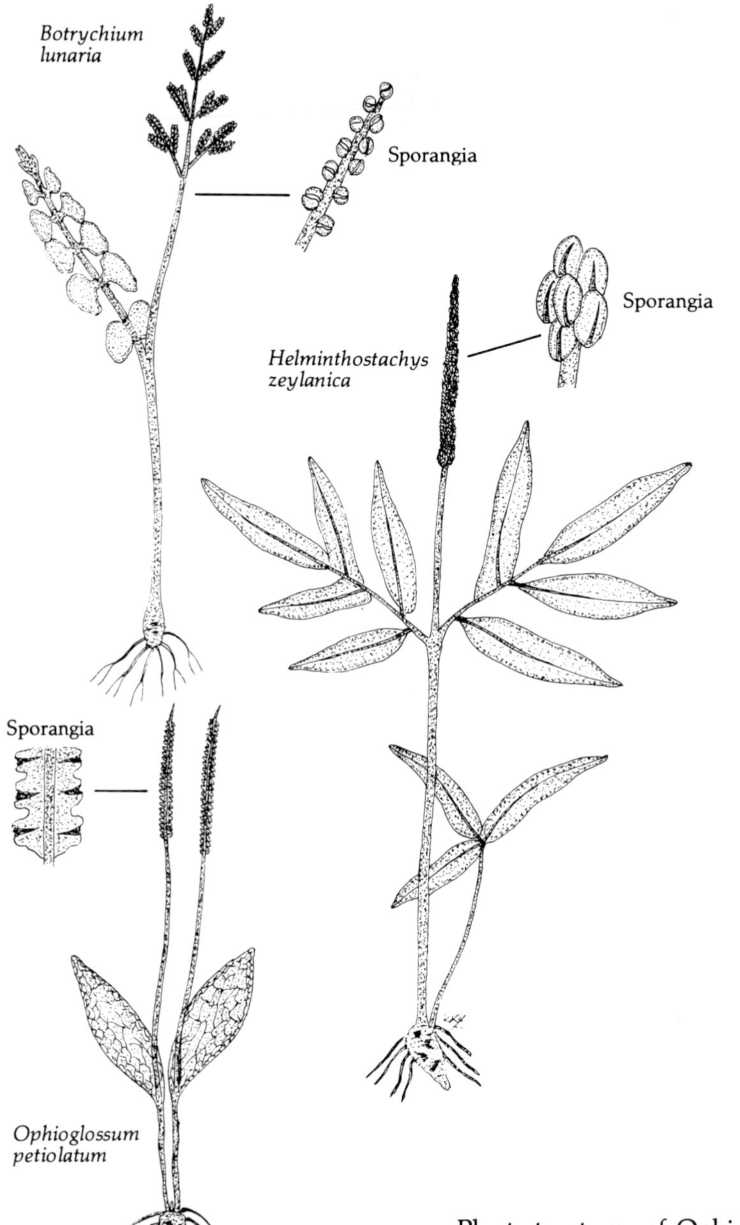

Plant structures of Ophioglossaceae

ORDER OPHIOGLOSSALES

This order comprises three genera (*Botrychium*, *Helminthostachys* and *Ophioglossum*) all placed in the family Ophioglossaceae. The family is an ancient one with links going back earlier than the Jurassic period.

Plant Structure

Ferns of this group have a fairly simple structure. The rhizome may be erect or creeping and bears fleshy roots. It is generally deeply buried in the soil and in most species gives rise to a solitary frond. Unlike most true ferns the fronds are not coiled when young. The frond may be completely sterile or may bear a fertile section. The sterile part may be simple, or divided, and is photosynthetic. The fertile part consists of a cylindrical spike or branched panicle bearing sporangia.

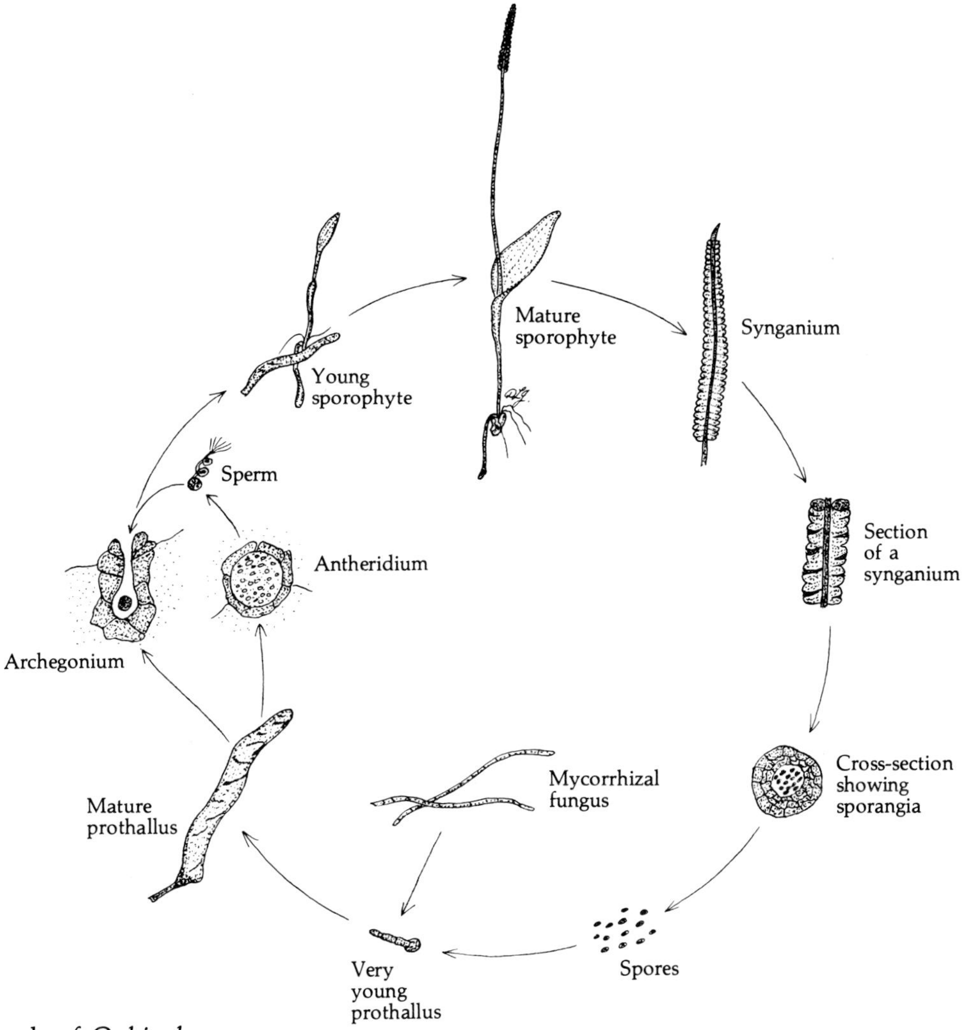

Life cycle of *Ophioglossum*

Life Cycle

Light acts as an inhibitor to the germination of the spores of the Ophioglossaceae, and they will only germinate in the dark. This means that in nature they must be covered with humus or washed into holes or cracks in the soil, or buried in some way. The spores germinate to form a slender prothallus which will not develop any further than a few cells, unless infected with mycorrhizal fungus. Once infected it develops into a cylindrical, colourless, subterranean prothallus which may persist in the soil for up to twenty years. The prothalli may be unisexual or bisexual. The sex organs are borne near the top of the cylindrical prothallus. After fertilization the sporophyte grows towards the soil surface. In these ferns the continued infection by mycorrhiza at all stages of development is essential for their successful growth.

ORDER MARATTIALES

This order comprises seven genera (*Angiopteris, Archangiopteris, Christensenia, Danaea, Macroglossum, Marattia* and *Protomarattia*), all in the family Marattiaceae. They are true ferns but are very primitive with links back to the Carboniferous period.

Plant Structure

The rhizome varies from an underground creeping structure to an erect, small trunk. In some species the trunk is greatly swollen and the roots are fleshy and arise in the leaf bases. Fronds are conspicuous, mostly pinnate, and may be massive – to over 8 m long in some species of *Angiopteris*. The stipe and rachis lack any strengthening tissue and are held erect by the turgor pressure of water in the cells. Thus the leaves

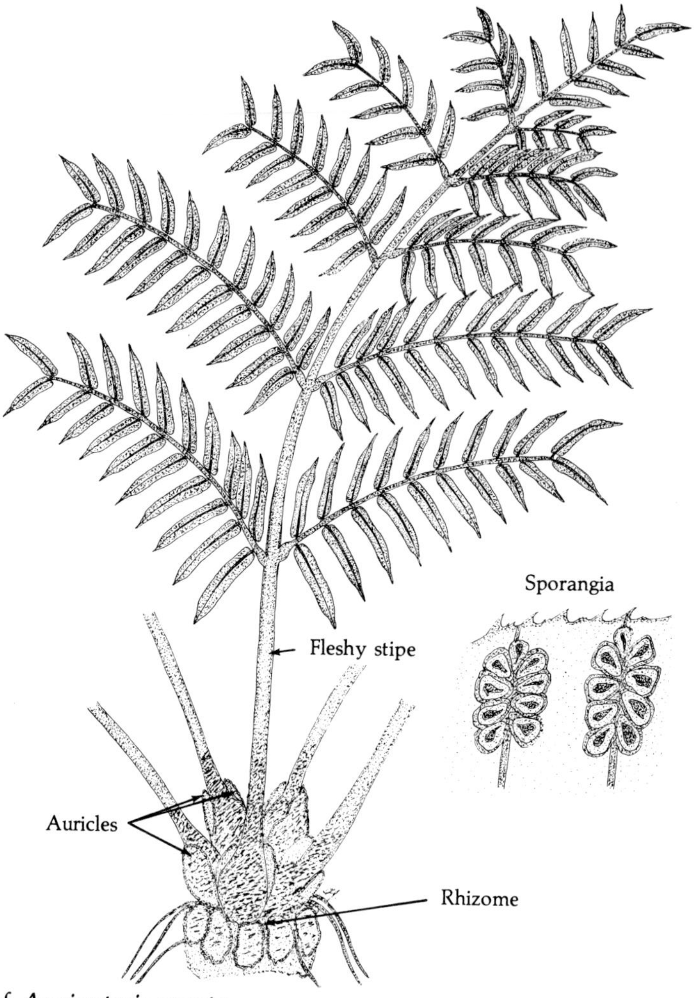

Plant structure of *Angiopteris evecta*

may sag when the plants are dry. The base of each stipe is surmounted by two ear-like structures (stipules or auricles), which in some species, persist on the trunk after the frond has died. In some species, e.g. *Angiopteris* these organs contain meristematic tissue and can act as a survival mechanism if the main meristem of the fern is destroyed. The undersurface of the fronds bears the sporangia which are grouped into sori (e.g. *Angiopteris*) or may be actually united into a structure known as a synganium.

Life Cycle

The spores germinate to form a relatively thick but flattened prothallus which branches to form a pinnate structure. The prothalli become infected with a mycorrhizal fungus and also develop chlorophyll and become photosynthetic. They are attached to the soil by rhizoids. Antheridia are borne on both the upper and lower surface; archegonia arise on the lower surface only (sometimes on a thickened pad). The motile sperm swim from the antheridia to the archegonia and effect fertilization. The young sporophyte develops a small, green, leaf-like structure and true roots. It has been shown that the act of fertilization inhibits further development of a prothallus. If, however, fertilization is not effected, the prothallus of Marattiaceae may live for up to six years and grow to over 5 cm in length. It has also been found that the prothallus of *Angiopteris* can continue development even if buried.

ORDER FILICALES

This order comprises the majority of true ferns and hence embraces an extraordinarily large, variable and complex group of plants. In size the ferns range from

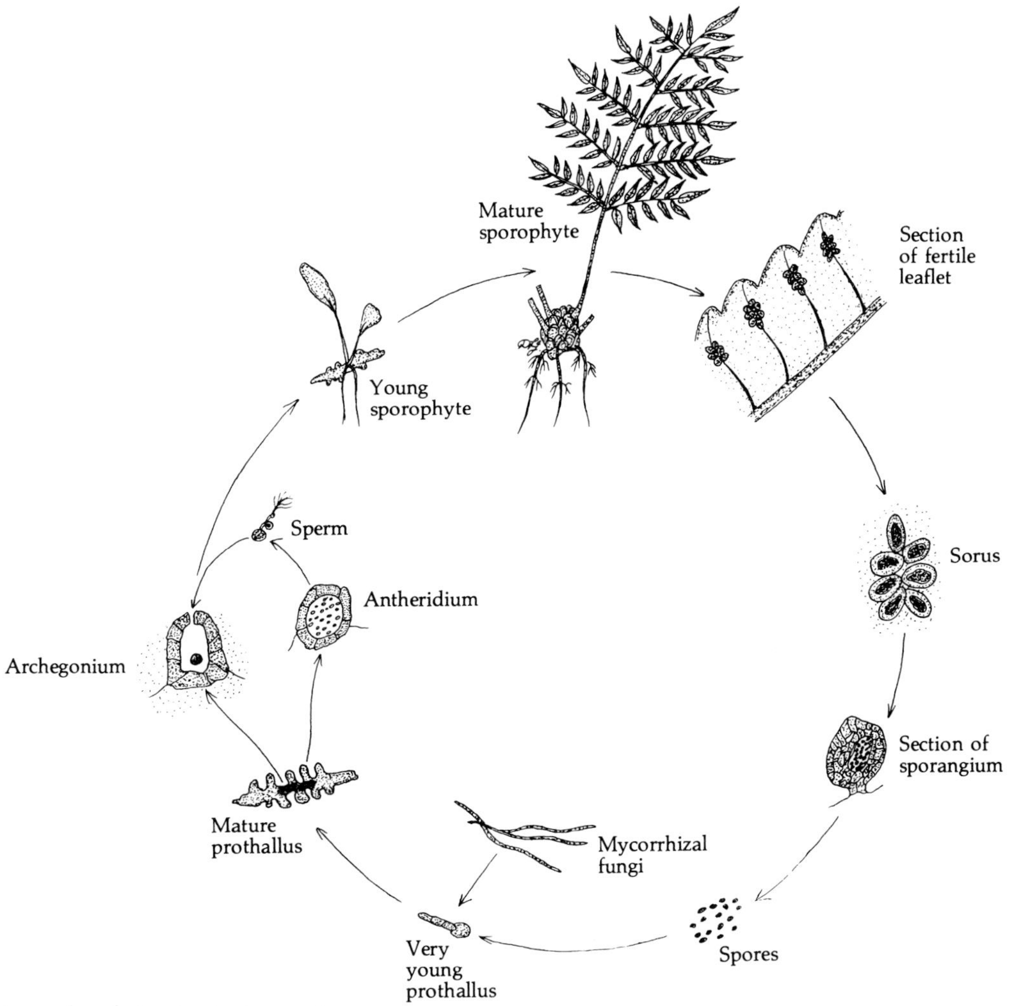

Life cycle of *Angiopteris evecta*

tiny species, which could easily be mistaken for a lowly moss or liverwort, to the arborescent giants of the realm of tree-ferns. In an evolutionary sense they range from the primitive relicts of the Schizaeaceae to the advanced members of the Marsiliaceae and Salviniaceae whose life cycle is almost so complex it is beyond understanding. Terrestrials, lithophytes, epiphytes, aquatics and even climbers are found in this diverse group of plants. Reproduction is mostly by spore, but some species have developed vegetative techniques to an extraordinary degree.

Being such a large group, a comprehensive coverage of the variations in form and life cycle is not possible in this book. Rather a select group is presented which will give an indication as to the variety of forms and life cycles found within this order. The families Osmundaceae and Schizaeaceae are included to illustrate primitive characters, Aspidiaceae as a representative of the majority of ferns, and Marsileaceae and Salviniaceae to illustrate the advanced state of evolution.

FAMILY OSMUNDACEAE

This family consists of three genera (*Leptopteris*, *Osmunda* and *Todea*) and about twelve species. They are true ferns but are regarded as the most primitive group of all living leptosporangiate ferns. They have a rich fossil record extending back to the Carboniferous period.

Plant Structure

The rhizome is erect or prostrate and is frequently woody, forming a trunk. Roots arise in pairs from the

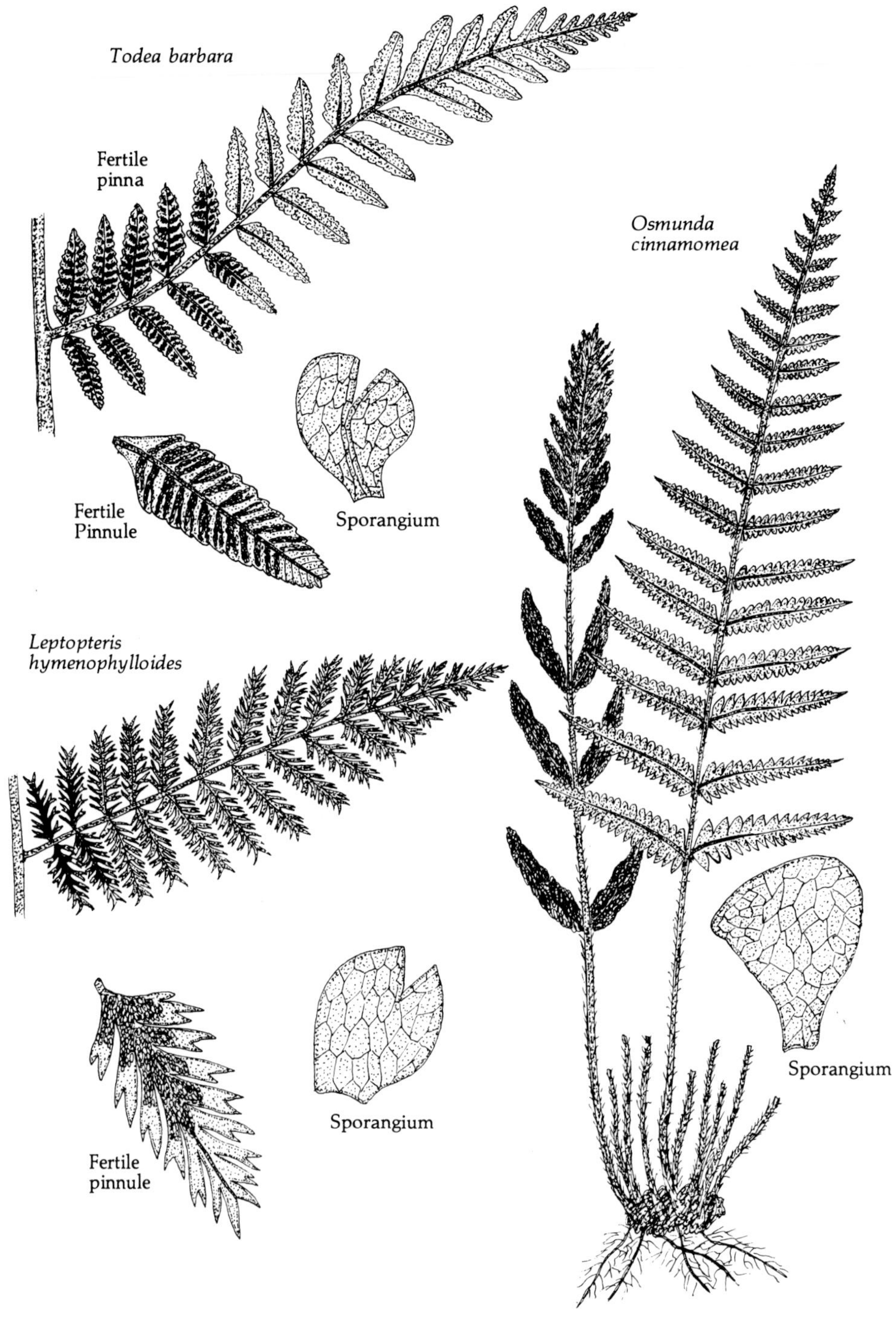

Plant structures of Osmundaceae

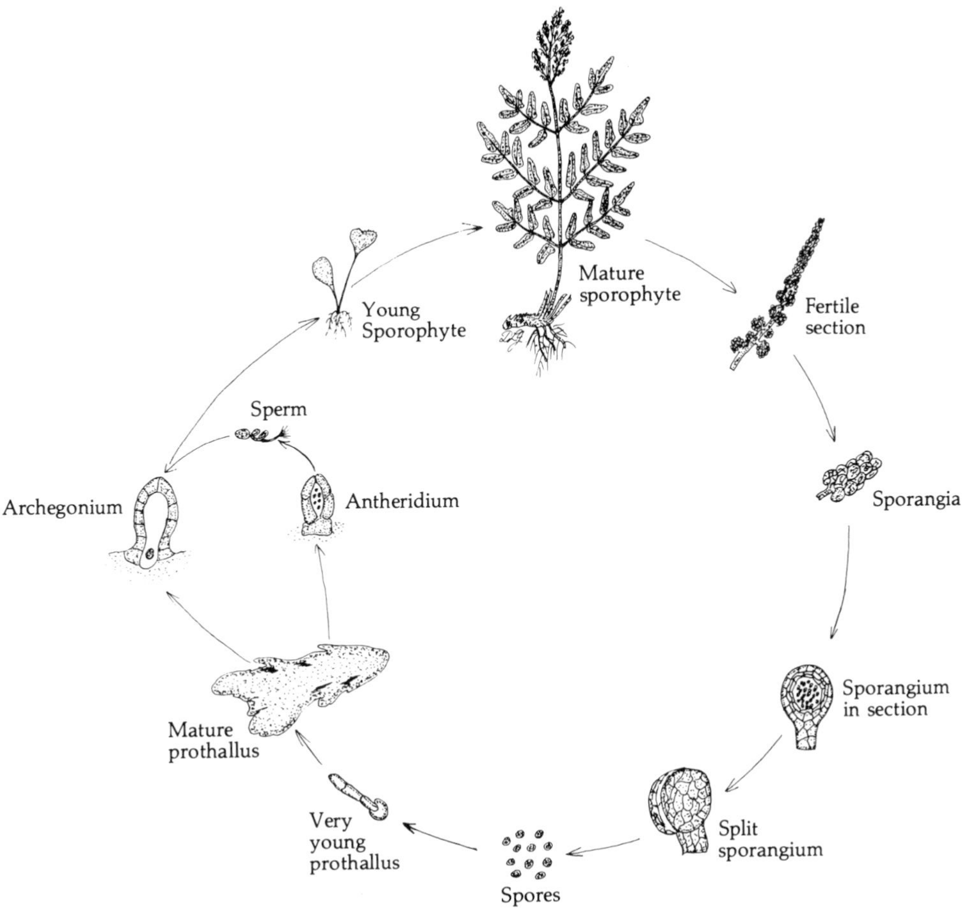

Life cycle of *Osmunda*

base of the fronds, and are tough and wiry and may form a covering over the trunk. The leaves are divided either once or twice, spread in a crown and are coiled when young. The stipe has an expanded, stipular base similar to members of the Marattiaceae. Species of *Osmunda* bear their sporangia on a specialized fertile section of the frond but in the other genera the sporangia are borne on the underside of the fronds. The sporangia of this group of ferns are relatively large and pear-shaped with a poorly developed annulus. All of the sporangia mature simultaneously and release green spores which are relatively short-lived.

Life Cycle

The spore is green and photosynthetic and germinates in the presence of light. It develops into an elongated prothallus which is anchored to the soil surface by rhizoids. The prothallus is green and capable of photosynthesis. It has a central thickened pad and is thin-textured around the margins and marginal lobes. The female sex organs are borne on the underside of the central thickened pad. The antheridia arise on the lower surface of the margins of the lobes. A tiny sporophyte develops after fertilization by motile sperm.

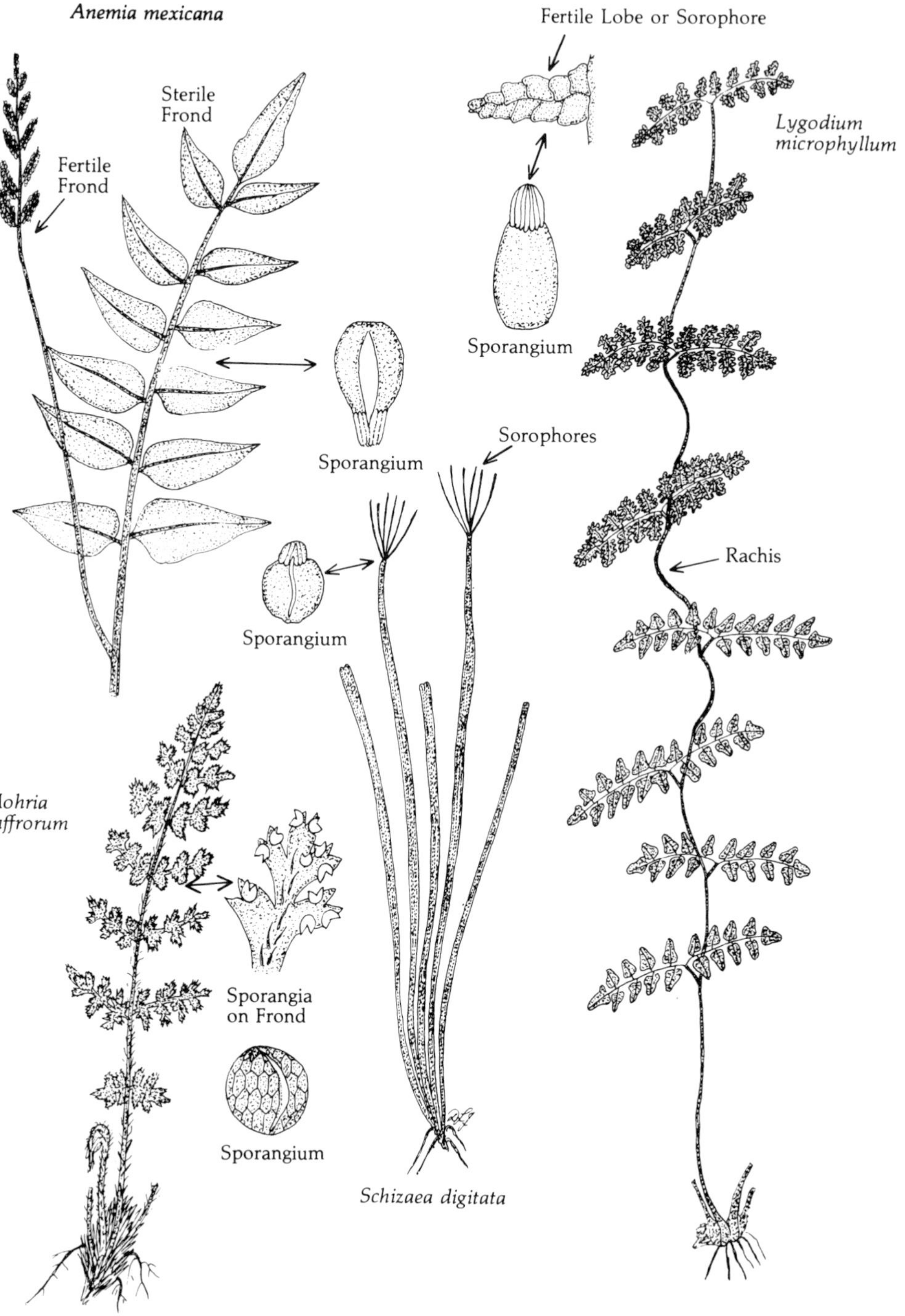

Plant structures of Schizaeaceae

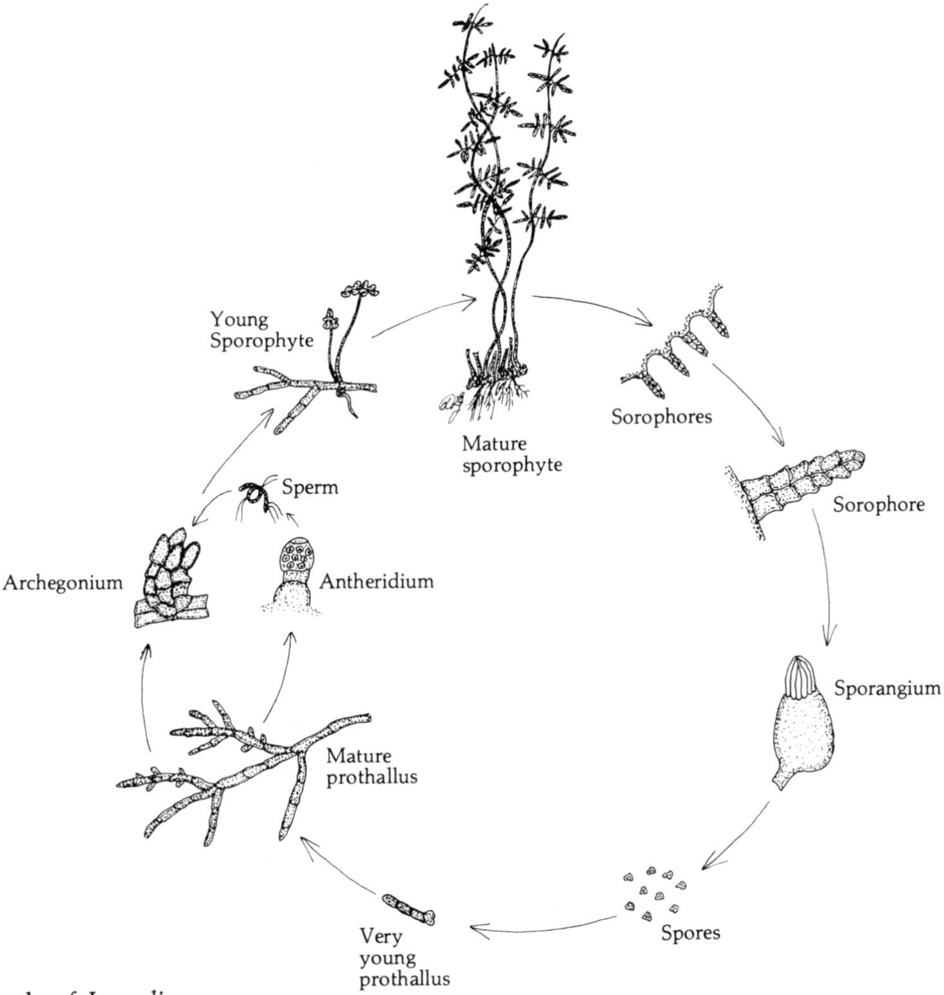

Life cycle of *Lygodium*

FAMILY SCHIZAEACEAE

This family consists of four genera (*Anemia*, *Lygodium*, *Mohria* and *Schizaea*). They are all true ferns but are generally considered very primitive and have links to the Jurassic period. Species of *Schizaea* have a mycorrhizal association whereby spores will not germinate successfully and plants will not survive in the absence of a specific fungus. The genus *Lygodium* is chosen as an example of the family.

Plant Structure

The rhizome, which is subterranean, varies from short to long-creeping and is frequently much-branched. The fronds are climbing and unbranched with a slender, wiry, twining rachis 1–10 m (40–400″) long. This rachis bears pinnae at intervals. Each pinna is branched pseudodichotomously and bears an arrested bud in its axil. Pinnae may be dimorphic. The fertile pinnae are often contracted, with lobes on the margins which bear sporangia, each covered by an overlapping flange of tissue (which acts as an indusium).

Life Cycle

The spore germinates to form a narrow, elongated prothallus which has marginal lobes which may develop into branches. The archegonia and antheridia are borne laterally on the lobes or branches. After fertilization the sporophyte develops a tiny frond with a solitary pinna or a pair of pinnae at the apex. New fronds arise in succession until the plant develops the slender, twining rachis characteristic of the genus.

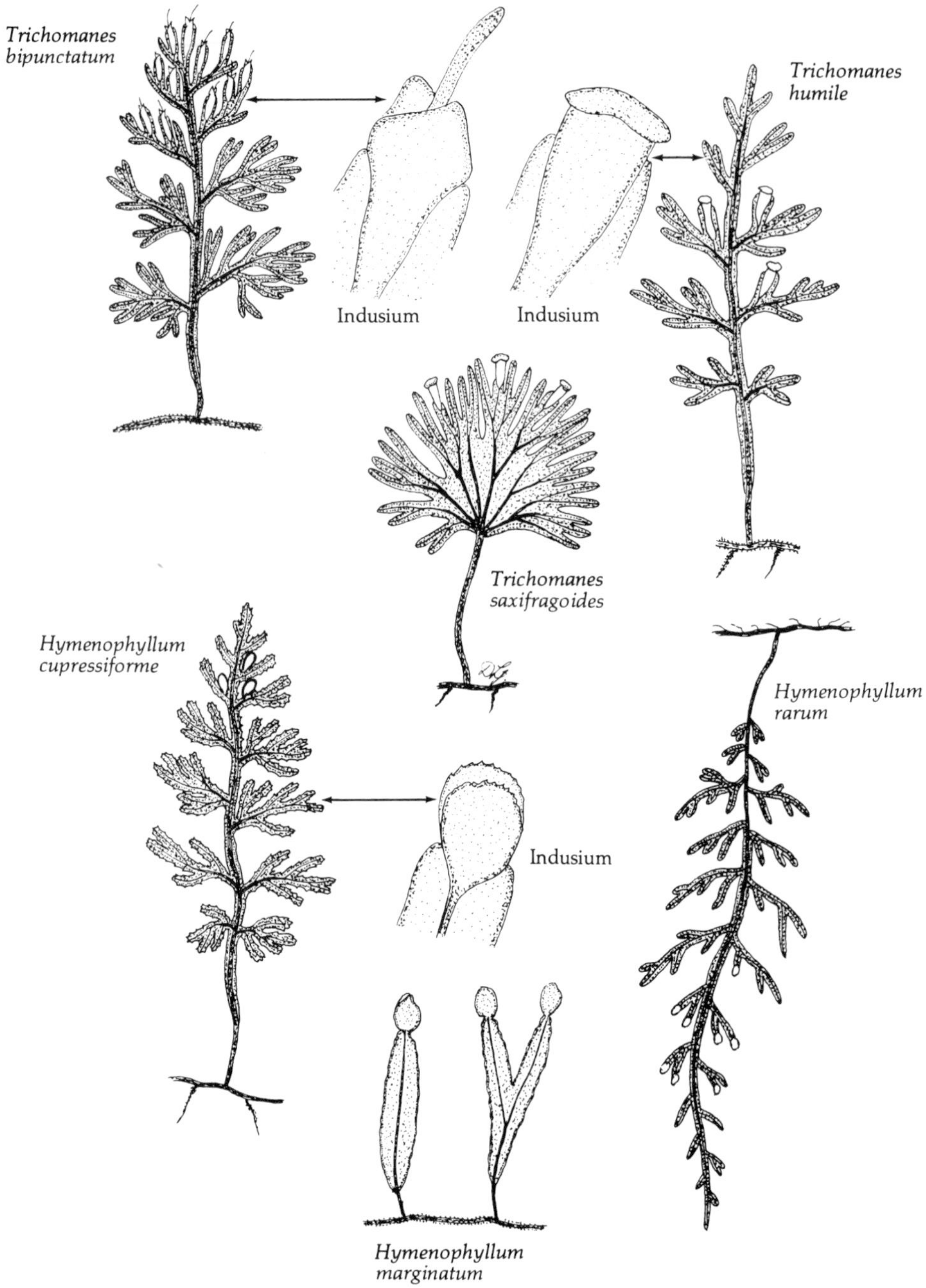

Plant structures of Hymenophyllaceae

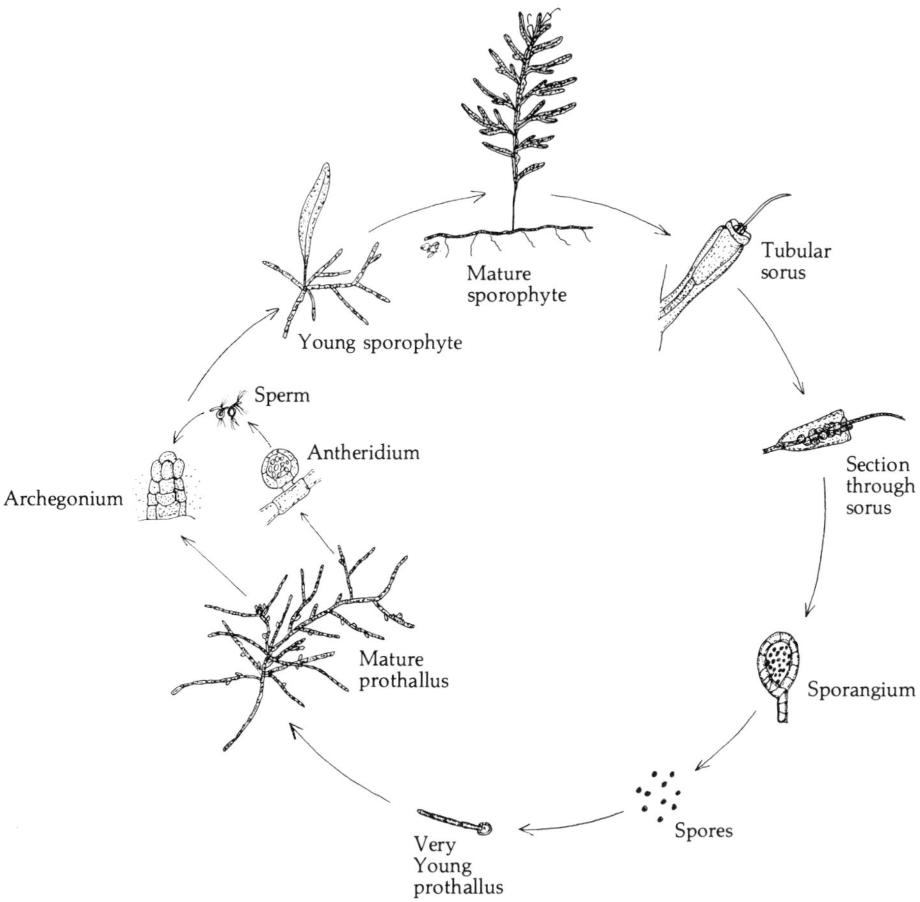

Life cycle of Hymenophyllaceae

FAMILY HYMENOPHYLLACEAE

The ferns grouped here are commonly known as the Filmy Ferns because of the diaphanous nature of the fronds of most species. The family is variously interpreted as consisting of two large genera with many subgenera, or as being comprised of up to 42 smaller genera. The Hymenophyllaceae is an ancient family with fossil records that date back to the Jurassic period, though because of their filmy nature the fossil record is generally poor.

Plant Structure

The rhizome is small and erect, or slender and creeping. Roots are absent in some species and are replaced by root hairs. In other species the roots are slender and wiry. The fronds vary from minute (less than 0.5 cm long) up to branched fronds over 1.5 m long. The sporangia are borne on a slender stalk called a receptacle, which is enclosed when young by a tubular indusium. As the sporangia mature the receptacle elongates and at maturity may protrude well beyond the indusium. Spores are of one type and are green and photosynthetic.

Life Cycle

The spores are short lived and must germinate within a few days of release. The prothallus is slender and filamentous, green and photosynthetic, and branches freely. It is attached to the surface by rhizoids which appear as modified branches of the prothallus. Specialized branches bear the sex organs, those bearing the archegonia are known as archegoniophores, and those with antheridia are termed antheridiophores. After fertilization the sporophyte develops as a tiny plant. In some species tiny vegetative buds (gemmae) are produced by the prothallus and these can germinate to produce new prothallial structures.

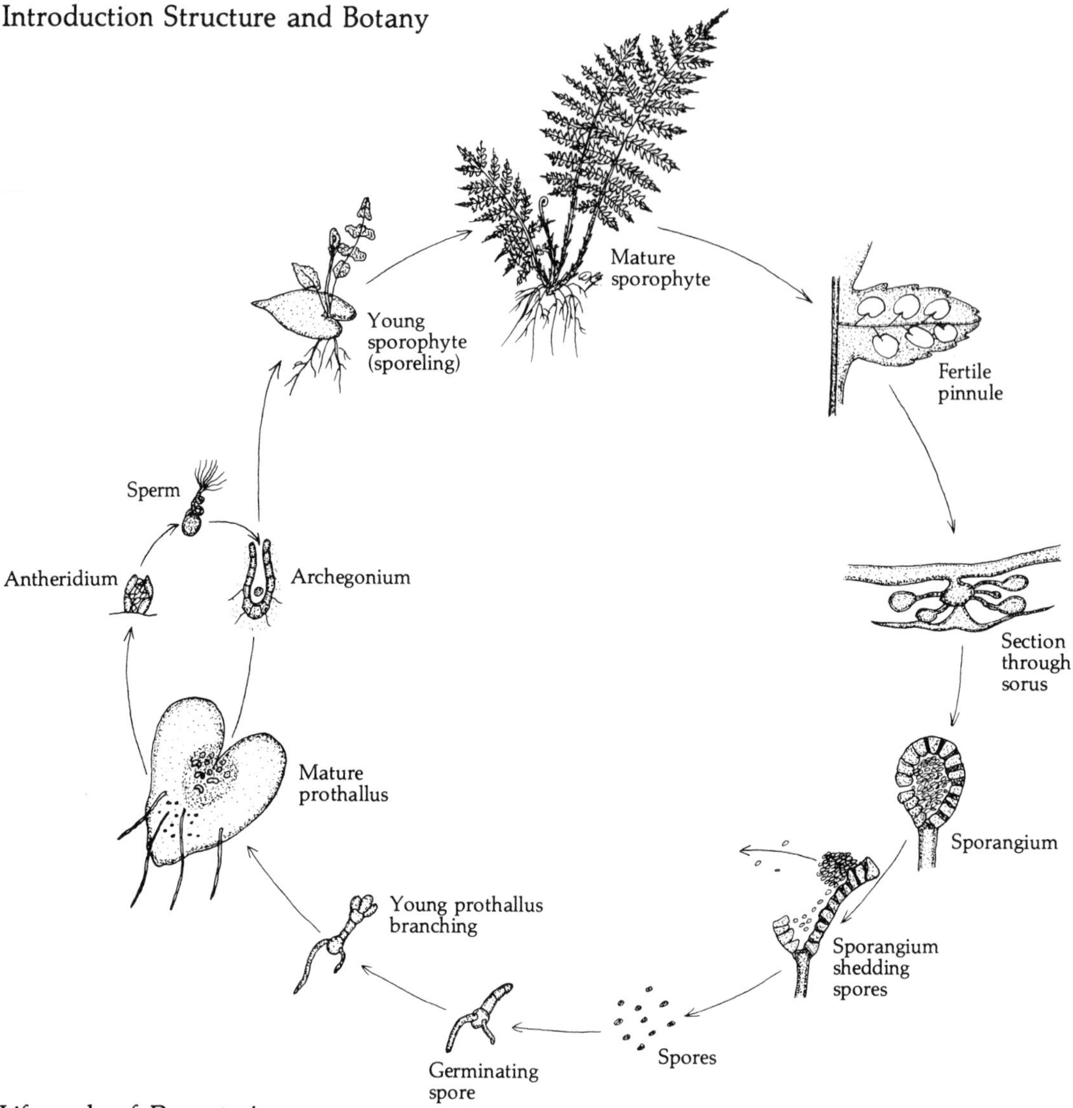

Life cycle of *Dryopteris*

FAMILY ASPIDIACEAE

This family is included simply as an example of the life cycle which the majority of true ferns pass through in their development.

Plant Structure

The typical fern structure is outlined in Chapter 3 (see also Chapter 4).

Life Cycle

The spore germinates to form a single green cell which divides a few times to form a filamentous prothallus. After an elongation phase to reach a certain length the apical cells divide laterally as well as longitudinally to form eventually a broad, green structure. This is the mature prothallus and it may be heart-shaped or lunar-shaped. The structure is flat green and photosynthetic and attached to the soil surface by rhizoids from the underside. The prothallus is one cell thick except at a thickened central point known as the cushion. Here the archegonia are borne on the underside, usually near the centre of the cushion, and the antheridia are separated and may arise on the margin of the cushion or on the basal margins of the prothallus. The antheridia release motile sperm cells which swim in water to the archegonia and effect fertilization. The sporophyte grows initially as an immature fern (sporeling) and eventually develops into a mature plant.

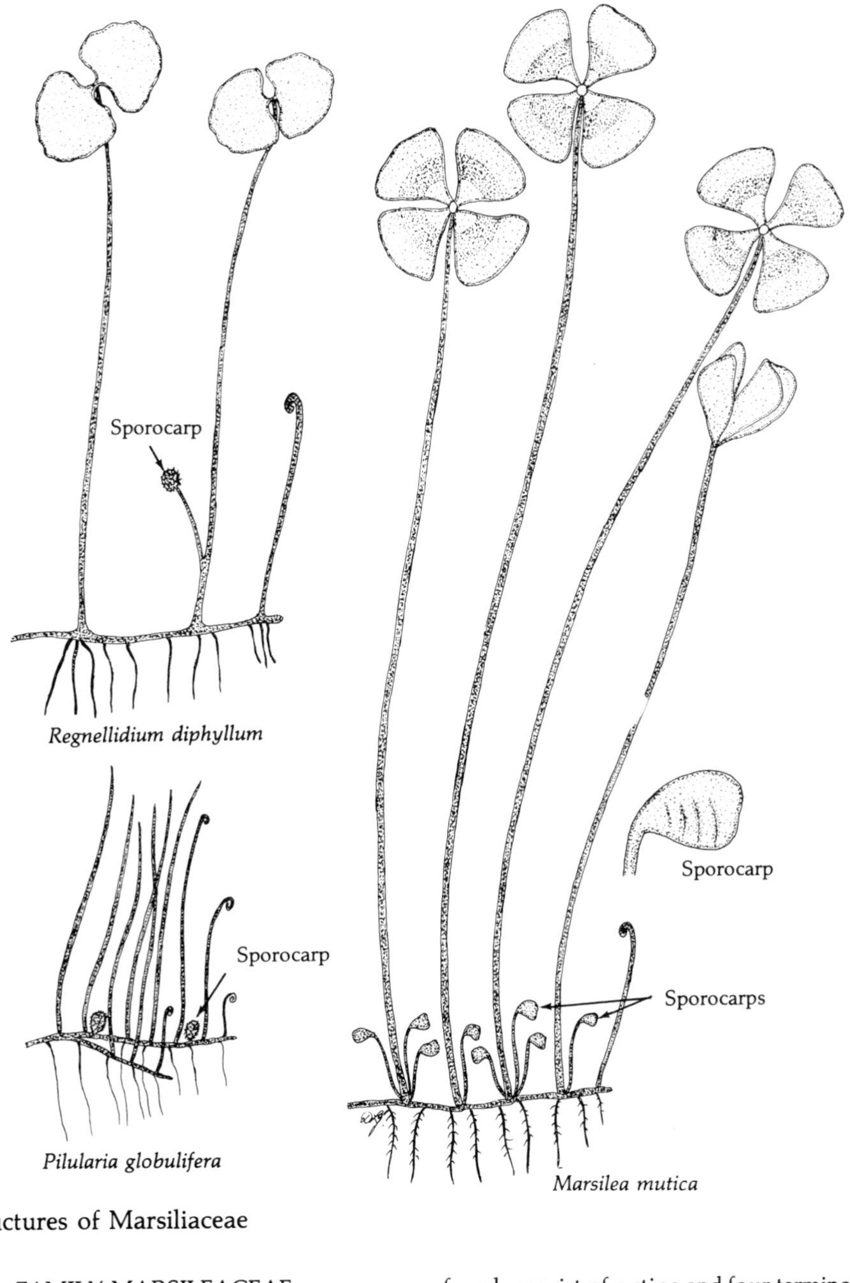

Plant structures of Marsiliaceae

FAMILY MARSILEACEAE

This family comprises three genera, *Marsilea*, *Pilularia* and *Regnellidium*. The three genera grow as aquatics in shallow water or root in mud. They have a fossil record dating back to the Cretaceous period. The genus *Marsilea* is chosen as an example.

Plant Structure

Rhizome slender, long-creeping, forking freely, producing fronds at intervals along its length. The fronds consist of a stipe and four terminal pinnae (or two pairs) which arise in a single whorl to form a clover-leaf pattern. Sporangia are borne within hardened structures known as sporocarps which arise on the rhizome in association with a frond.

Life Cycle

The sporangia are arranged in sori within the sporocarp. Each sorus is enclosed by a diaphanous indusium and bears two types of sporangia

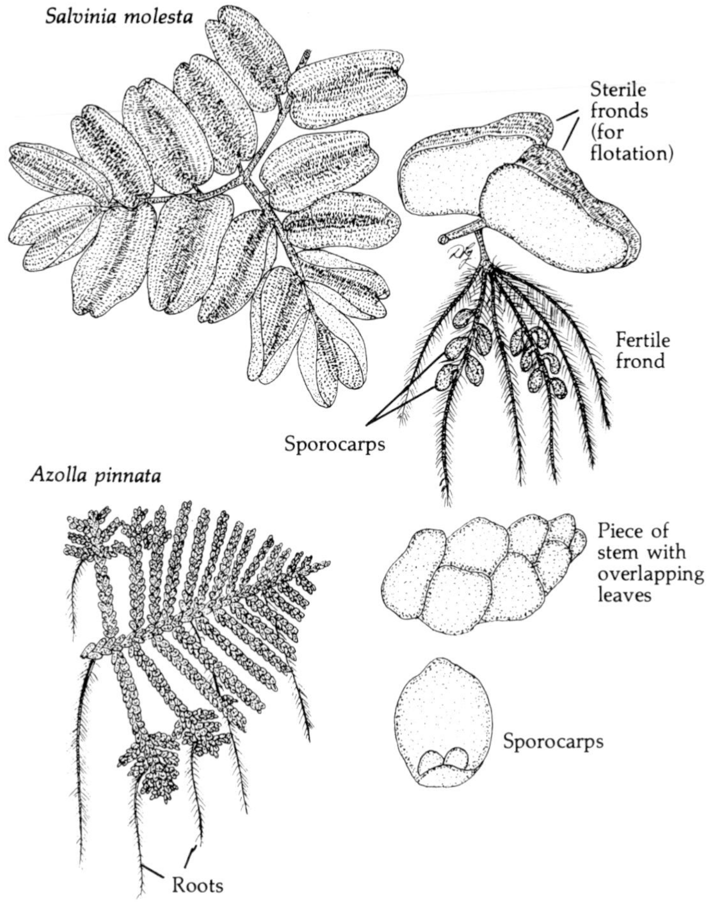

Plant structures of Salviniaceae

(megasporangia and microsporangia). The sporangia are borne on a ring-shaped receptacle which is gelatinous. As the sporangia mature, this receptacle absorbs water, expands, and eventually bursts the wall of the sporocarp. The sporangia, still clustered together, sink to the mud at the bottom. The megaspore germinates within the megasporangium to produce a minute prothallus containing a single archegonium which ruptures the sporangial wall. Each microspore germinates to form a minute prothallus which contain antheridia. These project through the sporangial wall and release free-swimming sperm cells which can effect fertilization in the archegonium.

FAMILY SALVINIACEAE

This family consists of two genera, *Salvinia* and *Azolla*. They are true aquatics, floating free and forming colonies on the surface of still water. They have numerous fossil links back to the Upper Cretaceous period. The genus *Salvinia* is chosen as an example.

Plant Structure

The much-branched stem bears dimorphic fronds in threes at a node. Two of the fronds at each node are rounded flotation structures which also carry out photosynthesis. The third type appears like a cluster of roots and is submerged in the water. This structure is colourless and bears small spherical bodies (sporocarps) which contain the spores. The spores are of two types, microspores in microsporangia and megaspores in megasporangia. Each sporocarp contains a single type of spore which is released into the water when the sporocarp wall breaks down.

Life Cycle

The megasporangium contains a single megaspore which germinates to form a tiny prothallus containing a single archegonium. The microsporangium contains many microspores which germinate within the sporangium. Each produces a tiny prothallus which contains two antheridia. These rupture the wall of the sporangium, and each releases four motile, free-swimming sperm which effect fertilization in the archegonia.

7 Fern cultivars

A cultivar is a horticultural variation of a species which differs from the usual forms of that species by some significant growth feature. This difference is not substantial enough for a botanist to classify the variation at variety or subspecies level, but the plants are of interest to the fern enthusiast. There may be some overlap with the botanical division of form or forma. This subdivision covers minor botanical variations which occur in nature. Modern botanists generally show little interest in such variants. Unless described as a form, minor variations may be best regarded as cultivars, and if they become well established in cultivation they can certainly be regarded as such.

Cultivars are of particular interest to horticulturists. Useful variations in ferns include ease of culture, patterns of growth habit (e.g. dwarfness or compactness), and frond features such as variegation, colour and the presence of lobes or crests.

It is usual for cultivars to be perpetuated by techniques of vegetative propagation such as tissue culture or division. Many fern cultivars, however, come true from spore or at least a percentage of the spore is the same as the parent. Some are also apogamous (see page 39). Thus an extensive number of fern cultivars can be propagated on a large scale. Those cultivars which are sterile (e.g. some hybrids) are limited to the numbers which can be produced by techniques of

A frond of the normal *Adiantum raddianum* (LHS) compared with a finely dissected cultivar 'Gracillimum'

vegetative propagation. Tissue culture is a possible means for their large-scale multiplication.

When a cultivar is cited in publications the abbreviation cv. should be placed before the cultivar name, or the cultivar name should be enclosed within single quotation marks. Capital letters must be used to start all words of a cultivar name and the names are not italicized. For example, a cultivar can be written *Adiantum tenerum* cv. Farleyense or *Adiantum tenerum* 'Farleyense'. Where a cultivar is known to be a form of a species the name is shown as in the example. Where the cultivar is of interspecific hybrid origin or its identity is uncertain, it is listed as a cultivar of the genus, e.g. *Platycerium* cv. European Hybrid or *Platycerium* 'European Hybrid'. Cultivars also occur in botanical varieties or subspecies, and they are then listed after the subspecific or varietal name.

Additional names may be attached to a cultivar if further selections are made from it, e.g. *Nephrolepis exaltata* cv. Bostoniensis Aurea. The latter name indicates that this fern is a golden-leafed form of cv. Bostoniensis. Frequently, commercial nurseries or specialist growers may add their own name to certain selections of a cultivar or even to individual well grown specimen plants.

The naming of cultivars is governed by the International Code of Nomenclature for Cultivated Plants. There is no international registration authority for ferns and all fern registration is handled, along with that of other plants, by local registration authorities. Popular names must be chosen for cultivars, and botanical terms are not to be used, to avoid confusion with botanical taxa such as subspecies and varieties. Many cultivar names retain a botanical flavour (e.g. *Adiantum raddianum* cv. Gracillimum) and these arose at a time when the concept of cultivars was unknown. Last century and earlier this century, it was common practice to name unusual forms (which we now recognize as cultivars) as botanical varieties. According to the International Code, such an epithet correctly published in accordance with the botanical code is to be retained as a cultivar name unless it duplicates an existing earlier cultivar name for that species. As these early names were correctly published the botanical spelling is retained.

Some botanical terms have been popularized by horticulturists. Thus, variegated forms are known as 'Variegata' and crested forms as 'Cristata' etc. Such terms must not be used in the naming of new fern cultivars. The International Code ruled in 1959 that common names must be in the common language and must not be Latinized.

Origins of Fern Cultivars

Fern cultivars can arise basically in four ways:
1. From variation within a species. Widely distributed species tend to vary as the plants adapt to the features of their environment. These changes may not be significant in a botanical sense but may be important in such features as vigour, growth habit and disease resistance.
2. As a genetic mutation or sport. Such changes are apparent in forms with lobed or crested fronds. These mutants may remain sporadic but, if they are fertile, they may become well established within an area, e.g. *Polypodium australe* cv. Cambricum.

An unusual cultivar, *Polypodium formosanum* 'Cristatum', which has flattened and divided rhizomes

Photo C. G. Goudey

Pteris cretica is subject to much variation. Illustrated is cv. Wimsettii

Osmunda regalis 'Cristata' Photo C. G. Goudey

Cristate variation in *Athyrium filix-femina*
Photo C. G. Goudey

3. From hybridization which can be natural or man-made. Natural hybrids tend to be recorded as botanical entities, although some may be regarded as cultivars. Most cultivars of *Adiantum raddianum* have arisen as the result of hybridization of plants in cultivation, either deliberately or accidentally.
4. From hybridization followed by apogamy. Many interspecific fern hybrids are naturally sterile but some may stabilize as the result of apogamy (see also page 39). These apogamous forms may or may not be sterile.

The Attractions of Fern Cultivars

Cultivars not only increase the range of ferns which can be grown, but they also add variety and interest to a collection. They can create tremendous excitement among fern fanciers, and there are some enthusiasts who avidly seek out new forms for their collections.

It is quite remarkable how some species of ferns are subject to extraordinary variations over their range, while other equally widespread species vary little. For example, *Athyrium filix-femina* has had more than 300 cultivars and forms named from it. These variants not only occur in the wild, as extra changes have been noted in gardens and private collections too; others have been stimulated by selection and hybridization. It seems, from this variation, that a species such as *Athyrium filix-femina* is unstable and may still be in the course of evolution.

The collection of cultivars reached feverish heights in the early 1900s, when enthusiasts scoured the fern localities of Europe and Britain for new variations which could be added to their already impressive collections. In 1903, in Britain alone, nearly 700 such variations were listed. Many of these have been lost to cultivation during the intervening years; however, today there is renewed interest by fern fanciers in such novelties.

Fern Cultivar Classification

The variations in the fronds of fern cultivars range from simple lobing to complex contortions and crestings which result in plants of vastly altered appearance. Basically, the variations occur either in the frond shape or on the divisions of the fronds.

A classification system of the frond variations is essential if any sense is to be made of the large number of fern cultivars which are now being grown. A suitable system must not only be straightforward and easy to follow, but also be capable of unravelling the complexities of the frond variations so that they can be understood. The following classification taken directly from the excellent book, *Hardy Ferns**, fulfils all of these requirements. It is reproduced here with the kind permission of the author, Reginald Kaye.

*Kaye Reginald, *Hardy Ferns,* Faber and Faber, London 1968.

Cristate – polydactylous variation, *Christella subpubescens* 'Keffordii'
Photo C. G. Goudey

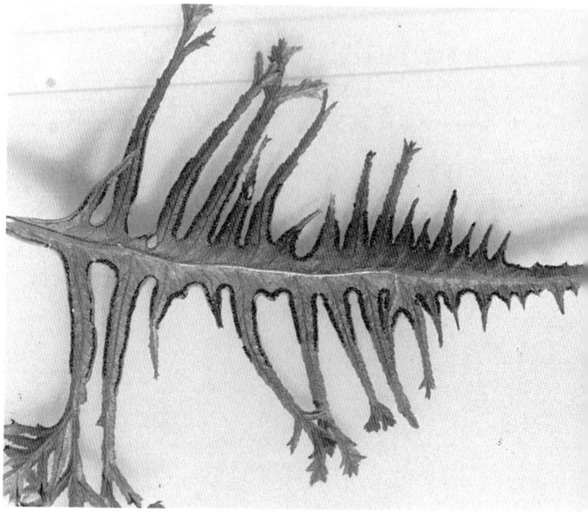

Cristate – foliose variation, *Pteris cretica* 'Rivertoniana'
Photo C. G. Goudey

Corymbose – glomerate variation in *Athyrium filix-femina*
Photo C. G. Goudey

Grandicipital variation, *Dryopteris filix-mas* 'Linearis Cristata'
Photo C. G. Goudey

Ramose variation, *Polypodium vulgare* 'Ramosum'
Photo C. G. Goudey

Cruciate variation, *Athyrium filix-femina* 'Victoriae'
Photo C. G. Goudey

Plumose variation *Nephrolepis exaltata* 'Childsii'
Photo C. G. Goudey

Foliose variation in *Blechnum nudum*
Photo C. G. Goudey

DIVISION A
Changes in frond shape
GROUP 1 CRISTATE

This is the commonest form of variation in which the frond apex, or the frond apex and pinnae, or the frond apex, pinnae and pinnules are divided to a varying degree at their tips into tassels or crests.

There being so many forms of cresting, this group has been subdivided into five sections:

a) CAPITATE The frond apex alone crested, pinnae not crested.

b) CRISTATE The frond apex crested in one plane like a fan, the pinnae also crested. The apical crest not as wide as the frond. When the divisions of the crest are slender and well separated they are termed polydactylous – many fingered.

c) PERCRISTATE The frond apex, the pinnae, and the pinnules are crested.

d) CORYMBOSE The frond apex divided in several planes to give a bunched tassel, not wider than the frond itself. The pinnae are crested. When the pinnae crests are wider than the pinnae themselves they are termed glomerate.

e) GRANDICIPITAL The terminal corymbose crest is wider than the frond itself. Pinnae crested, reduced or absent.

GROUP 2 OTHER CHANGES IN FROND SHAPE

a) CRUCIATE Each pinna reduced, usually to a pair of pinnules, set at right-angles forming a cross with the opposite pinna. Often combined with the cristate condition.

b) RAMOSE The lower part or the main frond axis divides once, to repeatedly, also often combined with the cristate condition.

c) CONGESTED Frond axis shortened so that the pinnae are very close, or overlap. Also combined with the cristate condition.

d) ANGUSTATE (Combining three of Lowe's sections.) Fronds very narrow with short pinnae which may be twisted (revolvens), reflexed, or reduced to small balls (lunulate).

e) DELTOID Frond triangular, more or less as in an equilateral triangle.

DIVISION B
Changes in pinnule shape

a) PLUMOSE Pinnules pinnate or bipinnate, sori scanty or absent. May be combined with the cristate condition.

b) FOLIOSE Pinnules wider, more leafy than normal, almost confluent, often overlapping. May be combined with cristate and cruciate condition.

c) DISSECT Pinnules finely divided into teeth or bristles – setigerous. Also may combine with the cristate condition.

d) DEPAUPERATE Pinnules reduced, irregular, or missing. Combines with cristate condition.

e) DIVISUM A special section referring to forms of *Polystichum setiferum* including:

a acutilobe, b divisilobe, c decomposite. The pinnules pinnatifid, pinnate, bipinnate, or even tripinnate. See Dyce, *British Fern Gazette*, IX. 4.

f) HETEROMORPHIC All other pinnule shapes, rounded, linear or jagged.

Part Two

The Cultural Requirements of Ferns

8 Fern likes and dislikes

People associate ferns with coolness, visits to ferny nooks and days in the country. These happy associations are a major factor in inducing people to grow ferns on their own plot of land, which may range from the postage stamp size backyards of terraces and tenements in the cities, to the rambling estates of the country. Ferns are also treasured for the beauty and delicate symmetry of their fronds; collectors find them irresistible, not only because of the large numbers available from various parts of the world, but also because of the mutations and sports which occur so freely in some species. There is, after all, always the chance of discovering a new fern.

Whatever the reasons for people wanting to grow ferns, the facts are that fern cultivation and study is again gaining impetus in many countries around the world. This may not reach the mania of the Victorian era, but nevertheless, it is a healthy trend.

Nowadays, ferns have to compete for gardener's favour with a wide range of colourful garden plants, from bedding annuals whose displays are brilliant, through a wide selection of herbaceous perennials to popular shrubs such as azaleas, rhododendrons and camellias. In the tropics we have the flamboyance of a vast range of plants to demand attention. Little wonder that the interest in ferns has waned somewhat from that enjoyed during the Victorian era. The relative popularity of ferns now is probably a position of strength since it recognizes and caters for their needs. After all, few plants can better liven a drab dark wall or line a shaded walk or survive in the root-filled soil under established trees. In the nursery trade, ferns are well entrenched and are grown by the thousands in various parts of the world, simply because they are unexcelled for their main purpose, that of decorating people's houses, verandahs and work places.

The successful fern grower is one who studies the ferns in their various natural environments and from this study learns to understand their needs and then translate this knowledge to all aspects of the garden including soil, exposure to sun and wind, pollution, competition from trees and shrubs and even to the niches which occur in any garden and which have their own microclimate.

FERN LIKES

Shade

Ferns as a group like shade. Some species will happily tolerate deep shade; others need much more light for their growth. Complete shade is the ideal situation for delicate ferns, however, the range that can be grown is greater if the site ranges from shade to brightly lit with parts perhaps even exposed to some sun.

Dappled shade, such as occurs when the sun is filtered through the canopy of established trees, is generally ideal for ferns. Situations exposed by large breaks in the canopy should not be planted with tender species which may burn, however, there are plenty of ferns which will tolerate this degree of exposure. Competition from roots is a problem under existing trees and the ferns will need extra watering, mulching and fertilizing if they are to cope, especially in the establishment phase.

Situations of partial sun and semi-shade can also be suitable for ferns providing that the sun is not too hot at the time of exposure. Morning sun is most suitable, however, the last hour in the afternoon may also be satisfactory for many species.

Humidity

Those who have been in a fern gully will immediately appreciate the atmosphere created by humidity rising from damp soil and not being dispersed by winds. It is this humidity which enables a wide range of ferns to proliferate and to grow in situations that would otherwise be unsuitable, e.g. on the trunks and branches of trees. The same is true of rainforests whether they be tropical or temperate. Even in woodlands the protection afforded by the trees and the moisture from the springy, humus-rich soil is enough to increase the humidity noticeably. Ferns growing in soaks, swamps and marshes, even though the situation may be quite exposed, are also growing in a very humid atmosphere.

Humidity then is greatly appreciated by ferns and fortunately this is readily catered for in a garden.

Humidity can be rapidly increased by watering or misting and a site protected from wind will reduce its dispersal. Planting ferns in groups helps create a congenial humid atmosphere since the transpiration from the fronds of one contributes to the atmosphere around another. Mulches on the soil surface also tend to increase humidity by presenting a larger surface area for evaporation.

Shelter and Warmth

These two factors generally go together. Ferns, like any other plants, appreciate warmth for growth. This even includes those very hardy species which have adapted to survive the rigours of an icy winter in cold climates. For tropical ferns the need is obvious. Warmth does not imply that a hot situation is needed, but rather a warm, sheltered situation that is insulated from the worst effects of a cold snap or a hot spell. Such a situation in cold climates may be against a brick wall which will catch the early rays of the sun or in the lee of a large boulder which will protect the ferns against the worst effects of winds, whether they be chilling or drying. Large ferns can provide shelter for small growing types and this is another reason why ferns like company and prefer to be planted in groups.

Soil Moisture and Aeration

Ferns love moisture and need it for their healthy growth and development. This moisture must be fresh and sweet and not the sour, wetness of a water-logged soil. Drainage then is of prime significance to most ferns and must be unimpeded, allowing excess water to drain rapidly through the root zone. This means that plenty of oxygen is available to the roots. Water is also still available to the fern because the soil retains it as a film around the smaller particles and within tiny pores. A certain proportion of this water is available to the fern roots and this level needs to be regularly topped up by watering or rainfall.

Mulches are very important for retaining soil moisture and the organic types add extra depth into which the fern roots can grow.

Few, if any, ferns will grow happily in a situation where the soil moisture stagnates. Such waterlogged soils lack oxygen and are generally cold and lifeless. People have difficulty in not equating this situation with that in a swamp or bog and wonder why ferns thrive under these conditions naturally. Appearances are deceptive however, for in a swamp or bog, the water is kept viable by the whole complex interchange that takes place between the various swamp plants and the animals large and small that inhabit such areas.

Although ferns do not like stagnant conditions they will thrive in wet situations where the water moves through the soil, even if this movement is slow and free water is visible. Such soakage areas in nature are commonly colonized by ferns and if they happen to occur in a garden well and good, for they can be converted into a fern oasis. Similar conditions can be created artificially by the controlled release of water from a hose or dripping tap. Where ferns are grown in such situations with the roots regularly bathed with moving water, the plants prove surprisingly hardy, and tolerant of adverse conditions such as strong sunshine and drying winds. The plants are also sturdy, often paler green with colourful new fronds, and may bear little resemblance in general appearance to those plants of the same species growing in shadier aspects (for more details on watering see page 165).

Mulches

Ferns are by nature shallow-rooting plants with a large percentage of the roots being found near the soil surface. Here they collect nutrients and moisture from that important layer where the active breakdown of organic material is taking place. They are therefore particularly susceptible to drying of the soil surface and greatly appreciate the application of mulches. These must be applied thickly and topped up at regular intervals to keep the plants healthy (for more details on mulching see page 85).

Fertilizers and Manures

Ferns, like any other plants, need nutrients from the soil and if for any reason the nutrient supply is poor then the soil should be treated with fertilizers or manures. For more details see Chapter 9.

FERN DISLIKES

Sun

The sun is a major enemy of ferns and the vast majority of species need shade for their successful culture. Hot sun can be particularly damaging even during brief periods of exposure. It kills delicate species and renders others unsightly by bleaching or scorching fronds and shrivelling new growth. There are of course hardy ferns which will tolerate considerable exposure to sun. Many of these, however, are not widely cultivated, and some indeed may be difficult to grow or have specific cultural requirements.

The scorching effects of the sun are influenced by a variety of factors including obvious ones such as the time of the year, the latitude and the altitude. Less obvious factors are fog, pollution and the garden surrounds. Reflective light-coloured surfaces or absorbent dark-coloured surfaces (such as brick walls) can aggravate the heating effects of summer sun and reduce the number of species that can be grown in their proximity. Similar surfaces exposed to winter sun, however, can create a warm environment which can allow some cold-sensitive species to survive winter conditions.

Wind

Ferns like air movement but dislike wind. Wind causes obvious physical damage from its buffeting effects and also causes less obvious but more insidious effects. Winds generally lower humidity by simple dispersal of the water vapour. Drying winds, especially if they are hot, may shrivel immature fronds and may damage young croziers, causing papery patches to appear in the fronds when they unroll. Cold winds stunt growth, and if they are especially chilling, may also cause papery patches to appear in unrolling fronds. Draughts cause insidious effects and are to be avoided if possible. Wind funnelling around buildings and through openings such as gateways and arches can retard the growth of ferns. Salt laden winds in coastal districts may cause salt burn on maturing fronds and damage delicate species. Many ferns though, are surprisingly tolerant of general coastal conditions and damage only follows severe winds when large quantities of salt may be deposited in a short time.

Dryness

Ferns are moisture-loving plants and dislike dry soils and dry atmosphere. Delicate species cannot tolerate dryness at all and shrivel and collapse quickly when such conditions even threaten. Some species are so sensitive to dryness (even when they are well established plants) that they collapse and die quickly if their roots dry out (e.g. *Ctenitis sloanei, Gleichenia* spp., *Pteris macilenta*).

Many ferns though, are surprisingly tolerant of dryness especially once they are established. Such plants will not withstand long dry spells and can in no circumstances be labelled as drought resistant. They also have a far better appearance if they are watered. A few hardy ferns prefer to be kept on the dry side and are able to cope happily with occasional long dry spells. These, however, are the exception and they are generally uncommon in cultivation (see Resurrection Ferns page 6).

Cold Weather

Ferns generally dislike cold weather and make all of their growth during the warm part of the year. Tropical species obviously have little ability to cope with cold weather but ferns from temperate regions have many adaptations which enable them to survive. Most species stop growth as the days shorten and the nights get colder and by the time the worst of the winter weather has arrived they are in a state of dormancy. Some species are deciduous and shed their fronds completely. Others are able to withstand freezing of their fronds without ill effect. It is perhaps not correct to say that these ferns dislike cold weather because they probably rely on the annual winter chilling for the formation or conversion of growth hormones within their cells.

Frosts cause damage to sensitive ferns and may even affect hardy types if they are in a susceptible stage of soft growth. Hardy ferns usually recover from the setback but sensitive species often collapse and die. Frosts cause a watery collapse and blackening of unfurling fronds and also cause black patches on hardened fronds which eventually become white and papery. Protection from mild frosts can be obtained by planting near buildings or large shrubs, or beneath the canopies of established trees. Sensitive species grown in areas with a cold winter must be protected by structures such as greenhouses.

Bare Soil

Because ferns are shallow rooted they resent a bare soil surface. Bare soils are subject to greater temperature and moisture fluctuations than are mulched soils and this means that the important top layer of soil is unsuitable and unavailable for fern root growth. The old practice of raking away all surface litter to present a neat appearance is fortunately dying out, for it had catastrophic effects on the soil and consequent fern growth.

SUN AND SHADE IN THE TROPICS

The conditions so far discussed in this chapter will vary somewhat depending on whether the ferns are being grown in a tropical or temperate region.

In the tropics, the winter sun can be nearly as damaging to tender plants as can the summer sun. This is because of the latitude combined with the generally clear skies and low humidity of the season, allowing the passage of a high incidence of burning ultraviolet rays. The effects of the summer tropical sun can also be very severe on tender plants, however, at the hottest time of the year, these effects are usually tempered by the higher prevailing humidity and frequent cloud cover. It is this high humidity which allows some sensitive ferns to survive summer conditions in the tropics.

Another problem in the tropics is encountered when shelter trees shed their leaves. Many tropical trees shed their leaves prior to flowering, and this occurs often during the late part of the dry season, when conditions are quite hot. While the leaf fall provides a beneficial mulch of leaves it also means that sensitive ferns are deprived of their protective cover and can suffer sunburn as a consequence. Trees which shed their leaves in the tropics often do so over a short period and with little prior warning.

A further problem encountered in the tropics is that the sun gets much hotter earlier in the day so that even those ferns in an easterly aspect can be damaged by excessive exposure.

SUN AND SHADE IN TEMPERATE REGIONS

In contrast to the tropics, winter sun in temperate regions is weak, and its effects on ferns are beneficial rather than harmful. Thus ferns growing under deciduous trees receive the dual benefit of a mulch of leaves plus winter sun (when it shines) for 3–4 months.

Summer sun, by contrast, can be quite hot and damaging, the particular effects varying with the latitude, altitude and proximity to the sea. In general, however, exposure to morning summer sun can be tolerated by more sensitive ferns in these regions than it can be in the tropics.

9 Soils for ferns

Ferns as a group are very adaptable plants and they can often be induced to grow in situations where they would not be found naturally and under conditions which would seem to be unsuitable. The latter is particularly true as far as the soils in which they will grow. Providing the soil is well drained, has a suitable pH and some organic content, ferns are not fussy about soil type.

It is impossible to define the ideal soil for ferns, because of the tremendous variation that occurs in soils around the world and the adaptability of ferns. A study of ferns in their natural habitats shows a distinct preference for well-structured soils rich in organic matter. Well-structured here means free drainage, adequate aeration and sufficient moisture retention for growth. The organic matter also plays a role in moisture retention as well as nutrition. Such soils in nature may be spongy or springy to touch. Although a soil of this type is ideal for fern growth many other common garden soils can be adequate for a wide range of species. Ferns also occur in nature in what would seem to be less than ideal conditions, e.g. rocky scree slopes where the organic matter is low.

Components of Soils

Soils are a complex system and though it is possible to classify various types it should be realized that changes can occur, even within a small area. Soils are made up of physical components which may be present in variable combinations. A knowledge of these components may aid the understanding of soils, and the processes which occur in them, including fern growth.

The major physical components of these soils are classified according to their particle size. They are as follows:

Name of Component	*Diameter*
Gravel	Greater than 2 mm
Coarse sand	2 mm–0.2 mm
Fine sand	0.2 mm–0.02 mm
Silt	0.02 mm–0.002 mm
Clay	Less than 0.002 mm

SOIL CLASSES

Soils are classified depending on the relative amounts of the components listed above. This classification is based on texture and relies on the feel of a moist sample of soil when worked between the fingers and palm of the hand. Soil classes arranged in increasing order of heaviness are: sand, loamy sand, sandy loam, loam, sandy clay loam, clay loam, sandy clay, clay.

Clay

This is the heaviest of the soil classes and is composed of very small particles that have strong cohesive properties. Clay can be poorly structured when the particles run together or well structured when the particles adhere in little aggregates. The former type drains poorly and lacks aeration while the latter clays can drain freely and be well aerated. Clays retain a greater percentage of water than other soil classes, but in many types only a small amount of this water is available for plant growth. Some clays are plastic and expand when wet and shrink when dry. In severe cases this results in cracking. Clays, despite their reputation have the ability to grow a wide range of ferns and their worst features can be reduced by cultural practices such as adding calcium and organic matter (see page 84).

Clay Loams

These soils are basically well structured clays, fortified with fine sand and silt particles. They are usually friable soils, but some types can lack aeration when wet. They are usually richer in organic matter than are clays and do not expand and shrink to the same extent. Depending on the depth of the topsoil and the pH, a wide range of ferns can be grown in soils of this type.

Loam

Loam is made up of the following components:

Silt	10–25%
Clay	10–25%
Sand	50–65%

Although there is a high proportion of sand this is not readily felt when the moist soil is tested in the hand. The organic content varies with different types of loam, but is usually fairly high. Appearances can be deceptive, as some loams which are dark coloured and appear therefore to be rich in organic matter, may in fact be quite low. Loams make an ideal garden soil with excellent drainage and moisture retentive properties. A very wide range of ferns can be successfully grown in them.

Sandy Loam

As the name suggests, this is a loam with a higher proportion of sand present. Drainage and aeration is excellent but in some sandy loams, especially those low in organic matter, moisture retention may be inadequate and plants may dry out quickly following rain or watering. Sandy loams are often very deep and frequently have ground water present. They also tend to be warmer than heavier soil types and this property may be helpful in cold climates. A good range of ferns can be grown in soils of this type.

Sand

In this soil class, the sand grains are visible. These granules may be fine, or large and coarse, resembling gravels. Although drainage is excellent, the organic matter is often low and mineral deficiencies are common. The range of ferns which can be grown in such soils is limited, although some hardy groups such as species of *Cheilanthes* may succeed very well.

SOIL PREPARATION PRIOR TO PLANTING

Soil preparation is not always necessary prior to planting ferns, however, it can aid in their quick establishment. This is especially true in poor soils or those depleted by the heavy growth of other garden plants or weeds. In poor soils, the better the soil preparation prior to planting, the quicker the establishment and resultant growth of plants.

Digging the soil to a depth of 20–30 cm ((8–12 in) is a simple and obvious preparation technique. Weeds can be removed at the time of digging and the soil will be loosened allowing rapid establishment of new fern roots. If perennial creeping weeds such as couch grass are present these should be removed completely by digging or spraying with an appropriate herbicide. The addition of well rotted manures or other organic material is beneficial to all soils and if it is dug in prior to planting so much the better. Lime will be of benefit in acid soils.

IMPROVEMENT OF PROBLEM SOILS

Heavy Clay

Heavy clay is difficult to cultivate no matter what its moisture content. It can be improved by the liberal incorporation of organic matter, gritty materials such as gravels, crushed rock and coarse sand, and by the addition of gypsum. The gypsum should be applied when the soil is slightly moist at the rate of 1–1.5 kg per square metre (2–3 lb per square yard) and worked into the top soil layer. It acts by causing the clay particles to clump together into small aggregates allowing better moisture penetration and aeration. Gypsum works best in the presence of organic matter, and for maximum improvement of clay soils, all the materials mentioned above should be used together. Repeat applications of gypsum may be needed every 4–5 years but the organic matter should be topped up every 6–12 months. Gypsum has a negligible effect on soil pH, and if the clays are very acid, liming may also be necessary.

Clay soils are prone to surface compaction and this may adversely affect fern growth. This problem can be overcome by maintaining an organic mulch on the soil surface. Clay soils generally have a shallow topsoil. The depth of a garden can be increased by the simple process of creating sunken paths and mounding up garden beds with the soil taken from the paths.

Waterlogged Soils

Ferns are quite happy in wet soil, where the water is moving, however, they do dislike waterlogged soils. In such soils the water is usually stagnant (and cold) and aeration is insufficient for root growth. Waterlogged soils can be improved by the use of surface drains, or underground drains, or by using tolerant plants which can help remove excess water. A simple technique is to excavate paths which can double as surface drains and the excavated soil can be used to raise garden beds.

Sandy Soils

Sandy soils generally have a low water holding capacity and ferns growing in them may wilt frequently and severely. The obvious answer is to water frequently and to add plenty of organic material, both by digging in and applying it as a surface mulch. In these soil types, organic manures and animal manures are better than inorganic fertilizers. Sandy soils often become water repellent when they become very dry. Again this can be overcome by liberal mulching with organic material.

Alkaline Soils

Soils which have an excess of calcium salts have a high pH, and are commonly referred to as limey or calcareous soils. Unhealthy plant growth is common in calcareous soils, usually because of the unavailability of elements such as zinc, iron and manganese. Some ferns, however, grow very well in calcareous soils and these are known as the lime lovers or calciphiles (see Appendix 9).

When there are large quantities of calcium present in the soil profile it is difficult to lower the pH, however, a few techniques can improve the soil and increase the range of species which can be grown. Once again the continued heavy application of organic matter will improve the soil structure and will have some acidifying effect. Elemental sulphur and aluminium sulphate are acidifying agents, but large quantities may be necessary for significant acidification.

Acid Soils

Soils with a pH less than 5.0 benefit from the addition of lime. Lime reduces acidity, supplies calcium which is often deficient in such soils, and reduces toxic levels of manganese and aluminium. The amount of lime to be added depends on factors such as the pH, soil type and the range of ferns to be grown. Some ferns are lime haters (calcifluges) and will only thrive in its absence (see Appendix 10). The majority of ferns, however, do respond to lime in acid soils. Soils with a pH of 4.5 will need more lime to reduce the acidity by one unit, than soils at a pH of 5.5. Clay soils have a capacity to buffer the addition of lime, without the corresponding pH change that occurs as when lime is added to sandy soils. It may also be very difficult to reduce the acidity of peaty soils because of their very acid nature and very high levels of organic matter.

ORGANIC SOIL ADDITIVES

Ferns like an organically rich soil and the addition of organic matter to the soil in which they are growing is beneficial, as it is to most garden soils. Some types of organic matter, however, are more beneficial than others.

Some organic materials are principally composed of carbon compounds such as cellulose and lignin and contain very little in the way of nitrogenous compounds. If these are added to the soil, without any prior treatment, they can impoverish the soil of nitrogen and cause deficiency in the surrounding ferns. This occurs simply because the bacteria which attack the cellulose compounds need nitrogen for their functions and reproduction. As there is insufficient nitrogen in the material being attacked, they use the reserves of nitrogen in the soil and they can compete very successfully for it with the fern roots. Such materials are described as having a high carbon : nitrogen ratio. Materials of this type can be successfully used as a mulch if nitrogenous fertilizers are added to the soil at the same time or if they are composted before being added to the soil. A large range of organic materials can be added to soils where ferns are to be grown.

Leaf Mould

Ferns love leaf mould both as a top dressing (or mulch) and when it is dug in prior to planting. A wide range of leaves exists and most of them seem to be beneficial as an organic additive. Those of the oak seem to be held in high esteem by fern fanciers, but even hard ligneous leaves like those of eucalypts can be satisfactory if treated correctly. Beech leaves are also good and they may be preferred by some ferns as they have an alkaline pH. Conifer leaves and pine needles are generally unsatisfactory because of resins and their ability to mat and shed water. Even these, though, may be appreciated by some ferns whose natural habitat is coniferous forest.

Leaves can be added directly as a mulch, however, if they are to be dug in to the soil it is best if they are first partially rotted and crumbly. This is simply achieved by stacking the leaves in a frame and keeping them moist. The leaves should be allowed to pack down under their own weight. For ligneous leaves such as eucalypts a light dressing of a nitrogenous fertilizer over each 30 cm (12 in) layer will aid in their partial breakdown. The leaves are usually ready for use after being stacked for 4–6 months. If first chopped with a rotary mower the time taken can be reduced by two thirds.

Peat Moss

Peat moss is the stable end product of sphagnum moss which has decayed over thousands of years under very acid conditions. It is very fibrous and has a high water holding capacity (peat moss can hold ten times its own weight in water, most of which is available for plant growth). It is an excellent soil additive and is appreciated by ferns. It is, however, very acid (pH 4.5–5.0) and lime loving ferns may need a lime additive. Peat moss is also very low in nutrients, but has the ability to hold added nutrients in a form available for fern growth. Peat moss is scarce and expensive in some countries but freely available in others. It is one of the best organic ameliorants which can be added to soil.

Spent Hops

Spent hops are a useful organic soil additive for those who live near a brewery. Fresh hops can be too strong, but if the material is left in a heap and kept moist for 2–3 months it can then be used safely.

Sedge Peats

Sedge peat is derived from the organic material which has accumulated in swamps and bogs where rushes and sedges grow. In general, sedge peats are inferior in all respects when compared with peat moss. Sedge peats are extremely variable, some being quite fibrous, others black and powdery.

Some sedge peats are stable when exposed to the air while others break down and lose their structure. Sedge peats are generally less acid than sphagnum peats (pH 4–6) and are higher in nitrogen (some samples have up to 1% nitrogen). Some sedge peats may be unsuitable as soil additives because they contain high levels of salt.

Rice Hulls

Rice hulls can be a useful additive to garden soils but they do have a fairly high carbon : nitrogen ratio and can use up nitrogen reserves from the soil. Because of this, they are best composted or stored for a couple of months in a heap after sprinkling lightly with a nitrogenous fertilizer.

Peanut Shells

Peanut shells are soft and break down quite easily. They are an excellent organic material to add to soils and are commonly used in tropical regions. Heavy applications may tie up nitrogen, making necessary the use of nitrogenous fertilizers.

Seaweed

Seaweed is available in quantities on some beaches especially after storms and onshore blows. It can be used to make compost, or as a mulch, or dug into the soil. Seaweed is an excellent source of organic material and is rich in potassium. It is especially useful as an additive to sandy soils and has proved to be beneficial to ferns. Some growers hose the seaweed thoroughly before use to remove any salt.

Compost

Digging in well prepared compost is an excellent way of boosting the organic reserves of a soil. The compost can be made from a variety of organic materials including those with a high carbon : nitrogen ratio. Grinding or chopping the organic materials speeds up decomposition because it increases the surface area available for attack by the micro-organisms. Fertilizers or manures may have to be added to keep the decomposition process going. The finished compost has a neutral pH after first being acidic then alkaline. It is not a good idea to add any form of lime to the compost as large amounts of nitrogen can be lost to the atmosphere.

10 The basics of fern nutrition

Ferns, like other plants, must extract nutrients from the soil so that they can grow and reproduce. These nutrients or elements are present in the soil in various chemical forms and are taken up through the roots of the fern. They are essential for normal fern growth and development and though some are needed in large quantities (the major elements) others are only required in small amounts (the minor or trace elements). The elements listed below are essential for normal growth and development in most plants and it is assumed that ferns are no different.

Major Elements	*Minor Elements*
Nitrogen	Iron
Phosphorus	Manganese
Potassium	Boron
Magnesium	Zinc
Calcium	Copper
Sulphur	Molybdenum
	Chlorine
	Cobalt
	Sodium

As well as nutrients, ferns also need carbon dioxide, water and oxygen. Carbon dioxide is taken in from the air through the small pores in the fronds called stomata. Inside the frond it is converted by the process of photosynthesis into sugars, using the energy of the sun. Water and oxygen, which are vital for fern growth, are taken in through the roots.

Carbon Dioxide Enhancement

Carbon dioxide is present in the atmosphere as about 0.033% of the air. This is adequate for normal plant growth outside, but carbon dioxide can sometimes be deficient in greenhouses where ventilation is inadequate, or when cold weather necessitates them being closed. The enrichment of the atmosphere of a greenhouse to about 0.1% carbon dioxide can actually promote growth. This enrichment is carried out by injecting carbon dioxide gas directly into the atmosphere or by burning materials which release carbon dioxide, e.g. natural gas.

Nutrients in the Soil

Healthy ferns need a balanced supply of all of the above elements. If only one is in short supply, growth will be reduced or malformed, despite an abundance of all the others. Most soils provide these elements in sufficient quantity for normal fern growth. Sometimes, however, they become short and we have to boost the levels present by the addition of manures or fertilizers. Sometimes an imbalance exists between different elements which disrupts growth and this is much more difficult to detect and correct. Strangely, although an element may be present in abundance in a soil, it may not be in a form available for plant growth. This is usually related to the acidity or alkalinity of the soil (see below). Waterlogging can also change the availability of elements to plants.

A rich soil promotes good growth because it has an abundance of elements present in forms which can be readily taken up by fern roots. This is particularly true of nitrogen which is required in good quantities for all plant growth. Soil reserves may be depleted by cropping, by the strong growth of grasses or weeds or by leaching following heavy rains. When soil reserves of nutrients are reduced, plant growth suffers. Normal growth resumes following the application of sufficient quantities of fertilizers or manures. Balanced applications are necessary since all plants grow better if a balance of nutrients is available to them, rather than if there is an excess of one particular element.

Acidity or Alkalinity

The acidity or alkalinity of a soil is extremely important since it critically affects the growth of ferns for the following reasons.

1. Ferns have acidity or alkalinity preferences. Many prefer to grow in acid soils, but there are a large number of species which will not tolerate such soils and will linger and die in them. These are the lime loving ferns or calciphiles and an alkaline soil is essential for their successful growth. Often an indication of their preference can be obtained from their habitat in nature and this can be confirmed by a simple test using a commercial kit (see below). Some ferns may have a very low tolerance of acidity or alkalinity yet others (the adaptable ones) will grow in a much wider range of acid or alkaline soils.
2. Extremes of acidity or alkalinity can influence the availability of some of the nutrients. Thus, in very

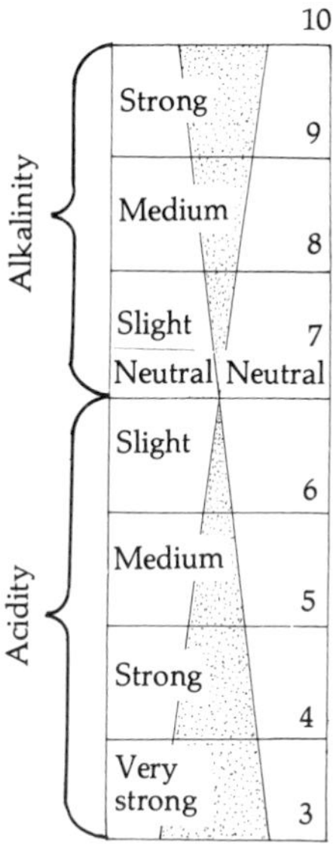

The soil pH scale

alkaline soils, iron and zinc may be unavailable to the ferns for growth, resulting in deficiency symptoms, and in very acid soils, manganese and aluminium may reach levels which are toxic.

The acidity or alkalinity of a soil can be measured by its pH. This is a logarithmic function of the hydrogen ions in the soil and its measure enables potential problems to be anticipated as well as allowing a direct comparison between soils. The pH scale ranges from 0–14 with 7 being neutral, 14 very alkaline and 1 very acid. Soils commonly range from pH4 to 9. The accompanying figure illustrates the pH scale. The pH of a soil can be measured accurately in laboratories using electronic apparatus. A very good field measure can be obtained by using a simple testing kit that is based on the colour changes in a mixture of dyes. These kits are generally cheap and can be quite effective.

DETAILS OF EACH ELEMENT

Nitrogen

Nitrogen is used in the fern for the formation of amino acids which are the building blocks of proteins. Nitrogen is also important in the formation of chlorophyll, which is the green pigment in fronds, essential for photosynthesis. Most of the air we breathe is composed of nitrogen (78%), but in this form it cannot be used by plants. Plants such as ferns can only absorb it from the soil as ammonium or nitrate which is released by the breakdown of organic materials. Nitrogen is readily lost from the soil by leaching following heavy rains or watering.

For vigorous growth, ferns need a steady supply of nitrogen throughout the growing season. Nitrogen encourages vegetative growth and produces a lush greenness in the fronds. If used in excess, however, it can weaken plants and may increase their susceptibility to some diseases and frost. Ferns suffering from a deficiency of nitrogen are usually stunted and have uniform, pale green or yellowish fronds which are smaller than normal.

Sources: Nitrogen is present in animal manures (see page 92), organic fertilizers (see page 90) and mixtures of inorganic fertilizers. The release of nitrogen from manures and organic fertilizers is usually slow and steady but that from inorganic fertilizers can be rapid. Nitrogen can be applied in a balanced mixture, or on its own as a specific chemical compound. These compounds are listed in the accompanying table. Applications of these materials must be used with care on ferns, especially slow growing types. They can be very useful on vigorous species (especially in the tropics) and the author has used materials such as urea with good effect on tree ferns.

Nitrogen can also be applied as a foliar spray (calcium nitrate 2 g/L [0.5 oz/gal] or urea 1.5 g/L [0.4 oz/gal]) or as a liquid fertilizer to the roots (ammonium nitrate 10 g/L [2.5 oz/gal], calcium nitrate (12 g/L [3 oz/gal]). For ferns in containers ammonium nitrate at 1 g/L (0.3 oz/gal) is adequate.

Nitrogen Compound	*% Nitrogen*	*Rate of Use* per square metre	per square yard
Ammonium nitrate	35	250 g	9 oz
Calcium nitrate	15	500 g	18 oz
Ammonium sulphate	20	500 g	18 oz
Potassium nitrate	13	500 g	18 oz
Sodium nitrate	15	500 g	18 oz
Urea	46	150 g	5 oz

Phosphorus

Phosphorus is virtually used in every important process in plants. It is particularly significant in the storage and supply of energy in respiration and photosynthesis. It is also important for root growth and reproduction. Phosphorus is deficient in the soils of many parts of the world. In some soils which are rich in iron or aluminium it may be present but is fixed in a form unavailable for plant growth. Phosphorus does not move readily through the soil and is not leached by rain or watering.

Phosphorus encourages strong growth in ferns and is important for a sturdy root system. Ferns deficient in phosphorus may be stunted with very dark green fronds and a reduced root system.

Sources: Phosphorus is present in animal manures (see page 92), organic fertilizers (see page 90), and mixtures of inorganic fertilizers. Phosphorus can also be applied as a specific fertilizer using materials such as superphosphate or ground rock phosphate. Ammonium phosphate, potassium phosphate and monocalcium phosphate are soluble compounds and can be used for foliar applications or as liquid fertilizers where rapid uptake is needed.

Potassium

Potassium is important for the lengthening of tissues such as stipes and stems, and also plays a major role in protection against disease by thickening the outer cell walls of plant tissues. It is also significant in chlorophyll formation, reproduction and root development. Potassium is commonly deficient in sandy soils and in soils that are cropped regularly.

Potassium is important for root development and disease resistance in ferns. Ferns deficient in potassium may show marginal patches or a border of dead tissue on the older fronds.

Sources: Potassium is present in animal manures (see page 92) and mixtures of inorganic fertilizers. Wood ash (3–10%) and seaweed (25%) are also a good source of potassium. Specific chemicals which can be used to supply potassium include potassium sulphate, potassium chloride and potassium nitrate. These are readily soluble. Liquid seaweed extracts are rich in potassium and can be useful for potted ferns.

Calcium

Calcium is an important element used in cell wall construction, cell division and protein formation. It is also very important for the development of a healthy root system. Calcium is commonly deficient in acid soils, especially the sandy types.

Ferns need calcium for sturdy growth and it is of special importance for the lime loving types. Ferns deficient in calcium develop stunted, distorted fronds which tend to die back from the tip. The root system is also reduced.

Sources: Calcium is present in some organic fertilizers (see page 90). It is also readily applied using ground limestone, hydrated lime, dolomite or gypsum. The first three are best used on acid soils since they also reduce the acidity. Gypsum does not alter the pH and also supplies sulphur (for details on forms of lime see page 93). Crushed egg shells and sea shells can be useful sources of calcium in potting mixes (see page 94).

Magnesium

This element is vital for photosynthesis since it is an important component of chlorophyll. Magnesium may be deficient in acid, sandy soils but is usually readily available in soils with a high clay content. It may be leached from sandy soils by rainfall or watering. Ferns deficient in magnesium may show a chlorosis on the older fronds with the main veins remaining dark green.

Sources: Magnesium can be applied as magnesium sulphate to the soil or as a foliar spray, 10–15 g/L (2–3 oz/gal) or by the use of dolomite. Successive foliar sprays may be necessary to correct severely deficient plants. Dolomite is useful on acid soils because it also reduces acidity.

Sulphur

Sulphur is an important constituent of some amino acids and chlorophyll, and is a necessary element in the formation of roots. Sulphur is commonly available in the organic matter of soils and is released as the organic matter breaks down. It may be deficient in sandy soils where the organic matter is low and the sulphur is readily leached.

Sulphur deficiency is not common and affected plants are a uniform pale green (similar to those deficient in nitrogen).

Sources: Sulphur, as a component of fertilizers such as superphosphate, or magnesium and potassium sulphate is frequently applied to ferns. It can also be applied as elemental sulphur or gypsum. It should be noted that elemental sulphur increases soil acidity and therefore perhaps should not be applied to acid soils. Gypsum on the other hand does not affect soil pH.

Iron

This element is needed in continuous small amounts for the functioning of chloroplasts and in enzymes. Iron is usually present in abundance in soils, however, it is not always available to plants because of interaction with other elements, particularly lime. In alkaline or calcareous soils a condition known as lime-induced iron chlorosis is common. Ferns that grow naturally on calcareous soils seem to handle this situation satisfactorily, however, those used to growing in acid soils may suffer severely. The symptoms in ferns are pale green to yellow new fronds with prominent dark veins. In severe cases brown patches appear in the fronds, which may eventually die.

Sources: The particular iron fertilizer used depends on the soil pH. Ferric sulphate is used if the soil pH is between 5 and 6, ferrous sulphate if between 6 and 7 and iron chelates if the pH is above 7. Iron chelates are mainly used to correct lime-induced iron chlorosis and are effective if applied to the soil around the plant and watered in.

Manganese

This element is required in small quantities for enzyme systems ard is also used in photosynthesis. It is commonly deficient in alkaline soils rich in organic matter. In very acid soils or those subject to waterlogging manganese may be present in toxic amounts.

Ferns suffering from manganese deficiency may

show curled or cupped fronds and chlorotic patches with the veins remaining green.

Sources: Very small amounts of manganese sulphate can be applied to the soil or used as a foliar spray, i.e. 2 g/L (0.4 oz/gal).

Boron

This element is required in small amounts for cell construction in actively growing parts such as meristems and root tips. Boron is frequently deficient in calcareous soils. On the other hand, soils formed from coastal sediments may have boron present in toxic amounts.

Ferns suffering from boron deficiency may show thickened, malformed fronds.

Sources: Small amounts of borax, i.e. 2-4 g/10 m^2 (0.05-0.15 oz/10 yd^2) can be applied or used as a foliar spray (boric acid at 1 g/L [0.2 oz/gal]).

Zinc

This element is of prime importance in plants for the production of growth hormones responsible for leaf and stem development and expansion. Zinc deficiency is common in calcareous soils and may also occur in heavily leached sands. Ferns with zinc deficiency produce markedly shortened, malformed fronds which may show irregular yellowish interveinal areas when young.

Sources: Small amounts of zinc sulphate can be added to the soil or applied as a foliar spray, i.e. 0.5 g/L (0.03-0.1 oz/gal).

Copper

This element is required in small quantities for use in enzyme systems. It is occasionally deficient in sandy soils and more frequently in calcareous soils. Ferns with copper deficiency may show wilting and dieback of young fronds or malformations.

Sources: Small amounts of copper sulphate readily correct this deficiency (about 10 g/10 m^2 [0.4 oz/10 yd^2]) or as a foliar spray of copper oxychloride 0.5 g/L (0.1 oz/gal).

The requirements of ferns for the elements molybdenum, chlorine, cobalt and sodium are uncertain.

11 Fertilizers, manures and lime

Despite some widely held beliefs to the contrary, ferns do respond to the artificial application of nutrients in the form of fertilizers and/or manures. The amount of these materials to be applied and the frequency of their application will vary with such factors as the richness of the soil and its organic content, the heaviness and frequency of rainfall and other climatic factors such as the temperature. Strong growing ferns need more nutrients and respond to manures and fertilizers more vigorously than do weaker or slow growing ferns.

Most ferns appreciate well-rotted animal manures or organic fertilizers such as bone meal, hoof and horn and blood and bone. Inorganic fertilizers can be very useful for strong, vigorous ferns such as tree-ferns, but should be used carefully on weak growing ferns. They are best applied in conjunction with organic mulches. Liquid fertilizers can be beneficial especially for ferns in containers, so too are organic extracts.

Fertilizers can be applied by digging into the soil prior to planting or by placing directly into the hole at planting time; slow release fertilizers are excellent for the latter method. After the ferns are established, fertilizers can be applied as regular top dressings on the soil surface, with several light applications in the growing season being preferable to one heavy application. The fertilizer should not be applied right against the active growing region or burning may result. The best times to apply fertilizers and/or manures is in spring or early summer while the plants have a long growing period ahead of them. An ideal time is when the fern is just starting on a flush of growth. Late applications of fertilizer or manures may interfere with the plants dormancy producing late growth and reducing its ability to survive a cold winter.

ORGANIC FERTILIZERS

Traditionally, organic fertilizers have been used in fern growing along with animal manures. As the name suggests, these materials are organic in origin and are composed of waste materials such as blood, blood and bone, bone meal, hoof and horn etc. All supply the major elements of nitrogen, phosphorus and calcium and, as well, have organic components which are useful in maintaining soil structure.

Organic fertilizers are favoured for ferns because they release their nutrients in a slow, gentle manner over quite a period of time; burning or plant damage is a rare occurrence. They are ideal for including in the hole at planting time or as a side dressing to maintain growth. They can also be added to potting mixes and are generally very beneficial to the growth of ferns in containers. Unfortunately, nowadays, they are not as commonly available as they used to be and are becoming more expensive. The nutrient composition of the commonly used organic fertilizers is shown in the accompanying table and a few details on each fertilizer follow.

Constituents of Commonly Used Organic Fertilizers

	% Nitrogen	*% Phosphorus*	*% Calcium*
Dried blood	12–15	–	–
Meat and bone	5–6	13–16	4–5
Blood and bone	4–7	4–7.5	5
Bone meal	2–4	2–8	3–5
Bone flour	0.5–1	6–12	2–4
Hoof and horn	12–14	1–2	3–5
Fish meal	7–9	3–8	–
Sewage sludge	4–6	2–4	–

Dried Blood

This material is obtained from abattoirs and killing works. It contains only nitrogen but is quite rich in this compound and promotes good, steady growth. It has a few drawbacks in that it is smelly, attracts dogs, rats etc. and may go mouldy if applied too thickly. These days dried blood is becoming very difficult to obtain. Application rates are about 50 g/m^2 of soil (2 oz/yd^2).

Blood and Bone

This material is a mixture of dried blood and crushed bone and supplies nitrogen, phosphorus and calcium. It is an excellent fertilizer for ferns, and is very commonly used by fern enthusiasts. It can be incorporated into the soil or potting mix or applied as a side dressing. It releases the nutrients slowly over a period of time and promotes steady growth. Blood and bone has a few drawbacks, one of the worst being the smell which prohibits its use on indoor ferns. It also attracts dogs and other carrion eaters such as rats and these animals may severely damage ferns in their efforts to get at the blood and bone. If applied too thickly to the soil surface, blood and bone may go mouldy and the resulting fungus can spread to sensitive ferns. It is commonly applied at about 50–100 g/m^2 of soil (2–4 oz/yd^2).

Meat and Bone

Most of the remarks made under blood and bone apply here especially the smells, attraction to vermin and the growth of moulds. This material is richer in phosphorus than blood and bone.

Bone Meal

This material is simply crushed bone and may be either of a floury or a gritty texture. It has proved to be quite useful for ferns especially if added to a potting mix. The nitrogen level is too low for strong growth and may need supplementing. Unlike dried blood and blood and bone, bone meal does not have an offensive smell or attract dogs. It can be safely used at a rate of 100–150 g/m^2 of soil (4–6 oz/yd^2).

Bone Flour

This material is made by finely crushing bones that have been extracted for glue production. As well as being more finely ground than bone meal it is richer in phosphorus but poorer in nitrogen, as protein is extracted in the glue making process. It can be used at similar rates to those of bone meal.

Hoof and Horn

This is a crushed mixture of animal bones, hooves and horns. It is an excellent fertilizer for ferns being quite rich in nitrogen, with a useful component of phosphorus and calcium. It releases the nutrient steadily over a fairly long period and promotes good growth. Hoof and horn is an excellent additive to potting mixes for ferns and can also be used as a dressing for plants in the ground. It does not smell or attract animals. It is usually applied at 50 g/m^2 of soil (2 oz/yd^2).

Fish Meal

This is ground up fish which may have been processed for a chemical use such as oil extraction. It is an excellent fertilizer but is smelly and attracts dogs, cats and vermin.

Sewage Sludge

Sewage sludge is frequently available from sewage disposal centres. It is an excellent fertilizer for vegetables and fruits but its effect on ferns is unknown to the author.

INORGANIC FERTILIZERS

Inorganic fertilizers are manufactured chemicals which supply one or more nutrients for plant growth. They are usually simple inorganic salts and are nearly all freely soluble in water, i.e. they dissolve readily when applied to the soil, following rain or watering, and supply nutrients quickly to plants. Inorganic fertilizers are widely used in agriculture and horticulture and are a cheap means of supplying nutrients for plant growth.

Manufactured fertilizers are regarded by some people as unnatural and as having an adverse effect on the growth of plants. This is not so, but it is true that they have no organic component and therefore are of no benefit to the structure of the soil or the microbial flora and fauna. If used in conjunction with heavy mulches or organic matter, however, this drawback is eliminated and a maximum response is obtained from their application.

Complete Fertilizers

As the name suggests, these fertilizers supply a range of nutrients for plant growth. They are virtually inorganic fertilizers which have been mixed together in different combinations. Some complete fertilizers only supply nitrogen, phosphorus and potassium, whereas others may supply all the major and some of the minor elements. By changing the ratios of nutrients, these complete fertilizers can be used for different purposes, e.g. high nitrogen, low phosphorus and potassium for frond growth; or low nitrogen, high phosphorus and potassium for root growth and sporing.

Complete fertilizers are very useful as maintenance dressings for established ferns, either in pots or in the garden, but they should be used sparingly and not at high rates without prior testing. This is especially true for potted plants because rapid solubility of the fertilizers can result in burning of the roots, with resultant damage to the fronds. Complete fertilizers are excellent for maintaining the growth of ferns under established trees where root competition is a major problem. In the tropics, where leaching of soil nutrients is severe, they are very useful for maintaining growth and colour in vigorous ferns such as *Nephrolepis* and tree ferns. In these conditions they can be applied as a surface dressing every 6–8 weeks during the growing season at a rate of about 50–100 g/m^2 of soil (2–4 oz/yd^2).

Slow-release Fertilizers

Slow-release fertilizers are excellent for container-grown ferns because their nutrients are released gradually rather than in one short burst. They can be included in a potting mix or applied as a dressing on the top of the potting mix of established ferns. All slow-release fertilizers are manufactured chemicals and they release their nutrients over a given period of time. Slow-release fertilizers in the simple form can be slowly soluble chemicals such as ureaformaldehyde. Most commonly, they are inorganic fertilizers coated with slowly soluble materials such as polymers or sulphur compounds. They are available in a variety of shapes and preparations from coarse lumps to granular pellets, rounded prills and even large tablets or plant pills.

Slow-release fertilizers are an ideal means of maintaining steady growth in ferns. In potting mixes, they are best distributed evenly through the mix, whereas for ferns in the ground they should be applied in small concentrations on the surface or buried shallowly. Some slow-release fertilizers only supply nitrogen, while others contain nitrogen, phosphorus, potassium and a few even include trace elements. Some of the polymer coated types operate on a timed release system with different coatings giving release rates from 3–4 months to 12–14 months. By mixing combinations of the different release rates, a steady release of nutrients can be maintained over a long period.

Liquid Fertilizers

Liquid fertilizers are a very popular form of promoting the growth of ferns in containers. There are many different commercial preparations available which are similar in their composition and effects on fern growth. Most of these consist of a balanced mixture of inorganic chemicals, although some organic extracts may also prove useful (see below). Liquid fertilizers must be readily soluble and easy to use. It is this solubility and ready availability to fern roots which makes them so suitable for ferns in containers or where a rapid response is needed for a fern in the ground. Application rates as recommended by the manufacturer should be followed.

Inorganic salts that are soluble in water can be applied in a liquid form. These can be specific chemicals used to correct a deficiency (e.g. potassium sulphate to supply potassium) or simply to promote strong growth (e.g. ammonium or calcium nitrate — see page 87 for rates).

Foliar Fertilizers

Some nutrients can be readily taken in through the leaves of plants, and hence ferns can be fed by foliar fertilizers through their fronds as well as their roots. Commercial mixtures are available for this purpose and should be used at the recommended strength. They are applied by spraying a dilute mixture onto the leaves. Some of the elements are absorbed rapidly within a few hours of application. The best time for foliar feeding is late in the evening or early in the morning when humidity is high. Uptake of nutrients is fastest in young fronds or those recently expanded, so be sure to wet them well. The fronds should be sprayed to run-off; any excess which drips on the soil can be taken up by the roots. The addition of a wetting agent at the recommended rate can help the material spread and stick to the fronds. A light spraying of water in between applications of nutrients can increase the uptake of remaining nutrients. Foliar feeding is best carried out during the warm, growing months at intervals of 2–4 weeks.

ORGANIC EXTRACTS

A few commercial products are available which are not strictly fertilizers but which, nevertheless, promote the growth of ferns. These are extracts of organic materials such as seaweed and fish. Seaweed extracts are used for a variety of plants and some specialist fern growers such as those growing maidenhairs and Boston ferns, swear by their use. Seaweed is rich in potassium, but growers claim that the growth responses from seaweed extracts are more than just an effect of this element. Fish emulsion is also used by fern growers and is also extremely popular with orchid enthusiasts. It has proved to be particularly beneficial to epiphytic species. One drawback of fish emulsion is the strong, distinctive smell which permeates the air where it has been used.

ANIMAL MANURES

Using animal manures to mulch or top dress ferns has the double benefit of providing plant nutrients as well as organic matter which is beneficial to soil structure and the microbial flora and fauna. The manures must, however, be old (at least 4–6 months) or well-rotted, because fresh manures can cause burning or result in soft, weak growth. Manures are very beneficial for problem soils. On sandy soils they provide important organic material and increase the water holding capacity and on clay soils they help aggregate the particles and improve drainage. Manures can also be used to make compost which can then be applied as a mulch or soil additive. Some manures, such as sheep manure, may contain grass and weed seeds and should be composted first.

Animal manures vary considerably in their chemical composition but all contain nitrogen, phosphorus and potassium. When fresh or in the early stages of decomposition, some are very rich in ammonia (e.g. chicken and horse manure). In this fresh form the ammonia will badly damage plant roots and can also be lost easily to the atmosphere. The chemical composition of commonly used animal manures is shown in the accompanying table.

Manure	*% Nitrogen*	*% Phosphorus*	*% Potassium*
Chicken	0.8–1.0	0.7–0.85	0.2–0.4
Horse	0.6–0.8	0.1–0.3	0.4–0.6
Cow	0.5–0.6	0.1–0.2	0.4–0.5
Pig	0.5–0.6	0.3–0.4	0.3–0.4
Sheep	0.8–0.9	0.3–0.4	0.8–1.0

Liquid Manures

Almost any animal manure may be applied to the soil around ferns in a liquid state. These liquid applications have the same advantages as liquid fertilizers but the disadvantages of being messy and smelly and hence are generally unsuitable for use indoors. Liquid manure can be simply made by adding solid animal manure to a drum of water and leaving it to steep until the nutrients are dissolved (usually 3–5 days is sufficient). The liquid fraction can then be removed and watered on direct or diluted further if it is very strong. The drum can be maintained by adding more manure and topping up with water as required. Liquid manure is best used as a side dressing every 6–8 weeks during the growing season and should not be applied so heavily that the roots become saturated.

LIME AND LIMING

Lime is of major importance to ferns, not only because it provides the element calcium, but also because it can reduce soil acidity and thus affect the availability of other elements for plant growth. Thus in very acid soils, levels of aluminium and manganese may be toxic, whereas deficiencies can occur in magnesium, calcium, sulphur and potassium. Lime is also useful in soils for maintaining structure (this is especially important in clay soils) and for bacterial and other microbial growth. It also offsets the acidity produced by chemical reactions when certain fertilizers are added to the soil, e.g. ammonium sulphate. Ferns in general seem to benefit from an annual dressing of lime with the exception of the lime haters, e.g. *Cryptogramma crispa* (see Appendix 10).

Forms of Lime

There are different forms of lime which can be used to raise the pH of soils. Lime occurs naturally as calcium carbonate and this may be present as limestone, seashells, marl or chalk. The lime commonly available for gardens is usually crushed or ground limestone. This is the easiest form to handle. When it is exposed to a hot, red flame the substance known as quicklime or calcium oxide is produced. Quicklime is extremely caustic to handle and it also causes rapid decomposition of animal and vegetable remains in the soil. It is therefore of considerable value in very acid soils or those very rich in stable, organic, fibrous materials such as peat soils. Quicklime takes up water from either the soil or the air to become slaked lime or calcium hydroxide. Over time, this calcium hydroxide reacts either with carbon dioxide in the atmosphere, or carbonic acid in the soil to form calcium carbonate once more. Dolomitic limestone is a mixture of calcium and magnesium carbonates and is mined from natural sources. Marble is metamorphosed limestone but is quite insoluble even when crushed, so it has limited value in supplying calcium.

The various forms of lime differ in their ability to reduce soil acidity. Quicklime is the most efficient, followed by slaked lime then ground limestone. Quicklime, however, is an unpleasant material to use and ground limestone is the commonest form applied to gardens. Dolomite is about half as effective as ground limestone in raising the pH, but can be valuable, as it also supplies the element, magnesium. In some countries, e.g. Spain and Portugal, Africa, USSR and USA, large natural deposits of calcium phosphate occur (termed phosphate of lime). When ground, these are a useful means of supplying phosphorus and calcium to the soil, but have a negligible effect on pH.

The amount of lime to be added to a soil to change the pH varies with the degree of acidity (see Acidity or Alkalinity page 86) and the soil type (see Acid Soils page 84). It is best to consult people with local experience before applying lime in any large quantities.

Limestone or Limerock

This is the naturally occurring rock which may be all calcium carbonate or have some other materials as impurities. Small limestone nodules, which occur naturally (e.g. in coastal sands), or limestone chips which can be obtained by breaking limestone with a hammer are useful for sprinkling around lime-loving ferns or adding to potting mixes. They should not be used to replace lime however, since their solubility is very slow and the amount of calcium they provide is minimal.

Chalk

This is a deposit of calcium carbonate usually mixed with clay and having other materials present. It may be hard, but usually crumbles on exposure to the air. It can be dug up, weathered and mixed with soil in the same way as lime.

Marl

These are materials which contain calcium carbonate bonded or mixed with other naturally occurring materials. Marls may be clayey, sandy, stony, chalky or shelly, depending on the material with which they are mixed. Some deposits are even found in peats. Marls frequently contain other useful plant nutrients such as phosphorus and potassium. They were amongst the earliest ameliorants to be added to soils and can be very beneficial. The amount of lime each contains varies with the location of the deposit and the type of marl. Chalk marl for example is much richer in calcium carbonate than is sandy marl. Clay marls can be of benefit in increasing the water holding capacity of sandy soils and sandy marls can open up heavy clays improving aeration and water penetration. Marls rich in shells may be advantageously added to potting mixes for ferns.

Calcareous Sands

These are a common form of calcium carbonate and may be found in inland regions or coastal districts where the deposits are rich in shells. They can be added to acid soils or used in potting mixes.

Egg Shells

These are a readily available form of calcium but should be crushed or powdered before use. A simple technique is first to dry the shells in an oven and then crush them in a mincer or blender. The powder can then be sprinkled on the soil or added to a potting mix.

Sea Shells

These are a convenient source of calcium for those who live near the sea. The shells are best broken or pounded before use. Some growers exclusively use oyster shells and claim that they are superior to any other shells.

Part Three

Pests, Diseases and Other Ailments of Ferns

12 Pest and disease control

Ferns are subjected to attacks by a wide range of pests and to a lesser extent, diseases. Most of these attacks are of a minor nature causing little significant damage to the plants and do not require drastic control measures. Sporadic attacks do occur however, which are of major significance and can result in stunting or even the death of the plant. Such attacks require rapid and effective control measures if the plants are to be saved.

In garden-grown ferns outbreaks of pests and diseases are infrequent and pest control occupies only a small proportion of the time spent on maintenance. In an artificial situation however, such as in a greenhouse or shadehouse, and particularly where the ferns are grown in pots, plants must be monitored for pests and diseases on a regular basis.

Vigorous, healthy ferns are able to withstand or tolerate pest or disease attack better than sick or weakened plants. If ferns are continually attacked by pests then perhaps this is an indication of some other ailment. The use of fertilizers often dramatically increases a fern's resistance to pests, especially if the plant has been previously starved.

Thrip damage on fronds of *Dryopteris*
Photo E. R. Rotherham

PEST CONTROL

Pest control can take the forms of handpicking and squashing, jetting with water from a hose and baiting, but most people resort directly to spraying with insecticides or fungicides. Before spraying, check the identity of the pest and ensure that it is still active. Identification of the pest is vital if the correct control procedure is to be used. Some pests rapidly build up in numbers, e.g. aphids. Pests should be dealt with as soon as they are noticed or they may quickly assume epidemic proportions.

With persistent or nasty pests such as fern scales it may be necessary to use drastic methods to eliminate them from a fern collection. Affected plants may be burnt, or quarantined and sprayed regularly, until the pest is eliminated. It is wise to check all new ferns before they are added to a collection, and quarantine them if necessary.

Pest control is basic commonsense. Not all insects are pests, so do not reach for the spray can every time you notice an insect crawling on your ferns. Make sure the ferns are being damaged, identify the culprit accurately and then use the appropriate control measures. Read the spray can labels carefully and do not spray at higher than the recommended strength. Remember, ferns can be damaged by some sprays even at the recommended strength (see Spray Damage, page 102) so, if in doubt two applications at reduced strength a few days apart may save a lot of heartbreak. Do not spray on windy days — the best time is in the morning or in the evening. Always use a mask, gloves and protective clothing when handling the chemicals, as well as when spraying. If spraying in a confined space, such as a greenhouse or shadehouse, be extra careful as the spray is not dispersed by wind.

Most pesticides are harmful to the environment and they affect birds and other wildlife, fish, spiders and beneficial insects such as bees. Therefore, it is important when spraying to spray only the plants being attacked and not to splash the spray about. If there is excess pesticide, dispose of it by digging a deep hole and pouring it in. Flatten and bury pesticide containers.

Pest Types

Pests feed on plants by either chewing the parts or sucking the sap. With the advent of wide spectrum pesticides the method of feeding adopted by the insect is not as important as it was when only specific insecticides were available. Some of the newer insecticides are not appropriate for ferns however, and the older, safer sprays can still give effective control if used properly. If the older-type sprays are to be used, it is important to determine how the pest is feeding as this will influence the choice of spray to be used. The major pests of ferns can be split into two groups:

Sucking Pests	Chewing Pests
Aphids	Caterpillars and grubs
Fern mirid bug	Cockroaches
Glasshouse thrips	Crickets
Mealy bugs	Earwigs
Mites	Fern weevil
Passion vine hopper	Fungus gnats
Scale insects	Grasshoppers
White fly	Millipedes
	Slaters
	Slugs and snails
	Staghorn beetle
	Staghorn borer
	Wireworms

PEST SPRAY TYPES

Sprays basically kill pests in one of three ways and an understanding of their mode of action is an important facet of effective control and also ensures that the correct spray is chosen for the job.

Contact Sprays

As the name suggests, these kill on contact. They are effective against both chewing and sucking pests and will kill virtually any insect contacted, either good or bad.

Stomach Poisons

These kill after they have been eaten by the insects. They are only effective against chewing insects.

Systemic Sprays

These sprays are absorbed into the sap stream and distributed throughout the plant. They are effective against sucking insects which feed on the sap. Unfortunately, many of these systemic sprays are very toxic and must be used carefully.

SAFER PEST SPRAYS

Some sprays are relatively safe to use and do not have a drastic effect on the environment. If used correctly they can give as effective a control as the more toxic sprays. For a list of the common and trade names of sprays mentioned in this book see Appendix 12.

Bacterial Spore Suspension

Commercial preparations of the spores of *Bacillus thuringiensis* are available under various trade names. These can be sprayed onto fronds where caterpillars are active, and when eaten, the spores germinate in the caterpillar's gut and kill it. The spores do not affect any other form of life and are safe for humans. The bacterial spores themselves are readily killed by ultraviolet light from the sun and to be effective should be applied in the evenings or during cloudy weather. For continuous protection, sprays must be applied every 10–14 days.

Clensel

This is a soapy type of solution of very low toxicity. It has some properties as a contact material and also kills by coating the insect and blocking its air supply. It is useful for controlling aphids and scales. Two or three sprays at intervals of 1–2 days may be necessary to clean up persistent attacks.

Derris Dust (Rotenone)

This material is a natural compound, obtained by crushing the roots of species of *Derris*, and is available in commercial preparations. It acts as a stomach poison and is effective when sprayed or dusted on foliage where caterpillars are active. It is broken down by sunlight and is best applied towards evening or during cloudy weather.

Garlic Spray

A natural spray made from cloves of garlic which is reputedly effective against a wide range of pests, including aphids and caterpillars. It is safe for the handler.

To make garlic spray crush 85 g (3 oz) of garlic cloves and mix with 10 mL (0.3 fl. oz) of paraffin oil. Leave for about 48 hours and then add 562 mL (nearly one pint) of water and 7 g (0.25 oz) of an oil-based soap. Mix thoroughly, filter out the lumps and store the concentrate in a plastic drum. This will keep for ever and can be used as needed. Dilutions range from 1 in 50 to 1 in 100 parts of water.

Pyrethrum

This is a naturally-occurring compound extracted from daisy flowers of the genera *Pyrethrum* and *Chrysanthemum*. It acts as a contact spray and is effective against a wide range of pests including aphids, caterpillars and bugs. Natural pyrethrum is broken down by sunlight but modern formulations are stabilized (see Permethrin).

Sulphur

Finely ground or micronized sulphur can be used as a dust against aphids and mites. Soluble sulphur, has some insecticide properties although it is mainly used as a fungicide.

White Oil

A viscous material which is effective against scale insects. It kills by coating the insect with a layer of oil which cuts off its air supply and the insect suffocates. A thorough coverage is essential for effective control. Two or three sprays at close intervals can also increase its effectiveness as can the inclusion of a contact insecticide such as pyrethrum or maldison. White oil may stunt the growth of ferns and also cause damage to young fronds and croziers. For ferns, it is best used at half to three quarters recommended strength. Damage is accentuated by high temperatures and white oil should not be sprayed when the ambient temperature is above 25°C (77°F).

LESS-SAFE PEST SPRAYS

Carbaryl

This is a manufactured chemical which acts as a stomach poison and is thus effective only against chewing insects. It is very persistent on the foliage and gives protection for 2–4 weeks. It is fairly safe to use but should still be handled with care.

Difocol

This is a manufactured chemical which is effective against mites. It is relatively safe but should still be handled with care.

Dimethoate

This is a manufactured chemical which is taken into the sap stream and distributed around the plant. It is thus a systemic insecticide and is only effective against sap-sucking pests. It is toxic and has a vile smell and must be handled with care. It should really be used only as a last resort for the control of persistent pests such as coconut scale.

Maldison

This is a manufactured chemical which kills any insect it contacts. It is effective against a wide range of insects including caterpillars, aphids and bugs and has some residual persistence on the foliage. Its effectiveness is increased if used in combination with white oil (see Combination Sprays below). It is toxic and should be used with due care.

Permethrin

This is a synthetically-manufactured pyrethrum compound which is resistant to breakdown by sunlight and will remain effective on the foliage for 10–14 days.

Tetradifon

This is a manufactured chemical which is effective in the control of mites. It is relatively safe to use and it does not kill beneficial insects nor damage foliage.

Combination Sprays

Some sprays are more effective when combined with other sprays than when used on their own. The effectiveness of white oil is increased by adding a contact insecticide such as maldison or pyrethrum. This combination also increases the effectiveness of the insecticide itself, because the white oil aids in its spreading and sticking powers. Remember, however, that ferns can be damaged by some sprays such as white oil and it would be a wise policy to use the combination at half to three quarters recommended strength of each material.

It should be noted that not all sprays are compatible and some should *not* be mixed together. Information on compatibility can be obtained from Departments of Agriculture or spray firms.

Baits

Baits containing stomach poisons are effective against pests such as cutworms, slugs, snails, earwigs and millipedes. The baits are generally scattered in the vicinity of the plants to be protected and may be effective for several weeks, although this depends on the weather conditions (baits often go mouldy when wet). Baits can be used strategically if something is known about the habits of the pest, for example, baiting dark humid areas for millipedes, baiting on rainy nights for slugs and snails, and baiting weedy areas for cutworms. Baits are poisonous and should not be placed where they can be eaten by pets or children.

Commercially-prepared baits are available and these are effective against a wide range of pests. An effective bait can be prepared at home by mixing 5 g (0.2 oz) of Paris Green or metaldehyde with 120 g (4.3 oz) of bran. Immediately before use sufficient water is added to form a crumbly mass and the bait can then be placed in small heaps. Another useful bait can be made by mixing one part pyrethrum powder or derris dust to two parts flour. Bran soaked in vinegar is an irresistible attractant to slugs and snails.

Dusts

Insecticides in powder form (dusts) can be applied to fern fronds or soil. Derris dust, which is widely used by vegetable gardeners to control caterpillars, is also very effective on ferns. Fine sulphur can be applied as a dust against aphids and, when used with equal parts by weight of hydrated lime it has been successful in controlling mites, but it must be applied to the underside of the fronds.

It should be noted that some dusts such as carbaryl

have been found to cause damage to the fronds of ferns. Foliage damage may result from using dusts when the ambient temperature is above 30°C (86°F).

DISEASE CONTROL

Diseases in ferns are a comparative rarity, especially serious diseases which cause widespread death. Most diseases which afflict ferns only cause limited damage and occur sporadically when a particular set of conditions favours an outbreak. At least one disease of ferns (that of hard crown) is insidious and causes stunted growth over many years.

Causative Agents

Diseases are primarily caused by three groups of pathogens – fungi, bacteria and viruses.

Soft brown scale on rachis and segments of *Asplenium cuneatum* Photo D. L. Jones

Fungi

Fungi can attack any part of the plant, but in ferns most attacks are centred on the roots, rhizome and fronds. Fungi spread by spores which drift around in the air currents. They are omnipresent and may only cause trouble when the ferns are weakened by some factor, or when conditions are optimum for their development. Some types are very troublesome during warm, humid, still weather. They can spread rapidly under these conditions and steps to control them should be taken immediately damage is noticed.

Elkhorn Tip Moth damage to fronds of *Platycerium bifurcatum* Photo D. L. Jones

Bacteria

Diseases caused by bacteria are uncommon in ferns. It is believed however, that some diseases which result in necrotic spots and patches of watery decayed tissue may be caused by bacteria. It is also a possibility that the damage to ferns caused by eelworms (see page 108) may be exacerbated by certain bacteria which are introduced to the fern from the gut of the eelworms. Experiments have shown, though, that the symptoms of damage may be produced by the bacteria alone in the absence of the eelworms. Bacterial diseases of plants can be very difficult to control and require different chemicals from fungal diseases.

Viruses

Viruses are minute particles which live and multiply within plant cells. Plant damage can result if they build up into sufficient numbers, or if they exist in certain combinations of different virus species. The presence of a virus in the plant cells causes symptoms in the leaves and shoots. Typical symptoms include irregular mosaic patterns on leaves and leaf distortion. Viruses are transmitted by sucking insects such as aphids and plant hoppers. Once established in a plant they are impossible to control.

Viruses are occasionally suspected as the cause of growth distortion and mosaic patterns in the fronds of certain ferns, however, to the author's knowledge

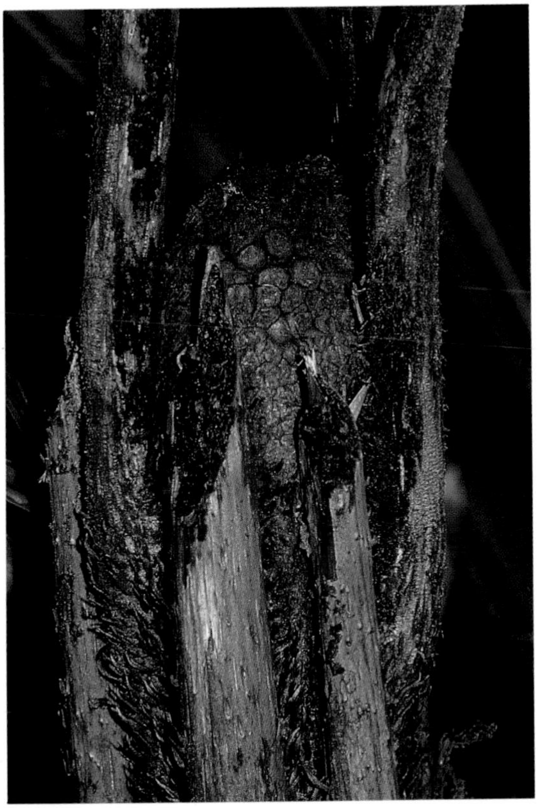

Deformed trunk apex on *Cyathea* caused by Hard Crown disease (*Rhizoctonia*) Photo D. L. Jones

Staghorn Borer damage in clump of *Platycerium bifurcatum* Photo D. L. Jones

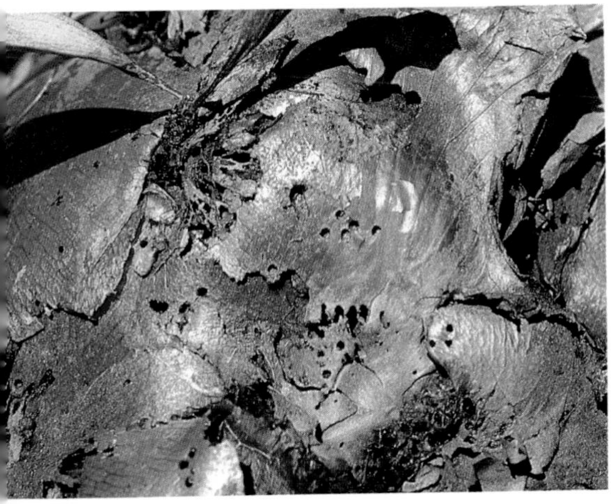

they have not been isolated as the causative agent. Plants suspected of being virus-infected should be destroyed, and aphids and other possible vectors should be controlled when noticed. Secateurs or knives should be sterilized if they have been used to cut plants suspected of being virus infected. Two commonly grown ferns which may be susceptible to virus are *Dryopteris erythrosora* and *Woodwardia orientalis*.

Symptoms of Disease

Leaf Spots

Small to large spots on the fronds and sometimes also on the stipes. The spots may be surrounded by a halo of lighter coloured tissue.

Blotches

When spots are large and irregular in shape they are usually called blotches.

Blights

A disease that kills young fronds, usually while they are in the process of unfolding.

Wilting

Young fronds wilt and rhizomes may die back from the tip. These symptoms indicate interruption to root growth or the water supply system.

Rots

Affected fern tissue goes slimy due to the disintegration of the cells.

Moulds and Mildews

Fungal threads obvious as a grey fluffy layer.

Practices to Reduce Disease Incidence

The best disease control relies on prevention rather than cure. The following points exemplify this.

1. Vigorous healthy ferns are better able to resist disease than are weak or unthrifty plants. When purchasing a fern only select from those which are healthy and vigorous. When growing ferns, attend to all factors such as drainage, fertilizing, watering and mulching and remember that any setback can contribute to the entry of disease.
2. Ferns like company, but avoid planting too thickly or crowding pots too close together, especially in sheltered, shady conditions. Air movement is an excellent control of some fungus diseases such as moulds. Thick planting of ferns may provide a rapid initial effect but thinning may be necessary later to maintain vigour.
3. When trimming back the rhizomes of spreading

ferns or when dividing ferns always seal any cuts in the rhizome by rubbing garden lime into the cut surface.
4. Remove and destroy any very weak or badly diseased ferns.
5. Initiate control measures as soon as diseases are first noticed. Use fungicidal treatments as a last resort and then in strict accordance with safety procedures and the manufacturer's directions.
6. Choose the correct fungicide for the job and wet the affected area thoroughly.

FUNGICIDAL SPRAYS

Fungicidal sprays, pastes or dusts can be used successfully for the control of diseases. They should, however, be handled carefully and with all due respect to the environment and health (as outlined earlier in this chapter). A fungicide generally controls a specific range of fungi, not a broad spectrum, hence the importance of identifying the fungus before choosing the chemical to be used. Not all fungicides are compatible with each other or with insecticides, and may cause problems if mixed together. Information on compatibility can be obtained from the Department of Agriculture or spray firms. Information on some commonly used fungicidal sprays follows. For a list of common and trade names see Appendix 12.

Benomyl

A systemic fungicide which has been promoted for controlling botrytis and other moulds. It is not very soluble in water and must be kept agitated while spraying. It is toxic to humans and may also damage ferns, especially prothalli. A combination fungicide or drench can be made by mixing benomyl with wettable sulphur (7.5 g sulphur, 1 g benomyl, 2 mL wetting agent, 2.25 L water).

Captan

A useful material against moulds and pythium. It is toxic and must be used with care but at the recommended strength it does not damage ferns.

Copper Oxychloride and Cupric Hydroxide

These are soluble copper sprays which are effective against a range of fungi. They are particularly good against leaf spots. Best used at about three quarter strength as they may damage foliage. Copper levels can build up following repeated spraying and may reach a concentration where they cause damage to ferns.

Dichloran

This is a manufactured fungicide which is useful as a soil drench against some soil-borne fungi. It is effective against damping off and may be useful for control of *Rhizoctonia*.

Dinocarp

This is a manufactured chemical which has been used effectively against mildews. It also has some effect as a miticide.

Fosetyl

A relatively new fungicide which is said to be effective against root-rotting fungi. It can be applied as a spray or drench. A mixture of fosetyl (1.25 g/L) and iprodione (1 g/L) is apparently very effective against many root-rotting fungi.

Iprodione

A useful fungicide for controlling damping off and grey mould.

Oxycarboxin

A fungicide which is effective at controlling rust diseases.

Propamacarb

A relatively new fungicide which is said to be effective against root rots caused by *Pythium*.

Sulphur

This material can be applied in a solution and is effective against a range of fungal diseases. It is available as a very fine powder (micronized sulphur) which is readily soluble in water. It is generally safe for ferns although it should not be applied on very hot days.

Thiram

Thiram can be a useful fungicide for the control of leaf spots and rusts. It does not damage foliage.

SPRAY DAMAGE

Ferns may be sensitive to concentrations of pesticides and fungicides. Some sprays can be very damaging and must be used at a reduced concentration or not at all. Spray damage usually shows up a few days after spraying and the plants may appear as if scorched or burnt. Young expanding fronds are particularly sensitive and usually show damage first. Not all species of ferns are sensitive to spray damage to the same extent. Some groups such as maidenhairs and fine, lacy *Nephrolepis* are sensitive to a wide range of sprays; others are rarely damaged, e.g. *Asplenium australasicum*.

It is a good policy to use all sprays on ferns at a reduced strength unless experience has shown them to be safe. In the author's experience, damage has resulted to ferns (mainly maidenhairs or young sporelings) from the following sprays applied at full strength

— carbaryl, maldison, diazinon, dimethoate, quintozen and thiram. Benomyl and pyrethrum may also cause damage to prothalli. White oil is safe to use in cool weather, but, if applied at full strength when the temperature is above 25°C (77°F), then stunting and damage can be expected. If white oil must be applied during warm weather then its strength should be reduced by one third to one half.

SPRAYING EQUIPMENT

A range of equipment is available for spraying pesticides onto plants. While a detailed coverage is beyond the scope of this book a few notes may be helpful.

Aerosol Sprays

Pesticide sprays in aerosol cans designed for use on plants are available from commercial outlets. These contain insecticides or fungicides and are safe for use on plants. Do not use aerosol sprays for household pests on plants as they contain chemical carriers which may damage leaves. Pressure packs for use on plants are relatively expensive but are useful to control sporadic outbreaks of pests such as aphids.

Atomizers

Efficient, small units that are suitable only for spraying indoor plants or small collections.

Hose Attachments

This very simple equipment consists basically of a valve attached to a hose and a container of concentrated solution. When the hose is turned on, the concentrate is sucked out and diluted with the water. Although simple and cheap, this equipment is not satisfactory for applying pesticides.

Slide Pump Sprayers

A range of simple sprayers use a moving cylinder to create pressure. Some slide pump sprayers such as stirrup pumps operate with the intake in a bucket; others have a sealed container which prevents spillage. Sprayers of this type are highly effective and ideal for fern collectors.

Compressed Air Sprayers

These sprayers are an extension of the previous group and have a pressure chamber which maintains spray delivery between pumps. The smaller types can be carried or worn on the back, and are designed primarily for home garden use. They are ideal for the enthusiast with a large collection of ferns.

13 Fern pests

Ants

Ants are not directly a pest of ferns, however, they foster the activities of honeydew producing pests such as aphids, scale and mealy bugs. The ants collect and feed on the sugary secretions of these pests and may farm them, moving them onto new plants or fresh new growth and guarding them against attack by predators. The widely distributed Argentine ant (*Iridomyrmex humilis*) is one of the worst offenders. In tropical and subtropical regions some ants may build a 'byre' to cover and protect the pests. This is usually made of chewed grass, pieces of leaves etc.

Control: Sticky solutions containing weak insecticides will reduce the incidence of ants. These should be smeared over the rhizome and base of the stipes or around the rim of the plant container.

Aphids

Aphids are very fond of ferns and usually congregate in colonies on young developing fronds. They are a familiar insect pest and feed by sucking the sap from young plant tissue. Most species which attack ferns are green or black, but sporadic attacks by pink, grey or yellow aphids are known. The nymphs are miniature versions of the adults and at certain times of the year winged males may be present. A common pest is the Fern Aphid (*Idiopterus nephrolepidis*) which is black with white legs. Winged adults have cloudy patches on their wings.

Aphids cause distortion of the plant tissue where they feed. Unexpanded fronds may open mis-shapen and frequently with papery patches in the tissue. Aphids secrete large quantities of honeydew and are usually attended and protected by ants. In severe infestations, sooty mould may grow on the honeydew, rendering the ferns very unsightly.

Control: Aphid colonies can be severely disrupted by hosing with a strong jet of water. Persistent attacks can be eliminated by spraying with reduced strength pyrethrum, maldison or dimethoate. Pressure pack sprays are available for control of this pest and work very effectively.

Caterpillars and Grubs

Quite a number of species of caterpillars and grubs feed on ferns. The attacks are usually of a sporadic nature and are most common in spring, summer and autumn. Some species can be troublesome because of persistent attacks by successive broods of the pest. The activity of caterpillars and grubs is obvious because of the large lumps eaten out of the fronds and sometimes the stipes. A close examination in the daytime will usually reveal the caterpillar sheltering on the underside of a frond. The presence of webbing or leaves joined together may also indicate a shelter used by the pest during the day. It is common for caterpillars to attack young expanding fronds. Damage to a frond can be very severe if the unrolled crozier is attacked.

Most caterpillars which feed on fern fronds are the larvae of moths. A grub that feeds on the roots of ferns is the larvae of a beetle. Other pests which cause damage of a similar nature are wireworms, earwigs, slugs and snails.

Details follow of the main species attacking ferns.

Leaf Roller or Light Brown Apple Moth (*Epiphyas postvittana*)

The caterpillars of this pest can be very destructive on a wide range of ferns, particularly near the tips of the fern fronds. The caterpillar usually constructs a simple shelter by joining adjacent leaves, pinnae or pinnules with a silken web. It hides in this shelter during the day and emerges at night to feed on surrounding fronds.

The caterpillars grow to about 13 mm (0.5 in) long, are very slender and are coloured light translucent green or pinkish, with a dark head. If disturbed from their shelter during the day they usually wriggle and jump actively, frequently falling to the ground in the process. The adult is a nondescript grey moth about 1 cm (0.4 in) across. Light brown apple moth caterpillars may be present throughout the year but are most troublesome in spring and summer months when a succession of broods is produced. Spraying is necessary when this pest becomes established in a fern collection.

Control: Spore suspensions of *Bacillus thuringiensis* are effective as are sprays of carbaryl or pyrethrum.

Painted Apple Moth (*Orgyia anartoides*)

The caterpillars of painted apple moth are very fond of ferns and attack a wide range of species. Fortunately, they are usually a solitary pest and therefore the damage they cause is fairly limited. They are a very conspicuous and distinctive caterpillar and feed actively during the day. They grow to about 2.5 cm (1 in) long, and are hairy with three or four dense hair tufts in the centre of the back. They may be present throughout the year but are often troublesome in the autumn and winter months. Spraying is rarely necessary for this pest and handpicking and squashing serves to keep numbers down.

Loopers

These are usually slender caterpillars which have the habit of alternately forming a loop and extending their body as they walk. They may be green or brown and are able to remain very still for long periods during the day and thus easily pass detection. They are voracious feeders and their activities can quickly cause significant damage to a fern. Fortunately their attacks are usually sporadic.

Control: They can be controlled by applications of spore suspensions of *Bacillus thuringiensis* or by spraying with carbaryl or pyrethrum.

Fleshy Green Caterpillars

The fleshy green caterpillars of small moths frequently feed on the fine, lacy fronds of such ferns as species of *Dennstaedtia*, *Hypolepis* and *Pteris tremula*. These caterpillars usually feed in groups and are very efficient at stripping the green tissue from a frond, leaving only a skeleton framework of the rachises and veins. They can be very destructive and in natural stands whole areas can be stripped bare. The caterpillars grow to about 1 cm (0.4 in) long and may be difficult to detect on the fronds.

Control: They can be controlled by applications of spore suspensions of *Bacillus thuringiensis* or by spraying with carbaryl or pyrethrum.

Cutworms

Cutworms are the fleshy grubs of dull moths belonging to the family Noctuidae. Their common name is derived from their habit of living in the soil and under debris and chewing off seedlings at ground level so that the whole plant topples over. The grubs grow to 3.5 cm (1.4 in) long, are fleshy and hairless and are mostly dull-coloured, although some tropical species are colourful. When disturbed, they coil and remain motionless for periods. They usually feed at night and hide during the day but may be active on cloudy days.

Cutworms are frequent pests of ferns. They are rather sluggish grubs which may feed near the ground or climb on mature fronds. They prefer the young tissues of developing fronds and croziers but also frequently feed on the fleshy stipes and chew out large, concave areas, thus weakening them.

Control: Small infestations can be handpicked and squashed. Baiting, dusting, or spraying with pyrethrum or carbaryl is effective.

Curl Grubs

Curl grubs live in the ground and feed on the roots of a wide range of plants, including ferns. They are the larval stage of a group of scarab beetles, in particular the colourful groups known as Christmas beetles and Japanese beetles (see below). The name curl grub is given, because they are usually semicircular or in the shape of a C, curling even more when disturbed. They are commonly found in pasture and lawns but can exist in most soils and are sometimes even found in fern containers. They can cause considerable damage to roots and on a favoured plant may congregate in large numbers.

Curl grubs' presence is advertised by a lack of vigour and the wilting of young fronds. Plants severely attacked may wobble in the soil; in pots, the soil mix appears wet and the surface may be disturbed. Examination will reveal the tunnels and the larvae.

Control: This can be difficult. If the curl grubs are found to be feeding on fern roots, the soils should be drenched with carbaryl at the recommended rate. In the USA, spores of the bacterial milky disease can be purchased for the control of scarabs.

Elkhorn Tip Moth

Frond tips of the Elkhorn (*Platycerium bifurcatum*) and some other polypodium ferns such as *Microsorum punctatum* are sometimes damaged by a small grub which feeds among the sori. The grub is the larva of a small, clear-winged moth. It feeds by tunnelling through the spore patches and into the leaf tissue causing browning and death of the frond tips. Outbreaks are rarely severe and mainly occur during the summer. The pest is restricted to tropical and subtropical regions.

Control: Readily achieved by spraying with maldison or pyrethrum at appropriate strengths.

Staghorn Borer

In tropical and subtropical regions, ferns of the genus *Platycerium* are sometimes attacked by a caterpillar which bores a short tunnel into the sterile fronds just near the crown where the fertile fronds emerge. The hole acts as a daytime shelter and is surrounded by a web which contains the insects droppings. The caterpillar emerges at night to feed on developing sterile and fertile fronds. Frequently the web is adorned with pieces of leaf which are presumably for camouflage purposes. The caterpillar is about 1.2 cm (0.5 in) long and dark grey. It matures into a small, grey moth.

This pest is seasonal, but persistent attacks can be very damaging. The Elkhorn *P. bifurcatum* is sometimes severely attacked even to the point where large clumps may be killed.

Control: By spraying with pyrethrum or maldison. Debilitated plants should be fertilized and watered regularly.

Florida Fern Caterpillar (*Callopistria floridensis*)

A large velvety caterpillar growing to about 5 cm (2 in) in length, which feeds voraciously on fern fronds. They usually feed at night and shelter in the soil or around the base of the plant during the day.

Control: By spraying with *Bacillus thuringiensis* spores. Baits may also be effective against this pest.

Fern Moth (*Euplexia benesimilis*)

Small green caterpillars of this moth feed actively on fern fronds in greenhouses and ferneries, causing appreciable damage. The caterpillars grow to about 1.5 cm (0.6 in) long and are well camouflaged in the fronds. The adult moth is about 2.5 cm (1 in) across and is deep red, mottled with grey.

Control: By spraying with carbaryl or *Bacillus thuringiensis*.

Yellow Woollybear (*Diacrisia virginica*)

A distinctive caterpillar which grows to about 3 cm (1.2 in) long. Its body is densely covered with long yellow, reddish, or white hairs. The adult is a shiny white moth about 3 cm (1.2 in) across with a small, black dot on each wing. Yellow Woollybear caterpillars are an occasional pest of ferns and can be very destructive.

Control: By spraying with pyrethrum or *Bacillus thuringiensis*.

Orange Tortrix (*Argyrotaenia citrana*)

This pest is similar in many respects to the leaf roller. The pale-green, fleshy caterpillars shelter in nests, made by joining leaflets together, and emerge at night to feed on the fronds. They grow to about 1.2 cm (0.5 in) long and are sparsely hairy. The adults are light-brown and about 1.2 cm (0.5 in) across.

Control: By spraying with pyrethrum or *Bacillus thuringiensis*.

Drynaria Butterfly (*Hypochrysops theon*)

This is a most attractive butterfly found in New Guinea, the Moluccas and Aru Islands and the northern part of Cape York Peninsula in Queensland. Its densely hairy larvae live in the ant galleries which exist in the rhizomes of ferns and emerge at night to feed on the recently mature sterile and fertile fronds. The larvae are attended by small, black ants which also live in the galleries. They can be very destructive of the fern but their ravages are offset by the beauty of the butterfly which they become.

Control: Rarely necessary but can be achieved by spraying with pyrethrum.

Japanese Beetle

The Japanese beetle (*Popillia japonica*) is a sporadic pest of ferns with the adults congregating on the fronds and stripping them of foliage. They are about 1.2 cm (0.5 in) long and are a metallic blue or green with coppery wing covers. The larvae are grubs living in the soil and feeding on plant roots.

Control: By spraying with maldison or carbaryl at appropriately reduced strength.

Cockroaches

It is perhaps surprising to think that cockroaches can damage plants, but in fact some of the larger species feed avidly on young plant tissue and are occasional pests of ferns. Most feeding is done at night and young fronds, roots and croziers are the favoured targets. Damage shows up as small to large chewed areas which turn brown. Two significant pest species are the smoky brown cockroach (*Periplaneta fuliginosa*) and the Surinam cockroach (*Pycnoscelus surinamensis*).

Control: Cockroaches can be very difficult to control. Baiting with some commercial snail baits can be effective as is spraying susceptible tissue with pyrethrum or carbaryl. Rubbish which provides shelter should be cleaned up and the area dusted with lime or naphthalene flakes.

Crickets

Crickets are related to grasshoppers and a couple of species can be occasional pests to fern growers in certain areas.

Black crickets are very widely distributed in temperate and subtropical regions. They are very active and familiar insects and in some years may be present in plague proportions. The insects are most active at night but are also frequently abroad during the day. They often hide in cracks in the soil, in mulches and under logs etc. They will eat plant tissue and have been known to severely damage young fern fronds and croziers.

Mole crickets are interesting burrowing insects that are not seen often. They have powerful forelegs which are developed for tunnelling and can also shear off roots. Mole crickets partly feed on plants and are an occasional pest of ferns loosening them by their burrowing activities and feeding on their roots.

Control: Black crickets can be controlled by baiting with a commercial preparation used for snails. In severe outbreaks spraying plant tissue with carbaryl or pyrethrum will give protection. Control of mole crickets is rarely necessary.

European Earwig (*Forficula auricularia*)

The European earwig is a widespread pest, very common in temperate regions. It usually hides among debris and weeds during the day and emerges at night to feed. These insects are fond of young plant tissues and may eat the green tips of fern roots, rhizomes and parts of developing fronds. Garden-grown ferns are not seriously affected but the pest may be a nuisance in pots and baskets, particularly in greenhouses and shadehouses.

Control: Populations of European earwigs can be effectively reduced by scattering balls of crumpled newspaper around the ferns, and on the floor of the greenhouse. The earwigs like to shelter in this paper which can be collected at regular intervals and burnt. Dusting the floor and benches with lime or naphthalene flakes is a useful deterrent. Commercial snail baits can also be effective against them. Fern tissues sensitive to earwig damage should be sprayed with carbaryl or pyrethrum.

Fern Mirid Bug (*Felisarcus glabratus*)

The fern mirid bug is a minor pest of ferns in tropical and subtropical regions. The adults are about 1.5 cm (0.6 in) long and are commonly shiny-green although they may be brown. Both the adult and immature forms feed by sucking sap and they attack ferns with lacy fronds such as *Hypolepis* and *Dennstaedtia* species. They concentrate their attack on the developing croziers and young fronds, causing white or grey papery patches. Frequently these damaged areas are not obvious until the croziers have unrolled and by then the bugs may have departed.

Control: Attacks are usually sporadic and spraying is rarely necessary.

Fern Weevils

Sudden wilting of parts of fronds or even whole fronds of lacy ferns can often be traced to attacks by the fern weevil (*Syagrius fulvitarsis*). Its larvae, which are small fat white grubs, tunnel in the stipes and rachises of fern fronds causing the affected parts to wilt, wither and die back. The dark tunnels can be seen if the affected areas are split open. The weevil attacks such ferns as Soft Tree-fern (*Dicksonia antarctica*), False Bracken (*Culcita dubia*), Bats-wing Fern (*Histiopteris incisa*) and Bracken (*Pteridium esculentum*), amongst others. Attacks are usually of a sporadic and minor nature and natural control is by a small black wasp.

Weevils in the related genus *Neosyagrius* also feed on ferns in a similar manner.

The vine weevil (*Otiorhynchus sulcatus*) is a serious pest of ferns in many countries. The larvae feed on the roots and rhizomes causing stunting, dieback and death. In some years they are present in large numbers and dozens may be found in the root system of a single fern. The grubs grow to about 0.5 cm (0.2 in) long and are white with a brown head, the adults are stout black beetles of similar length.

Control: Control of weevils can be very difficult. Regular spraying with permethrin may be successful. Effective control of tunnelling weevils is not practical.

Fungus Gnats (Sciarids)

Fungus gnats are tiny insects which resemble small mosquitoes. They obtain their name because some species are known to breed in fungi. Scientifically, they belong to the family Mycetophilidae and they commonly gather in moist, sheltered areas. There are many species of fungus gnats, especially in Australia, however they are a poorly studied group. The adults often gather in colonies and may be seen flying close to the ground or running actively over the soil surface. Shadehouses and greenhouses create ideal conditions for them.

The larvae of the fungus gnat is a small maggot, and for most species it feeds on decaying plant tissue. Some species, however, feed on live plant tissue and they are particularly fond of ferns. Adult ferns may be damaged, but the effects are usually most severe on prothalli and sporelings.

Adult ferns in pots are susceptible to fungus gnat attack but it is rare for plants in the ground to be damaged. Damaged plants lack vigour but there is no sign of damage to the above-ground parts. The surface of the potting mix, however, appears disturbed and close examination may show damage to below-ground parts of the crown or rhizome and particularly the roots. The potting mixture frequently appears wet and the plants may look as if they are suffering from waterlogging. The presence of small white maggots in the mix, or of adult flies running around or flying near the soil surface, is a sure indication as to the cause of the problem.

Fungus gnats are a headache for enthusiasts and commercial growers who raise ferns from spores. If fungus gnats get into the propagation mixture they can quickly destroy all prothalli and sporelings that are present. Affected containers appear wet and the surface of the mix appears as if it has been turned over and ploughed by a miniature tractor. Careful sifting will reveal the small white maggots and the adults are usually obvious, flying about or running over the soil surface. Odd adults may also emerge from the soil when it is disturbed.

Control: Fungus gnats are extremely difficult pests to control. Affected potted plants are best repotted after first washing all of the old potting mix away and dipping the root system in a solution of carbaryl. The pests are all but impossible to control when entrenched in a pot of sporelings and the whole lot is best destroyed. Thorough sterilization of the propagation mix and sealing of the container after sowing should prevent attacks. Dusting with micronized sulphur or drenching with carbaryl provides some degree of control. Adult numbers can be reduced by trapping on fly-paper.

Thrips

Ferns are frequently damaged by these tiny pests which graze on the surface of young fronds and lap up the sap which leaks out. This feeding leaves small white, brown or papery patches visible and extensive attacks can result in deformed fronds. In suitable conditions, thrips can build up in numbers very rapidly and severe damage follows. Attacks are usually of a transient nature and mostly occur during spring and summer.

Examination of damaged areas with a hand lens will reveal the thrips as tiny, slender insects which are pale green when immature, changing to brownish or black when adult. The adults are about 1.5 mm long and have narrow wings which are delicately fringed on the margins.

Greenhouse thrips (*Heliothrips haemorrhoidalis*) attack garden-grown ferns in tropical and subtropical regions, but in temperate areas are only a pest in greenhouses. They favour warm, moist conditions and their numbers are drastically reduced by hot, dry weather. Onion thrips (*Thrips tabaci*) may be severe on ferns in some seasons.

Control: Infestations can usually be controlled by 1–3 applications of maldison or pyrethrum at ten-day intervals. Badly damaged fronds should be removed and burnt.

Grasshoppers and Locusts

Grasshoppers and locusts are common and well known insects that feed on a wide variety of plants by chewing large lumps out of the leaves. Grasshoppers are generally regarded as solitary insects but locusts are gregarious. Specialized forms such as katydids are usually included with the grasshoppers.

There are many different types of grasshoppers, especially in tropical regions, and most of these will feed on ferns if given the opportunity. They are mainly active from spring to autumn.

Control: Solitary grasshoppers are best controlled by squashing or at least disturbing them so that they leave the valuable plant. Spraying with pyrethrum or carbaryl can be effective, but a continual cover is needed as the insects are nomadic.

Leaf Nematodes

Nematodes, which are also known as eelworms, are microscopic, round worms. The vast majority of species are harmless to plants but a few are parasitic attacking roots, rhizomes or leaves. They are capable of penetrating cell walls and feed on the contents. Root-feeding nematodes are not known to attack ferns but leaf nematodes can be a serious pest.

Leaf nematodes (*Aphelenchoides fragariae*) are common parasites of ferns, destroying patches of tissue on the fronds and in severe cases debilitating or even causing the death of plants. They penetrate the cells through the leaf surface and feed internally, spreading from cell to cell. The damaged areas collapse and may take on brown, red, grey or orange tonings. Their spread is limited by the larger veins and on some ferns their feeding causes characteristically-shaped damaged areas, e.g. between the parallel veins of *Asplenium australasicum* and *A. nidus*. Further spread is on the surface of wet fronds and they can be transferred to other plants by splashing from rain or during watering.

Leaf nematodes are a serious pest and can attack a wide variety of ferns. They are a potential threat to fern collections and once established can be very difficult to control and impossible to eliminate.

Control: Cut off and burn all infected fronds including old ones, which can be sources of infection. Reduce overhead watering to a minimum so as to prevent their spread. Pot into sterilized mixtures. Do not purchase any plants that have suspicious leaf patches. Some chemical nematicides are available but these are generally too toxic to be recommended for home use. Hardy ferns may be treated by immersion in hot water (43°C [110°F]) for 10–15 minutes.

Mealy Bugs

Mealy bugs are one of the most persistent pests of ferns. They are easily recognized by the white mealy covering over the body and the long tail-like processes which project from the margins and the rear. They feed by sucking the plant's sap. The adults grow 2–4 mm long and cluster in dry sheltered sites such as in the crown, at the base of petioles, at rachis junctions and on the underside of fronds. They are gregarious and are usually to be found in colonies. Wherever they feed, their waxy secretions litter the surface and sooty mould commonly grows on the

Long-tailed Mealy Bugs (*Pseudococcus longispinus*) feeding on under-side of frond Photo C. G. Goudey

honeydew. Mealy bugs are a common pest of ferns in greenhouses, and severe infestations can weaken a plant. Colonies are frequently attended by ants, which may also discourage natural enemies.

Mealy bugs are capable of a rapid build-up in numbers. The long-tailed mealy bug (*Pseudococcus longispinus*) is the commonest species and it has been shown to produce about 200 young in 2–3 weeks. The young mealy bugs resemble the adults and usually feed with them. Each young mealy bug progresses through three nymphal moults before it becomes an adult. Mealy bugs attack a wide variety of ferns and are widely distributed in tropical, subtropical and temperate regions.

Control: By spraying with a mixture of maldison and a suitable strength of white oil (see page 99). Systemic sprays such as dimethoate can also be used with success. A simple means of dealing with scattered individual mealy bugs is to dab them with a cotton bud dipped in methylated spirits.

Millipedes

Millipedes are slow-moving animals with numerous legs. Their bodies are very slender and are covered with many overlapping joints which are very hard and act like armour. These animals have a characteristic habit of coiling when disturbed, and when in danger or crushed emit an obnoxious smelling fluid. There are numerous species of millipedes but the commonest types are dull brown or shiny black and vary from 2.5–4 cm (1–1.5 in) in length. They favour damp, humid situations where there is an abundance of decaying organic matter. Greenhouses and shadehouses provide ideal conditions for them. Millipedes mainly feed on rotting vegetation but they will also eat fleshy tissue such as the root tips, young fronds and parts of the rhizomes of ferns. They mostly hide during the day and emerge at night to feed, but are often seen moving about on cloudy or rainy days.

Control: Populations can be reduced by collecting and squashing the pests at night (with the aid of a torch). Commercial snail baits can also be effective against them. Dirty areas should be cleaned up and dusted with lime or naphthalene flakes as a deterrent. Sensitive tissues should be sprayed with carbaryl or pyrethrum.

Passion Vine Hopper

The passion vine hopper (*Scolypopa australis*) is a leafhopper which is particularly fond of passionfruit, but which can also severely damage developing fern fronds. The adults are about 0.8 cm (0.3 in) long, roughly triangular in outline (especially when viewed from the side), with clear wings which are bordered and mottled with brown and black. The immature stages are greenish-brown and have a conspicuous tuft of white, waxy filaments at the tip of the abdomen. Both adults and nymphs can hop if disturbed but the immature stages are particularly active in this respect earning the apt name of 'hairy rockets'.

The nymphs frequently congregate when feeding and are then quite conspicuous. They are commonly to be found on developing fern fronds in spring. They suck the sap of the young frond as it unrolls and cause distortion of the growth with associated dead papery patches. They may also feed amongst the sporangia and there is some evidence that they may destroy spores and fertile tissue. Though they may attack a variety of ferns, they are particularly fond of the soft tree-fern (*Dicksonia antarctica*). They are also common on Bracken Fern (*Pteridium esculentum*). There is considerable seasonal variation in the numbers of this pest. It is widely distributed in temperate and subtropical regions.

Control: These can be controlled by spraying with pyrethrum or maldison when the pests are active. Hosing young fronds disperses them effectively.

Scale Insects

Scale insects are immobile pests which shelter beneath a waxy covering that varies from species to species in shape and colour. A variety of scale insects attack ferns, usually congregating in colonies on the stipes and the underside of fronds. They feed by sucking the sap and severe attacks can debilitate ferns. Their feeding is accompanied by the exudation of honeydew, and sooty mould often follows severe attacks. Ants are attracted to some species of scales to feed on the honeydew they produce. The ants may guard the scales against predator attack and move them to new feeding sites.

Control: This consists of spraying with white oil at a suitable strength to avoid damage to plants (see page 99). Some ferns such as maidenhairs are very sensitive to white oil damage and a better alternative may be two sprays of half strength maldison, 7–10 days apart. At certain times of the year scales reproduce and produce numerous tiny young called crawlers. At this stage they are very susceptible to spraying.

Details follow of the main species attacking ferns.

Nigra Scale (*Parasaissetia nigra*)

Outbreaks of Nigra scale occur sporadically on ferns, usually in temperate regions. They may live in colonies on the stipes, but also frequently exist as solitary individuals on the rachises and underside of the fronds. They are particularly fond of ferns with leathery fronds, such as species of *Asplenium*. Damage is usually of a minor nature and control is only needed when the numbers build up to colony proportions.

Control: Spraying with white oil at a suitable strength (see page 99) is usually sufficient.

Cottony Cushion Scale (*Icerya purchasi*)

This common scale is an occasional pest of ferns of subtropical regions. It favours dry conditions and is most often to be found on weakened ferns growing under eaves etc. where insufficient moisture penetrates. The adults are easily recognized by their plump bodies which are soft and can be squashed between the fingers.

Control: This is not a major pest of ferns, and colonies can be easily disrupted by hosing or squashing. Spraying is rarely necessary as a predatory ladybird also feeds actively on the scale.

Fern Scale, Coconut Scale or Snow Scale (*Pinnaspis aspidistrae*)

This tiny scale is a severe and persistent pest of ferns and once established in a collection is difficult to eliminate. The adult female scales have a slender covering 1–1.5 mm long. This is white, and an infestation has the appearance of desiccated coconut scattered on the fronds. The pest mainly feeds on the underside of fronds and is frequently to be found among the sori of the fertile fronds. It mainly occurs in tropical and subtropical regions, but in temperate areas is a common greenhouse pest.

Despite its tiny size this pest is particularly destructive and an infestation severely debilitates a fern and may even cause its death. The tissue around where the scale feeds yellows, and scattered feeding on a frond results in a mottled appearance. Fronds usually die back. The scale attacks a wide variety of ferns but seems to be particularly fond of species of *Asplenium*, *Platycerium* and Tassel Ferns. Sporadic outbreaks also occur on fine, lacy *Nephrolepis* cultivars and usually cause their death. Bird's Nest Ferns (*Asplenium australasicum* and *A. nidus*) are very commonly attacked by this pest.

Control: Because of its destructive capability this scale

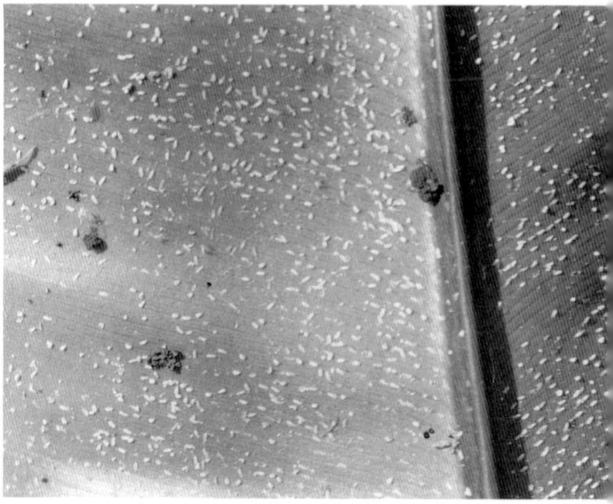

A colony of Fern Scale or Coconut Scale (*Pinnaspis aspidistrae*) Photo D. L. Jones

must be controlled as soon as it is noticed. Badly infected plants are best destroyed by burning, and all neighbouring plants should be sprayed with dimethoate or a mixture of white oil and maldison. Spraying should be repeated at intervals of about ten days, until all scales are eliminated. Any outbreaks that follow should be treated immediately they are noticed. Collectors are advised to maintain a quarantine area where newly-acquired ferns can be observed regularly for this scale, before the plants are incorporated in the collection. The scale covering of this pest remains attached to the frond long after it has been killed, making it difficult to determine the efficacy of the spraying.

Soft Brown Scale (*Coccus hesperidium*)

This scale is a serious enemy of ferns, usually congregating in colonies on the fleshy stipes. It is a particularly dirty scale, secreting copious quantities of sticky honeydew which becomes covered with a growth of sooty mould. The adults can be recognized by their soft, flat, oval, waxy, pale-brown coverings which are about 0.3 cm (0.1 in) long. Infested ferns are very unsightly and should be cleaned up by hosing and then sprayed with white oil and maldison at a suitable concentration (see page 99).

Pink Wax Scale (*Ceroplastes rubens*)

Pink wax scale attacks a wide variety of fruit trees and garden plants including ferns. Although it occurs in temperate regions, it is most prominent in subtropical and tropical regions. The scales have an almost globular waxy covering up to 0.5 cm (0.2 in) long. This is quite hard, is of a pinkish colour and has four prominent lobes around the margin. The pest congregates in colonies, and on ferns feeds on the fleshy stipes, rachises and occasionally the lamina of the fronds themselves. The scales' feeding activities appear to do little damage but the heavy growth of sooty mould on their copious secretions renders the plants very unsightly.

Pink wax scale thrives in humid conditions and spreads rapidly on suitable hosts. Dark purplish crawlers move actively to new sites in December and May, and once established, grow fast.

Control: Spraying with suitable concentrations of white oil (see page 99) and maldison in December and May greatly reduces the incidence of the pest. Adult scales can be easily removed by handpicking.

Indian White Wax Scale (*Ceroplastes ceriferus*)

This scale is very similar in appearance and habits to the pink wax scale. The adults covering may be up to 0.8 cm (0.3 in) long, is domed (although somewhat irregular in shape), with a short, down-turned horn at one end, and is waxy white in colour. On ferns it congregates on fleshy stipes and rachises. Like pink wax scale, this species secretes copious quantities of honeydew which supports a strong growth of sooty mould, rendering the plants very unsightly. Adults can be easily dislodged by hand or hosing. Severe infestations must be controlled by spraying with white oil at a suitable concentration for ferns (see page 99).

Oleander Scale (*Aspidiotus nerii*)

A persistent scale which can be bad on ferns in some countries. Scales are circular, pale yellow and about 0.25 cm (0.1 in) across. They congregate in dense colonies on the stipes and fronds, and can severely debilitate a plant.

Control: By regular spraying with maldison at an appropriately reduced strength.

Slaters, Woodlice, Sow Bugs and Pillbugs

Slaters are also known as woodlice and those types that can curl into a ball are often called pillbugs. The adults are about 1 cm (0.4 in) long, dull grey, more or less elliptical in shape and with seven pairs of legs. Juveniles are scaled-down versions of the adult. Pillbugs are sturdier animals than slaters with an armoured appearance and the habit of curling into a tight ball when disturbed. Both slaters and pillbugs favour cool, moist conditions and usually congregate around rubbish, debris etc. Shadehouses and greenhouses provide ideal conditions for them and they mostly hide during the day and emerge at night to feed.

Slaters and pillbugs mostly feed on decaying plant tissue, but the author has seen them on numerous occasions grazing the soft green tissue of young fern roots, croziers and even the exposed apices of rhizomes. They seem particularly fond of the surface tissue (especially of Platyceriums) and the areas where they have fed shrivel and turn brown or black. They are frequently a problem on epiphytic ferns because of the coarse potting mixture and structures in which these are grown. They shelter in baskets, slats and the fibres of tree-fern slabs and emerge at night to feed on the ferns. The pads of Platyceriums provide an ideal refuge.

Control: Slaters and pillbugs are overall a minor pest of ferns, however, they can build up in numbers and become a nuisance if not controlled from time to time. Because they favour dirty areas, all rubbish and debris should be removed. Naphthalene flakes are an effective deterrent and should be sprinkled around benches and cleaned areas. Dusting with insecticides such as carbaryl, pyrethrum and derris is also effective. If slaters are present in large numbers, sensitive plant tissue should be sprayed with carbaryl or pyrethrum.

Slugs and Snails

Slugs and snails are a common and often severe pest of ferns. They generally hide during the day and emerge at night to feed. They are particularly active during rainy weather but also emerge on dewy nights and in shadehouses and greenhouses seem to be perennially active. They feed by grazing the surface of young, succulent tissue and can do significant damage in a relatively short period. Sap leaks from the damaged tissue, which may go slimy or dry and wither. The movements of the slugs and snails are marked by a prominent silvery trail which is the dried mucus which they lay down as they travel.

There are many species of slugs and snails but not all are destructive of plants and some may indeed be beneficial carnivores. The commonest and worst snail is *Helix asper* originally from Europe. This pest is now well-entrenched in subtropical and temperate regions of many countries and is very fond of ferns wherever they may be growing. The small, conical garlic or onion snail *Oxychilus alliarius* (so called because of its smell when crushed) is also a common pest of ferns in some areas. Many species of slugs also feed avidly on ferns, one of the worst being the fern slug (*Deroceras laeve*). This species grazes in strips and does not leave a trail of slimy mucus.

Control: Regular baiting with commercial preparations is the best means of controlling slugs and snails. Baits should be applied before rain to coincide with maximum activity. Hand collection and squashing at night (with the aid of a torch) is also a very useful measure. Some growers spread tobacco dust with good effect.

Spider Mites (red spider etc.)

Spider mites, as the name suggests, have eight legs and are therefore not insects. They are tiny animals, some species of which attack ferns. They generally congregate in colonies on the underside of leaves and feed by sucking the sap. The undersurface of the leaf is coated with a very fine web, which helps to protect them, and aids in their movements. Adult mites are so small that they are difficult to detect, even with the aid of a magnifying glass. Young mites are miniature, scaled-down versions of the adult.

Spider mites favour warm, dry weather and can reproduce very rapidly when conditions are suitable. Symptoms of their attack are a dryish, mottled appearance of the fronds. Sometimes the fronds may go silvery and in severe infestations they may yellow prematurely. Two species of spider mite may attack ferns. These are the red spider mite, also called two spotted mite (*Tetranychus urticae*) and the bryobia mite (*Bryobia arborea*).

Control: Spider mites are sporadic rather than persistent pests of ferns. Their presence may be an indication that the plants are too dry or the humidity is too low. Control measures should be initiated when the pests are first noticed because they can increase in numbers very quickly. Dusting with a mixture of equal parts by weight of fine sulphur and hydrated lime has been used with some success. Predator mites are available from some commercial outlets. Miticides may be needed to clean up persistent infestations (difocol or tetradifon).

Staghorn Beetle

This species (*Halticorcus platyceryi*) is a small beetle of the family Chrysomelidae which feeds on the fronds of species of the fern genus *Platycerium*. The beetles are about 0.4 cm (0.15 in) long, almost round, and are very distinctive; being a shiny black with four prominent dull red spots on the wing covers. The larvae are small, fleshy pink grubs. Both the adults and larvae feed by chewing small sunken areas of an irregular oval shape in the surface of the fronds. At first, these eaten areas appear as distinct brown spots, but in persistent attacks these coalesce into larger areas. In severe attacks, large areas may be destroyed and the fronds themselves may die. This pest is most prominent in tropical and subtropical regions.

Control: Infestations can be controlled by spraying with pyrethrum or maldison.

White Fly

White fly is an occasional pest of ferns grown in greenhouses in temperate and subtropical regions. It is a rather conspicuous although tiny pest for the adults are white and rise in clouds when infested plants are disturbed. The adults are about 0.15 cm long and congregate on the underside of fronds where they suck the sap. Immature stages are oval, black or yellowish with waxy fringes and resemble scale insects.

White flies are usually found in colonies and secrete quantities of honeydew which allows the development of sooty mould. They mainly attack ferns with soft, lacy fronds and can be a problem on *Nephrolepis* cultivars. Affected fronds may develop papery patches, become limp, and yellow prematurely. This pest favours humid conditions and is most noticeable during spring and autumn. Greenhouse white fly (*Trialeurodes vaporarium*) is the commonest species encountered. The fern white fly (*Aleyrodes nephrolepidis*) is a significant pest in some countries.

Control: A wasp parasite has reduced the incidence of white fly dramatically in recent years. Spraying the underside of infested fronds with dimethoate, maldison or pyrethrum at weekly intervals will give effective control. Soap solutions may also be useful.

Root Coccids

These pests are sometimes called root aphids. They feed on the roots of plants and usually congregate in colonies. The adults are about 0.2 cm (0.1 in) long and grey. As they feed, they secrete waxy threads and these give the colonies an untidy appearance. Root coccids may debilitate a fern, especially if they are present in large numbers. They are most noticeable on pot-bound ferns, where the roots seem to be always on the dry side.

Control: Root coccids dislike wet conditions and immersing the pot completely in water for a few hours may serve to control them. The addition of a weak concentration of a contact insecticide such as maldison will ensure control.

Wireworms

Wireworms are the larvae of click beetles, and are found in soil, rotting wood etc. These animals are so-called because of their slender body and hard, wiry texture. They may grow to about 3 cm (1.2 in) long and are usually a cream to pale brown in colour. They are not particularly active animals since their legs are very short, however, they are equipped with a formidable pair of mandibles.

Outbreaks of wireworms are very sporadic and they are occasional pests of ferns. They are very fond of young plant tissue and may feed on new roots and developing croziers. They usually shelter by day in the top layer of soil or beneath debris and may feed on roots and below-ground tissue, emerging at night to feed on the plant parts above-ground. Fortunately, with ferns they are only a minor problem as they can be difficult to control.

Control: Drenching the soil with carbaryl provides some control.

Birds

Some birds feed actively by scratching through litter and searching for grubs, worms etc. During this feeding process they not only disturb mulch, but can also cause considerable damage to small ferns, even uprooting them. They can even be very damaging to potted ferns in ferneries etc. A wide range of birds can be damaging, including the English blackbird, ground thrushes, mound builders related to the domestic fowl, and bower birds. There is no control apart from the destruction of the birds, however, stout sticks inserted around the ferns will disrupt their feeding habits and reduce the damage caused.

Earthworms

Earthworms are among the most beneficial of all animals with their constant tunnelling and distribution of organic matter through the soil. Their presence in a potted fern, however, is not beneficial and their activities can quickly disrupt the drainage of the potting mixture and cause the death of the fern by waterlogging. Worms mainly enter a pot through the drainage holes and this is one of the disadvantages of placing pots directly onto the soil surface. The worms live where conditions are moist and in a pot this is at the bottom. By tunnelling, feeding and moving organic matter they interfere with the drainage and the potting mix becomes churned and soggy.

Control: Worms are difficult animals to discourage. The problem is reduced by growing potted plants on benches. Ferns in which the potting mix has been disrupted by worms should be repotted. Worms can be discouraged by weak solutions of copper or iron salts. Copper though may damage plants and should be used carefully. Immersing the pots in a weak solution of copper sulphate is effective. Carbaryl may also be effective against worms.

14 Fern diseases

Armillaria Root Rot

Armillariella mellea is an unusual fungus which becomes established in dead stumps or other large pieces of rotting wood. Once established it sends out thick fungal strands through the soil. These resemble boot laces and are technically known as rhizomorphs. These strands can enter the roots of healthy plants and cause dieback or death. Thus the damage can occur at a considerable distance from where the fungus is established.

Armillaria attacks a very wide range of plants but is particularly severe on trees and shrubs. In some areas it can also attack large ferns such as *Cyathea australis, Dicksonia antarctica, Polystichum proliferum* and *Todea barbara*. The symptoms of attack are premature death of fronds, a starved dry look and general debilitation. Affected ferns usually appear as if they are suffering from dryness yet they do not respond to watering. This is because part, or all, of their root system has been destroyed by the fungus. Ferns infected by this fungus often linger for many years and may recover if the fungus is destroyed.

Control: Armillariella mellea is a rather difficult fungus to control. If its presence is suspected, then the complete removal and destruction of all stumps, large roots and pieces of decaying wood is essential. Apart from the rhizomorphs the fungus advertises its presence by dense clusters of orange or honey-coloured fruiting heads. The appearance of these around the base of a plant indicates an advanced state of infection by the fungus. Chemical control of this fungus is impractical and in cases of severe infection soil fumigation is the only answer.

Staghorn Rot

Ferns of the genus *Platycerium*, particularly *P. coronarium, P. grande, P. holttumii* and *P. superbum* are subject to a blackening and rotting of the pads enfolding the root mass. This blackening starts on the outer pads, often near the central growing point, as a sunken black spot and spreads. When it reaches the growing point the fronds usually fall prematurely and eventually the whole central mass of the fern may turn black and die. The disease is believed to be caused by a species of the fungus genus *Rhizoctonia*. The effects of the disease are worse in plants that are kept too wet in cold weather and it is more of a problem in the tropical species when they are grown out of their environment.

Platyceriums are very drought resistant ferns and can be kept dry for long periods without ill effects. In cold weather the plants should be placed in a situation sheltered from rain and watered sparingly until the weather warms up again. The condition of staghorn rot can also indicate insufficient air movement and resulting stale conditions.

Control: In afflicted plants, especially in those where the central core has been damaged, it is difficult. The plants should be placed in a warm, dry situation and they should be watered sparingly, if at all, until growth recommences. The affected areas should be liberally dusted with garden lime to dry the tissue out and arrest the spread. Wettable sulphur may also be useful for controlling this disease.

Fern Rusts

Various species of rust fungi are occasional parasites of some ferns such as *Lunathyrium japonicum, Lygodium* spp., and some polypodies. In *Lunathyrium japonicum* the fungus can be readily recognised by small round orange or rust-coloured blobs on both surfaces of the frond as well as the rachis and main veins. As the disease advances these pustules become powdery from spore production and may coalesce to form patches. The plant tissue around the site of the fungus becomes yellow and severely-attacked fronds die prematurely. Rust fungus is more severe on weakened plants and vigorous specimens seem to be able to withstand attacks for many years although they may appear unsightly. As *Lunathyrium japonicum* is a weedy fern a simple means of control is to destroy all affected plants. Species of *Lygodium* may occasionally exhibit similar symptoms with patches of rust-coloured spores being prominent. This is caused by the fungus *Puccinia lygodii*. A whitish powdery covering on the fronds of some *Osmunda* species is due to the rust *Uredinopsis osmundae*.

Control: Rust fungi may be difficult to control and severely affected plants are probably best culled. A thorough coating with the fungicide oxycarboxin may give some measure of control.

Root Rot

Ferns may sometimes collapse dramatically and die, leaving a soggy mass of tissue which has an unusual sour smell. If the plant is noticed in the early stages of decline, an examination will show that the roots and some outer parts of the crown are dead and rotted but the inner parts of the crown and undeveloped croziers are still quite healthy. This disorder is caused by root rotting fungi of such genera as *Pythium* and *Phytophthora*. The attack usually starts in the roots and spreads into the crown. Frequently plants still appear fairly healthy until the attack is well advanced and then they collapse completely over a very short period. Periods of stress such as hot weather often precipitate the collapse. One puzzling aspect of root rot is that the fronds appear dry but the soil mixture or soil around the plants is usually still moist. This is because of the inability of the dead roots to take up water for the plant, which leads to the dehydrated appearance.

Root rot is most frequently caused by overwatering or potting into a heavy, poorly-drained mixture or a combination of both. Too much water means lack of oxygen in the root zone rendering the roots susceptible to invasion by the fungi. It is not uncommon for large specimens of epiphytic ferns such as Davallias or Polypodiums to collapse from root rot when the coarse mixture they have been growing in for years loses structure and becomes gluggy. Worms may hasten this collapse and interfere further by blocking the drainage holes of the container. There are some suggestions that lime-loving ferns may be more susceptible to root rot when grown in an acid mix low in calcium salts.

Control: Root rot is easier to prevent than to control, and afflicted plants are best destroyed. Prevention is by ensuring good drainage in the pot and the mixture, watering with care and regular repotting when the mixture is beginning to decline. The fungicides fosetyl and metalaxyl are recommended for control and should be used as a drench if replanting into affected areas. A mixture of fosetyl and iprodione is worth trying (see page 102).

Leaf Spots and Blotches

Various species of fungi cause spots and blotches on the fronds of ferns. The spots may be small or coalesce into larger blotches. They usually have characteristic concentric rings around the margins. A variety of ferns are affected by leaf spots, with, in some cases, the fungus being peculiar to a species or genus of fern. Leaf spots are at their worst under still, humid, warm conditions especially where the surface of fronds is regularly wet. Large brown blotches on the fronds of *Nephrolepis* spp. and *Rumohra adiantiformis* are cause by *Cylindrocladium pteridis*. Small, circular brown spots on the margins of fronds are usually caused by *Alternaria polypodii*. Spots on the leaves of aspleniums may be caused by *Septoria asplenii*, on royal ferns by *Gloeosporium osmundae* and on the walking fern by *Cercospora camptosori*.

Control: The most efficient way to control leaf spots is to improve ventilation, space plants further apart and remove and burn affected tissue. Spraying with captan or thiram may give effective cover.

Moulds

Moulds are primitive, rapidly spreading fungi which thrive under very humid or damp conditions. Grey mould (*Botrytis cinerea*) is the species which commonly causes problems in ferns although *B. longibrachiata* may also be damaging in some countries.

Under certain conditions grey mould attacks a wide variety of plants including some ferns. The fungus spreads over the foliage as a fine cobwebby network of threads which are generally inconspicuous except when they catch droplets of water. Later, when the fungus spores, it becomes conspicuous by virtue of masses of sporing bodies which give it an overall grey woolly appearance. The damaged plant tissue blackens and may go slimy.

This disease is very common under still, humid conditions and in temperate regions is frequently prevalent during the first cold nights of the autumn. It is a severe problem for ferns with very fine, crowded foliage such as some cultivars of *Nephrolepis* (e.g. 'Childsii', 'Suzi Wong') and Maidenhair ferns (e.g. *Adiantum raddianum* 'Bridal Veil' and 'Gracillimum'). It also attacks the young, developing, hairy fronds of species such as *Pyrrosia* (e.g. *P. lanuginosa*) and *Platycerium* (e.g. *P. grande, P, superbum*). In the latter genus the developing pads of many species are covered with fine, woolly hairs and if these remain too wet, or if the pads are damaged, then grey mould can completely destroy the pad and may even damage the crown. In very bad conditions (stagnant humid atmospheres) grey mould may infest a wide variety of ferns, including sporelings.

Control: Moulds should be sprayed as soon as they are noticed with benomyl, captan or iprodione. A couple of good, drenching sprays a few days apart may be necessary. Damaged tissue should be trimmed off and the plants observed regularly to be certain all of the disease has been effectively controlled. The presence of moulds is an indication that growing conditions provided for the ferns are unsatisfactory. Under conditions of adequate ventilation, providing sufficient air movement and with controlled watering, the disease is not a problem. Where conditions are stale and moisture remains on fine foliage for long periods, the disease can be expected to proliferate.

Ferns with a compact growth of finely divided

fronds should be watered carefully so that the water reaches the potting mix and root system but does not lodge on the fronds. Such ferns should never be misted or watered with jets and must be placed carefully so that they are not dripped on from neighbouring pots. Dead fronds should be removed regularly so that they do not rot and provide a starting point for the disease. Staghorns affected by grey mould should be sprayed and moved to a position where they receive more air movement.

Acid Rot

This is a condition which affects ferns sporadically. It has very similar symptoms to those described for hard crown and it may in fact be the same problem. The rhizome and the basal parts of the fronds become swollen and distorted and are very brittle. The plants lack vigour and produce limited new growth. Any fronds that are produced are generally weak and may often be distorted. Frequently the top of the pot is covered by a dark green to blackish slime.

Ferns with this condition invariably die slowly, unless treated. Some growers claim that this problem is caused solely by acid conditions and that no fungus is present. This is supported by the observation that lime-loving ferns frequently suffer badly from acid rot and usually when they are grown in a lime-deficient mixture.

Control: Watering with limewater (3 tablespoons ground limestone/9 litres [2 gal] of water) can provide some relief, but severely affected plants should be repotted completely into a new potting mix containing adequate lime and limestone chips.

Greenhouse Frond Rots

A variety of fungi may damage ferns grown in greenhouses because the growing conditions are ideal for them as well as the ferns. Such attacks may be much worse if ventilation is inadequate, and under very stale and moist conditions even innocuous fungi can cause damage. The symptoms are usually discoloured fronds which may go slimy, and a mould-like growth of fungus mycelium. Spread of the fungi is usually rapid and attacks can quickly assume epidemic proportions. Fungi responsible include *Cladosporium herbarum* (bad on *Pteris*), *Coniosporium filicinum* and *Moniliopsis aderholdii*. The simplest means of control is to improve greenhouse aeration either by opening ventilation or installing fans. Spraying with a mixture of benomyl and sulphur may check bad outbreaks (see page 102). Dinocarp and thiram may also be effective.

Cibotium Frond Rot

This disease occurs in some countries on species of *Cibotium*. It usually affects plants grown in greenhouses and attacks young developing fronds and recently mature fronds, causing them to blacken and die. The causative agent is a specific fungus, *Pestalozzia cibotii*.

Control: No effective control has been reported.

Damping-off

Damping-off is a disease which attacks sporelings, especially when they are weakened from overcrowding. Affected sporelings tend to fall over easily and quickly blacken or turn watery. The disease spreads rapidly and soon a patch of infected plants is noticeable in the pot. Unless treated, the fungus will spread and kill all sporelings in the container. Damping-off is commonly caused by fungi in the genera *Pythium* and *Rhizoctonia*. The disease is frequent in still, humid weather and may start following damage from drips etc.

Control: This can be achieved by drenching with a mixture of benomyl and sulphur (see page 102) or other chemicals such as dichloran, iprodione and propamacarb. Sowing into completely sterilized mixture and thinning out regularly is the best means of avoiding the disease.

Crown Rot or Hard Crown

Crown rot is a common disease of ferns and is believed to be caused by a species of the fungus genus *Rhizoctonia*. It attacks a wide variety of fern species. Afflicted plants are characterized by severely stunted growth. New fronds which appear are often distorted and usually have black wet-looking patches on the fronds and stipes. Frequently, fronds abort while still quite small and this gives the crown a crowded, irregular, hard, appearance. Another common symptom is the collapse of mature fronds caused by a watery rot in the stipe at ground level.

Control: Ferns affected with this malady frequently linger for years and seem to lack the ability to recover. Such ferns are best destroyed. If the plant is particularly valuable, it can be sometimes restored by the following treatment. Tip the plant from the container (or dig up) and wash all soil from the roots. Submerge the plant in a solution of captan until all parts are thoroughly soaked. Allow to dry and pot into a small container of peat moss or sphagnum moss. Place in a sheltered position and water normally. Spray regularly with captan or wettable sulphur until root and top growth has recovered. Crown rot may be induced or made worse by placing the crowns too deep when potting or planting and is also worsened by overwatering. *Rhizoctonia* readily infests soil mixes and infected plants and their potting mix must be discarded or destroyed and not allowed to contaminate clean mix. The chemical dichloran, or a mixture of fosetyl and iprodione (see page 102) may offer some control.

Sooty Mould (*Fumago vagans*)

This is a fungus disease which, as the name suggests, causes a black, sooty covering on the leaves and shoots of plants. It is common on some shrubs and trees, but is rarely seen on ferns. It is always of a secondary nature, growing on the sweet exudates of fast growing shoots, or on honeydew secreted by sucking insects such as scales, aphids etc. On ferns, it usually follows the attacks of aphids or scales, but in tropical regions the author has seen sooty mould induced on ferns by drips from overhead trees such as eucalypts and Umbrella Trees (*Schefflera actinophylla*). Sooty mould is unsightly, but is not a serious disease.

Control: If the source of the secretion is controlled, then the sooty mould usually disappears within a week or two. Hosing quickly improves an affected plant's appearance.

Water Spots

Many ferns, especially those types with leathery fronds, may suffer from diseases which cause watery spots on the fronds. These spots have been noticed on many different ferns in many different countries and are caused by a wide variety of fungi. The spots are usually less than 0.5 cm (0.2 in) across and are often sunken with a water-soaked appearance.

Control: Such spots are usually of a minor nature and control measures are rarely warranted. Improving aeration and spacing plants can be helpful. Severe attacks may be sprayed with wettable sulphur, dinocarp, or a soluble copper compound such as copper oxychloride.

Brittle Frond

A very wide range of ferns are susceptible to attacks by the fungus *Corticum anceps*. This damages the fronds (or sometimes only the pinnae) and the affected parts become somewhat thickened and very brittle. They readily break off and the fronds or plants take on a lop-sided appearance. Sometimes whole fronds may fall off. This fungus is of a sporadic nature and is worse in very humid conditions. Susceptible ferns include *Blechnum spicant*, *Cystopteris fragilis*, *Dryopteris filix-mas*, *Phyllitis scolopendrium*, *Polypodium vulgare* and *Polystichum aculeatum*.

Control: No effective control measures have been reported.

Frond Malformation

The fungus *Taphrina laurencia* induces an unusual malformation in the fronds of certain species of *Pteris* (e.g. *P. quadriaurita*) and *Polystichum* (e.g. *P. aristatum*). On the underside of the fronds, buds are initiated which develop into a cluster of outgrowths resembling much-reduced abnormal fronds. This cluster can become quite large and eventually parts of it become powdery as the fungus produces spores.

Control: Sporadic outbreaks can be controlled by cutting off and burning affected fronds. Severe outbreaks may be controlled with a spray containing soluble copper such as copper oxychloride.

Osmunda Fern Smut

In some seasons species of *Osmunda* may be blackened by the smut fungus *Ustilago osmundae*. This is a dirty fungus which mars the appearance of the plants. Affected fronds should be removed when the disease is first noticed. As the fungus develops and begins to spore, the affected fronds may contract and curl.

Control: No effective control measure has been reported.

Young Frond Blight

At certain times of the year (particularly summer) young developing fronds may wither and die. This is caused by a fungus known as blight. The disease is usually of a minor nature and control is rarely warranted.

Control: Severe attacks may be sprayed with wettable sulphur or copper oxychloride.

Frond Tip Blight

This fungus, *Phyllosticta pteridis*, attacks the tips of fronds causing dieback. Frequently, grey spots which have dark margins, are to be found on affected leaves.

Control: By spraying with a copper spray such as copper oxychloride or cupric hydroxide.

Fern Anthracnose

Cultivars of the Boston Fern (*Nephrolepis exaltata* cv. Bostoniensis) may be damaged by the fungus *Glomerella nephrolepis*, during still, humid conditions. The unrolling tips of young fronds collapse, turn brown and wither. Badly affected plants look very unsightly. The disease is worst on fine-leaved cultivars, especially where the fronds become wet.

Control: Remove and burn affected leaves, improve ventilation, spray with captan.

Frond Blisters

Areas of yellowish blistered or pulpy tissue on the fronds of ferns usually indicate an attack by a species of the fungus genus *Taphrina*. This disease, which is very difficult to control, is usually sporadic and confined to a few fronds. The commonest fungus species is *T. filicina* which attacks *Dryopteris* spp., *Onoclea sensibilis* and *Polystichum acrostichoides*. Other species are specific to a few ferns.

Control: Remove and burn affected fronds.

15 Disorders and other miscellaneous fern ailments

Ferns suffer damage from a variety of environmental factors many of which are related to the climate or human activities. The symptoms and severity of damage resulting from these factors vary considerably and all are grouped together in this chapter.

Sweating

Sweating is a physiological condition common in some ferns during certain climatic conditions. The commonest symptoms are a blackening of all or part of the fronds. The condition is caused when the outside conditions are so still and humid that normal transpiration cannot take place. Black patches appear on the leaves, and in severe circumstances, whole fronds may collapse. This not only renders the plants unsightly, but they are also weakened and left open to attacks by other pests and diseases. Death from sweating can be quite common in some seasons.

In temperate regions sweating is most common in the autumn with the onset of still days and cold dewy nights. It is prevalent in greenhouses and shadehouses but can also occur in crowded garden situations. In subtropical regions the condition can occur in the autumn but also is frequent during the hot, humid conditions of the wet season. In the latter season sweating is much worse if the plants are crowded or overgrown with weeds. Not all ferns are affected by sweating to the same degree. Sensitive ferns include various species of *Blechnum*, *Doodia* and *Pteris*. Ferns in transit that are packed in plastic frequently sweat badly.

Dryness

Most ferns appreciate moisture and dislike dryness intensely. Dry ferns initially lose the healthy lustre in their fronds and look drab by comparison with well-watered ferns. The older fronds may yellow and die prematurely. If soft young growth is present this will wilt and may die. Wilting is the most common symptom of dryness and is an indication that the roots cannot supply water fast enough to the fronds to keep up with transpiration losses. Some ferns do not wilt but turn a pale whitish green, e.g. *Nephrolepis* species and cultivars.

Ferns that do not receive sufficient water will continually struggle and will have a poor appearance. They will also be susceptible to attack by pests such as mealy bugs and spider mites. Though most ferns will recover (after a setback) from transient dryness caused by neglect, certain species invariably die following such an occurrence, e.g. *Pteris comans*, *P. macilenta*, *Ctenitis sloanei*, *Diplopterygium longissimum*, *Gleichenia dicarpa* and *G. microphylla*. Some growers claim that they notice a peculiar smell in a greenhouse when the ferns are dry. In the case of maidenhairs this has been described as resembling 'tea leaves'.

Sun Scorch

Hardy ferns tolerate, and even welcome, exposure to sun, however, tender species which are shade-lovers may suffer bleached fronds and scorching if planted in an exposed situation. Scorching can also occur when protection is suddenly removed, such as when overhead trees are damaged in a storm. The drying effects of the sun are exaggerated by hot winds.

Sun scorch may also occur on indoor ferns thoughtlessly left out in the open, or on those ferns removed from greenhouses during hot weather and not conditioned before being placed outside. Damage from scorching may be temporary, however, tender ferns may have to be moved to a more sheltered situation if they are to survive.

Frost Damage

Frost is a common killer of sensitive ferns. Frost causes damage by freezing plant tissue, although most problems occur during thawing. As the tissue in fern cells freezes, it contracts and expels water into the spaces between the cells. This water freezes to form ice crystals. When thawing begins, the ice melts and the water is absorbed back into the cells by osmosis. If thawing occurs quickly, there is little damage to the leaves, but if the ice melts slowly, the cells collapse and the surface frond tissue desiccates. This effect is aggravated because the atmosphere on a frosty night is dry, due to all the moisture being frozen.

Frost damage is more severe on young soft growth than on mature hardened growth. Frost can damage hardy ferns, but in these species the setback is temporary and the plants grow again in the spring. Sensitive species, such as those from the tropics, may collapse dramatically and usually rot away to nothing.

Wind Burn

Wind burn commonly shows up on young fern fronds following periods of windy weather. Drying winds, especially if they are hot, may shrivel developing fronds and may damage unrolling croziers so that papery patches show up in the fronds when they expand. Cold winds stunt growth and very chilling winds may damage fronds resulting in papery patches. Constant draughts may buffet ferns and retard their growth. Salt-laden winds may cause damage in coastal districts (see below).

Hail Damage

Hail causes obvious physical damage to ferns such as punching holes in the fronds, bruising and smashing stipes and young croziers. Hail may also chill ferns if it collects in sufficient quantities around the growing apex and, if large quantities of hail collect, the fern may actually be killed by this chilling effect.

Salt Damage

Salt damage may occur by windborne salt in coastal areas or by a build-up of salt in the soils of low-lying areas.

Windborne Salt

Salt is picked up from the sea and transported inland by onshore winds. Ferns growing in coastal districts may be damaged as the result of salt deposition on exposed fronds. Damage is more severe following strong winds associated with storms because larger quantities of salt are picked up and deposited. Symptoms of windborne salt damage are brown papery patches on the fronds. Young fronds, especially, may be damaged. Some ferns, particularly those that grow naturally in maritime situations, are quite resistant to salt damage, e.g. *Asplenium marinum, A. obtusatum, A. difforme, A. terrestre, Blechnum banksii, Acrostichum speciosum.*

Soil Salt

Soils in low lying zones, where drainage water collects, are subject to salting because the water is continually evaporating during warm weather and the dissolved salts become concentrated. The water need not appear on the soil surface for salting to occur, for, if the water table rises near enough for capillary action to take place, salt can build up in the surface layer of the soil. In severe cases, salt may appear as a white encrustation on the surface; few ferns will survive in such saline soils. Most will die or suffer severely reduced fronds which tend to curl and have patches of dead tissue. Some hardy ferns of the genera *Notholaena* and *Cheilanthes* may have some tolerance of saline soils.

Smog Damage

Smog is a large-city problem that is created primarily by pollution. Smog is a variable material that may be composed of many different chemical compounds and may consist of a mixture of liquids, solids and gases. Smog damage to plants is quite common in and near large cities and ferns are among the plants affected. The damage is mainly caused by peroxide products resulting from hydrocarbon pollutants reacting with ozone in the atmosphere, and to a lesser extent sulphur compounds.

Early symptoms of smog damage in ferns are the presence of numerous small brown spots on the fronds. These fronds may die prematurely with the frond browning completely and becoming brittle. Sometimes these effects are also associated with wilting of the frond. Usually the growing apex, stipes and roots remain unaffected, although in areas of severe smog pollution whole plants may die.

Fog Damage

Continuous fogs may cause sweating in sensitive ferns such as species of *Pteris* and *Blechnum*. The symptoms and cause are identical with those outlined under the heading 'Sweating' earlier in this chapter.

Waterlogging

Ferns like moisture, however, many species are surprisingly sensitive to overwet soils. Waterlogging of soils occurs when water replaces air in the soil pores for long periods. Waterlogging usually occurs in low lying areas or in heavy soils. In waterlogged conditions, fern roots may not be able to extract sufficient oxygen for normal growth and the plants suffer. Waterlogging should not be confused with natural conditions such as those which occur in soaks and swamps, where the water is frequently moving and kept aerated by the complex of life forms which have evolved to survive in such conditions. Though many ferns will thrive in these natural areas, they may linger unwillingly in the waterlogged conditions created by man.

Waterlogging can be complicated by the presence of iron or sulphur compounds which may be chemically converted to toxic substances, and also by the presence of vigorous root fungi such as *Phytophthora*.

Symptoms of waterlogging damage are usually wilting of young fronds, distortion of growth and the appearance of papery patches in the frond. Some ferns seem able to cope very well with waterlogged conditions (see Appendix 7).

Nutritional Disorders

Unusual growth in ferns caused by nutritional

disorders such as incorrect soil pH, deficiencies or toxicities are dealt with in Chapter 10.

Lack of Mycorrhiza

Some ferns have a symbiotic association with certain fungi which infect their roots. This is a controlled infection and the fungi aid in the ferns' nutrition. These ferns cannot grow in the absence of the fungi and if the mycorrhizal balance is destroyed, for example if the plant is shifted from its natural habitat, then it lingers and dies slowly. Such ferns do not respond to the application of fertilizers and are usually classed as being very difficult to grow. Examples of pteridophytes which have a mycorrhizal relationship include species of *Schizaea* and perhaps some species of *Ophioglossum, Botrychium, Lycopodium* and *Selaginella*.

Mosses and Liverworts

Mosses and liverworts require the same growing conditions as ferns and are common components of greenhouses and ferneries. They are most noticeable under benches and on walls etc., but they also may invade pots and are dangerous competitors for sporelings.

Liverworts have a flat thallus-like growth attached to the soil surface by numerous root hairs. They reproduce vegetatively and quickly build up into colonies. These colonies can completely smother the surface of the soil so that water is shed from the pot and the ferns suffer from dryness. There are many different types of Liverwort but those of the genus *Marchantia* are among the worst pests.

Mosses come in a wide range of types, however, only a few species are nuisances to the fern enthusiast. Odd plants will occur in most pots, however, the presence of a thick crop of mosses on the surface of a pot is usually a sign that the fern is in need of repotting.

Both mosses and liverworts can be disastrous to fern sporelings as they grow much faster, and can quickly smother, the young fern plants. Control in these instances is difficult and the problem is best avoided by careful sterilization of the sowing mix and, if necessary, disinfection of the spores.

Algae

Algae are a primitive form of plant life closely related to ferns. They require the same conditions for germination and development as do ferns but they are usually faster growing. If present in a pot of sporelings algae may completely smother the young ferns, resulting in a blackened slimy mass over the surface of the pot. If only a few algae are noticed in a pot of sporelings they should be removed or else the young ferns should be transplanted. If algae have gained a strong hold, then the pot is best discarded. Chemicals such as physan may provide some algae control but may also damage the young ferns. Efficient sterilization is the best answer.

Part Four

Propagation and Hybridization of Ferns

16 Vegetative propagation

Ferns can be propagated by a number of vegetative techniques; some are very simple to perform, others are complex and require sterile techniques and specialized equipment. The simple techniques are useful and are widely employed by fern enthusiasts to increase the numbers of their favourite ferns.

DIVISION

Division is a very useful means of propagating those ferns which are amenable to it and, being a straightforward process, it can be carried out with a minimum of experience and equipment. Division is probably the most frequently used and effective method of vegetative propagation of ferns. The only equipment needed is a sharp knife or, perhaps, a spade for larger specimens.

The division process is simply that of taking a suitable clump of a fern and dividing it into two or more parts which are capable of existing as separate plants. A suitable fern is a clump which has more than one growing point, each of which is separated by sufficient distance to be divided. There are some variations on this theme and these are dealt with under separate headings below.

After dividing a fern, the separate pieces must be

Divided clump of *Doodia aspera* prior to potting

Potted division of *Doodia aspera*

Dividing a clump of *Doodia aspera* with a spade

handled carefully if the process is to be successful. This is known as aftercare. Dead fronds and dead or damaged parts of the rhizome should be removed. The rhizome can be trimmed until live tissue is evident and this is then sealed by rubbing with a small amount of garden lime. An excessively large root system should be trimmed back, and decaying or damaged roots should be removed completely. Fronds should be trimmed back to achieve a balance with the reduced root system of the division. New croziers and young, unfolding fronds should be carefully protected and encouraged to develop, for they will provide much of the photosynthetic material needed for the establishment of the division.

Divisions of very hardy garden ferns can be planted directly into a suitable position in the garden. For most ferns however, especially the more delicate species, or for small weak divisions, the best alternative is a period of pot culture. This promotes better and more rapid establishment of the division which, when suitably advanced, can be planted out with little or no disturbance. The divisions should be potted into an open, fibrous mixture of free drainage and kept moist and warm until new growth is well established. The performance of the growth above ground is obvious but the root system should be checked by examination. Once established, the propagated fern can be planted into the garden or potted into a larger container.

Notes on the various types of division in ferns follow.

Creeping Rhizomes

Any fern with a creeping rhizome can be propagated by division. For this group of ferns division is an obvious method of propagation and it generally works satisfactorily. The main requisites are that the clump should be large enough to provide divisions of sufficient size that will survive, and that the rhizomes removed should have roots attached. Rootless sections of rhizomes can be very difficult to start (see treatment under offsets, below).

Not all ferns with creeping rhizomes have the same growth habit and the major variations are further grouped below. In each of these groups however, the rhizomes may be short, medium or long-creeping (see Figure p.22). This is a genetic characteristic that is constant for any species. It is not necessary to expose the rhizome to determine this feature, for ferns with long-creeping rhizomes generally have widely spaced fronds and those with short-creeping rhizomes are crowded. Ferns with long-creeping rhizomes can, in general, be divided more readily than those with a short rhizome, however, both types can be equally successful if the plants to be divided are big enough.

Subterranean Creeping Rhizomes

These are terrestrial ferns with rhizomes which are below ground and are not generally visible. The best time for dividing ferns of this group is when they are in active growth, usually in spring or early summer. On the surface this growth shows as the appearance of a succession of new fronds and croziers. Exposing the rhizomes will show active tips which may be either green or covered in young scales. New roots will also be obvious and these will have long, fleshy, often green tips. Divisions made when growth is at this stage usually establish quickly and grow away strongly.

The technique of dividing these ferns is simple. After deciding where the divisions are to be made, the covering soil is scraped away to expose the rhizome which can then be cut with a knife or spade. The surfaces of the rhizome exposed by the cut should be sealed by rubbing with garden lime. The division should then be carefully lifted with a spade and planted direct or potted as outlined in Chapter 20.

Dormant bulbils on rachis of *Callipteris prolifera*
Photo E. R. Rotherham

Tissue culture of *Davallia mariesii* Photo D. L. Jones

Plantlets on frond segments of *Asplenium bulbiferum*
Photo E. R. Rotherham

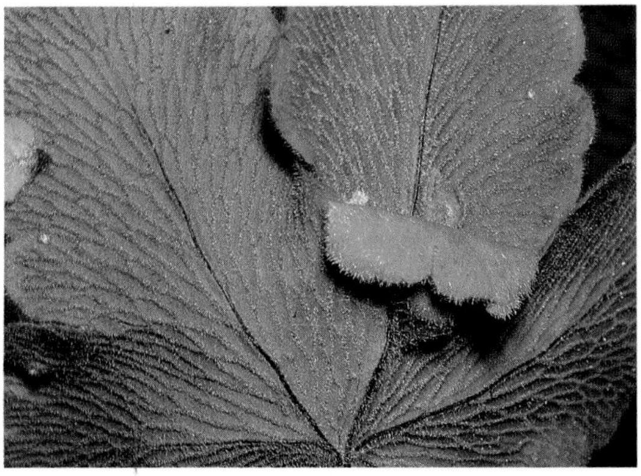

Plantlets developing on underside of frond of *Hemionitis palmata*
Photo E. R. Rotherham

Some ferns with subterranean-creeping rhizomes grow rapidly and the rhizomes branch freely, e.g. species of *Hypolepis*. Such ferns develop quickly into a clump and may spread too rapidly. They are, however, very easy to divide. Other ferns such as *Cyrtomium falcatum* may grow for years but, because they have a short-creeping rhizome that rarely branches, they do not develop into large clumps. As may be expected, there are all sorts of growth habits between these extremes.

An interesting form of vegetative increase has been observed in some ferns which have short-creeping rhizomes, e.g. *Bolbitis taylori, Cyrtomium falcatum*. Such plants usually have a long piece of old, barren

Sporelings of *Marattia salicina* developing on an earth bank
Photo D. L. Jones

rhizome attached which slowly withers away. This has vegetative buds present but, while it is attached to the plant, they usually remain dormant presumably because of hormones produced from the growing tip. If a substantial section of the old, live rhizome is removed and placed in a pot of sphagnum moss, one or more of these buds can often be induced to grow and will eventually form roots and become a separate plant. In old plants the long length of barren rhizome sometimes sprouts new plantlets from these dormant buds. This is probably as the distance from the growing apex increases and the effect of the hormones lessens. Once the plantlets start they usually grow away strongly and become separate plants.

Exposed Creeping Rhizomes

These are epiphytic or lithophytic ferns, the rhizomes of which clamber over the surface of the tree or rock on which they grow and the roots wander amongst accumulated litter and debris. In cultivation the rhizomes always remain visible on the surface of the potting mix and may rot if buried. This is a common group of ferns in cultivation and most species are readily propagated by division. When dividing the

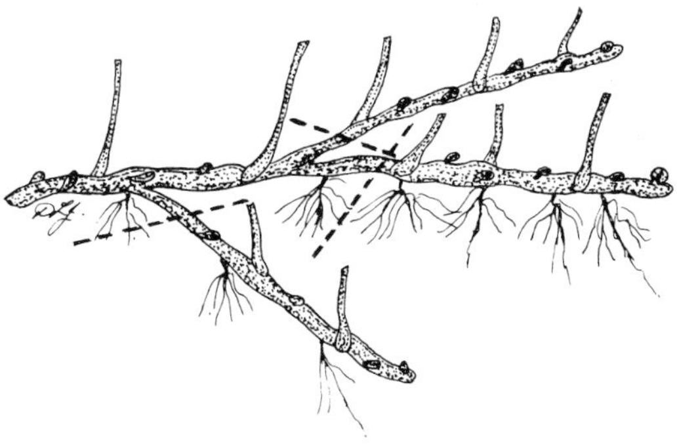

Subterranean creeping rhizome

The exposed creeping rhizomes of *Humata tyermanii* can be divided with care Photo C. G. Goudey

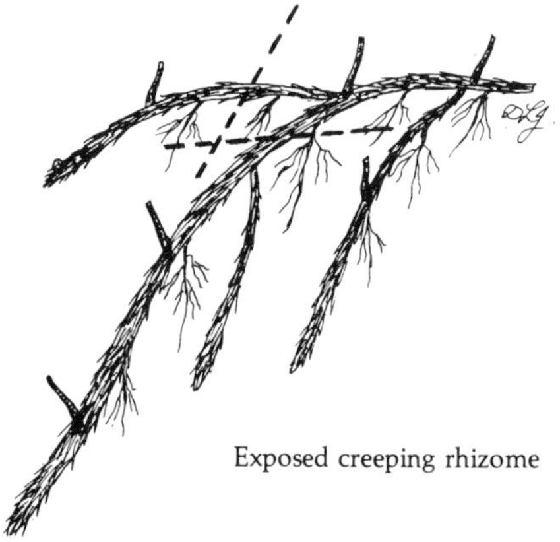

Exposed creeping rhizome

clumps several rhizomes may need to be cut to make a division of sufficient size that will survive transplanting. In some species the rhizome may elongate for a distance before roots are produced. If this is the case it is important that the rhizomes are cut behind where the roots are produced so that each division has some roots to help it get started. Rootless sections of rhizomes can be very difficult to get started and tend to wither and collapse (see treatment under offsets, below).

The best time of the year for dividing ferns with visible-creeping rhizomes is in spring and early summer. The plants should be in active growth with growing tips on the rhizomes and new roots and fronds being produced. As plants of this group grow strongly over the warm summer months the division should be carried out sufficiently early so that the plants can become established before the cold winter months slow growth.

Aerial Rhizomes

Ferns of this group are typically epiphytic or lithophytic and often grow in large clumps. The basal parts of the rhizomes are surrounded by a thick mat of roots while the upper parts of the rhizomes are erect

Plant of *Platycerium bifurcatum* which can be divided

or semi-erect and grow through the air. This part of the rhizome is usually rootless. This group of ferns is typified by some species of *Davallia* (*D. solida, D. pyxidata*) and *Phlebodium decumanum*. The growth habit acts as a litter-collecting device.

When dividing ferns of this group care should be taken to ensure that basal parts of the rhizome with

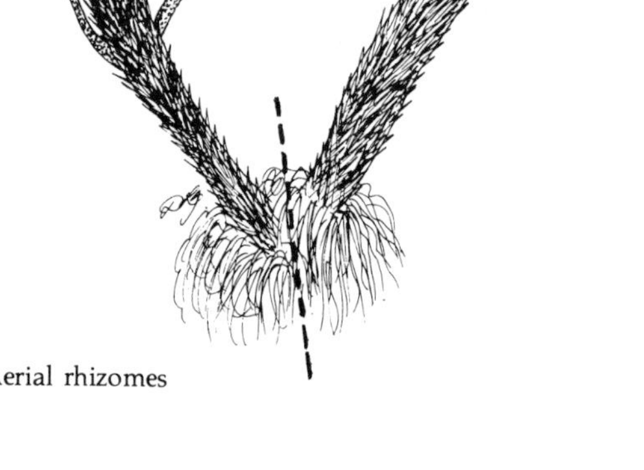

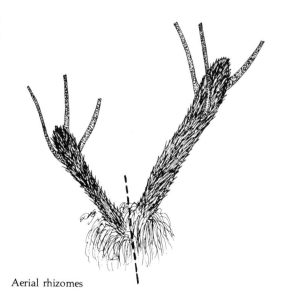

Aerial rhizomes

Materials necessary for division including tree fern slab

Tying division onto slab with a generous pad of sphagnum moss

roots attached are included in the division. Rootless pieces of rhizome can be very difficult to start and frequently wither and rot. Spring and early summer is the best time to divide ferns of this group and the divisions must be potted into a coarse mixture (see also Aerial Layering below).

Platycerium Division

Ferns of the genus *Platycerium* are commonly known as Staghorns or Elkhorns. Many species and hybrid cultivars are very popular in cultivation. Most of them are clumping ferns with a creeping, branching

The division finally mounted and hung

rhizome which is hidden beneath layers of specialized sterile leaves called pads. New pads are produced at intervals from the top of the rhizome and are pressed closely against the older ones beneath. The very old pads decay and the fern's roots ramify through these and any litter which has been collected.

Clumping species and hybrids of *Platycerium* can be successfully divided, but, because of their greatly modified appearance, people are sometimes loathe to carry out this simple operation. In the clumping species each separate group of fronds is the end point of a branch in the rhizome. By carefully cutting far enough into the old, dead pads the rhizome can be severed and the piece separated. The simplest technique is to run a sharp knife around the back of the plantlet. This must be sufficiently deep so that it cuts into dead pads as well as severing the rhizomes and roots.

The severed plantlet can be tied or wired securely onto a support such as a slab of tree-fern trunk or weathered hardwood. A pad of moist material such as sphagnum moss, placed beneath the severed part will help retain moisture and aid in the development of new roots and the establishment of the piece. Separated pieces should be watered regularly until they are obviously growing strongly. The best time to divide Platyceriums is in spring and early summer, thus allowing the divisions all of the warm summer months to become established.

Clumps of vigorous species such as *P. bifurcatum* may need to be divided when they get too big. This

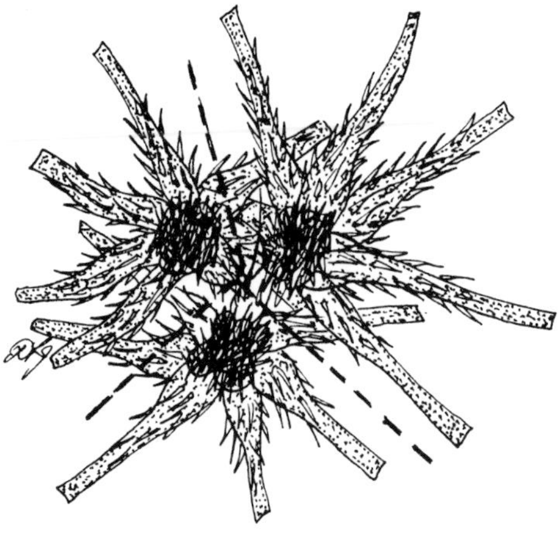

Crown division

Dormant bulbils on *Tectaria gemmifera*
Photo C. G. Goudey

is slightly different from removing a plantlet for propagation and involves much harsher methods. Because of the years of accumulated litter and old pads the major part of an elkhorn clump is a tough mass of fibrous tissue. Separating such clumps requires rugged tools such as a bow saw and a sharp axe or cane-knife plus plenty of energy. The technique is simply to make a start in the upper part with the saw and then chop downwards with the axe or cane-knife until the two pieces are separated. Establishing such large divisions is very easy compared with separated plantlets and they generally need very little aftercare.

Crown Division

Many ferns with a tufted rhizome develop a large crown of fronds at the soil surface. As the plant ages, so the crown increases greatly in size. Eventually, a maximum size is reached and the single crown divides into two. These crowns grow side by side and eventually one or the other of them will also divide. A large clump of these types of ferns then consists of several distinct crowns all closely placed and at first sight appearing as if one. Such clumps can be lifted and readily divided by slicing the root system between them with a sharp knife. After appropriate trimming of roots and fronds the divisions can be potted or planted in the ground.

Ferns which can be divided in this manner include *Polystichum formosum, P. fallax, P. lentum, P. aculeatum, P. setiferum.*

It should be noted that not all tufted or crown-forming ferns can be divided in this manner. For

Bulbil on frond apex (*Polystichum lentum*)

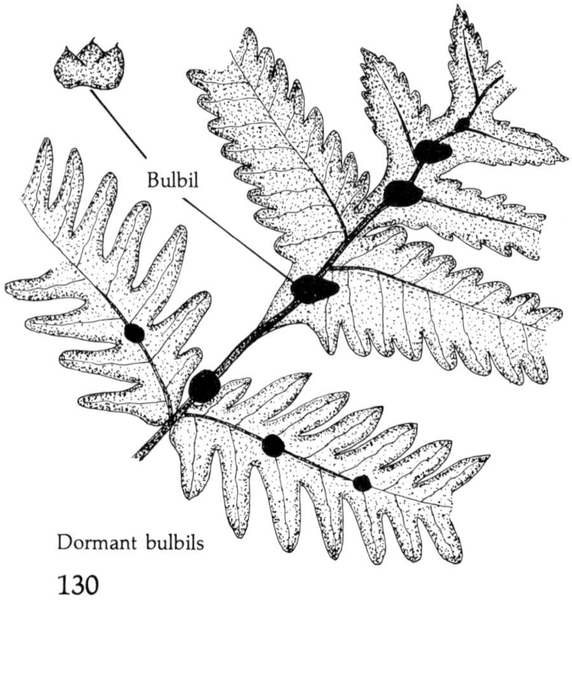

Dormant bulbils

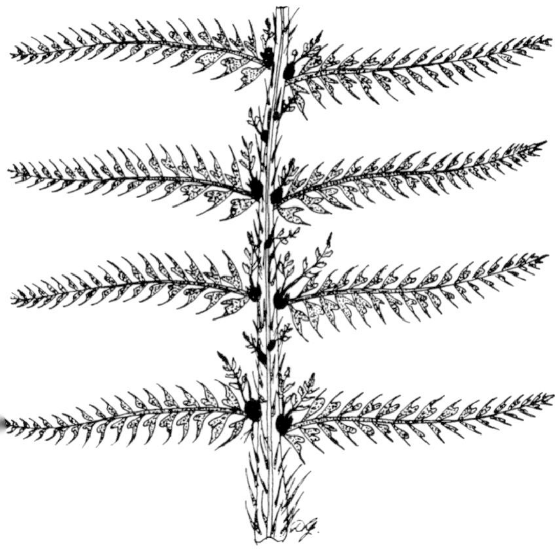

Bulbils along rachis (*Polystichum setiferum*)

Bulbils on frond surface (Asplenium bulbiferum)

instance, it is widely believed that the Birds-nest type ferns, e.g. *Asplenium australasicum* and *A. nidus*, can be propagated by splitting the crown down the middle. Propagation by this method is difficult to achieve with these ferns and such an act usually results in the death of one, or both, parts of the plant.

BULBILS OR PLANTLETS

Some ferns have the ability to produce miniature plants on their fronds. These tiny plants usually have a bulbous base and are termed bulbils or plantlets. In the young stage they are usually present as small rounded leafless structures but as they develop, miniature fronds and even roots are produced. Ferns which produce bulbils are usually colony formers in nature, the colonies being maintained and increased by their production.

Two types of bulbils may be distinguished depending on their activity while on the plant. They are:

1. Dormant bulbils — these are fleshy tuber-like swellings which do not develop any roots or leaves while attached to the frond. When mature they fall, and, if conditions are suitable, will immediately develop roots and fronds. If conditions are not suitable they can remain dormant for up to six months until rains come and they begin growth. The best example of this type is *Tectaria gemmifera*.

2. Active bulbils or plantlets — these develop fronds and may even form roots while still attached to the plant. They do not generally fall from the plant but remain attached to the frond until it contacts the ground and decays.

Bulbils may be produced from one of three positions on the frond.

(i) From near the tips of the fronds, e.g. *Polystichum lentum*, *P. proliferum*, *Asplenium paleaceum*, *Woodwardia radicans*. In these ferns usually only one or a couple of plantlets are produced. In nature the plantlets on this type of fern develop until the frond ages and the tip eventually touches the ground, then the plantlets take root and grow as separate plants.

Propagation of these ferns involves pegging the

Pegging down plantlet on the frond apex of *Polystichum proliferum*

frond tip into the ground or in a pot until the plantlet is established and then severing the top part of the parent frond.

(ii) Bulbils scattered along the length of the midrib (rachis), e.g. *Polystichum setiferum*. In this type numerous plantlets develop on each frond and they increase in size as the frond matures. Eventually, the old frond rots or becomes covered with humus and a few of the plantlets survive to grow into new ferns.

Ferns of this type can be propagated by cutting off the frond completely and lying it on a shallow tray of sand-peat mixture (3 : 1). The bulbils must be sufficiently large to withstand the cutting of the frond and the period until they become established.

(iii) Bulbils produced all over the surface of the frond, e.g. *Asplenium bulbiferum, Woodwardia orientalis*. In this type plantlets of various stages are scattered over the upper surface of the frond. They usually begin to appear 6–12 months after the fronds develop and slowly increase in size as the frond ages. The frond is slowly forced down by the development of younger ones and, when it touches the ground, the bulbils become independent plants while the frond rots.

Mature plantlets can be removed and, if potted and kept in a humid atmosphere, will eventually become separate plants. If the bulbils are removed while too young, they collapse and die. Those bulbils which have developed roots are usually ready for removal. An alternative to removing the bulbils is to layer the frond while it is still attached to the plant and separate the plantlets as they begin to grow strongly.

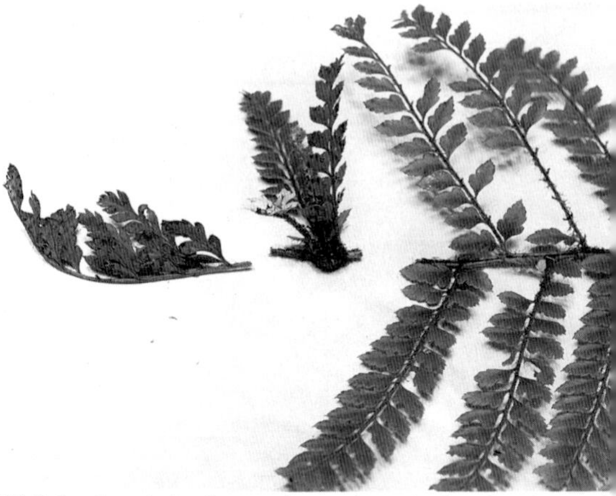

Well developed plantlets can be cut from the frond and potted separately

Plantlets on rachis of *Callipteris prolifera*
Photo D. L. Jones

Plantlets on rachis of *Polystichum setiferum*
Photo C. G. Goudey

Plantlets on frond of *Asplenium daucifolium*
Photo C. G. Goudey

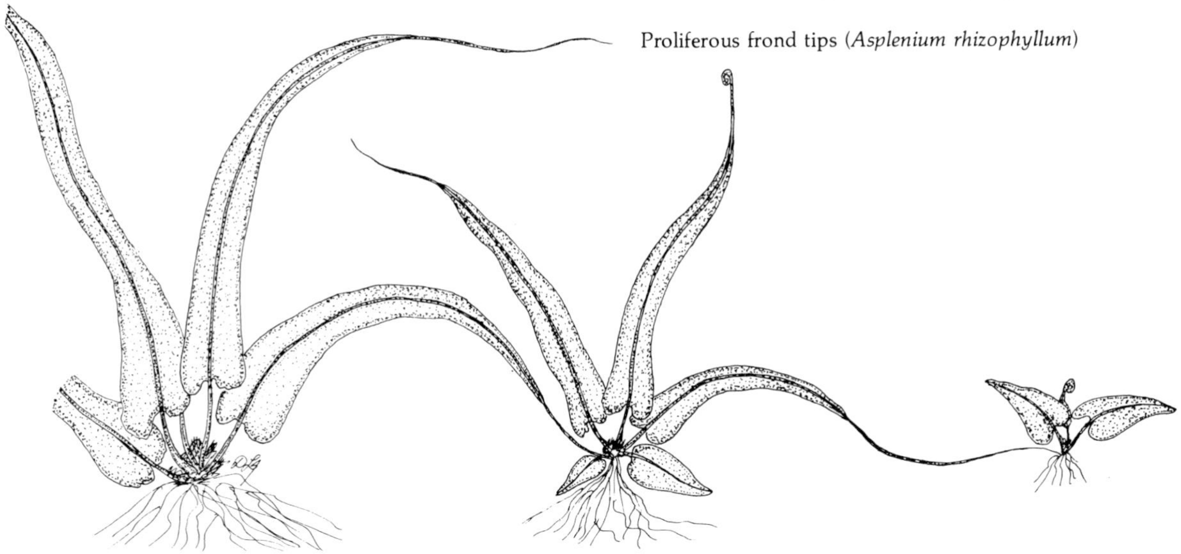

Proliferous frond tips (*Asplenium rhizophyllum*)

Commercial propagation of *Hemionitis arifolia* from proliferous leaves Photo D. L. Jones

Commercial propagation of *Hemionitis palmata* from proliferous leaves Photo D. L. Jones

Proliferous Frond Tips

In a few species of ferns the rachis continues elongating past the last part of the lamina or pinna. If this slender rachis extension contacts soil, it becomes proliferous and a small plant with roots is formed. This small plant quickly becomes independent, but usually remains attached to the parent frond for many months and sometimes a chain of interconnecting plants is formed. Ferns of this type can be readily propagated and are generally popular in cultivation. Examples include *Adiantum caudatum, A. edgeworthii, A. philippense, Asplenium rhizophyllum.*

Aerial Growths

Some species of Tassel Fern, e.g. *Lycopodium proliferum, L. phlegmaria,* produce aerial growths

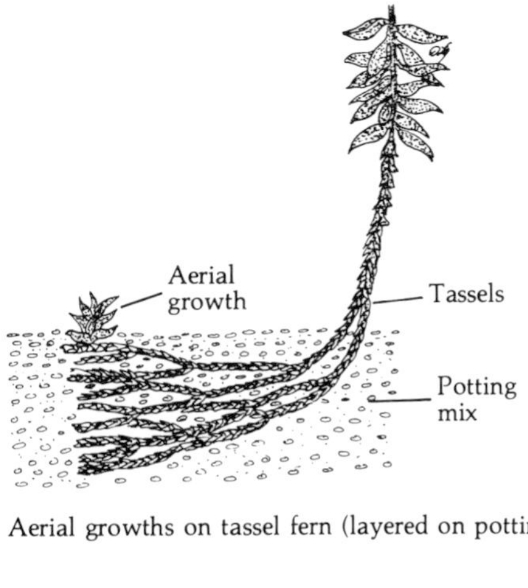

Aerial growths on tassel fern (layered on potting mix)

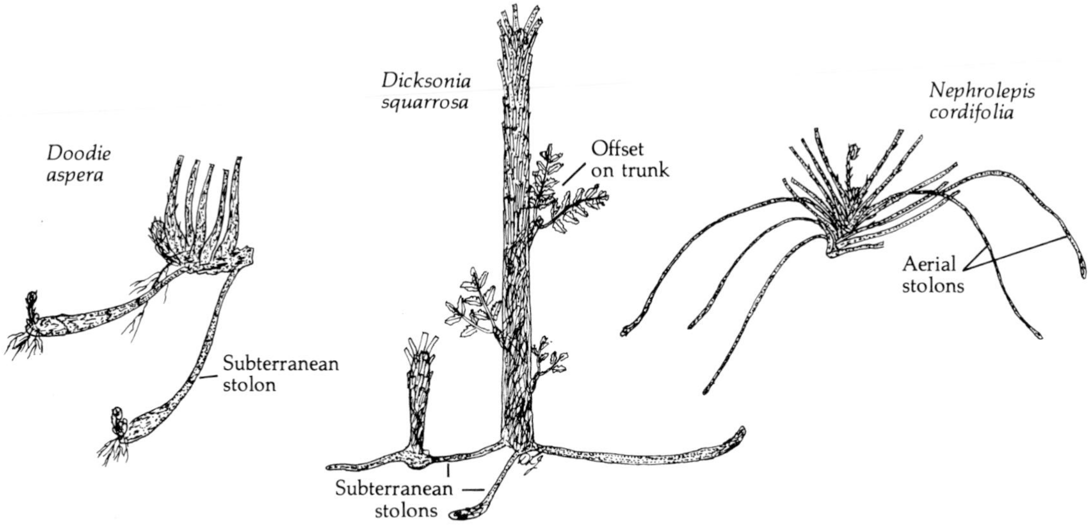

Stolons and offsets

from among the tassels or near the tips of the fronds. These growths develop and may even form roots. If they come into contact with a suitable surface they may become established and eventually become separate plants. In nature *L. proliferum* usually grows in colonies and often this technique of vegetative increase can be traced through the plants established on a tree, with the adult plants being at the top and the progeny in a series below.

STOLONS

Many clumping ferns reproduce prolifically by the production of lateral growths called stolons. These are a specialized stem which resembles a root, but which bears nodes, buds and roots. The stolons of most ferns are subterranean, but species of *Nephrolepis* produce wiry, specialized stolons which grow through the air for a considerable distance before contacting the soil. These root where they touch the soil and can also produce plants at intervals along their length.

Subterranean stolons grow from the side of the parent rhizome and emerge from the soil at various distances. The tip of the stolon produces fronds and these appear in a clump near the main plant. The stolon generally remains attached to the parent plant for at least twelve months, but eventually the base rots away and the small clump becomes a separate entity. Most species of *Blechnum* and *Doodia* reproduce by the production of subterranean stolons.

Separation of stolons is a relatively simple procedure. The base of the stolon should be severed near where it joins the parent rhizome and the whole of the young plant (including roots and leaves) should be carefully lifted and potted or planted in a new position. Only those stolons which have produced expanded leaves should be separated. Stolons cut prior to this stage often struggle and may simply wither and die. Spring and summer are the best times for separating stolons.

OFFSETS

A few species of tree fern produce offsets which may arise on the trunk (*Cyathea rebeccae, Dicksonia youngiae, D. squarrosa*), or from the base among the roots (*Cyathea baileyana, C. rebeccae*). These offsets are small shoots which are firmly joined to the vascular system of the plant. They are usually rootless and at the apex may have only one or two small fronds plus a cluster of undeveloped croziers. They are maintained in a quiescent or very slow-growing state until the situation is right for their growth. Their dormancy is probably maintained by the production of hormones from the growing apex. If the top of the trunk is killed or, as in the case of *D. youngiae* it falls over, then the offsets can grow away strongly.

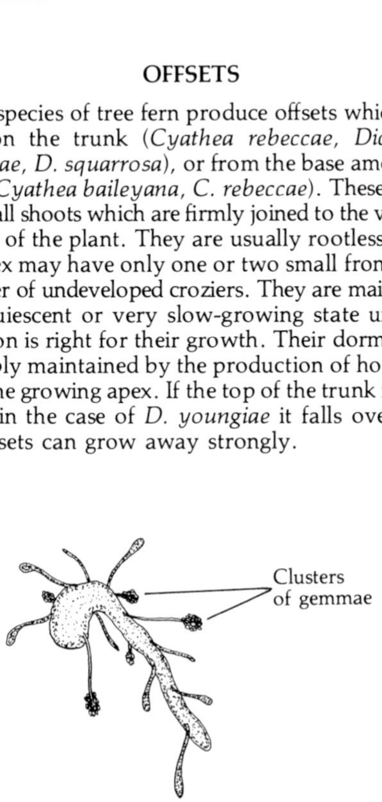

Gemmae on *Lycopodium* prothallus

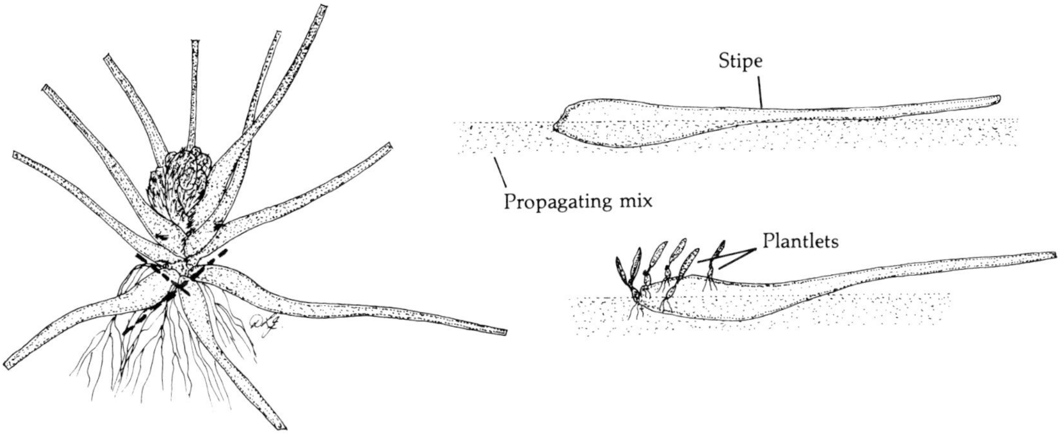

Crown showing old stipes ready for removal

Specialized layering of *Asplenium scolopendrium*

Offsets can be used as a means of propagation but they can be tricky to re-establish as separate plants. Because they are usually rootless they must be coddled until roots are formed. They can also be very hard to remove and a sharp knife or a chisel may be necessary. Once removed, they should be potted in a small pot of coarse mixture or sphagnum moss and kept in a humid position until established. An aquarium is a useful place in which to maintain humidity, or the whole pot and plant can be sealed in a plastic bag until growth is obvious. Offsets should only be removed during the warm growing months so that conditions are ideal for their establishment. Well-developed offsets usually establish readily, however, immature offsets can be difficult.

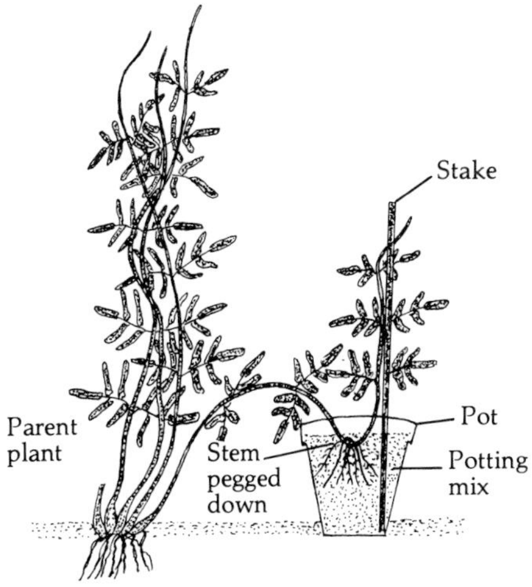

Technique of layering *Lygodium*

GEMMAE

A gemma is a small vegetative bud by which a plant can reproduce itself. The vegetative buds produced on the fronds of some ferns could perhaps be termed gemmae, but here are treated separately as bulbils. True gemmae are produced by the gametophytes of various filmy ferns and species of *Psilotum*, *Tmesipteris* and the epiphytic Lycopodiums. As the prothallus develops, it forms clusters of numerous tiny gemmae, often on specialized growths. When mature these can be splashed about by rain. If they lodge in a suitable situation in the bark of the host tree or in the soil, they can develop into another tiny prothallus. Some species of epiphytic *Lycopodium* may produce gemmae in the leaf axils of the sporophyte.

LAYERING

Simple Layering

Layering is a propagation technique used for many plants but it is not commonly adopted for ferns, although the pegging down of bulbil-bearing fronds is a form of layering. Layering can also be used to good effect for the propagation of Tassel Ferns and also species of *Lygodium*. In this technique, no tissue is detached until new plants are established.

For Tassel Ferns, a shallow container filled with a coarse, moist material such as river gravel or a mixture of coarse sand and peat moss (3 : 1) is placed so that the tips of the growths and/or the clusters of tassels are in contact with it or lie along its surface. These can be held in contact with the surface of the material by pinning or placing small rocks on top of the tissue. After a few months plantlets will appear from the tips of the growth and among the tassels. These can be allowed to develop and are separated only when they have good root and top growth.

In *Lygodium* the climbing rachis can be pegged down into a pot of sandy mixture and lightly covered at a nodal joint (from where the pinnae arise). This will eventually produce roots. When sufficiently well-established it can be separated from the parent and grown on its own.

Specialized Layering

The Hart's-tongue Fern, *Asplenium scolopendrium*, can be propagated by a specialized technique which seems to be unique to it. The bases of the old fronds and part of the rachis remain fleshy and green for long after the rest of the frond has withered and died. For propagation, these frond bases are detached close to the rhizome, cleaned of any dead material and are then laid on a tray of washed sand and peat moss (3 : 1). The tray is covered with a sheet of glass and left in a warm, but not sunny situation. After 6–10 weeks tiny white bulbils develop in a cluster around the base. These are allowed to develop until they begin to form good roots when they can be detached and potted into community pots or individually in small containers. Sometimes bruising the stipe will result in areas of bulbil formation other than at the base. This technique is simple to perform and is especially valuable for those cultivars of the Hart's-tongue which are sterile.

Aerial Layering

Some ferns of the *Davallia* alliance produce long rhizomes which grow through the air, e.g. *Davallia solida*, *D. fejeensis* and also *Phlebodium decumanum*. These are often woody and are attached to the host at the base. The roots of each stem are usually well developed at the base but are nearly always absent along the rhizome. If such a woody rhizome is severed it can be sometimes induced to grow but more often than not shrivels and dies. Such rhizomes can be propagated by the technique known as aerial layering or marcotting. This is more usually applied to ornamental shrubs and fruit trees, but can also be used on some palms and will work for ferns of the type under discussion. The best time for aerial layering is in the warm, growing months.

A pad of moist-to-wet sphagnum moss or peat moss is wrapped around the stem and squeezed to hold its shape. The area covered should include at least one node. The moist pad of moss is then wrapped tightly with a piece of polythene film which is then sealed at each end to form a watertight bundle. After 8–12 weeks roots should show through the polythene and, when a good root system is formed in the moss, the section of rhizome can be severed and potted as a separate plant.

AURICLES

Auricles are thick, fleshy, ear-like structures which enclose the base of the stipe of fronds of the genera *Angiopteris* and *Marattia*. They are technically termed stipules. One auricle is found on each side of the stipe, and buds or meristematic tissue occur in the axil of the stipe and the auricle. The auricles remain fleshy and persist on the trunk for many years after the fronds have died. In some species the vascular buds may develop and eventually produce separate plants.

The old auricles can be carefully cut from the trunk

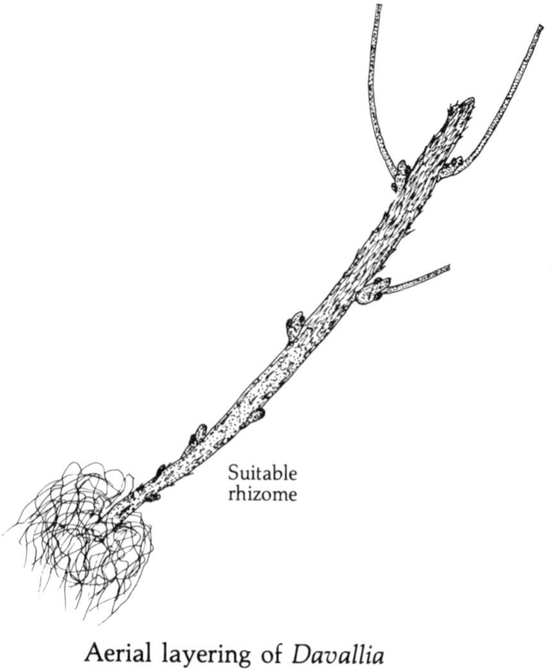

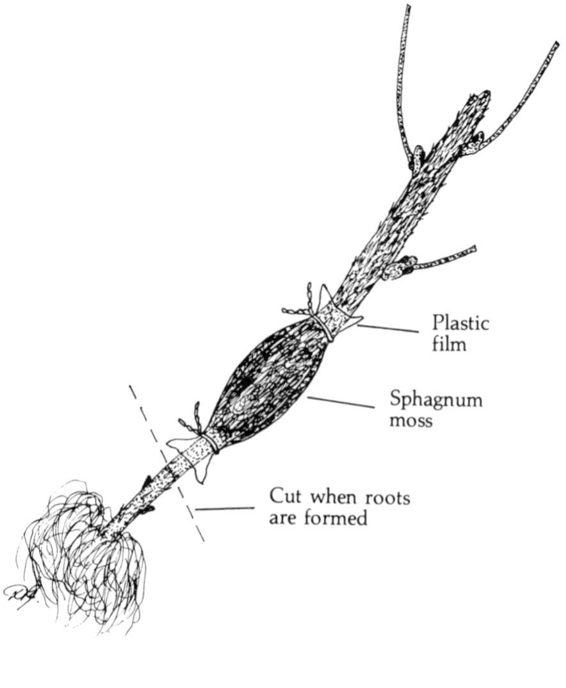

Aerial layering of *Davallia*

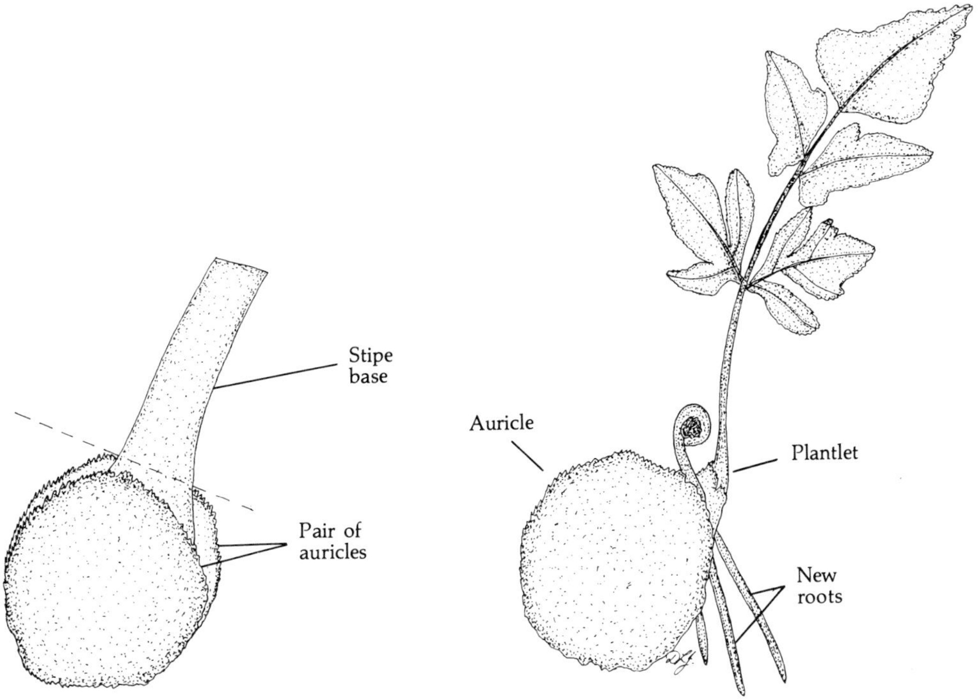

Auricle propagation

and if buried in a mixture of sand and peat (3 : 1) with the tips of the auricles just exposed, will eventually produce one or two plants from the base. The auricles generally take 6–12 months to form plants and should be kept warm and moist in this time. Auricle cuttings are best taken in spring or early summer.

Auricle cuttings can also be taken from live fronds using those which are overmature or senescing. The frond is cut from the rhizome below the auricles and the stipe is cut off below the pinnae. The auricles and base of the stipe are then planted in a coarse, propagating medium (or sphagnum moss) with the top of the auricles slightly exposed. The stipe base rots leaving the auricles which eventually produce a plant each. Some growers split the stem before planting and put each auricle in separately.

Auricles on a young plant of *Angiopteris evecta*
Photo D. L. Jones

TUBERS

Tubers are swellings which develop on underground stems or stolons. They are a modified structure and act as both a storage organ and a reproductive unit. Very few ferns produce tubers. Perhaps the best known are the very widespread *Nephrolepis cordifolia*, the South American *N. occidentalis*, and the remarkable Potato Fern (*Solanopteris tuberosa*). The species of *Solanopteris* are epiphytes and the tubers are crowded along the rhizomes. These are hollow and filled with water which may act as a reserve for the fern during times of shortage.

The tubers of *Nephrolepis cordifolia* and *N. occidentalis* can be used for propagation if removed with a small piece of stolon and potted separately, however, the author does not know if those of *Solanopteris* respond in the same way.

STEM PROPAGATION

Some epiphytic Tassel Ferns can be propagated by a technique which is termed stem propagation or even

Tubers on the stolons of *Nephrolepis cordifolia*

'cuttings'. Apical sections of 5–8 cm (2–3 in) long are cut off and laid horizontally in peat moss or sphagnum moss. These are kept moist, humid and warm (some growers use aquariums or terrariums) and after a period (varying from 6–15 months) lateral growths may develop which form roots at the base and become separate plants. The technique is slow but invaluable, since Tassel Ferns cannot be raised from spore. Experienced growers can tell which stems will make suitable cuttings. One good indication is the apex of the stem turning and beginning to grow upright. Some species such as *Lycopodium proliferum* can be readily propagated by this method but others such as *L. carinatum* and *L. dalhousianum* are extremely difficult.

As well as the tips of the stems, the sporing clusters or tassels of some species, e.g. *Lycopodium phlegmaria* and *L. phlegmaroides*, can sometimes be induced to form plantlets when removed and treated as above.

APOGAMY AND APOSPORY

These are sometimes included as techniques of vegetative propagation, though they are in fact better discussed as abnormalities in the life cycle. For more details see Chapter 4.

ROOT BUDS

Some terrestrial species of *Ophioglossum* reproduce vegetatively by producing buds on thick roots which wander through the humus. While still attached to the parent these buds produce a small leaf and a few roots. They become independent in a few months however,

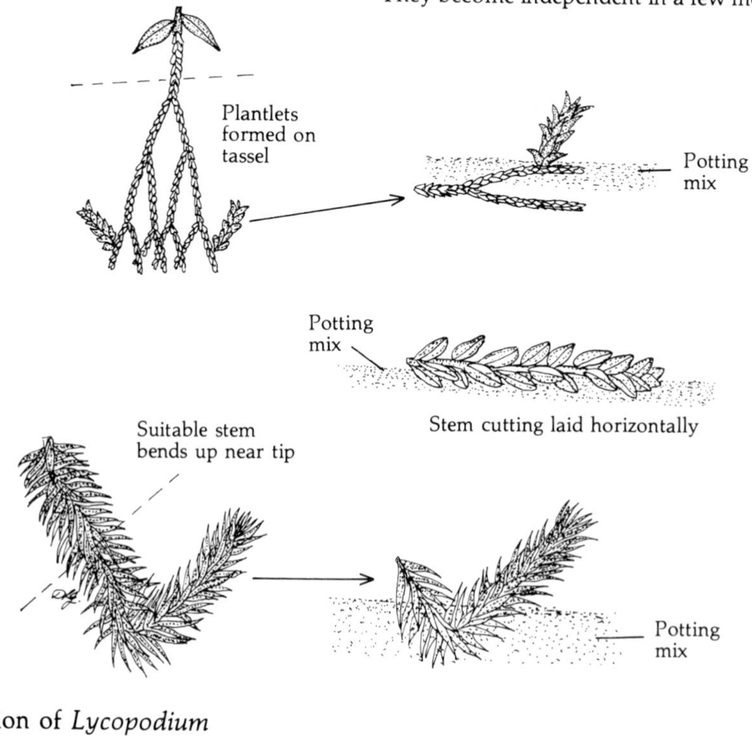

Stem propagation of *Lycopodium*

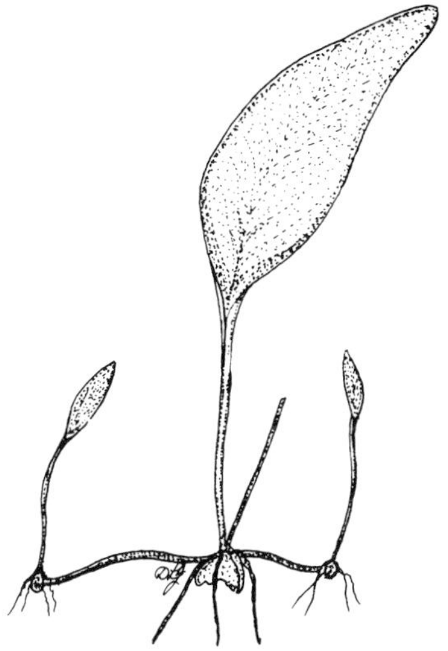

Root buds on *Ophioglossum*

when the root attaching them to the parent rots away. They increase in size until they themselves are sufficiently developed to produce bud bearing roots of their own.

It is also reported that new buds may be formed on the roots of clumping species of *Platycerium* and, as these develop sufficiently, they emerge as offsets on the clump. Whether these arise on roots or rhizomes is uncertain.

TISSUE CULTURE

Tissue culture is a modern innovation for the rapid propagation of large numbers of uniform plants. It may also be known as meristem culture or as a technique of micropropagation. It involves a laboratory type set-up, specialized equipment, special nutrient solutions and sterile techniques. The technique, therefore, is the province of specialized tissue culture laboratories or well-set-up nurseries and is not for the average fern enthusiast.

Technique: Basically tissue culture involves the successful separation and sterilization of a small piece (termed explant) of a parent plant. In ferns this is usually a rhizome tip or section of a rhizome containing buds. More recently, small sporelings and apogamous sporophytes have been used successfully as starting tissue. Whatever starting tissue is used, the most important initial step is to sterilize it and successfully introduce it into a sterile flask of nutrient agar media, without contamination. Once past this hurdle (which can be considerable) the explant can develop in the sterile flask and produce callus growth and shoots. The growing flasks are usually placed in warm, well-lit cabinets where conditions are optimum for growth and development.

As shoots proliferate on the explant, they can be cut from the original tissue and transferred to new culture flasks where they themselves will begin to proliferate. By maintaining this cutting and transfer process, a large build-up of the fern can be obtained (multiplication factors of 30 times to 100 times are quite common). This can be termed the build-up stage.

Having obtained sufficient numbers the next stage is to induce the development of the shoots and callus tissue into small plants with leaves and roots. This is achieved by manipulating the contents of the growing medium. The addition of hormones such as naphthalene acetic acid (NAA) or 2-4-dichlorophenoxy acetic acid (2, 4-D) stimulates root formation on some species and shoot formation may be promoted by NAA and/or Kinetin. This can be termed the stage of plant development.

Once the plants are well developed with small leaves and roots, they are ready for transference to a growing medium. The plants are removed from the flask and rinsed thoroughly in warm water to remove any agar followed by a weak solution of fungicide. They are then placed on the surface of community pots containing a sterilized potting mix, e.g. 2 parts peat moss : 1 part coarse sand. They are moistened and maintained in very humid conditions (e.g. under intermittent mist) for at least one month and are then gradually hardened off. When strong root and frond growth is obvious the small plants can be separated into community trays or potted singly. This can be termed the stage of adjustment.

Many species and cultivars of ferns have been propagated successfully by tissue culture and it is likely that more will be propagated by this method in the future. The technique offers the advantages of rapid propagation of large quantities of plants and freedom from disease. As the propagation is vegetative, all plants produced by the technique should be identical with the original, unless mutation has occurred in the flask.

The technique has been spectacularly successful with weedy type ferns such as species and cultivars of *Nephrolepis*. In the USA and Australia the majority of these ferns are now produced by tissue culture and the old system of large stock beds containing parent plants has been replaced by a modern laboratory. Many other ferns have been raised by tissue culture, although not with quite such spectacular results as for *Nephrolepis*. In a number of cases propagation has been successful, but difficulty has occurred in the transition stage from the sterile flasks to the growing media and, in some cases, subsequent growth has been poor.

The real benefits of tissue culture should lie in the propagation of choice sterile cultivars such as *Drynaria* rigidula cv. Whitei, *Goniophlebium subauriculatum* cv. Knightiae and *Pteris* cv. Childsii, or of species which are slow or difficult to propagate by conventional means, e.g. the single-crowned Platyceriums such as *P. grande*, *P. holttumii*, *P. superbum* and *P. wandae*. While success has been obtained with some Platyceriums and a growth rate approximately twice that of sporelings has been achieved, the results obtained with some of the choice cultivars have been quite disappointing.

17 Propagation from spores

Spores are tiny objects by which ferns reproduce themselves. A spore is actually a tiny vegetative structure which contains only half the normal complement of chromosomes and no embryo. Although the spore itself is a vegetative unit, the reproduction which it supports is actually sexual since it involves the union of sex cells. In mass, spores look like a fine dust and may be green, grey, brown, black, or yellow. They are produced from the specialized sites known as sori which occur on the underside or around the margins of fronds (see Chapter 3, page 34). These sites of spore production are usually quite obvious as round or elongated brown or blackish fluffy areas. To the uninitiated, they are often mis-identified as a pest or disease attacking the fern. Sometimes, they are borne separately on specialized fronds.

The propagation of ferns from spores is the most efficient and economical means of raising large numbers of any species. Unfortunately, propagation of ferns from spores is not always reliable and the results are often far from predictable. This unreliability may be exasperating for amateurs, but it is costly to commercial growers and is one of the major reasons why many beautiful ferns are not propagated in large numbers and made available for general sale. Wholesale nurseries tend to propagate those hardy species which are easy to grow from spore.

Materials needed for sowing fern spores

Sterilizing sowing mixture with boiling water

Technique of Spore Sowing

The technique of raising ferns from spores is basically simple and can be mastered by anyone. The steps are outlined below and should be followed if success is desired. This is basically the information needed, however, for the reasons behind some of the steps and if any problems are encountered the detailed notes which follow should be consulted.

Steps

1. Prepare the sowing medium, making sure that it is moist (for media see page 148).
2. Wash second-hand pots or (preferably) use new pots (for containers see page 149).
3. Fill the pots to one third full with washed coarse propagating sand.

A small sterilizer useful for sterilizing propagating mix

Moistening spores after sowing

Sowing spores by gently tapping paper

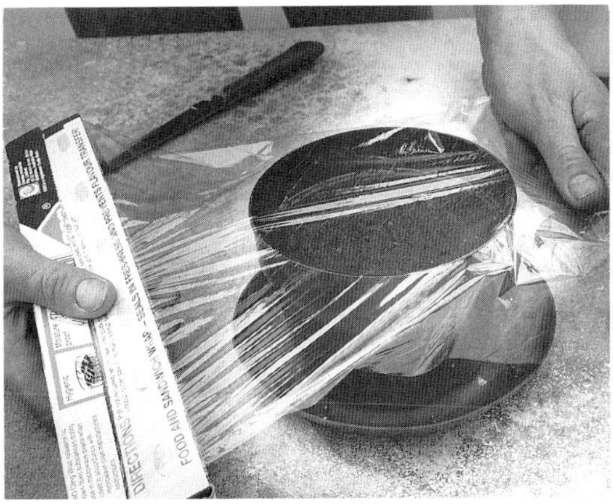

Sealing spore container with plastic film

Sowing spores from the tip of a knife

The final product, note the reservoir of water the pot is standing in

4. Fill the remainder of the pot with sowing medium, press it down to make it firm and leave a catchment of at least 3 cm below the rim of the pot.
5. Pour boiling water over the pot and sowing medium until the whole mix has been thoroughly moistened and the top 2 cm becomes very hot (90°C [190°F]). An alternative is to place the pot containing the medium in an oven at 93°C (200°F) for at least 30 minutes. Exposure for 10 minutes in a microwave oven will kill foreign spores.
6. Allow to cool until the mixture is just warm.
7. Sow the spores thinly using a spoon or the blade of a knife.
8. Dampen the freshly sown spores with a fine mist of previously boiled water (such as from the type of hand-pump spray used for dampening or starching ironing).
9. Cover immediately with a sheet of glass or polythene.
10. Stand the pot to about one third of its depth in clean water.
11. Cover the glass or plastic with a sheet of newspaper for 2–3 weeks, (this ensures more uniform germination in some species).
12. Maintain water level and the glass or polythene cover until germination is completed and the first true fronds are beginning to appear.
13. Remove the glass or polythene and allow the plants to harden off.
14. After hardening, prick the seedlings out into trays or pots. They are usually pricked out in small clumps or groups. When these have developed into a mass of healthy plants they can be further split up. Once they have reached 5–10 cm (2–4 in) high they are hardy little plants that are easily handled.

Notes on the Technique

The use of boiling water on the sowing mixture or heating in the oven at 93°C (200°F) for 30 minutes is to kill the spores of algae, mosses, fungi and alien ferns which may be present in the mixture. These spores germinate faster than the sown fern spores and unless destroyed smother the young ferns before they have developed.

The mixture must be allowed to cool before sowing but it is advisable to sow while the mix is still warm. If the mix is too hot, the spores can be damaged. If it is still warm then the upward convection of air will prevent contaminating spores from entering until the pot is sealed.

Collection of Spores

Fern spores can be collected by taking a fertile frond, or a piece of frond, placing it in a folded sheet of paper and storing in a warm, dry atmosphere. The spores appear as a fine dust on the paper, but not all of the

Spore collection – mature frond on white paper

Spores have shed from frond – note pattern formed

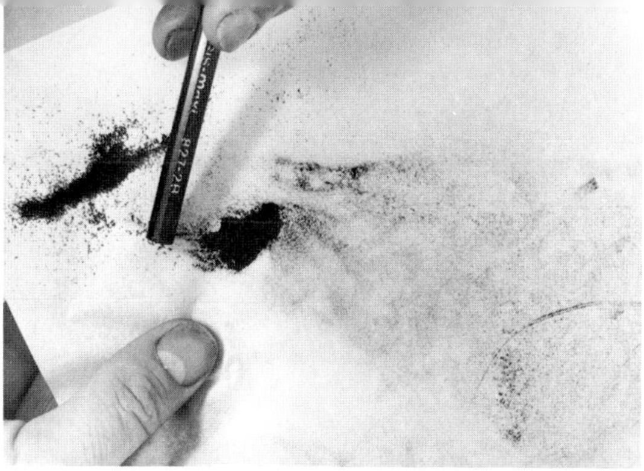

Tapping spores to separate from coarser debris (on LHS)

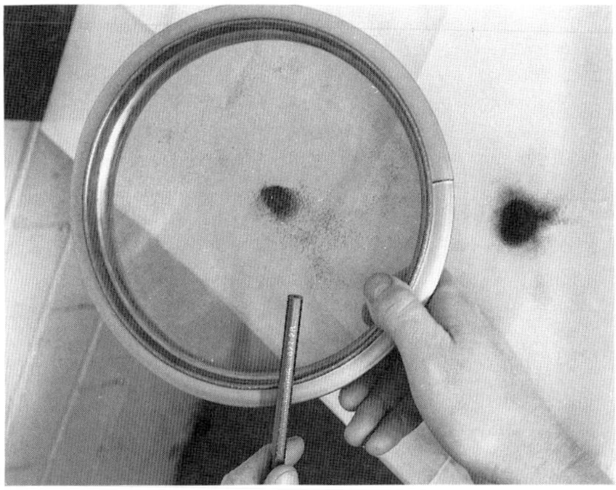

Sieving spores to remove debris

Collecting spores in packet for storage

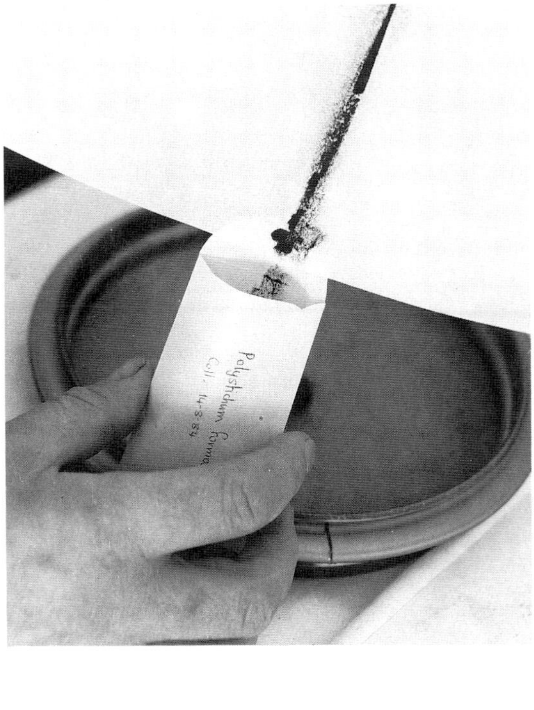

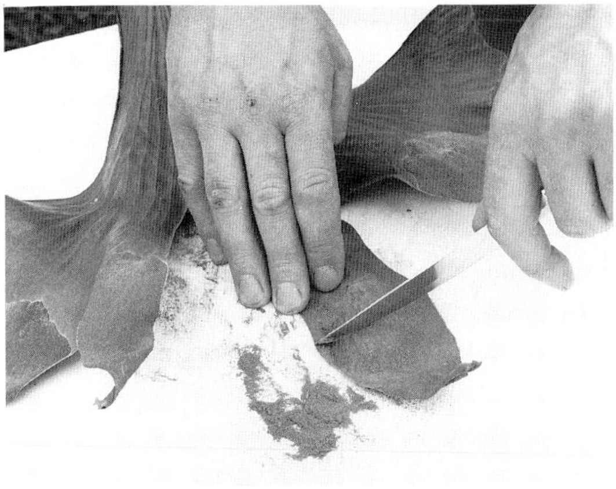

The spores can be scraped off large species such as *Platycerium superbum*

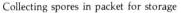

dust is spores, as other material is also shed, particularly debris from the indusia and sporangia, and also scales, hairs etc.

White paper shows up the spores well and is frequently used, but clean newspaper will suffice. Some growers use envelopes or paper bags with success, but each must be properly sealed at the bottom. Some spore is always lost or difficult to recover from the corners and folds of bags and envelopes. Fronds should not be held in plastic bags as moulds may develop in the humid atmosphere and these can damage the spores or run rampant in the pots after sowing.

A warm dry atmosphere encourages quick and complete shedding of the spores. During cold or excessively humid weather the shedding process is slowed down considerably and the spores may become damp and contaminated with fungi. Under such conditions, the papers around the fronds may need to be changed regularly or dried by occasional spells in front of a radiator. Spores which have been kept damp during collection frequently have a low viability. Some growers may dry spores over a desiccant prior to storage.

The fronds should remain in the paper for at least three days, to allow sufficient time for the spores to be shed. Ripe, mature spore will shed rapidly, often beginning within a few minutes of collection. Other spore will take longer. Immature or old spore may not shed at all.

When the spores have been shed, remove the dusty material carefully, sow immediately or collect in a paper envelope. The envelope should be labelled as to species and date and then stored in cool, dry conditions until needed for sowing.

Choosing Suitable Fronds

Many people experience difficulty in judging when the sporangia are ripe and the fronds are suitable for

Immature — Mature — Over Mature

Stages of spore maturity in *Rumohra adiantiformis* — Photos C. G. Goudey

cutting for spore collection. Collection of viable spores is one of the major requisites for successful fern propagation. Experience is the best guide but a few notes may avoid some pitfalls.

Sori which are immature to mature have a granular appearance like grains of sugar, whereas those which have shed most of their spores have a fluffy appearance. Immature sori are usually pale green or brown and the sporangia are small and tightly clustered. Mature sori are much darker, are often shiny and the sporangia are swollen and beginning to spread apart from each other. Mature sporangia may be pink, e.g. *Lastreopsis rufescens*, grey, brown, yellow or orange. Small sori with shrivelled or sparse sporangia indicate infertility, a common problem in hybrid ferns.

A close examination of the sporangia under a hand lens will tell whether the spores are being shed or if the sporangia are immature or overmature. Split or cracked sporangia will have dispersed their spores, whereas fat, whole sporangia are mature and ready to shed. The ideal stage for collection is when just a few of the sporangia have split to release their spores. A useful trick is to hold a piece of the fertile frond underneath an incandescent light. If the sporangia are mature the heat from the light will quickly trigger their release and this can be observed under a hand lens.

If the ferns are indusia-bearing, then the state of the indusium can also be a guide to the frond's maturity. An immature indusium is green and completely covers the sorus. As it matures it turns brown or black and begins to curl in at the edges revealing the outer sporangia. This is the ideal stage for collection. Curled or shrivelled indusia are overmature and indicate that the spores have probably been shed.

Another guide is the speed of release of spores from collected fronds. Ripe mature spore will be shed rapidly and freely, whereas immature or old sporangia will shed spore slowly, if at all.

Once the correct stage of maturity has been determined, the other factors necessary in choosing fronds are basic commonsense. Only healthy fronds from good plants should be selected for spores. Very strong, vigorous fronds taken in the peak of a flush of growth produce the best spores and in large quantities. Spores taken from weak plants or during periods of low growth activity, often germinate poorly. Some ferns produce spores for most of the year, others are very seasonal, producing spores on fronds when conditions are optimum. Avoid fronds that are very dirty or mud-spattered. If the fronds are wet, then it is necessary to dry them before placing them in paper for the spores to shed.

Spore Life

The length of time during which collected spores remain viable varies from species to species. The fresher the spores the higher the percentage of germination and the more quickly they germinate. As a general rule, those ferns with green spores have a very short life and to be certain are best sown within a few hours of collection. Such spore may, perhaps, last two or three days, (some may last for three to six months) but the author has noticed a rapid decline in others after 10–12 hours (e.g. *Leptopteris*) and best results are obtained by sowing quickly after collection. Ferns with green spores include species of *Onoclea*, *Osmunda*, *Todea* and *Leptopteris* and filmy ferns (see Appendix 11). Because of the short viability of such ferns, some growers place pieces of fertile fronds on the sowing medium and allow the spores to shed directly on to the propagating surface. The life of green spores can be increased by dry storage in a refrigerator at 4.5°C (40°F).

Ferns that do not have green spores generally have a much longer viability period. There is still variation from species to species, however, good spore, properly collected and stored, will retain its viability for 3-5 years and perhaps even longer (some spores have been germinated after more than 80 years storage). The author knows of many instances of tree ferns such as *Cyathea australis* and *Dicksonia antarctica* retaining viability for 10–15 years as well as other species such as *Adiantum hispidulum*, *Asplenium nidus*, *Pellaea viridis*, *Pteris tremula* and *P. vittata*.

Much is still to be learnt about the viability of spores and their storage. Wise growers always sow fresh spore, or at least a sample while it is fresh, and store the rest. This way, at least, they are eliminating one of the factors which can cause difficulty in spore raising: that of spore which has lost its viability.

Spore Storage

Storing spores under cool dry conditions prolongs their life. A simple system is to store the sealed envelopes containing the spores in an airtight plastic container in the non-freezing compartment of a refrigerator. Green spores can be stored for 2–4 weeks under these conditions (longer in some species), and non-green spores can be stored for many months or years. Damage will occur to the spores if they freeze and an optimum temperature seems to be about 4.5°C (40°F).

If spores are to be stored for long periods, they should be freed of all detritus by sieving (see page 146). This removes the material which can harbour pests and fungi. Stored spore can be eaten by pests such as psocids and silverfish. These may not be present on the fronds at collection, but could enter the bags while the spores are being shed. They can then be transferred to the storage envelopes with the spore and can cause considerable destruction in a short time. A few naphthalene flakes, sprinkled around the area where the bags are stored, will deter these pests and will not affect the viability of the spores.

A pot of spores covered with glass.

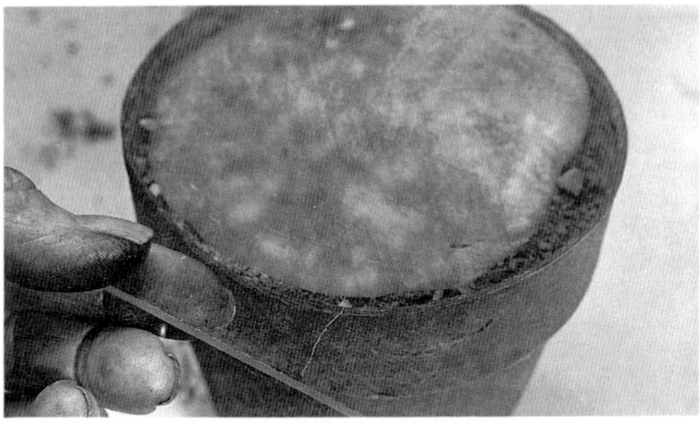

A simple spore sowing technique.

A simple spore sowing system using ice-cream containers
Photo C. G. Goudey

A collection of spore pots Photo D. L. Jones

Spore Contamination

One of the most frustrating aspects of fern spore collection and propagation, and one that is often not appreciated by enthusiasts, is the contamination of the spores by dirt, mosses, algae, fungi and even other weedy-type ferns. It is often difficult to understand how this contamination can occur, especially when the spores have been collected and not purchased. Contamination is common and arises primarily because of air-borne spores of algae, mosses, fungi and other ferns lodging on the fern fronds while they are still growing on the plant. Thus the fronds are contaminated before collection and some of these foreigners find their way into the spores. They themselves are present also as spores and these are usually mixed in the detritus obtained during spore collection. Dirt splashed onto fronds during rainstorms or blowing in as dust can also contain fungal spores, and certainly bacteria, some of which may be harmful.

Contamination is common in commercial samples of spores purchased from dealers. This is because large quantities of fronds are collected and they may be held in open areas while the spores are shed. Under these circumstances air-borne spores of ferns, mosses, fungi and algae can blow in and be readily dispersed from one species to another.

The significant factor in spore contamination is that it shows up after the spores have been sown. The algae, mosses and weedy ferns inevitably grow faster than the ferns being propagated and smother them before they get a chance to develop. The fungi also grow rapidly and, if they are saprophytic, may smother developing prothalli; if they are parasitic, then they are purely antagonistic and will kill the prothalli outright.

Contamination is a common problem, but its effects can be reduced by disinfecting fronds prior to spore collection (see below) and sieving the spores prior to sowing.

Cleaning Spores

One of the major problems of successful spore propagation is the contamination by algae, mosses and fungi (see above). These nuisances are present as spores, most of which are mixed with the non-spore detritus which consists of pieces of the shedding mechanism, indusia, scales, hairs and even bits of the frond. This detritus is larger than the spores, is of uneven shape and because of this can be separated leaving a collection of pure spores and removing much of the contamination.

A simple technique of separating the detritus from the spores is to use a folded sheet of paper. Tip the collected material into the groove, tilt the paper slightly and tap it gently with a finger or pencil. As the material moves down the groove the larger detritus moves forward faster than the spores which cluster behind. When the two groups are separated, the detritus can be brushed away and the spores collected.

Sowing fern spores on a brick is an old technique. Water evaporates through the porous brick

Another more accurate technique is to sieve the material using very fine meshed sieves (74μ [0.0029 in] or 100–150 mesh screen) (Figure p.143). If a lot of debris is present, a nest of sieves can be used with the coarsest on the top and the finest mesh on the bottom. The spores should be sieved over clean white paper so they can be observed and readily transferred to an envelope for storage. If fine sieves are not available, then fabric with fine holes (e.g. muslin or cheesecloth) can be used as a substitute. This is more difficult to use than a metal sieve as many of the spores stick to the cloth because of electrostatic attraction.

Disinfecting Spores

A further step on from cleaning spores is to disinfect them. This process is designed to kill any contaminating fungi, algae and mosses without damaging the fern spores themselves. It is not an essential process for enthusiasts or commercial growers but is mainly employed by scientific workers. It can be a useful step for those people raising spores on agar media. The disinfection techniques are always carried out on sieved spore (see above).

The fern spore is disinfected in solutions of sodium or calcium hypochlorite (10 g/140 mL of water [0.5 oz/0.25 pint]). Commercial disinfecting or bleaching materials containing hypochlorite can also be used. A small quantity of spore is soaked or shaken in a small bottle about two thirds full of the hypochlorite solution for 5–10 minutes. The excess hypochlorite solution is then drained off and replaced with one or two washings of sterile water. The fern spore (mixed in water) can be sown onto the agar with an eye-dropper or collected on filter paper, air dried and stored as outlined earlier.

A modification used by research workers is to disinfect the soral area of the frond and the sporangia while they are still mature, but before the majority

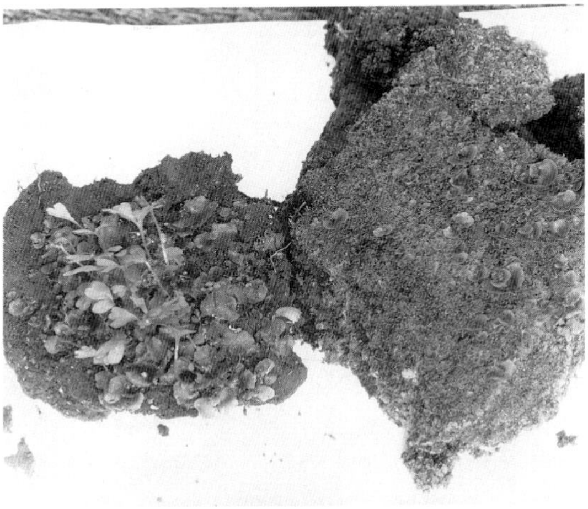

These prothalli and young sporelings have germinated on moist soil in the garden

of spores have been shed. The collected frond is immersed in a solution of hypochlorite to which has been added a few drops of a wetting agent (a mild household detergent is satisfactory). The frond is dunked for a short time (merely to wet it) and then allowed to air dry after which it is placed in clean, white paper for spore dispersal. The spores collected from fronds treated in this way should be free of contamination. One problem with this technique is that the spores usually begin to shed while the frond is air drying after being dipped. The loss of spores, however, is usually minimal.

Materials Used for Spore Raising

Fern spores can be sown on a variety of materials such as sphagnum moss, peat moss, tree-fern fibre, scoria, coarse sand, crushed terra-cotta, fly-ash, staghorn peat, decomposed coral and even soil. Not all of these materials are successful for all fern species though, and some growers obtain good results mainly because they find that certain materials suit their techniques and the particular species they grow. To be useful, a material must be able to hold water, must be well drained and with a sufficiently rough surface for aeration, and must be of the right pH (acidity and alkalinity).

Some details on each of the materials follows:

Sphagnum Moss

This moss grows in large colonies in boggy situations and is an important component of water catchments. Chopped sphagnum moss has been used to raise spores, but the author has found it disappointing for this purpose. It holds a considerable amount of water and is useful for mixing with other materials.

Sphagnum Peat Moss

This is the commonest material used for raising fern spores. It is the decayed remnants of sphagnum moss which has decomposed over a very long period of time and under acid conditions, until it has reached a stable end product. Large deposits are found in Europe and Canada and it is available as a shredded material. Peat is very light in weight, but has a considerable water-holding capacity, absorbing up to ten times its weight in water. Once wet, it remains so for a considerable period, but at the same time has excellent aeration properties. It has a pH of about 4.5 which is very acid. This pH does suit many species of ferns but some like much less acidity. The pH can be raised by the addition of lime to the peat. Most importantly, peat moss is virtually sterile and does not provide a good growing medium for pathogenic bacteria and fungi. Peat is packed dry and, initially, is difficult to wet. It must be mixed around constantly while being wetted, to achieve uniform uptake and distribution of water. *Note:* Sedge peats are also available but are more granular and have a pH about 5.5. Their physical properties are not as good as sphagnum peat and they are inferior for fern spore propagation.

Scoria or Sponge Rock

Scoria is crushed basalt pumice. It is a very coarse, granular material with the particles being of very uneven shape and with an internal pore system. It has a high pH ranging from 7–10, the variation depending on the locality of the basalt. Scoria is available in a range of particle sizes but the most useful grade for spore propagation has particles up to 0.5 cm (0.2 in) across. Scoria retains moisture and has good aeration because of its uneven surface and internal pore system. It is not suitable for spore raising on its own, but is very useful when added to other materials in a mixture.

Coarse Sand or Grit

This material is derived from the weathering of rocks and is composed of silica. It is found in many soils and can be easily collected from the beds of streams where it accumulates. It is a variable product and a coarse grade with granules up to 0.3 cm (0.1 in) across is useful for fern spores. It is usually dirty and should be washed thoroughly before use. It may also contain many weed seeds and fungal spores. Sand does not hold any water, nor does it have any nutrient value, but it provides excellent drainage and aeration. It is useless on its own for fern spores but must be mixed with water-holding materials such as peat moss.

Crushed Terra Cotta

Terra cotta is the material obtained when clay is baked for bricks or flower pots. The crushed waste is very porous and has many properties similar to scoria. It needs to be sieved to provide some uniformity of particle size. It has a pH of about 6 and has proved to be a very useful material on which to raise maidenhairs. It can be used on its own, but is best when added to other materials in a mixture.

Fly-ash

This material is the residue from furnaces and large boilers. It is granular, with an internal pore system and in many respects is similar to scoria, only the surface is much smoother. It has a pH of 6.5–8 and can be used for spore raising, but is best when added to other materials in a mixture.

Tree-fern Fibre

These are the chopped up fibres which make up the lower and outer parts of a tree-fern trunk. They are mostly roots and of course are very fibrous in nature with excellent drainage, moisture retention and aeration. Their pH is about 4.7, but varies somewhat with the species.

The species commonly used for fibre are *Cibotium glaucum*, *Cyathea australis*, *C. cooperi*, *C. medullaris*, *Dicksonia antarctica* and *D. fibrosa*. The *Cibotium* tends to have a wiry fibre, the Cyatheas are thicker and much coarser. The fibre of *Dicksonia* is fine and soft with numerous root hairs. Tree-fern fibres have proved to be an excellent medium for raising fern spores. Because of their fibrous nature, air circulation is better around the spores than in peat moss. One disadvantage is that they are usually contaminated with tree-fern spores. They can be used alone or mixed with other materials. Some growers claim that soaking the fibres of *Cyathea australis* in a strong lime solution for a week before sowing is beneficial.

Staghorn Peat

This is the peaty fibrous material of old staghorn and elkhorn clumps which have died. When shredded, the material consists of small, fluffy, fibrous particles of similar appearance to peat moss. It has a pH of 5.5 and is an excellent material for raising spores, but it must be mixed with some coarse material such as scoria or sand, as it loses its consistency. Samples are also usually freely contaminated with fern spore, as well as mosses, algae and fungi.

Decomposed Coral

It is a common sight in nature to see ferns germinating freely on old weathered coral. If such material is crushed and sieved through a 0.5 cm (0.2 in) mesh, it makes an excellent medium for raising fern spores. The pH varies from 6.5–7.5 and can be used alone, or mixed with other materials. Decomposed coral has proved to be excellent for the germination of species of *Adiantum*, *Asplenium* and *Pteris*.

Soil

Though this is the commonest material on which ferns germinate in nature, its performance for propagation is less than satisfactory. Soil is usually riddled with fungi and bacteria not to mention mosses, algae, liverworts and other ferns. When in a pot and treated with boiling water, the soil loses its structure and runs together, creating aeration problems. At best, good quality sandy loam can be added to a propagating mixture, but only at about one third to one quarter by volume.

Mixtures Used for Spore Raising

We have seen that some materials such as peat moss, decomposed coral, and Tree-fern fibre can be used on their own to raise fern spores. Most growers, however, use a mixture of the materials already discussed and this has the following advantages:

1. A mixture can make use of the good properties of a material and reduce the effects of bad properties, e.g. in a mixture of sand and staghorn peat, the sand ensures that drainage and aeration will be good and the staghorn peat ensures that the mixture will hold water.

2. In a mixture of two or three materials, there is an increased chance that the fern sown will find one of the materials to its liking, e.g. a mixture of equal parts tree-fern fibre, peat moss and scoria. If this mix is sown with a range of ferns, some species will grow best on one or other of the ingredients and some may grow equally well on each material. Such a broad spectrum mixture is useful for sorting out fern likes and dislikes and improves the chances of successful propagation.

Useful Mixes

The following mixes have proved to be successful (ratios by volume):

1. Equal parts peat moss, tree-fern fibre and scoria or fly-ash.
2. One part staghorn peat : two parts coarse sand.
3. One part peat moss : two parts crushed terra cotta.
4. One part tree-fern fibre : two parts coarse sand.
5. One part peat moss : two parts fly-ash or coarse sand.

Commercial growers may use 100% peat moss, or more commonly, a mix of one part peat moss to two parts coarse sand.

Whatever the mixture chosen, it must be realized that factors such as variation in the ingredients, the climate of the particular area and the species of ferns being grown, will all affect the results. Once a suitable system is worked out it should be adhered to and only changed when necessary.

Some growers screen their mix to give a uniform, fine product. The author believes a rough mix gives better germination and this is reinforced by observations in nature which show ferns commonly

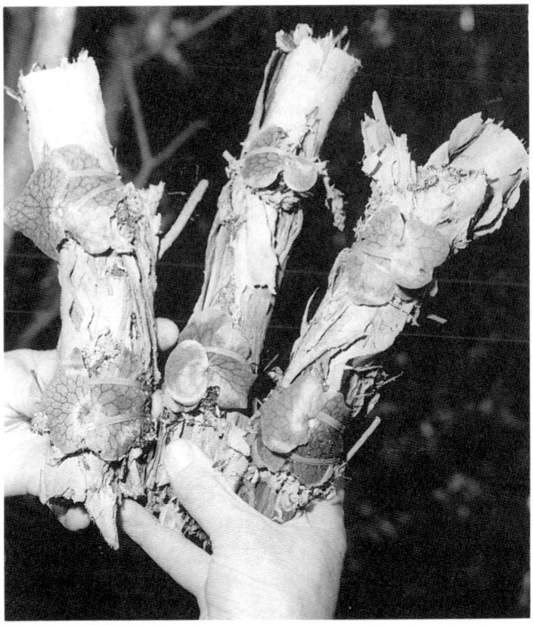

Platycerium sporelings tied onto paperbark branches

germinating on rough surfaces. All mixes or ingredients must be sterilized prior to sowing as outlined under Sowing Technique (page 142).

Containers for Sowing Spores

There are a variety of containers which can be used for sowing ferns but the most commonly used are pots or trays. The container used for sowing does not need to be too deep as the sporelings are usually pricked out before they have developed a deep root system.

Pots

These may be plastic or terra cotta. Some growers claim better success with terra cotta but plastic can be equally successful. New pots will not need sterilizing but second-hand pots will need thorough washing before sterilizing in boiling water or in hypochlorite solution (see page 146). Pots from 8 cm to 15 cm (3–6 in) diameter are usually satisfactory.

Trays

These are commonly used by nurseries and may also be called flats. They are usually 6–8 cm (2–3 in) deep and may be square or rectangular in shape. They have a large surface area and can hold many sporelings. They are mostly used by commercial growers. Prior to 1960 the flats were commonly made of wood but today they are nearly all plastic.

Ice-cream Containers

These can make a very useful spore container and they are readily available and cheap. The inner part of the lid is cut out leaving the rim and about 1 cm (0.4 in) of plastic all round for strength. A piece of polythene film, large enough to cover the top of the container and protrude about 1 cm all around, is cut and acts as a sealing insert for the lid. Sterilized mixture can be placed in the container, the spores sown and the lid sealed. The whole lot can be left undisturbed as a unit until germination takes place.

Sealing the Container

After sowing the spores the pot must be covered as quickly as possible to prevent contamination by algae, mosses or alien ferns. Glass and polythene film are the two materials most commonly used. Glass has the drawback of being hard to handle, brittle and expensive. Polythene is much cheaper and easier to use. Both materials are satisfactory for the purpose.

Watering the Spores

Once the spores are sown and the pot is sealed, the mixture and the spores are kept moist by watering from the bottom. The easiest method is to stand the pot in a tray or container of water which is about one third the depth of the pot. The water rises through the sowing mixture by capillarity and the spores are kept continually moist.

There are a couple of points to watch with this system. Firstly, it is a good idea to use boiled water for the first watering as this eliminates any chance of contamination. Topping up can then be by tap water. Secondly, the water should not rise too high in the outside container, as the spores inside may become flooded. A couple of small holes bored in the side of the outside container will ensure that the correct level is not exceeded. Used ice-cream containers are excellent for standing the pots of spores in.

Development of Sporelings

If the spores are fertile they germinate to form the prothalli. These first appear on the surface of the medium as a green scum. They continue to develop and, eventually, the edges lift free of the surface and each can be distinguished as a moon-shaped or heart-shaped prothallus. After a further period of time the first true leaves and roots appear and the plants are then known as sporelings. Development from then on can be rapid or slow, depending on how starved or crowded the sporelings are.

The time of development varies considerably with the species and also depends on the time of the year, how crowded the prothalli are, and their growing conditions. It is noticeable that spores sown in the spring develop much faster than those sown at other times of the year. The development of sporelings is slowed and impeded if they are too crowded. Fast growing species such as *Christella dentata, Histiopteris incisa* and *Pteris tremula* may develop the first true leaves within eight months of sowing and be established plants a further ten months later. On the other hand, slow growing species such as *Asplenium nidus, Blechnum patersonii* and *Platycerium superbum* may take 12–18 months before developing the first true leaf and a similar period to become established small plants. Spores sown in greenhouses or held on bottom heat units can be expected to develop more rapidly than those in less privileged conditions.

Aftercare

After the containers are sown, they should be placed in a warm situation where they receive adequate light but not direct sun. Most ferns germinate well at a fairly low light intensity (200–500 foot-candles) but the author has noticed that species of *Cyathea* (particularly the Sphaeropteris group), *Pteris* and *Blechnum* germinate far better at a higher light intensity (about 800 foot-candles). Some growers maintain that a period of darkness for 10–14 days after sowing is beneficial and promotes more even germination. Accordingly, they cover the glass with sheets of newspaper or black plastic. Several weeks of darkness may be necessary before the spores of *Botrychium* will germinate.

Commercial growers raise their spores in glass or polythene greenhouses, or sheds specially constructed for the purpose. Enthusiasts may find window sills or verandahs equally suitable. A common site for fern raising is under the benches of greenhouses. This can be suitable providing sufficient light can reach the sporelings. Artificial lights can be used over spore pots (suspended 60 cm [24 in] above) and should be left on for about 12–15 hours a day. These can be of a commercial type such as a Gro-lux tube. If fluorescent lights are used, they should be supplemented at intervals with an incandescent globe as this provides more light from the red end of the spectrum.

Spores germinate best with an increasing day-length and a temperature range between 24°–27°C (75°–85°F). This approximates to spring and early summer conditions. Remember that sporelings from tropical ferns detest cold and will be damaged or killed at temperatures below 10°C (50°F).

Fertilizing Sporelings

Many growers do not realize that sporelings will respond to the use of fertilizers from a very early age. Only liquid solutions should be used and they should be weak (one half to two thirds full strength) and applied regularly, but not in large doses. In the prothalli stage, it is best to apply the solution with an atomizer and, as the sporelings develop, the solutions can be poured on carefully. Applications every 3–4 weeks are highly beneficial. The fertilizers can consist of complete commercial, liquid preparations. The author, however, has found that the major response is to nitrogen and solutions of 2 teaspoons of ammonium nitrate/9 litres (2 gal) of water, work just as effectively.

A healthy batch of sporelings ready to be pricked out

Transplanting Sporelings

The initial transplanting from the container where the spores were sown is usually in clumps. A plastic tray or pot of open fibrous mixture is prepared (many growers use the same mix as for sowing the spores) and it should be sterilized prior to transplanting. The clumps are transferred to this mix and placed 1–2 cm apart. The mix must be moist and should be firmed around each clump after transplanting. When a few clumps are moved, the whole lot should be misted with boiled water from an atomizer as the young ferns can dry out very rapidly. When the tray or pot is filled cover with glass or polythene film.

Some growers like to transplant when well-developed prothalli can be discerned. At this stage however, they require ideal conditions during handling and for further development. Plants which have developed true fronds, i.e. sporelings, are much hardier and easier to handle and it is recommended that beginners wait till this stage of growth.

After the first transplanting the clumps are left until they consist of individual, sturdy little plants. The glass is removed and the plants allowed to harden before the next transplanting. If the plants are sufficiently well developed they can be potted individually into small (5 cm [2 in]) tubes and the smaller, weaker ones can be planted into another community tray. Some growers break up the clumps in another step before finally potting into tubes.

The small ferns in the tubes must be given warmth, moisture and sufficient light to allow them to develop into sturdy plants. They should be protected from extremes of temperature and wind and fertilized regularly with weak liquid solutions. Once they have developed new fronds and a good root system, they can be potted on or even planted out into a protected garden situation.

Pricking out a sporeling using a knife

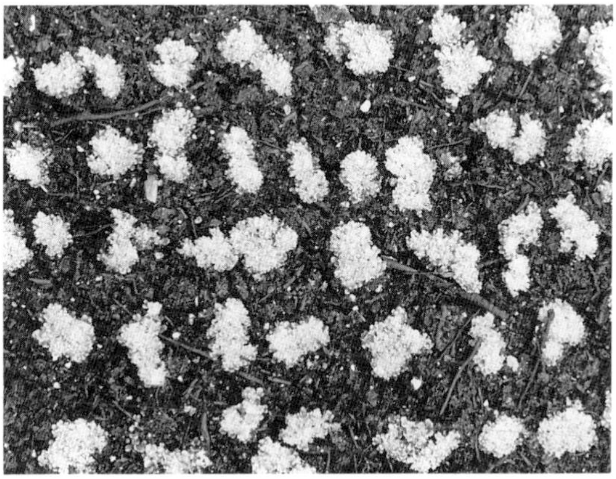

Prothalli pricked out in clumps for further development

Potting a sporeling into a small tube

Sporelings becoming established in tubes, compared with original batch

Healthy sporelings in different stages of growth

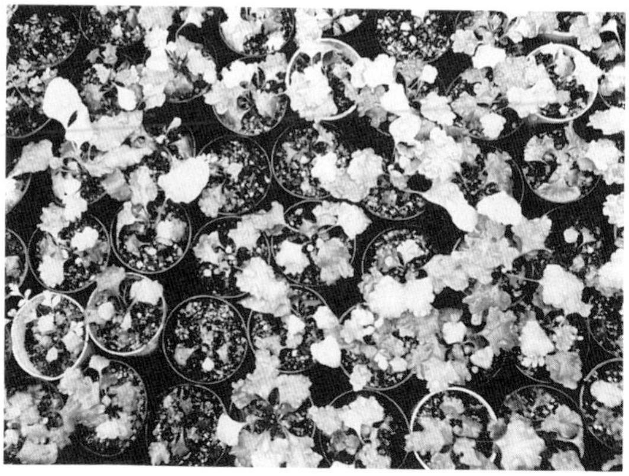

Young sporelings in tubes

Well developed sporelings ready for potting into a larger container
Photo D. L. Jones

Problems with Spore Raising

Disappointments can be common with spore raising and they occur both with amateurs and commercial growers. The major causes of failure are outlined below.

1. Infertile spores are the commonest cause. Spores may be infertile because they are collected from immature or overmature fronds (when in fact little of the collected material will be spore), or because they have been stored too long or incorrectly, or because they are hybrids. The commonest causes are from incorrrect collection (see page 142) and improper storage (see page 145).

A close examination of the material to be sown, with the aid of a hand lens, or better still, a microscope, will show whether there are spores present and if they are healthy (non-viable spores appear shrivelled or empty). Green spores have a limited viability period and, as a general rule, must be sown within a few days of collection.

2. Algae, mosses, liverworts or weedy ferns such as *Christella dentata, Dryopteris carthusiana, Histiopteris incisa, Hypolepis punctata* or *Lunathyrium japonicum* may gain a hold and smother the ferns that have been sown. This may be an indication of incomplete sterilization of the media before sowing, or contamination. Contaminants can be present in the spores prior to sowing or enter during the sowing process.

3. The spores are sown too thickly and the prothalli become crowded, misshapen and weakened. They are then susceptible to damage, such as by drips of condensation from the plastic or glass and the entry of diseases. Whole containers of prothalli can be wiped out quickly if they are too crowded. Another problem is that crowded prothalli produce mainly antheridia and very few archegonia and thus fertilization is impeded.

4. Attacks by pathogenic fungi or bacteria (see Chapter 14). Fungi may develop in spite of all precautions and can quickly devastate a pot of prothalli. Water drips from condensation can damage delicate tissue and lead to their entry. Even mildly pathogenic fungi can be devastating in the closed conditions required in a spore container. If an area does become affected the prothalli rapidly change colour (often dark and water-soaked). The infected site should be removed, together with about 1.5 cm (0.6 in) of the mix all around it, and drenched with a suitable fungicide (see Chapter 14).

5. Attacks by fungus gnats (see page 107). The maggots of these tiny flies feed on prothalli and churn up the soil surface. Once they are in a pot they are very difficult to control. Prevent their entry by effective sterilization and sealing.

6. Incorrect temperature and light. Sporelings being propagated in cold temperatures and/or dark conditions are usually very slow and sporadic in developing. Cold periods, and particularly frosts, are disastrous to sporelings of tropical ferns. It is better to have sporelings develop rapidly as they are less prone to attack by fungi, and to competition from algae, mosses and liverworts.

Spores have been sown too thick and the prothalli are weak and drawn-out
Photo C. G. Goudey

A healthy batch of sporelings with grey mould (*Botrytis*) just starting at two points near the centre

Grey mould (*Botrytis*) is spreading through these sporelings. Liverworts (*Marchantia*) are also present

Too much light will cause the sporelings to bleach badly so that their fronds are pale yellow or even whitish; frequently, the margins may turn brown. The pots should be moved to a shadier position. Treatment of bleached sporelings with a weak fertilizer solution will regreen them rapidly (see page 92).

Sporelings of some species are particularly sensitive to high temperatures (above 30°C [86°F]). High temperature exposure results in whole containers of

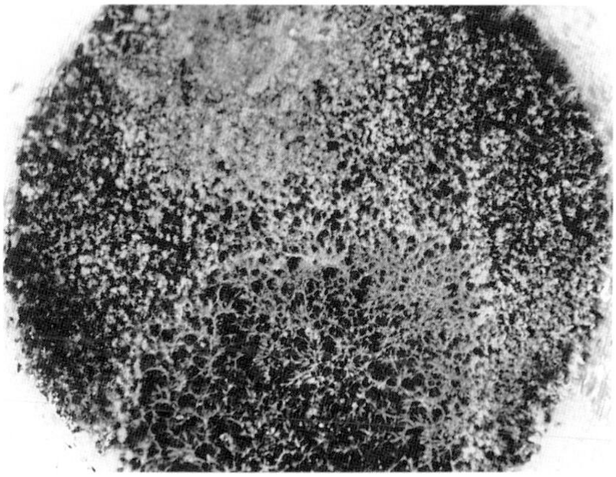

These sporelings were devastated by grey mould (*Botrytis*)

sporelings collapsing and dying within a very short period of time. Usually, there are no survivors from a whole potful and this is an indication of the cause of the problem.

7. Some ferns are impossible to raise from spores by conventional methods because they rely for their establishment on a delicate mycorrhizal balance with a fungus. Examples are species of *Botrychium* (except *B. virginianum*) *Schizaea* spp., *Ophioglossum palmatum* and some other species, and possibly species of *Ctenopteris*, *Grammitis* and *Scleroglossum*.

8. Sometimes healthy prothalli develop, but true fronds are produced sporadically. This indicates lack of fertilization and can be corrected by a shallow covering of luke warm water (18–21°C [65–70°F]). (See Chapter 18.)

9. Occasionally, prothalli and sporelings may be attacked by leaf nematodes. These pests can be disastrous on small plants, causing brown patches on the fronds and prothalli, and eventually spreading and killing patches. Spore pots with leaf nematodes present should be destroyed by burning (see also page 108).

SPECIALIZED SOWING TECHNIQUES

Spores on Agar

Fern spores can be successfully raised on an agar medium, in a manner similar to that for orchid seeds. The agar is fortified with nutrients, but lacks the sugars (such as sucrose, dextrose or fructose) which are essential for orchids. These sugars encourage fungal and bacterial growth and their deletion from the mixture means that the fern spores do not have to be sown under sterile conditions. Better results are obtained if fern spores are sieved and disinfected prior to sowing on agar than if they are sown as collected.

An agar medium is liquid while hot but sets to the

consistency of jelly at air temperature. It retains a thin film of water over the surface in which the fern spores can germinate. A suitable agar mixture is as follows.

Chemical	*Formula*	*Quantity*
Ammonium sulphate	$(NH_4)_2SO_4$	1 g
Calcium nitrate	$Ca(NO_3)_2$	500 mg
Potassium chloride	KCl	250 mg
Potassium dihydrogen phosphate	KH_2Po_4	250 mg
Magnesium sulphate	$MgSO_4{:}7H_2O$	250 mg
Iron chelate	–	42 mg
Manganese sulphate	$MnSO_4$	7.5 mg
Agar	–	12 g
Water to make up one litre (1.8 pints)		

All of these chemicals can be purchased from chemists or chemical supply companies. The chemicals must be weighed accurately using a sensitive balance because the concentrations of each element are critical.

Sown spores smothered by a growth of weedy ferns

Preparation of Media

Take one litre of water and warm it gently. Add the ingredients one at a time and stir until each is dissolved before adding the next. Add the agar last and stir thoroughly until it is dissolved. The medium is now mixed but must be adjusted to the correct pH. Most ferns germinate happily at pH 6–6.5, alkaline lovers may prefer 7–7.5.

A small sample of the liquid agar mixture is tested by a colour indicator or litmus paper. If too acid, a drop of 0.1 normal potassium hydroxide is added to the bulk solution, mixed thoroughly and the pH re-tested. Further additions may be necessary, although the pH usually changes rapidly with the addition of small quantities. If the solution is too alkaline, it is adjusted with drops of 0.1 normal hydrochloric acid in a similar manner to that outlined above. When the pH is correct, the solution is ready for pouring into the culture flasks.

Agar Flasks

Fern spores are best sown on wide, shallow containers such as Petri dishes. Erhlenmeyer flasks and cream bottles can also be satisfactory. Petri dishes are ideal because they are shallow, have a readily removable, but effectively sealing lid and they are transparent. They are available in glass or disposable plastic, in a range of sizes. Disposable Petri dishes are sterile when purchased, are quite cheap and are available at chemical supply firms.

Sowing

The agar is poured into the culture flasks while it is still hot. It is allowed to cool and solidify and is then ready for sowing. The agar solution has a pink tinge and the spores are readily visible. They are sprinkled thinly over the surface and the lid replaced. The flask or Petri dish can be placed in a warm well-lighted situation for the spores to germinate and prothalli to develop.

Germination of fern spores on agar can be fairly rapid, but is not much faster than in pots. The technique is very useful for very rare species where it is often only possible to obtain a small quantity of spore. It has also been used successfully to hybridize ferns (see chapter 18).

Prothalli smothered by algae

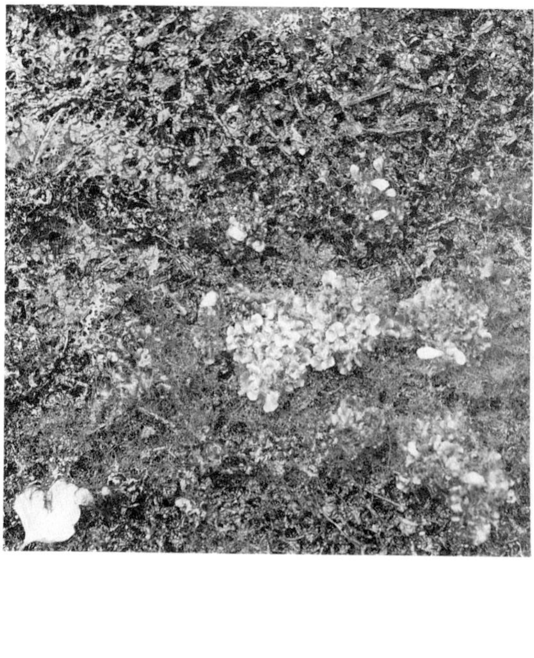

Prothalli smothered by mosses and algae

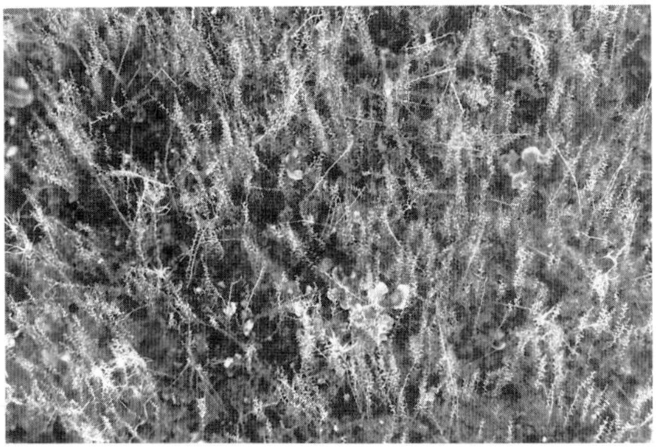

Prothalli smothered by a vigorous growth of mosses

Poor germination of spores

Spores on Nutrient Solution

Fern spores can also be raised on a nutrient solution although this is mainly a novel technique used by the research worker. This is a similar system to the one discussed previously, except that the agar is deleted and the material remains liquid. The ingredients listed under the previous heading can be used to make a satisfactory nutrient solution with the agar left out. Another one which is often used in research facilities for a variety of purposes is the Hoogland solution. Its ingredients are:

Chemical	*Formula*	*Quantity*
Potassium phosphate	KH_2PO_4	140 mg
Potassium nitrate	KNO_3	510 mg
Calcium nitrate	$Ca(NO_3)_2$	1.18 g
Magnesium sulphate	$MgSO_4 7H_2O$	490 mg
Ferrous tartrate	$FeC_4H_4O_6$	5 mg
Water to make up one litre (1.8 pints)		

These chemicals are all easy to obtain from chemists or chemical-supply companies. A high quality is not necessary for this purpose and technical grade will suffice. The chemicals should be weighed fairly accurately.

Prepare the solution as outlined in the previous heading, but using tap water. Test and adjust the pH if required. Sterilize by boiling for a few minutes and then pour the solution into sterilized Petri dishes or some other shallow container. The solution need only be 0.5–1 cm (0.2–0.4 in) deep. After cooling, the spores can be sprinkled on the surface and the cover is replaced on the container. The spores float and germinate on the surface so avoid moving or bumping the flask. Better results will be obtained if the spores have been previously sieved and disinfected (see page 146).

Spores on Distilled Water

Some growers sow fern spores on the surface of distilled water that has been previously boiled and allowed to cool. The pH of the water should be checked prior to sowing and, if necessary, adjusted as outlined under Spores on Agar (above).

The Towelling Technique

The towelling technique is a simple method which was developed to raise orchids symbiotically from seed. It relies on cleanliness and the presence of the specific orchid fungus to ensure successful germination. The technique could be useful for ferns which have a symbiotic germination requirement.

A new terra cotta pot, 15–20 cm (6–8 in) across, is boiled in water for about 15 minutes. While it is boiling, a mixture of chopped sphagnum moss, peat moss and tree-fern fibre is made up and moistened. After the pot has been sterilized, it is filled to about one third with the above mixture. Another quantity

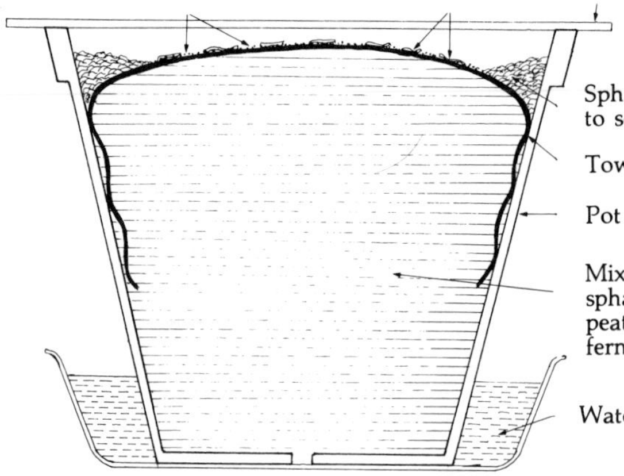

Towelling method of sowing fern spore symbiotically

of the mixture is then compacted into a tight ball, partially wrapped with a piece of new towelling and forced into the top of the pot with the towelling uppermost. A gap of 2–3 cm (1.25 in) is left between the top of the towelling and the top of the pot. Some sphagnum moss is forced around the edge of the pot to reduce evaporation. The towelling and mixture are then sterilized by pouring copious quantities of boiling water over the whole lot.

When cool enough fern spores can be sprinkled over the surface of the towelling. A few tips of live roots of the fern being sown are scattered among the spores to provide the important mycorrhizal fungi necessary for successful germination. A glass cover is then placed over the surface of the pot and the pot stood in a container of boiled water which is maintained at about 3 cm (1.25 in) high. The pots are then placed in a warm, well-lit position, protected from full sun and observed for germination and development.

18 Fern hybridization

Ferns do hybridize, although in nature the occurrence of hybrids is sporadic and they are generally rare. Ferns can be deliberately hybridized however, and there is considerable interest in this process. Generally, only closely-related ferns will produce hybrids and the progeny are usually sterile. This sterility can be seen by microscopic examination of the sporangia of hybrids, which are frequently imperfectly-formed or contain shrivelled or empty spores. Although intergeneric hybrids are known in ferns, these only occur between very closely-related groups and are probably a reflection of the inadequacy of the classification systems adopted by man.

Fern hybridization is of use to the researcher to determine relationships between various genera and species. It is of major interest to the enthusiast, since it increases the range of ferns available for cultivation and there is always the chance of a really worthwhile hybrid turning up. Not all artificially raised fern hybrids are worth keeping however, and the majority are probably best discarded. Those which are superior in features of ornamental appeal or ease of growth should be maintained and cultivated. If they become established in cultivation, man-made hybrids are usually classed as cultivars (see page 71).

Fern hybridization was a popular pastime in the late 19th Century and early 20th Century and hundreds of hybrids were raised during this period. The prime mover of this hobby was Edward J. Lowe who recorded his achievements and those of others in a fascinating book entitled *Fern Growing, Fifty Years Experience in Crossing and Cultivation* (published 1895).

Lowe, in fact, appears to be the first person to realize that ferns could actually hybridize, and even after producing the first hybrids in the 1870s, the process was not acknowledged by prominent botanists of the day.

Prior to these first experiments with fern hybridization, Lowe had noted that spores collected from an abnormal frond produce a high percentage of that abnormality in the progeny. By careful selection of spores he was able to produce these oddities in greater quantities than was previously possible. During this propagation new forms came to light which he was able to perpetuate and introduce into cultivation.

Following this initial selection and propagation work, Lowe then set up a large series of experiments to prove that ferns do hybridize and that genetic characters can be transferred from one fern to another by this hybridization. It is interesting to note that the techniques he used nearly 100 years ago are still in use today.

Important Factors in Fern Hybridization

Five useful facts will aid in the understanding of the hybridization process and may increase the chances of success for those who wish to produce their own hybrid ferns.

1. Antheridia and archegonia can be discerned easily under a good dissecting microscope. Examination of prothalli to ensure that the sex organs are at the correct stage of development is wise prior to treatment.

2. Antheridia are produced first on a prothallus, frequently developing 4–6 weeks earlier than the archegonia. It is wise to sow a succession of cultures of each parent so that the correct stage of development of each can coincide.

3. Crowded prothalli produce mainly antheridia and very few archegonia but well-spaced prothalli produce an abundance of archegonia. Thus the density of sowing or later transplanting can be used to determine which prothalli are to be the male and female parents.

4. The sperms of ferns are attracted to low concentrations (0.1–0.01%) of malic acid and those of the fern allies are attracted to citric acid.

5. Hybrid fern sporophytes will not appear for 4–6 weeks after fertilization. Any sporophyte appearing up to three weeks after fertilization will probably be the product of self-fertilization and will not be a hybrid.

Techniques of Hybridization

There are a number of techniques available by which ferns can be hybridized. These vary in their complexity and effectiveness, but all basically rely on the sperm from one parent fertilizing the egg of another.

1. The simplest technique is to sow mixed spores of two ferns together and hope that hybridization will occur. This technique relies on the same developmental time of the prothalli for each species and this often does not happen. It also has the problem of locating and identifying any hybrid that occurs and all plants may have to be grown until they can be identified. The technique can be improved slightly by just covering the prothalli with luke warm water, 21°C (70°F), for about thirty minutes. If the prothalli are at the correct stage, the water induces sperm release (visible under a microscope) and these can be dispersed among the prothalli by gentle swirling.

2. A refinement of the above technique involves sowing spores of each species in distinct but overlapping bands. At the right stage of development, the water technique mentioned above will aid dispersal of the sperm. If the process is successful, hybrids will appear where the two species overlap and hopefully can be distinguished while quite young.

3. A further refinement is to raise separate prothalli of each fern and then to transplant them together when they are at the correct stage of development.

4. A more exacting technique involves regular microscopic examination of sample prothalli. The male sex organs or antheridia are mostly found on the tapered part of the prothallus and the female sex organs or archegonia occur on the lower cushion which is that part which is indented or notched. When the antheridia open, the upper third of the prothallus can be excised transversely with a razor blade or scalpel and matched with an excised lower third of another prothallus containing the archegonia. Water will then aid the release and transfer of sperms.

5. A crowded culture of prothalli is placed in warm boiled water, 25–35°C (77–95°F), when the antheridia mature to give a solution of sperms. This liquid can then be doused onto the female prothalli. The chance of success will be increased if the section containing the antheridia is removed first from the receptive prothalli.

6. A modification of the above technique is to transplant and clean several prothalli which have mature archegonia present, and actually float these on the solution of water containing the sperm. The female prothalli can be left to float for several hours and then can be removed, washed and planted in fresh potting mix. Hybrid sporophytes will appear 6–8 weeks after this treatment. Any sporophytes that appear earlier will probably have been fertilized prior to treatment and will not be hybrids. This technique is frequently used in laboratories to good effect.

Part Five

Specialized Fern Culture, Repotting, Fern Containers and Housing

19 Ferns for containers, indoors and out

FERNS AS INDOOR PLANTS

Some fern species and cultivars adapt well to indoor conditions and add grace and beauty to houses, flats, tenements, units, commercial offices etc. In fact, many ferns make excellent indoor plants and have been used for this purpose for centuries in some countries. In Japan, species of *Davallia* are popular subjects and have been grown indoors for hundreds of years. They may be grown in open-weave baskets which are in turn adorned with banners, streamers etc. or else the rhizomes are trained into fern balls or shapes. Old plants are highly prized.

The English, and later the Americans, were quick to size up the virtues and adaptability of *Nephrolepis exaltata* as an indoor and greenhouse plant and it rapidly became a favourite. It arrived in England at about the time that ferns were experiencing an enormous popularity boom which became known as the Victorian fern craze. During this time, ferns became almost an obsession and were widely-used for decorating the large airy rooms and hallways of stately homes as well as the smaller, more cramped parlours and rooms of the less affluent. Ferns were not only used to decorate rooms, but also adorned banquets and dinners.

In the mid to late 1800s a structure known as the Wardian Case became a very fashionable household item in which to grow ferns. It was invented by Nathaniel Bagshaw Ward, a London surgeon and, more importantly, a fern enthusiast. He was prompted by difficulties with growing ferns outside in London's polluted atmosphere and designed a sealable glass case which took his name. The idea was modified and expanded by various people until some of the models were more like miniature conservatories than cases. The principles involved are the same as those employed in modern-day terrariums. Within these Wardian Cases a vast range of ferns flourished.

Today's modern housewife is well aware of the decorative value of plants in the home and a very wide range of ferns is grown for this purpose. Commercial firms also realize the importance of indoor decoration using plants, and ferns are prominent in offices, showrooms and even shops.

Although people tend to think of any fern as being suitable for indoor use, many species, in fact, do not respond favourably to indoor conditions. A wider range of species can be used to decorate houses in the tropics than in temperate zones because of the open, airy design of the houses and the warmer climate. There is little doubt that it is during the cold months of winter that indoor ferns in temperate climates suffer most. This need not necessarily be because of the cold, more likely it is caused by the heating system used to keep the people inside comfortable. Ferns, in general, resent the dry atmosphere of forced draught systems that are commonly used for heating. House design can also play a part. The rooms of older houses tend to be compact and crowded, but many modern houses are designed for a more open living style and provide ideal conditions for the growth of plants.

Suitable Ferns

When choosing a fern to grow indoors, it is wise to select a species or cultivar that is known to tolerate indoor conditions. In general, ferns which grow well indoors are those that tolerate fairly dark situations, an often dry atmosphere, and some degree of neglect. The best of these are undoubtedly some of the tried and trusted ferns which have been proven over the decades. Particularly prominent in this group are cultivars of *Nephrolepis exaltata* especially cv. Bostoniensis and *N. cordifolia* and its cultivar, Plumosa. Others which are especially hardy are *Asplenium bulbiferum*, *Cyrtomium falcatum*, and some forms of *Pteris cretica*. These ferns can be expected to survive fairly poor conditions but naturally will grow better in surroundings that provide their needs. A much wider range of ferns can be grown if the conditions indoors are good (draught free, bright indirect light, some humidity) and if they receive regular attention. A list of suitable indoor ferns is presented in Appendix 1.

Choice of a Fern Plant

Having decided on the right species of fern the next step is to select a suitable plant. This need not be difficult, in fact the selection is basic common sense. Look for a sturdy, healthy plant in active growth. Avoid those with dull lustreless leaves, or those with a wilted appearance as they have probably been neglected in the store or held there too long. Plants with very lush, soft growth should also be avoided as they may have just been taken out of a greenhouse and will deteriorate when placed indoors. One area which people often do not check is the fern's root system. It is often not practical to tip the plant out and observe its roots directly, however, if it is very wobbly in the pot then it should be discarded in favour of one that is anchored securely.

Buyers should be especially wary of plants which have pests already established on them. A few holes in the leaves from caterpillars or slugs and snails is acceptable, but colonies of scale, mealy bugs or spider-mites can be expected to proliferate in the indoor environment. These pests are difficult to eradicate once established and it is better to start with clean stock. When checking for mealy bugs or scale, it is advisable to look under the fronds and in the folds at the base of the stipe.

This large specimen plant of *Adiantum raddianum* brightens a hallway

Indoor Conditions

Light

Ferns indoors prefer a situation where they receive fairly bright indirect light or direct or filtered morning sun. Sun filtered through shrubs and trees is generally ideal except where it is westerly summer sun. Screened light coming through an archway, window, skylight or doorway can often provide a suitable position for an indoor fern. Bright light through coloured or frosted glass provides an attractive background for a group of ferns and can be quite suitable for their growth. Such glass, however, may also transmit heat and the ferns will require more frequent watering and attention to humidity than would be the case in other situations. Bathrooms, especially those in some of the modern homes, are often ideal for ferns because of both the good light through the frosted glass and the enhanced humidity of the atmosphere. In tropical regions, it is a common practice to apply solar films to windows to reduce the glare and heat transmission. These films are generally detrimental to indoor plants, including ferns, although in some sunny or brightly lit rooms, conditions may still be satisfactory.

Every house or apartment is different and the keen grower will soon find the position that suits a particular plant best (once found, leave it there). The choice will be influenced by the prevailing climate where one lives and also to some extent the Hemisphere.

Easterly Aspect

A room facing east receives the early rays of the morning sun and warms more quickly than the rest of the house. Such a room may not be suitable as a bedroom for those who wish to sleep late, but it can create a congenial atmosphere for indoor plants including ferns. In tropical climates, however, even early morning sun in summer can be hot and burning, and the plants may need some protection or else hardy species chosen for most exposure. By contrast, direct early morning winter sun in cold temperate climates may do little to warm or stimulate the growth of even hardy ferns. In areas where fogs are frequent or in cities with polluted atmospheres a position close to a window may be necessary so that the plant can receive sufficient light just to survive.

Westerly Aspect

A room facing west receives afternoon sun and contrasts in most respects to the east-facing room. It is generally dark and cool in the morning but is warm to hot in the afternoon because the ambient temperature is high. Such a room exposed to winter sun in temperate or even tropical regions can be excellent for ferns. A room exposed to westerly summer sun, however, would generally be unsatisfactory for ferns because of the bright light and the dry heat. Modifying the environment by slat blinds or solar films on the glass can produce a more suitable atmosphere.

Northerly Aspect

A north facing room in the Southern Hemisphere is usually well lit and can be suitable for ferns, although they may need some protection in the summer. A north facing room in the Northern Hemisphere can be well lit depending on the latitude but in northerly regions will generally be too dark, especially during the short days of the winter.

Southerly Aspect

A south facing room in the Southern Hemisphere may be bright enough for ferns, depending on the latitude. In more southerly regions a room with this aspect will generally be too dark during the winter. In the Northern Hemisphere a south facing room is brightly lit and can be suitable for a range of plants.

Modifying Indoor Light

High light levels can be reduced by obvious modifications such as slatted blinds or solar film on the windows or using darker paint on the walls. The only practical means of increasing light is by the addition of artificial lighting. The light sources chosen must be suitable for plant growth, that is, they must be of the correct wavelengths which can be used by

The Boston fern (*Nephrolepis exaltata* 'Bostonensis') is widely acclaimed around the world as an indoor plant

Adiantum raddianum is an excellent fern for growing near windows

plants. They also must be applied in sufficient intensity and left on for periods long enough to be of benefit to the ferns (day lengths of eight hours minimum in the winter, 12–14 hours in the summer).

Ordinary fluorescent lights can be suitable, provided they are not too far from the ferns and are encased in a reflector to direct the light onto the plants. Growth is even better if the fluorescent tubes are supplemented with one or two incandescents of low wattage. Specialized growing tubes which supply all the correct wavelengths can be used, but they are generally quite expensive.

Commercial kits are available for creating an artificially-lit small garden indoors. The same situation can be created easily enough using planter boxes and lights. The lights should be close enough to the plants to be effective (40–60 cm [16–24 in] above the foliage) and should be on adjustable stands to allow for growth. The amount of light required can be calculated from the approximation that a plant in a 150 cm pot needs about 10 watts. The globes should be cleaned regularly and if they are used daily (on a time switch) should be changed annually.

Humidity

Indoor atmospheres are generally of low humidity and tend to fluctuate considerably with changes in the outdoor environment. The atmosphere is also affected by indoor activities such as cooking, winter heating appliances and summer air conditioning. Ferns generally dislike low humidities and if they are to be grown successfully need some modifications at least to the environment immediately surrounding them. Ferns held in atmospheres of low humidity tend to wilt readily and their fronds have a dull, lustreless appearance. Frequently such plants are severely attacked by pests such as spider mites and mealy bugs.

Increasing the humidity around the ferns is the most successful answer to the problems caused by low humidities indoors. This does not necessarily mean increased watering, although the plants must not be allowed to dry out. Many an indoor fern has been killed by overwatering at the roots because its leaves seemingly advertise that it is dry. The dryness is caused by the low humidity in the atmosphere and cannot be compensated for by increased watering of the potting mixture.

Increasing the humidity around the ferns can be achieved by a few simple techniques. Grouping indoor plants or ferns so that each contributes to the atmosphere around the other is a very simple means. For the same reason a number of plants in each pot can be more successful than a solitary one. Standing the pot on a large saucer or tray of a wet evaporative material such as scoria or pebbles is also a useful technique to increase the surrounding humidity. The two techniques can be combined and the plants grouped on a large tray containing the pebbles. Syringing the foliage and surrounding atmosphere with a fine spray (as that produced from an atomizer or hand pump) can boost the humidity quickly.

This frilly lace fern (*Nephrolepis exaltata*) 'Elegantissima' makes a fine indoor plant

Temperature

Ferns from the tropics are generally sensitive to cold spells and dislike intense cold such as frosts. Frosts are not a problem to indoor ferns (although those plants close to windows may suffer damage), however, the temperatures can become low enough for them to suffer some damage. Tropical ferns can be damaged by temperatures of 10°C (50°F) but hardier ferns will tolerate much lower temperatures. The length of time during which the plant is exposed to low temperatures also exerts considerable influence on its behaviour. Low temperatures are rarely a problem in tropical regions, but in highland districts and temperate zones the winter temperature indoors can drop to a level which damages sensitive species.

Houses fitted with internal heating avoid the problems of cold damage to indoor ferns but the very dry atmosphere emanating from forced draught heating systems may cause excessive water loss or shrivelling. Open fires and bar radiators may provide too much radiant heat. Often an indoor fern is subject to a tremendous range of heating and cooling in the winter, and these fluctuating temperatures and humidities may lead to their demise. Indoor ferns, in winter, generally grow slowly or are dormant, not only because of the low temperature but also from reduced light intensity and short photoperiods. If difficult growing conditions prevail in a house during the winter it may be better to move the plants to a sheltered situation outside until the weather conditions improve (see Rest and Recuperation page 166).

Hazards to Indoor Ferns

While some indoor environments are good for ferns many are totally unsuitable. In some cases it is expecting a lot for a fern to even survive the transition from a nursery to an indoor environment. Apart from the problems outlined in the above paragraphs ferns can face other hazards. Lack of ventilation is a common one and this can be significant in winter when houses tend to be shut up against the cold. At the other end of the scale draughts can be very drying or chilling. Another common problem is to place ferns right next to windows. These plants can be burnt by direct sun or chilled by cold spells as the glass is an excellent conductor of heat. Ferns can also suffer from being continually moved from place to place. If a situation is found that suits a particular fern, leave it there. Closing blinds and drawing curtains cuts down the light available to a fern and can drastically reduce its growth. Fumes from smoking or cooking can also be detrimental. Light from a single source may cause the fern to grow in that direction and this can only be offset by turning the pot at regular intervals. Poor light may result in drawn out, spindly pale growth. Indoor ferns may also be attacked by pests (see page 166).

Care of Indoor Ferns

Watering

Watering indoor ferns, or indeed indoor plants in general, is a practice which is often approached with uncertainty, and creates far more problems than it needs to. Watering indoor ferns is basic common sense and it is a matter of catering for an individual fern's needs in a particular situation. Healthy, actively-growing ferns need regular watering and the frequency depends upon the light intensity, prevailing temperatures and humidity. In summer, indoor ferns can be safely watered daily, whereas in winter they need less water. The same parameters for decision-making are used as those which apply to any indoor plants, i.e. vigorous-growing plants will need more water, more frequently than those growing slowly or not at all; plants will need watering more regularly in the summer than in the winter and plants growing in bright light will dry out more quickly than those in dim situations.

Other factors must also be considered such as the type of potting mix, the size of the container and how full it is of roots and the situation of the plant in the room in relation to light and air movement. The potting mixture must drain freely but should also retain sufficient moisture for the fern's growth. Heavy soil mixtures that become soggy when watered or potting mixes that have broken down, are useless for indoor ferns and cause rotting of the roots and stunting or death of the plant.

Dunking pot in a container of water is an excellent way to water indoor ferns

The ideal watering régime keeps the potting mixture sufficiently moist to provide adequate oxygen and water to the roots for growth. Regular topping up can be quite satisfactory but at intervals the potting mixture should be thoroughly soaked so that water flows out of the drainage holes. This ensures a thorough wetting of the root system and also leaches out salts which may accumulate from the breakdown of fertilizers. This leaching process should be performed out of doors, or in a bath or sink, so that the excess water drains away without creating a mess.

In any group of indoor plants some specimens are going to require more regular watering than others. It is a temptation to water all of the plants at the same time, but this practice should be avoided and individual needs catered for. For example, if all of the plants are watered each time the most vigorous plant dries out then the least vigorous ones will receive too much, and will suffer from waterlogging. Conversely, if they are watered to the demands of the slowest grower then the strong ones will receive insufficient water and their progress will be retarded.

Ferns that are kept too dry wilt frequently, and generally lose the sheen on their leaves and take on an unthrifty appearance. Ferns that are kept too wet may also wilt but will not recover after watering and the soil will appear moist. This is because the ferns have suffered damage to the root tips from the waterlogged potting mix and they are unable to extract water from the soil. Waterlogging quickly leads to the death of a fern. If a waterlogged plant is tipped out the soil is excessively wet and gluggy and the root tips will have more than likely rotted. Healthy fern root tips are green or brown and firm-textured.

The number of waterings required by indoor ferns can be cut down by techniques such as mulching the top of the potting mix with sphagnum moss, leaf mould or even cut-outs of material such as thin cardboard or foil. Such a technique reduces the evaporation of moisture from the surface of the potting mix but does not cut down transpiration from the leaves, which is the main way any plant loses water. It also has the disadvantage that one cannot tell if the soil mix is dry because the surface cannot be seen. A better technique is to encase the pot in a larger container and fill the area between the two with peat or sphagnum moss (termed double potting). The same system can be applied with indoor planting boxes. Using techniques such as these the number of waterings can be reduced by one third to one half.

Repotting

Indoor ferns need regular repotting but the intervals between pottings will depend on the species and its vigour. Vigorous ferns will need repotting more often than slow-growing ferns or those which do not mind being potbound (e.g. *Asplenium simplicifrons*). Indoor ferns should only be repotted when reasonable growing conditions can be expected so that the fern can become established again in the new mix. The most suitable times for repotting are during spring and early summer.

For details on repotting techniques and potting mixes see Chapter 20.

Rest and Recuperation

Indoor ferns appreciate a freshen up at intervals and it is a good idea to give them a spell in a protected situation outside from time to time. Indoor ferns get quite a tonic from a gentle hosing of the foliage. This not only refreshes the plant but it washes the dust off the leaves and discourages the build up of pests such as spider mites. For the same reasons it is also a good policy to put ferns outside in rainy or drizzly weather. Keep a watch on the weather though, for ferns grown in a sheltered indoor environment can be easily burnt by sudden exposure to sun.

A recuperation process can work very well for indoor ferns or for that matter for any indoor plants. The plants are simply moved outside to a suitable shady situation in the garden. Here they are well watered, repotted or fertilized if necessary, and generally encouraged to recuperate and put on new growth. By this means, a system can be developed where plants are alternated between indoors and out and those inside will always present a bright, healthy appearance.

Fertilizers

Indoor ferns benefit from the application of fertilizers. These should only be applied during the warm, growing months of the year and can be readily used when the ferns are outside being spelled. Fertilizers for indoor ferns are best applied in small doses at regular intervals rather than one large dose. Fertilizers applied during winter, when growth is slow, or sudden applications of quick-release fertilizers to starved or weakened ferns may be of no benefit and indeed may result in severe fertilizer burn. Fertilizers should not be applied to plants where the potting mix is dry, otherwise foliage burn may result. Quick-release fertilizers should never be applied to indoor ferns because they can damage the roots, which in turn results in wilting or damage to the fronds.

A wide range of commercial products are available to fertilize indoor ferns and most of these will be successful for ferns. Some fertilizers are usually incorporated into the potting mix to encourage initial growth and these may be supplemented with surface dressings when it is felt that the growth is in need of a boost. Complete fertilizer mixtures are usually added to the potting mix and these may be quick or slow releasing. Organic manures and organic fertilizers can be very beneficial to ferns but some such as blood and bone, have the drawback of being smelly and attractive to dogs. Rotted cow manure is excellent for ferns and some growers add dollops of it to the surface of the potting mix during spring and summer. Bone meal and hoof and horn provide a slow release of nitrogen and, as well, are rich in calcium which is important for ferns such as maidenhairs which like high levels of this element.

This young *Cyathea cooperi* is a decorative subject

Supplementary fertilizing of indoor ferns can make use of slow release fertilizers, plant pills or liquid preparations. Various commercial preparations are available, most of which are quite suitable. Liquid fertilizers are particularly popular and are usually quite safe except where the plant is suffering from overwatering. If there is doubt or concern that the plant may suffer damage then reduce the strength of the liquid fertilizer to three-quarters of that recommended. Some growers regularly use organic materials such as fish emulsion or seaweed extracts. While these can produce excellent growth in ferns they are best used outside because of the smell. Some nutrients can be applied through the leaves in a process known as foliar feeding (see page 92). This is generally a much less satisfactory and more expensive way of boosting growth compared with root applications.

Pests

Pests are dealt with in detail from page 104 onwards, but it should be mentioned here that indoor

Davallia bullata is an excellent container fern for indoors or out

ferns may be more susceptible to certain pests than those ferns grown in the garden. In particular, this refers to mealy bugs, spider mites and scale insects all of which can proliferate in the indoor environment. Spider mites revel in dry conditions and their effects can be reduced by frequent syringing or hosing. Mealy bugs and scale may be present on any fern but become very severe on those ferns weakened from some cause such as being potbound, short of nutrients, overwatered or underwatered. Healthy plants resist pests far better than weakened ones.

FERNS AS OUTDOOR CONTAINER PLANTS

Some of the larger growing, hardy ferns make excellent container plants for outdoor decoration of areas such as terraces, patios, verandahs, pools and around barbecues. Because the plants are outdoors they do not have to tolerate the restricted environment of indoor ferns, however, in most cases they will be exposed to sun and only a limited range of hardy species can be grown. Almost any large fern will make a suitable container specimen, but some may be vigorous and will need regular attention and repotting (e.g. *Cyathea* spp.). Others can be grown in the same container for many years (e.g. *Asplenium australasicum*). A selection of ferns suitable for large containers is provided in Appendix 6. Remember, however, that because these ferns are being grown outdoors the species chosen must be able to tolerate the climatic regime of the area. Container grown ferns can usually be repotted (page 169) often back into the same container. If they have become too big or unwieldy they can always be planted in the garden or sold.

Outdoor Conditions

Sun

Container grown ferns can be used to decorate sunny or shady areas. Naturally, the range of suitable species is greater in the latter conditions compared with a sunny situation. A guide to the species tolerance to sun is included in Appendix 6 but remember it is only a guide and ferns grown in the sun will need more attention, especially with regard to watering, than those grown in the shade. Ferns will need hardening off before being placed in full sun, especially if they have previously been grown in a greenhouse or shadehouse. Hardening consists of increasing the exposure to sun the plant receives each day, while keeping it well watered. Prolonged exposure to sun without prior hardening, especially in summer, will lead to severe burning of the fronds and a setback to the plant. Ferns grown in the sun may have yellower fronds and a tougher appearance than those plants grown in the shade, however, they can still look very decorative.

Wind

Ferns in outdoor containers should not be placed in a windy or draughty situation. Cold winds may cause chilling which affects young fronds and will show up subsequently as stunted or deformed growth. Hot winds cause wilting and desiccation, resulting in dry papery patches in the fronds and a ragged appearance.

Frost

Frost can be very damaging to tropical ferns but those hardy types from temperate regions generally tolerate them with little or no damage. Ferns in containers have the advantage that they can be moved to a protected situation if environmental conditions such as frost are imminent.

Care of Outdoor Container Ferns

Watering ferns in outside containers is generally easier than watering indoor ferns because hoses are available and there is less need to worry about the mess. Because they are outside however, there is greater danger of them being forgotten and their watering neglected. If container ferns are to grow and maintain a good appearance they must be regularly watered and at no stage allowed to dry out completely.

Watering needs will vary with the weather conditions prevailing. In summer a daily watering may be needed whereas in winter once or twice a week may be sufficient. Windy weather dries plants out and extra watering may be needed. Heavy rain will water the ferns for you, but do not fall into the trap of thinking that light rain will do the same job. Rain needs to be fairly heavy and persistent to penetrate into the potting mix and many a plant has died because the owner thought that rain had watered the plant sufficiently.

In addition to normal waterings it is a wise policy to thoroughly soak the plants every two weeks. This prevents dry spots developing in the potting mixture and also leaches out excessive fertilizer salts. Hosing down the foliage at intervals refreshes the fern, reduces the build up of dust, and discourages pests.

Polypodium formosanum will grow for many years in a container

Potting Mix

For details on suitable potting mixes and repotting techniques for outdoor containers see Chapter 20.

Fertilizers

Slow-release fertilizers are incorporated in the potting mixes detailed in Chapter 20 and these will maintain growth for up to nine months. After this time surface dressings of slow-release fertilizers, manures or liquid fertilizers will be necessary. If the fern is completely potbound it can be potted on into a larger container or repotted into a new potting mix in the same pot. For more details on fertilizers types see Chapter 11.

Pests

The pests and diseases which affect ferns in outdoor containers are dealt with in detail in Chapters 13 and 14.

Miscellaneous Considerations

Some ferns, such as *Cyathea cooperi* and *Dicksonia youngiae*, have hairs or scales which may be irritating to the skin of sensitive people. Similarly, some ferns are very prickly, e.g. *Cnemidiaria horrida, Cyathea celebica*. While all of these species make excellent tub plants they should not be placed where people will come into regular contact with them.

Tubs or containers should not be placed directly on soil, but rather should be supported on concrete or bricks above the soil surface. This is to prevent the entry of pests via the drainage holes (e.g. beetles, worms and grubs) which can churn up the potting mix or feed on the fern roots. It also prevents the roots of the ferns from growing through the drainage holes and becoming entrenched in the soil beneath the pot.

Some large ferns have a very strong root system and/or rhizomes and it is quite within their capacity to burst the container if they are not repotted regularly. This applies particularly to plastic containers, but may also occur with other types.

20 Potting and repotting ferns

Repotting is a routine activity in which the old potting mix of a container-grown fern is replaced with a fresh, new mixture. Container-grown ferns require repotting to maintain their appearance and growth. Repotting can be necessary for a variety of reasons (see below), but most commonly because the container has become filled with roots. Such plants are referred to as being potbound and watering them can be very difficult. To some extent repotting potbound ferns can be offset by the application of liquid or slow-release fertilizers, but eventually repotting becomes necessary.

Repotting will be necessary every 6 months to 18 months depending on the species and the circumstances. Vigorous-growing plants such as tree ferns will fill a container with roots very rapidly and will need regular repotting, whereas slow-growing ferns which do not mind being potbound (e.g. *Asplenium australasicum*), will happily go for long intervals without repotting. Such plants may only need repotting every 2–3 years.

At the repotting stage two options are open. The plants can be put into a larger sized container with little disturbance to the root ball (termed potting on). In this case fresh potting mixture is packed into the spaces around the root ball (formed in the previous pot). The alternative is to put the fern into a container of the same size after removal of most of the old potting mix and some of the fern's root system. Fresh potting mixture is then used to fill in the gaps. As a general guide, vigorous ferns are generally potted on into larger containers while slow-growing species with a limited root system can be put back into the same sized container.

Repotting is best carried out after a period of dormancy. This stage is indicated by flushes of new croziers and numerous new green root tips. For most ferns, the optimum time for repotting is during spring and early summer while there is still ample growing time ahead for them to become re-established in the container.

Repotting Technique

1. Water the fern thoroughly 12–24 hours before repotting (soak in a bucket if necessary).
2. Tip the plant from the container by tapping the edge of the pot against a solid object. Do not pull the fern

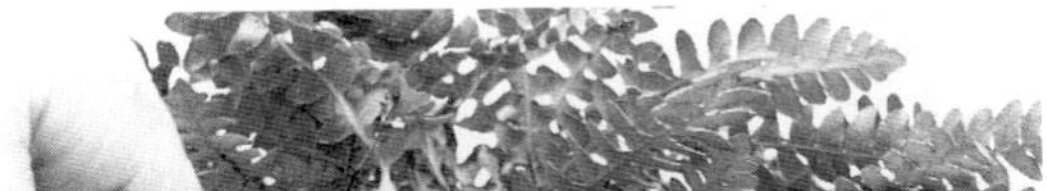

Plant of *Blechnum penna-marina* in need of division and repotting — note rhizome at bottom of root mass

Dividing clump of *Blechnum penna-marina*

Trimming dead fronds from clump

Filling pot with fresh potting mixture

by the fronds or stipes as this can result in damage to the roots or rhizomes.
3. Tease the edges of the root ball to remove old or dead roots and up to one third of the old potting mix. In particular, remove all of the surface soil as this is probably compacted.
4. In the base of the new container, cover the drainage hole with gauze to prevent the entry of worms and then place crocks or pieces of rubble at the bottom to ensure good drainage. Although crocking is no longer carried out in commercial establishments because of the cost, it is still a wise precaution, especially where valuable ferns are concerned. Then put enough fresh potting mix in the base to cover the crocks.
5. Place the fern in the container and fill with fresh potting mix to just above the desired level (allow for some settling). Firm potting mix gently. A gap of about 3 cm (1.25 in) should be left between the top of the soil mix and the rim of the container. This allows a good catchment for watering.
6. Water thoroughly and place in a sheltered situation.

The Need to Repot

Repotting is necessary to keep container-grown ferns healthy and sometimes to correct a problem which is impairing growth. A simple check can be made on the health of a fern's root system by tapping it from the pot and observing the mixture and the root tips.
1. If growth is stunted because of the exhaustion of nutrient reserves in the potting mix, either the plant must be fertilized or repotted.
2. If the pot has become so full of roots that they are a solid mass and are also protruding from the drainage holes, the fern needs potting on. Frequently the new fronds of such potbound ferns are reduced in size compared with the older fronds and may even develop improperly or become distorted.
3. If the potting mix is soggy and/or even smelling sour and the roots are poorly-developed with the potting mix falling away from them readily, such ferns need potting into a new mix in the same size container or even into a smaller container.

The cause of the soggy potting mixture is due to excess water and insufficient aeration. This may be from too much fine material in the potting mix, the activities of worms, overwatering or the breakdown of materials in the mix resulting in the formation of fine, cloggy debris. Soggy potting mix can also result from an unsuitable potting mix (commonly too acid) which discourages root growth.

Newly potted plant of *Blechnum penna-marina*

Potting-on a fern from a 100cm (4 in) pot to a 150cm (6 in) pot

Newly potted fern (*Blechnum brasiliense*)

Repotting Epiphytic Ferns

Epiphytic ferns, especially those with creeping rhizomes tend to wander all over a container and can be difficult to repot. If the plant is healthy, delay repotting for as long as possible and maintain growth by the application of liquid or slow-release fertilizers. If the fern dies out in the centre, the old potting mix can be scooped out in this area and replenished with fresh material. If repotting is essential, then a sharp knife may be needed to cut any roots that grip the container tenaciously. For some specimens the original container may have to be sacrificed so that the fern can be removed safely and repotted.

POTTING MIXES FOR FERNS

Ferns grown in containers require a growing medium which will produce strong healthy plants. The problem is that there seems to be almost as many different growing media as there are species of ferns, and each fern fancier has his own particular favourite. Perhaps this can be interpreted as an indication of the adaptability of ferns. Although it was once widely believed that a special potting mixture had to be used for each type of fern it is now known that ferns are far more adaptable than this and a potting mixture can be created that will grow a very wide range of species.

Certainly there are some factors which must be considered which will greatly influence the mixture used. These include whether the fern is an epiphyte or a terrestrial and whether it appreciates lime in a potting mix or whether this material will have an adverse effect on its health. Terrestrial ferns will grow with soil in a potting mix but epiphytic ferns will not.

Whatever materials are used to make up a potting medium, that mixture must meet the following criteria if it is to be successful.

1. It must supply suitable anchorage for the fern.
2. It must be free-draining and supply adequate oxygen for healthy root growth.
3. It must hold sufficient water for fern growth.
4. It must hold adequate nutrients for plant growth.
5. It must be free of any organisms that may be detrimental to the plant (this includes pathogenic fungi, pathogenic bacteria, nematodes, slaters, grubs, weed seeds and earthworms).

Potting mixes are usually a combination of more than one material, because it is difficult to find a single material which has all of the above features. Soil comes closest to meeting these requirements but today it is becoming very difficult to get the good quality loams necessary for potting ferns. This fact, particularly, has imposed constraints on commercial nurseries and modern potting mixes frequently contain little or no soil. Many materials have been tried for the growth of plants in containers and new materials are constantly being tested. Some of these are suitable for ferns, others are not.

MIXES BASED ON SOIL

The traditional fern potting mixes are based on a good quality loam, coarse sand and partially-rotted leaf mould. These mixes still produce excellent fern growth and if the ingredients can be obtained then it is a very safe mix to use.

The problems inherent in a soil-based potting mix are:

1. Variability of the material used, particularly the soil and leaf mould.
2. Obtaining suitable soil.

A good quality loam is generally dark-coloured, rich in organic matter and has a pleasing friable feel and an earthy smell, which an experienced grower can recognize instantly. Suitable loams can be obtained from under pasture or in woodland or forests. Sandy loams rich in organic matter can be quite satisfactory and even the clay loams found in mountainous districts can be suitable providing they are well structured and rich in organic matter.

Poor quality loams must not be regarded as a

substitute for good quality loams and are best avoided completely. Their behaviour in a pot leaves much to be desired, with poor drainage and clogging, or setting hard like concrete being common problems.

Some fern growers ensure a continued supply of good loam by cutting sections out of pasture or lawns and stacking these upside down for 6–12 months before use. These 'turves' provide a good fibrous soil material upon which a suitable potting mixture can be based.

Soil should not be used by itself as a potting material, but should be mixed with coarse sand which ensures aeration and drainage, and an organic material which increases water retention and nutrient availability. Complete details of these materials are provided in the following section dealing with soil-less mixes but some discussion about their suitability for mixing with soil is warranted here.

Sand

The sand added to soil for a potting mix should contain a predominance of coarse particles. It should be added at more than 1½ times the volume of the soil or else the fine particles of soil merely fill in between the particles of sand and negate its drainage and aeration properties.

Sand Substitutes

Materials such as perlite and polystyrene balls or chips are generally unsatisfactory in soil-based mixes. They separate readily and are difficult to mix because of the big differences in their shape, weight and specific gravity.

Soil Substitutes

Materials which can act as soil substitutes (e.g. brown coal, scoria and fly ash) are best used in a soil-less mix and should not be incorporated with soil in a potting mixture. This is because their properties are too similar to those of the soil and poor results may be obtained from the combinations.

Organic Materials

A wide range of organic materials can be used in potting mixes, but these are not all suitable for mixing with soil. The best organic materials for use in a soil-based potting mix are undoubtedly leaf mould, sphagnum peat moss and milled pine bark. Other materials which can be used satisfactorily include sedge peats, rice hulls, peanut shells, coffee grindings and spent hops (see next section for more details on these materials). Organic materials which are unsatisfactory for including in soil-based mixes are: vermiculite, charcoal, cocoa husks, sawdust and fibres of osmunda, todea and tree ferns. They are generally unsuitable because when combined with the soil they increase the waterholding capacity of the mixture far too much.

SUMMARY OF SOIL-BASED MIXES

A potting mix based on good loam still promotes the best growth of ferns. If good loam cannot be obtained then a soil-less mixture should be used (see next section).

A useful and safe potting mixture based on soil is
- 5 parts coarse washed sand
- 4 parts organic material
- 3 parts friable loam.

For ferns, two suitable fertilizer mixtures which could be added to a potting mix of this type are as follows.

Mix A

Fertilizer	per cubic metre	per cubic yard	per 12 shovels
Ammonium nitrate	1 kg	2 lb	5 g (0.2 oz)
Superphosphate	1–1.5 kg	2–3 lb	5–8 g (0.2–0.3 oz)
Potassium sulphate	0.5 kg	1 lb	3 g (0.1 oz)
Dolomite	1–2 kg	2–4 lb	5–10 g (0.2–0.4 oz)
Iron sulphate	0.5 kg	1 lb	3 g (0.1 oz)

Mix B

Fertilizer	per cubic metre	per cubic yard	per 12 shovels
Organic fertilizer (blood and bone etc.)	1–2 kg	2–4 lb	5–10 g (0.2–0.4 oz)
or			
Slow-release fertilizer	2–3 kg	4–6 lb	10–15 g (0.4–0.5 oz)
Dolomite	1–2 kg	2–4 lb	5–10 g (0.2–0.4 oz)

(Note that 12 shovels can be made up easily on the 5 : 4 : 3 mix.)

Lime may be needed to adjust the pH of the potting mix to 6, or whatever is desired. Trace elements can be added as a prepared mixture but may not be needed because of sufficient reserves in the soil. Slow-release fertilizers or liquid fertilizers can be added later to maintain growth.

SOIL-LESS POTTING MIXES

Because of the difficulty of obtaining continued supplies of good quality loam, and because of disease problems associated with soils, the nursery industry in various countries around the world has switched to soil-less potting mixtures. Researchers at the University of California were the first to initiate the trend away from soil in potting mixes. Their mixes were based on a fine sand and sphagnum peat moss obtained from Canada, and fortified with necessary nutrients. The results of these experiments showed conclusively that a wide range of plants could be grown in soil-less mixtures and the growth was as healthy and as vigorous as plants grown in soil-based mixes. The fine grade of sand so useful in California is not available in many parts of the world and peat moss may be very expensive. Hence the search has continued for suitable materials, and it has been shown that a range of soil-less mixtures based on different ingredients can be satisfactory for plant growth.

SOIL SUBSTITUTES

Some materials have similar properties to those of soil and can be used as soil substitutes in potting mixes.

Brown Coal

This has properties intermediate between soil and organic matter. Poorly-structured samples composed mostly of dust are useless, but samples composed mostly of small nuggety aggregates have good properties. The pH of brown coal is about 6.0. It has a high water-holding capacity and should not be used above 25% by volume of the mix. Ferns have been grown satisfactorily in mixtures containing this material.

Scoria, Crushed Pumice, Sponge Rock and Lava Rock

These porous rock materials have properties very similar to soil. Unfortunately they are rather variable, not only in colour which is from orange to black, but also in porosity and pH which ranges from 7–10. Samples with a very high pH are generally unsatisfactory because they create iron deficiency. Samples which are freshly mined, and those with too much dust, may also cause problems. Drainage, aeration and moisture retention of these materials are generally excellent. They have proved to be useful soil substitutes for potting mixes, and ferns have been grown satisfactorily using them. Some samples can also be very useful for spore propagation (see page 147).

Basic Slag and Fly Ash

These materials are waste products from furnaces and boilers. They have good aeration and water holding properties and may serve as a substitute for soil. The pH varies from 6.5–7.7. These materials are very high in calcium and iron but need the addition of other fertilizers for good growth.

SAND AND SAND SUBSTITUTES

Sand or Grit

This material is added to potting mixes to provide drainage and aeration. It is inert and very stable and is best used in a coarse grade which can be referred to as a gravel. It is mostly alluvial in origin. Fine sands can be useful providing they have no tendency to pack and impede aeration. For the same reason, sands with angular particles are far better than those with rounded particles. Frequently sand is dirty or contains weed seeds and may need washing before use. Sands are also commonly used in mixtures prepared for spore propagation (see also page 147).

Perlite

Perlite can be used in soil-less mixtures as a substitute for sand. It is a naturally occurring material of volcanic origin. In its preparation it is heated to 725°C (1337°F) and forms into sterile greyish-white particles which are very light and have a sponge-like texture. It is sterile because of the heating process used in its preparation and is available screened into various sizes (grades) from fine to coarse. It has some water-holding capacity. Because it is light in weight it will not mix with heavy materials and is best used in mixtures with peat moss, vermiculite or pine bark.

Polystyrene Foam

This material is available in both a shredded form (which has angular or irregular-shaped particles) and as polystyrene balls which are especially prepared for packaging and soil mixes. It has most of the properties of perlite, but has no worthwhile water-holding capacity. Because of its lightness it can only be mixed with similar light materials. It tends to wash readily from a mix and may even be blown out of a pot by wind.

ORGANIC MATERIALS

Leaf Mould

Leaf mould is one of the best organic materials which can be used in a fern potting mix whether it be with soil or soil-less. Unfortunately, leaf mould is often not readily available and it can be an extremely variable material. Experience has shown that the leaves of oak and beech trees make the best leaf mould. These are only available to the fortunate few however, and they are certainly rather scarce in many parts of the world, for example in the tropics. Fortunately, a range of leaves seems to be suitable for adding to potting mixes, the main criterion being that they be in a crumbly, partially-rotted state when used. Hard leaves such as those obtained from evergreen trees, are not as suitable as the softer fibrous types from deciduous forests. They can, however, be used after suitable preparation. Even very hard leaves such as those from eucalypts can be used with some benefit. Pine needles and conifer needles are much less satisfactory than broad leaves, because of the presence of resins and the difficulty of mixing. Even these, though, may be useful to ferns which occur naturally in conifer forests. It may be a wise policy to check the pH of leaf mould before use as some leaves have an alkaline reaction, though most are neutral to acid.

All leaves should be partially broken down before they are used in a potting mix. Leaf mould which is crumbly in the hand yet retains a spongy fibrous texture is ideal. This is simply prepared by stacking the moist leaves in loose heaps. A simple wire frame can be used to hold the heaps together, however, they should not be compressed as air in the presence of moisture is vital to their decomposition. A few shovels of soil will suffice to keep the top leaves in place. This is all that is needed for soft leaves, however, hard leaves or those of conifers should have a light dressing of a nitrogenous fertilizer such as ammonium sulphate spread over each 30 cm (12 in) layer of leaves. Leaf mould is usually ready to use after stacking for 6–12 months.

Sphagnum Peat Moss

This is the stable end product of sphagnum moss which has decayed over thousands of years under very acid conditions. Sphagnum peat is available as a shredded material and has a very fibrous consistency. It is sterile, light in weight, and has a tremendous water-holding capacity while still having good aeration. It is very acid with a pH of about 4.5. Peat moss is also very low in nutrients, but has the ability to hold added nutrients in a form available for fern growth.

Peat moss is one of the best organic materials which can be added to potting mixes. It mixes readily with other materials and is valued for its lightness, water-holding capacity and its ability to store nutrients for later use by ferns. When dry, it can be difficult to wet and only moist to wet samples should be used in potting mixes. Wetting can be achieved by pre-soaking the peat moss or rubbing a sample between the hands under water. Mixtures containing peat moss need the addition of lime to counteract the acidity, unless acid-loving ferns are being grown. Peat moss is available in large natural reserves in various countries of Europe and Canada and New Zealand. It is available in many other countries as an imported material but is becoming very expensive.

Sedge Peats

This is a peaty material which is derived from the organic matter which has accumulated over hundreds of years in swamps and bogs where rushes and sedges grow. Some samples of sedge peats can have very useful properties, but in general they are inferior in most respects when compared with sphagnum peat. A good sample is fibrous, with a nuggety texture and little dust. Sedge peats are extremely variable in structure and texture some having good consistency like that just mentioned others being mainly powdery. When exposed to the air, some sedge peats are stable, others break down and lose their structure. Sedge peats are generally less acid than sphagnum peats (pH 4–6) and are higher in nitrogen (some samples have up to 1% nitrogen). Salt contamination may be a problem with sedge peats mined in low-lying coastal districts.

Pine, Redwood and Fir Bark

These barks are waste products of the softwood industry which cuts mainly species of *Pinus*, *Sequoia* and *Abies*. Finely-ground pine bark (particles less than 0.5 cm (0.2 in) diameter) has proved a useful peat moss substitute for potting mixes and may sometimes be sold as pine peat. Fresh bark contains toxins which inhibit plant growth. These, however, can be removed by a very simple process. The coarse bark is milled and then the milled bark is wetted and stored moist in a heap for 6–8 weeks. After this time the strong resinous smell is lost and the material can be used in potting mixes.

Milled pine bark has good water-holding and aeration properties and mixes well with other materials. Its pH is initially about 5 but rises in time to about 6.5. Lime is not needed for its amelioration. Pine bark retains its structure and breaks down slowly. It can tie up nitrogen initially in a mix but this effect is readily offset by the use of liquid fertilizers.

Tree-fern Fibre

Details of this material are included in the chapter on spore propagation (page 148). As well as being very useful for raising ferns, tree-fern fibre can also be an excellent additive to potting mixes. The long fibres provide good aeration and, as well, have some water-holding capacity.

Peanut Shells

A waste product of the peanut industry. It can be used in a coarse grade or hammer milled into a fine grade with a particle size less than 1 cm (0.4 in). The coarse grade is very useful for epiphytic mixtures (see page 176). The finer grade has a higher water-holding capacity. Peanut shells can be successfully added to mixes for growing ferns. The material has a couple of drawbacks, namely that some samples may contain weed seeds and it may also be attractive to vermin such as rats, mice and birds.

Sawdust

Sawdust is a waste material from the timber industry and may be derived from hardwood or softwood trees. Both types of sawdust may behave similarly except that softwood sawdust tends to rot quicker than hardwood sawdust. The drainage, aeration and water-holding capacity of sawdust is excellent, however, chemically the material has many problems. Fresh sawdust contains toxins but the amount and type varies with the species of tree. Some toxins can be removed by wetting the sawdust and keeping it in a heap for 2–4 months. Others may benefit from the addition of lime at 3 kg per cubic metre (6 lb per cubic yard). The pH of sawdust is about 4.5.

Chemically, sawdust is very poor and has the extra problem of tying up added nitrogen so that it is unavailable for plant growth. This can be offset by adding a nitrogenous fertilizer to the sawdust heap when it is being aged to remove the toxins. While sawdust has been used successfully in mixes to grow ferns, it is a difficult material to handle and others should be used in preference.

Vermiculite

This is a naturally occurring mica, which is treated by exposure to temperatures of 1110°C (2030°F). The heat treatment causes expansion and the resultant vermiculite is a light, spongy material which has the ability to take up and hold large quantities of water. It can also take up and retain nutrients for extended periods before releasing them for plant growth. The pH ranges from 6.5 to 7.5. Vermiculite is a useful material but it should not be used at above 10% by volume of a mixture because of its high water-holding capacity. It can also be short lasting and may break down after 12–18 months.

Spent Hops

Spent hops are best used as a mulch or dug in as a soil conditioner, but they can be used in a potting mix. They are best stored in a heap for 2–4 months prior to use. They have some water-holding capacity and do not appear to tie up added nutrients.

Rice Hulls

A waste product of the rice industry available in some areas in large quantities. It is a light-weight material with a very low water-holding capacity and may tie up nitrogen. Composting rice hulls with fertilizers greatly improves the product. Seeds present in some samples may attract vermin such as birds and mice.

Sunflower Husks

These are best used after hammer milling through a 1 cm screen. They have good physical properties but require extra nitrogen. They have been successfully used in mixes for ferns. Seed remnants present in some samples may attract vermin such as birds and mice.

Cocoa Husks

This material is very rich in nitrogen and may be toxic when fresh. It is best used after storing moist in a heap for a couple of months.

Coffee Grindings

This material has good physical properties and also has a high level of nitrogen. It is best used after storing moist in a heap for a couple of months.

Mushroom Compost

Spent mushroom compost can be very useful in a potting mix, however, it should be well rotted. Some samples may be high in salt and should be leached before use. It should not be used above 20% of a mix for ferns.

Charcoal

Charcoal is manufactured by burning wood in a limited supply of oxygen. It is a useful material for potting mixes, in particular for epiphytes. It is renowned for its ability to absorb gases and can also hold nutrients for plants. Charcoal is available in various grades and its properties vary somewhat with the wood from which it is produced.

Suggested Proportions of Soil-less Materials in a Mix

Mix A
- 2 parts organic matter
- 1 part soil substitute or coarse sand

Mix B
- 1 part organic matter
- 1 part soil substitute
- 1 part sand or sand substitute

Mix C
- 4 parts organic matter
- 5 parts sand or sand substitute
- 3 parts soil substitute

Suggested Fertilizers for Soil-less Mixes

The following base fertilizers are suggested for use with soil-less potting mixes. Note that the levels of each will vary with the materials used and some experimentation is needed. The pH of the mix should be adjusted to about 6 but the amount of lime to add, if any, will depend on the materials used and the ferns to be grown. Also, the nitrogen levels used will depend on whether the organic material was aged in the presence or absence of nitrogen.

Fertilizer	per cubic metre	per cubic yard	per 12 shovels
Ammonium nitrate	1 kg	2 lb	5 g (0.2 oz)
Dolomite	1 kg	2 lb	5 g (0.2 oz)
Iron sulphate	0.5 kg	1 lb	2.5 g (0.1 oz)
or			
Iron chelate	120 g	6 oz	55 mg (0.002 oz)
Trace elements	recommended rate		trace
Organic fertilizer	1–2 kg	2–4 lb	5–10 g (0.2–0.4 oz)
or			
Slow-release fertilizer	2–3 kg	2–6 lb	10–15 g (0.4–0.5 oz)

Note that twelve shovels can easily be made up from a 5 : 4 : 3 mix. Slow-release fertilizers or liquid fertilizers can be added later to maintain growth.

SUMMARY OF SOIL-LESS POTTING MIXES

A range of materials is available which can substitute for soil and sand and combine with an organic material to form a suitable potting mix. Traditional fern growers raise doubts that ferns will grow in such soil-less mixtures. The author has grown many thousands of healthy ferns in such mixes and similar mixes are being used by commercial growers in many countries around the world.

The material to choose depends on local availability and cost. Do not change your growing medium if you are presently getting good results. If you are, however, having problems getting quantities of good loam, or feel that better growth is possible, then experiment first on a small scale. Remember that ferns are adaptable.

POTTING MIXES FOR EPIPHYTIC FERNS

Epiphytic or lithophytic ferns grow on trees or rocks in nature. They exhibit a range of growth habits from erect rosettes to widely-creeping rhizomes, however, in all cases their roots wander over the surface of the tree or rock on which they grow. These roots search in crevices or amongst accumulated litter etc. for nutrients. The roots of ferns of this type are somewhat specialized and like access to adequate supplies of oxygen and air movement. Thus, they generally perform poorly if grown in a soil-based potting mixture where aeration may be at a premium. If overwatered or if the soil mix is poorly aerated, the roots quickly collapse and rot and the fern suffers as a consequence.

Epiphytic ferns generally grow very well in soil-less potting mixtures because of the improved aeration and drainage of these media. Not all of the materials used in soil-less potting mixes are suitable for these ferns and the best ones are detailed below. It should be pointed out that epiphytic ferns need plenty of aeration around their roots and hence coarser grades than would normally be used in potting mixes can be very satisfactory for their growth (e.g. pine bark and charcoal in chunks ranging from 0.5–1.5 cm [0.2–0.6 in] across). As a general rule, the larger growing and coarser the epiphytic fern, the coarser the chunks used in its potting mixture.

Suitable Materials

Coarse Sand, Gravels and Grit

This material is added to epiphytic mixes as a safeguard, for if the potting mix should break down, the coarse sand will ensure adequate drainage. Perlite and polystyrene foam can be used in such mixes for similar reasons.

Leaf Mould

Leaf mould can be added to epiphytic fern mixes with advantage, but only coarse material should be used and not more than 20% of the mix by volume.

Sphagnum Peat Moss

Peat moss tends to be lost in an epiphytic mixture. It can, however, be added to boost water-holding capacity if the potting mix dries out too rapidly.

Pine, Redwood and Fir Bark

These materials are excellent for epiphytic ferns. They should be used in grades which have particle sizes from 0.5–1.5 cm (0.2–0.6 in) across and with a low percentage dust. Excess dust should be sieved or washed out prior to use. If fresh, the pine bark should be aged in a moist heap as outlined on page 174. Other barks such as spruce can also be quite satisfactory if treated.

Tree-fern Fibre

This is one of the best materials which can be used in an epiphytic mixture. Its long fibres keep the mix open ensuring aeration and drainage while at the same time having some water-holding capacity. The qualities of the fibre depend on the species of tree fern and whether living or dead (see also page 148, Fern Propagation). Material obtained from long-dead stumps may be acid and require pre-soaking in a solution of lime prior to use.

Osmunda Fibre

Osmunda fibre is the black wiry root systems obtained from large clumps of species of fern genus *Osmunda*. It has been traditionally used for orchids but can also be successfully employed for epiphytic ferns. Unfortunately, unless chopped, it does not mix well with other materials. It can be used as a potting material on its own.

Todea Fibre

This material is obtained from the bulky trunks of the fern *Todea barbara*. It is an excellent material for epiphytic fern culture and most of the remarks in the previous section apply here.

Peanut Shells

Peanut shells can be successfully used in mixes for epiphytic ferns. The coarse grade is best. Peanut shells have a limited life and mixes containing them should be observed regularly for signs of breakdown.

Charcoal

Charcoal is an excellent material to incorporate in a potting mix for epiphytes. Only good quality chunky material should be used and this grade should have little or no dust present.

Moss

Mosses can be used to line baskets and slabs so that they improve the moisture-holding properties around the base of the fern and its root system. Not all mosses are suitable, however those species which form spreading interwoven clumps can be useful. Sphagnum moss is by far the best moss for the purpose and is the one most commonly used for ferns. It can be used either dead (when it is often known as brown moss) or while still living when it is commonly called green moss. As well as being used for lining baskets and slabs, sphagnum moss can be used as a potting medium for epiphytic ferns. It is also an excellent material for starting offsets and sections of rhizome.

Suitable Epiphytic Potting Mixes

Mix A

1 part pine bark
1 part tree-fern fibre
1 part charcoal
1 part peanut shells

Mix B

1 part chopped todea or osmunda fibre
1 part peanut shells
1 part pine bark

Mix C

1 part coarse sand
1 part pine bark
1 part peat moss

Mix D

1 part tree-fern fibre
1 part pine bark
1 part coarse sand

The above mixes can be fortified with bone meal, (2–3 kg per cubic metre [4–6 lb/cubic yard] or 10–20 g/12 shovels) or slow-release fertilizers at the same rate. The pH should be checked and may need to be adjusted with lime or dolomite.

21 Specialized containers and systems of culture

Ferns can be grown in a variety of containers including baskets and other hangers, terrariums, aquariums and bottles, as well as on slabs or attached directly to trees. Because the growing requirements may vary from the normal, as outlined in other parts of the book, these systems of culture are all grouped together here in a single chapter.

Types of hanging containers clockwise from bottom RHS: tree fern basket, plastic basket, plastic coated wire basket, ceramic pot, hanging plastic pot

HANGING BASKETS AND OTHER HANGING CONTAINERS

Some species of ferns adapt well to hanging baskets. Although people tend to associate hanging baskets with those ferns having strongly weeping fronds, there are many other types of ferns which look good, and grow well in them. These include rosetting types (*Asplenium nidus, A. simplicifrons*), those with arching fronds (*Asplenium bulbiferum*) and those with a creeping growth habit (e.g. *Pyrrosia* spp. and various other polypodies). Weeping ferns of course are well suited to basket culture and can look graceful or even spectacular (for a list see Appendix 4).

A variety of containers can be suspended in a similar manner to a hanging basket and today many specialized types are produced. These include metal, ceramic and terra cotta pots fitted with chains, and moulded plastic containers which have their own saucer attached. Baskets are also cut from Tree-fern trunk sections. These make excellent baskets for all types of ferns as the roots can penetrate between the fibres. Baskets made from slatted hardwood can be very decorative and are ideally suited for the culture of Davallias and their relatives. Add to this collection the traditional wire basket and some idea can be gained into the variety of containers which may be used for hanging.

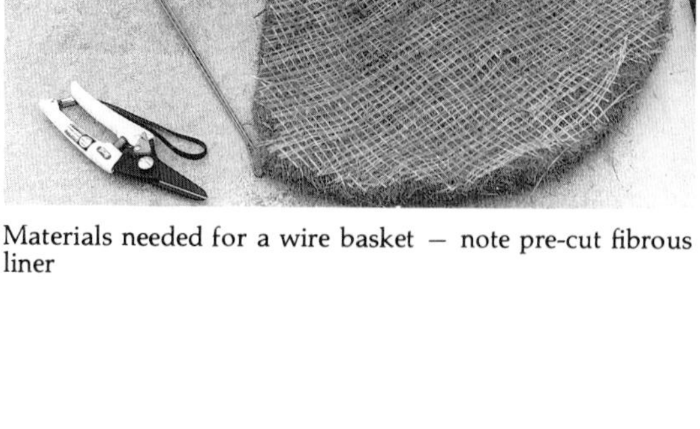

Materials needed for a wire basket — note pre-cut fibrous liner

Wire Baskets

Wire baskets have been used for hanging plants for over 100 years and they are still one of the most reliable containers for the job. Wire baskets must be lined with some material to prevent the potting mix from falling out. A variety of lining materials can be used but whatever is chosen it should look attractive, be congenial to the fern and be sufficiently long lasting to support the fern for many years. Suitable materials

Lining basket with fibrous material

Fern after planting and ready for watering

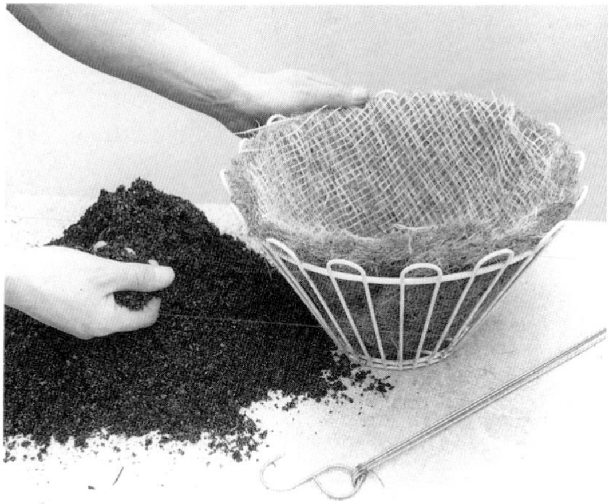
Basket completely lined, ready for planting fern

The finished product

Planting fern into basket

include moss, elkhorn peat, paperbark and coconut fibre.

Sphagnum moss is the traditional lining used for wire baskets and is still one of the best materials available. It should be pre-soaked and applied in the wet state so that it packs together. A thick layer 6–8 cm (2–3 in) deep around the basket should ensure good results. Other mosses which grow in thick fibrous pads can also be suitably employed for basket linings.

Elkhorn peat is freely available in some tropical regions and can be excellent for lining baskets because it handles easily and is often curved. It is best if the layers (which are the old pads) are separated and these can be used to line the basket. They can be rendered more pliable by a quick dip in hot water. Each pad should freely overlap the next to prevent the potting mix running out. Gaps can be plugged with fibre or moss. Irregular edges at the top of the basket can be easily trimmed to give a neat appearance.

Pyrrosia rupestris in a wire basket lined with sphagnum moss

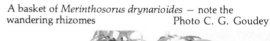

Vittaria elongata in a wire basket lined with elkhorn peat and moss Photo D. L. Jones

Paperbark is the outer papery bark of trees of the genus *Melaleuca*, some species of which are distributed through the tropics. It is pliable, especially if wet, and hot water does wonders for its handling qualities. It can be shaped around the basket, once again allowing plenty of overlap on the joints. The excess bark can be trimmed off to provide a neat finish.

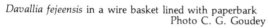

Davallia fejeensis in a wire basket lined with paperbark Photo C. G. Goudey

A basket of *Merinthosorus drynarioides* – note the wandering rhizomes Photo C. G. Goudey

A specimen of *Pyrrosia longifolia* well established in a wire basket lined with coconut fibre Photo C. G. Goudey

Coconut fibre is the lining of the husk which surrounds the nut. It consists of coarse, interlacing fibres and is an excellent material for lining baskets. It can be applied in layers until the overlapping fibres are sufficiently dense to prevent the mix from washing through. Many other palms also have fibrous materials which can be usefully employed in basket linings.

The Rock Tassel (*Lycopodium squarrosum*) is a magnificent basket plant for a greenhouse or conservatory

Lycopodium phlegmaria in a slatted basket

Those of the Chinese Windmill Palm (*Trachycarpus fortunei*) form a fibrous covering on the trunk and make an excellent dense lining for baskets.

The materials so far discussed are the best for lining baskets, however, they may not always be available and substitutes may be needed. Carpet underfelt and hessian can be usefully employed, as also can durable fabrics such as canvas. Some growers use polythene sheeting but it lacks any aesthetic appeal and is best camouflaged by some other material. Thin sections of tree-fern fibre make an excellent, pliable basket lining but are somewhat tedious to fashion.

Other Baskets

Slatted wooden baskets can be a successful container for some types of ferns. The timber should be hardwood, preferably redwood or red cedar, which are resistant to rotting. The gaps between the slats should be lined or plugged with a material such as sphagnum moss or coconut fibre. Davallias and polypodies generally grow well in this type of container. Large slabs of cork bark can be hung horizontally or moulded into an attractive container for epiphytic ferns.

Tree-fern baskets are excellent for ferns. They drain freely, have plenty of aeration and yet provide some water-holding capacity within their fibres. They can, however, dry out excessively in a windy or sunny situation. Epiphytic ferns with a creeping rhizome love creeping over the surface of Tree-fern baskets and establishing themselves between the fibres. Tree-fern baskets may have a limited life, particularly if they are kept continually wet. They are, however, sufficiently long-lasting for a fern to grow to perfection in them.

Plastic hanging pots are available in a variety of

Asplenium simplicifrons in a tree fern basket

A young plant of *Davallia pyxidata* in a simple tree fern basket

Pyrrosia lanceolata in a tree fern basket

A specimen of *Nephrolepis cordifolia* in a plastic basket
Photo C. G. Goudey

shapes and sizes. Frequently the drainage holes are too small and need enlarging. Some types have a saucer attached to prevent water dripping onto furniture or other objects below. Ceramic pots are also commonly used for hanging containers but these have the problem of drying out very quickly. Ceramic containers which have been glazed dry out more slowly than those which haven't been treated.

A large plant of a cultivar of *Nephrolepis exaltata* in a plastic container. Note attached saucer

An unusual method of growing *Platycerium bifurcatum* on a terra cotta pot. The fern will eventually envelop the pot

Potting Mixes

The potting mix to be used in a hanging container will vary somewhat with the type of container, the fern to be grown and/or the material used to line it. As a general rule, however, the potting mix must be very well drained. For lined wire baskets and ceramic containers the potting mix should also be moisture retentive and rich in well rotted organic components. For plastic hanging containers, a light, open mix as used for epiphytes may be needed, as these containers do not dry out as quickly as the other types. For terrestrial ferns, a soil-based mix will be suitable and for epiphytes a coarse mix is needed (for more details on potting mixes see Chapter 20).

When planting baskets, the soil mix should be pressed down to leave an adequate catchment of about 3 cm (1.25 in) for watering.

Watering and General Maintenance

Baskets and hanging containers dry out rapidly because of the continual circulation of air around them. This is especially true if they are hung in windy or sunny areas. Ideally, baskets should only be hung in protected situations, but if they must be exposed only hardy ferns should be chosen and they must be regularly monitored for watering. Baskets must be watered regularly, and if a well-drained potting mix is used, they are almost impossible to overwater. If drying is a major problem, the plant may have to be potted into a mix rich in well-rotted organic matter. A mulch of moss on the soil surface will reduce evaporation and the number of waterings necessary. Ferns grown in baskets and hanging containers respond to the occasional applications of slow-release or liquid fertilizers.

Repotting and Rejuvenating

Tired, old basket plants look terrible and are best

Watering a specimen basket of *Pyrrosia lingua*

replaced with a fresh subject. The old fern can be planted in the ground or rejuvenated by potting into a new mix and carefully tending to its watering and nutritional needs. Once it has regained some strength and vigour and has a good appearance it can again be potted into a basket.

Established baskets of creeping ferns usually die off and begin to look tatty in the centre while the outside is still fresh and vigorous. The centre part can be rejuvenated by cutting out the potting mix including the dead part of the roots and rhizomes of the fern and replacing it with fresh potting mix. After a short period new rhizomes of the fern will creep into the mix and fill in the gap. For repotting procedures see Chapter 20.

Suitable Species and Cultivars

A wide range of ferns is suitable for baskets and hanging containers. Epiphytes adapt particularly well to this type of culture as they appreciate the air movement and do not mind the frequent lower humidities experienced by basket plants. A basket can be used for a single species or a mixture. Combining ferns with different growth habits can impart a pleasing effect. Baskets can also be devised with pockets or openings in the sides from which smaller ferns can protrude.

Fern species and cultivars suitable for baskets are listed in Appendix 3.

TERRARIUMS

A terrarium is a sealable container made of glass or clear plastic. It is usually round but can be of any shape. A terrarium is designed for the growth of tender plants and as a decorative addition to the indoor decor. The idea is to establish a miniature glade or garden inside the terrarium and this will in turn be an attractive conversation piece. Because of the nearly constant high humid atmosphere inside a terrarium, ferns as a rule grow well in them.

Any good potting mixture can be used for plants in a terrarium, although the more successful mixes have a fairly chunky texture with good aeration and water-holding properties. Dead sphagnum moss is an excellent potting material for terrariums providing it is not kept too wet. Mixes containing high proportions of soil and/or compost are best avoided as they can create many problems. The potting mix should be sterilized before use to destroy weed seeds and any pest and disease organisms which may be present. Sterilizing in a pressure cooker can be successful, so can baking in an oven at 93°C (200°F) for 30 minutes. After cooling, the mix should be introduced into the terrarium and moistened evenly before planting. Some growers include a layer of pebbles and/or coarse charcoal in the bottom of the terrarium before adding the potting mix. It is critically important that the soil is evenly moist but not overwet because a terrarium has no means of losing moisture once it is all set up. If extra moisture is necessary, use cool boiled water to avoid introducing pests and diseases.

Terrariums should only be planted with small-growing ferns as small plants of suitable species are easier to handle and adapt better to the conditions. In fact the smaller the fronds and the more compact the growth habit, the more suitable the fern will be for terrariums. Do not make the mistake of planting any young fern as some will grow too large and any weedy species may take over and smother everything else. A list of ferns suitable for terrariums is presented in Appendix 2.

Planting and Maintaining a Terrarium

Planting ferns in a terrarium can involve much ingenuity and dexterity. All sorts of instruments such as long tweezers, chopsticks, kitchen spatulas, wooden spoons, bamboo slivers and cotton threads can be used to scrape holes, manoeuvre the ferns, plant them and cover any exposed roots with potting mix. It is a good idea to pre-soak or treat the ferns to be planted with solutions of a fungicide and/or insecticide.

After planting moisten the ferns with the fine spray of an atomizer, seal the terrarium, and place it in a shady situation for a few days. A moisture balance will be established and humidity will condense on the sides of the container and run down the sides to the potting mix. This indicates a good balance. If the soil and atmosphere is too wet excessive condensation will continually cover the sides. This is remedied by leaving the top off until some of the excess moisture has evaporated. If the condensation is very fine or sparse or disappears altogether then the system is too dry. A light watering or misting will help restore the balance. Once a terrarium is properly set up, little attention to watering is needed and the plants may go for many weeks or months without any addition.

Maintenance of a terrarium consists of ensuring that the plants receive adequate indirect light but not excessive levels, removing any dead tissue which may lead to rotting and ensuring that vigorous species do not take over and dominate the whole scene. Fertilizers are not necessary for plants in a terrarium. Occasional opening of the lid will ensure that oxygen and carbon dioxide levels of the atmosphere are maintained.

A well-set-up terrarium is very decorative and can be a source of interest for children and a topic of conversation. Unfortunately, failures with terrariums are far more common than are successes. Most failures can be traced to overwatering, with the potting mix becoming sour and the ferns unhealthy. Pests, diseases and weeds are another common failure and are caused by inefficient sterilization of the potting mix prior to planting.

Terrariums for Specialized Ferns

Terrariums can be a means of cultivating difficult ferns. Those species which in nature grow in a delicate balance between moisture, humidity and dryness are difficult to cultivate by conventional means (e.g. *Cheilanthes* spp., *Doryopteris concolor, Notholaena* spp. and *Paraceterach* spp.). In a terrarium set up with a stony potting mix and kept on the dry side (by sparse watering and leaving the lid off for long periods), these tricky ferns can sometimes be grown to perfection. They may need brighter light than other ferns usually grown in terrariums.

Terrariums can also be set up to grow successfully amphibious ferns from marshy habitats such as *Ceratopteris* spp., *Isoetes* spp., *Marsilea* spp. and *Pilularia* spp. For these species, the potting mix is kept wetter than normal. Condensation of moisture on the sides can be a problem reducing visibility, however, the terrarium can be left open at the top providing it is observed regularly and watered when necessary.

Small epiphytic ferns also can be grown in terrariums with the potting mix being fern fibre or dead sphagnum moss. Filmy ferns and *Leptopteris* species, in particular, adapt well to terrarium culture but need constant high humidity. Difficult epiphytes such as *Ctenopteris* spp., *Grammitis* spp. and *Scleroglossum* spp. can sometimes be induced to survive in a terrarium, but rarely thrive.

Small ferns from limestone habitats can be successfully grown in a terrarium providing that the potting mixture is suitably alkaline. Chips of limestone and shells are useful ingredients to add to such mixtures.

BOTTLE GARDENS

Ferns can be successfully grown in large bottles with the principles and techniques of terrarium culture being applied in the same way. Because of size limitations, frequently only a solitary fern may be grown in a

Mounting a piece of Elkhorn (*Platycerium bifurcatum*) on a tree fern slab. Note pad of sphagnum moss

Attach Elkhorn to slab with strong galvanized wire

The Elkhorn is securely attached to the tree fern slab

bottle. Because they are smaller than terrariums, bottles have the advantage that they can be placed on shelves, mantlepieces etc. and moved about readily, until a congenial situation is found for the ferns.

Bottles are useful for the culture of specialist groups such as filmy ferns. Because of the small stature of some of these ferns, quite small bottles can be employed with the limitation being the size of the opening.

Platycerium veitchii growing on a slab of tree fern.

SLAB CULTURE

Some epiphytic ferns adjust well to growing on a slab e.g. *Drynaria* spp., *Platycerium* spp. They seem to prefer this situation where some or all of their roots are exposed to the atmosphere, rather than in a container where all of their roots are buried in potting mix. In nature epiphytic ferns are used to having their roots exposed and some may even grow through the air. Such ferns usually grow in humid conditions however, and this is a major factor in their successful cultivation on a slab.

Suitable materials for slabs include tree fern, weathered hardwood, corkbark and compressed cork. Of these, slabs of tree-fern trunk are the most commonly used for ferns. Tree-fern slabs are fibrous and drain freely while still retaining water for growth between the fibres. If possible, orientate the slab with the fibres running vertically so that they will catch water and rain rather than shedding it. A range of tree ferns in the genera *Cibotium*, *Cyathea* and *Dicksonia* provide suitable material for slabs. Old dead trunks may have become acid and require soaking for 1–2 weeks in a solution of lime prior to attaching the fern. One disadvantage of tree-fern as a slab material is that pests such as slugs, slaters, earwigs and cockroaches can hide between the fibres.

Hardwood slabs are very suitable for platyceriums and may also be successful for other large epiphytes such as species of *Aglaomorpha* and *Drynaria*. A variety of hardwoods can be used but it is important that they be weathered by long exposure to the elements before they are used. Hardwood slabs shed water and dry out quickly after watering. Slabs of compressed cork can be used in a similar manner to weathered hardwood except that they do not need weathering before use.

Some growers modify hardwood slabs so that they retain nutrients and moisture for the fern roots. The simplest way to do this is to nail three pieces of slender hardwood to the bottom and sides of the slab. This is then covered with fine chicken- or bird-wire thus forming an open pocket which can be stuffed full of potting mix and/or sphagnum moss.

Plants to be grown on slabs can be secured with nylon fishing line, thin copper wire, plastic-coated wire or pliant material such as strips of stockings or panty hose. A pad of sphagnum moss beneath the plant helps the ferns get started and can act as a water reservoir on hardwood and cork slabs.

Once established on a slab the ferns are relatively hardy requiring regular watering to maintain growth. The intervals between waterings vary with the degree of exposure and the climate and weather conditions, however, it is generally difficult to overwater a fern growing on a slab. Watering should be thorough so that the fern's roots are soaked. Occasional doses of liquid fertilizers maintain healthy growth.

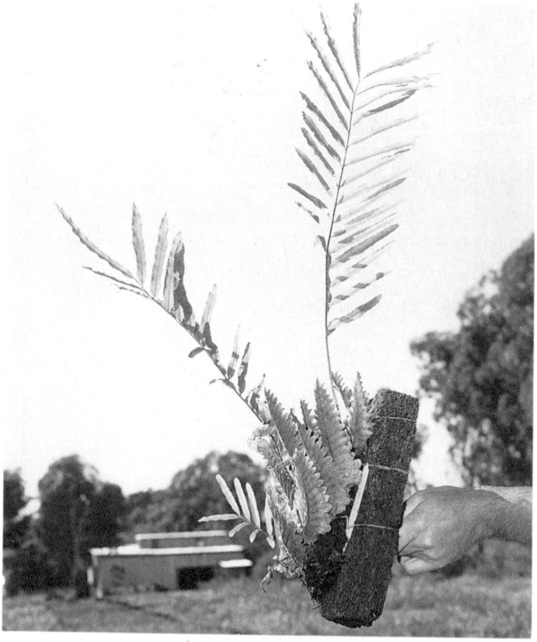
Drynaria rigidula growing on a slab of tree fern

Pyrrosia longifolia grown on a slab of tree fern fibre

Slabs should be hung in a protected situation where they do not receive too much sun and wind. Some air movement is necessary but this should not be excessive.

TREE CULTURE

If the prevailing macroclimate of the region is satisfactory, epiphytic ferns can be induced to grow on trees in parks or gardens providing niches with suitable microclimates exist. In fact, in ideal climates, some ferns may appear spontaneously, and colonize garden trees of their choice. Epiphytic ferns are most common in tropical zones but a few species also occur in temperate regions.

Epiphytic ferns require conditions of protection, humidity and air movement. Some species prefer deep shade, others require bright light. Sunshine is best avoided except for the hardy and adaptable species. Humidity and air movement are closely linked and though epiphytic ferns resent the stagnant conditions of high humidity they also dislike the draughts and strong winds of low humidity.

Not all trees are suitable for epiphytic culture. Species that shed their bark regularly are obviously a poor choice. Those with a tessellated or rough bark may be ideal but it should be realized that some trees have resins, toxins or inhibitors present in their bark and these chemical compounds may discourage or even kill epiphytes, e.g. walnuts. Solutions to this problem can only be obtained by trial and error or by observing which trees in the area support epiphytic plants. A wide range of garden trees are suitable

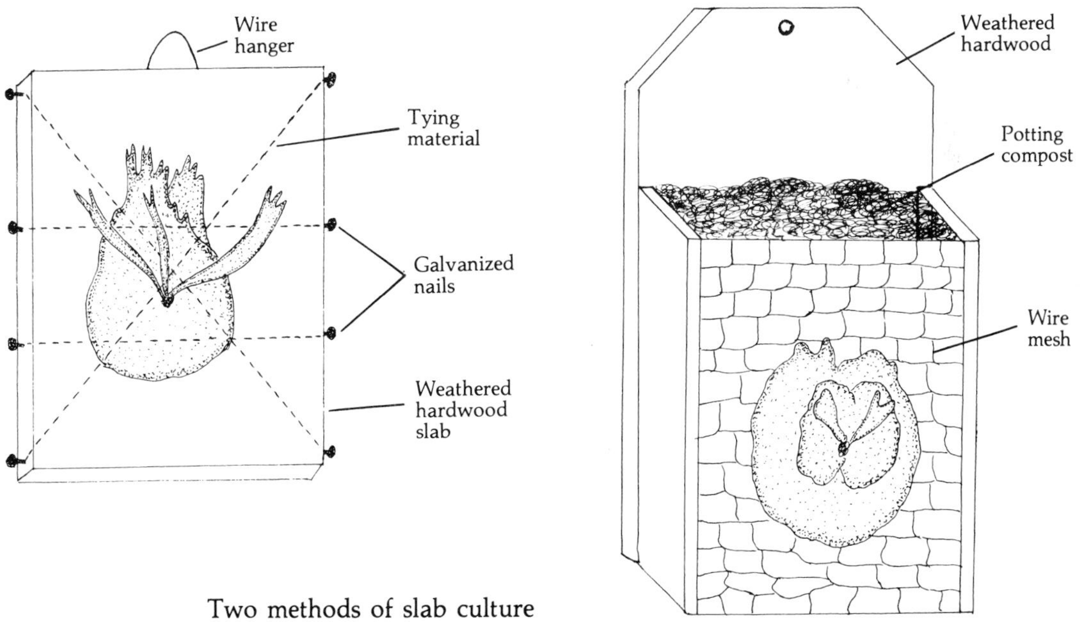

Two methods of slab culture

A magnificent specimen of Elkhorn Fern (*Platycerium bifurcatum*) growing on a tree

including many commonly grown subjects. Tree ferns are usually excellent for the culture of epiphytes, as their fibrous trunks provide an ideal growing medium.

Epiphytic ferns, especially the larger ones such as species of *Platycerium*, are best placed where their beauty can be appreciated. They should not be too far out of the way, as they will need some watering during dry periods, and especially early in their establishment. Siting large ferns so that they are supported in a fork may be an advantage as these plants can become very heavy after periods of rain. Knowledge of the most common direction of the prevailing rain and observing the selected trunks during periods of rain can save much anguish. Attaching epiphytic ferns to the side sheltered from most of the rain will only lead to their death, whereas a suitable channel or runnel on the other side of the trunk may prove excellent by guiding rainwater to the roots of the fern.

Epiphytic ferns are attached to the tree by materials such as nylon fishing line, copper wire or plastic-coated wire. The material should not be wrapped right around the trunk as it may cut in and damage the expanding bark and lead to the entry of pests or diseases. Materials which can be stretched, e.g. strips cut from nylon stockings or panty hose can be excellent because they expand as the trunk grows. An alternative method is to hammer one or two nails into the trunk on either side of where the plant is to be attached. The plant can then be held in place by the wire which is wound across it and around the nails. The nails should be galvanized to prevent rusting. A pad of sphagnum moss immediately below the fern may aid in its establishment. The attachment of creeping ferns such as species of *Pyrrosia* need only be superficial as in favourable conditions they will quickly spread and anchor themselves.

BLISTER CULTURE

Blisters are a knobbly outgrowth found on the trunk and larger branches of various species of eucalypts. These blisters are generally hollow inside or filled with partly rotten wood. When cut from the tree and cleaned out, these blisters make a very durable and decorative container for various plants including ferns. They are especially attractive when planted with large growing ferns such as *Asplenium australasicum* or weeping species like *Goniophlebium verrucosum*.

Before planting it may be necessary to drill a number of holes in the blister to ensure unimpeded drainage. The ferns can then be potted in a normal manner using a well drained but moisture retentive mixture. The blister should then be hung in a suitable, airy protected situation.

STUMP CULTURE

In nature ferns are frequently to be seen growing on dead trees and in rotting stumps. Dead trees may be a health hazard in a garden and are best removed, however, stumps can be readily employed for growing ferns. The rosetting types of *Asplenium* commonly known as Bird's Nest Ferns are ideal for this situation but others can be equally suitable (e.g. *Microsorum punctatum*, *M. pappei*, *Aglaomorpha* spp., *Drynaria* spp. etc.). If the stump is large enough a mixture of large and small growing ferns can be planted. The stump should be hollowed prior to planting and checked for drainage by pouring in a bucket of water. The hollow can be filled with appropriate potting mix prior to planting.

FILMY FERNS

For specialized structures used in the cultivation of Filmy Ferns see Chapter 38.

ROCKERIES AND ROCK WALLS

In nature, many ferns grow among rocks and on ledges and crevices where they sometimes seem to have a tenuous existence. It is also noticeable that old rock walls may become colonized with ferns, with some species preferring the weathered mortar to the rocks. Ferns blend in well with rocks and a rockery or rock wall is another place in which to grow them.

A rockery is usually constructed of medium-sized rocks placed so that pockets of soil can be created where ferns can be planted. The ideal rockery is simply a pile of rocks with all of the gaps filled with soil. This construction is not always possible, however, and the common alternative is to start with a mound of soil and work the rocks in to create pockets where the soil will not be washed away. The ferns can then be planted in these pockets. The soil used in rockeries should drain freely. A shady rockery will support a variety of ferns, whereas in a sunny aspect fewer types can be grown.

A rock wall is usually constructed of smaller rocks than a rockery and these rocks commonly have flat interfaces so that they can interlock together. The crevices and niches between the rocks provide a suitable home for the ferns. In a dry wall these crevices are packed with soil. If support is needed, some of the crevices can be filled with mortar and as the mortar ages some ferns may volunteer and establish on it.

Rock walls can be free-standing constructions or else they can be built to stabilize and batter earth banks. In the latter situation seepage areas will form and the fern roots can grow into the soil behind the wall. In a free-standing wall provision should be made for watering prior to construction. Trickle and spray systems are very suitable.

Rock Types

Rockeries and rock walls can be constructed from a wide variety of rocks and the selection will generally depend on what material is locally available. Sandstone is an excellent material for rock walls because it is easy to work and tends to be porous. Basalt is also frequently used. Granite is brittle by comparison, but is an excellent material for those ferns which like acid conditions. Lime-loving ferns adapt well to rockeries and walls constructed of limestone and will also grow on mortar used to hold rocks together. Decomposing coral is an excellent material for walls and rockeries since it is light, porous, easy to use and a wide range of ferns adapt well to it.

MOSS POLES

Pieces of hardwood or Tree Fern covered with moss or coconut fibre can be effectively used to grow epiphytic ferns. The moss or fibre is held in place by plastic mesh or even wire netting. Moss poles can be suspended horizontally or vertically or placed upright with the base buried in the ground. The ferns growing on moss poles require similar treatment to those on slabs or in hanging baskets.

ROCK CULTURE

Porous rock such as pieces of pumice, tufa or coral can be used as a support for epiphytic ferns. The ferns can be tied or wired to the rock with a small pad of moss to help them get started. The ferns require similar treatment to those on slabs.

A tree fern with the epiphyte *Phymatosorus diversifolius* growing on its trunk

22 Housing for ferns

In suitable climates a good range of ferns can be grown in a garden, however for the keen enthusiast this range may be too limited and a greenhouse or shadehouse may be used to house those species which demand the extra protection. In temperate and subtropical regions either greenhouses or shadehouses can be useful, however, in the tropics the choice is really limited to a shadehouse because a greenhouse is generally unsuitable for the climate. The purpose of any fern structure is to encourage their growth by providing protection from the extremes of climate encountered in the area.

A magnificent collection of ferns and other foliage plants grown in a fernery

FERNERIES OR SHADEHOUSES

A fernery may also be known as a lathe-house, a shadehouse or a bush-house. It is designed principally to protect tender ferns from the ravages of hot sun and to a lesser extent winds. It is also an airy place where the humidity is higher than outside and where it fluctuates less. Thus it creates a congenial atmosphere for ferns. Constructions of this type are common in tropical and subtropical climates where protection from the burning sun is required. They can also be successful in temperate zones, however, it should be realized that structures of this type give little or no protection from frosts, certainly not from heavy ones.

Siting

In a home garden there is often little choice as to the site where a fernery can be built. People frequently make the mistake of putting a fernery in a shady location which only serves to emphasize the shade, especially in winter. Where a fernery is situated is perhaps not so important in the tropics where light is present in abundance even in the winter, but in temperate zones the lack of light is often a limiting factor for growth in winter. As well, a shady fernery will be cold in winter, reinforcing the effects of frost and cold weather and greatly reducing the range of ferns that can be grown. The best position for a fernery is where it is exposed to the maximum amount of winter sun.

Construction

Ferneries do not have to support much weight and are usually structures of simple construction. Wood or galvanized pipes are the materials most commonly used for the frames. Rot-resistant hardwood or pressure-treated softwoods should be used where possible, because of the wet conditions maintained in a fern house. Galvanized pipes are the most functional structural material but probably have the least aesthetic appeal and are expensive in the short term.

Covering Materials

Once the frame is erected it must be covered with some shade-inducing material. The modern fern grower is very fortunate in having a whole range of commercial fabrics available that are specially pro-

Lathe roof of a fernery. Photo D. L. Jones

duced for this purpose. These are made from black synthetic threads which may be woven or knitted to form the final fabric. The number of threads per centimetre and their individual thickness determines the amount of shade supplied and it is possible to buy samples ranging from 33% to 90% shade. In temperate regions, 50% shade cloth is satisfactory, but in tropical regions 90% may be needed. In very hot areas such as some inland zones, two layers of 90% shade cloth, 15–30 cm (6–12 in) apart, may be needed to create sufficient shade for ferns to survive.

Shade cloth is quite aesthetic but may not appeal to everyone. Wooden lathes about 5 cm (2 in) wide running north–south, and spaced 3–5 cm (1–2 in) apart, provide dappled shade which is appreciated by ferns. If they are painted in brownish or greenish tones they blend in well with the surrounds and can be an attractive addition to the outside decor. Such slatted ferneries can be built to make use of small areas such as walkways between buildings or between buildings and fences, thus improving what may be otherwise drab areas.

The sides of a fernery may be covered with the same material as that used on the roof. If, however, one side is exposed to a prevailing wind then it may be useful to fill this side in completely with some solid building material. The ferns will benefit from the added protection.

Inside a fernery with the plants grown in the ground. Note the path and the mist unit in action. Photo C. G. Goudey

The Ferns

As a fernery is designed primarily for ferns these can be grown in garden beds and/or in containers such as pots, tubs and hanging baskets. The ideal is to fill the fernery without overcrowding. The plants should be able to grow to their potential without too much interference from their neighbours, and while still being able to benefit from the congenial atmosphere created.

Ferns in containers need more watering and maintenance than ferns planted in garden beds. If time is limited it may be a wise idea to plant the majority of ferns in the ground. The beds should be raised to ensure good drainage and to give the ferns a good start in the absence of competition. Ferns mix well with rocks so consider constructing a rockery. Ferns also mingle well with water and a pond or stream will enhance the atmosphere and have a pleasant, cooling effect on the environs. A well-set-up fernery will be a source of pleasure for many years and once established will require little maintenance.

Layout

If it is decided to plant the ferns in garden beds or rockeries then some thought should be given to the layout and planting to be used. The maximum visual impact of a fernery should be gained upon entering and walking along a path, therefore the fern's growth habits and planting should be considered in order to achieve the desired effect.

Those ferns with a very bushy habit, such as species of *Microlepia*, *Gleichenia* and *Pteris*, should not be placed where they will hide ferns of lesser stature from view. Tree ferns are excellent in that they eventually lift their crowns well above the ground and then do not obscure anything. Remember, however, that in the early stages they develop large spreading fronds and need plenty of room. Later when the trunk begins to form, new ferns can be planted beneath the canopy of fronds. Be wary of ferns with a vigorous, creeping growth habit such as species of *Hypolepis*. They can spread very quickly, often to the detriment of their neighbours. Similarly, weedy ferns which voluntarily appear may have to be ruthlessly culled or eventually they will dominate the fernery.

The ideal layout for a fern bed would be to have the larger bushy ferns at the back along with some tree ferns, although these can also be scattered about to provide a pleasing, aesthetic effect. The smaller-growing ferns can be placed close to the path where they can be readily seen. The larger growing ferns with an open habit, such as some of the species of *Blechnum*, can be scattered about. Observe each fern closely after watering to ensure that each is receiving its share of the water and it is not being sheltered by a neighbour or missing out altogether.

As well as the growth habit, consider the individual fern's requirements in relation to the fernery. Some species will grow better in a lighter situation, others prefer the shade. For calciphiles a special limy soil may have to be created. If a wet situation exists, be sure to plant a fern that revels in such a position rather than one that grows in drier soils.

Watering

In these days of plastic technology it is a comparatively simple matter to set up a watering system for the fernery. If required this can be automated so that it can be turned on at the same time each day by a time clock or else by a sensory device which measures evaporation and humidity.

Trickle or drip watering systems can be satisfactory for a fernery and may be of particular value if water is limited. Ferns, however, benefit from having their fronds moistened and a system employing sprinklers fits in better with the environment created. The sprinklers should be of a fine misting type so that they do not damage delicate fronds but at the same time enhance the humidity. The latter effect may be very important on hot, dry days when the watering effects may be minimal, but the beneficial effects of increasing the humidity may be enormous. A suitable mist spray should have some coarse droplets for watering or else insufficient water will reach the roots of the ferns.

The sprinklers may be supported on stands in which case some provision will need to be made for their placement prior to planting. Alternatively, they can be supported from the roof or walls of the structure and for this arrangement must be able to work upside down. Special sprinklers which do not drip when not in use are available for this purpose.

GREENHOUSES

A greenhouse is needed to modify the environment so that a greater range of ferns can be grown. The main purpose of such a structure is to provide shelter and extra warmth for cold periods of the year but other benefits also accrue, e.g. shelter from winds, maintenance of humidity when the atmosphere outside may be dry, and an enhancement of growth due to the earlier start and later finish of a season. Obviously, protection from climatic extremes such as frosts are a major factor in deciding whether the expense of a greenhouse is worthwhile.

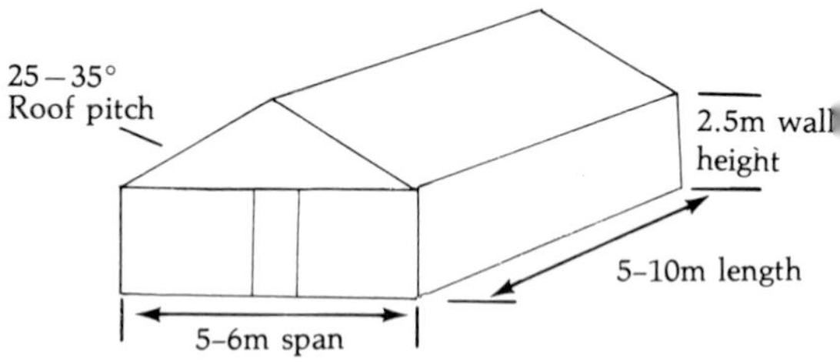

Efficient dimensions of a gable roof greenhouse

One of the many factors to be considered before building a greenhouse is its size. A small greenhouse will look like a palace for a while, however, as the collection increases (and it does!!) then space quickly is at a premium. If a larger greenhouse is possible financially, then it is a wise policy to choose the bigger size, because a small greenhouse can be difficult to manage. Small greenhouses are very subject to rapid fluctuations in temperature, caused by the heating and cooling of the small volume of air. Ventilation too, may be inadequate, causing unhealthy growth. These conditions are not conducive to good fern growth.

A greenhouse is composed of a structural frame clad by a translucent material of which many different types are available. The minimum dimensions of a typical gable roof greenhouse are shown in the accompanying diagram. Such a structure has sufficient volume to buffer severe fluctuations in temperature, transmits adequate light and provides enough room both to work in, and for plant growth. It is also an efficient unit for heating if that is an important consideration.

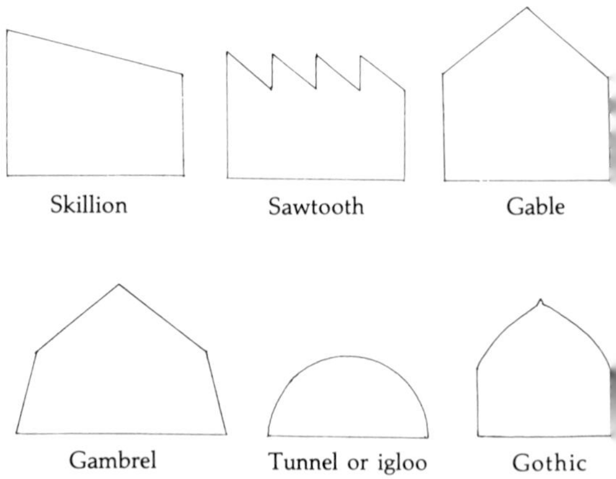

Greenhouse profiles

Greenhouse Shape

Greenhouses are available commercially as pre-fabricated kits or they can be constructed on site by a handyman to suit the particular situation. A range of shapes can be suitable and cross sections of some of these are shown in the accompanying diagram. Certain shapes may be more suitable in some climates, however, the major factors of cost and ease of construction must also be considered. Aesthetic appeal also plays an important role in the choice of structures to be built in a home garden. Another factor that should be considered is that the shapes tried and tested over many years may be more economical and efficient than novelties. Most greenhouses are free-standing units, however lean-tos attached to a wall of a building can be very efficient and useful.

Greenhouse Orientation and Siting

Much has been written about the significance of the orientation of greenhouses, i.e. whether they should run east-west or north-south. Studies have shown that this consideration is only of significance at high latitudes (cold temperate zones) where the amount of available sunlight is low. The shape of the greenhouse is also of major significance in such areas, since maximum light transmission occurs when the greenhouse shape and orientation is such that it presents its translucent surface at right angles to the sunlight. In warm temperate and subtropical regions the total amount of light received in a greenhouse is largely independent of its orientation.

As well as the total amount of light entering a greenhouse, its actual distribution within the house may be of significance. This can be seen at higher latitudes where the ridge on a gable construction may cast a shadow which remains stationary when the house is orientated east–west, whereas it moves throughout the day when the house runs north–south. This effect is particularly noticeable in greenhouses clad with non-diffusing materials such as glass and is less apparent in diffuse light transmitted for example by fibreglass.

The obvious aim in locating a greenhouse is to choose a spot where it will receive as much light as possible throughout the day. Winter sun is a major factor in all but tropical areas. Constraints such as slope, available space and shading caused by nearby trees and buildings must be considered. Shading by trees can be useful in summer but detrimental in winter. Exposure to winter sun becomes of greater significance the higher the latitude where the greenhouse is located. In northern hemispheres a clear exposure to the south is important in the winter but in southern hemispheres the reverse is true.

Construction

Greenhouses require a more solid and intricate construction than do ferneries. In many respects the construction is similar to that of a house and in most cases must conform to local building codes and regulations. Some cladding materials such as glass are heavy and the supporting structures must be strong. The frames should also not be too bulky and should not cause more than 8% shading.

Commonly-used framing materials include pressure-treated timber, galvanized steel and aluminium. Timber is easy to work, but is bulky and requires some maintenance. Steel is strong but heavy, is expensive and requires maintenance against rusting. Aluminium is strong, light in weight, maintenance free but expensive.

For the roof, an adequate pitch is required, so that condensation formed on the interior of the structure does not drip onto the ferns and cause damage. Studies have shown that an angle of 25–35 degrees avoids this problem.

Covering Materials

A range of greenhouse cladding materials are available and the pros and cons of each are discussed below. One of the most important factors of these materials is light transmission and comparative details are presented in Table 6.

TABLE 6
Comparative Light Transmission of Greenhouse Cladding Materials (Flat Sheets)

Material	*Percent Transmission of Visible Light*
Glass	90
Film Plastics	86
Rigid Plastics	70
Fibreglass	65

Glass: This is the traditional material used for glasshouses and it still has many proponents. Glass provides the maximum degree of light transmission and does not deteriorate with age. For ferns it may require shading by painting or covering with shade cloths. Glass is rigid and can only be used in flat sheets. It is also fragile (subject to hail damage) and heavy, requiring a strong supporting structure and separate glazing system.

Film Plastics (polythene): These materials are very light and relatively cheap, but are unfortunately short-lived. Their breakdown is caused by the sun's ultra-violet rays and even those plastics which are stabilized against ultra-violet breakdown last only 2–2½ years maximum. Plastic films are easy to use and can cover any shape frame. Because of their light weight, the supporting structures can be simple. Plastic films can be very successfully used as an inner lining for greenhouses and will greatly increase the humidity and reduce the heat loss. Some plastic films may be strengthened by including a sparse lattice of reinforcing threads in their structure. Others may be bonded to include air bubbles and are not only stronger but also have good insulating properties. Both of these types last considerably longer than the single films.

Rigid Plastics: These materials include poly vinyl chloride (PVC), high density polythene and polypropylene. Most are available in corrugated sheets but some may be available in flat sheets. The former profile is stronger than the latter. All of these materials transmit diffuse light and are lighter and stronger than glass. Some suffer from a deterioration in light transmission and ultra-violet breakdown. There is a considerable amount of developmental work being carried out with these materials to improve their durability and performance.

Fibreglass: This material is actually plastic based, being known technically as glass fibre reinforced polyester. It has been treated separately from plastic materials in this book however, because it is fast becoming the popular and suitable substitute for glass in greenhouse cladding. Fibreglass is lightweight and is commonly available in a corrugated profile in sheets of almost any length. It is also sometimes available as flat sheets or films and, more recently, the corrugated profile has been produced in rolls.

Fibreglass is available in a range of weights, colours and quality. Cheap fibre glass is to be avoided at all costs as the glass fibres may quickly separate from the resin and the material darkens within a short time greatly reducing light transmission. The heavier grades (about 170 g or 6 oz) are more expensive initially but are long lasting and are best used for greenhouse cladding. Some fibreglass is now available which is bonded on the inside with a film of poly vinyl chloride. This greatly increases its stability and life. One problem with fibreglass is that the material itself heats up with light transmission and ferns hung too close to it may burn.

Fibreglass is available in a range of colours, however, only clear or white should be used for greenhouse cladding. Light colours can be suitable, but for the best growth choose the opaque white or clear (for ferns the latter may need to be painted). At all costs avoid very dark colours as they result in abnormal growth and upset growth processes such as photosynthesis.

Layout

The greenhouse should be laid out so as to obtain the most efficient use of the available space. Walks and lanes should be at least 70 cm (28 in) wide to allow for easy passage and room for those ferns which always hang into the aisle. The arrangement of benches should be given critical examination, for, after all, the greenhouse is built for the plants and one wishes to grow to perfection the maximum number possible. Paths can waste up to 40% of the floor space unless careful planning reduces this. A simple planning technique is to draw a scale plan of the greenhouse floor on graph paper and juggle a series of bench cut outs (to scale) until the most efficient use of space is obtained. The arrangement of benches so that several tiers of potted plants can be included, and the hanging

View inside a greenhouse

of containers from overhead supports, also increases the productive area within the greenhouse.

Benches are best constructed from galvanized pipe frames with tops made from wire mesh or corrugated asbestos sheeting. Wood can be used but tends to rot quickly in the wet conditions and also provides a haven for pests and diseases. Mesh benches allow air movement around the ferns. Asbestos benches create humidity around the ferns especially if the corrugations are filled with crushed stone or gravel. The benches should be about 80 cm (32 in) high and no more than 1 m (40 in) wide.

The paths should be concreted, bricked or adequately drained and surfaced with a solid material such as crushed stone, pumice or ant-bed. On no account should materials such as sawdust or shavings be used as these will break down in the wet conditions and become gluggy. They are also cold and breed worms. The area under the benches can be kept bare or planted with small ferns.

Ventilation

Ventilation provides fresh air from outside and is very important in a greenhouse. Ferns appreciate fresh

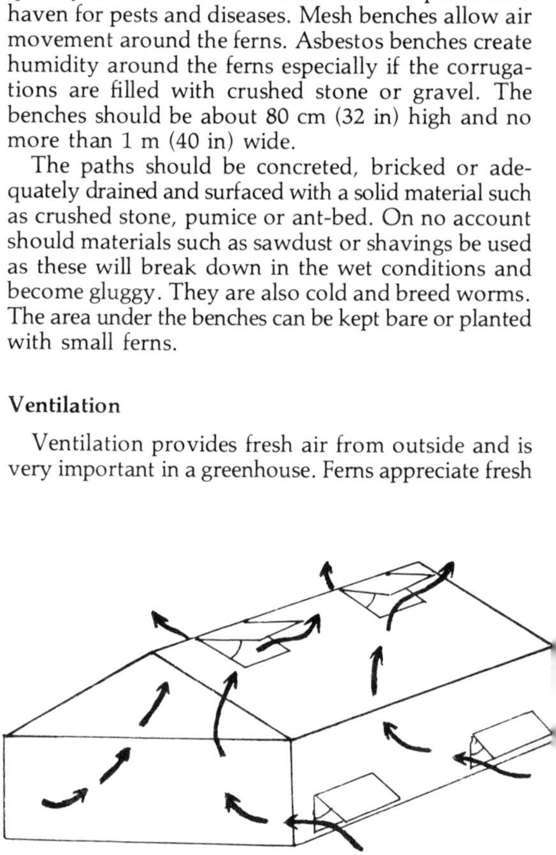

Principles of greenhouse ventilation

Greenhouse ventilator Photo C. G. Goudey

rather than stale or stagnant air, and where ventilation is adequate, growth is stronger and disease problems are fewer. Carbon dioxide is an important gas used by plants in photosynthesis and the atmosphere in closed greenhouses may become deficient in it, thus temporarily stopping growth. Ventilation ensures a good supply of this gas. Ventilation is also important for cooling the structure during hot weather.

The shape of the greenhouse influences the way which air moves within it. Narrow greenhouses with low wall inlets and outlets near the ridge of the roof are very effective at creating a natural air movement within the structure. This is caused by the heated air rising, flowing out the vents near the ridge and so drawing fresh air in from the open vents in the walls. Large greenhouses, especially some of the modern designs where the ridge is sealed, sometimes do not have efficient ventilation and forced ventilation may be needed.

Forced ventilation involves the use of fans to distribute air around the greenhouse and thus avoid any stale pockets. The use of long polythene tubes, sleeves or ducts with holes at intervals can help distribute the air evenly around the greenhouse. These are simply attached to the fan either under the benches or in the roof and will direct the air flow. The same ducts can also be used for heating or cooling if needed.

Watering

Watering ferns in a greenhouse is no different to watering ferns in containers inside or out. Ferns in a greenhouse are protected from extremes of the weather but they do still dry out. Thus, if the sun is hot and the ventilators of the greenhouse are open, the ferns will have to be watered because of the heat and the movement of dry air into the greenhouse. In windy weather, greenhouses tend to lose humidity even if they are closed and attention to watering will be necessary. During the warm summer months it is difficult to overwater ferns, especially if they are potted in a freely draining mix. Daily watering is usually the case at this time of the year. Watering in winter is much more tricky and individual attention may be necessary. Most ferns slow down their growth over winter, with some becoming completely dormant and a few even deciduous. Watering during this time of the year must be just sufficient to keep the potting mix moist.

Watering systems can be installed and are best used for watering over summer because in winter ferns need more individual treatment. Such systems are an excellent means of quickly humidifying a greenhouse.

Greenhouse Heating

Owning a greenhouse means an increase in the range of ferns which can be grown by an enthusiast. Heating that greenhouse increases this range and means that the enthusiast can begin tapping that vast resource of ferns which grow naturally in the world's tropics.

Heating though, can be a costly exercise both in terms of the initial capital outlay for equipment and installation and also in running costs. The capital costs are nearly fixed, however, the running costs will vary greatly depending on a range of factors including the size and shape of the greenhouse, its cladding material, the type of fuel used for energy and the temperature to be maintained inside the greenhouse in relation to the outside temperature. Some discussion on how a greenhouse loses heat may be pertinent at this stage.

The major source of heat loss from a greenhouse is by the direct loss of heated air through the ventilation system. Naturally during cold weather the ventilators are closed and this heat loss is eliminated. Heat still flows out of a closed greenhouse because of a variety of physical processes. Convection and conduction are the main processes and occur because of the differences in temperature between the air inside the greenhouse and the air outside. The greater this difference (i.e. the temperature gradient) the greater will be the heat loss and the higher will be the energy input needed to maintain a given temperature. Wind also influences heat loss and the stronger the wind the greater the rate of loss. Cloud, high humidity, dust or atmospheric pollution tend to reduce heat loss, however, in regions with a clear dry atmosphere considerable radiation losses occur because of the differences between the sky temperature and the air temperature.

The heat loss is also strongly influenced by the properties of the materials used in the construction of the greenhouse. A double brick wall loses less heat than a single brick wall, which in turn loses less than a wall clad with asbestos sheeting. Double glazing of a greenhouse reduces heat loss through the glass by 40–50% because the included air acts as an insulator. The simple act of lining a greenhouse with polythene film reduces heat requirements by 35%.

The fern grower with a heated greenhouse must decide on the temperature to be maintained in the house. The higher the temperature the greater will be the heating costs but the bigger will be the range of ferns that can be grown to perfection. An excellent range of ferns can be grown if the temperature is maintained at 10°C (50°F) and these ferns will tolerate occasional short periods of temperatures as low as 5°C (41°F). Flamboyant tropical species and cultivars are very sensitive to cold and prefer temperatures about 15°C (50°F), tolerating drops to 10°C (50°F). Some growers may have special small greenhouses for their tropical treasures. Another alternative is to partition off a section of the ordinary heated greenhouse and supplement the heating in that section with a small electric or kerosene heater.

Heating Systems

The traditional heating of greenhouses was based on hot water flowing through black steel pipes beneath the benches. The water was heated by boilers which were fired by solid fuels such as wood, coal or coke. This system resulted in a gentle, humid, heating of the greenhouse and created an excellent atmosphere for the cultivation of ferns. Today, hot water systems are still used by fern enthusiasts but with some modern innovations. The boilers may be fired by heating oil or gas and the hot water distributed through finned tubing which releases up to four times the heat per unit length of ordinary pipes. The author considers the hot water system of heating to be vastly superior to any others for fern growth, however, it suffers from high capital and running costs.

The alternative to heating water in pipes is to heat the air directly. Warm air heaters, fired by either gas or oil, are now commonly used by commercial growers for heating their greenhouses. The heat is distributed evenly through the greenhouses by means of the polythene sleeves or ducts mentioned in the section on ventilation. The initial warm air heating systems produced dry air which was unsatisfactory for fern growth. The simple technique of misting fine sprays of water into the polythene tube solved this problem. Recent improvements to air heating systems, which are cheaper to install and run than hot water units, have meant a viable heating alternative is available to greenhouse fern growers.

The technology developed for tapping solar energy can be adapted to supplementing the heating of greenhouses and thus reducing heating costs. The greenhouse itself can be used as a solar collector. On hot days, instead of diverting the excess heat out through the ventilators, it is passed through a rock pile situated in an attached shed. The heated air heats up the rocks and creates a store of heat that can be used for heating the greenhouse at night. The principles of the system are shown in the accompanying figure. By reversing the flow of the system in the summer and passing the air over wet rocks a cooling system can be obtained.

Greenhouse Cooling

In areas with a hot summer climate, the overheating of a greenhouse and subsequent damage to ferns is a common problem. Proper use of an efficient ventilation system can eliminate this problem, but further problems can arise if the outside air is very dry or if windy conditions prevail. If such conditions are present for a substantial part of the year then it may be necessary to install a cooling system.

The cooling system most commonly used in greenhouses involves evaporation. Commercial evaporative coolers can be successfully used and are mounted in the wall so that they draw fresh air in from the outside and to some extent pressurize the air in the greenhouse. The cooled air can also be distributed by the polythene ducts already discussed.

A simple evaporative cooling system can be constructed by a handyman. This consists of a pad which contains wood wool or some suitable material and a fan. Water is trickled over the pad and the fan blows or sucks air over the moistened material. The air is cooled by evaporation as it passes over the moistened pad and the greenhouse is cooled.

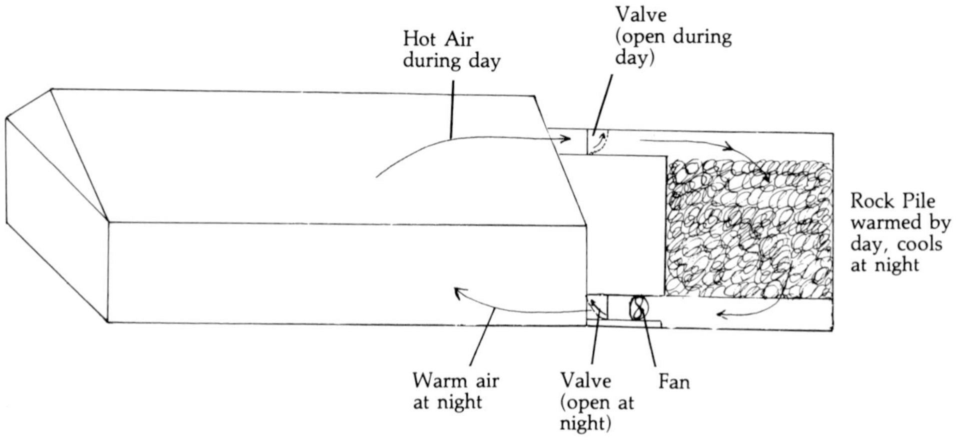

Principles of heating a greenhouse using a rock pile thermal storage unit

Greenhouse Shading

In areas with a very hot summer climate, shading will be necessary on the cladding to prevent burning of the fern fronds. The simplest method is to paint a white, reflective solution over the outside of the cladding material. Traditionally, this has been a mixture of lime, water and a little linseed oil, however this material washes off in heavy rain. Commercial greenhouse paint is available or a water-based house paint can be used if it is diluted (about 2 parts water : 1 paint).

Shading paints are efficient and cheap but messy and sometimes it is difficult to apply the desired degree of shade. The shade cloth used for ferneries and shade-houses is a very suitable alternative and provides an accurate and uniform shade. The shade cloth should not be laid flat on the glass but should be supported on a frame 15–30 cm (6–12 in) above. This allows an air gap which acts as an insulator. Laying the cloth directly on the glass causes extra heat build-up in the greenhouse, since the cloth is black and absorbs heat readily from the sun. Much of this heat is transferred into the greenhouse.

Humidifying a Greenhouse

If a greenhouse is well-set-up and the plants regularly cared for, an atmosphere builds up over time. Much of this atmosphere is created by the humidity. An experienced fern grower can tell if this atmosphere is agreeable, or needs some attention, immediately upon entering the greenhouse.

Greenhouses which have an earthen floor and are lined with polythene sheeting generally maintain good humidity. In those which have a concrete floor, the humidity may fluctuate markedly. In regions where it is commonly low, the maintenance of a humid greenhouse can be a problem. Commercial humidifying units can be purchased or a simple system based on mist sprays can be installed. These can be regulated by a sensor. The mist sprays can be placed under the bench or along the roof so that the mist drifts downwards over the plants.

Air Circulation

Air circulation in a greenhouse is vital to the health of the ferns. In most cases the ventilation system creates adequate air circulation. For periods when the ventilators are closed the installation of a couple of small, cheap fans will keep the air moving and prevent the formation of stale pockets.

Part Six

Ferns to Grow

Explanation of text

In this section information is provided for more than 700 species of ferns. It also includes numerous cultivars. They have been grouped together into chapters, these groupings being either of species with obvious relationships, or a much looser arrangement with a common theme such as cultural requirements. Within each chapter the species are arranged in alphabetical order.

For the majority of species a standardized layout has been used to facilitate comparisons.

Example of Layout

Genus and species name (alternative name) Common Name
World Distribution Frond length: Frond shape or division Suitable Growing Regions: Terrestrial or Epiphytic.

Simplified information and cultivation requirements.

Cultivars.

Notes on Layout

Genus and species name — this is as up-to-date as possible but some errors can be expected and changes will occur during publication.
Alternative name — because of differences in interpretation by botanists, a fern species may have a couple of different generic and/or specific names which are valid depending upon the classification system adopted. Fern fanciers from various countries may grow a fern under different (but technically correct) names and for this reason the well-known alternative has been provided in brackets. A cross reference of these names is also supplied in alphabetical order. These entries contain the word 'see'.
Common Name — only well-known names in common use have been included. There is no standardized convention for such names and to list them all would add bulk and considerable confusion.
Distribution — as accurate as possible but in some cases regions have been used instead of specific countries e.g. Polynesia.
Frond length — this feature is included to give some idea of the space required by the fern. Note, however, that the fronds may be erect, sprawling or pendulous. For obvious reasons the terms 'climber' or 'creeping' replace frond length for some species. In tree ferns the approximate trunk height is given as well as frond length. Frond lengths are not given for species of *Platycerium* and some aquatics.
Frond shape or division — included simply as an indication of what the frond may be expected to look like.
Suitable growing regions — these are only meant to be a rough guide as to the regions in which the fern can be expected to be successfully cultivated, i.e. in an outside environment offering the usual fern requirements. It does not take into account local factors such as altitude.
Terrestrial or Epiphytic (Terr. or Epi.) — this entry is included merely as a guide to the potting mix and cultural requirements a species may require. The term aquatic is used for water ferns.
'Cultivars' — as a general rule only commonly grown or well known cultivars are included. The cultivar names are presented in quotation marks and listed in alphabetical order under the species.
Synonyms (=) — major and recent entries are included in a cross reference to facilitate the use of the book. For these entries an equals sign is used.

23 Squirrel's-foot, rabbit's-foot, hare's-foot ferns and their relatives

genera *Araiostegia, Davallia, Davallodes, Gymnogrammitis, Humata, Leucostegia Scyphularia* and *Trogostolon*

Ferns of this group are of great appeal to fern enthusiasts and are also popular with professional growers. They are valued for their dissected fronds and wandering rhizomes which are covered with prominent woolly scales of various colours. The appearance of the rhizomes is the explanation for many of the popular names applied to this group of ferns, e.g. Hare's-foot.

Habitat

These ferns are most commonly epiphytes on trees or mossy boulders, although a few species grow as terrestrials. In some of the epiphytic species the base of the plant is firmly attached to the support, while the rhizomes grow through the air. Ferns of this group are found in or along the margins of rainforests, along the banks of streams and amongst boulders and on cliff faces in quite exposed situations. Many species grow in areas with a seasonally dry climate and are deciduous. *Davallia denticulata*, for example, avoids extremes of heat and dryness by means of its subterranean rhizomes and with the fronds dying at the start of the dry season. *D. tasmanii* grows close to the sea in the partial protection of large rocks.

Cultivation

Uses

Ferns of this group are generally very easy and rewarding to grow. They are most suitable for container culture and can be used for indoor decoration, or on verandahs, patios or in bush-houses or greenhouses. In the tropics many species can be grown on suitable garden trees or even among rocks in the garden. The Japanese mould the long flexible rhizomes of *D. mariesii* into shapes such as balls, spheres and monkeys. These are hung indoors for decoration and the more intricate shapes are highly prized objects.

Soil Types

Most ferns in this group are not suited to growing in soil. The few terrestrial species need soils of unimpeded drainage.

Potting Mix

These ferns require a coarse, epiphytic type potting mix, which must be well drained and aerated, and which provides sufficient moisture for the roots. The mix should be based on materials such as milled pine bark, fern fibre, peat moss, charcoal and coarse river sand. Sphagnum moss can also be very successful. Ferns of this group do not generally make a large root system and are best underpotted rather than overpotted. Repotting will be necessary immediately the mix begins to break down. When potting, the rhizomes (especially the tips) should not be buried.

Watering

Ferns of this group like plenty of water during the warm, growing months. They must be watered more carefully during the winter, especially those species which become dormant. At this time, they should receive just sufficient water to keep them moist, but must not be allowed to dry out to the stage where the rhizomes shrivel as this can lead to dieback. Overwatering is a common winter problem in these ferns, with the rhizomes turning watery and then rotting. The same thing happens when the compost breaks down and becomes soggy. Affected plants can be saved by cutting off most of the root system together with any pieces of rotting rhizome and laying the good pieces in a tray of moist sphagnum moss. The fronds of some species are also subject to sweating if overwatered at certain times of the year (see page 119).

Fertilizing

Ferns of this group are not heavy feeders and even slow-release fertilizers should be used with care. Dollops of old animal manure incorporated in the potting mix are appreciated, as are occasional applications of liquid fertilizer during the growing period.

Situation

Most of these ferns like bright but indirect light or filtered light. All need air movement, preferably with humidity. Most species favour tropical conditions and are sensitive to frosts and long periods of cold, wet weather. A few species are quite tolerant of the cold and will even withstand periods of freezing, e.g. *Davallia bullata, D. mariesii, D, pyxidata*. In regions with a cold winter climate a heated greenhouse is essential if a range of these ferns is to be grown.

Pests

Attacks by Fern Scale and Hard Brown Scale may be a nuisance but rarely persist. Aphids may congregate on developing fronds, and slugs, snails and caterpillars may be occasional pests.

Propagation

Ferns of this group can be tricky to raise from spores and are most commonly propagated vegetatively. Results with spores seem to be best when they are sown during periods of increasing day length. Some species show a preference for a particular sowing medium, e.g. staghorn peat (*Davallia fejeensis*), tree-fern fibre (*D. pyxidata*), or milled bark (*D. solida*).

Vegetative propagation is by division or layering. Creeping rhizomes which root as they grow can be easily divided, however, those species with aerial rhizomes must be handled more carefully. They can be severed so that each piece contains a section of basal roots or they can be pegged into a container of moss and separated when roots are formed. They can also be propagated by aerial layering (**see page 136**). Species such as *D. mariesii* lend themselves well to tissue culture.

Davallia bullata

SPECIES AND CULTIVARS

Araiostegia hymenophylloides
India, Sri Lanka, Malaysia, Philippines
60–120 cm (24–48 in): 4–5 pinnate Trop.: Epi.

A delightful fern with finely dissected lacy fronds of a most delicate nature. Plants can be grown in a large basket or a tub of coarse mixture. They like warm, humid conditions with air movement. Plants are deciduous with the fronds shedding in the winter months.

Araiostegia pseudocystopteris
India
40–60 cm (16–24 in): 3–4 pinnate S.Trop.–Temp.: Epi.–Terr.

A species from the mountains of northern India where it is common on trees and rocks at high elevations. Can be grown as a basket fern or in a pot. The fronds are finely divided and attractive.

Araiostegia pulchra
India, Sri Lanka
40–50 cm (16–20 in): 2–3 pinnate S.Trop.–Temp.: Epi.

An attractive fern from mountainous regions growing in shady situations. The slender rhizomes are covered with blunt, whitish scales and the fronds tend to be spreading or weeping. Easily grown in a pot or basket. Fronds may be deciduous.

Davallia bullata Hare's-foot Fern
India, Sri Lanka, China
15–20 cm (6–8 in): 3–4 pinnate S.Trop.–Temp.: Epi.

Although subject to much confusion in identity this fern has been a favourite with growers for many decades. It grows readily in a basket or pot of coarse mixture. Plants become deciduous over winter and should be kept on the dry side until new fronds appear.

Davallia bullata-mariesii = D. mariesii var. **stenolepis**

Davallia canariensis Canary Island Hare's-foot
Portugal, Spain, Canary Islands
40–60 cm (16–24 in): 3 pinnate Temp.–S.Trop.: Epi.

A delightful hare's-foot fern which looks graceful in a basket or hanging pot. Its finely-divided lacy fronds are nearly as broad as they are long and the rhizomes are stout and thick. Plants tend to be more slow growing than other species but are long-lived. Useful for indoor decoration.

Davallia canariensis

A very attractive davallia prized for its large, finely-divided, deep green fronds and its rhizomes covered with coarse, dark-coloured, spreading scales. New fronds are red to crimson. Makes an excellent basket plant and can be developed into a large specimen.

Davallia elegans = D. denticulata

Davallia embolostegia
Philippines, Borneo
80–120 cm (32–48 in): 4 pinnate S.Trop.–Trop.: Epi.
A delightful fern with large, lacy, light green fronds which are produced in abundance from the spreading rhizomes. The young tips of the rhizomes are covered with conspicuous, tangled, reddish-brown scales. Can be grown in a large container or basket. Each frond is quite long-lived.

Davallia epiphylla
New Guinea, Polynesia
60–90 cm (24–36 in): 3–4 pinnate Trop.–S.Trop.: Epi.
A little-known davallia which is similar in general appearance to *D. embolostegia*. Its young rhizomes are also covered with a soft mass of reddish scales and the fronds are finely-divided and handsome. Coarse

Davallia embolostegia Photo D. L. Jones

Davallia corniculata
Malaysia
30–70 cm (12–28 in): 3–4 pinnate Trop.–S.Trop.: Epi.
A rare species with slender rhizomes densely covered by brown scales. The fronds are finely-divided and much longer than they are wide, giving a narrow triangular appearance. Plants can be grown in a pot or basket of coarse mixture.

Davallia denticulata
India, Malaysia, New Guinea, Australia
60–100 cm (24–40 in): 3 pinnate Trop.–S.Trop.: Terr.–Epi.
A widely distributed and locally common species usually found in exposed situations. This fern grows as an epiphyte, also frequently among rocks and often as a terrestrial in sandy soil with the rhizomes deeply buried. Plants grow readily in a pot or in the ground but the fronds are deciduous during the winter. Sporelings of this species are particularly attractive.

Davallia dissecta = D. trichomanoides

Davallia divaricata
South China, South-East Asia, Malaysia, Indonesia
60–120 cm (24–48 in): 3 pinnate Trop.–S.Trop.: Epi.–Terr.

Davallia embolostegia

and fine fronds may be present on the one plant. It grows easily but requires protection from excess sun and wind.

Davallia griffithiana — see **Humata griffithiana**

Davallia fejeensis Lacy Hare's-foot
Fiji
20–100 cm (8–40 in): 3–5 pinnate Trop.–S.Trop.: Epi.
A choice, extremely popular fern which is favoured for basket culture and can be grown into large specimens. Plants are very long-lived and individual fronds on healthy plants may last 2–3 years. The thick rhizomes usually grow through the air. The species is variable and a number of forms are grown. The commonest form has large, extremely finely-divided fronds with very small segments.

'Major' — a vigorous form with large, coarse fronds which tend to be pale green.

'Plumosa' — a finely-divided form with graceful, drooping fronds.

'False Plumosa' — a finely-divided form, the rhizomes of which do not grow through the air, but cling to the substrate.

'Dwarf Ripple' — a dwarf form with finely-divided fronds. Grows very easily.

Davallia hymenophylloides — see **Araiostegia hymenophylloides**

Davallia mariesii Hare's-foot Fern
Japan, Korea
20–35 cm (8–14 in): 3–4 pinnate S.Trop.–Temp.: Epi.
This is one of the most popular ferns in cultivation and it has been a favourite for decades. It can be grown in a basket or pot and the long, furry rhizomes wander at will. These rhizomes can be trained into shapes and this makes it a popular subject in Japan. Plants are quite hardy and cold resistant and the fronds are shed each year. The var. *stenolepis* is a robust variety with conspicuous white scales on the rhizomes. It is more popular in cultivation than the typical variety because of its vigour.

Davallia pentaphylla — see **Scyphularia pentaphylla**

Davallia plumosa Black Caterpillar Fern
Samoa
20–45 cm (8–18 in): 2–3 pinnate Trop.–S.Trop.: Epi.
This fern makes an exceptionally fine basket plant.

Davallia fejeensis Photo D. L. Jones

Davallia plumosa

The fronds have relatively large leathery dark green segments and the young rhizomes are covered with spreading black scales. Plants need a fibrous or coarse mixture, warmth, humidity and air movement.

Davallia pycnocarpa — see **Scyphularia pycnocarpa**

Davallia pyxidata Australian Hare's-foot
Australia
30–80 cm (12–32 in): 2–3 pinnate Trop.–Temp.: Epi.–Terr.

An easily-grown fern with woody, erect or spreading rhizomes and leathery, dark green fronds. Juvenile or sterile fronds may be coarsely-divided, while fertile fronds are much finer. Can be grown in a pot or basket or among rocks in the garden.

Davallia pyxidata

Davallia solida Giant Hare's-foot
Asia, Malaysia, New Guinea, Australia, Pacific Islands
60–120 cm (24–48 in): 3–4 pinnate Trop.–S.Trop.: Epi.

A handsome fern, with large leathery fronds that are usually dark green and shiny. These are coarsely-divided and are often a dark purple when young. The

Davallia pyxidata

Davallia solida Photo D. L. Jones

thick rhizomes grow stiffly away from the compost. Makes an attractive basket plant. There is considerable range in the degree of frond division.

'Ornata' — a coarse form with very broad segments.

'Ruffled Ornata' — as above but the margins of the segments are conspicuously ruffled. A very attractive form.

Davallia stenolepis=**D. mariesii** var. **stenolepis**

Davallia tasmanii
Three Kings Islands (New Zealand)
20–50 cm (8–20 in): 3–4 pinnate Temp.: Terr.
A very hardy and cold-resistant fern which can be grown as a ground cover among rocks or in a basket. It is a handsome species with its closely placed, finely-divided leathery fronds. Plants grow readily in temperate regions, but do not thrive in hotter climates.

Davallia trichomanoides Hare's-foot or Squirrel's-foot Fern
Malaysia, New Guinea, Indonesia
20–40 cm (8–16 in): 3–4 pinnate S.Trop.–Temp.: Epi.
A popular fern with fern enthusiasts and general gardeners alike. Valued for its neat habit, refreshing lacy fronds and interesting furry rhizomes which wander at will. Excellent for baskets or pots. Plants are deciduous for a short period but new fronds are quickly produced. In the typical form, the rhizome scales are yellowish-brown and in forma *barbata* they are reddish-brown and the frond margins are less deeply incised. The var. *lorrainii* has dark-coloured rhizome scales and sparser fronds than other forms.

Davallodes hirsutum
Philippines
20–40 cm (8–16 in): 2–3 pinnate Trop.: Epi.
A very attractive fern with narrow, lacy, hairy fronds which tend to be pendulous. These are closely spaced on thick rhizomes, which are green and bear numerous, slender dark-coloured scales. Plants grow easily, but resent disturbance and are slow to establish from pieces. They like warm, humid, airy conditions.

Davallodes membranulosum
India
30–40 cm (12–16 in): 2–3 pinnate Trop.–S.Trop.: Epi.
An interesting fern, with sparsely scaled, creeping rhizomes and narrow, lacy fronds which are quite hairy on the underside, especially on the main veins. Plants like warm, humid, airy conditions.

Davallia solida 'Ornata'

Davallia trichomanoides

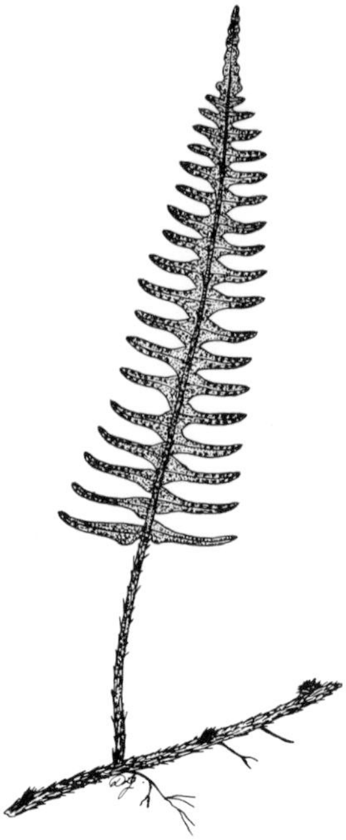

Humata pectinata

Davallia trichomanoides

Gymnogrammitis dareiformis
North India, China
30–60 cm (12–24 in): 3 pinnate S.Trop.: Epi.
An interesting fern with bright green, deeply segmented fronds arising from a densely scaly, strongly creeping rhizome. Can be grown in a basket of coarse mixture. Plants come from high altitude and would be worth trying in temperate regions.

Humata angustata
Malaysia
10–25 cm (4–10 in): entire Trop.–S.Trop.: Epi.
A novelty fern, with simple, leathery, dark green fronds closely placed on a long, slender rhizome. Can be grown in a pot or basket of coarse mixture. Grows well in a tree-fern basket.

Humata falcinella – see **Trogostolon falcinellus**

Humata griffithiana
India, China, Taiwan
30–50 cm (12–20 in): 3–4 pinnate S.Trop.–Temp.: Epi.
This fern, which is sometimes included in the genus *Davallia*, could be easily mistaken for *D. mariesii*. It can, however, be distinguished by its roundish indusium which is not attached on the upper margins. Plants are easily grown and are suitable for baskets or pots.

Humata heterophylla
Malaysia, Indonesia
5–15 cm (2–6 in): entire Trop.–S.Trop.: Epi.
A novelty fern, which has a long slender rhizome and spaced fronds which are of two types. The sterile fronds are broadly oblong, with entire, or sometimes scalloped, margins and the fertile fronds are deeply-lobed. Rhizome tips are sometimes purplish. Grows easily in a small pot or basket.

Humata parvula
Malaysia, Borneo
2.5–5 cm (1–2 in): 2–3 pinnate Trop.–S.Trop.: Epi.

A delightful dwarf fern which forms clumps of lacy fronds. The rhizomes are thread-like and the fronds quite closely spaced. Likes warm, humid conditions and is best grown in a small pot.

Humata pectinata
Malaysia, New Guinea, Australia
10–20 cm (4–8 in): 1 pinnate Trop.–S.Trop.: Epi.
A distinctive dwarf fern with erect, leathery fronds. Grows in spreading patches usually in exposed situations. Fronds are quite resistant to dryness. Very sensitive to disturbance and can be difficult to establish in cultivation. Likes warm, humid but airy conditions.

Humata repens
India, Japan, Malaysia, New Guinea, Australia
10–20 cm (4–8 in): 1–2 pinnate Trop.–S.Trop.: Epi.
A widespread dwarf fern which grows in large, spreading patches on rocks and trees. Makes a very desirable basket plant, but is somewhat slow growing and sensitive to disturbance. Likes warm, humid but airy conditions.

Humata tyermanii Silver Hare's-foot
China
20–30 cm (8–12 in): 3–4 pinnate S.Trop.–Temp.: Epi.

Humata pectinata Photo D. L. Jones

Humata tyermanii in paperbark-lined basket
Photo D. L. Jones

Humata tyermanii

Leucostegia immersa Photo D. L. Jones

A choice fern, with widely creeping silvery rhizomes and neat, finely divided, dark green fronds which are often purplish when young. Makes an excellent basket specimen especially in tree-fern baskets where the rhizomes contrast with the dark material. A dwarf growing form with smaller, more widely spaced fronds is also grown.

Leucostegia immersa
India
40–70 cm (16–28 in): 3–4 pinnate Trop.–S.Trop.: Terr.–Epi.

In nature, this fern grows on trees or rocks or in humus-rich soil in fairly exposed situations and often at high elevations. It adapts readily to cultivation and makes an effective basket or pot plant. Needs good drainage and some warmth.

Leucostegia pallida
Philippines, Borneo
60–120 cm (24–48 in): 3–4 pinnate Trop.–S.Trop.: Epi.

A very attractive fern with a delicate appearance which belies its nature. Its large, broad, pale-coloured fronds are divided into small lobes and present a lacy effect. Plants can be grown easily in a basket or pot of coarse mixture and like warm, humid conditions.

Scyphularia pentaphylla Black Caterpillar Fern
Malaysia, Indonesia, New Guinea, Polynesia
30–50 cm (12–20 in): 1–2 pinnate S.Trop.–Temp.: Epi.

A popular fern, usually grown in hanging baskets where it shows off its features to perfection. The fronds are coarse and leathery and with an arching or drooping habit which adds to its appearance. The rhizomes are covered with coarse, black scales, a feature which gives rise to its common name.

Scyphularia pycnocarpa
Fiji
20–60 cm (8–24 in): Trop.–S.Trop.: Epi.

An appealing fern with fairly open, bright green, somewhat leathery fronds and widely creeping rhizomes, densely clothed with black, bristle-like scales. An excellent basket fern which will tolerate a fair degree of exposure to sun.

Scyphularia simplicifolia
Borneo
10–20 cm (4–8 in): entire Trop.: Epi.

Leucostegia pallida Photo D. L. Jones

Scyphularia pycnocarpa Photo D. L. Jones

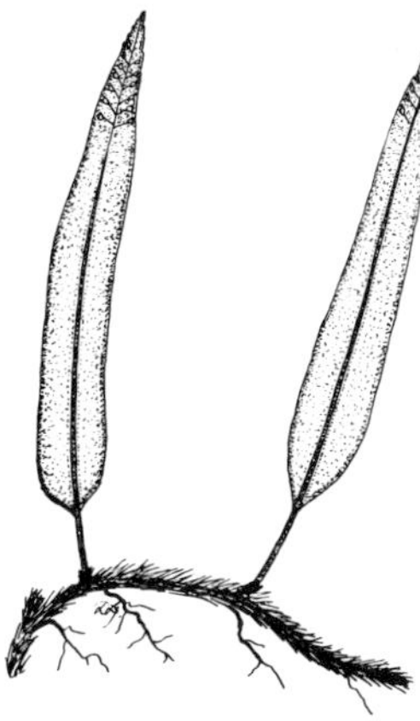

Scyphularia simplicifolia

A novelty fern, which can be grown in baskets, especially those made from tree-fern trunks. Plants have a slender, scaly rhizome and simple leathery fronds. They need warm, humid, airy conditions.

Scyphularia triphylla
Malaysia, Indonesia
15–35 cm (6–14 in): 1 pinnate Trop.–S.Trop.: Epi.
This fern resembles a weak form of the Black Caterpillar Fern with a slender, very scaly rhizome and smaller, well spaced fronds which usually have only three leaflets. Easily grown as a basket fern in a coarse mixture. Needs warm, humid conditions.

Trogostolon falcinellus
Philippines
10–15 cm (4–6 in): 3–4 pinnate Trop.–S.Trop.: Epi.
The finely-divided lacy fronds of this fern are a refreshing green and are a most ornamental feature. They are borne at intervals, along a slender, creeping rhizome, which is covered with dark brown scales. An attractive basket specimen. Grows readily in warm humid conditions.

Leucostegia pallida

24 Maidenhair ferns

genus *Adiantum*

The Maidenhairs probably have the largest and most enthusiastic following of any group of ferns. They are known and grown by a cross section of the community from housewives with a casual interest to ardent enthusiasts who specialize in their culture. They are also an important group of ferns for commercial growers. Maidenhairs are valued for their dissected fronds of delicate appearance and infinite variety of species and cultivars. They are generally regarded as a difficult group to grow to perfection, however, this need not be the case.

Habitat

Maidenhairs grow in a variety of habitats but always where there is adequate moisture. A number of species occur in shady forests but many more grow in brightly lit to quite sunny situations. Maidenhairs are frequent along streams and around soaks and waterfalls, as well as in crevices, among rocks and on earthen embankments. Quite a number seek out limestone rocks and calcareous soils. Some species are colonizers and especially in the tropics may be weedy, appearing in nurseries, on old mortar and disturbed earth.

Cultivation

Uses

Maidenhairs are most commonly grown in pots and are used for decoration indoors, on verandahs or in greenhouses and conservatories. Those with long weeping fronds can be used for hanging pots or baskets. Some grow easily while others are quite tricky. Most of the species and some of the hardy cultivars can be grown in the ground providing the prevailing climate is suitable for their survival. New fronds are frequently quite colourful.

The range of Maidenhairs available for cultivation is greatly increased by the propensity of some species to hybridize or mutate (particularly *A. raddianum*, *A. tenerum* and *A. capillus-veneris*). The resulting cultivars embrace a tremendous range of segment size and dissection including skeletonized and crested forms. A few have variegated fronds. These various forms are of interest to specialists but may lack general appeal or be difficult to grow.

Soil Types

Maidenhairs prefer a well-drained soil rich in organic matter and treated with lime on a regular basis. Many garden soils will be suitable for their growth but will generally require the addition of lime and organic matter.

Potting Mix

Maidenhairs need excellent drainage, and an open fibrous mixture based on friable sandy loam is usually very suitable. Added materials such as peat moss, milled pine bark or chopped fern fibre improve water holding capacity and lime or dolomite reduces acidity. Some growers also find benefit from limestone or marble chips, shell grit or crushed coral added to the mix.

Maidenhairs are better underpotted rather than overpotted and usually need repotting only once a year.

Watering

Maidenhairs require regular (almost daily) watering during the summer but require much less during the winter when growth is slow or even absent. Those Maidenhairs with clustered or finely-divided fronds must be watered carefully so that the foliage is not wet. If the fronds are kept wet patches of dead tissue can appear and these may spread or else lead to the introduction of Grey Mould. Enthusiasts water their prized Maidenhairs by hand and keep all water off the foliage. They also move them away from drips (condensation) and allow room between plants for aeration purposes.

Standing Maidenhairs in a saucer of water is a common practice and it works well. It must be realized, however, that salts can build up in the saucer and the basal part of the soil mix and, at a critical level, may cause damage to the fern. A heavy watering about once a month will flush out the salts and avoid the problem.

Adiantum capillus—veneris

Fertilizing

Maidenhairs like fertilizers but only in small doses at a time. They are easily damaged by overfertilizing or by concentrations that are too strong. Some growers get excellent growth by packing weathered cow manure on the surface of the potting mix. Liquid solutions of cow manure are also reported to be excellent. Slow-release fertilizers can be successful in a potting mix as can applications of fish emulsion and seaweed extracts.

Situation

Most Maidenhair species and cultivars resent too much shade and prefer a well lit situation. This belies their delicate appearance. Exposure to morning sun or filtered sun is ideal for the majority. In a greenhouse or fernery, plants should be placed where they will receive plenty of light but not so much as to cause burning. Some Maidenhairs are exceptions, preferring shade, e.g. *A. diaphanum, A. silvaticum.*

Maidenhairs like air movement but must be protected from wind. A small fan to lightly circulate air is of benefit in a greenhouse.

Pests

Healthy Maidenhairs do not suffer greatly from pests. Slugs, snails, earwigs and caterpillars can damage croziers and young fronds while aphids are a common pest on uncurling fronds. Grey Mould (Botrytis) can be a serious disease in stagnant, wet conditions. A condition known as Acid Rot may develop where the potting mix becomes too acid (see page 116).

Propagation

Maidenhairs are surprisingly easy to raise from spores and sporelings can be quite fast growing. Spores are best sown on a coarse mixture with a neutral to alkaline reaction (pH 7–8.5). Suitable materials include crushed terra cotta, decomposed coral, scoria and fly ash, mixed with peat moss or platycerium peat. Commercial growers find mixtures of sand and peat moss or sandy loam and peat moss to be quite satisfactory.

Most Maidenhairs can also be propagated by division and one particular group (*A. caudatum* etc.) by plantlets formed on the elongated tip of each frond. Maidenhairs that spread by stolons can be divided readily (*A. aethiopicum*) but others may be more difficult. Small pieces of plant may be very hard to re-establish and only large divisions should be made (except for *A. venustum* when the reverse is true).

SPECIES AND CULTIVARS

Adiantum aethiopicum Common Maidenhair
Australia, Africa, New Zealand
20–80 cm (8–32 in): 2 pinnate Temp.–Trop.: Terr.

A widely-distributed fern which extends over a range of climates. It commonly grows in a semi-shady situation in wet soils and has the ability to spread rapidly in a suitable position by the production of rhizomes. Can be grown easily in a pot or established in the ground in moist soil in a situation exposed to some sun. Plants from temperate regions are very cold hardy.

Adiantum anceps
Ecuador, Peru
40–100 cm (16–40 in): 2 pinnate Trop.: Terr.

A large maidenhair with coarse pinnules which may be up to 8 cm (3 in) long, and each characteristically drawn out into a long, pointed apex. Fronds have an arching or even weeping aspect. This is an attractive species which is very cold sensitive. Requires an open mix with an alkaline pH and is best underpotted rather than overpotted.

Adiantum capillus-junonis
Japan, China
10–25 cm (4–10 in): 1 pinnate S.Trop.–Temp.: Terr.
A little-known species which may become more widely grown, because it adapts well to cultivation. Plants have slender fronds with large pinnae. The fronds arch and can be proliferous on the tip. Requires an acid, loamy mix.

Adiantum capillus-veneris Venus-hair Fern
Pantropical
30–60 cm (12–24 in): 2–3 pinnate Trop.–Temp.: Terr.
A fern which is widely distributed from warm temperate to tropical regions but which is commonest in the latter zones and may naturalize itself in greenhouses and bush-houses. It often grows in limestone, usually in a fairly sunny situation. Plants are prized for their attractive fronds of delicate appearance and in some countries the species is the subject of myths and folklore. Plants can be grown easily in pots of mixture fortified with lime or among rocks in the ground, on walls etc. In temperate regions a greenhouse may be necessary for its cultivation.
The species is quite variable and a number of cultivars have been selected or produced by deliberate hybridization.

'Banksianum' – strong grower well suited to specimen culture. Upright growth habit. Cold hardy. True from spore.

'Fimbriatum' – segments deeply cut into finger-like lobes. Plants are cold sensitive. Partially fertile.

'Imbricatum' – small growing decorative form with cascading fronds. Segments large and deeply cut into lobes. Partially fertile.

'Scintilla' – unusual twisted segments which are deeply skeletonized. Best in a shallow pot. Sterile.

Adiantum cardiochlaena = A. polyphyllum

Adiantum caudatum Trailing Maidenhair
Africa, India, Asia, Malaysia, Philippines, Indonesia, New Guinea
10–30 cm (4–12 in): 1 pinnate Trop.–S.Trop.: Terr.
A fine maidenhair for culture in a hanging pot or basket. It has prominently pendulous fronds with attractively lobed segments. A well grown plant is a thick mass of fronds and is a very decorative addition to a fernery. Can also be grown among rocks. Plants favour a neutral to alkaline mix. They can be propagated readily by plantlets produced from the frond tips.

Adiantum chilense = A. capillus-veneris

Adiantum concinnum Brittle Maidenhair
Central and South America, Mexico, West Indies
30–80 cm (12–32 in): 2–3 pinnate Trop.–S.Trop.: Terr.

Adiantum diaphanum is a colony-forming fern
Photo D. L. Jones

A neat fern which has characteristic yellowish-green fronds. In nature it grows in rocky situations that are sometimes quite exposed. Grows easily in cultivation but is very cold sensitive. Plants are best grown in a pot of slightly acid to neutral mix. The species is variable and a few forms have been selected in cultivation.

'Edwinii' – tall erect fronds with broad segments.

'Noaksii' – compact form with arching fronds.

'Upright Noaksii' – similar to above but with erect fronds.

Adiantum cultratum
Central and South America, Mexico, West Indies
60–90 cm (24–36 in): 2–3 pinnate Trop.: Terr.
A large, coarse maidenhair which is uncommonly grown. Plants are very cold sensitive and require a neutral to alkaline soil mix of unimpeded drainage.

Adiantum cultrifolium = A. cultratum

Adiantum cuneatum = A. raddianum

Adiantum curvatum = A. cultratum

Adiantum cunninghamii
Australia, New Zealand, New Guinea
60–100 cm (24–40 in): 2–3 pinnate Trop.–Temp.: Terr.
A handsome, robust maidenhair with spreading fronds and prominent segments which are distinctly glaucous. The new fronds are very colourful varying from salmon-pink to deep purplish-red. Likes a cool shady situation in organically-rich acid soil. Plants resent disturbance.

Adiantum deflectens
Central and South America, Mexico
10–30 cm (4–12 in): 1 pinnate Trop.: Terr.
A small species with slender fronds which are some-

Adiantum diaphanum

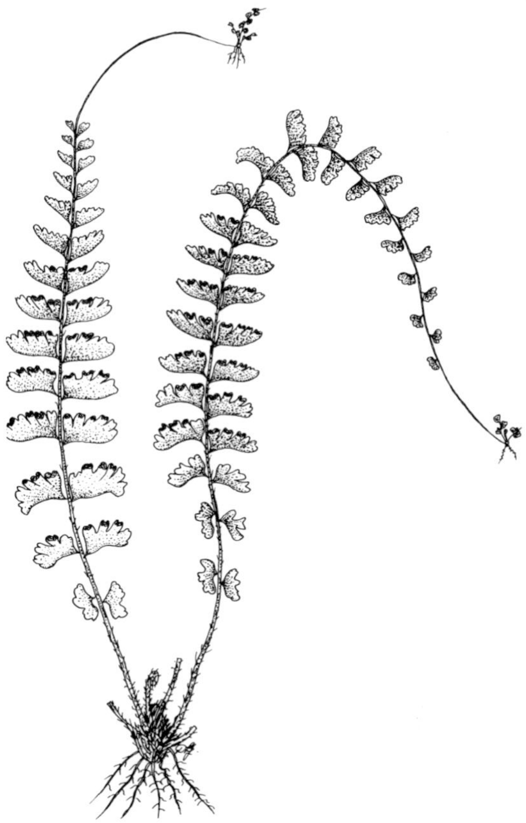

Adiantum edgeworthii

times proliferous at the tip. It grows in rock crevices and on clay embankments, frequently in colonies. The segments have very sharply-toothed margins. Plants are easily grown but are very cold sensitive.

Adiantum diaphanum Filmy Maidenhair
Australia, New Zealand, Fiji, Norfolk Island, New Guinea, China, Japan
5–25 cm (2–10 in): 1–2 pinnate Trop.–Temp.: Terr.
A small growing, colony-forming species which favours moist to wet and shady conditions. Plants are often to be seen on dripping boulders and cliff faces close to streams. Despite its delicate appearance this species is a surprisingly hardy fern and one which really thrives in cultivation. It reproduces prolifically and quickly fills a container with fronds. Likes shady conditions, an acid soil mix and plenty of moisture. Propagates easily from division.

Adiantum edgeworthii
China, India, Thailand, Japan, Philippines
10–30 cm (4–12 in): 1 pinnate Trop.: Terr.
This species is very similar to *A. caudatum* and the two are frequently confused in cultivation. The pinnae of *A. edgeworthii* are much more shallowly lobed and the plants are more tropical in their requirements. New fronds are reddish. This species makes a very attractive specimen for a hanging container.

Adiantum excisum Chilean Maidenhair
South America
30–50 cm (12–20 in): 2 pinnate Trop.–S.Trop.: Terr.
The specific name of this species arises from the deeply cut margins of the broad segments. It is a handsome fern with prominently flexuose rachises. Grows easily in cultivation, with the plants needing ample light in a neutral to alkaline soil mix of free drainage. A few forms are grown.

'Rubrum' — a striking form with dark reddish-brown mature fronds. New fronds by contrast are pale yellow-green. Plants are fertile.

Adiantum formosum Black-stem Maidenhair
Australia, New Zealand
60–120 cm (24–48 in): 2–3 pinnate S.Trop.–Temp.: Terr.
This is a truly beautiful maidenhair which forms extensive colonies by virtue of its long-creeping underground rhizomes. The tall, freely branched fronds are borne at widely spaced intervals and are a lovely verdant green. Plants like acid, organically rich loam in a shady situation.

Adiantum formosum Photo D. L. Jones

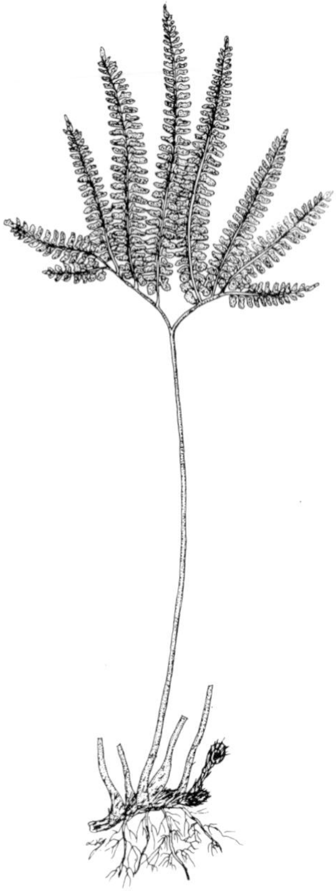

Adiantum hispidulum

Adiantum formosum

Adiantum henslovianum
South America, Galapagos Islands
20–50 cm (8–20 in): 2 pinnate Trop.: Terr.

A rarely cultivated species which is characterized by its very thin-textured, even membranous segments which overlap the rachis. Plants grow easily in cultivation but are very tropical in their requirements and need a neutral to alkaline potting mix.

Adiantum hispidulum Rosy Maidenhair
Australia, India, Malaysia, New Zealand, Polynesia, Africa
30–50 cm (12–20 in): 2–3 pinnate Trop.–Temp.: Terr.

A widespread and rather variable fern that is highly regarded in cultivation because of its hardiness and adaptability. It will grow in good or poor soils providing the drainage is unimpeded and from shady to exposed situations. Also makes an attractive container plant. Plants are generally very cold hardy. New fronds are a bright rosy pink and in spring may be produced in a flush.

Adiantum jordanii Californian Maidenhair
North America (west coast), Mexico
40–60 cm (16–24 in): 2 pinnate Temp.–S.Trop.: Terr.

Adiantum hispidulum Photo D. L. Jones

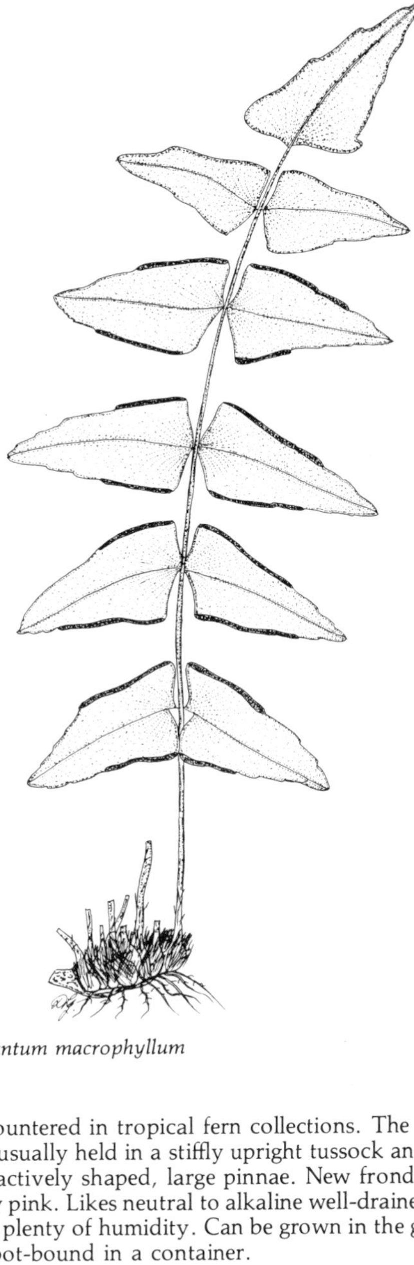

Adiantum macrophyllum

This maidenhair has the reputation of being difficult to grow and it is certainly very intolerant of any change or disturbance in its environment. Plants are very sensitive to over-wet or waterlogged soils. They can be grown in a pot or the ground and need brightly lit conditions.

Adiantum latifolium
Central and South America, Mexico, West Indies
30–70 cm (12–28 in): 2 pinnate Trop.: Terr.

A large maidenhair with a long-creeping, cord-like rhizome. The fronds are conspicuously glaucous underneath and are carried on a long, thick stipe. Cultivation requirements are for bright light, warmth and a neutral to alkaline soil.

Adiantum macrophyllum
Central and South America, Mexico, West Indies
20–50 cm (8–20 in): 1 pinnate Trop.–S.Trop.: Terr.

A distinctive maidenhair which is commonly encountered in tropical fern collections. The fronds are usually held in a stiffly upright tussock and have attractively shaped, large pinnae. New fronds are a rosy pink. Likes neutral to alkaline well-drained soils and plenty of humidity. Can be grown in the ground or pot-bound in a container.

Adiantum hispidulum

Adiantum × 'Mairisii'
Cultivar
30–60 cm (12–24 in): 2–3 pinnate Temp.–S.Trop.: Terr.

A hybrid maidenhair raised at an English nursery in the 19th century. It has as one of its parents *A. capillus-veneris* but the other parent is uncertain. It has proved to be a hardy fern tolerating cold climatic conditions and succeeding well in pots or a protected situation in the garden.

Adiantum monochlamys
Japan, China, Korea
20–60 cm (8–24 in): 2–3 pinnate S.Trop.–Temp.: Terr.

In nature this species often grows on earth banks with the fronds hanging. It is a neat maidenhair with wedge-shaped pinnules which are strongly toothed on the outer margins. Requires an acid, loamy soil in a protected situation. New growth is reported to be pinkish.

Adiantum pedatum 'Japonicum' Photo W. R. Elliot

Adiantum patens
Central and South America
20–80 cm (8–32 in): 2–3 pinnate Trop.: Terr.

This maidenhair grows in deciduous forests at medium to high altitudes. Plants can be grown in a pot of well-drained neutral to alkaline mixture and prefer high humidity with adequate air movement. They are very cold sensitive.

Adiantum pedatum American Maidenhair
North America, Canada, Alaska, North India, Japan
30–50 cm (12–20 in): 2–3 pinnate Temp.: Terr.

A hardy fern which thrives in cold districts, but which is very difficult to grow in areas with a warm to hot climate. Plants may be deciduous in cold regions. They like shady conditions and plenty of moisture and are best grown in the ground as they dislike being pot-bound. Acid organically-rich loams are very suitable and the plants appreciate applications of surface mulches. This is a variable species consisting of two botanical varieties and a subspecies. Many forms are in cultivation and there seems to be much confusion as to their identity.

var. *aleuticum* – a form from Canada, Alaska and the states of north-western USA in which the branches of the fronds are strongly ascending and have fewer, more deeply-lobed pinnules. Deciduous and very cold hardy.

var. *subpumilum* – a dwarf form originating from north-western North America and Vancouver Island off Canada. Fronds are somewhat glaucous and pinnules overlap to give a crowded impression. Very adaptable in cultivation. Comes true from spore.

ssp. *calderi* – an upright form from north-eastern North America. Plants form a crowded clump and the fronds are glaucous with fairly small pinnules.

'Asiaticum' – a form with drooping fronds.

'Imbricatum' – another form often confused with var. *aleuticum*. It has crowded, stiffly erect fronds which are markedly glaucous. Attractive when planted among rocks.

'Japonicum' – a form from Japan with pinkish-bronze new fronds.

'Miss Sharples' – a form with yellowish-green new fronds.

'Montanum' – compact grower.

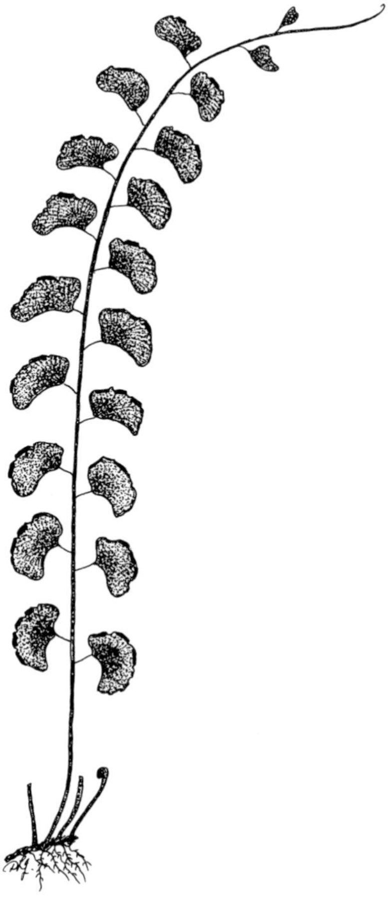

Adiantum philippense

Adiantum peruvianum is commonly called the Silver Dollar Fern Photo D. L. Jones

Adiantum pentadactylon
South and Central America, Mexico
60–80 cm (24–32 in): 3 pinnate Trop.: Terr.
A large growing, coarse maidenhair for the tropics. It is similar in many respects to *A. trapeziforme* but has deeply-lobed segments with toothed margins. Plants are very cold sensitive and can be grown in a large container or in the ground. Fronds may be damaged by excessive overhead watering, turning an unattractive rusty brown.

'Funkii' — a form with pendulous fronds and deeply lobed segments.

'Sanctae Catherinae' — erect fronds with deeply cut segments. Fronds have a distinctive, strong smell.

Adiantum peruvianum Silver Dollar Fern
South America
80–100 cm (32–40 in): 2 pinnate Trop.–S.Trop.: Terr.
A beautiful maidenhair which is prized for its new fronds which are silvery pink, almost with a metallic sheen. Plants like humidity and air movement in a brightly lit situation and neutral to alkaline soils. They are dormant during winter and at this time must be watered sparingly.

Adiantum philippense
Pantropical
10–50 cm (4–20 in): 1 pinnate Trop.: Terr.
This is a very widespread fern that is popularly grown in the tropics, where it may freely naturalize gardens, ferneries etc. In nature it grows around rocks and on embankments and is usually deciduous. Frequently, the frond tips take root and produce a plantlet on each. Plants are very cold sensitive and look particularly appealing in a hanging container.

Adiantum poiretii
Africa, Madagascar, Central and South America, India
20–80 cm (8–32 in): 2–4 pinnate Trop.–S.Trop.: Terr.
A widely distributed maidenhair found in rocky forested areas. It is an attractive species with entire, rounded segments but is not commonly grown. Requires well-drained soil and bright light.

Adiantum polyphyllum
South America, West Indies
80–150 cm (32–60 in): 2–3 pinnate Trop.: Terr.
New fronds of this species are pale pink and contrast with the bright green of mature fronds. Plants grow readily in the tropics and may even become weedy. Can be grown in a large container but because of its size and vigour should perhaps be grown in the ground.

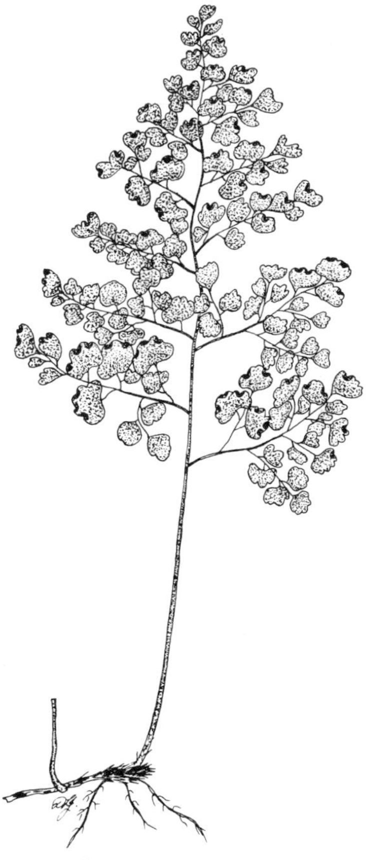

Adiantum poiretii

Adiantum princeps
Central and South America
60–120 cm (24–48 in): 3–4 pinnate Trop.: Terr.

A large growing maidenhair found in shaded forests. It is unusual in that the pinnules are shed completely from ageing fronds leaving only the skeletonized framework of rachises. Plants grow readily in an alkaline soil mix but need warmth and brightly lit conditions.

Adiantum pubescens
Australia, New Zealand, Sri Lanka, Fiji, New Caledonia, New Hebrides
20–50 cm (8–20 in): 2 pinnate Trop.–S.Trop.: Terr.

This species is similar in most respects to *A. hispidulum*, and can only really be distinguished by the thin, much less rigid hairs. It is a very hardy fern that forms an attractive clump of fronds. Likes an acid, organically rich soil and a brightly lit or partially sunny situation.

Adiantum polyphyllum Photo D. L. Jones

Adiantum raddianum

Adiantum pulverulentum
Central and South America, Mexico, West Indies
30–100 cm (12–40 in): 2 pinnate Trop.: Terr.

A species belonging to rainforests and usually growing along stream banks. The stipes and rachises are covered with a mixture of hairs and scales and each frond ends in a long segment. Fronds are dark green and attractive. Plants are very tropical in their requirements and need a neutral to alkaline soil mix.

Adiantum raddianum Maidenhair Fern
Central and South America, Mexico, West Indies
15–60 cm (6–24 in): 2–3 pinnate Temp.–S.Trop.: Terr.

This is the most commonly grown maidenhair in the world and it is now naturalized in many countries. It is renowned for its variability, with over 60 cultivars named and more selected or produced each year by fern fanciers. In nature it grows in rocky situations and frequently on bluffs and cliff faces. The cultivars vary in their cultural requirements with some liking acid soils and the majority liking neutral to alkaline soils. All need good drainage and fairly bright light. They are commonly grown in pots but some of the hardier cultivars can be grown in the ground.

'Bridal Veil' — drooping fronds with small, tear-drop shaped segments. Useful in a basket. Fronds rot readily if overwatered. Fertile.

'Dissected Leaflet' — upright fronds with skeletonized segments. Requires some warmth. Alkaline soil. Fertile.

'Elegans' — lobed, wedge-shaped segments, the terminal segments deeply-lobed. Easy to grow. Raised in England in 1885. Fertile.

'Fragrantissimum' — vigorous form with deep green fronds and toothed segments. Can be grown in the ground or a pot. Fertile.

'Fritz Luth' – very popular cultivar with bunched, stiff erect fronds and overlapping segments. Cold hardy. Decorative in a pot. Originated in Switzerland. Fertile.

'Goldelse' – large form with deeply-lobed, wavy segments, pink to red new growth. Sterile.

'Gracillimum' – pendulous, finely-divided fronds with small to large segments. New fronds pink. Good in hanging basket. Fertile.

'Lambertianum' – finely-divided segments with prominent yellow veins which give a variegated appearance. Segments often twisted or contorted. Fertile.

'Lawsonianum' – strong grower with delicate lacy fronds. Good for specimen culture or in the ground. Fertile.

'Micropinnulum' – long weeping fronds with tiny segments. Useful in hanging baskets. Fronds rot easily if kept too wet. Fertile.

'Old Lace' – lacy segments due to lobing. Doesn't like hot weather. Fertile.

'Pacific Maid' – large, erect fronds with broad, overlapping, deeply-lobed segments. Spectacular flush of fronds in spring. Fertile. Very hardy in temperate regions.

'Pacottii' – small form with erect, compact congested fronds with deeply-lobed segments. Hardy and easy to grow. Fertile.

'Variegatum' – upright fronds, the segments flecked with white variegation. Grows easily. Collect spore only from strongly variegated fronds. Fertile.

'Weigandii' – compact form with congested, erect fronds and small, deeply-cut segments. Hardy and easily grown. Fertile.

Adiantum reniforme
Africa (Kenya), Tenerife, Madeira, Canary Islands
5–15 cm (2–6 in): entire Temp.: Terr.

An unusual maidenhair with simple, undivided fronds. Each is rounded to kidney-shaped and terminates a slender, wiry black stalk. Plants can be grown easily in an alkaline potting mix well fortified with leaf mould. They like an open airy position and greatly resent hot, stuffy weather (cold nights are very acceptable). In nature the species grows in colonies in the scant protection of rocks and boulders.

Adiantum seemannii
Central and South America, Mexico
30–60 cm (12–24 in): 1–2 pinnate Trop.: Terr.

A very attractive maidenhair with large ovate pinnae which are prominently glaucous underneath. The pinnae of the sterile fronds have prominently toothed margins while those on fertile fronds are entire. Plants are very tropical in their cultural requirements and need a neutral to alkaline soil mix.

Adiantum silvaticum Photo D. L. Jones

Adiantum silvaticum
Australia
40–80 cm (16–32 in): 2–3 pinnate S.Trop.–Temp.: Terr.

An attractive maidenhair with bright green spreading fronds and thinly-textured segments. In nature it grows in cool shady forests and likes similar conditions in cultivation. Plants do not like to dry out and prefer organically-rich acid soil.

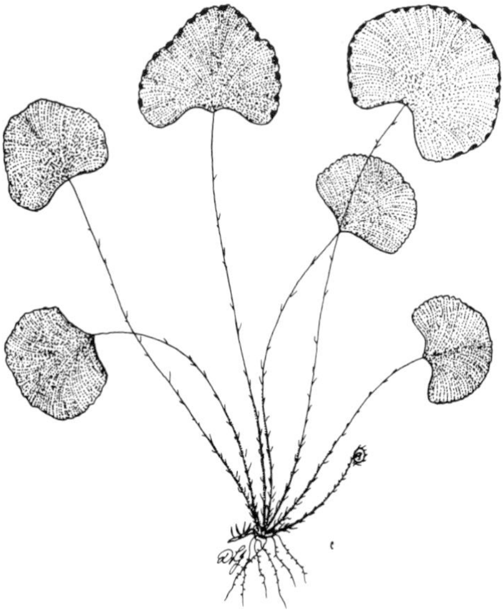

Adiantum reniforme

Adiantum tenerum
Florida, Central and South America, West Indies
30–90 cm (12–36 in): 3–5 pinnate Trop.–S.Trop.: Terr.

This maidenhair is a favourite in tropical regions, and in such conditions it thrives almost to the extent of becoming weedy. It can be grown easily in a pot of fibrous mixture with an alkaline to neutral reaction. Plants like plenty of light but for best appearance should be sheltered from hot sun. In the tropics the species frequently colonizes the mortar in old walls. This is a variable fern with many choice cultivars selected by fern fanciers.

'Bessoniae' – stiff erect leathery fronds with congested segments. Fertile.

'Farleyense' – found naturally in 1865 at Barbados. Renowned for its drooping fronds and large segments with beautifully ruffled and crisped margins. Difficult to grow to perfection. Partially fertile.

'Fergusonii' – deeply-lobed segments with the terminal ones fused together. New growth pink. Fertile.

'Gloriosum Roseum' – arching to pendulous fronds with relatively small, wavy segments. New growth a colourful pink. Fertile.

'Lady Moxam' – large weeping fronds with broad, wavy segments. Partially fertile.

'Marsha's Pride' – segments deeply cut into lobes, terminal segments fused. Easy to grow. Fertile.

'Scutum Roseum' – upright fronds with very broad, crowded segments. New growth a very colourful pink. Easy to grow but likes warmth. Fertile.

Adiantum × tracyi
North America (west coast)
40–60 cm (16–24 in): 2–3 pinnate Temp.–S.Trop.: Terr.

A sporadic natural hybrid between *A. jordanii* and *A. pedatum*. The progeny are sterile but adapt well in cultivation and are very tolerant of cold conditions. Because plants are sterile they must be propagated by vegetative techniques.

Adiantum trapeziforme Diamond Maidenhair
Central and South America, Mexico, West Indies
50–200 cm (20–80 in): 2–3 pinnate Trop.–S.Trop.: Terr.

A very large and attractive maidenhair which is commonly grown in the tropics, where it may readily naturalize itself in gardens and ferneries. Because of its large size plants are best grown in the ground. Will tolerate considerable sun and likes neutral to alkaline soils.

Adiantum venustum Evergreen Maidenhair
India, Canada
30–80 cm (12–32 in): 3–4 pinnate Temp.–S.Trop.: Terr.

Adiantum tenerum 'Farleyense'

Adiantum tenerum 'Lady Moxam'

An attractive fern of the Himalayas where it grows among rocks at high altitudes. The fronds are large and coarsely divided with the segments prominently toothed and glaucous beneath. Plants are very cold hardy and can be grown in pots or sheltered situations in the ground. A useful ground covering species. Flushes of new croziers are very decorative.

Adiantum villosum
Central and South America, West Indies
60–150 cm (24–60 in): 2 pinnate Trop.: Terr.

A tall species which forms tussocks of erect fronds, each of which bears large, dark green, sharply pointed segments. In nature it occurs on shady stream banks and among rocks. Plants are somewhat slow growing and are very cold sensitive.

25 The spleenworts

genus *Asplenium*

A popular group of ferns prized for their frond symmetry, frond texture and sheen and neat growth habit. They generally succeed very well in cultivation and include many highly decorative ferns.

Habitat

Aspleniums may grow as terrestrials, especially along stream banks, but their favoured habitat is on large, mossy boulders. Epiphytes are also common in the genus and grow attached to the bark of trees or in branch junctions or in the fibrous root system of clumps of larger epiphytes. A unique group of terrestrials grows in exposed sites on the coastlines of many countries. A distinctive tropical group (the Bird's-nest Ferns) has large entire fronds which radiate in a tussock and act as litter collectors, e.g. *A. nidus*. These types mainly grow in rainforest. Aspleniums are generally common in rainforests, ranging from lowland to montane. A few species grow in exposed alpine regions, e.g. *A. trichomanes*. Most aspleniums grow in a moist, humid environment but a few can withstand 4–6 months of dry weather.

Cultivation

Uses

Many species of *Asplenium* have been introduced into cultivation and some have become firmly entrenched in the nursery trade and are sold in many countries. Some species of *Asplenium* have proved to be very difficult to grow and others are very slow growing. Most are long-lived ferns.

Aspleniums make excellent pot subjects and prefer to be underpotted rather than overpotted. The larger growing types can be used in tubs, e.g. *A. oblongifolium, A. australasicum*. Many epiphytic species are well suited to basket culture, especially those with drooping fronds, (e.g. *A. bulbiferum, A. polyodon*). Some species are excellent for indoor decoration (*A. dimorphum, A. simplicifrons*). Robust, large growing species are useful subjects in a general garden situation (*A. oblongifolium, A. scleroprium*), and the more delicate types can be grown in rockeries, walls etc. (*A. adiantum-nigrum, A. trichomanes*).

Soil Types

In the garden Aspleniums and their relatives need well-drained loam fortified with organic matter. Most species like an acid pH (5.5–6.5) but some require neutral to alkaline conditions. Organic mulches are very beneficial.

Potting Mix

An open but fibrous mix well endowed with organic matter is generally suitable. A mix well fortified with tree-fern fibre or osmunda fibre is usually to their liking. As a group they resent poor drainage and must be repotted as soon as the mix shows signs of breaking down.

Watering

Aspleniums like plenty of water during the warm growing months but are best kept on the dry side during winter. This is especially important in temperate regions where winter temperatures are low and the photoperiod short.

Fertilizing

Slow-release fertilizers in the potting mix are beneficial. Potted plants also respond to liquid fertilizers applied during the warm, growing months. Plants in the ground like a spring dressing of blood and bone, well-rotted animal manure or compost.

Situation

Aspleniums generally like well lit conditions but must be protected from excessive hot sun. Exposure to morning sun or filtered sun is ideal. They also need fairly high humidity and appreciate air movement, but not excessive wind, draughts or stagnant conditions. Frosts are tolerated by the hardy species from temperate regions but are very damaging to those from the tropics. In temperate regions these types will need the protection of a heated greenhouse.

Asplenium adiantum-nigrum

Propagation

Aspleniums can be readily raised from fresh spore. Some people have difficulty with these ferns in determining when the sporangia are ripe for picking. Each sorus is elongated and protected by an indusium attached by one margin. The best time to collect spores is when a few sporangia are protruding from the edge of the indusium. Sori that have a fluffy appearance are well past dispersal.

Many spleenworts produce plantlets on their fronds and these are a very useful means of propagation (see page 131).

SPECIES AND CULTIVARS

Asplenium adiantum-nigrum Black Spleenwort
Europe, Africa, Asia, North America, Hawaii
20–50 cm (8–20 in): 2–3 pinnate Temp.: Terr.

A very widespread spleenwort which usually grows in rock crevices and shady, dry earth banks. It is a favourite among fern growers because it is fairly easy to cultivate and has an attractive neat appearance. The fronds are dark shiny green and thick-textured. Plants can be grown in a rockery or small pot of fibrous neutral to slightly alkaline mixture.

Asplenium aethiopicum Shredded Spleenwort
Africa, Australia, Asia
20–50 cm (8–20 in): 2 pinnate Temp.–Trop.: Terr.–Epi.

A variable fern, some forms of which are adaptable to cultivation, others are difficult. Plants are notable for their finely-dissected leathery fronds. An open fibrous mixture and a relatively small pot are needed. Plants appreciate air movement and should not be overwatered.

Asplenium alternans (alt. **Ceterach dalhousiae**)
North India, Mexico, North America (Arizona)
5–15 cm (2–6 in): pinnatifid Temp.–S.Trop.: Terr.

A neat little fern which forms a small rosette of dark green fronds. Plants are attractive when planted among rocks. They need well drained, friable soil and protection from frosts. This species may be included in the genus *Ceterach* or *Ceterachopsis* by some authors.

Asplenium antiguum
Japan
50–100 cm (20–40 in): entire Temp.–S.Trop.: Epi.

A fairly cold-hardy fern, the fronds of which form a loose rosette. Each frond is fairly narrow and tapers gradually to each end. Plants grow readily in a pot

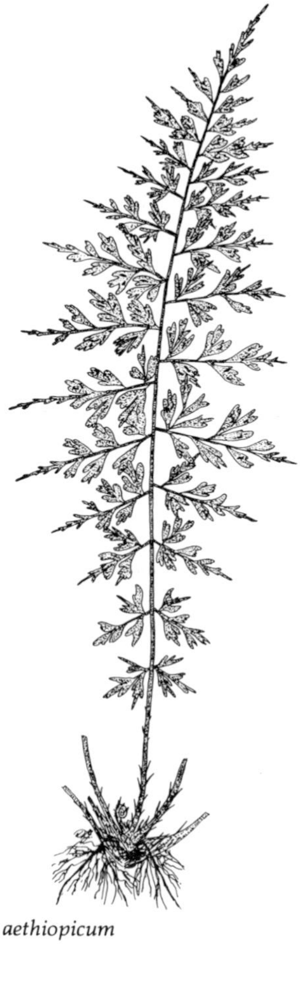

Asplenium aethiopicum

Asplenium auritum

of coarse, fibrous mixture and could perhaps be grown on rocks in a garden.

Asplenium attenuatum Slender Spleenwort
Australia
15–30 cm (6–12 in): entire–1 pinnate Temp.–Trop.: Terr.

A colonizing fern which produces a plantlet from the tip of each frond resulting in linked chains. Forms with entire or variously lobed fronds are known. Attractive as a rockery plant or in a small pot or basket of fibrous mixture.

Asplenium aureum (alt. **Ceterach aureum**)
Canary Islands, Madeira
10–45 cm (4–18 in): pinnatifid Temp.–S.Trop.: Terr.

This species is similar in appearance to *A. ceterach*, but is generally larger growing. The leathery fronds are yellow-green with the underside densely scaly. Plants can be grown in a small pot of neutral mix or perhaps a limestone rockery.

Asplenium auritum
Florida, Central and South America
20–40 cm (8–16 in): 1 pinnate Trop.–S.Trop.: Epi.

An attractive fern with thick leathery fronds of a dark green or slightly glaucous colouration, borne in a compact clump. Plants require excellent drainage in a coarse mix and should not be overpotted. An extremely variable species of many forms.

Asplenium australasicum growing in a blister cut from a eucalypt Photo D. L. Jones

Asplenium australasicum Bird's-nest Fern
Australia, Norfolk Island, New Caledonia, Fiji, Tahiti
50–200 cm (20–80 in): entire Trop.–Temp.: Epi.–Terr.

A very robust and strong growing Bird's-nest Fern which adapts extremely well to cultivation. Can be grown in the garden on rocks or in a dryish position or as a tub plant in a coarse mixture. Very adaptable and long-lived.

'Multilobum' — is a cultivar with lobed fronds. A form with forked frond tips is also known.

Asplenium belangeri
Malaysia, Indonesia, Borneo
20–50 cm (8–20 in): 2 pinnate Trop.–S.Trop.: Epi.

An outstanding fern prized for its delicately-dissected fronds which radiate in a rosette. The fronds

Asplenium australasicum

Asplenium bulbiferum Photo D. L. Jones

are somewhat leathery in texture and are quite shiny on well-grown plants. An ideal basket or pot fern, the species requires a fibrous free-draining mixture and continual protection from slugs and snails which find its tissues very appetizing.

Asplenium billotii
Europe
10–30 cm (4–12 in): 2 pinnate Temp.: Terr.

A dwarf to small species with bright green fronds. Plants can be grown in a small pot of fibrous, acid mix, or in a shady position outside. They will tolerate very cold climates (remaining green) but need continual protection against slugs and snails.

Asplenium bulbiferum Mother Spleenwort/Hen and Chicken Fern
Australia, New Zealand
50–120 cm (20–48 in): 2–3 pinnate Temp.–S.Trop.: Terr.–Epi.

A very familiar fern which is a popular item of the nursery trade in many countries. Excellent for indoor decoration and makes an impressive basket specimen. Very forgiving of neglect and adaptable to many garden situations including those in very cold climates. Attractive in a rockery. Easily propagated from plantlets.

Asplenium ceterach (alt. **Ceterach officinarum**) Rusty-back Fern
India, Africa, Europe
5–20 cm (2–8 in): pinnatifid Temp.: Terr.

A dwarf fern which grows in rock crevices and frequently naturalizes the mortar in old walls. Fronds are yellow-green, leathery and the underside is densely clothed with silvery brown scales. It is a very drought resistant little fern which can be grown in a small pot or limestone rockery. It may be included in the genus *Ceterach* by some authors.

Asplenium cheilosorum
Thailand, China, Japan, Philippines, Borneo, Malaysia
25–40 cm (10–16 in): 1 pinnate Trop.–S.Trop.: Terr.

The slender fronds of this species have overlapping pinnae the margins of which are deeply toothed or lobed. The rhizome is creeping and the species forms clumps on rocks or earth banks. It can be grown in a small pot of coarse, fibrous mixture.

Asplenium cristatum
Florida, Central and South America, West Indies
30–60 cm (12–24 in): 2 pinnate Trop.: Epi.

Young fronds of this species are pale, yellowish green and they mature to dark green. They are thinly-textured, delicately divided and are borne in a clump at the end of an erect rhizome. Plants can be grown in a pot of coarse, fibrous mixture fortified with lime.

Asplenium cuneatum
South America, Malaysia, Philippines, Indonesia, New Guinea, Australia, Polynesia
30–75 cm (12–30 in): 2–3 pinnate Trop.–S.Trop.: Epi.

An extremely variable fern which is found in a range of forms; some with broad fronds, others relatively narrow; some proliferous; some with erect fronds, others weeping. A few of the forms are excellent for cultivation in baskets, others grow well in the ground in a loamy soil.

Asplenium cymbifolium
Indonesia, Borneo, Philippines, New Guinea, Samoa
50–100 cm (20–40 in): entire Trop.–S.Trop.: Epi.

Tropical jungles are the home of this Bird's-nest Fern

A nice potful of the Rusty Back Fern, *Asplenium ceterach*
Photo W. R. Elliot

Asplenium cuneatum is an attractive basket fern
Photo D. L. Jones

Asplenium dimorphum has variable-shaped fronds
Photo D. L. Jones

Asplenium dimorphum

which has very broad, dilated bases to the fronds. In large plants these bases overlap and form a watertight receptacle. Plants are very decorative in a pot or tub and can be grown as a garden plant in the tropics or a greenhouse plant in cold climates. Requires a fibrous, acid mixture.

Asplenium daucifolium Mauritius Spleenwort
Mauritius, Madagascar
30–60 cm (12–24 in): 3–4 pinnate Trop.–S.Trop.: Terr.

A handsome spleenwort with long, arching, finely dissected fronds which are liberally sprinkled with plantlets in the manner of *A. bulbiferum*. It makes an excellent basket plant but can be equally well grown in a dry, shady position in the ground.

Asplenium dimorphum Three-in-one Fern
Norfolk Island
50–80 cm (20–32 in): 3 pinnate Trop.–S.Trop.: Terr.

A very popular fern in cultivation especially in tropical regions where it grows readily as a garden plant. The sterile fronds have broad bright green segments and contrast markedly with the fertile fronds which are finely dissected and lacy. Plants grow readily in a loose open potting mix or in well drained garden soil.

Asplenium ebenoides (alt. **Asplenosorus×ebenoides**)
Scott's Spleenwort
North America (eastern states)
25–50 cm (10–20 in): 1 pinnate Temp.: Terr.

A sporadic natural hybrid between *Asplenium platyneuron* and *A. rhizophyllum* (*Camptosorus rhizophyllus*). The progeny may be sterile or fertile and both types are in cultivation. Requires a fibrous, humus-rich mixture of neutral to alkaline reaction.

Asplenium excisum Scalloped Spleenwort
Japan, Malaysia, New Guinea, Australia
20–60 cm (8–24 in): 1 pinnate Trop.: Terr.-Epi.

A very slow growing but beautiful fern found in intermediate to highland rainforest, often in wet soil. The fronds are dark green, leathery in texture and with a pleasant arching habit. Plants need warm moist conditions in a pot or basket and must not be overpotted.

Asplenium falcatum=A. polyodon

Asplenium flabellifolium Necklace Fern
Australia, New Zealand
10–30 cm (4–12 in): 1 pinnate Temp.-S.Trop.

In nature this species forms large spreading colonies frequently in the protection of boulders. The fronds have a weak trailing habit and root at the tip. A decorative fern for a rockery or small container, but readily damaged by slugs and snails. Very cold hardy. Forms with attractively lobed segments are known.

Asplenium flaccidum Weeping Spleenwort
20–100 cm (8–40 in) 1–2 pinnate Temp.-S.Trop.: Epi.

This delightful fern is renowned for its strongly weeping and delicately lobed fronds. An excellent basket plant in a coarse, fibrous mixture. Likes humid conditions with some air movement. Extremely variable in growth habit with some forms having a few long slender fronds, others being shorter and compact.

Asplenium fontanum Smooth Rock Spleenwort
Europe
8–12.5 cm (3–5 in): 1–2 pinnate Temp.: Terr.

A hardy dwarf fern from mountainous areas where it grows in rock crevices (often limestone). Plants form a dense small clump of slender dark green fronds with toothed segments. They can be grown amongst rocks or in a small pot of alkaline mix. Very susceptible to attack by slugs and snails.

Asplenium hookerianum
New Zealand, Australia
10–25 cm (4–10 in): 1–2 pinnate Temp.: Terr.

A delicate fern with finely-divided lacy fronds of a thin texture. It is quite variable with some attractive forms known. Plants prefer moist conditions and do not like to dry out. Well suited to terrarium or Wardian Case culture. Plants are very cold tolerant.

A large plant of *Asplenium oblongifolium*
Photo D. L. Jones

Asplenium flaccidum

Asplenium milnei Photo D. L. Jones

Asplenium hybridum
Mediterranean
5–20 cm (2–8 in): pinnatifid Temp.: Terr.
This is a sporadic natural hybrid between *A. ceterach* (*Ceterach officinarum*) and *A. sagittatum* (*Phyllitis sagittatum*). The progeny are fertile and can be grown readily in an acid, humus-rich loam.

Asplenium incisum
China, Japan, Korea
10–30 cm (4–12 in): 1–2 pinnate S.Trop.–Temp.: Terr.
A delightful small fern with narrow, shiny green arching fronds which have deeply incised pinnae and shiny black stipes and rachises. Plants can be grown in a small pot of fibrous, acid mix or in a protected rockery.

Asplenium laserpitiifolium Maidenhair Spleenwort/ Johnstone River Fern
Africa, Seychelles, Indonesia, Australia, Japan
50–150 cm (20–60 in): 3 pinnate Trop.: Epi.
A very decorative fern with large, weeping fronds of a chartaceous texture. It grows in well lit situations in lowland humid rainforest. Plants need heat, humidity and plenty of air movement. A coarse, epiphytic mixture is essential. This species is difficult to grow to perfection, but a well grown plant is eye-catching.

Asplenium lucidum = A. oblongifolium

Asplenium majoricum
Majorca
7.5–15 cm (3–6 in): 1–2 pinnate Temp.: Terr.
A dwarf, dainty fern which is very cold-hardy. Can be grown in a fibrous alkaline mix in a small pot or a shaded rockery.

Asplenium marinum Sea Spleenwort
United Kingdom, Europe, North Africa
20–50 cm (8–20 in): 1 pinnate Temp.: Terr.
Crevices, cliffs, caves and rocky outcrops close to the sea are the haunts of this coastal fern. Plants are most attractive with their glossy, thickly-textured fronds but they can be rather tricky to grow. They require well-drained soil and continual protection from slugs and snails which devour the fronds eagerly. Plants also resent excessive overhead watering.

Asplenium milnei Shining Spleenwort
Lord Howe Island
50–80 cm (20–32 in): 1 pinnate S.Trop.–Temp.: Terr.
A beautiful spleenwort which is characterized by forming dense clumps of shiny dark green, almost leathery fronds. It adapts well to cultivation provided the drainage is free and unimpeded and the soil is fortified with lime or limestone.

Asplenium musifolium
India, Malaysia, New Guinea
50–150 cm (20–60 in): entire Trop.–S.Trop.: Epi.
This fern is frequently propagated and wrongly sold as *A. nidus*. It closely resembles that species but has much broader fronds (to 35 cm [14 in]) that are broadly rounded at the tip, rather than drawn out. It makes a handsome pot subject or garden plant in the tropics.

A small plant of *Asplenium musifolium* Photo D. L. Jones

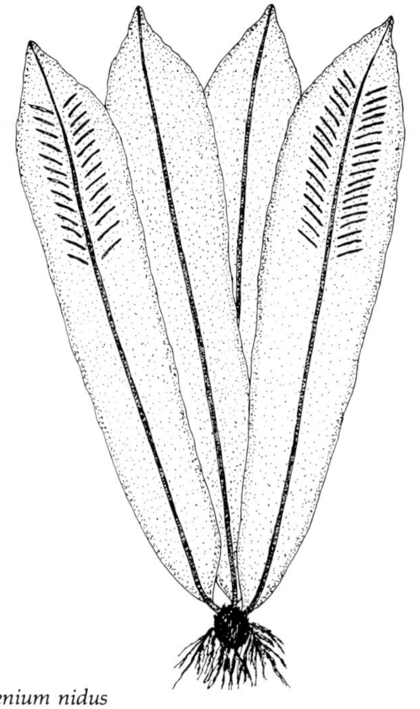

Asplenium nidus

Asplenium nidus Bird's-nest Fern
Pantropical
50–150 cm (20–60 in): entire Trop.–S.Trop.: Epi.

A very widely distributed fern that commonly colonizes trees, rock faces and boulders in tropical jungles. It is a spectacular fern which is popular for its neat rosette of spreading fronds. Readily grown in pots, tubs or among rocks in the garden but needs warm, humid conditions. *A. nidus* is rather variable and forms with lobed fronds are known. Perhaps the most distinctive variation is var. *plicatum* (Lasagne Fern) which has narrow, dark green, distinctly convoluted and pleated fronds.

Asplenium normale
Africa, Asia, Malaysia, New Guinea, Australia, Hawaii, China, Japan
10–30 cm (4–12 in): 1 pinnate Trop.–S.Trop. Terr.–Epi.

A delightful small fern which occurs in rainforests often at high altitudes. Plants are usually found in colonies, often in crevices or among rocks. Fronds are narrow and dark shiny green. Plants adapt well to cultivation, requiring shady moist conditions and can be grown in small pots of acid, humus-rich mix, or in the garden.

Asplenium oblongifolium Shining Spleenwort
New Zealand
30–120 cm (12–48 in); 1 pinnate Temp.–S.Trop.: Terr.

A large, coarse but handsome fern which develops a slowly spreading clump. Fronds are erect or arching, dark green and leathery with purple-black stipes. An excellent long-living fern for a filtered sun situation in the ground or a tub. An annual application of lime is beneficial. It was previously known as *A. lucidum*.

Asplenium oblongifolium

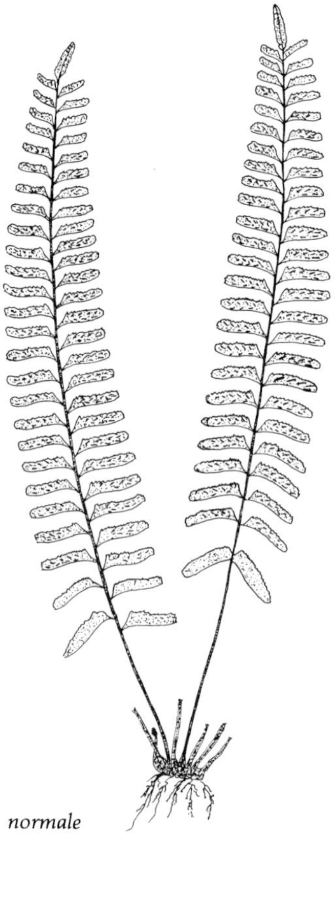

Asplenium normale

Asplenium obtusatum is a very tough fern
Photo D. L. Jones

Asplenium obtusatum Shore Spleenwort
South America, Australia, New Zealand, Pacific Islands
10–60 cm (4–24 in): 1 pinnate Temp.–S.Trop.: Terr.
This species is found on the coastline of many countries, growing within the influence of salt spray. Plants have thick, fleshy, often brittle fronds and may be somewhat difficult to grow to perfection. Requires very well-drained soil fortified with lime or shell grit. Very susceptible to slug and snail damage.

Asplenium oligophlebium
Japan
15–30 cm (6–12 in): 1 pinnate S.Trop.–Temp.: Terr.
This is a colonizing fern which spreads by tip-rooting of the fronds. It is a delightful small species with arching fronds and deeply incised, narrow pinnae. Plants make a useful ground-cover fern for shady conditions in humus-rich soil.

Asplenium paleaceum Chaffy Spleenwort
Australia, New Guinea
20–50 cm (8–20 in): 1 pinnate Trop.–S.Trop.: Terr.
A colony-forming fern proliferating by a vegetative bud located near the apex of each frond. A useful fern for a rockery or a hanging container. Needs an open fibrous mix in a small pot. Once established, plants are quite hardy to dryness. The fronds have a harsh chartaceous texture.

Asplenium paleaceum Photo D. L. Jones

Asplenium pellucidum
Madagascar, India, Malaysia, New Guinea, Australia
30–100 cm (12–40 in): 1 pinnate Trop.: Epi.
A delightful fern from lowland tropical rainforest where it forms clumps of long, graceful fronds. Plants like warm to hot, moist but airy conditions in a fibrous, free-draining mixture containing lime or limestone chips. An ideal basket fern.

Asplenium pinnatifidum (alt. **Asplenosorus** × **pinnatifidus**)
North America (eastern states)
10–15 cm (4–6 in): pinnatifid Temp.: Terr.
This species is a fertile natural hybrid between *A. montanum* and *A. rhizophyllum* (*Camptosorus rhizophyllus*). Plants grow easily in cultivation preferring an acid, humus-rich soil and a shady aspect. Its fronds are sometimes proliferous.

Asplenium platyneuron Ebony Spleenwort
North America (eastern states)
30–50 cm (12–20 in): 1 pinnate Trop.–S.Trop.: Terr.
The herringbone-shaped fronds of this fern impart a general appearance similar to *Nephrolepis cordifolia*. It is, however, a much more desirable fern than that species, with its dark green somewhat glossy fronds. The fertile fronds are more erect and with narrower segments than the sterile fronds. Can be grown in a well-drained rockery or small pot. Plants are very sensitive to waterlogged soil or overwatering and prefer to be kept on the dry side.

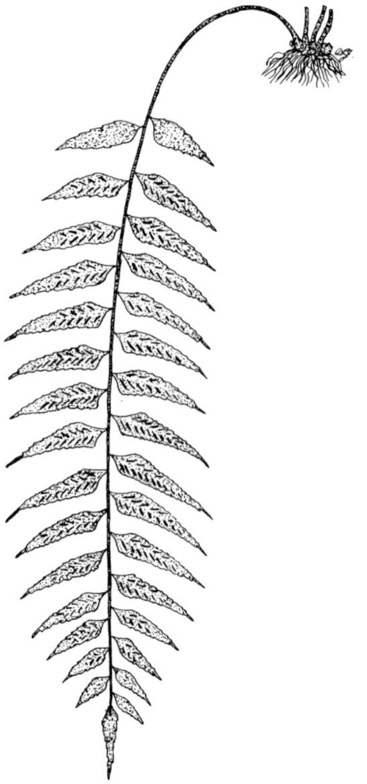

Asplenium polyodon

Asplenium polyodon Weeping Spleenwort/Mare's-tail
Madagascar, India, Malaysia, New Guinea, Australia, New Zealand
30–100 cm (12–40 in): 1–2 pinnate Trop.–Temp.: Terr.–Epi.

This is a most variable fern existing in a wide variety of forms some of which are very beautiful. Those with weeping, pinnate fronds (formerly called *A. falcatum*) make a delightful basket specimen. Plants may be slow growing but are long-lived and require a coarse, well-drained mixture.

Asplenium praemorsum
Mexico, Central and South America
10–50 cm (4–20 in): 2 pinnate Trop.: Epi.

This species has been confused with *A. aethiopicum* but the two are quite distinct although similar. Its fronds are dark green and somewhat leathery or chartaceous in texture and rise up in a fairly sparse rosette. Plants can be grown in a small pot of coarse, fibrous mixture.

Asplenium prolongatum
Japan, China, North India
20–40 cm (8–16 in): 2 pinnate S.Trop.–Temp.: Terr.

A very attractive species which in nature forms colonies by tip-rooting. The relatively narrow, deeply dissected, dark green fronds are leathery to rigid in texture and have an extended proliferous rachis. An excellent ground-cover fern requiring humus-rich acid soil in a shady position.

Asplenium resiliens Black-stemmed Spleenwort
North America (southern states), Central and South America, West Indies
20–30 cm (8–12 in): 1 pinnate Trop.–S.Trop.: Terr.

This is a small species similar in general appearance to *A. trichomanes*. It occurs naturally in shady forests on calcareous rocks. Plants can be grown in a small pot of fibrous, neutral to alkaline mix.

Asplenium rhizophyllum (alt. **Camptosorus rhizophyllus**) Walking Fern (Figure p.133)
North America
5–20 cm (2–8 in): entire Temp.–S.Trop.: Terr.

The most outstanding feature of this fern is the long drawn-out fronds which lie flat on the ground, take root at the tip and produce plantlets. These plantlets develop while still attached and eventually congested colonies form, plants of which will be linked together in series. The species favours shallow soils over rocks, particularly limestone. Plants can be grown readily in a pot or in the garden but need lime added to the soil or potting mix.

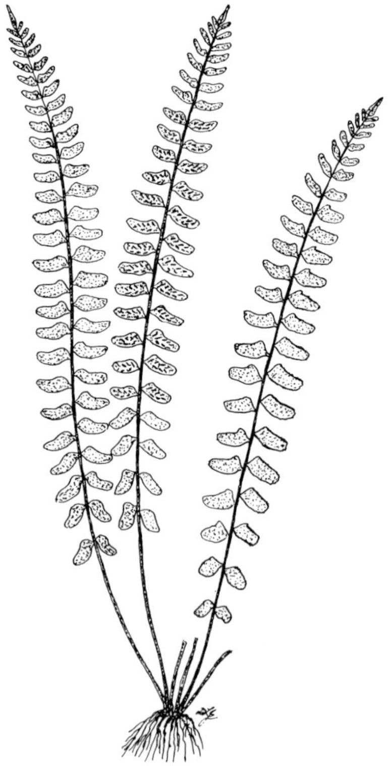

Asplenium resiliens

Asplenium scolopendrium Photo W. R. Elliot

Asplenium ruprechtii (alt. **Camptosorus sibiricus**)
Japan, China, Siberia
5–20 cm (2–8 in): entire Temp.–S.Trop.: Terr.
This fern is very similar in appearance and habit to *A. rhizophyllum* but with narrower fronds which taper more to the base. It is a colony-forming species that likes shady, moist conditions in loamy soil.

Asplenium ruta-muraria Wall Spleenwort
Europe, Asia, North America (northern states)
5–12.5 cm (2–5 in): 2–3 pinnate Temp.: Terr.

Asplenium scleroprium

A dwarf fern which grows in rock crevices and frequently colonizes man-made walls. It is especially fond of limestone and mortar. Can be somewhat tricky to grow in a pot and resents disturbance. Best suited to wall culture, among limestone or weathered mortar.

Asplenium scleroprium
New Zealand
50–80 cm (20–32 in): 1 pinnate Temp.–S.Trop.: Terr.
A coarse, hardy fern which when established will tolerate a fair amount of sun and neglect. In particular it thrives in the sandy soils of coastal regions. Plants are quite attractive with their thickened, fleshy fronds, the segments of which are prominently toothed. In suitable situations they are very long-lived.

Asplenium scolopendrium (alt. **Phyllitis scolopendrium**) Hart's-tongue Fern/Scollies
Europe, Asia, North America (north-eastern states)
20–60 cm (8–24 in): entire Temp.–S.Trop.: Terr.
An extremely widely distributed fern which is one of the most popular in cultivation. In nature it is most common on limestone and calcareous soils although it does also occur on acid types. It is also known as *Phyllitis scolopendrium*. Plants are excellent for pot culture in a lime fortified mix or in a rockery in the garden where they appreciate an annual topdressing of lime. Hart's-tongue Ferns are rather variable and hundreds of cultivars are known, some originating in the wild and others in cultivation.

'Capitatum' — the fronds end in a heavy crest.

'Crispum' — a sterile form with the frond margin deeply frilled like a ruff.

'Crispum Golden Queen' — a form with golden-green frilled fronds.

'Cristatum' — the fronds divide many times and each division ends in a spreading crest.

'Digitatum' — the fronds divide many times and each ends in a flat segment.

'Marginatum' — a form with narrow fronds which have deeply lobed margins.

'Muricatum' — the surface of the frond is pleated and wrinkled.

'Ramo-cristatum' — a crested form with narrow fronds which branch from the base.

'Sagittatum' — the bases of the fronds are strongly lobed imparting a shape like an arrow head.

Asplenium septentrionale Forked Spleenwort
Europe, North Asia, North America (western states)
5–15 cm (2–6 in): forked Temp.: Terr.
A dwarf spleenwort with unusual leathery, forked grass-like fronds. It grows in small compact clumps on rock crevices, frequently at high elevations. Plants are very cold-hardy and can be grown in small pots of well-drained, acid mixture.

Asplenium serratum American Bird's-nest Fern
North America (Florida), Central and South America
30–60 cm (12–24 in): entire Trop.–S.Trop.: Epi.

A large growing, decorative fern with a massive rhizome surrounded by numerous woolly roots. The fronds form an erect rosette and are entire or, more usually, have coarsely toothed margins. They can be grown readily in a pot of coarse mixture and require warm, humid conditions.

Asplenium shuttleworthianum
Polynesia
15–45 cm (6–18 in): 3 pinnate Trop.–S.Trop.: Epi.

This species occurs on a number of islands usually growing on trees or rocks in shady forests. It is similar in general appearance to many other aspleniums. Plants can be grown in a pot or basket of fibrous mix in warm, sheltered conditions.

Asplenium shuttleworthianum Photo D. L. Jones

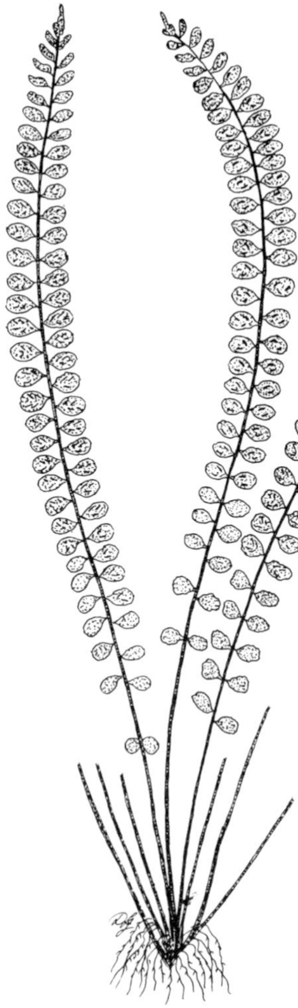

Asplenium trichomanes

Asplenium simplicifrons Narrow-leaf Bird's-nest Fern
Australia
20–60 cm (8–24 in): entire S.Trop.–Trop.: Epi.

A very distinctive spleenwort which grows in moist, shady situations from lowland to highland regions. Plants form an attractive upright rosette of dark green, slender fronds. An ideal pot or basket plant excellent for indoor decoration tolerating quite dark conditions and neglect. Forms with lobed and lacerated fronds are known.

Asplenium tenerum
Malaysia, Sri Lanka, Polynesia, Australia, New Guinea, Japan
40–60 cm (16–24 in): 1 pinnate Trop.–S.Trop.: Epi.

This attractive fern is common in rainforests, growing on trees or rocks. It is rather variable in texture (though usually thick) and some forms may be proliferous while others are not. The fronds are held in a stiff rosette and collect litter. Plants can be grown in a pot of coarse, well-drained mixture.

Asplenium trichomanes Common or Maidenhair Spleenwort
Cosmopolitan
15–40 cm (6–16 in): 1 pinnate Temp.: Terr.

A familiar and popular fern that forms a neat rosette of narrow, dark green fronds. Can be grown in a small pot but is best in a dryish rockery or crevice in a wall, where it receives a fair amount of light. The most commonly grown forms require lime or limestone for best growth, however, ssp. *trichomanes* is a lime-hater. A very cold-hardy fern.

'Cristatum' — a form found in the UK with the apex of each frond repeatedly branched into a crest. Plants are fertile.

'Incisum' — a form with deeply incised segments.

Asplenium unilaterale
Africa, India, China, Japan, Malaysia, New Guinea, Australia
20–30 cm (8–12 in): 1 pinnate Trop.: Terr.–Epi.
Sheltered stream banks and sheltered boulders are the favoured haunt of this attractive spleenwort which has a long, slender, creeping rhizome and neat pendulous fronds. It frequently grows in areas of limestone formation and can be grown in a pot or basket of coarse mixture fortified with lime. Plants need warm, humid conditions and air movement. They are very slow growing.

Asplenium viride Green Spleenwort
Europe, Asia, North America (northern states)
10–15 cm (4–6 in): 1 pinnate Temp.: Terr.
A dwarf fern which is prized for its neat character and verdant green fronds. It is found only on limestone or in calcareous soils and must be grown in soil containing lime. An excellent rockery plant or one for a small pot or a limestone wall.

Asplenium viviparum = A. daucifolium

Asplenosorus × ebenoides – see **Asplenium ebenoides**

Asplenium simplicifrons Photo D. L. Jones

Asplenosorus × pinnatifidus – see **Asplenium pinnatifidum**

Camptosorus rhizophyllus – see **Asplenium rhizophyllum**

Camptosorus sibiricus – see **Asplenium ruprechtii**

Ceterach aureum – see **Asplenium aureum**

Ceterach dalhousiae – see **Asplenium alternans**

Ceterach officinarum – see **Asplenium ceterach**

Ceterachopsis dalhousiae – see **Asplenium alternans**

Phyllitis hybrida – see **Asplenium hybridum**

Phyllitis scolopendrium – see **Asplenium scolopendrium**

26 The polypodies

genera *Anarthropteris, Belvisia, Campyloneurum, Colysis, Crypsinus, Dictymia, Gonophlebium, Lecanopteris, Lemmaphyllum, Loxogramme, Microgramma, Microsorum, Niphidium, Phlebodium, Phymatosorus, Pleopeltis, Polypodium, Pyrrosia, Selliguea*

The ferns dealt with in this chapter all belong to the very large family Polypodiaceae and are affectionately grouped as Polypodies. They are a very important group of ferns with many species being cultivated including a number which are commercial nursery lines. Most species grow easily and are rewarding subjects for cultivation (for the larger growing species in this family see Chapter 27).

Habitat

Polypodies occupy a great range of habitats, from regions with a pronounced dry season to equatorial forests. Most species grow on trees or rocks but many are terrestrial. They are frequently noticeable in brightly lit situations but many species also seek shade and shelter. Some species grow as rheophytes in the beds of streams and others prefer rocks of limestone origin.

Cultivation

Uses

Polypodies are among the most popular of all ferns with growers. This is probably because of their diversity of form and ease of culture. Many species are ideal for baskets and well-grown specimens are highly decorative. They are also quite long-lived and once specimen status is achieved the plants are easy to maintain. Some species can be successfully grown in the ground and add interest because of their different growth form, e.g. *Phlebodium aureum*.

Soil Types

Those Polypodies which will grow in the ground invariably demand excellent drainage. A friable loam is most suitable with the pH varying from acid to slightly alkaline, depending on the species.

Potting Mix

Polypodies (even the terrestrial types) grow well in a coarse epiphytic mixture. Drainage must be excellent and aeration around the roots adequate (see page 176 for suitable materials). Some growers, especially in tropical regions, use pads of *Platycerium* peat to good effect. Those species with a creeping rhizome can also be effectively grown on blocks of tree-fern fibre. Although some Polypodies have an extensive root system most are quite tolerant of periods of dryness and regular repotting is not necessary unless the mixture begins to break down.

Watering

Polypodies like plenty of water while in active growth during warm weather. Plants should not be overwatered during cold spells however, and this is especially true in winter when photoperiods are short and the growth slows or may even stop. During such times the plants may be kept quite dry.

Fertilizing

Polypodies respond to the use of manures and fertilizers particularly during the warm months. Slow-release fertilizers in the potting mix are especially beneficial as are occasional applications of liquid fertilizers. Well-rotted animal manures applied to the surface of the potting mix of specimen plants help to maintain growth. Blood and bone, well-rotted animal manures and compost are suitable for plants in the ground.

Situation

Most Polypodies seem to require exposure to bright light without excessive sun which can cause unattractive bleaching of the fronds. A few (such as species of *Colysis*) seem to need shade but these are in the minority. Species from temperate regions will tolerate light to mild frosts but the tropical species are generally very sensitive to cold. Air movement is important, especially for epiphytic polypodies which will not thrive in stagnant conditions.

Pests

Fern scale seems to be a persistent pest of Polypodies and once established is very difficult to eradicate.

Belvisia mucronata growing in a basket
Photo D. L. Jones

Attacks by caterpillars and aphids are sporadic. Slaters and earwigs may live in the crevices of baskets or in the coarse potting mixture and feed on young roots and rhizomes.

Propagation

Some Polypodies are easy to raise from spore, others are quite difficult. Most sporelings are slow to develop. Many species prefer a coarse, rough surface on which to germinate and the pH could be significant. Sporelings of very hairy species may rot if kept too wet. Judging when the fronds are ripe for spore collection can be very difficult and may require regular examination with the aid of a hand lens. Sori that have a fluffy appearance are well past dispersal.

Polypodies with a creeping rhizome can usually be divided readily. Fast growing types, however, may not form roots on the younger sections of rhizome and it is wise to check that the rhizome has roots attached before severing.

SPECIES AND CULTIVARS

Anarthropteris lanceolata
New Zealand
5–25 cm (2–10 in): entire Temp.–S.Trop.: Epi.

This fern grows in dense patches and looks attractive with its dark green, leathery fronds. Plants can be cultivated but resent disturbance and are very slow to re-establish. Once growing strongly they are easy to maintain. They need a coarse mixture, humidity and air movement.

Belvisia mucronata Needle Fern/Tailed Fern
Malaysia, Sri Lanka, Polynesia, Australia
30–60 cm (12–24 in): entire Trop.–S.Trop.: Epi.

A distinctive fern because of the long slender tailed section at the end of each fertile frond. This is actually the fertile segment of the frond. Makes an attractive basket specimen but plants frequently resent disturbance and may be slow to re-establish after a setback such as division. Needs a coarse mixture, warmth, humidity and air movement.

Campyloneurum angustifolium (alt. **Polypodium angustifolium**) Central American Strap Fern
Mexico, Central and South America
20–70 cm (8–28 in): entire Temp.–Trop.: Epi.

An excellent basket fern with pendulous, dark green, leathery fronds. Although slow, plants are steady growers and once developed as a specimen are easily maintained. Likes a coarse, open mixture in a humid shady situation.

'Corkscrew' — fronds prominently twisted.

'Fimbriatum' — margins of fronds lobed and lacerated.

Campyloneurum phyllitidis (alt. **Polypodium phyllitidis**) Florida Strap Fern
Florida, Mexico, Central and South America, West Indies
30–120 cm (12–48 in): entire Trop.–S.Trop.: Epi.

This species has erect fronds of papery texture that are usually a pale, yellowish green. Plants are easily grown in pots or baskets of a coarse mixture and will tolerate exposure to sun.

Colysis elliptica (alt. **Polypodium ellipticum**)
India, Japan, China, Korea, Philippines
30–100 cm (12–40 in): pinnatifid S.Trop.–Temp.: Terr.

A spreading fern of similar habit and appearance to *C. pothifolia* but the fronds have fewer segments. The fronds are widely separated on the creeping rhizomes imparting a sparse appearance to the clumps. Excellent for planting on banks. Likes shady, moist conditions.

Colysis hemionitidea Photo D. L. Jones

Colysis hemionitidea
China, Japan, Korea, North India
10–30 cm (4–12 in): entire S.Trop.–Temp.: Epi.

This fern has slender, dark green, thickly-textured fronds with wavy margins and prominent veins. The fronds are held erect, are crowded, and have a lustrous appearance when wet. Plants are easily grown in a pot or basket of coarse mixture and like shady, humid conditions.

Colysis pothifolia
Japan, China, Korea
30–100 cm (12–40 in): 1 pinnate S.Trop.–Temp.: Terr.

A spreading fern with erect to arching, deeply lobed dark green fronds. Fronds are widely spaced on the rhizome and the clumps are sparse. An easily grown fern which likes shady, moist conditions.

Colysis pothifolia Photo D. L. Jones

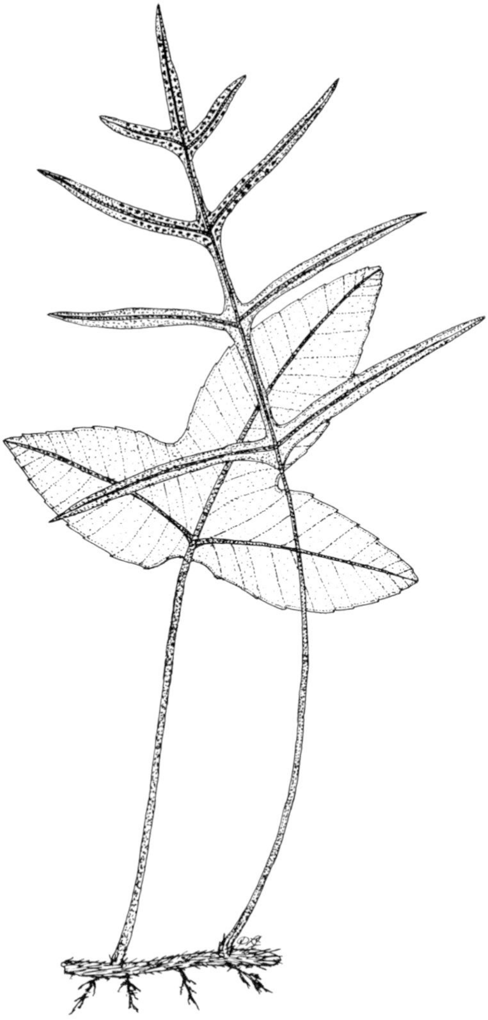

Crypsinus trilobus

Colysis sayeri
Australia, New Guinea
30–80 cm (12–32 in): pinnatifid Trop.–S.Trop.: Epi.

A fern with a remarkable, though superficial resemblance to *Microsorum scandens*. The two can be easily distinguished by the venation and sori. Makes an admirable, long-lived basket plant. Requires a coarse mixture and shady, moist conditions.

Crypsinus trilobus
Malaysia, Philippines, Indonesia
15–25 cm (6–10 in): pinnatifid Trop.–S.Trop.: Epi.

The fertile and barren fronds of this fern are remarkably dissimilar. The barren fronds are most noticeable being broadly tri-lobed, thickly-textured, dark green and shiny. The fertile fronds, by contrast, have 2–4 pairs of narrow segments and are carried erect on long stalks. An easily grown species requiring good light, warmth and humidity in a coarse mixture.

Colysis sayeri in a basket Photo D. L. Jones

Dictymia brownii growing in a tree-fern basket
Photo D. L. Jones

Goniophlebium subauriculatum has strongly weeping fronds
Photo D. L. Jones

Goniophlebium persicifolium Photo D. L. Jones

Dictymia brownii Strap Fern
Australia
15–40 cm (6–16 in): entire Trop.–Temp.: Epi.

The fronds of this fern are slender, leathery and dark green, and are held stiffly erect. They are borne closely on a creeping, very scaly rhizome and are excellent for pots or baskets. Growth is slow but steady. Prefers to be underpotted. Needs a coarse mix, shade, humidity and air movement.

Drymoglossum piloselloides – see **Pyrrosia piloselloides**

Goniophlebium persicifolium (alt. **Polypodium persicifolium**)
South-East Asia, Malaysia, Philippines, Indonesia
100–200 cm (40–80 in): 1 pinnate Trop.–S.Trop.: Epi.

A delightful fern with long, weeping, light green fronds. The segments are spreading and have toothed margins. An excellent basket fern for a warm position. Needs a coarse mixture, humidity and air movement.

Goniophlebium subauriculatum (alt. **Polypodium subauriculatum**)
North India, China, Malaysia, New Guinea, Australia
100–200 cm (40–80 in): 1 pinnate Trop.–Temp.: Epi.–Terr.

One of the best basket ferns available. This species is prized for its long willowy fronds. Plants are very fast growing and adaptable. For best development they need warm, humid conditions with plenty of air movement. Can also be grown in the ground in the tropics and will take sun. Old rhizomes are an interesting chalky-white colour.

'Knightiae' – a form renowned for its deeply-incised and broader segments which may overlap. Highly ornamental and can be developed as a basket specimen. Fronds last well after cutting.

Goniophlebium verrucosum (alt. **Polypodium verrucosum**)
Malaysia, New Guinea, Indonesia, Australia
100–200 cm (40–80 in): 1 pinnate Trop.–S.Trop.: Epi.
An excellent basket fern with long, weeping, dark green fronds. Specimen plants are eye catching and are long-lived and easily maintained. Requires warmth, humidity and air movement and a coarse, epiphytic mixture.

Lecanopteris carnosa Ant Fern
Malaysia, Indonesia, Philippines
20–45 cm (8–18 in): pinnatifid Trop.–S.Trop.: Epi.
The rhizomes of this fern are quite remarkable, for not only are they hollow and inhabited by ants, but they also undergo a remarkable transformation from young to old. Young rhizomes are bluish-green and fleshy and the old rhizomes are black, tough and wizened. This is an interesting fern which can be grown in a coarse epiphytic mixture.

Lecanopteris crustacea (alt. **Polypodium crustaceum**) Ant Fern
Malaysia, Borneo, Indonesia
20–45 cm (8–18 in): pinnatifid Trop.–S.Trop.: Epi.
The rhizomes of this fern are fleshy, swollen and hollow. The hollows are inhabited by ants in nature but this relationship is not essential for the fern's cultivation. Makes an interesting basket fern in a coarse epiphytic mixture.

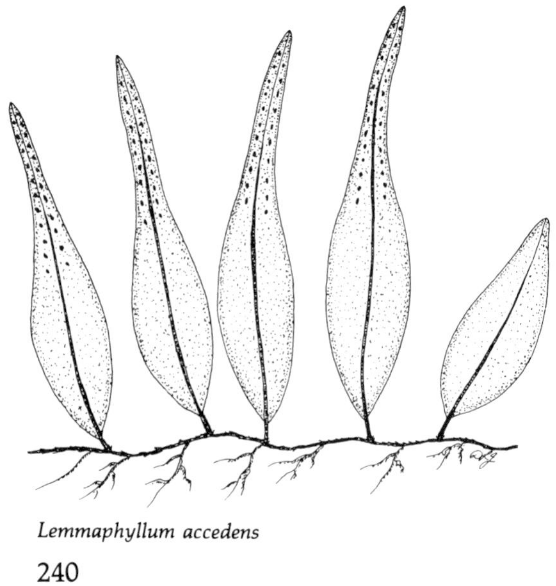

Lemmaphyllum accedens

Goniophlebium verrucosum is an excellent basket fern
Photo D. L. Jones

Lecanopteris sinuosa – see **Phymatosorus sinuosa**

Lemmaphyllum accedens
Malaysia, New Guinea, Polynesia
2.5–15 cm (1–6 in): entire Trop.–S.Trop.: Epi.
A common fern with small dimorphic fronds and long-creeping rhizomes. Plants can be grown on slabs, in pots or baskets and, in the tropics, even on suitable garden trees. They are fast growing and easy to establish. Needs a coarse mixture, bright light, moisture and air movement.

Lemmaphyllum microphyllum Green Penny Fern
India, China, Japan, Korea, Taiwan
1–3.5 cm (0.5–1.5 in): entire Trop.–Temp.: Epi.
A lovely little fern with bright, shiny green, fleshy, dimorphic fronds. Sterile fronds are rounded and produced in abundance and the fertile fronds are long and slender and occur less frequently. Plants are well suited to tree-fern slabs and baskets and will cover the whole surface with a mass of fronds. Also very good in a terrarium. Surprisingly cold hardy.

Lepisorus clathratus
China, Japan, Siberia, Afghanistan
12–20 cm (4–8 in): entire S.Trop.–Temp.: Epi.
This fern has a fairly thick, creeping rhizome covered with scales and narrow, widely spaced, blue-green fronds which have large, brown sori. Can be grown in a pot or basket of fibrous epiphytic mixture.

Lepisorus thunbergianus
China, Japan, Korea
10–20 cm (4–8 in): entire S.Trop.–Temp.: Epi.

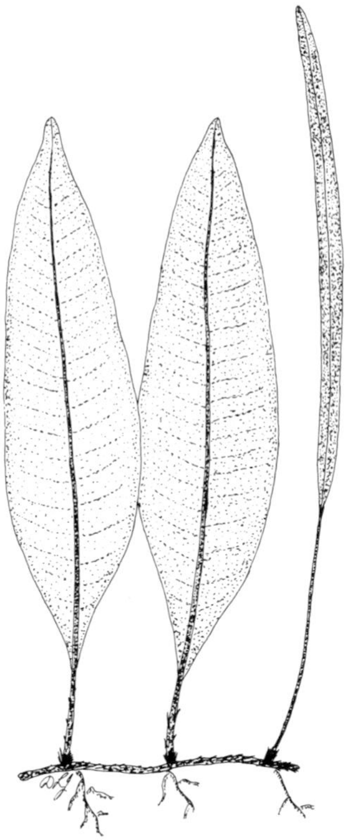

Leptochilus decurrens

A clumping fern with a short-creeping rhizome and narrow, dark green fronds which arch or hang. Easily grown in a small pot or basket of fibrous epiphytic mixture.

Leptochilus decurrens
India, China, Malaysia, Polynesia
10–35 cm (4–14 in): entire Trop.–S.Trop.: Epi.
A novelty fern with long slender rhizomes and fronds which are remarkably dimorphic. The sterile fronds are fairly broad and taper to each end; the fertile fronds are long and slender (usually less than 1 cm [0.5 in] wide) and covered with brown sporangia. Can be grown in a small pot of coarse mixture.

Loxogramme involuta
India, Sri Lanka
15–45 cm (6–18 in): entire Trop.–S.Trop.: Epi.
An interesting fern with broad, lanceolate, simple fronds borne on a creeping rhizome. Makes a decorative basket fern especially in baskets of tree-fern fibre. Needs a coarse mixture and air movement.

Marginaria formosana = Polypodium formosanum

Microgramma lycopodioides (alt. **Polypodium lycopodioides**)
Mexico, Central and South America, West Indies
5–20 cm (2–8 in): entire Trop.–S.Trop.: Epi.

Microgramma nitida Photo D. L. Jones

A spreading fern with a freely branching rhizome and simple slender fronds of a firm, papery texture. The rhizome is covered with rusty brown scales. Plants are easily grown in pots or baskets of a coarse mixture or on a slab of tree fern. Likes warm, moist, airy conditions.

Microgramma nitida (alt. **Polypodium palmeri**)
Mexico, Central America
10–20 cm (4–8 in): entire Trop.–S.Trop.: Epi.
A small fern with fairly stiff, shiny fronds and a long-creeping, freely-branched rhizome. It is a fairly fast grower and likes humid but airy conditions. An ideal basket fern.

Microgramma piloselloides (alt. **Polypodium piloselloides**) Snake Polypody
Mexico, Central and South America, West Indies
6–9 cm (2–3 in): entire Trop.–S.Trop: Epi.
A small species with a long-creeping, wiry rhizome bearing oval sterile fronds and longer, narrower fertile ones. Fertile fronds often have an irregularly-toothed margin. Grows very easily in a pot or basket of coarse mixture and prefers humid but airy conditions.

Microgramma vaccinifolia (alt. **Polypodium vacciniifolium**)
South America
5–10 cm (2–4 in): entire Trop.–S.Trop.: Epi.
A freely creeping little fern with a conspicuous scaly rhizome and dimorphic fronds. Rhizome scales are white. Ideal for a basket and requires warm, humid conditions with air movement. Slower growing than other species of *Microgramma*.

Microsorum diversifolium — see **Phymatosorus diversifolius**

Microsorum linguiforme
Borneo, Philippines, New Guinea, Fiji
20–50 cm (8–20 in): entire Trop.–S.Trop.: Epi.
An interesting fern with erect, dark green, fairly thin textured fronds with a prominent venation. The fronds

trap litter which rots down and provides nutrients for the roots. Plants are easily grown in a basket of coarse mixture but are rather cold sensitive and need warm, humid, airy conditions.

Microsorum musifolium (alt. **Polypodium musifolium**)
Malaysia, Philippines, Indonesia, New Guinea
50–100 cm (20–40 in): entire Trop.–S.Trop.: Epi.
A striking fern with pale green entire fronds which have a prominent network of dark veins. Makes a very decorative pot or basket plant and grows easily in a coarse mixture. Likes warmth, air movement and humidity.

Microsorum normale
North India, China (South), Malaysia, New Guinea, Australia
20–40 cm (8–16 in): entire Trop.–S.Trop.: Epi.
This fern is similar in many respects to *M. pappei* but the fronds are more thinly textured and end in a short point. It adapts well to cultivation and can be grown in baskets or pots of a coarse mixture. In the tropics plants can be grown on rocks or suitable garden trees.

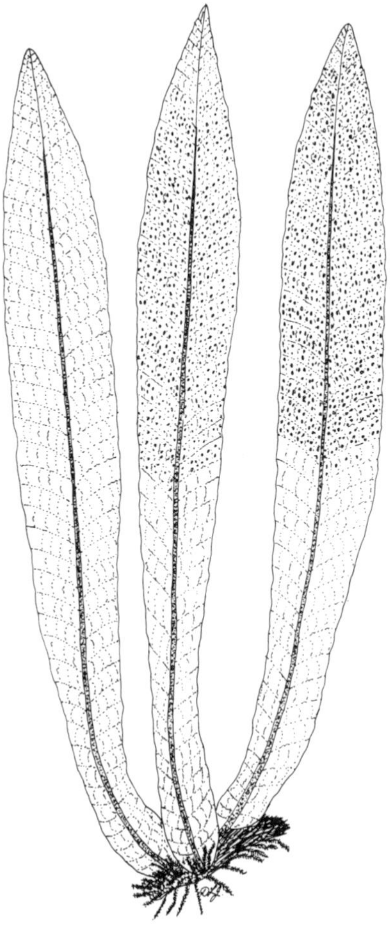

Microsorum musifolium

Microsorum pappei Photo D. L. Jones

Microsorum pappei (alt. **Polypodium pappei**)
Africa
30–90 cm (12–36 in): entire Trop.–Temp.: Epi.
A commonly grown fern with tall, dark green, slender fronds on long stipes. Usually grown in pots or baskets of a coarse mixture. Grows easily and looks best when given shade rather than too much light.

Microsorum parksii — see **Phymatosorus parksii**

Microsorum polycarpon=**Microsorum punctatum**

Microsorum pteropus (alt. **Polypodium pteropus**)
India, South China, Malaysia, Philippines
20–40 cm (8–16 in): pinnatifid Trop.–S.Trop.: Epi.
A coarse fern with erect, simple or tri-lobed dark green, thinly-textured fronds. In nature plants grow close to streams and may become submerged during floods. They grow easily in a basket of coarse mixture and need warm, moist conditions. Can also be grown as an aquatic and with care as an aquarium plant.

Microsorum punctatum (alt. **Polypodium polycarpon**)
Africa, Asia, China, Malaysia, New Guinea, Australia, Polynesia
40–120 cm (20–48 in): entire Trop.–S.Trop.: Epi.
A coarse fern with large leathery simple fronds which are usually a pale yellowish-green. In nature it forms large spreading colonies commonly on boulders and in very sunny but humid situations. An easily grown fern usually in baskets or large containers. In the tropics it is frequently grown as a garden plant. Needs coarse, free draining mixture, bright light,

A clump of *Microsorum punctatum* perched on a boulder
Photo D. L. Jones

warmth and humidity. This is a variable species which has given rise to many commonly grown forms.

'Climbing Bird's Nest' — fronds entire, the margins undulate to slightly crisped, arching to strongly pendulous. Fronds dark green above, paler beneath.

'Compactum' — entire fronds much shorter than the typical form. Usually light green to yellow green.

'Cristatum' — form with slender but erect, branching fronds each branch ending in a slender crest. Fronds light green to yellow green.

'Grandiceps' — leathery strongly pendulous fronds ending in heavy, spreading much-branched crests. An excellent basket plant.

'New Guinea' — long, slender entire fronds. May be a form of *Microsorum superficiale*.

'Pendulum Grandiceps' — arching to pendulous olive green fronds with widely spreading branches crested on the tips.

'Ramosum' — erect fronds densely branched and crested close to the apex. Generally dwarf growing. Fronds light green to yellowish.

'Serratum' ('Laciniatum') — fairly thinly-textured

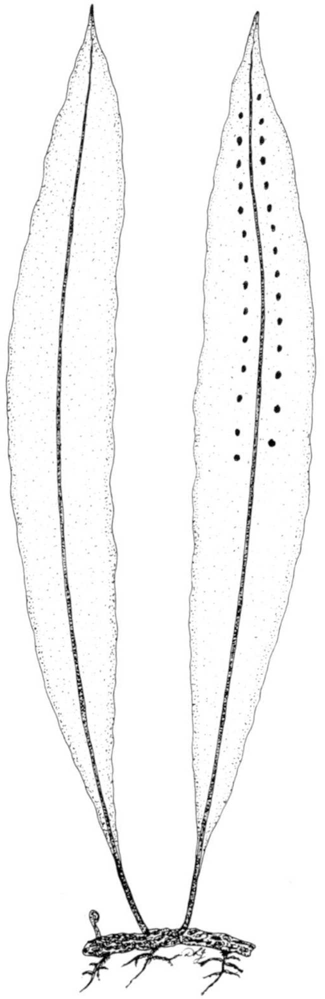

Microsorum pappei

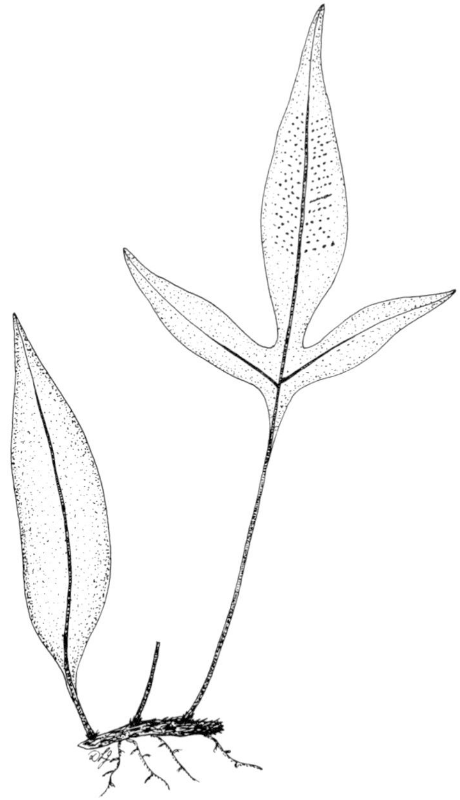

Microsorum pteropus

Microsorum punctatum 'Serratum' Photo D. L. Jones

fronds, the margins undulate and are heavily toothed. Fronds erect, dark green.

'Lobatum' – undulate margins and variable lobes, some long and pointed, others short and blunt.

Microsorum scandens – see **Phymatosorus scandens**

Microsorum scolopendrium – see **Phymatosorus scolopendria**

Niphidium crassifolium (alt. **Polypodium crassifolium**)
Mexico, Central and South America
30–150 cm (12–60 in): entire Trop.–S.Trop.: Epi.

A most attractive fern with dark green, fairly broad, strap-like fronds which are distinctly and heavily veined. It is a neat fern ideal for pots or baskets in a coarse mixture. Needs warmth, humidity and air movement.

'Monstrosum' – fronds unusually contorted and lobed.

Phlebodium aureum (alt. **Polypodium aureum**)
Rabbit's-foot Fern/Golden Polypody
Florida, Mexico, Central and South America, West Indies
20–150 cm (8–60 in): pinnatifid Trop.–Temp.: Epi.–Terr.

A widely grown fern, which varies tremendously; some of the forms appear to bear little relation to others. Plants adapt to cultivation readily and can be grown in the ground (in well-drained soil), or in containers or baskets. A large growing variety (var. *areolatum*) with greenish-grey fronds makes an excellent border plant or a 'fill-in' in gardens. A number of choice cultivars are grown.

'Cristatum' – erect to arching distinctly bluish fronds which have slender, loosely-spreading crests on the tips of the lobes.

'Ekstrand' – a very fine form with weeping, heavily ruffled fronds of a deep, bluish-green colour. The final lobes are blunt to rounded.

'English Crested' – fronds blue green, lobes with crested tips, not congested.

'Glaucum' – a large growing form with distinctly glaucous fronds. May be identical with var. *areolatum*.

'Leatherman' – a form with falcate lobes drawn out into long slender tips.

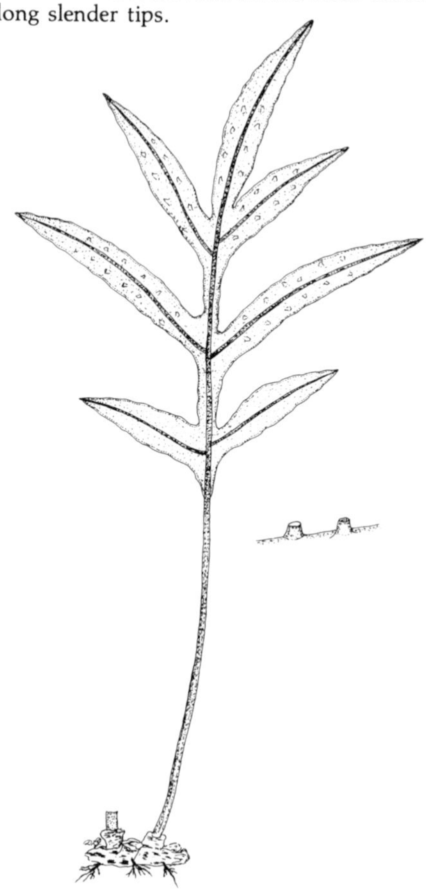

Phymatosorus nigrescens

Phlebodium aureum 'Ekstrand' Photo D. L. Jones

Phlebodium decumanum in a basket Photo D. L. Jones

'Mandaianum' – strong grower with curly margins on the segments and some lobes. A very popular form.

'Mexican Tasseled' – fronds are deep bluish-green, weeping with incredibly crested tips which resemble a frilly pompom.

'Undulatum' – margins of the segments undulate or crisped.

'Variegatum' – fronds have yellowish bands and blotches. May be a form of 'Mandaianum'.

Phlebodium decumanum (alt. **Polypodium decumanum**)
Mexico, Central and South America
30–120 cm (12–48 in): pinnatifid Trop.–S.Trop.: Epi.
An interesting fern with thick rhizomes which are covered with soft, brown, woolly scales. These wander over the surface of the potting mixture and also through the air. Only a few, large, leathery, bluish-green fronds are carried on each rhizome and the plants often present a sparse appearance. Difficult to grow to perfection needing warm, moist conditions in a coarse mixture.

'Giant' – a very large-growing form.

Phymatosorus diversifolius (alt. **Microsorum diversifolium**) Kangaroo Fern
Australia, New Zealand
10–60 cm (4–24 in): pinnatifid Temp.–S.Trop.: Epi.–Terr.
This fern has proved to be very adaptable and can be grown in the ground or in pots, baskets or on slabs. In shady humid situations plants will also grow on garden trees. A striking fern with leathery, dark green fronds.

Phymatosorus longissimus (alt. **Polypodium longissimum**)
Northern India, Thailand, Vietnam, Malaysia
60–100 cm (24–40 in): pinnatifid Trop.–S.Trop.: Epi.
A large species with a fleshy rhizome and tall, broad, deeply lobed fronds with bumps on the upper surface of the fertile segments. Can be grown in large pots of coarse mixture and requires warm, humid conditions.

Phymatosorus nigrescens (alt. **Polypodium nigrescens**)
Pimple Fern
Southern India, Sri Lanka, Malaysia
40–80 cm (16–32 in): pinnatifid Trop.–S.Trop.: Epi.
An attractive large fern with deeply lobed fronds of a dark bluish-green and segments with prominently crisped margins. Plants make a decorative pot subject and require a coarse mixture.

Phymatosorus parksii (alt. **Microsorum parksii**)
Fiji, Samoa, Lord Howe Island
30–90 cm (12–36 in): pinnatifid Trop.–Temp.: Terr.
A clumping fern with erect, coarsely lobed, shiny green fronds. Plants like a sandy soil and will tolerate considerable exposure to sun. They grow very well in coastal districts. Also makes an attractive pot plant.

Phymatosorus diversifolius can grow as a ground cover or climber on suitable trees Photo W. R. Elliot

Phymatosorus scandens (alt. **Microsorum scandens**) Fragrant Fern
Australia, New Zealand, Norfolk Island
20–50 cm (8–20 in): pinnatifid Temp.–Trop.: Epi.

A vigorous scandent fern which forms clumps on trees in shady, moist situations. Fronds have an elusive but perceptible fragrance. Plants grow easily and are excellent for baskets. Need a coarse mixture, shade and humidity.

Phymatosorus scolopendria (alt. **Microsorum scolopendrium**)
Tropical Africa, Asia, Malaysia, New Guinea, Australia, Polynesia
15–30 cm (6–12 in): pinnatifid Trop.–S.Trop.: Epi.

Phymatosorus parksii is a hardy fern that will tolerate much sun Photo D. L. Jones

Phymatosorus scolopendria Photo D. L. Jones

A coarse, fairly commonly grown fern that can look decorative in a basket and will also grow well as a garden plant. Plants grow easily in a coarse mixture and like warmth, humidity and air movement. Will tolerate considerable sun but fronds become bleached and unattractive.

Phymatosorus sinuosa (alt. **Lecanopteris sinuosa**) Ant Fern
Malaysia, Philippines, Indonesia, New Guinea, New Hebrides
20–40 cm (8–12 in): entire Trop.–S.Trop.: Epi.

The rhizomes of this fern are somewhat flattened and have hollow chambers which are inhabited by ants. Plants can be grown in the absence of ants and in fact they are quite easy to grow if given warm, humid conditions and a coarse mixture.

Pleopeltis clathratus = Lepisorus clathratus

Pleopeltis macrocarpa
Mexico, Central and South America, West Indies, Africa, India
10–40 cm (4–16 in): entire Trop.–S.Trop.: Epi.

This fern has a long-creeping, scaly rhizome and erect, leathery fronds, the fertile ones with two rows of prominent large sori. It is a variable species but makes an attractive subject for a pot or basket. Plants require a coarse mixture and humid, airy conditions.

Pleopeltis normale = Microsorum normale

Pleopeltis percussa (alt. **Polypodium percussum**)
Mexico, Central and South America
15–40 cm (6–16 in): entire Trop.–S.Trop.: Epi.

This fern has long-creeping scaly rhizomes and leathery, dark green fronds which have numerous small round whitish scales on their surface. Makes an attractive basket plant (especially in a fibre basket). Requires a coarse mixture and humid but airy conditions. It will succeed as an indoor plant.

Pleopeltis thunbergianus = Lepisorus thunbergianus

Polypodium adnatum
Central and South America
30–60 cm (12–24 in): 1 pinnate Trop.–S.Trop.: Epi.
An attractive species with hairy grey fronds. The pinnae are relatively wide but are well separated imparting a sparse appearance. Plants are relatively slow growing.

Polypodium amoenum
India, China
30–60 cm (12–24 in): 1 pinnate S.Trop.–Trop.: Epi.
Similar in general appearance to *P. formosanum* but with the rhizomes more prominently scaly and greener fronds with fewer, wider pinnae. Tends to be slow growing and is sensitive to overwatering. An attractive basket plant.

Polypodium angustifolium – see **Campyloneurum angustifolium**

Polypodium aureum – see **Phlebodium aureum**

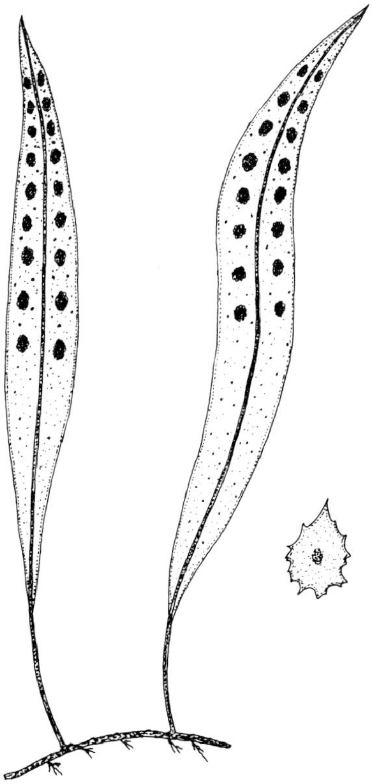

Pleopeltis percussa

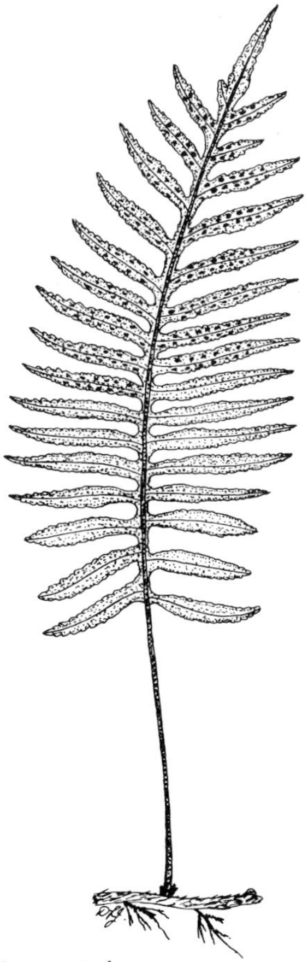

Polypodium australe

Polypodium australe Southern Polypody
Europe, Atlantic Islands
20–50 cm (8–20 in): pinnatifid Temp.–S.Trop.: Terr.–Epi.
A widespread deciduous species often confused with *P. vulgare* but with broader, less leathery fronds. Plants are easily grown in a humus-rich loam in a semi-shady situation or in a pot or basket. A few cultivars are grown.

'Cambricum' – margins of segments attractively lobed and dissected. An excellent basket fern. Occurs naturally in Wales but plants are sterile.

'Pulcherrimum' – fronds attractively lobed, the lobes extending nearly to the mid-ribs and blunt. Plants are fertile.

'Semilacerum' – lower segments of the frond are deeply lobed, the upper ones are normal.

Polypodium crassifolium – see **Niphidium crassifolium**

Polypodium crustaceum – see **Lecanopteris crustacea**

Polypodium decumanum – see **Phlebodium decumanum**

Polypodium diversifolium – see **Phymatosorus diversifolius**

Polypodium ellipticum – see **Colysis elliptica**

Polypodium fauriei
Japan, Korea
30–60 cm (12–24 in): 1 pinnate S.Trop.–Temp.: Epi.
Similar in general appearance to *P. formosanum* but with a more slender, scaly rhizome. Fronds arch or weep attractively. Would make an excellent basket fern. Requires a coarse, epiphytic mixture.

Polypodium formosanum Grub Fern/Caterpillar Fern
Japan, Taiwan, China (South)
30–60 cm (12–24 in): pinnatifid Temp.–S.Trop.: Epi.
A handsome fern prized for its drooping, light green fronds and long-creeping, lime-green to chalky white rhizomes. It is unexcelled as a basket plant and looks particularly ornamental in baskets made of tree-fern fibre. Likes humid but airy conditions in a coarse mixture. Plants are slow to recover from disturbance.

'Cristatum' – an unusual form with flattened rhizomes, which produce several branches from a single point, giving a crested impression.

Polypodium fraxinifolium – see **P. meniscifolium**

Polypodium glaucophyllum
Central and South America
10–30 cm (4–12 in): entire Trop.–S.Trop.: Epi.
A delightful fern with slender, greenish rhizomes and arching fronds which are dark, shiny-green on their surface and bluish underneath (from a powdery coating). Grows easily in a pot or basket and likes humid, airy conditions.

Polypodium glycyrrhiza Licorice Fern
North America (Alaska to California)
10–40 cm (4–16 in): pinnatifid Temp.–S.Trop.: Terr.–Epi.
The unusual common name arises from the sweet taste of the rhizomes. A hardy, deciduous fern that can be grown in a sheltered garden situation or in containers. Easily raised from spore but sporelings are generally slow to develop.

Polypodium integrifolium=Microsorum punctatum

Polypodium interjectum
Europe
30–60 cm (12–24 in): pinnatifid Temp.–S.Trop.: Terr.
This species has a fairly broad frond like *P. australe* but of leathery texture like *P. vulgare*. Plants grow easily in the garden or fernery or in a container (useful in a basket). Likes freely draining, humus-rich soil and good light.

Polypodium formosanum is a popular basket fern
Photo D. L. Jones

Polypodium irioides=Microsorum punctatum

Polypodium longissimum – see **Phymatosorus longissimus**

Polypodium loriceum
Mexico, Central and South America, West Indies
25–50 cm (10–20 in): pinnatifid Trop.–S.Trop.: Epi.
This fern is commonly confused with *P. formosanum* by fern fanciers but has larger, more erect fronds and smaller sori set close to the midrib. The rhizomes are dark green and they frequently curl. Makes an attractive basket plant in a coarse mixture. Needs shade, humidity and air movement.

Polypodium lycopodioides – see **Microgramma lycopodioides**

Polypodium meniscifolium
Mexico, Central and South America
30–120 cm (12–48 in): pinnate Trop.–S.Trop.: Epi.
A fern with long, arching, leathery, dark green fronds that have attractive undulate margins. Cultivated plants often do not develop long fronds and remain fairly compact. Easily grown in a pot or basket of coarse mixture. Has been confused with *P. fraxinifolium* by fern growers.

Polypodium musifolium – see **Microsorum musifolium**

Polypodium nigrescens – see **Phymatosorus nigrescens**

Polypodium palmeri — see **Microgramma nitida**

Polypodium pappei — see **Microsorum pappei**

Polypodium pectinatum Comb Fern
South America, West Indies
15–45 cm (6–18 in): 1 pinnate Trop.–S.Trop.: Epi.
A very cold-sensitive species that is also slow growing. Plants should be started in a small pot of coarse mixture and when well established can be transferred to a basket.

Polypodium percussum — see **Pleopeltis percussa**

Polypodium persicifolium — see **Goniophlebium persicifolium**

Polypodium phyllitidis — see **Campyloneurum phyllitidis**

Polypodium piloselloides — see **Microgramma piloselloides**

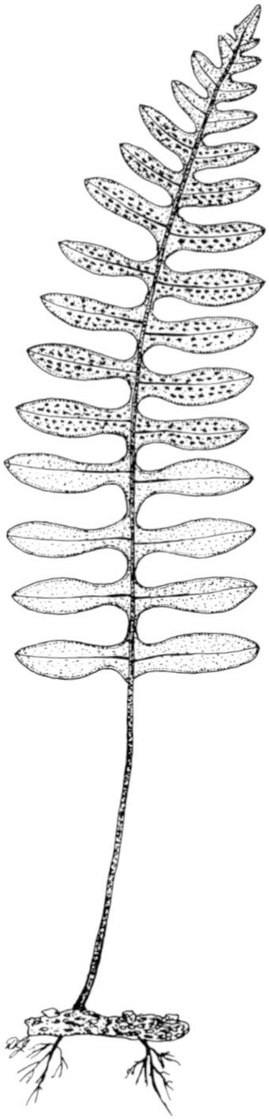

Polypodium meniscifolium

Polypodium pectinatum Photo D. L. Jones

Polypodium polycarpon — see **Microsorum punctatum**

Polypodium polypodioides Resurrection Fern
North, Central and South America, West Indies, South Africa
10–30 cm (4–12 in): pinnatifid Trop.–S.Trop.: Epi.
A widely distributed and variable fern which consists of five botanical varieties. Plants are very tolerant of dryness being very scaly and the fronds curling to reduce water loss (expanding again after rain). Can be grown in a pot or basket of coarse, humus-rich mixture.

Polypodium pteropus — see **Microsorum pteropus**

Polypodium punctatum = Microsorum punctatum

Polypodium sanctae-rosae
Mexico, Central America
25–75 cm (10–30 in): pinnatifid Trop.–S.Trop.: Epi.
An interesting fern with the frond surface covered with small, tawny scales. The fronds are erect and have numerous spreading lobes. Requires a coarse epiphytic mixture and warm, humid conditions with plenty of air movement and good light.

Polypodium scouleri Leathery Polypody
North America (British Columbia to California)
20–50 cm (8–20 in): pinnatifid Temp.–S.Trop.: Terr.
A hardy fern, restricted to near-coastal regions and not extending any distance inland. Plants are slow

Polypodium polypodioides ssp. *ecklonii*
Photo D. L. Jones

growing, with glossy-green, leathery fronds and a glaucous rhizome. Can be grown in a basket of coarse mixture or in the ground in freely-draining soil.

Polypodium subauriculatum – see **Goniophlebium subauriculatum**

Polypodium thyssanolepis Scaly Polypody
North America (Arizona, Texas), Mexico, Central and South America, West Indies
5–50 cm (2–20 in): pinnatifid Trop.–S.Trop.: Epi.

A widely distributed and often common fern with deeply-lobed, somewhat leathery fronds which on the lower surface are covered with pale scales. Rhizomes are slender, long-creeping and much branched. Looks attractive in a basket and requires a coarse mixture.

Polypodium vaccinifolium – see **Microgramma vaccinifolia**

Polypodium verrucosum – see **Goniophlebium verrucosum**

Polypodium virginianum American Wall Fern
North America
10–25 cm (4–12 in): pinnatifid Temp.–S.Trop.: Terr.–Epi.

A hardy deciduous fern that colonizes moist sites. Plants have a creeping rhizome and arching or hanging leathery fronds. An attractive subject for a partial sunny situation in the garden or fernery, or in a pot of well-drained, humus-rich soil.

Polypodium vulgare Common Polypody
Europe, North America, Japan, China, Africa
10–40 cm (4–16 in): pinnatifid Temp.–S.Trop.: Terr.–Epi.

A very widely distributed deciduous fern with erect, lobed, leathery fronds which are slender throughout. Adaptable to garden situations as well as ferneries, pots and baskets. Plants require an organically-rich, well-drained mixture. Many cultivars are grown.

'Bifidum' – the lower segments prominently notched.

'Cornubiense' – the segments are lobed so that the fronds appear 3–4 pinnate. May revert.

'Cristatum' – segments and frond tip have a spreading crest.

'Ramosum' – the fronds fork repeatedly in an attractive manner.

'Ramosum Hillman' – the fronds one to several times forked and with some cresting on the tips.

Pyrrosia adnascens=**P. lanceolata**

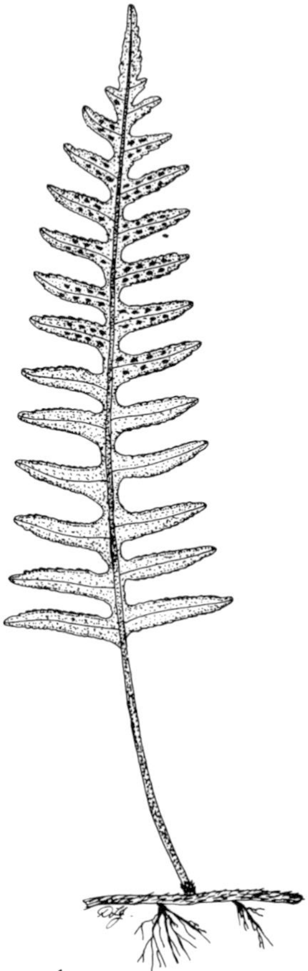

Polypodium vulgare

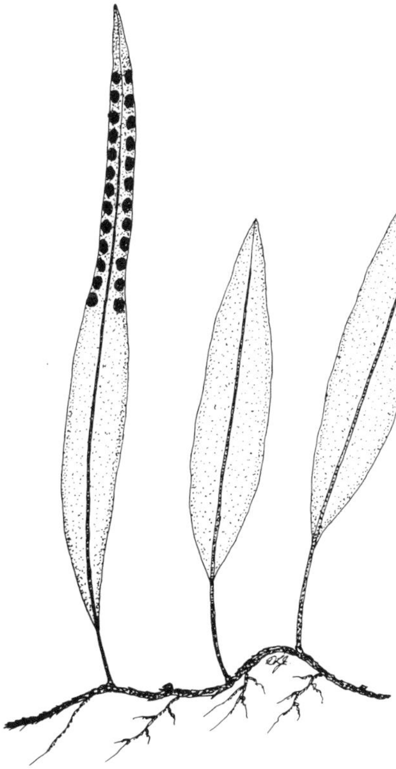

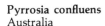

Pyrrosia angustata

The colonizing *Pyrrosia confluens* Photo W. R. Elliot

Pyrrosia confluens
Australia
10–30 cm (4–12 in): entire Trop.–Temp.: Epi.
An adaptable species which can be established on garden trees or grown in pots or baskets. Will tolerate sun but plants in shade are much greener. Plants require plenty of moisture, humidity and air movement.

Pyrrosia hastata
Japan, China, Korea
15–25 cm (6–10 in): entire Temp.–S.Trop.: Epi.
A hardy fern with distinctive, tri-lobed fronds which are closely set on a short-creeping rhizome. In suitable areas it can be grown as a garden plant (among rocks) but looks its best in a basket. Needs a coarse, freely draining mixture.

Pyrrosia lanceolata
India, China, Malaysia, New Guinea, Polynesia, Australia
15–25 cm (6–10 in): entire Trop.–S.Trop.: Epi.
A very widely distributed fern which forms clumps on trees and rocks in brightly lit situations. Makes a good basket plant and can also be established on trees in tropical gardens. Needs bright light, warmth, humidity and air movement.

Pyrrosia lingua Tongue Fern/Japanese Felt Fern
Japan, China, Taiwan, Laos, Thailand
10–20 cm (4–8 in): entire Trop.–Temp.: Epi.–Terr.
A widely cultivated, popular fern that is excellent in pots and baskets and can also be grown as a ground cover in suitable positions. Once established plants are very tolerant of dryness and neglect. Plants need good drainage, bright light, humidity and air movement. A number of cultivars are prized, some with fancy variations.

'Contorta' (Eboshi) — with unusual twisted or contorted fronds.

'Cristata' (Shisha) — frond tips repeatedly and irregularly forked to impart a crested appearance.

'Monstrifera' — irregular deep lobes and lacerations on the frond margins.

'Nana' — a dwarf form with short fronds.

'Nankin-Shisha' (Kujaku) — a heavily-crested form with the crests congested and twisted.

'Nokogiri-ba' (Serrata) — frond margins are crinkled and bluntly toothed.

Tsunomata' — tips of fronds divided into 2–3 branches.

'Variegata' — pale oblique bands on the fronds which have bluntly-toothed margins.

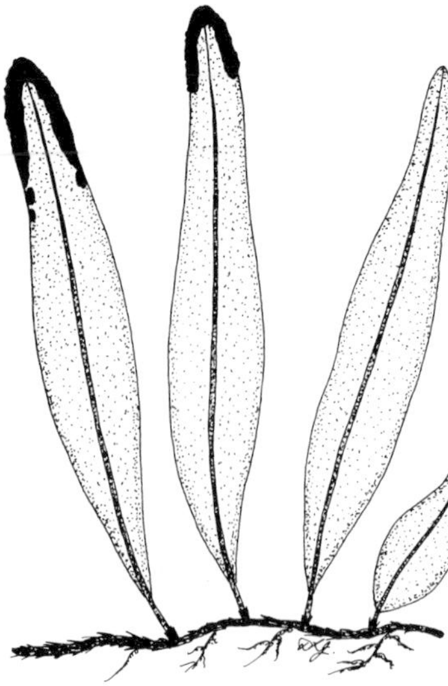

Pyrrosia confluens

Pyrrosia lingua 'Cristata' Photo D. L. Jones

Pyrrosia longifolia Photo D. L. Jones

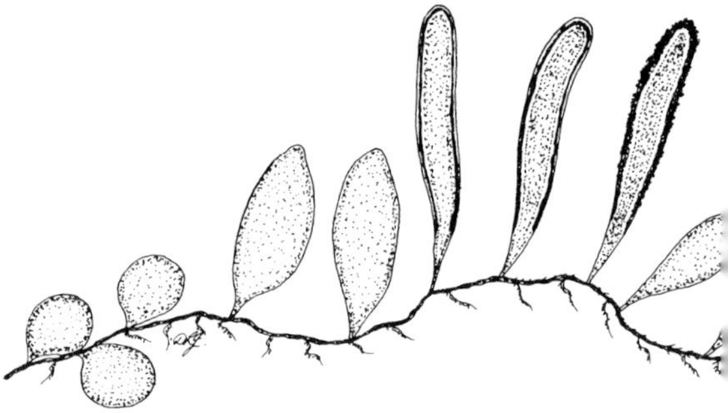

Pyrrosia piloselloides

Pyrrosia lingua is a versatile fern Photo W. R. Elliot

Pyrrosia varia Photo D. L. Jones

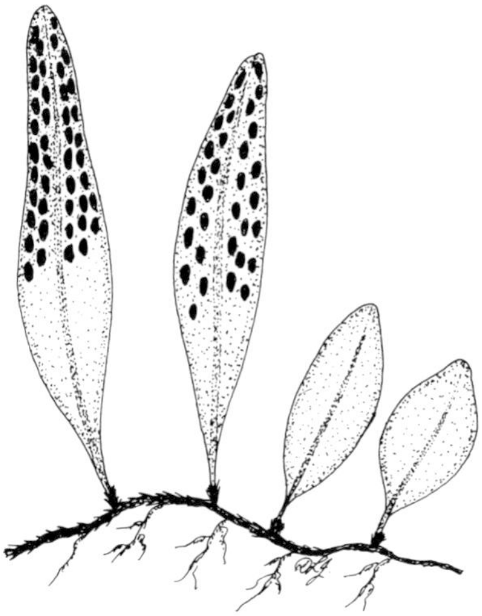

Pyrrosia serpens

Pyrrosia longifolia
Thailand, Malaysia, New Guinea, Polynesia, Australia
20–100 cm (8–40 in): entire Trop.–S.Trop.: Epi.
A spectacular fern with long, fleshy, shiny fronds and wandering rhizomes. Plants are easily established on trees in tropical regions. They make an impressive basket plant and require warmth, good light, humidity and air movement.

Pyrrosia polydactylis has unusual fronds for the genus Photo D. L. Jones

Pyrrosia nummularifolia Creeping Button Fern
India, Malaysia, Philippines
2.5–7.5 cm (1–3 in): entire Trop.–S.Trop.: Epi.
The sterile fronds of this creeping fern are like small green buttons, the fertile fronds are long and slender. An interesting species for a pot or basket. Needs a coarse mixture, good light, humidity and air movement.

Pyrrosia piloselloides
India, Malaysia, Philippines, Indonesia, New Guinea
2.5–10 cm (1–4 in): entire Trop.–S.Trop.: Epi.
A miniature fern with long, slender, creeping rhizomes and dark green, fleshy fronds. Ideal for pots or baskets. Needs a coarse mixture, good light and humidity.

Pyrrosia polydactylis
Taiwan
5–20 cm (2–8 in): palmate Trop.–S.Trop.: Epi.
A most ornamental fern, with the fronds divided like a hand into finger-like lobes, and with a creeping rhizome. Makes a most appealing basket plant. Needs a coarse mixture, good light, warmth and air movement.

Pyrrosia rupestris Rock Felt Fern
Australia
2.5–10 cm (1–4 in): entire Trop.–Temp.: Epi.
A hardy little fern, easily established on suitable garden trees and can also be grown in baskets or pots of a coarse mixture. Very tolerant of dryness. Succeeds best in bright light and needs humidity and air movement.

Selliquea feei
India, Indonesia
10–15 cm (4–6 in): entire S.Trop.–Temp.: Epi.

A harsh-textured but attractive fern, with glossy, bright green fronds and wandering rhizomes that are covered with golden-brown scales. Excellent for pots or baskets and very easy to grow. Needs a coarse mixture, shade, humidity and air movement.

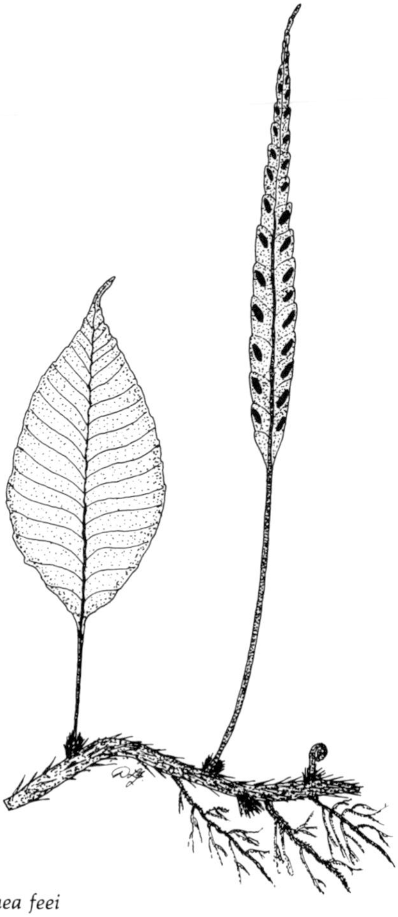

Selliguea feei

Pyrrosia serpens
New Zealand
2.5–15 cm (1–6 in): entire Temp.–S.Trop.: Epi.

A hardy sun-loving fern which grows in congested colonies on suitable trees. Sterile fronds are shorter and more rounded than fertile fronds. Easily grown in a pot or basket of coarse mixture.

Pyrrosia tricuspis = P. hastata

Pyrrosia varia
Malaysia, Indonesia, New Guinea
5–15 cm (2–6 in): entire Trop.–S.Trop.: Epi.

The long-creeping rhizomes of this fern branch freely, so that the fronds end up overlapping, and present a crowded appearance. Each frond is long, tapered and light green with even lighter veins. An appealing fern for a pot or basket. Needs coarse mixture and good light.

27 Staghorns, elkhorns and other large epiphytes

genera, *Aglaomorpha, Drynaria, Merinthosorus, Platycerium* and *Pseudodrynaria*

A number of large ferns in the family Polypodiaceae have considerable cultural appeal and are grouped together here. Chief among these are the various species of *Platycerium* which have a special attraction for fern fanciers and may be a common garden plant in some tropical countries.

Habitat

Ferns of this group grow on large rocks, cliff faces or trees and may look spectacular because of their size. They favour humid, brightly-lit situations, from dense rainforest to more open vegetation. Many occur in climates which have a distinct dry season and the ferns exhibit seasonal growth patterns which they retain in cultivation.

Cultivation

Uses

Most of these ferns are easy to grow given suitable conditions. They are highly decorative or interesting ferns and in warm climates can be grown on garden trees or rocks. Many are also excellent for large containers and tubs and, once established, are hardy and long-lived. They are particularly well-suited to specimen culture.

Soil Types

The ferns discussed here cannot be grown in soil.

Potting Mix

Ferns of this group like a coarse, very well-drained potting mix (see page 176). Mixes made from coarse pieces of bark, gravel, fern fibre and charcoal can be suitable. Many of these ferns can also be mounted on slabs of tree-fern fibre or weathered hardwood. A pad of sphagnum moss between the fern and the slab ensures moisture for the fern and aids attachment. Some growers use specially constructed slabs with wire-mesh reservoirs which are filled with potting mix and/or sphagnum moss (see slab culture page 186).

Watering

All ferns of this group need plenty of water during the warm growing months but over the winter, the need varies with the species. Many species cease growth as the photoperiod shortens and their requirements for water at this time are much less than in the summer. All species must be watered sparingly and carefully during these conditions, especially those plants grown in heated greenhouses in temperate climates. In the latter situation plants can be left unwatered for 4–6 weeks at a time, whereas in warm climates watering every 1–2 weeks in winter may be needed.

Fertilizing

These ferns respond to the application of organic fertilizers and well-rotted manures. They should only be applied during the warm growing months of the year, the best time being spring or early summer just prior to a flush of growth. Liquid fertilizers can also be usefully applied in the summer.

Situation

All ferns in this group like good to bright light but for best appearance need protection from excessive hot sun. Filtered sun and light transmitted through opaque fibreglass is most suitable. Exposure to periods of sun can be very beneficial and if the plants are regularly watered they may withstand long exposures without detriment.

Hardy species of *Drynaria* and *Platycerium* (e.g. *P. bifurcatum*) will tolerate considerable cold weather and even mild frosts. Many of the tropical species are, however, very sensitive to cold and require the protection of a heated greenhouse (some species of *Platycerium* need a minimum temperature of 15°C [60°F]).

Pests

As a general rule ferns of this group do not suffer much from attacks by pests or diseases. A few specialized pests may damage platyceriums and species of

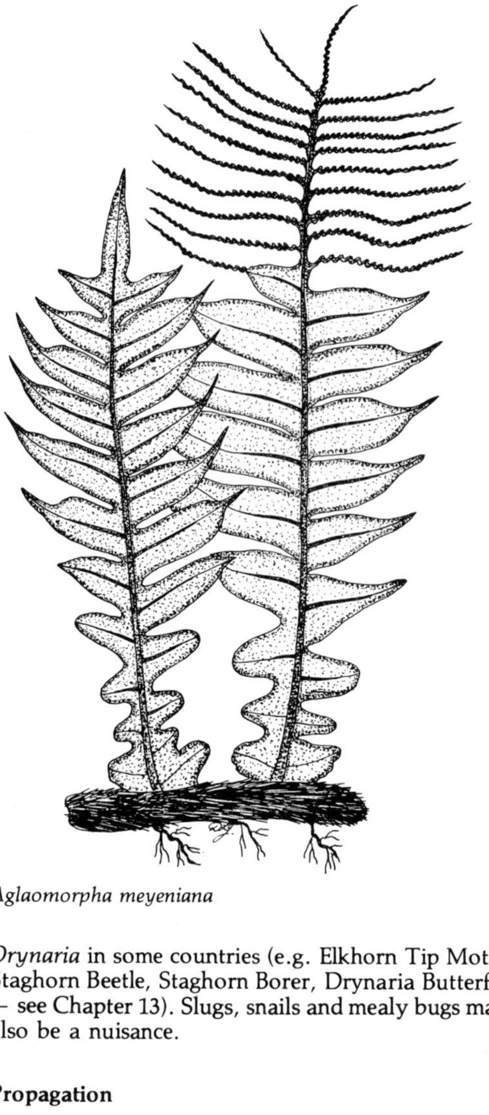

Aglaomorpha meyeniana

Drynaria in some countries (e.g. Elkhorn Tip Moth, Staghorn Beetle, Staghorn Borer, Drynaria Butterfly — see Chapter 13). Slugs, snails and mealy bugs may also be a nuisance.

Propagation

The majority of ferns considered here can be propagated from spores. Some may be very easy (e.g. *Drynaria rigidula*) but others are quite difficult (*Merinthosorus drynarioides*). As a group, Platyceriums appear to be difficult, especially for beginners. Growers specializing in their culture have more success, some germinating them on distilled water or mineral solutions. Frequently the spore of Platyceriums germinates well but the sporelings are difficult to handle and sometimes die at a later stage.

Most of the large growing ferns can be propagated by division and this includes species of *Platycerium* that have a multiple crown (see page 129). Only large divisions are successful and a suitable time is when rhizome growth is active (usually spring or early summer). Some species and cultivars of *Platycerium* have been successfully propagated by tissue culture.

SPECIES AND CULTIVARS

Aglaomorpha coronans = Pseudodrynaria coronans

Aglaomorpha heraclea
Malaysia
100–250 cm (40–100 in): pinnatifid Trop.–S.Trop.: Epi.

A coarse fern with large, leathery, dark green fronds and a broad, brown woolly rhizome. The fronds are placed close together on the rhizomes and their bases are expanded and overlap to trap litter. This large species is attractive in a container and can be decorative in a large basket. Plants need a coarse mixture, bright light and humidity.

Aglaomorpha meyeniana Bear's-paw Fern
Philippines, Taiwan
50–80 cm (20–32 in): pinnatifid Trop.–Temp.: Epi.

This is a most desirable fern with attractively-lobed, dark green, leathery fronds. The fertile fronds have an unusual terminal fertile section where the segments are constricted into a series of bead-like lobes. The species is easily grown in a pot or basket of coarse epiphytic mixture. It has proved to be rather cold-hardy and will adapt to a variety of regions.

Aglaomorpha 'Roberts'
cultivar
60–150 cm (24–60 in): pinnatifid Trop.–S.Trop.: Epi.

This fern cultivar is unusual in that all its plants are sterile and it appears to be of unknown origin. It may have arisen in horticulture as the result of a chance hybrid or it may be a sterile cultivar of *A. meyeniana*. Certainly it is a very handsome fern with large, leathery, dark green fronds and is well worth growing. Plants succeed in a warm environment and must have a coarse, well-drained potting mixture.

Aglaomorpha splendens
India
60–90 cm (24–36 in): pinnatifid Trop.–S.Trop.: Epi.

A robust fern with coarse fronds and a thick rhizome covered with greyish scales. Fertile fronds have a terminal section of slender segments. Makes an attractive basket fern in a coarse potting mixture.

Drynaria bonii
Thailand, Vietnam, Laos
30–60 cm (12–24 in): pinnatifid Trop.–S.Trop.: Epi.

An interesting species with fairly widely spaced fronds on a creeping rhizome. The nest leaves and true fronds have blunt, almost rounded segments. Plants grow well on a slab of tree-fern fibre or in a basket of coarse mixture.

Drynaria fortunei
China, Taiwan, Vietnam, Thailand, Laos
20–40 cm (8–16 in): pinnatifid Trop.–S.Trop.: Epi.

This species is rather like *D. quercifolia* but has smaller nest fronds and the typical fronds are also

Drynaria quercifolia Photo D. L. Jones

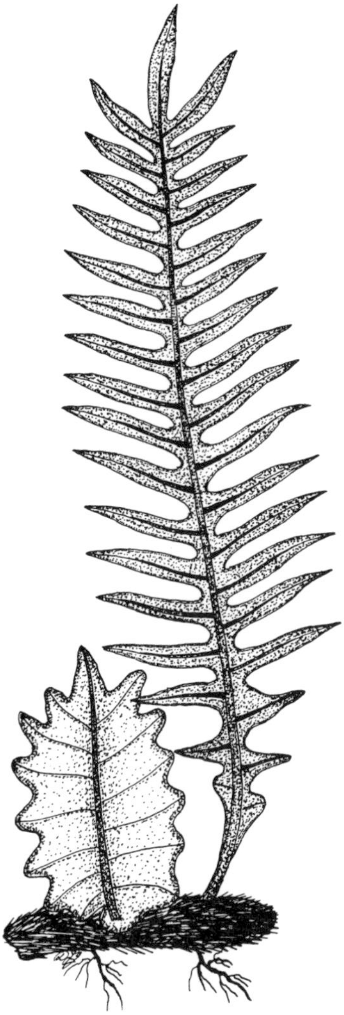

Drynaria quercifolia

smaller and thinner textured. Plants can be grown in a container of coarse mixture and need humid, airy conditions.

Drynaria mollis
India
20–50 cm (8–20 in): pinnatifid Trop.–S.Trop.: Epi.

An extremely ornamental fern with thick creeping rhizomes covered with golden, hairy scales. The sterile fronds (which are smaller) persist for many years and act as litter accumulators; the fertile fronds are produced in a new crop each year. The fertile fronds are softly hairy and the sori are dark and conspicuous. Plants can be grown in a pot or basket of coarse mixture.

Drynaria propinqua
India, Thailand
60–120 cm (24–48 in): pinnatifid Trop.–S.Trop.: Epi.

A species with very broad, deeply-lobed, leathery fronds the segments of which have finely-toothed margins (also present on the nest leaves). Plants look attractive in a large pot or basket of a coarse, epiphytic mixture.

Drynaria quercifolia Oak Leaf Fern
India, China, Malaysia, New Guinea, Polynesia, Australia
30–120 cm (12–48 in): pinnatifid Trop.–S.Trop.: Epi.

Widely distributed and common, this fern forms spreading patches in brightly lit but humid situations. Plants have very broad, furry rhizomes and dark green leaves. They can be readily grown on rocks or trees in tropical gardens or in a large pot or basket. A coarse epiphytic mixture is suitable. Once established, plants are very tolerant of dryness.

Drynaria rigidula Basket Fern
Malaysia, Philippines, Indonesia, Polynesia, New Guinea, Australia
50–250 cm (20–100 in): 1 pinnate Trop.–Temp.: Epi.

A widely distributed and very common fern that is almost a tropical weed readily colonizing garden trees, walls, pots in ferneries, greenhouses etc. This is an attractive fern with long weeping fronds, and plants in nature can develop to huge dimensions. The nest leaves produce an interesting effect especially when green and brown stages are present together. Plants can be grown on rocks, garden trees, in large pots and baskets and need a coarse mixture, bright light, humidity and air movement. Once established

Drynaria rigidula Photo D. L. Jones

The sterile fronds (or nest fronds) of *Drynaria rigidula* Photo D. L. Jones

they are quite drought resistant. A couple of cultivars are known.

'Vidgenii' — segments are lobed but are much narrower than the above. Has long, hanging, dark green fronds.

'Whitei' — fronds have very broad segments which are deeply-lobed to impart a ruffled appearance. The segments are crowded and overlap each other. A very beautiful and prized fern.

Drynaria sparsisora
Malaysia, Sri Lanka, Polynesia, New Guinea, Australia
30–90 cm (12–36 in): pinnatifid Trop.–S.Trop.: Epi.

This fern is similar in most respects to *D. quercifolia* but has different rhizome scales, nest leaves and soral arrangement. Plants grow readily with the same requirements as for that species.

Merinthosorus drynarioides
Malaysia, Philippines, Polynesia, Solomon Islands
80–120 cm (32–48 in): pinnatifid Trop.–S.Trop.: Epi.

A large fern with coarse fronds the fertile ones of which have an intriguing terminal section of narrow, fertile lobes. Plants can be attached to trees or rocks in tropical gardens and they also make a decorative specimen for a tub or large basket. They require a coarse mixture, bright light and humidity.

Platycerium alcicorne
Madagascar, Mauritius, Seychelles
clumping Trop.–S.Trop.: Epi.

This staghorn is similar in many respects to *P. bifurcatum* but has much tougher, leathery shield fronds and marginal hairs on the rhizome scales. The fertile fronds are grey-green, carried erect and are divided 3–4 times. Plants are adaptable to cultivation but are not quite as cold-hardy as *P. bifurcatum*. In cold climates they are best kept dry over winter (minimum temp. 5°C [40°F]).

Drynaria rigidula 'Whitei' Photo D. L. Jones

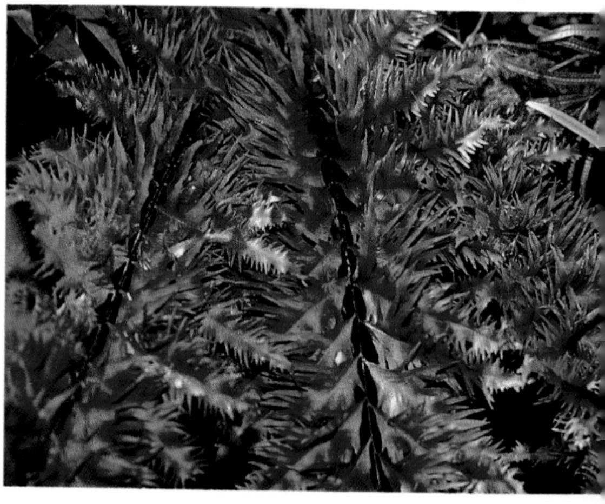

Drynaria rigidula 'Vidgenii' Photo D. L. Jones

Platycerium andinum South American Staghorn
South America
clumping Trop.–S.Trop.: Epi.

A handsome and easily grown species. The shield fronds, which are loosely sheathing, are erect with prominent veins and irregularly lobed upper margins. The pendulous fertile fronds are pale grey-green and divided 1-3 times into narrow segments. Plants require warmth and humidity (min. temp. 15°C [60°F]).

Merinthosorus drynarioides Photo D. L. Jones

Merinthosorus drynarioides

Platycerium angolense = P. elephantotis

Platycerium bifurcatum Elkhorn Fern
Australia, New Guinea, New Caledonia, Indonesia, Lord Howe Island
clumping Temp.–Trop.: Epi.

A widespread and common *Platycerium* which grows vigorously and is very rewarding in cultivation. In Australia the species extends into temperate regions and plants from such southerly collections are very cold-hardy and will tolerate severe frosts. Those from the tropics are less cold-hardy but are still adaptable and easily grown. This fern is tremendously variable and many forms and hybrids are grown, mostly under cultivar names.

'Majus' – fertile fronds erect and prominently lobed, the segments drooping.

'Netherlands' – a form with relatively short arching fronds that are deeply-lobed, the segments narrow and drooping.

A large clump of *Platycerium bifurcatum*

Platycerium bifurcatum Photo D. L. Jones

'Roberts' — fertile fronds thick-textured, grey-green, and much more deeply-lobed than 'Majus'.

'San Diego' — fertile fronds deeply divided with long, slender segments.

'Ziesenhenne' — a small, weak form with slender dark green fertile fronds that are deeply-lobed.

var. *willinckii* (Indonesia, New Guinea, Trop.–S.Trop.)
A variety with long, pendulous fertile fronds with the fertile segments mostly confined to the tips. Seems to integrate with typical *P. bifurcatum* and a range of confusing forms are cultivated. Plants grow readily but are somewhat more cold sensitive than typical *P. bifurcatum*. The following cultivars seem to be of this variety.

'Payton' — the fertile fronds have only 2–4 divisions and these spread stiffly apart.

'Pygmaeum' — an unusual dwarf form with compact shield fronds and short spreading fertile fronds. Believed to originate from New Guinea.

'Scofield' — the fertile fronds divide at a wide angle and the segments are broader than normal.

Platycerium 'Cass Hybrid'
Cultivar
clumping Trop.–S.Trop.: Epi.
This hybrid was deliberately made in Florida by mixing the spores of three or four species of *Platycerium*. It appears to be the result of a cross between *P. alcicorne* and *P. hillii* and is a vigorous, attractive form.

Platycerium coronarium
Malaysia, Indochina, Philippines, Indonesia
non-clumping Trop.: Epi.
A truly beautiful staghorn with bright green, closely embracing shield fronds which are deeply-lobed at the top. The fertile fronds are deeply divided and hang for 1–3 m (40–120 in). Plants are very cold sensitive and suited only to the tropics or a heated greenhouse with a minimum temperature of 15°C (60°F).

Platycerium elephantotis Cabbage Fern
Afria (tropics)
non-clumping Trop.: Epi.
A distinctive staghorn, readily recognized by its broad, undivided fertile fronds which have prominent, raised veins. As well, the shield fronds have entire, but very wavy margins and sweep upwards and outwards in a very distinctive manner. Plants are cold sensitive but grow readily in a heated greenhouse with a minimum temperature of 15°C (60°F).

Platycerium ellisii
Madagascar
non-clumping Trop.: Epi.
A small staghorn with roundish, closely embracing shield fronds which are entire or shallowly-lobed. The light green fertile fronds are held erect and widen suddenly toward the apex where they are divided into two lobes. An easily grown species that is somewhat cold sensitive needing a heated greenhouse with a minimum temperature of 10–15°C (50–60°F).

Platycerium holttumii Photo B. Gray

Platycerium hillii
Australia
clumping Trop.–S.Trop.: Epi.

Some authorities consider this a variety of *P. bifurcatum*. It is easily distinguished by its shallowly-lobed closely appressed shield fronds, and although plants may hybridize in cultivation they vary little in nature. The fertile fronds are held semi-erect and are shallowly lobed near the tips. Plants grow readily but are more cold sensitive than *P. bifurcatum* (minimum temperature 10°C [50°F]). A number of cultivars are known.

'Bloomei' — a distinct form with short deeply-lobed fertile fronds which impart a crowded impression.

'Drummond' — fertile fronds very broad, the apex divided into ten or more segments.

'Drummond Diversifolium' — fertile fronds even broader than above with the segments longer and drawn-out.

'Pumilum' — short fronds deeply-lobed with the lobes widely spreading.

Platycerium holttumii
Thailand, Vietnam, Laos
non-clumping Trop.: Epi.

Platycerium grande Staghorn Fern
Philippines
non-clumping Trop.: Epi.

A beautiful species which is basically similar to *P. superbum* except that the fertile leaves have two large spore patches instead of a solitary one. Plants are much more cold sensitive than *P. superbum* however, and need warmth and humidity (heated greenhouse with a minimum temperature of 15°C [60°F]).

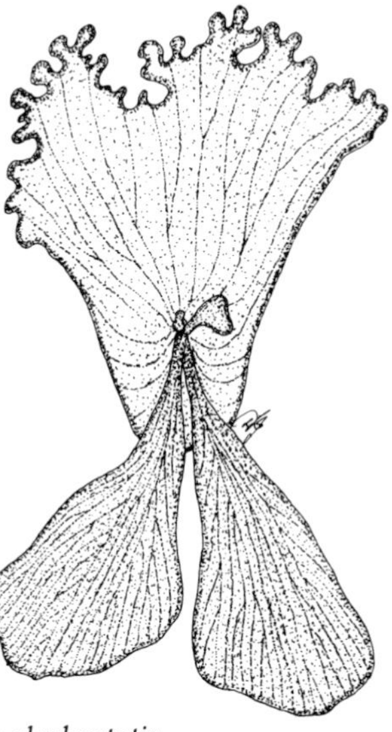

Platycerium elephantotis

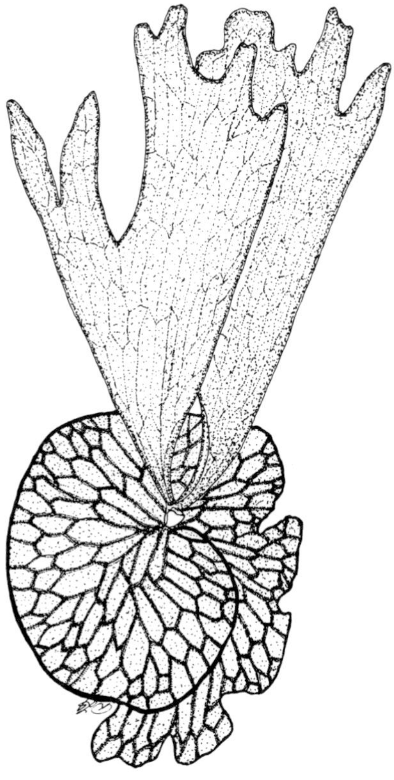

Platycerium madagascariense

This species is similar to *P. grande* but is light grey-green and has much shorter, sparsely-branched fertile fronds which are very broadly wedge-shaped at the base. Plants have proved to be cold sensitive and are best suited to the tropics or a heated greenhouse (minimum 15°C [60°F]).

Platycerium 'Lemoinei'
Cultivar
clumping Trop.–Temp.: Epi.

This cultivar was developed at the nursery of V. Lemoine and Son, in France and is reputedly a hybrid between *P. veitchii* and *P. bifurcatum* var. *willinckii*. The fertile fronds tend to be erect, especially at the base and are whitish-grey and much-branched. Plants grow easily in warm, humid conditions.

Platycerium madagascariense
Madagascar
non-clumping Trop.: Epi.

An interesting species with hygroscopic fronds which respond to large fluctuations in humidity. The shield fronds of this species are unmistakable, for they have prominently raised veins with sunken areas in between, creating an interesting pattern. Fertile fronds are very broad and pendulous with a few shallow lobes at the tip. The whole plant is very dark green. It is stringent in its requirements of heat (15–18°C [60–65°F]) and humidity.

Platycerium quadridichotomum
Madagascar
non-clumping Trop.: Epi.

A rarely grown species that is very tropical in its requirements (minimum temp. 18°C [65°F]). The shield fronds are loosely appressed with the upper margins shallowly-lobed and undulate. The fertile fronds are narrow and covered thickly on the underside with yellowish stellate hairs. These fronds hang and are divided 3–4 times.

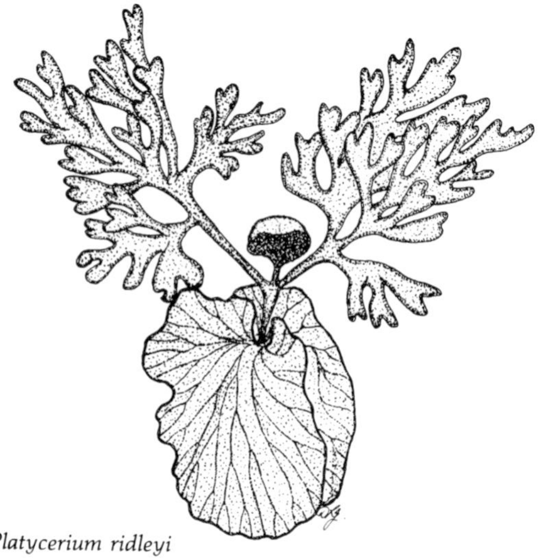

Platycerium ridleyi

Platycerium superbum Photo D. L. Jones

Platycerium ridleyi
Malaysia, Indonesia
non-clumping Trop.: Epi.

In cultivation this species has proved to be very cold sensitive and impossible to maintain in the absence of heat (18°C [65°F]). It is a beautiful fern with slightly-lobed shield fronds which are patterned by raised veins with sunken areas in between. The fertile fronds are held erect and fork many times, finally ending in rounded or expanded tips.

Young plants of *Platycerium superbum*
Photo D. L. Jones

Platycerium stemmaria Triangular Staghorn
Africa (tropics)
clumping Trop.: Epi.

A fairly small growing species with bright green, loosely enfolding sterile fronds which have shallowly-lobed and undulate margins. The fertile fronds are short and very broad. It requires tropical conditions for cultivation with a minimum temperature of 18°C (65°F). A well grown plant is highly ornamental.

Platycerium superbum Staghorn Fern
Australia
non-clumping Trop.-Temp.: Epi.

One of the most beautiful and easily grown members of the genus. Shield fronds are greyish-green, closely embracing and deeply-lobed at the apex. Bright green fertile fronds are deeply divided with a large, central spore patch and hang for 1-2 m (3-6 ft). Readily grown on trees in tropical and subtropical gardens. In cool climates plants need to be kept dry over winter.

Platycerium vassei = P. alcicorne

Platycerium veitchii Silver Elkhorn
Australia
clumping Trop.-S.Trop.: Epi.

A remarkable species which colonizes boulders and cliff faces in situations exposed to blazing hot sun.

Two plants of *Platycerium superbum* growing back to back

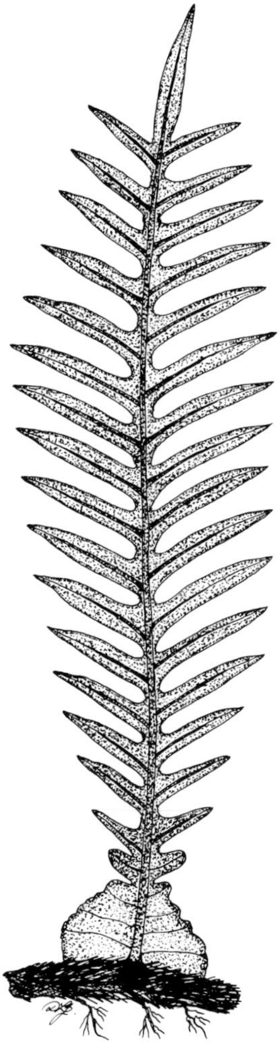

Pseudodrynaria coronans

Plants have a dense covering of white, woolly stellate hairs so as to avoid desiccation. The sterile fronds are closely appressed with the tips deeply divided. The fertile fronds are held stiffly erect and are divided near the apex into a few slender lobes. This species grows easily but needs much more light than most other platyceriums. Plants will happily tolerate sun. They will take a fair amount of cold but are best kept dry over winter.

Platycerium wallichii
Thailand, Malaysia
non-clumping Trop.: Epi.

A tropical fern which appears to be rather difficult to maintain in cultivation. The usual response is a slow decline of collected plants which appear to have a dormant period. Plants are cold sensitive requiring a minimum temperature of 15°C (60°F). This is the only *Platycerium* species with green spores.

Pseudodrynaria coronans Photo D. L. Jones

Platycerium wandae
New Guinea
non-clumping Trop.-S.Trop.: Epi.

A beautiful species which closely resembles *P. superbum,* but which can be distinguished by an unusual patch with toothed or laciniate margins situated just above the growing bud. Plants adapt well to cultivation requiring warmth and humidity (minimum temperature 10°C [50°F]).

Platycerium wilhelminae-reginae = P. wandae

Platycerium willinckii — see **P. bifurcatum** var. **willinckii**

Pseudodrynaria coronans
North India, China, Hong Kong, Taiwan
50–200 cm (20–80 in): pinnatifid Trop.-S.Trop.: Epi.

A large, coarse fern with a thick, woolly rhizome and a rosette of erect to arching dark green, leathery fronds. Bases of the fronds are expanded for the trapping of litter. This is a very adaptable and easy fern to grow either in the garden or in a container. Will tolerate a fair amount of cold (especially if kept dry) and needs good light.

28 The brakes

genus *Pteris*

The common name 'Brake' is a diminutive of bracken and arises because of the resemblance of some species to that fern. Brakes are an important and popular group of commercial ferns with many species and fancy cultivars propagated by nurseries throughout the world.

Habitat

Brakes are invariably terrestrial ferns and grow in a variety of habitats from shaded forests (*P. umbrosa*) to open sites (*P. vittata*). Many species are colonizers appearing on disturbed earth and sites of man's activity (*P. orientalis, P. tremula*). A few species commonly grow on limestone (*P. vittata, P. cretica*). Some species favour situations that are continually moist and humid (*P. comans*); others grow where dry seasons are a regular occurrence. *P. ensiformis* can colonize the mud among mangroves in large tidal rivers and estuaries of the tropics.

Cultivation

Uses

Species and cultivars of *Pteris* are popular with fern fanciers because of their adaptability and ease of culture. Many are useful for indoor decoration. Fast growing species are excellent for filling in gaps in the fernery (*P. biaurita, P. tremula*) and the larger types provide protection for smaller ferns beneath their umbrella-like fronds (*P. tripartita, P. wallichiana*). The smaller growing *Pteris* look attractive when planted among rocks.

Various species and cultivars of *Pteris* are ideal for containers with the smaller growing types succeeding in pots (*P. ensiformis, P. cretica* cultivars) and the larger types suitable for tubs (*P. quadriaurita*). *P. multifida* grows surprisingly well in a hanging basket.

Soil Types

Most Brakes are not fussy as to soil and will grow in a range of well-drained loams. Species such as *P. comans* and *P. umbrosa* will grow in wet to boggy soils providing the water is not stagnant. Most species prefer an acid soil but some need neutral to alkaline conditions (*P. cretica, P. vittata*).

Potting Mix

An open mix based on well-structured loam is usually suitable. Mixes containing peat moss or milled pine bark produce good growth. Cultivars of *P. cretica* and some others such as *P. vittata* respond to lime or limestone chips in the mix. *Pteris* ferns generally have a strong root system and quickly fill a pot with roots. Vigorous plants will need repotting once or twice a year.

Watering

Brakes like plenty of water while in active growth but should not be overwatered during the winter. Getting sufficient water to the roots can be a problem with potbound plants. Some *Pteris* are very sensitive to drying of the root system and generally die following such an occurrence, e.g. *P. comans, P. macilenta*.

Fertilizing

As a group these ferns are strong growers and respond to the use of manures and fertilizers. Liquid fertilizers applied during the warm months and slow release fertilizers in the potting mix are beneficial. Blood and bone, well-rotted animal manures and compost are suitable for plants in the ground and should be applied in the spring or the summer.

Situation

Exposure to morning sun or filtered sun is ideal for most species. Some like shady conditions and must be protected from direct, hot sun (*P. comans, P. umbrosa*), others resent shade and need at least some sun (*P. tripartita, P. vittata*). Species from temperate regions will tolerate light to mild frosts but the tropical species are generally very sensitive to cold.

Pests

Caterpillars may eat the fronds of some of the finely divided species such as *P. tremula* and *P. macilenta*. Aphids may attack unrolling fronds in spring.

Propagation

Pteris are generally very easy to raise from spores and they are an ideal group for beginners learning to propagate. Sporelings and young plants can be surprisingly fast growing. Judging when fronds are ripe for spore collection can be very difficult as the sporangia are hidden by a long indusium. The optimum time is when the indusium turns dark-brown to black and when a few sporangia are visibly protruding from the edge. These will be more readily seen under a hand lens. Sori which have a fluffy appearance are well past dispersal.

Species of *Pteris* with a creeping rhizome can be divided, however, some resent disturbance and are best left as specimen plants (*P. comans, P. macilenta*).

SPECIES AND CULTIVARS

Pteris altissima Forest Brake
Mexico, Central and South America
100–250 cm (40–100 in): 3 pinnate Trop.–S.Trop.: Terr.

A large fern of shaded stream banks and rocky situations. Fronds are delicately dissected and lacy. Plants can be grown in a large pot or shady situation and they appreciate plenty of water, mulch and well-rotted manure.

Pteris argyraea Silver Brake
India
60–100 cm (24–40 in): 1–2 pinnate Trop.–Temp.: Terr.

One of the most popular brakes in cultivation, this species is grown for its ornamental foliage in many countries. The striking, silver variegation of the fronds attracts immediate attention. Plants can be grown in the ground or in a pot and can be used for indoor decoration. In the garden a semi-shady position is satisfactory. Sometimes included as a variety of *P. quadriaurita*.

Pteris biaurita
Pantropical
60–150 cm (24–60 in): 1–2 pinnate Trop.–S.Trop.: Terr.

A strong growing and adaptable *Pteris* that can be grown in a variety of situations, but with best appearance under moist, shady conditions. The fronds have a pleasing symmetry and clumps can be quite dense. Once established plants are very hardy and can tolerate dry spells. They respond well to mulches and manures.

Pteris buchananii
South Africa
50–150 cm (20–60 in): 3–4 pinnate Temp.–S.Trop.: Terr.

A species with broadly triangular dark green fronds arising from a widely creeping rhizome. It grows in moist, shady forests, sometimes with its roots in water. An attractive fern which forms a spreading clump. Requires organically rich, acid soil.

The striking variegated fronds of *Pteris argyraea* Photo D. L. Jones

Pteris biaurita is a clumping fern Photo D. L. Jones

Pteris 'Childsii'
cultivar
30–50 cm (12–20 in): 2 pinnate S.Trop.–Temp.: Terr.

This fern is of unknown origin and apparently arose as the result of accidental hybridization. It has affinities with *Pteris cretica* and is sometimes regarded as a cultivar of that species. It has attractively crisped and lacerated fronds which are crested on the ends of the segments. It grows easily in a pot of fibrous well-drained mixture but since it is sterile it can only be propagated by division or perhaps tissue culture.

Pteris comans Netted Brake
Australia
100–200 cm (40–80 in): 3 pinnate Temp.–S.Trop.: Terr.

In nature this brake favours boggy soils in shady locations. In appearance it resembles a vigorous *P. tremula* but can be distinguished by the netted venation. The fronds are very thinly-textured and a lush, dark green. Plants are somewhat difficult to maintain in cultivation and are very sensitive to drying of the root system (see also *P. microptera*).

Pteris cretica Cretan Brake
Africa, Southern Europe, Asia
40–70 cm (16–28 in): 1–2 pinnate Temp.–S.Trop.: Terr.

A very widespread species which readily extends its range by naturalization. Its fronds are markedly dimorphic with the fertile ones having thinner segments and being held stiffly erect. It is an easy and

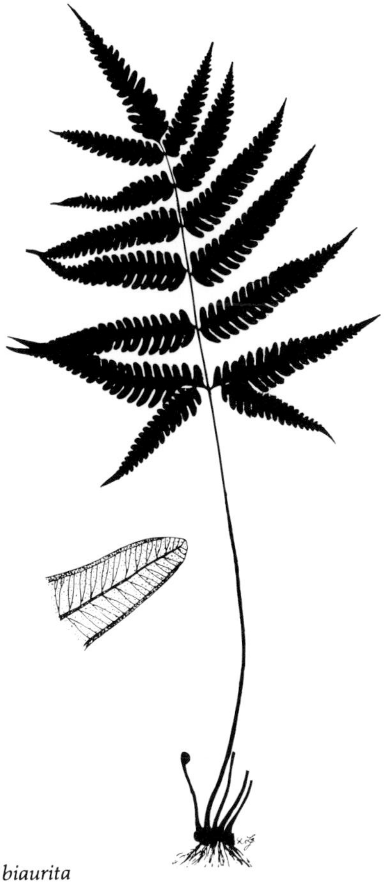

Pteris biaurita

Pteris 'Childsii'

Pteris cretica 'Distinction'

A clump of *Pteris cretica* 'Albo-lineata'
Photo D. L. Jones

rewarding fern to grow in a pot or in a variety of situations in the ground but needs lime in the soil or potting mix. It is extremely variable and is perhaps best known for its cultivars, some of which are important nursery plants in various countries.

'Albo-lineata' – readily distinguished by a broad, white stripe running the length of each segment. Often regarded as a botanical variety.

'Albo-lineata Alexandrae' – as above but the segment tips have small, narrow crests.

'Albo-lineata Cristata' – as above but the segment tips are very broadly crested. A very beautiful fern.

'Albo-lineata Cristata Mayi' – as above but the segment tips broad and flattened or with finger-like lobes.

'Angustata' – a form with very narrow segments which are heavily and deeply crested at the tips.

'Distinction' – a compact form with lobed margins and the tips irregularly divided into finger-like lobes.

'Grandis' – a dwarf growing form with the segment margins deeply-lobed and lacerated.

'Ouvrardii' – a vigorous form with broad segments.

'Parkeri' – a very handsome, strong-growing form with very broad segments.

'Rivertoniana' – a vigorous form with deeply and irregularly lobed margins to the segments.

'Wilsonii' – a popular form with heavily crested tips to the segments.

'Wimsettii' – one of the most popular forms grown, the segments of which have numerous long marginal lobes.

Pteris dentata Toothed Brake
Africa, Mauritius, Aegean Islands, Mascarene Islands
50–180 cm (20–72 in): 3–4 pinnate S.Trop.–Trop.: Terr.

A very attractive fern which forms a clump of bright green fronds which are finely dissected and lacy. The ultimate segments have conspicuous teeth on their margins. Plants like a well lit but protected situation such as under a sparse canopy of trees. A well grown clump is most ornamental.

Pteris dispar – see **P. semipinnata** var. **dispar**

Pteris ensiformis Slender Brake
India, China, Japan, Sri Lanka, Malaysia, Australia, Polynesia
15–30 cm (6–12 in): 2 pinnate Trop.–S.Trop.: Terr.

A widespread fern found in a variety of habitats from the fringes of mangroves to the margins of forests. It frequently colonizes disturbed areas and man-made structures such as brick walls. Plants look attractive in a container or in a garden setting among rocks. They are frequently quite long-lived. A couple of attractive cultivars are commonly grown in the tropics.

'Evergemiensis' – segments have a striking silver-white band down the centre contrasting with the dark green margins. Comes true from spore.

'Victoriae' – segments have a white zone on either side of the midrib. Comes true from spore.

Pteris cretica 'Wilsonii'

Pteris fauriei Photo D. L. Jones

Pteris hendersonii Photo D. L. Jones

Pteris dentata

Pteris fauriei
Japan, China
20–60 cm (8–24 in): 1–2 pinnate S.Trop.: Terr.

A fairly small growing brake found on shaded forest floors. The fronds arch, are attractively lobed, and are light green in colour. Plants respond well to cultivation but are fairly slow growing and prefer a well-drained fibrous soil. They like a shady situation and appreciate mulches.

Pteris hendersonii
China
60–80 cm (24–32 in): 3 pinnate S.Trop.–Temp.: Terr.

Although of uncertain origin, this fern is well entrenched in the nursery trade of a few countries. It is prized for its neat clump of light green, finely dissected fronds. Plants look attractive in a container or in a garden setting among rocks and they can be quite fast growing.

Pteris kingiana
Norfolk Island
60–150 cm (24–60 in): 3–4 pinnate Temp.–S.Trop.: Terr.

A strong growing fern reminiscent of *P. tremula* but with coarser segments and thicker textured, dark green fronds. It adapts very well to cultivation in situations from partial sun to shade. Plants prefer loamy, well-drained soils.

Pteris kiuschiuensis
Japan
50–80 cm (20–32 in): 1–2 pinnate S.Trop.: Terr.

This fern is very similar to *P. biaurita* but the fronds are relatively wider and have an attractive arching habit. They are fairly thinly-textured and are sensitive to desiccation and hence the plants should be grown in a moist, protected position.

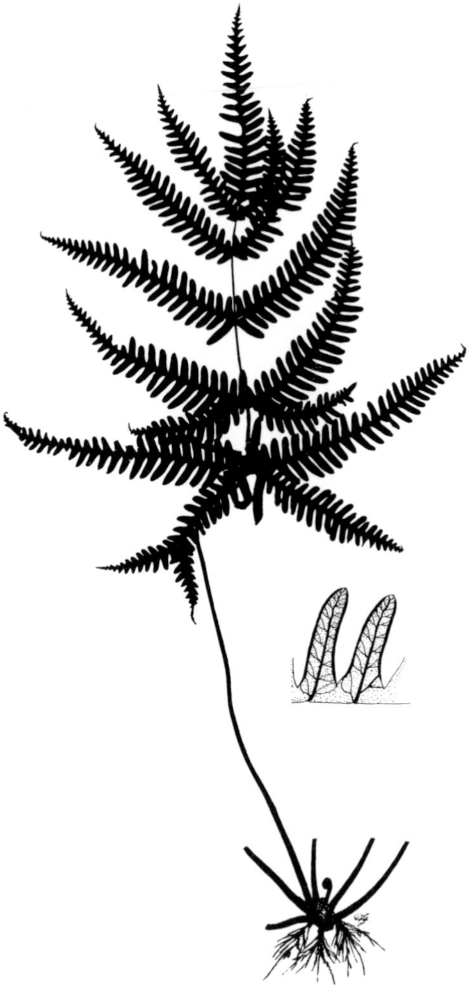

Pteris kiuschiuensis

Pteris longifolia
Florida, Central America, West Indies
60–80 cm (24–32 in): 1 pinnate Trop.–S.Trop.: Terr.

This species has been confused for many years with *P. vittata*, however, it has generally more segments per frond with the margins slightly crenate rather than deeply toothed. Plants can be grown in a partially exposed to protected situation and like plenty of water during dry periods.

Pteris macilenta New Zealand Brake
New Zealand
50–100 cm (20–40 in): 3 pinnate Temp.–S.Trop.: Terr.

A very fast growing fern which has a remarkable sensitivity to drying of the root system. Established plants rarely recover from such an occurrence. The species is best planted in a moist semi-shady situation which is well mulched. It can be propagated readily from spores.

Pteris microptera has very shiny fronds
Photo D. L. Jones

Pteris microptera
Lord Howe Island, Fiji, Pacific Islands
60–100 cm (24–40 in): 3 pinnate Trop.–S.Trop.: Terr.

This fern has been confused with *P. comans* but can be distinguished by its more compact growth habit and fronds of much thicker texture. Plants are much more reliable in cultivation and are long-lived in a shady situation.

Pteris macilenta

Pteris multifida Spider Brake
China, Japan
15–45 cm (6–18 in): 1–2 pinnate Temp.–Trop.: Terr.

A very popular fern which grows into a compact dense clump of bright green fronds. It can be grown easily in a pot or semi-shady garden situation and frequently colonizes and becomes weedy. Plants look quite decorative in a hanging basket and can be used indoors. A few cultivars are known.

'Cristata' – tends to be smaller growing than the typical form and each segment ends in a broad crest. Comes true from spores. A variegated form is much sought after.

'Corymbifera' – has the apex of each segment very finely crested.

'Tenuifolia' – is a form with very slender segments.

Pteris nipponica
Japan
20–45 cm (8–18 in): 1 pinnate Temp.–S.Trop.: Terr.

This is a relatively small species with a strong superficial resemblance to *P. cretica*. Margins of the juvenile fronds are toothed and a pale band runs down the centre of each segment. An easily grown species requiring humus-rich, loamy acid soil and a shady situation.

Pteris orientalis Oriental Brake
Philippines, New Guinea, Australia
80–120 cm (32–48 in): 1 pinnate Trop.–S.Trop.: Terr.

A weedy fern of the tropics which readily colonizes roadsides, nurseries, greenhouses etc. Plants are very fast growing and adaptable, tolerating nearly full sunshine as well as a fair degree of shade. They appreciate watering during dry periods.

Pteris pacifica
Australia
60–80 cm (24–32 in): 2 pinnate Trop.–Temp.: Terr.

Pteris pacifica is a graceful fern Photo D. L. Jones

Pteris pacifica

A truly delightful fern which grows in dense, neat clumps. The fronds are pleasantly divided with spreading segments. New fronds are frequently pale green and contrast with the much deeper green of mature fronds. Plants grow readily in a pot or shady situation and appreciate mulch and manure.

Pteris propinqua
Mexico, Brazil, Venezuela, Peru, West Indies
50–150 cm (20–60 in): 3 pinnate S.Trop.–Temp.: Terr.

An easily grown species which occurs naturally along the margins of rainforests in highland areas. Plants prefer well-drained but moist soil in a semi-shady situation. They can be quite fast growing and are easy to raise from spores. One unusual feature of this fern is the long stipe which occupies about two thirds of the length of the fronds.

Pteris pteridioides
Africa
60–120 cm (24–48 in): 2–3 pinnate Trop.–Temp.: Terr.

An attractive species with broad (almost palmate) finely divided, dark green fronds arising from an erect rhizome. It grows in wet, shady forests at medium altitudes. Requires moist to wet shady conditions in humus-rich, acid soil.

Pteris semipinnata var *dispar* Photo D. L. Jones

Pteris tremula Photo D. L. Jones

Pteris quadriaurita
Pantropic
60–100 cm (24–40 in): 1–2 pinnate Trop.–S.Trop.: Terr.

This is a very widely distributed and complex fern which consists of many different forms, quite a number of which are in cultivation. The typical form has thinly-textured fronds, which have long prominent spines along main veins on the underside and the tips of the segments have serrated margins. Some of the forms in cultivation may be of hybrid origin and are difficult to identify with any accuracy. All forms of the fern seem to adapt very well to cultivation (see also *P. argyraea* and *P. tricolor* which are regarded by some authors as varieties of *P. quadriaurita*).

Pteris ryukyuensis
Ryukyu Islands (Japan)
20–40 cm (8–16 in): 1 pinnate S.Trop.–Temp.: Terr.

In general appearance this little fern resembles *P. ensiformis*. It occurs naturally in rock crevices; the sterile fronds are short and crowded and the fertile fronds are tall and tend to be straggly. It grows easily in a pot but may be slow to establish in the garden.

Pteris semipinnata
Japan, China, Taiwan, Malaysia
50–80 cm (20–32 in): 2 pinnate Trop.–S.Trop.: Terr.

This graceful fern is distinctive for its one-sided pinnae, a feature which gave rise to its specific epithet. It succeeds admirably as a garden plant or in a rockery and can also be grown in a pot. Plants appreciate organic litter and mulches. The var. *dispar* is a compact, smaller growing variety. Some botanists regard it as a distinct species.

Pteris tremula Tender Brake
Australia, New Zealand, Norfolk Island, Fiji
60–120 cm (24–48 in): 3 pinnate Temp.–S.Trop.: Terr.

A very attractive fast growing fern that is valued because of its delicate lacy fronds which are a verdant green. It grows readily in a variety of situations and can naturalize itself freely. Plants will tolerate considerable sun but for best appearance should have some protection.

Pteris tricolor Painted Brake
Malacca
60–80 cm (24–32 in): 1–2 pinnate S.Trop.–Trop.: Terr.

The colourful fronds of this fern make it popular with fern fanciers. New fronds unroll a deep purplish-red and fade to bronze and then green as they mature. The stipe and main veins retain a purplish colouration and provide a patterned contrast. Plants can be grown in a pot or a warm, protected position.

Pteris tripartita Giant Brake
Pantropical
100–250 cm (40–100 in): 4 pinnate Trop.–S.Trop.: Terr.

This hardy fern is almost a tropical weed and is a frequent colonizer of disturbed areas, greenhouses etc. Plants will tolerate considerable exposure to sun and because of their large size can be useful for sheltering other plants. Spores germinate easily and young plants are fast growing.

A young frond of *Pteris tricolor* Photo D. L. Jones

Pteris tripartita Photo D. L. Jones

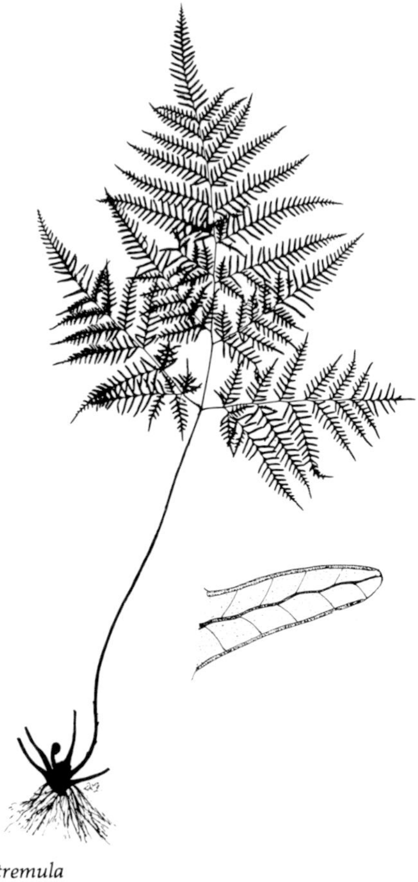

Pteris tremula

Pteris umbrosa Jungle Brake
Australia
60–120 cm (24–48 in): 2 pinnate Temp.–Trop.: Terr.

A fern of jungle flats and rainforests, often colonizing stream banks. Plants form a very dense clump of dark green shiny fronds. They look very attractive in a fernery or a shady garden position, and appreciate an abundance of water and organic mulch. In suitable situations they are very long-lived.

Pteris vittata growing on mortar in a sandstone wall Photo D. L. Jones

Pteris umbrosa

Pteris vittata Chinese Brake
South Africa, Madagascar, Asia, Japan, Malaysia, New Guinea, Australia
60–100 cm (24–40 in): 1 pinnate Temp.-Trop.: Terr.

A very widely distributed fern usually found in sunny situations, often among rocks which are sometimes of limestone formation. It is a hardy garden plant which shuns shade and revels in sunshine. Requires free drainage but appreciates watering during dry periods.

Pteris wallichiana
India, China, Japan, Malaysia, New Guinea, Samoa
200–300 cm (80–120 in): 4 pinnate Trop.-Temp.: Terr.

A giant fern which has tall, attractively divided, umbrella-like fronds. Spores germinate readily and young plants are very fast growing. They thrive in the tropics but have also proved to be adaptable and will succeed in warm temperate regions.

29 The tree ferns

genera *Cibotium, Cnemidaria, Cyathea, Dicksonia, Nephelea* and *Trichipteris*

Tree Ferns are a popular group with fern enthusiasts and some growers specialize in their collection and cultivation. A few species such as *Cyathea cooperi* and *Dicksonia antarctica* have become important landscape subjects and are propagated by commercial nurseries.

Most Tree Ferns have a distinctive arborescent growth habit and consist of a woody or fibrous trunk topped by a crown of spreading fronds. Many are massive ferns, however, some species may be quite small growing. A few interesting ones have a creeping or prostrate trunk. Young Tree Ferns are notable for their rounded crown of fronds.

Habitat

Tree Ferns are distributed in a wide range of habitats from cool temperate forests to tropical rainforests. In some situations they may be the dominant component of the vegetation. Some species grow in shade; others occur in very open situations. Many species grow as shade plants while they are small but when older the crowns emerge from the forest canopy and may be exposed to full sun. In the tropics, Tree Ferns are abundant in lowland situations and also have a significant development on tropical mountains. Some species are colonizers of disturbed earth.

Cultivation

Uses

As a general rule, Tree Ferns adapt very well to cultivation. They are valued for their decorative appearance and are frequently used in commercial landscaping around pools etc. Some species are widely planted in private and municipal gardens in temperate, subtropical and tropical regions. Established Tree Ferns provide excellent shelter for tender ground ferns and epiphytic plants can be established on their trunks. Some, particularly species of *Dicksonia*, make very ornamental tub plants and will grow for many years in the one container if regularly watered and fertilized. Such plants can be a prized addition to the indoor decor of large rooms, hallways etc.

Soil Types

Tree Ferns will grow in many soil types but generally appreciate acid loams rich in organic matter. Some species of *Cyathea* and *Dicksonia* will withstand wet soils (e.g. *C. australis, D. antarctica*) but as a general rule free drainage is necessary. (Species of *Cibotium* may be quite sensitive to badly drained soils.)

Potting Mix

Container-grown Tree Ferns like an open, free draining mix rich in organic matter. Most Tree Ferns are very strong growers and quickly fill a container with roots. Young Tree Ferns should be moved to the next size container as soon as a substantial number of roots appear on the outside of the potting mix. This procedure maintains strong growth and avoids setbacks to the plants.

Watering

Tree Ferns like an abundance of water especially during the warm growing months. Once established, many species are quite resistant to dryness but look better with supplementary watering.

Fertilizing

As a general rule Tree Ferns are heavy feeders. This is especially true of the vigorous growing types such as *Cyathea cooperi*. Regular dressings of organic or inorganic fertilizers and manures maintain strong growth. These are best applied in the spring or early in the summer months. Potting mixes for Tree Ferns should contain manures or slow-release fertilizers.

Situation

Being such a large group of ferns, a species can be found to grow in many situations. Some species such as *Cyathea cooperi* are very adaptable and will grow in a variety of positions from shade to full sun. Others like *C. baileyana* demand shade and protection and will not succeed in an adverse situation. Tree Ferns from tropical regions are sensitive to cold and frost whereas species from temperate regions are generally hardy to these occurrences. Strong or buffeting winds may damage Tree-fern fronds.

Pests

One of the commonest problems with young Tree Ferns is the disease known as hard crown. This results from attacks by the fungus *Rhizoctonia* and it causes stunting and badly distorted fronds (see page 116). Passion vine hoppers may also damage Tree-fern fronds, particularly the unrolling croziers, where their feeding results in papery patches in the pinnae. Attacks by this pest are sporadic.

Propagation

Tree Ferns are generally very easy to raise from spores. Some, particularly species of *Cyathea*, can be quite fast growing while others may be slow (e.g. *Dicksonia* species). Tree-fern spore can be successfully stored for many years, however, freshly collected spore gives more certain results. Tree-fern spores germinate best on a rough surface and many species prefer a near neutral sowing medium (pH 6.5–7.5). A proven mixture for sowing is equal parts tree-fern fibre, scoria or fly ash and peat moss.

The sporangia of species of *Cyathea* and related genera take on a granular or sugary appearance when they are mature and ready for collection. This stage can be much more difficult to judge with species of *Cibotium* and *Dicksonia* since the sorus is hidden by two indusia. A change in colour of the indusium from green to brown is a useful indicator. The appearance of the first few empty sporangia (as seen under a hand lense), signals a good time for collection.

Some species of Tree Fern reproduce by basal suckers or stolons, or growths on the trunk. These growths when separated can be a useful means of propagating the species.

SPECIES AND CULTIVARS

Alsophila australis — see **Cyathea australis**

Alsophila baileyana — see **Cyathea baileyana**

Alsophila brevipinna — see **Cyathea brevipinna**

Alsophila capensis — see **Cyathea capensis**

Alsophila colensoi — see **Cyathea colensoi**

Alsophila cunninghamii — see **Cyathea cunninghamii**

Alsophila dregei — see **Cyathea dregei**

Alsophila gigantea — see **Cyathea gigantea**

Alsophila hornei — see **Cyathea hornei**

Alsophila kermadecensis — see **Cyathea kermadecensis**

Cibotium regale Photo D. L. Jones

Alsophila loheri — see **Cyathea loheri**

Alsophila rebeccae — see **Cyathea rebeccae**

Alsophila robertsiana — see **Cyathea robertsiana**

Alsophila smithii — see **Cyathea smithii**

Alsophila spinulosa — see **Cyathea spinulosa**

Alsophila tricolor — see **Cyathea dealbata**

Alsophila vieillardii — see **Cyathea vieillardii**

Alsophila woollsiana — see **Cyathea woollsiana**

Cibotium barometz
India, China, Malaysia
prostrate: fronds 100–200 cm (40–80 in): Trop.–S.Trop.: Terr.

This species has an interesting growth habit, for the trunk creeps along the surface of the ground with the fronds arising in a crown at the apex. Plants are hardy and easily grown. They will grow in sun or shade, need good drainage and respond to mulches and extra water during dry periods.

Cibotium chamissoi Man Fern
Hawaii
trunk 200–500 cm (80–200 in): fronds 200–300 cm (80–120 in) Trop.–S.Trop.: Terr.

Cibotium schiedei Photo W. R. Elliot

Cyathea albifrons Photo W. R. Elliot

A huge tree fern with a widely-spreading crown of fronds and a thick trunk. The upper part of the trunk and the stipes are covered with a thick mass of light brown hairs. This is a truly beautiful fern which needs warm, sheltered conditions and must be supplied with plenty of water.

Cibotium glaucum Hawaiian Tree Fern/Hapu
Hawaii
trunk 200–600 cm (80–240 in): fronds 200–300 cm (80–120 in) Trop.–S.Trop.: Terr.

An interesting species with spreading, thick-textured, almost leathery fronds which are markedly glaucous or even waxy beneath. Plants like warm sheltered conditions with plenty of moisture. In some cases plants may be slow growing, but others are fast. Young plants are sensitive to wind damage.

Cibotium regale
Mexico, Honduras, Guatemala, El Salvador
trunk 100–400 cm (40–160 in): fronds 300–400 cm (120–160 in) Trop.–S.Trop.: Terr.

A decorative tree fern which has a crown of fairly coarse fronds which range from grey to prominently glaucous on the underside. Plants are slow growing and some enthusiasts have reported them as being difficult to establish. They need shade, moisture and a well-drained acid soil.

Cibotium schiedei Mexican Tree Fern
Mexico
trunk 200–400 cm (80–160 in): fronds 200–300 cm (80–120 in) S.Trop.–Temp.: Terr.

A graceful tree fern with long, drawn-out pinnae and matted brown hairs on the upper parts of the trunk and on the frond bases. Plants grow in clumps and adapt well to cultivation. They prefer shade and moisture.

Cnemidaria horrida Prickly-stemmed Tree Fern
Central and South America, West Indies
trunk 30–120 cm (12–48 in): fronds 150–240 cm (60–96 in) Trop.–S.Trop.: Terr.

A tree fern which develops a short woody trunk and a crown of coarse, dark, glossy-green fronds. The stipes are covered with large black thorns hence the common name. This is an easily grown fern which likes shady conditions and plenty of moisture.

Cyathea albifrons
New Caledonia
trunk 100–300 cm (40–120 in): fronds 150–250 cm (60–100 in) Trop.–S.Trop.: Terr.

A beautiful tree fern with a moderately stout trunk covered with prominent white scales. The under-surface of the fronds is conspicuously white, almost with a waxy lustre. Plants are rarely cultivated but have outstanding ornamental features. They are relatively fast growing and like good light with some protection.

Cyathea arborea West Indian Tree Fern
Central and South America, West Indies
trunk 500–1000 cm (200–400 in): fronds 300–400 cm (120–160 in) Trop.–S.Trop.: Terr.

A very fast growing tree fern which in nature is a colonizer, growing on disturbed earth, landslips, embankments etc. Young plants have yellow-green, lacy fronds. As they form a trunk the fronds spread in a lacy crown and retain the yellow-green colouration. The trunk is slender, naked (with leaf scars) and the apex is covered with large, pale scales. Plants grow easily with warmth, moisture and bright light (partial to filtered sun).

Cyathea australis (alt **Alsophila australis**) Rough Tree Fern
Australia, Norfolk Island
trunk 100–300 cm (40–120 in): fronds 200–300 cm (80–120 in) Temp.–S.Trop.: Terr.

A popular, cold-hardy tree fern that has proved to be adaptable to a variety of soils and climates. Plants are also excellent for tub culture and can be maintained in good condition with little effort. In temperate climates they will tolerate considerable exposure to sun, however, in hotter climates they need some protection. Plants respond to plenty of water in an acid, loamy soil.

ssp. *norfolkiensis* from Norfolk Island has shiny green fronds.

Cyathea australis with a flush of new fronds; the old ones have been flattened by snow Photo D. L. Jones

Cyathea australis — on left showing specimen suitable for transplating, on right as often sold but with little chance of growing

Cyathea baileyana (alt. **Alsophila baileyana**) Wig Tree Fern
Australia
trunk 100–300 cm (40–120 in): fronds 200–300 cm (80–120 in) S.Trop.–Temp.: Terr.

A curious, clustering, wig-like growth covers the trunk apex of this tree fern and is formed by specialized basal segments of the fronds. Apart from the wig, plants closely resemble *C. rebeccae* and, like that species, are quite slow growing. They need shade, good loamy soil and plenty of water. This species has proved to be extremely difficult to raise from spores.

Cyathea borinquena = Trichipteris borinquena

Cyathea brevipinna (alt. **Alsophila brevipinna**)
Lord Howe Island
trunk 50–150 cm (20–60 in): fronds 60–100 cm (24–40 in) Temp.–S.Trop.: Terr.

An unusual tree fern with short densely-crowded fronds. The stipe of each frond is very short or almost absent and the basal segments overlap and crowd the centre of the trunk. Fronds have a stiff spreading habit. Plants are very slow growing and require bright light, moisture and protection from strong wind.

Cyathea brownii (alt. **Sphaeropteris excelsa**) Norfolk Island Tree Fern
Norfolk Island
trunk 200–500 cm (80–200 in): fronds 200–300 cm (80–120 in) S.Trop.–Temp.: Terr.

Vigorous young plants of this tree fern develop a

The delicate wig which covers the upper part of the trunk of *Cyathea baileyana* Photo D. L. Jones

Cyathea brevipinna with *Blechnum* aff. *oceanicum* growing on its trunk Photo D. L. Jones

massive trunk, the apex of which is covered with pale brown scales. The stipes are also thick and croziers imposingly large. The whole plant looks like a very vigorous *C. cooperi* and the two species are quite closely related. Plants of *C. brownii* thrive in a partial sun situation and appreciate adequate moisture. They can be very fast growing.

Cyathea capensis (alt. **Alsophila capensis**) Cape Tree Fern
Africa
trunk 100–400 cm (40–160 in): fronds 150–250 cm (60–100 in) Temp.–S.Trop.: Terr.

A hardy tree fern with dark-green, somewhat shiny fronds on long dark-brown stipes. A mixture of scales and hairs is present on the underside of the fronds. Plants like shady to semi-shady situations in well-drained soil and plenty of moisture.

Cyathea celebica (alt. **Sphaeropteris celebica**)
Australia, New Guinea, Celebes
trunk 100–400 cm (40–160 in): fronds 200–300 cm (80–120 in) Trop.–Temp.: Terr.

Unfurling fronds of this tree fern are delightful, for they are covered in cobweb-like hairs. This is a magnificent species with one major drawback to its wider cultivation — the presence of brittle black spines on the stipes and rachises. Plants grow easily in a sheltered situation and like plenty of water.

Cyathea colensoi (alt. **Alsophila colensoi**)
New Zealand
prostrate: fronds 50–150 cm (20–60 in) Temp.–S.Trop.: Terr.

An interesting tree fern with a creeping, subterranean trunk. Fronds arise in a crown at the soil

Cyathea colensoi (two pinnae)

surface and are short, broad and shiny green. Plants can be grown readily in a tub but are best planted in the ground in a semi-shady aspect. They like plenty of moisture and well-drained soils.

Cyathea contaminans (alt. **Sphaeropteris glauca**)
New Guinea, Indonesia, Philippines, Malaysia
trunk 300–600 cm (120–240 in): fronds 300–400 cm (120–160 in) Trop.–S.Trop.: Terr.

This is a very widespread tree fern that commonly grows as a colonizer in the tropics. Plants can be very fast growing and always occur in a sunny situation. The stipes and rachises are prickly and the underside of the fronds is grey to glaucous. Previously known as *C. glauca*.

Cyathea cooperi (alt. **Sphaeropteris cooperi**) Lacy Tree Fern
Australia
trunk 200–500 cm (80–200 in): fronds 200–300 cm (80–120 in) Trop.–Temp.: Terr.

A very popular tree fern that is commonly grown in many tropical and subtropical areas. Plants have a characteristic spreading crown of light-green, lacy fronds and a slender, 'coin spotted' trunk. Young croziers and stipe bases are covered with large, pale-coloured papery scales. Plants are very fast growing and like a sunny aspect and plenty of moisture. They also respond to heavy applications of manures and fertilizers (urea spread over the ground and watered in is very good in the tropics). This is an extremely variable tree fern with some plants having a massive trunk apex similar to *C. brownii*. The colour of the scales is variable (from silver white to brown) as is the length of time they are retained on the plant. A couple of cultivars have been selected in the USA but these are probably no more than normal variations as found in the wild.

'Brentwood' — a robust form with coppery scales and light-green fronds.

'Robusta' — fronds are dark green and the scales are a dark coppery colour.

Cyathea costaricensis = Trichipteris costaricensis

Cyathea cunninghamii (alt. **Alsophila cunninghamii**)
Slender Tree Fern
Australia, New Zealand
trunk 100–300 cm (40–120 in): fronds 50–150 cm (20–60 in) Temp.: Terr.

This tree fern is stringent in its requirements of humus-rich acid soils, shade and moisture and detests sun and especially wind. Plants are rather slow-growing and only develop a small crown.

Cyathea dealbata (alt. **Alsophila tricolor**) Silver Tree Fern/Ponga
New Zealand
trunk 100–300 cm (40–120 in): fronds 150–250 cm (60–100 in) Temp.–S.Trop.: Terr.

Cyathea dealbata Photo D. L. Jones

A popular tree fern well known for the silvery white undersides to the fronds and stipes. Plants like an abundance of water and for best appearance need a sheltered situation. They develop a crown quickly but trunk growth is generally slow. Very effective if planted where the fronds are illuminated by lights at night.

Cyathea dregei (alt. **Alsophila dregei**)
Africa, Madagascar
trunk 100–400 cm (40–160 in): fronds 150–300 cm (60–120 in) Temp.–S.Trop.: Terr.

A large tree fern with a very stout, dark trunk, glossy brown scales and spreading, deep green fronds. Plants are fairly slow growing. They need shady to semi-shady situations in well-drained soil and must be well-watered during dry periods.

Cyathea gigantea (alt. **Alsophila gigantea**)
India, China, Sri Lanka, Burma, Thailand, Laos, Vietnam
trunk 100–500 cm (40–200 in): fronds 200–300 cm (80–120 in) Trop.–S.Trop.: Terr.

A widely distributed tree fern which has long stipes which are densely covered with shiny, dark-brown scales. Fronds are bright-green and fairly thinly-textured. Plants will tolerate exposure to sun in a sheltered, moist situation.

Cyathea glauca = C. contaminans

Cyathea hornei (alt. **Alsophila hornei**)
New Guinea, Fiji
trunk 100–300 cm (40–120 in): fronds 150–200 cm (60–80 in) Trop.–S.Trop.: Terr.

An attractive tree fern with dark-green, lacy fronds in a spreading crown (the basal pinnae are reduced to a wig) and a slender trunk topped with masses of dark scales which have a pale margin. Fertile segments are much smaller than sterile ones giving the fronds a dimorphic appearance. Likes shady conditions and plenty of moisture.

Cyathea howeana
Lord Howe Island
trunk 100–200 cm (40–80 in): fronds 150–200 cm (60–80 in) S.Trop.–Temp.: Terr.

A delightful tree fern with a spreading crown of soft, lacy, light-green fronds atop a slender trunk. On older plants the new fronds are produced in a spectacular, unfurling flush. Plants resent disturbance and may be somewhat slow to re-establish. They like cool, moist conditions in a shady to semi-shady situation.

Cyathea kermadecensis (alt. **Alsophila kermadecensis**)
Kermadec Islands
trunk 100–300 cm (40–120 in): fronds 100–250 cm (40–100 in) Temp.–S.Trop.: Terr.

A beautiful but rarely-grown tree fern. Plants have a slender, woody trunk with a conspicuous mass of light-brown scales over the croziers and stipes. The crown of fronds is dark green and spreads almost at right angles to the trunk. Plants have proved to be quite fast growing and like strong light, humidity and plenty of moisture.

Cyathea leichhardtiana (alt. **Sphaeropteris australis**)
Australia
trunk 200–400 cm (80–160 in): fronds 150–250 cm (60–100 in) Trop.–Temp.: Terr.

A tall slender tree fern with white woolly scales and long, shiny-green fronds which have numerous black spines on the stipes and rachises. It can be a handsome plant, but in adverse conditions quickly loses character and becomes tatty. Plants need shade, plenty of moisture and protection from wind.

Cyathea lepifera (alt. **Sphaeropteris lepifera**) Flying Spider-monkey Tree Fern
Taiwan, Philippines, Japan
trunk 100–300 cm (40–120 in): fronds 200–300 cm (80–120 in) S.Trop.–Temp.: Terr.

A beautiful tree fern which has the apex of the slender trunk covered with white to brown scales. Developing croziers twist slightly and resemble a monkey hence the unusual common-name. This is an easily grown species which likes a protected situation and adequate water during dry periods.

Cyathea howeana Photo D. L. Jones

Cyathea loheri (alt. **Alsophila loheri**)
Taiwan, Philippines, Borneo
trunk 200–400 cm (80–160 in): fronds 200–300 cm (80–120 in) Trop.–S.Trop.: Terr.

A large tree fern with prominent, pale-coloured, papery scales on the trunk and frond bases. Fronds are lacy, bright-green and spread in a graceful crown. Plants have proved to be somewhat cold sensitive and for best growth require warm, moist conditions.

Cyathea lunulata (alt. **Sphaeropteris lunulata**)
Fiji, Solomon Islands, New Hebrides, Tonga, Samoa
trunk 200–500 cm (80–200 in): fronds 200–300 cm (80–120 in) Trop.–S.Trop.: Terr.

A large tree fern with a stout trunk, the apex of which is covered with a mixture of dark and light coloured scales. Plants like warm, sunny conditions and plenty of moisture. Once established they can be quite fast growing.

Cyathea medullaris (alt. **Sphaeropteris medullaris**)
Black Tree Fern/Mamaku
New Zealand, Fiji, Polynesia
trunk 200–500 cm (80–200 in): fronds 200–300 cm (80–120 in) Temp.–S.Trop.: Terr.

A splendid robust tree fern renowned for its massive head covered with black scales and huge, spreading crown of lacy fronds. Plants can be very fast growing and need a sheltered situation with plenty of moisture. They are adaptable and easy to grow.

Cyathea mexicana — see **Nephelea mexicana**

Cyathea rebeccae (alt. **Alsophila rebeccae**)
Australia, Flores
trunk 100–300 cm (40–120 in): fronds 200–300 cm (80–120 in) Trop.–Temp.: Terr.

Fronds of this tree fern have quite large segments which are a dark glossy-green. Young specimens are particularly decorative when they develop a lustrous, spreading crown. Plants grow easily but are unfortunately rather slow growing. They require acid loamy soils and plenty of moisture. Once established, plants are quite hardy to exposure to sun.

Cyathea rebeccae Photo D. L. Jones

Cyathea robertsiana (alt. **Alsophila robertsiana**)
Australia
trunk 100–400 cm (40–160 in): fronds 100–150 cm (40–60 in) Trop.–Temp.: Terr.

In nature, this species colonizes landslips, embankments and other areas of disturbance in rainforests and moist forests. Sporelings appear in large numbers and are very fast growing but soon thin out with the competition. This species is remarkable for its slender trunk which may be less than 3 cm thick and yet can grow many metres tall. Plants need exposure to some sun and can be somewhat tricky to keep growing unless conditions are suitable.

Cyathea robusta (alt. **Sphaeropteris robusta**)
Lord Howe Island
trunk 100–300 cm (40–120 in): fronds 100–200 cm (40–80 in) S.Trop.–Temp.: Terr.

Juvenile plants of this tree fern are most attractive as the stipes and young trunk are covered with masses of large white scales. Older plants are less appealing but nevertheless are still quite ornamental. They like shady conditions with plenty of moisture and freely draining soil.

Cyathea smithii (alt. **Alsophila smithii**)
New Zealand
trunk 200–500 cm (80–200 in): fronds 200–300 cm (80–120 in) Temp.–S.Trop.: Terr.

A large tree fern, well suited to temperate districts with a cold, moist climate. Young plants need protection from direct sun but older plants are more tolerant. They like an abundance of moisture, loamy soils and organic mulch.

Cyathea spinulosa (alt. **Alsophila spinulosa**)
India, Thailand, China, Taiwan, Japan
trunk 100–300 cm (40–120 in): fronds 200–300 cm (80–120 in) S.Trop.–Temp.: Terr.

A graceful tree fern which has brittle spines on the frond bases, which may be covered by shiny-brown scales. Fronds are dark green and finely divided. This species does not appear to be widely cultivated but can be grown in a moist, sheltered position.

Cyathea vieillardii (alt. **Alsophila vieillardii**)
New Caledonia, New Hebrides
trunk 100–400 cm (40–160 in): fronds 100–200 cm (40–80 in) Trop.–S.Trop.: Terr.

An attractive tree fern with a slender dark trunk, warty stipes and spreading, crowded, dark green fronds. Plants grow easily but need warmth or else the fronds tend to abort. Needs shade to partial sun, well-drained, humus-rich soils, and water during dry periods.

Cyathea woollsiana (alt. **Alsophila woollsiana**)
Australia
trunk 100–300 cm (40–120 in): fronds 200–300 cm (80–120 in) Trop.–Temp.: Terr.

A very reliable tree fern for cultivation which will grow well in a wide variety of soil types, climates and situations from shade to considerable sunshine. Plants develop a graceful, dense crown of light green fronds. Once established, plants are quite hardy to dryness.

Cyathea robertsiana Photo D. L. Jones

The upper trunk of *Cyathea woollsiana*
Photo D. L. Jones

Dicksonia antarctica Soft Tree Fern
Australia
trunk 100–300 cm (40–120 in): fronds 150–250 cm (60–100 in) Temp.–S.Trop.: Terr.

A majestic fern which is popular in cultivation. It thrives in cool, moist conditions and, if given plenty of water, will tolerate a fair degree of exposure to sun. Plants have a spreading crown of many, dark green, harsh-textured fronds and a large fibrous trunk. Advanced specimens are easily transplanted.

Dicksonia antarctica Photo D. L. Jones

Dicksonia brackenridgei
Fiji, Samoa
trunk 100–200 cm (40–80 in): fronds 100–150 cm (40–60 in) Trop.–S.Trop.: Terr.

This species is hardly known in cultivation, however, those plants which have been introduced grow easily. In nature, plants occur in moist rainforests, sometimes in colonies. The slender trunk is covered with long reddish hairs and the fronds are finely lobed and coarse-textured. They require a moist, sheltered situation.

Dicksonia fibrosa Wheki-Ponga
New Zealand
trunk 100–300 cm (40–120 in): fronds 200–250 cm (80–100 in) Temp.–S.Trop.: Terr.

An attractive tree fern with a large, spreading crown of dark green, firm-textured fronds. Old fronds frequently persist as a brown skirt which covers the fibrous trunk. This is a very easily grown and adaptable species that likes cool, moist conditions.

Dicksonia herbertii
Australia
trunk 100–300 cm (40–120 in): fronds 150–250 cm (60–100 in) S.Trop.–Temp.: Terr.

A species of highland rainforests, often growing in wet soil. Young parts are covered with coarse, brownish prickly hairs. This can be a fairly fast growing species preferring light shade and an abundance of water.

Dicksonia lanata
New Zealand
prostrate: fronds 100–200 cm (40–80 in) Temp.–S.Trop.: Terr.

An unusual tree fern with a creeping trunk and a crown of fronds at the apex. The fronds are relatively short but quite broad and thickly-textured. Plants reproduce vegetatively and usually develop in clumps. They can be easily grown in a moist, shady situation in acid, well-drained soil.

Dicksonia mollis
Malaysia, Philippines, Indonesia
trunk 100–300 cm (40–120 in): fronds 200–300 cm (80–120 in) Trop.–S.Trop.: Terr.

A slender tree fern of highland rainforests where it may grow in exposed situations. Frond bases are covered with reddish, shiny hairs. This species is not generally cultivated but can be grown in moist, protected conditions in good light.

Dicksonia sellowiana
Mexico, Central and South America
trunk 100–300 cm (40–120 in): fronds 60–100 cm (24–40 in) Trop.–S.Trop.: Terr.

This is an attractive species with a slender trunk, and with the apex and bases of the stipes covered with conspicuous yellow hairs. Fronds are dark green, fairly

Dicksonia lanata

Dicksonia squarrosa Photo W. R. Elliot

narrow and firm-textured. Plants have proved to be very adaptable in cultivation preferring shady, moist conditions.

Dicksonia squarrosa Wheki
New Zealand
trunk 100–300 cm (40–120 in): fronds 100–200 cm (40–80 in) Temp.-S.Trop.: Terr.

This is a clumping tree fern which develops a series of slender trunks and spreads by underground rhizomes. The trunks are woody and covered in the upper parts by conspicuous, long, pale hairs. Fronds are harsh-textured but spread in a graceful crown. This is a very cold-hardy and easily grown species in a moist situation exposed to filtered or partial sun.

Dicksonia youngiae
Australia
trunk 100–300 cm (40–120 in): fronds 150–250 cm (60–100 in) Temp.-S.Trop.: Terr.

The trunks of this species are fairly weak and fall readily. Adventitious plantlets develop and grow so that a series of interconnected trunks is formed which eventually become separate plants. Young parts of the trunk are covered with coarse, reddish tangled hairs. Plants grow easily in moist, sheltered conditions.

Nephelea mexicana (alt. **Cyathea mexicana**)
Mexico, Central and South America
trunk 200–600 cm (80–240 in): fronds 200–300 cm (80–120 in) Trop.-S.Trop.: Terr.

A stout tree fern with a thick trunk which is armed with numerous long black spines, and a spreading crown of bright green, lacy fronds. The stipes are also similarly spiny and this detracts somewhat from its horticultural appeal. Plants need warmth, moisture and bright light to partial sun.

Sphaeropteris australis — see **Cyathea leichhardtiana**

Sphaeropteris celebica — see **Cyathea celebica**

Sphaeropteris cooperi — see **Cyathea cooperi**

Sphaeropteris excelsa — see **Cyathea brownii**

Sphaeropteris glauca — see **Cyathea contaminans**

Sphaeropteris lepifera — see **Cyathea lepifera**

Sphaeropteris lunulata — see **Cyathea lunulata**

Croziers of *Dicksonia youngiae* covered in reddish hairs
Photo D. L. Jones

Sphaeropteris medullaris – see **Cyathea medullaris**

Sphaeropteris robusta – see **Cyathea robusta**

Trichipteris borinquena Creeping Tree Fern
Puerto Rico
trunk prostrate 100 cm (40 in): fronds 100–200 cm (40–80 in) Trop.–S.Trop.: Terr.

This is an interesting tree fern with a leaning to prostrate woody trunk and a crown of dark green, deeply-dissected fronds. It is a very easily grown species requiring cool, loamy soils, shade, and an abundance of moisture.

Trichipteris costaricensis
Mexico, Central America
trunk 100–500 cm (40–200 in): fronds 200–300 cm (80–120 in) Trop.–S.Trop.: Terr.

A large attractive tree fern with relatively broad, bright green fronds. Plants are cold sensitive and need warm, sheltered conditions and plenty of water. In general they prefer bright light and will tolerate considerable exposure to sun especially if the roots are kept moist.

30 Shield ferns, buckler ferns, holly ferns and their relatives

genera *Arachniodes, Cyrtomium, Dryopteris, Lastreopsis, Matteuccia, Polystichum Rumohra, Tectaria* and *Woodsia*

A loosely related group of ferns which includes many species which are favourites of enthusiastic gardeners and fern specialists alike. As a group they are hardy ferns of easy culture and are rewarding to grow. They are known by a range of common names some of which are related to herbal or medicinal uses. A few species are in demand as commercial ferns.

Habitat

The vast majority of these ferns grow as terrestrials but *Rumohra adiantiformis* can grow as a terrestrial or an epiphyte and a few species of *Dryopteris* are epiphytes. Most ferns in this group commonly grow in wet, shady situations in forests and along stream banks. Hardy species from northern latitudes may be covered in snow during winter.

Cultivation

Uses

These ferns are excellent for gardens, ferneries and containers and there is a wide range available for selection. A few are suitable for indoor decoration. Some have colourful new fronds (*Dryopteris erythrosora*) or spectacular flushes of new fronds (*Dryopteris wallichiana*) and should be planted where these features can be appreciated. Many from cold regions are dormant over winter and may even be deciduous. A wide range of frond shape and dissection is available in these ferns and they are ideal for filling gaps in a fernery.

Soil Types

Most of these ferns are adaptable to a variety of soils providing that drainage is unimpeded. Loams fortified with organic matter are particularly suitable. The majority prefer acid soils but some from limestone areas need a neutral to alkaline reaction.

Potting Mix

An open mix based on a well-structured loam and fortified with peat moss, milled pine bark or chopped tree-fern fibre is usually satisfactory for their growth. Some may respond to lime or limestone chips in the mix. Many species have a vigorous root system and can quickly fill a pot. Repotting for most species will be required annually.

Watering

Ferns of this group like plenty of water while in active growth over spring and summer. Those species which are dormant over winter should be watered sparingly until new fronds appear. Some species may suffer frond sweating if kept too wet during still, cool weather (see page 119).

Fertilizing

Fertilizers and manures are very beneficial to these ferns and promote strong healthy growth. Those in the ground can receive supplementary dressings at intervals during the growing season. A spring dressing on those species that become dormant will help a strong flush of new growth. Slow-release fertilizers incorporated into potting mixes help maintain growth.

Situation

Most of these ferns need protection from direct hot sun and like shade or perhaps filtered sun. In temperate regions a situation under deciduous trees is ideal. Species from the tropics may be sensitive to cold, especially frosts.

Pests

Brown Scale and Fern Scale may kill fronds on species of *Dryopteris, Cyrtomium* and *Tectaria*. Passion Vine Hoppers can also damage developing fronds.

Propagation

Ferns of this group are generally very easy to raise from spores and some such as the cultivated forms of *Cyrtomium falcatum* may be apogamous. Spores can be sown fresh and if stored correctly will last for many years. Some fancy cultivars of *Dryopteris* may be sterile or produce only a low percentage true to type.

Cyrtomium falcatum has very shiny fronds
Photo D. L. Jones

It is relatively easy to judge when spores of this group are ready for collection. On indusiate species the indusia darken as the sporangia mature and when the first few sporangia are visible at the margin of the indusium, the frond should be cut. Species of *Lastreopsis* can be tricky to judge and should be collected when the sori have a black, crystalline appearance.

Various species can be propagated vegetatively by division, e.g. *Lastreopsis microsora, Rumohra adiantiformis* and bulbils (*Tectaria gemmifera*).

SPECIES AND CULTIVARS

Arachniodes aristata Prickly Shield Fern
Malaysia, South-East Asia, Polynesia, Sri Lanka, New Guinea, Australia
30–100 cm (12–40 in): 3–4 pinnate Trop.–Temp.: Terr.

An attractive but harsh fern which has triangular, glossy, dark green, almost prickly fronds and a creeping rhizome. It can be grown easily in a shady situation and will adapt to most well-drained soils. Once established, plants will tolerate periods of dryness.

Arachniodes aristata 'Variegata' — see **A. simplicior**

Arachniodes simplicior Variegated Shield Fern
Japan, China
30–80 cm (12–32 in): 2–3 pinnate S.Trop.–Temp.: Terr.

An attractive, but slow growing fern, which is popular with fern fanciers. It is notable for its glossy-green fronds which have a prominent yellowish band on each side of the midrib. Plants can either be grown in a shady situation in loamy soil or in a container. It is often incorrectly sold as *A. aristata* 'Variegata'.

Arachniodes standishii Upside-down Fern
Japan
60–100 cm (24–40 in): 3 pinnate Temp.–S.Trop.: Terr.

This fern forms a rosette of pleasant, bright green fairly narrow fronds. The fronds are thinly-textured and the dense black sori are visible from the upper side, hence the unusual common name. Plants grow easily in a semi-shady situation in well-drained loamy soil and like plenty of moisture.

Byrsopteris aristata — see **Arachniodes aristata**

Cyrtomium caryotideum Dwarf Holly Fern
North India, Sri Lanka, Japan, China
15–30 cm (6–12 in): 1 pinnate S.Trop.–Temp.: Terr.

A desirable fern with attractive leathery fronds of a verdant green. Plants have a compact growth habit and succeed well in pots or among rocks. Grows readily in acid, humus-rich soils and likes a semi-shady position.

Cyrtomium falcatum Japanese Holly Fern
Japan, Korea, China
30–50 cm (12–20 in): 1 pinnate Temp.–S.Trop.: Terr.

An exceedingly popular fern which is propagated by the nursery industry in many countries. It is prized for its decorative, dark green, leathery fronds. Plants are hardy and long-lived and succeed equally well in containers or in the ground. Will grow in acid or alkaline soils and the species frequently colonizes sites

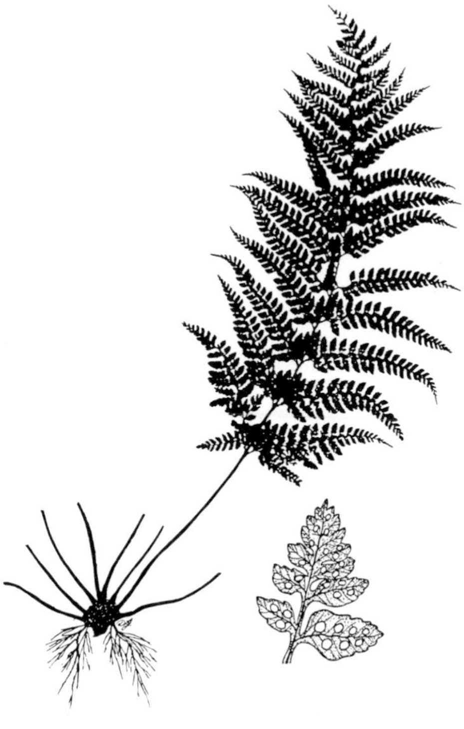

Arachniodes standishii

that suit its requirements. A variety of positions from shade to full sun can be suitable. It is also a useful indoor fern. A few cultivars are known.

'Butterfieldii' – segments have toothed margins and the tips tend to be drawn out.

'Mayi' (Cristata) – pinnae strongly crested, fronds often forked and with a terminal crest.

'Rochfordianum' – segment margins lobed or coarsely toothed. Commonly grown.

Cyrtomium fortunei
Japan, Korea, China
20–40 cm (8–16 in): 1 pinnate S.Trop.–Temp.: Terr.
Similar in many respects to *C. falcatum* but with narrower, more erect, shiny, dark green fronds that have longer drawn-out segments. A very handsome species that does well in a shady position in acid, humus-rich loamy soil.

Cyrtomium macrophyllum
Japan, China, North India
20–40 cm (8–16 in): 1 pinnate S.Trop.–Temp.: Terr.
This species is generally like *C. caryotideum* but has fewer and much larger segments on each frond. The frond colour tends to be light green and a clump has a much sparser appearance than *C. caryotideum*. Plants grow well in a shady position in acid, humus-rich soil.

Cyrtomium macrophyllum var. **turkusicola** – see **C. turkusicola**

Cyrtomium turkusicola
Japan, China
30–50 cm (12–20 in): 1 pinnate S.Trop.–Temp.: Terr.

Cyrtomium macrophyllum Photo D. L. Jones

A decorative fern with narrow, upright deep-green fronds that have close, almost crowded segments. New fronds are light green and contrast with the mature ones. Grows easily in a shady position in acid, humus-rich loamy soil. This species is included by some authors as a variety of *C. macrophyllum*.

Dryopteris aemula Hay-scented Buckler Fern
Europe
20–60 cm (8–24 in): 2–3 pinnate Temp.: Terr.
A pleasant fern with reddish-purple stipes and yellow-green deltoid, scented fronds carried in a spreading tussock. Plants are easily grown in the shade and they prefer a humus-rich loamy soil and plenty of water during dry spells.

Dryopteris affinis Scaly Male Fern
Europe, South-West Asia
50–150 cm (20–60 in): 1 pinnate Temp.–S.Trop.: Terr.
This fern thrives in cool climates and can be grown

Cyrtomium turkusicola

Cyrtomium turkusicola Photo D. L. Jones

A colony of *Dryopteris affinis* 'Cristata The King'
Photo W. R. Elliot

in a shady garden position or a fernery. It likes moist conditions and well-drained soil. The flush of new fronds in the spring is very decorative, as each is densely covered with coppery scales. Plants are generally dormant in winter. A number of cultivars are known.

'Cristata The King' — a fine form with large crests on the pinnae and on the end of each frond. Fertile.

'Grandiceps' — fronds with a much-branched terminal crest.

Dryopteris affinis 'Cristata The King'

Dryopteris carthusiana

'Ramosissima' — fronds fork repeatedly and each branch ends in a large crest.

Dryopteris atrata — see **D. cycadina**

Dryopteris austriaca = **D. dilatata**

Dryopteris borreri = **D. affinis**

Dryopteris carthusiana Narrow Buckler Fern
Europe, North America, Canada, Alaska
30–120 cm (12–48 in): 2–3 pinnate Trop.–Temp.: Terr.

A weedy fern which commonly naturalizes ferneries, greenhouses, nurseries and moist sites in gardens. Plants may become deciduous in very cold areas. A hardy garden fern which grows easily in a variety of soil types and situations. Fronds are yellowish-green.

Dryopteris clintoniana
North America
50–100 cm (20–40 in): 1–2 pinnate Temp.: Terr.

This fern apparently originated as a natural hybrid between *D. goldiana* and *D. cristata* and is now established as a species; growing in wet soils. Plants develop a tussock of spreading fairly broad fronds. They are cold-hardy and retain their fronds throughout the year even in a severe winter. They grow easily in a shady position with plenty of moisture.

Dryopteris crispifolia
The Azores
30–90 cm (12–36 in): 3–4 pinnate Temp.–S.Trop.: Terr.

A distinctive species, well-named for its curled frond

segments which impart a distinctive, crisped effect. The fronds are also scented like hay. An attractive fern easy to grow in a shady position in loamy soil.

Dryopteris cristata Crested Shield Fern
Europe, Siberia, Japan, North America
60–100 cm (24–40 in): 1 pinnate Temp.: Terr.
An attractive fern of wet areas. Fronds develop in an open rosette, with the fertile fronds being held erect and the sterile ones spreading. Plants grow easily in an acid soil in a shady position and need plenty of moisture.

Dryopteris cristata var. **clintoniana**=**D. clintoniana**

Dryopteris cycadina Shaggy Shield Fern
India, Sri Lanka, Thailand, Japan, China
20–40 cm (8–16 in): 1 pinnate Temp.–S.Trop.: Terr.
This distinctive species can be recognized by the masses of long, slender, black scales which clothe the stipes and underside of the rachises. Plants require well-drained soil, shade to partial sun, and plenty of moisture. An easily grown species very hardy in a cold climate. Plants grown as *D. hirtipes* and *D. atrata* are probably this species.

Dryopteris dilatata Broad Buckler Fern
Europe, Asia, North America, South Africa, Greenland, Japan
30–150 cm (12–60 in): 2–3 pinnate Temp.–S.Trop.: Terr.
A vigorous fern which forms a spreading rosette of broad, triangular, dark green fronds. Plants are easily grown in a loamy soil in a shady or partially sunny aspect. A few cultivars are known.

'Grandiceps' – crests on the pinnae and also a prominent one on the end of each frond. Fertile.

'Lepidota' – segments finely-cut, imparting an open appearance.

'Lepidota Cristata' – finely-cut segments which are crested on the ends.

Dryopteris erythrosora Autumn Fern
China, Japan, Korea
20–45 cm (8–18 in): 2 pinnate Temp.–S.Trop.: Terr.
The young fronds of this fern are an unusual coppery colour and contrast pleasantly with the older fronds. In cold climates thay may be bright red. This is a very adaptable and easy fern to grow. Plants will succeed in situations from deep shade to partial sun and in a range of soils providing the drainage is adequate. Also makes a good pot subject.

Dryopteris filix-mas Male Fern
Europe, Central and North America, Asia
60–150 cm (24–60 in): 1–2 pinnate Temp.–S.Trop.: Terr.
A widely distributed fern which is a firm garden favourite because it is easy to cultivate and has a large variation in form. It does well in a semi-shaded situation, and a neutral to acid soil, rich in humus. Plants cease growth in autumn and may become completely deciduous before producing a vigorous flush of new fronds in spring. Many cultivars have been selected.

Dryopteris erythrosora Photo D. L. Jones

'Barnesii' – fronds are long and arching with short, broadly-triangular, toothed segments. Fertile.

'Crispa' – dwarf grower with compact, crested fronds.

'Cristata' – fronds and pinnae crested.

'Cristata Martindale' – a remarkable form with terminal crests on the pinnae and a confluent series of crests at the apex of the frond. Fertile.

'Grandiceps' – apex of frond with heavy terminal crest. Vigorous and clumping. Fertile.

'Linearis' – tall erect fronds with slender segments.

'Linearis Cristata' – as above but the segments crested.

'Linearis Polydactyla' – slender segments with long, divergent crests. Fertile.

Dryopteris formosana
Japan
45–60 cm (18–24 in): 2 pinnate Temp.–S.Trop.: Terr.
Similar to *D. erythrosora* but with narrower, more drawn out segments and the young fronds yellowish-green rather than coppery or red. Easily grown in a protected situation in loamy soil.

Dryopteris goldiana Giant Wood Fern
North America
60–120 cm (24–48 in): 1–2 pinnate Temp.–S.Trop.: Terr.
The new fronds of this fern are covered with prominent white and brown scales and the flush on a large plant in spring is quite decorative. Plants grow easily in a shady position with plenty of moisture. In cold climates the fronds are deciduous.

The fronds of *Dryopteris sieboldii* are distinctive for the genus
Photo D. L. Jones

Dryopteris hirtipes – see **D. cycadina**

Dryopteris intermedia Evergreen Wood Fern
North America (eastern states)
45–90 cm (18–36 in): 2 pinnate Temp.–S.Trop.: Terr.
Similar in most respects to *D. carthusiana* but with blue-green rather than yellowish fronds. Very hardy and easily grown in a shady situation in loamy soil.

Dryopteris lepidopoda
North India, China
30–60 cm (12–24 in): 2 pinnate Temp.–S.Trop.: Terr.
A striking fern of mountainous areas. Croziers arise in a flush and are covered with numerous, narrow, black scales. Young fronds are coppery-bronze and mature dark green. Requires loamy, acid soils.

Dryopteris ludoviciana Southern Shield Fern
North America
60–120 cm (24–48 in): 1 pinnate Temp.–S.Trop.: Terr.
A hardy fern of wet soils; in forests sometimes growing on limestone. Plants form an erect tussock of dark green, leathery fronds. Cultivated plants need plenty of water.

Dryopteris marginalis Marginal Shield Fern
North America
20–60 cm (12–24 in): 1–2 pinnate Temp.–S.Trop.: Terr.
In nature this fern occurs in shady woodland, and is sometimes known as the Leather Woodfern. Fronds are dark blue-green and are carried in a tussock. Plants grow easily in shade in a loamy soil.

Dryopteris montana = Oreopteris limbosperma

Dryopteris oreades Mountain Male Fern
Europe
30–60 cm (12–24 in): 1 pinnate Temp.: Terr.
A very hardy fern of mountainous regions, growing among rocks. Plants form an upright tussock of fairly narrow, pale green fronds. Deciduous in cold climates. Easily grown in a sheltered position in loamy soil.

Dryopteris oreopteris = Oreopteris limbosperma

Dryopteris paleacea – see **D. wallichiana**

Dryopteris parallelogramma
Mexico, Central and South America, India, Hawaii, New Guinea
50–120 cm (20–48 in): 1–2 pinnate Trop.–S.Trop.: Terr.
This fern likes plenty of moisture in well-drained soil in a shady aspect. The fronds are carried in a spreading rosette. Each is quite broad and is dark green and shiny above and paler on the underside. An

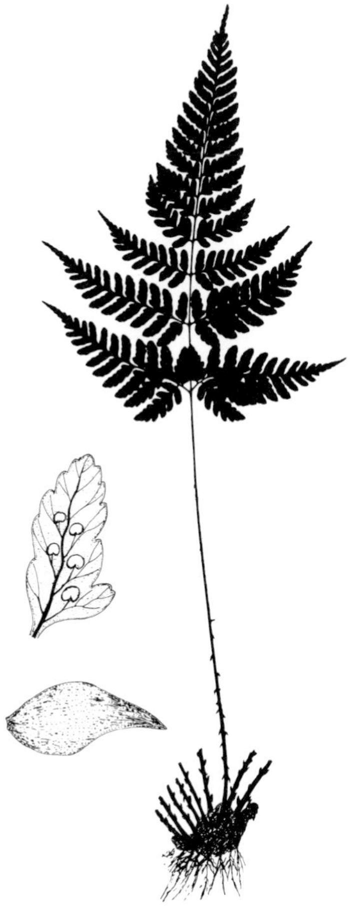

Dryopteris sparsa

attractive fern for the garden or in a container. The species is included by some authors in *D. wallichiana*.

Dryopteris patentissima — see **D. wallichiana**

Dryopteris pseudomas=D. affinis

Dryopteris sieboldii
Japan, China
20–45 cm (8–18 in): 1 pinnate Temp.–S.Trop.: Terr.
The fronds of this fern are unusual in the genus in that each consists of a few large pinnae which are leathery in texture and may be glaucous on the underside. They also have an arching or drooping appearance that is quite distinctive. Plants are rather slow but steady growers and like a shady situation in acid, well-drained loamy soil.

Dryopteris sparsa
India, China, Japan, Malaysia, New Guinea, Australia
20–80 cm (8–32 in): 2–3 pinnate Trop.–S.Trop.: Terr.
A pleasant fern found in rainforests and shady forests sometimes colonizing disturbed earth. Plants adapt to cultivation readily but need protection from excessive sun and wind. The fronds are very brittle and easily damaged. Likes humus-rich loamy soil.

Dryopteris tokyoensis

Dryopteris spinulosa=D. carthusiana

Dryopteris submontana
Europe, North Africa
15–20 cm (6–8 in): 2 pinnate Temp.: Terr.
A small rigid fern of mountainous areas, growing on limestone. Fronds are blue-green, relatively broad, stiff and leathery and covered with glandular hairs. Easily grown but requires neutral to alkaline soil.

Dryopteris tokyoensis
Japan, Korea
30–45 cm (12–18 in): 1 pinnate Temp.–S.Trop.: Terr.
A hardy fern which forms an erect rosette of fairly narrow, dark green fronds. Very attractive when planted among rocks. Requires humus-rich acid soil and a shady aspect.

Dryopteris uniformis
Japan, China, Korea
15–20 cm (6–8in): 2 pinnate Temp.: Terr.
A dwarf fern, attractive when planted among rocks. Fronds are quite broad relative to their length and have slender, drawn-out segments. Requires acid, loamy soil.

Dryopteris varia
Japan, Korea, China, India, Philippines
50–75 cm (20–30 in): 2–3 pinnate Trop.–S.Trop.: Terr.
A widely distributed fern with leathery, dark green, deltoid fronds, which have numerous dark-coloured papery scales on the stipes and rachises. Plants require acid, loamy soil in a shady situation. Well grown plants are very decorative.

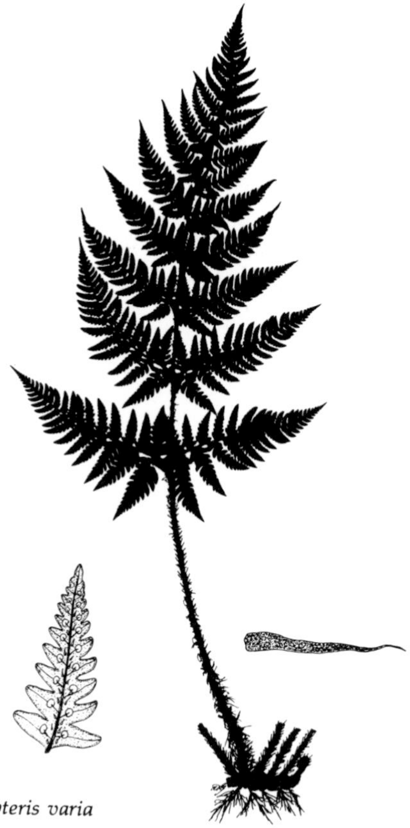
Dryopteris varia

Lastreopsis marginans Photo D. L. Jones

Dryopteris wallichiana
India, China, Japan, South and Central America, Africa, Madagascar
60–100 cm (24–40 in): 2 pinnate S.Trop.–Temp.: Terr.

In its native state this is a fern of the high mountains growing beneath the shelter of shrubs and trees. Plants form an open tussock with a small trunk and are notable for the strong flush of new fronds in the spring. These are of light green to golden hues with numerous dark reddish-black scales. Plants are easily grown in a shady situation and adapt well to temperate areas. Some authorities include other *Dryopteris* species (*D. paleacea*, *D. parallelogramma*, *D. patentissima*) under *D. wallichiana*, recognizing it as a widespread and variable species.

Lastreopsis calantha
Norfolk Island
40–80 cm (16–32 in): 3–4 pinnate S.Trop.–Temp.: Terr.

Although only grown by enthusiasts this fern is deserving of wider cultivation. It develops into a clump of light blue-green to grey-green, lacy fronds with the new fronds almost yellowish. Likes shade and plenty of moisture but is not difficult to grow.

Lastreopsis decomposita Trim Shield Fern
Australia, Norfolk Island
50–90 cm (20–36 in): 3–4 pinnate S.Trop.–Temp.: Terr.

A coarse, strong growing fern which will grow in shady or partially shady conditions. Once established, plants are quite hardy of dryness. They are sensitive to excessively wet soil. Fronds are often light green and the stipes are liberally covered with large brown scales.

Lastreopsis hispida Bristly Shield Fern
Australia, New Zealand
30–80 cm (12–32 in): 3–4 pinnate Temp.: Terr.

This fern is appreciative of cool, shady, moist conditions and does not like to dry out. It prefers acidic loams rich in organic matter and resents disturbance. Once established, plants grow steadily and are long-lived. Plants from New Zealand appear to be more adaptable to cultivation than those from Australia.

Lastreopsis marginans Glossy Shield Fern
Australia
60–120 cm (24–48 in): 3–4 pinnate S.Trop.–Trop.: Terr.

Prized for its glossy dark green fronds, this species adapts well to cultivation. Likes a shady situation in acid, humus-rich soil. Once established plants are quite hardy to dryness but for best appearance should be watered regularly.

Lastreopsis microsora Creeping Shield Fern
Australia
30–90 cm (12–36 in): 3–4 pinnate Trop.–Temp.: Terr.

An attractive fern, with soft lacy fronds, which grows in spreading colonies. Easily contained and never a nuisance. Likes shady conditions and plenty of moisture but plants are surprisingly tolerant of dryness once established. Plants are variable and forms with soft, brown hairs are attractive.

Lastreopsis hispida

Lastreopsis munita
Australia
20–30 cm (8–12 in): 2–3 pinnate Trop.–Temp.: Terr.
A useful ground-cover fern forming spreading colonies of dark green, deltoid fronds. Excellent for a shady situation in loamy, acid soil. Plants will tolerate dry spells once they are established.

Lastreopsis tenera Broad Shield Fern
Australia, Philippines, India, Sri Lanka, Indonesia, Fiji, New Caledonia
60–150 cm (24–60 in): 3–4 pinnate Trop.–S.Trop.: Terr.
A very widely distributed species which commonly grows in well lit situations such as along forest margins. Fronds are lacy, pale green and soft to the touch. Grows in slowly spreading patches. Hardy and adaptable to a variety of soils and situations.

Lastreopsis velutina Velvety Shield Fern
New Zealand
30–60 cm (12–24 in): 3–4 pinnate: S.Trop.–Temp.: Terr.
A delicate-looking fern with soft, lacy fronds which are liberally coated with brown, velvety hairs. Somewhat slow growing. Likes shady conditions in organically rich soil.

Matteuccia orientalis
China, Japan, Korea
30–90 cm (12–36 in): 1 pinnate Temp.: Terr.
This species is similar to *M. struthiopteris* but with smaller fronds, the sterile ones of which are almost prostrate. Spreads by underground rhizomes. Easily grown in acid, loamy soil.

Lastreopsis velutina

Lastreopsis munita Photo D. L. Jones

Matteuccia pennsylvanica = M. struthiopteris

Matteuccia struthiopteris Ostrich Fern
North America, Europe, Japan, China
60–150 cm (24–60 in): 1 pinnate Temp.: Terr.
A vigorous fern which spreads by underground rhizomes, producing clusters of new fronds at

A clump of *Matteuccia struthiopteris* in spring
Photo W. R. Elliot

Polystichum lentum Photo D. L. Jones

intervals. Each cluster eventually develops a small trunk. Flushes of new fronds are most decorative. Requires acid, loamy soil.

Polystichum acrostichoides Christmas Fern
North America, Canada
30–90 cm (12–36 in): 1 pinnate Temp.–S.Trop.: Terr.
A very hardy fern which adapts well to a moist, shady garden situation or fernery. New fronds are produced in a spectacular, silvery flush. Plants will tolerate considerable cold and still remain evergreen. The fronds are used for cut foliage in some states of the USA.

'Crispum' – fronds with strongly-crisped margins.

'Incisum' – fronds with deeply-lacerated pinnae.

Polystichum aculeatum Hard Shield Fern
Europe, North India
60–120 cm (24–48 in): 1–2 pinnate Temp.–S.Trop.: Terr.
A hardy fern with stiff, leathery, dark glossy-green fronds. It occurs in shady situations frequently in mountainous regions and often on limestone rocks. Young fronds may be light green and provide a pleasant contrast to the mature rosette. Plants are very hardy in a shady, moist situation and may benefit from the addition of lime to the soil. A number of attractive cultivars are known.

'Acutilobum' – segments narrow and sharply pointed.

'Cambricum' – segments ovate or sickle-shaped with coarsely toothed margins.

'Pulcherrimum' – a beautiful form with graceful silky fronds with the segments tailed. Sterile.

'Pulcherrimum Gracillimum' – described as the most beautiful British fern. Fronds are delicately divided and the segments end in slender almost hair-like divisions. Sterile.

Polystichum andersonii Anderson's Holly Fern
North America, Canada, Alaska
30–100 cm (12–40 in): 2 pinnate Temp.–S.Trop.: Terr.
An attractive fern with hard, holly-like fronds. In nature, it grows in cool wet woodlands and shaded, rocky hillsides. Plants are proliferous having a vegetative bulbil at the apex of each frond. They can be grown easily in a moist, shaded fernery or similar garden situation.

Polystichum aristatum = Arachniodes aristata

Polystichum braunii Holly Fern
North America, Canada, Europe, Japan, China
30–100 cm (12–40 in): 2 pinnate Temp.: Terr.
A hardy fern which will tolerate considerable cold, although in severe climates plants may be deciduous. New fronds are produced in a spectacular, silvery flush. Likes shady, moist conditions in acid, loamy soils.

Polystichum cystostegia
New Zealand
10–25 cm (4–10 in): 2 pinnate Temp.: Terr.
A very hardy little fern from alpine regions. Plants are very cold tolerant and are ideal for a rockery. The stipes and rachises are covered with conspicuous, brown scales.

Polystichum imbricans
North America
30–60 cm (12–24 in): 1 pinnate Temp.–S.Trop.: Terr.
This species was formerly regarded as a variety of *P. munitum*, but is smaller growing than that species and has crowded, overlapping pinnae. It is a hardy fern for a shady, moist position.

Polystichum lentum
India
20–40 cm (8–16 in): 1 pinnate Temp.–S.Trop.: Terr.
A fern which is common in the Himalayas growing on shady, humus-rich, rocky slopes. It forms an attractive sprawling rosette of slender, dark green fronds which are proliferous on the tip. Grows easily in a variety of soils but likes shade.

Polystichum lonchitis Holly Fern
Europe, North Asia, North America, Canada, Greenland
20–50 cm (8–20 in): 1 pinnate Temp.: Terr.
A rarely grown fern confined to mountainous regions. Plants resent moving and are very slow to establish following such disturbance. Sporelings establish easily in a loamy soil to which lime has been added. They like shady, moist conditions and are very cold-hardy.

Polystichum longipaleatum
North India, China
60–120 cm (24–48 in): 2 pinnate S.Trop.–Temp.: Terr.

A large fern of mountainous areas, prized for its spectacular flush of densely scaly fronds. The underside of the fronds is also covered with fine hair-like scales. Requires moist loamy soil and shady conditions.

Polystichum munitum Sword Fern
North America
30–100 cm (12–40 in): 1 pinnate Temp.–S.Trop.: Terr.

This fern is similar in many respects to *P. acrostichoides*, however, the segments are longer and narrower. Like that species, it is a hardy fern for a shady, moist situation in the garden or fernery. Plants are quite cold tolerant.

Polystichum munitum var. **imbricans** — see **P. imbricans**

Polystichum polyblepharum
Japan, Korea, China
60–120 cm (24–48 in): 1–2 pinnate S.Trop.–Temp.: Terr.

Polystichum munitum Photo D. L. Jones

An attractive fern which forms a rounded rosette of harsh-textured, glossy, dark green fronds (somewhat scaly beneath). New fronds are scaly and interesting. Grows easily in shade and humus-rich acid soil.

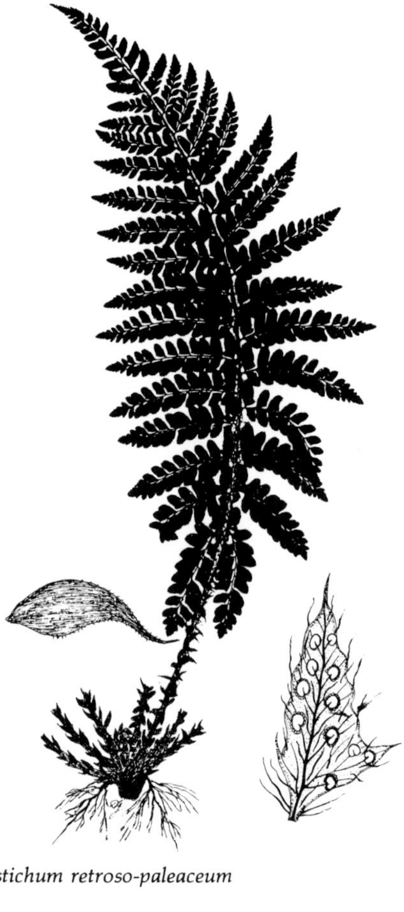

Polystichum retroso-paleaceum

Polystichum proliferum Mother Shield Fern
Australia
50–100 cm (20–40 in): 2–3 pinnate Temp.–S.Trop.: Terr.

An attractive shield fern which grows in colonies, the fronds characteristically developing plantlets near the end which take root while still attached. Flushes of new fronds are covered with brown scales and are eye-catching. Plants grow easily in a shady, moist situation and are also useful in a large pot.

Polystichum retroso-paleaceum
Japan, Korea
50–100 cm (20–40 in): 2 pinnate S.Trop.–Temp.: Terr.

A beautiful fern with a spreading rosette of bright green, shiny fronds. Flushes of new fronds are scaly and interesting. Plants are easily grown in a shady, moist garden position and are also ideal for a tub or large container.

Polystichum richardii
New Zealand
20–45 cm (8–18 in): 2 pinnate Temp.: Terr.

A neat fern forming a rounded rosette of dark green, somewhat harsh fronds which often have a bluish caste. Easily grown in a shady or partial sun aspect in loamy soil. Looks particularly attractive when planted among rocks.

A colony of *Polystichum setiferum* 'Divisilobum' in spring
Photo W. R. Elliot

Polystichum setiferum Soft Shield Fern
Europe
60–150 cm (24–60 in): 2 pinnate Temp.-S.Trop.: Terr.

Widely grown in temperate gardens of the world, this fern is deservedly popular. It forms a ground-hugging rosette of spreading fronds which are attractively dissected and generally quite soft to the touch (forms with harsh fronds are known). Numerous plantlets are produced along the length of the rachis. Plants can be grown readily in moist soil in a shady to partially sunny aspect. This is an extremely variable fern and over 300 cultivars have been selected by enthusiasts.

Polystichum retroso-paleaceum Photo D. L. Jones

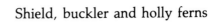

Polystichum triangulum is a neat fern for a pot or rockery
Photo D. L. Jones

'Acutilobum' – narrow fronds with sharply-pointed segments. Compact growth.

'Congestum' – upright dense fronds with overlapping segments. Compact growth to 20 cm tall. Fertile.

'Cristatum' – segments prominently crested.

'Divisilobum' – large fronds 3–4 times divided with finely cut segments.

'Foliosum' – fronds have a leafy appearance caused by numerous overlapping segments.

'Plumoso-divisilobum' – fronds divided into slender, mossy segments which are crowded or overlap each other. A very beautiful form.

'Polydactylum' – the segments end in divergent crests.

'Rotundatum' – the segments are almost circular. A crested form is also known.

'Tripinnatum' – erect finely-divided feathery fronds. Strong grower. Fertile.

Polystichum scopulinum Western Holly Fern
North America, Canada
15–35 cm (6–14 in): 1 pinnate Temp.: Terr.

This fern apparently originated as a hybrid between *P. lemmonii* and *P. imbricans*, but is now established as a species. A small leathery fern suitable for planting among rocks.

Polystichum triangulum
South America, West Indies
20–40 cm (8–16 in): 1 pinnate Trop.-S.Trop.: Terr.

This is an interesting species which forms a spreading rosette of narrow, bright green fronds; the pinnae being deltoid to triangular in shape. Although reported as being associated with calcareous rocks, this species grows well in acid, loamy soils.

Polystichum tsus-simense

Polystichum tsus-simense
China, Japan, Korea
20–50 cm (8–20 in): 2 pinnate Temp.–S.Trop.: Terr.

A neat fern valued for its compact, spreading rosette. The fronds are fairly stiff and leathery and an interesting dark, purplish colour when young. Makes an excellent pot plant and can also be grown in a shady position among rocks.

Polystichum vestitum Prickly Shield Fern
New Zealand
50–150 cm (20–60 in): 2 pinnate Temp.: Terr.

A large, tough fern with harsh, prickly fronds of an attractive dark green colouration. Plants are very cold-hardy and will withstand severe frosts and snow. Likes plenty of moisture and will tolerate shade to partial sun.

Polystichum whiteleggei
Lord Howe Island
30–80 cm (12–32 in): 2 pinnate S.Trop.–Temp.: Terr.

A beautiful fern which is only grown by a few enthusiasts but which deserves to become more widely known. Plants have long and broad bright green fronds attractively divided, with the stipe and young fronds covered with large, papery scales. They like shady conditions in moist but well-drained soil.

Polystichum vestitum is a large coarse fern
Photo D. L. Jones

Rumohra adiantiformis Leathery Shield Fern
Africa, Australia, New Zealand, Polynesia, South America
60–150 cm (24–60 in): 2–3 pinnate S.Trop.–Temp.: Epi.–Terr.

A very widely distributed fern which is somewhat variable. The form common in Australia and New Zealand grows on trees (particularly tree ferns) and has long-creeping, slender rhizomes and medium-sized fronds. It is excellent for slab or basket culture. The Cape Form from South Africa is really a giant with broad rhizomes and large, thick, leathery fronds. It grows very easily as a terrestrial in a shady to semi-shady position in well-drained loamy soil.

Polystichum vestitum frozen in a heavy frost
Photo D. L. Jones

The very handsome *Polystichum whiteleggei*
Photo D. L. Jones

The Cape Form of *Rumohra adiantiformis*
Photo D. L. Jones

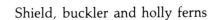

Polystichum vestitum

Tectaria brachiata
China, North India, Malaysia, New Guinea, Australia
60–90 cm (24–36 in): 1 pinnate Trop.–S.Trop.: Terr.

An interesting fern with markedly dimorphic sterile and fertile fronds. The sterile fronds are broad, much dividing and with a spreading habit; the fertile fronds are erect and much contracted. Plants are cold sensitive but in the tropics are easily grown in a shady situation.

Tectaria cicutaria Button Fern
West Indies
40–100 cm (16–40 in): 2 pinnate Trop.–Temp.: Terr.

The common name of this fern arises from the fleshy, button-like bulbils which are produced in abundance on the upper surface of the frond. These fall to the ground, take root and become separate plantlets. A coarse but ornamental fern easily grown in shady moist conditions. It is often confused with *T. gemmifera* but can be distinguished by the red hairs on the stipe and rachis.

Tectaria crenata Samoan Tectaria
Polynesia
60–80 cm (24–32 in): 1–2 pinnate S.Trop.–Trop.: Terr.

A large growing, coarse fern with attractively lobed, fairly thickly-textured fronds. Can be easily grown in a shady situation but is somewhat cold sensitive. Needs well-drained soil and plenty of moisture.

Tectaria gemmifera
Africa, Malagasy, Seychelles
60–150 cm (24–60 in): 2–4 pinnate Temp.–S.Trop.: Terr.

A coarse, easily grown fern which produces an abundance of bulbils on the upper surface of its fronds. Fronds are dark green and thinly-textured. Plants favour shady situations (they will grow in deep shade). The species is often confused with *T. cicutaria* but can be distinguished by the stipes and rachises bearing sparse, short, white hairs.

Tectaria heracleifolia Halberd Fern
Texas, Mexico, Central and South America
50–80 cm (20–32 in): entire–1 pinnate Trop.–S.Trop.: Terr.

A coarse, fairly commonly grown fern with fairly leathery, bright-to-dark-green fronds. The juvenile fronds may be entire or partly lobed; the mature fronds are deeply lobed with a large terminal section. Plants grow easily in a pot but are best established in a shady situation in the ground.

Tectaria incisa
Mexico, Central and South America, West Indies
60–180 cm (24–72 in): 1 pinnate Trop.–S.Trop.: Terr.

A large fern with attractively lobed, very broad fronds. Plantlets are occasionally produced in the axils of the leaves. Plants are cold sensitive and need a warm position with a shady aspect.

Tectaria mexicana
Mexico, Central and South America
50–100 cm (20–40 in): 1–2 pinnate Trop.–S.Trop.: Terr.

An attractive fern with broadly deltoid, dark green fronds. Plants are very cold sensitive. Can be grown in a shady situation in well-drained soil with plenty of moisture.

Tectaria muelleri
Australia, New Guinea
30–90 cm (12–36 in): 2 pinnate Trop.–Temp.: Terr.

This very attractive fern is always found in shady locations often growing along stream banks. It is common in both lowland and highland areas. It is a handsome fern with fronds of an appealing shape. Plants grow readily if given shelter and moisture.

Woodsia ilvensis Rusty Woodsia
Europe, North America (northern states), Asia
10–20 cm (4–8 in): 2 pinnate Temp.: Terr.

A small fern which forms a clump usually consisting of only a few fronds. It grows in rocky situations and is uncommonly cultivated. Reported to be easily raised from spores.

Tectaria crenata Photo D. L. Jones

Woodsia obtusa Blunt-lobed Woodsia
North America (eastern states)
15–20 cm (6–18 cm): 2 pinnate Temp.–S.Trop.: Terr.

A deciduous small fern of shaded situations among rocks (sometimes limestone). An easily grown species in a well-drained, neutral to alkaline soil mix.

Woodsia polystichoides
China, Japan, Korea
15–35 cm (6–14 in): 1 pinnate Temp.–S.Trop.: Terr.

A cold-hardy, deciduous fern that produces a flush of new fronds in spring. The fronds are narrow, dark green and held erect. Attractive when planted among rocks. Requires an acid, loamy soil.

Tectaria gemmifera Photo D. L. Jones

Tectaria muelleri Photo D. L. Jones

31 Boston ferns, fishbone ferns, lace ferns and sword ferns

genus *Nephrolepis*

Ferns of this genus are extremely popular with fern enthusiasts, and their cultivars are among the most widely propagated commercial ferns in the world. One species, *N. exaltata*, is very prone to mutation, and has resulted in hundreds of cultivars some of which are so radically altered that it is difficult to relate them to the species.

Habitat

Nephrolepis is a very adaptable group of ferns and species can be found growing in a wide variety of habitats from shade to full sun and as terrestrials or epiphytes. A few species prefer wet or boggy situations (*N. biserrata*) but others are found in hot, dry situations among rocks (*N. acutifolia*). Many are colonizers of disturbed sites, and weeds of nurseries and gardens in the tropics. Most are colony formers. Once a sporeling is established, a colony can build up by the production of stolons.

Cultivation

Uses

Nephrolepis are generally easy ferns to grow, some embarrassingly so. They can be used for a wide range of purposes in gardens and in a variety of containers including pots, tubs and hanging baskets. Most species can be grown in the tropics but only the hardy types are suitable for temperate regions. Some species and cultivars make excellent indoor plants, tolerating considerable neglect and still managing to look decorative. In fact they are among the best of all ferns for indoor use. *Nephrolepis* are particularly well suited for specimen culture in tubs and large baskets and with careful culture they will retain each frond for many years.

Soil Types

Nephrolepis will grow in a range of soil types providing the drainage is free and unimpeded. They particularly favour loose soils rather than those which are packed tightly. Most prefer soils of an acid pH but species such as *N. dicksonioides* may need the addition of lime.

Potting Mix

Ferns of this group are very adaptable as to the potting mix in which they will succeed. The only requirement is that the mixture must be very well-drained and open. One based on a well-structured loam supplemented with peat moss or pine bark is usually satisfactory. Some cultivars, especially the finely divided forms, tend to be weak growing and are more demanding in their potting mix. A soil-less mix based on coarse sand, milled pine bark, peat moss and/or tree-fern fibre will be suitable.

Vigorous *Nephrolepis* quickly fill a container with roots. Unlike many ferns though, they can last well in a pot-bound condition provided they are watered regularly and fertilized occasionally. Weak growing cultivars are better underpotted and do not need frequent repotting.

Watering

Species and cultivars of *Nephrolepis* like plenty of water especially during the summer months. Greenhouse grown plants in temperate regions are best kept on the dry side over winter to avoid rotting. Established plants, especially those in the ground, are quite tolerant of dry periods, and species such as *N. cordifolia* are extremely resistant to dryness.

The very finely dissected cultivars must be watered carefully as frond rots may develop if the compact mat of foliage is kept too wet. Such plants should be watered so that the roots only are wet and must be placed out of the reach of drips, condensation etc.

Fertilizing

Inorganic and organic fertilizers and manures are useful for plants in the ground; in pots, slow-release and liquid fertilizers can be used. Fertilizers should only be applied during the warm, growing months. Avoid sprinkling solid fertilizer or solutions of liquid fertilizer onto the foliage of finely divided cutlivars as it can cause rotting.

Situation

Ferns of this group like a well lit situation such as

A colony of *Nephrolepis acutifolia* Photo D. L. Jones

Nephrolepis biserrata Photo D. L. Jones

that provided by partial sun or filtered through sparse canopies. In the tropics, many species and some cultivars can be grown in full sun, although their colour may be somewhat bleached.

Most *Nephrolepis* are sensitive to severe cold weather, and frosts in particular. They have no reserves in their rhizomes and the tropical species usually collapse and die following such weather. Species which extend into warm temperate regions are much more cold tolerant.

Pests

Nephrolepis species suffer little from attacks by pests or diseases and because of their vigour usually grow out of any damage. Cultivars by comparison are very sensitive to damage by fern scale and on the finely dissected types these attacks may be persistent and very difficult to control. Affected tissue yellows and dies and whole fronds or patches may collapse leading to rotting.

Propagation

Species of *Nephrolepis* can be propagated readily from spores, however, most cultivars are sterile and the commonest means of propagation is from stolons. These can be pegged into pots or grown in special benches and the small plants detached when they are sufficiently developed. *Nephrolepis* adapt particularly well to tissue culture and millions of plants can be produced in a short time starting from a single piece of tissue. This has meant that new cultivars can be quickly multiplied and distributed as new releases. The tubers produced on the stolons of *N. cordifolia* and *N. occidentalis* can also be used for propagation providing a section of rhizome is attached.

SPECIES AND CULTIVARS

Nephrolepis acuminata
Malaysia, Indonesia
100–200 cm (40–80 in): 1 pinnate Trop.–S.Trop.: Terr.–Epi.

The fertile pinnae of this species are much narrower than the sterile and are deeply lobed and attractive. Both types are usually present on a frond with the basal part sterile. This fern can be grown as a garden plant in the tropics, as well as in a large container. Some forms may have drooping fronds.

Nephrolepis acutifolia
Africa, South-East Asia, Malaysia, New Guinea, Australia, Polynesia
100–200 cm (40–80 in): 1 pinnate Trop.–S.Trop.: Epi.–Terr.

An interesting fern that forms large scattered colonies often in full sun. It may grow on rocks or as an epiphyte, favouring palms. Plants have a creeping rhizome the old parts of which are densely covered with dead, wiry stipes. There is a remarkable difference between sterile and fertile pinnae and usually both occur on the one frond. Plants are rather cold sensitive but in the tropics can be grown in the garden or in containers.

Nephrolepis biserrata Coarse Sword Fern
Pantropical
90–250 cm (36–100 in): 1 pinnate Trop.–S.Trop.: Terr.–Epi.

A large coarse fern which is very widespread and has escaped from cultivation, becoming naturalized in many countries. It grows in huge colonies in a variety of situations (usually shady) and as a terrestrial or an epiphyte. It can be easily grown as a garden plant but tends to become invasive. Can be a useful coastal fern as it tolerates considerable exposure. For cv. Furcans see under *N. falcata*.

Nephrolepis cordata = N. cordifolia

Nephrolepis cordifolia Fishbone Fern
Pantropical
40–80 cm (16–32 in): 1 pinnate Trop.–Temp.: Terr.–Epi.

A very widely distributed fern which occurs naturally in a variety of situations from shade to full sun and grows in soil, among rocks or as an epiphyte

Nephrolepis cordifolia

Nephrolepis cordifolia is a very hardy fern
Photo D. L. Jones

Nephrolepis cordifolia 'Duffii' Photo D. L. Jones

Nephrolepis cordifolia 'Plumosa' is an excellent basket fern
Photo D. L. Jones

(particularly on palm trunks). It is a colony former and plants frequently bear small scaly tubers on their roots. It is popularly grown in temperate regions but in the tropics is generally regarded as a weed. It can be grown in gardens, pots or baskets. A number of cultivars are known.

'Compacta' — a dwarf-growing, compact form.

'Duffii' — a sterile form with small, button-shaped pinnae and crested frond tips. Very cold sensitive. Common garden fern in the tropics.

Nephrolepis exaltata 'Hillii' is a vigorous fern for tropical gardens
Photo D. L. Jones

'Petticoat' — an interesting form with pinnate fronds. The tips of the pinnae are forked once or twice and the ends of the fronds also fork from one to many times. The older fronds are pendulous, the younger ones erect. Ideal for baskets.

'Plumosa' — a graceful cultivar with the outer part of the pinnae divided and lobed. An excellent pot or basket fern.

Nephrolepis dicksonioides
Malaysia, New Guinea
300–500 cm (120–200 in): 1 pinnate Trop.–S.Trop.: Epi.

A giant fern which grows in large colonies among rocks (often limestone) in sunny situations. It has thick, leathery fronds which have crowded pinnae. Plants appear to be cold sensitive but behaviour in cultivation is largely unknown. May require the addition of lime to a potting mix.

Nephrolepis exaltata Sword Fern
Florida, Mexico, Brazil, West Indies
50–250 cm (20–100 in): 1 pinnate Trop.–S.Trop.: Terr.

The typical form of this fern is not remarkably different from many species of *Nephrolepis* and is not eagerly sought after for cultivation. It is, however, grown to some extent and it has proved to be a very hardy and easy fern to cultivate. The species is indeed adaptable for it has become commonly naturalized in the tropical parts of many countries after escaping from cultivation.

N. exaltata is undoubtedly best known for its mutant forms many of which are important nursery plants in various countries. Hundreds of mutants have occurred and these range from simple pinnae-margin variations to complex and bizarre developments which may be best labelled monstrosities. These finely divided forms are generally much slower growing than the coarser types. Some of these mutants have proved to be unstable, however, the more stable and attractive ones have been taken up by fern fanciers around the world. They are well suited to pot culture and are generally ideal for indoor decoration. The very finely divided forms with lacy fronds are aptly known as lace ferns. Most fancy cultivars of *N. exaltata* are sterile and must be propagated vegetatively. Early this century this was achieved by stripping stolons from specially grown stock plants, today, however, the various cultivars are successfully propagated by tissue culture.

Considerable confusion exists as to the correct naming of *Nephrolepis exaltata* cultivars. This confusion has arisen from a variety of factors, not the least of which is the difficulty of describing the differences between, or the distinct features of each cultivar, accurately. It is compounded by the use of different names in various countries and the practice of renaming an old cultivar and passing it off as new, for marketing purposes.

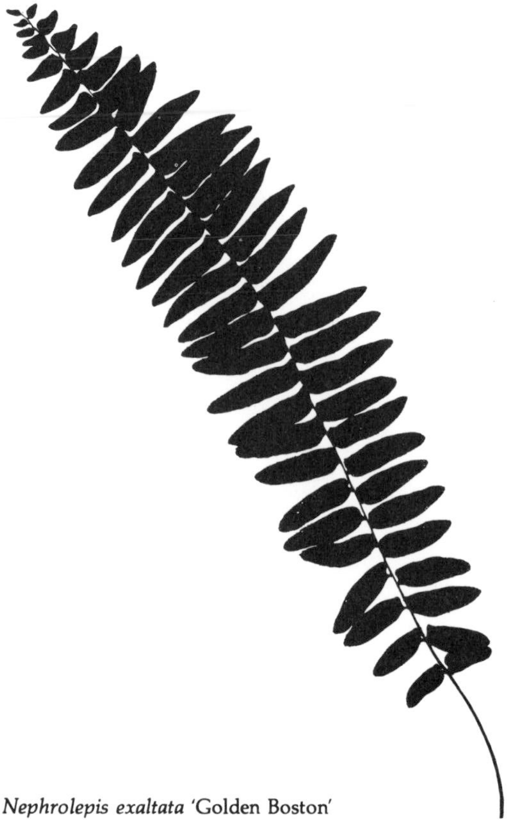

Nephrolepis exaltata 'Golden Boston'

'Amerpohlii' – a form with 3-pinnate fronds which are quite finely divided but not as compact as 'Smithii'.

'Anna Foster' – a tall growing form with bipinnate fronds. Arose from 'Piersonii'.

'Barrowsii' – a tall growing form with bipinnate fronds. Arose from 'Piersonii' in 1905.

'Childsii' – a form with very broad, almost triangular, dense fronds. Frond are 3–4 times pinnate and overlap others. Very sensitive to water damage.

'Clarkii' – a form with 3-pinnate fronds which are very finely divided and lacy. Arose from 'Smithii'.

'Craigii' – an extremely finely divided form which has 4-pinnate fronds. The ultimate segments are long and slender. Fronds are soft and very subject to rotting. Arose from 'Smithii'.

'Elegantissima' – this is a handsome bipinnate form which was developed by careful selection of good forms of 'Piersonii'. It makes a handsome basket plant but can show reversion to the pinnate type. Strong growing.

The first mutant of *N. exaltata* was noticed about 1870 in a batch of plants shipped from Philadelphia to Massachusetts. This form was eventually recognized under the name 'Bostoniensis' and was in fact the famous Boston Fern. All later mutants arose from this form (or cultivar) and strictly the name 'Bostoniensis' should be included in their cultivar names, although in practice this is never followed. A selection of *Nephrolepis exaltata* cultivars follows. Those names included in brackets indicate possible synonymy or perhaps a further development of that particular form.

'Bostoniensis' (Boston Fern) – this is the original mutant which had slightly broader and more graceful fronds than the species. It is also more vigorous in cultivation and quickly became the major cultivar grown. It is still a very popular fern in the USA today.

'Bostoniensis Aurea' (Golden Boston) – a form with pinnate fronds which are a most attractive golden yellow.

'Bostoniensis Compacta' – a compact growing form of 'Bostoniensis'. The pinnae sometimes have irregularly wavy margins especially towards the ends.

'Dwarf Boston' – a compact growing form with erect pinnate fronds. Quite vigorous and popular. Arose from 'Elegantissima Compacta'.

Nephrolepis exaltata 'Randolphii'

'Elegantissima Compaca' — a form of 'Elegantissima' with a denser, more compact growth habit. Fronds 2–3 pinnate. Shows less reversion. Arose in 1909.

'Elegantissima Improved' — an improved selection of 'Elegantissima' which shows less tendency to revert to the pinnate form.

'Elmsfordii' — a compact form with spreading 2–3 pinnate fronds.

'Erecta' — an unusual form with stiffly erect fronds, the leaflets of which are tightly curled with undulate margins. Croziers have a mass of conspicuous, silvery scales.

'Falcata' — a dwarf growing form with pinnate fronds the tips of which are once or twice forked. Arose from 'Scottii'.

'Fandancer' — a registered name for 'Bostoniensis Aurea'.

'Fish-tail' — see *Nephrolepis falcata* forma *furcans*.

'Florida Ruffle' — a form with stiff dense fronds that are 2–3 pinnate. Can be large growing. Fronds have a ruffled appearance. Good basket plant.

'Fluffy Ruffles' — a compact form which develops into dense clumps. Fronds are narrowly triangular, 2–3 pinnate with a conspicuous ruffled appearance.

'Giatrasii' — a compact dwarf growing form with pinnate fronds, and a graceful growth habit. Slow growing. Arose from 'Bostoniensis' in 1909.

'Gracillima' (Irish Lace) — a form with 3-pinnate fronds which are very finely divided and lacy.

'Harrisii' — an attractive pinnate form which has prominent wavy margins to the pinnae. Arose from 'Bostoniensis'.

'Hillii' — a very vigorous form with fronds to 1.5 m (60 in) long. These are pinnate and the pinnae are variously lobed and with crisped and wavy margins. An excellent fern for a large basket. Commonly grown as a garden plant in the tropics.

'Lycopodioides' — a compact growing form with very dense, finely divided 3–4 pinnate fronds which are irregularly twisted. Very slow growing.

'Magnifica' — a form with 3-pinnate fronds which are held erect. Has an open growth habit and the fronds are pale green. Arose from 'Whitmanii'.

'Milleri' — a form with 3-pinnate fronds which are finely divided and lacy.

'Mini Ruffle' — a miniature form with fronds that do not grow much more than 6 cm (3 in) long. These are 2–3 times divided with ruffled margins and are held erect. Very compact growth. Useful for pots or terrariums.

'M.P. Mills' — a compact slow growing form with bipinnate fronds and well-separated segments. Reverts easily. Arose from 'Scottii'.

'Muscosa' — a dwarf growing form with very dense 3-pinnate fronds, the segments of which are overlapping and irregularly twisted. Very slow growing. Arose from 'Superbissima'.

'Neubertii' — a form with 3-pinnate fronds which are finely divided and lacy. Arose in Germany.

'New York' — a smaller growing pinnate form of 'Bostoniensis' with slightly wavy margins to the pinnae. Can be slow growing. Arose from 'Giatrasii'.

'Petticoat' — see *Nephrolepis cordifolia*.

'Piersonii' — this was the first mutant to arise from 'Bostoniensis' in 1902. The fronds are twice pinnate but tend to revert readily to the pinnate form. Gave rise to 'Elegantissima' and most of the bipinnate forms.

'Rams Horn' — see *Nephrolepis falcata*.

'Randolphii' — slender, pinnate fronds which are strongly pendulous. Pinnae are prominently lobed at the base. Excellent for baskets.

'Robusta' — a form with 1–2 pinnate fronds which are extremely broad (25–30 cm [10–12 in]) and arching. It has a fairly open growth habit and suffers less from rotting. Arose from 'Elegantissima'.

'Rochfordii' — a form with 3 pinnate fronds which are finely divided and lacy. Arose in England.

'Rooseveltii' — a dwarf to intermediate growing form with pinnate fronds which have prominent wavy margins and auricles at the base. Arose from 'Bostoniensis'.

'Scholzelii' — an intermediate sized form with bipinnate fronds which have fairly large segments. Arose from 'Scottii' in 1908.

'Scottii' — a compact dwarf growing pinnate form with closely placed, recurved pinnae. The fronds tend to be succulent. Arose from 'Bostoniensis'.

'Shadow Lace' — a form with fronds 3–4 times divided. Fronds are very broad and almost triangular with the leaflets tightly clustered. New fronds sometimes have golden tints.

'Silver Balls' — an erect growing form with 1–2 pinnate fronds. Pinnae are crinkled or lobed. New croziers are covered with conspicuous silvery scales.

'Smithii' — a form with 3-pinnate fronds which are very finely divided and lacy. Growth is so dense that fronds rot readily if over-watered.

'Superbissima' — a form with 3-pinnate fronds with the segments closely overlapping and irregularly twisted. Fronds have a spreading habit and are fairly thick textured and dark green. Very slow growing. Arose in 1908 from 'Elegantissima'.

'Suzi Wong' — an extremely dense form with fronds which are 3–4 times pinnate. Each frond may be very broad and overlaps others. Fronds are very soft and sensitive to over-watering.

'Teddy Junior' – a dense, compact growing pinnate form with broad pinnae which have conspicuous wavy margins. Young fronds are often yellow-green. Very attractive and strong growing. Arose from 'Rooseveltii'.

'Todeoides' – a form with 2–3 pinnate fronds. Similar to 'Elegantissima' but with more elongated segments. Selected in England.

'Verona' (Lace Fern) – a compact growing form with 3–4 pinnate fronds. These are usually of a light green colouration and the older ferns are strongly pendant. An excellent basket fern, but fronds are sensitive to water damage.

'Viridissima' – an unusual compact growing form with pinnate fronds. These are held rigidly erect and have deep green overlapping twisted pinnae. Slow growing. Arose from 'Superbissima'.

'Wagneri' – a dwarf, compact growing pinnate form with the pinnae crowded, curved and with wavy margins. Arose from 'Scottii'.

'Wanamaker Boston' – a dwarf growing form with narrow, erect pinnate fronds. The pinnae are irregular being wavy and sometimes lobed or pinnatifid in the upper half and auriculate at the base. Arose from 'Scholzelii' in 1915.

'Whitmanii' – a form with 2–3 pinnate fronds similar in many respects to 'Elegantissima' but with the ultimate segments rounder and the fronds more open. Arose from 'Barrowsii'.

'Whitmanii Compacta' – a form of 'Whitmanii' with a denser, more compact growth habit. Fronds softly textured, very attractive.

'Whitmanii Improved' – a selection of 'Whitmanii' which shows less tendency to revert to the pinnate form.

'Willmottae' – a form with 3-pinnate fronds which are very finely divided and lacy. Compact grower.

Nephrolepis falcata Weeping Sword Fern
Thailand, Vietnam, Malaysia
100–250 cm (40–100 in): 1 pinnate Trop.–S.Trop.: Epi.–Terr.

A very desirable species valued horticulturally for its long, strongly-weeping fronds. Plants are excellent for a large basket and grow vigorously, quickly developing into an attractive specimen. They like plenty of light but should be protected from direct sun.

The forma *furcans* can be easily recognized by each pinna being regularly forked like a fish tail, and is commonly known as the Fishtail Fern. It is reported to be of cultivated origin in New Guinea but is now naturalized in many countries. It will grow in full sun and makes an unusual fern for a large border.

'Ram's Horn' – a form with strongly curved pinnae.

Nephrolepis falcata has strongly weeping fronds
Photo D. L. Jones

Nephrolepis falcata 'Ramshorn' Photo D. L. Jones

Nephrolepis falcata forma *furcans* is commonly called the Fishtail Fern Photo D. L. Jones

Nephrolepis hirsutula Rough Sword Fern
Asia, Malaysia, New Guinea, Australia, Central and South America
60–150 cm (24–60 in): 1 pinnate Trop.–S.Trop.: Terr.

A coarse fern usually found growing in colonies in exposed situations. It is a strong growing species that can be used as a garden plant in warm climates but it may become invasive. It also makes a decorative tub specimen which can be used outdoors or in a well-lit situation indoors.

Nephrolepis occidentalis Annual Sword Fern
Central and South America, West Indies
20–60 cm (8–24 in): 1 pinnate Trop.–S.Trop.: Terr.

A weak growing fern which apparently dies back annually to tubers. A plant consists of a few fronds which have a lax or weak habit and a slender, small rhizome. Appears to have been cultivated only on a limited scale.

Nephrolepis pectinata
Central and South America, West Indies, Cuba
30–50 cm (12–20 in): 1 pinnate Trop.–S.Trop.: Terr.

In this species the fronds grow in a stiffly erect, tight cluster and arise from an upright rhizome which in old plants becomes a wiry trunk. Plants grow in large colonies usually in shady forests. They can be grown easily as a garden or tub plant.

Nephrolepis pendula
Mexico, Central and South America
30–150 cm (12–60 in): 1 pinnate Trop.–S.Trop.: Epi.–Terr.

This species has been confused with *N. cordifolia* but differs in its polished, brown, scale-less stipes and the entire-margined pinnae which are blunt at the apex. It is a handsome fern with strongly-weeping fronds and looks very attractive in a basket or any hanging container.

32 Lady ferns and their allies

genera *Allantodia, Athyrium, Callipteris, Cornopteris, Cystopteris, Diplazium, Lunathyrium* and *Pseudocystopteris*

An attractive group of ferns which contains some very decorative species of delicate appearance. Some of this group are common commercial ferns. The Lady Fern itself (*Athyrium filix-femina*) has been responsible for hundreds of fancy-leaved cultivars many of which are grown by dedicated fern enthusiasts.

Habitat

Ferns of this group are invariably terrestrials and are mostly shade lovers. A few hardier types grow in sunny situations but usually where there is an abundance of soil moisture, or at high altitudes. Some species have very brittle fronds easily damaged by wind or rough handling. Ferns of this group are to be found in temperate and tropical regions, although they are most abundant in the tropics.

Cultivation

Uses

Many species of this group are valued for their delicate and finely divided fronds. They mingle well with other ferns and can also be grown as garden plants in shady positions. A few species are amenable to cultivation in containers although generally ferns of this group have a strong root system. The unusual growth patterns in cultivars of *A. filix-femina* add diversity to a fern collection.

Soil Types

Most of these ferns are very appreciative of humus and like well-drained organically rich loams. They also appreciate regular applications of organic mulch to the soil surface. Species such as *Diplazium dilatatum* and *D. dietrichianum* will grow in wet to boggy soils providing the water is not stagnant. Most species need an acid soil; a few, such as *Lunathyrium japonicum*, appreciate the addition of lime.

Potting Mix

An open mix based on well-structured loam and fortified with peat moss or milled pine bark is usually suitable.

Many ferns of this group have a very strong root system and quickly outgrow a container. Such species are best planted in the ground otherwise their appearance suffers because of the confined root system.

Watering

Ferns of this group generally like moist conditions and appreciate plenty of water, especially during periods of hot or dry weather. They also respond to water sprayed onto their foliage during such weather. Their fronds quickly become tattered if the plants dry out at the roots or are exposed to dry, buffeting winds.

Fertilizing

As a group, these ferns are strong growers and respond to the use of fertilizers and manures. Blood and bone, well-rotted animal manures and compost are particularly beneficial and should be applied during the spring or summer. Slow-release fertilizers can be added to a potting mix and/or the plants supplemented with applications of liquid fertilizer.

Situation

Most ferns in this group are shade lovers. They will tolerate brief exposure to direct sun or filtered sun, but they are readily damaged by over-exposure and this must be borne in mind when choosing a position. A few species will tolerate nearly full sun (*Callipteris prolifera, Diplazium dietrichianum, Lunathyrium japonicum*) but need plenty of moisture around their roots. The tropical species are generally very sensitive to cold, and frosts in particular.

Pests

Young fronds of most species are eagerly attacked by slugs and snails. Grubs may be a problem on those with finely divided fronds and aphids may congregate on croziers and uncurling fronds.

Propagation

Ferns of this group are generally very easy to raise from spores and present no problems with spore

A colony of *Athyrium filix-femina* 'Minutissimum'
Photo W. R. Elliot

collection. A limited number are proliferous and can be propagated from plantlets. Some species produce multiple crowns or have a creeping rhizome and plants of these species can be divided when sufficiently large.

SPECIES AND CULTIVARS

Allantodia australis (alt. **Diplazium australe**)
Australia, New Zealand
100–200 cm (40–80 in): 3–4 pinnate Temp.–S.Trop.: Terr.

A large handsome fern which is always found in shady areas sheltered from the wind. The broad lacy fronds are extremely brittle and easily damaged. Old plants develop a prominent trunk. Grows very easily in a shady position but likes plenty of moisture and appreciates regular mulching.

Allantodia squamigera (alt. **Diplazium squamigerum**)
Japan, China, North India
60–90 cm (24–36 in): 2–3 pinnate S.Trop.–Temp.: Terr.

This is a large-growing fern with broad, finely divided, dark green fronds of a lacy appearance. The fronds have long stipes and arise in a rosette. Readily damaged by wind, plants need a sheltered aspect.

Anisogonium esculentum — see **Diplazium esculentum**

Athyrium accedens=**Callipteris prolifera**

Athyrium alpestre=**A. distentifolium**

Athyrium asplenioides Southern Lady Fern
North America
50–100 cm (20–40 in): 2 pinnate Temp.–S.Trop.: Terr.

This fern forms a rosette of patterned fronds that spread and arch in an attractive manner. It is a deciduous fern with the fronds dying after the first frost. Plants are very cold-hardy and can be grown in a shady situation in loamy soil. This species is sometimes included as a variety of *A. filix-femina*.

Athyrium atkinsonii — see **Pseudocystopteris atkinsonii**

Athyrium crenatoserrulatum — see **Cornopteris crenatoserrulatum**

Athyrium deltoidofrons
China, Korea, Japan
30–60 cm (12–24 in): 2 pinnate S.Trop.–Temp.: Terr.

An unusual fern with pale, yellow-green fronds which contrast pleasantly with other ferns of darker hues. Plants can be grown in a shady situation, but seem to prefer more light than other ferns of this group.

Athyrium distentifolium Alpine Lady Fern
Europe, Iceland, North America, Canada, Scotland
30–70 cm (12–28 in): 2 pinnate Temp.: Terr.

This is a fern of high mountains and alpine scrubs and meadows. Plants have erect thinly-textured, light green fronds and are fully deciduous in winter. The species is very cold-hardy and ideal for temperate climates. It can be readily grown in a shady situation in loamy soil.

Athyrium falcatum
India
15–40 cm (6–16 in): 1 pinnate S.Trop.: Terr.

A hardy little fern from mountainous areas where it grows in partially sheltered situations. Very attractive in a rockery. Needs a partially sunny but protected aspect in humus-rich soil.

Athyrium filix-femina Lady Fern
India, China, Japan, North Africa, Canada, North America, Mexico, Peru
60–150 cm (24–60 in): 2–3 pinnate Temp.–S.Trop.: Terr.

A graceful fern which is valued for its hardiness, ease of culture and its ability to produce a large range of cultivars which have bewildering frond variations. It grows best in the ground rather than a container and requires a shady to semi-shady situation in loamy, humus-rich soil. Plants are dormant in winter and in cold regions they may be completely deciduous. A vigorous flush of new growth in the spring is very decorative. In all, over 300 cultivars have been named from this fern.

Athyrium filix-femina 'Frizelliae Cristatum'

Athyrium filix-femina 'Glomeratum'

'Acrocladon' — a form in which the fronds branch many times to form a spherical clump. Partially fertile.

'Angusto-cruciatum' — a form with narrow fronds each of which has a terminal crest. Partially fertile.

'Clarissima' — a form with large and remarkably broad fronds (to 100×60 cm [40×24 in]) which are very finely cut. This is an excellent form but, unfortunately, it can only be propagated by crown division which is very slow.

'Congestum Cristatum' — a dwarf form with densely-congested crested pinnae and a large terminal crest. Partially fertile.

'Congestum Minus' — a dwarf form with congested fronds 10–15 cm (4–6 in) tall.

'Corymbiferum' — a form with bunched fronds which are heavily crested. Partially fertile.

'Craigii-cristatum' — a narrow-fronded form with terminal crests.

'Cristatum' — a variable group with crested pinnae which are held flat rather than erect or in bunches. Partially fertile.

'Fieldii' — a tall growing form with narrow fronds with the pinnae paired so as to form crosses. Strong grower.

'Frizelliae' — in this distinctive form the pinnae are reduced to rounded structures giving the fronds the appearance of a necklace. Fertile.

'Glomeratum' — slender fronds with large terminal crests, the pinnae are also crested.

'Grandiceps' — a variable form, each frond having a large crest on the end. Partially fertile.

'Minutissimum' — a dwarf clumping form with compact fronds 10–15 cm long. Partially fertile.

'Plumosum' — a variable group of forms with light green fronds each divided 3–4 times and with a delicate, feathery appearance. Fertile.

'Setigerum' — a group of forms in which the pinnae are reduced to slender segments. Strong growing. Fertile.

'Setigerum Cristatum' — a form with slender segments which have terminal crests. Fertile.

'Victoriae' — a very distinctive form with fronds up to 1 m (40 in) tall and narrow pinnae which are paired so as to form crosses, with each having a terminal crest. Fertile.

Athyrium flexile
Europe
20–30 cm (8–12 in): 2 pinnate Temp.: Terr.

A relatively small species similar to *A. distentifolium*, but with prostrate fronds and smaller segments. A hardy species which may be deciduous in very cold areas. Attractive among rocks.

Athyrium frangulum is an excellent small fern for a rockery
Photo D. L. Jones

Athyrium frangulum
Japan
15–45 cm (6–18 in): 2–3 pinnate S.Trop.–Temp.: Terr.

This is a neat fern with triangular, lacy, light coloured fronds and a distinctly reddish to purple rachis. The frond segments are closely placed giving a crowded appearance. A very easily grown species attractive among rocks.

Athyrium goeringianum = A. niponicum

Athyrium filix-femina 'Victoriae'

Athyrium frangulum

Athyrium japonicum – see **Lunathyrium japonicum**

Athyrium niponicum var **pictum** Japanese Painted Fern
China, Korea, Japan
20–50 cm (8–20 in): 3–4 pinnate S.Trop.–Temp.: Terr.

This fern is prized for its delicately coloured new fronds which are of a soft metallic grey colour suffused with reddish or bluish hues. The colour is maintained in old fronds, however the young fronds contrast pleasantly with the mature ones. Plants are very cold-hardy, withstanding quite heavy frosts. They can also be grown in subtropical regions. A shady location in humus-rich loam is suitable for their culture although plants in good light develop the best colour.

Athyrium otophorum
China, Japan, Korea
50–70 cm (20–28 in): 2 pinnate Temp.–S.Trop.: Terr.

This is a distinctive fern with fairly broad, deltoid fronds which have dark green segments and a reddish to purplish stipe and rachis. Plants prefer a shady location in humus-rich loam.

Athyrium pycnocarpum American Glade Fern
North America
60–120 cm (24–48 in): 1 pinnate Temp.–S.Trop.: Terr.

A graceful fern with the fronds spreading in a rosette. It grows naturally in moist woodlands frequently in small colonies. Plants are very cold-hardy and are dormant during winter with the fronds being deciduous. New fronds are an attractive light green while the old fronds frequently turn russet-brown before they shed. Slugs and snails can be very damaging to young fronds.

Athyrium spinulosum – see **Pseudocystopteris spinulosum**

Athyrium squamigerum – see **Allantodia squamigera**

Athyrium thelypterioides – see **Lunathyrium thelypterioides**

Athyrium umbrosum
India, Thailand
50–150 cm (20–60 in): 3–4 pinnate S.Trop.: Terr.
This species is rather confused botanically, however, the fern that is cultivated under this name is highly ornamental and deserves to be much more widely grown. It has large, finely divided lacy fronds which are light-to-bright-green and shiny. Plants grow well in loamy soil in a shady situation.

Callipteris prolifera
Malaysia, Philippines, Indonesia, Australia, Polynesia
50–120 cm (20–48 in): 1 pinnate Trop.–S.Trop.: Terr.
A large growing, fleshy fern which forms an impressive rosette of fronds. On old plants these arise from a short trunk. The fronds bear numerous plantlets along the rachis, which can be used for propagation. An excellent tub fern and also useful for ferneries or gardens in the tropics.

Cornopteris crenulatoserrulatum (alt. **Athyrium crenulatoserrulatum**)
Japan
45–90 cm (18–36 in): 2–3 pinnate S.Trop.–Temp.: Terr.
This species has finely divided, broad fronds with long, overlapping segments which create a crowded impression. It favours cool, shady conditions in humus-rich soil.

Cystopteris bulbifera Berry Bladder Fern
Canada, North America
30–75 cm (12–30 in): 2 pinnate Temp.–S.Trop.: Terr.
A most distinctive fern with lax or pendant fronds and which produces numerous bulbils from the underside. These fall and develop into new plants on the ground. The species characteristically grows in crevices of limestone rocks, often in colonies. It adapts easily to cultivation and in fact may be weedy. Likes moist conditions in a semi-shady aspect and responds to the use of lime.

Cystopteris dickieana – see under **C. fragilis**

Cystopteris fragilis Brittle Bladder Fern
Cosmopolitan
10–35 cm (4–14 in): 1–2 pinnate Temp.: Terr.
This is one of the most widely distributed of all ferns. It is a dwarf species which grows among rocks and in crevices frequently in mountainous areas. The delicate fronds are easily damaged and in cold climates die off with the onset of winter. Plants can be grown in a small container but if grown in the ground are best planted among rocks. Can also be successfully grown in a terrarium. Likes shade and moisture. This fern is quite variable and consists of a number of forms which some workers regard as distinct species, e.g. *C. dickieana*, *C. montana* and *C. regia*.

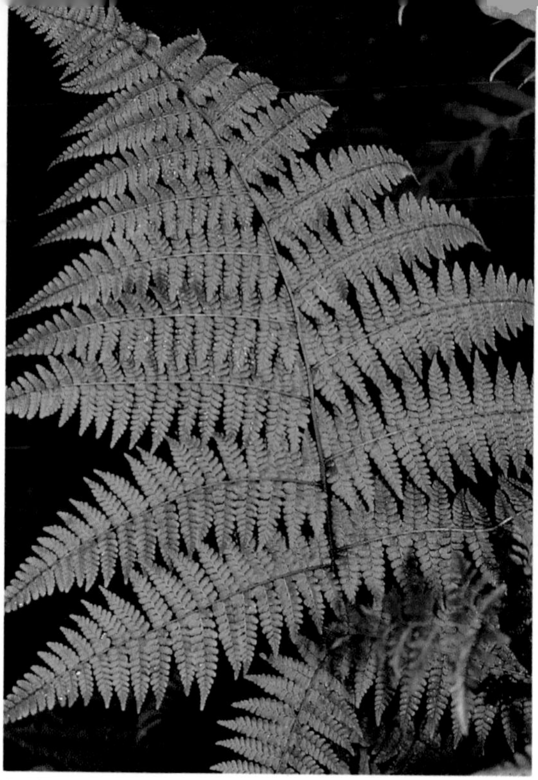

Diplazium assimile Photo D. L. Jones

Cystopteris montana – see under **C. fragilis**

Cystopteris regia – see under **C. fragilis**

Diplazium accedens=**Callipteris prolifera**

Athyrium umbrosum Photo D. L. Jones

Diplazium asperum
Malaysia, Philippines, Indonesia, New Guinea
60–150 cm (24–60 in): 2–3 pinnate Trop.–S.Trop.: Terr.

In nature, this fern grows along stream banks and forest margins and commonly colonizes road embankments etc. It is a distinctive species with prickly stipes and large, broad attractively divided fronds. Plants can be cultivated easily in a semi-shady situation and require plenty of water.

Diplazium assimile
Australia
50–150 cm (20–60 in): 3–4 pinnate Temp.–Trop.: Terr.

This fern has finely divided lacy fronds which arch in a rosette. The fronds are membranous and easily damaged. Plants are decorative and fast growing. They are adaptable to most soils and need shade and plenty of moisture.

Diplazium australe — see **Allantodia australis**

Diplazium cordifolium
Malaysia, Philippines, Indonesia, New Guinea, Australia
20–80 cm (8–32 in): entire-pinnate Trop.–S.Trop.: Terr.

A delicate fern always found growing in moist shady situations usually near streams. Forms with simple and pinnate leaves are known. This is a very slow growing fern which requires warm, humid, shady conditions for its cultivation. It is best grown in a small container of humus-rich mixture and should not be overpotted. Occasional fronds produce plantlets.

Diplazium crenatum
Europe, Asia, Japan
20–45 cm (8–18 in): 2–3 pinnate Temp.: Terr.

A delicate-looking fern from mountainous regions where it grows among rocks. Fronds are thinly-textured, light-green and almost triangular in outline. Plants are very cold-hardy and will withstand heavy frosts without damage. They are dormant during the winter months. Useful in a shady rockery.

Diplazium dietrichianum
New Guinea, Australia
100–200 cm (40–80 in): 2–3 pinnate Trop.: Terr.

A weedy-type fern which forms large colonies in low lying areas subject to inundation. Plants usually grow in full sun and spread freely by means of stolons. The large fronds are very brittle. Can be grown easily in a sunny, moist situation but plants are very sensitive to cold.

Diplazium dilatatum
Malaysia, Philippines, Indonesia, New Guinea, Australia
100–200 cm (40–80 in): 2–3 pinnate Trop.–Temp.: Terr.

A large fern with very decorative fronds. These have

Diplazium dilatatum Photo D. L. Jones

Diplazium dilatatum

Diplazium esculentum

Diplazium esculentum Photo D. L. Jones

an arching habit and are divided into coarse segments. The arrangement of the sori on the underside of the fertile fronds is very beautiful. Likes a shady situation and will grow in quite wet soils where the water is not stagnant.

Diplazium esculentum alt. **Anisogonium esculentum**
Edible Fern/Vegetable Fern
India, Philippines, Indonesia, New Guinea, Polynesia
50–120 cm (20–48 in): 1–2 pinnate Trop.–S.Trop.: Terr.

The developing croziers and young fronds of this fern are eaten as a cooked vegetable or raw in salads in many countries of the Pacific regions and are even sold in local markets. Plants grow vigorously and spread by stolons. Juvenile plants are slender with pinnate fronds but on mature plants the fronds are broad and bipinnate. The species grows easily but prefers moist to wet soils.

Diplazium japonicum — see **Lunathyrium japonicum**

Diplazium lanceum = D. subsinuatum

Diplazium lanceum var. **crenatum = D. tomitaroanum**

Diplazium melanochlamys
Lord Howe Island
50–100 cm (20–40 in): 2–3 pinnate S.Trop.–Temp.: Terr.

This is a coarse fern which grows naturally in shady and sunny areas among rocks. Plants are strong growing and will adapt to a variety of soils but for best appearance require shade. Very easily grown. Older plants tend to develop a short trunk.

Diplazium pallidum
India, Indonesia, New Guinea, Australia
50–80 cm (20–32 in): 1 pinnate Trop.–S.Trop.: Terr.

A slender fern found on shady stream banks. Makes an attractive subject for pot culture and can also be grown in a shady position in the ground. Plants tend to be slow growing but are very long-lived.

Diplazium silvaticum
India, Malaysia, New Guinea, Australia
40–60 cm (16–24 in): 1 pinnate Trop.–S.Trop.: Terr.

A somewhat slow growing species that forms a rosette of bright green fronds. Occasional plantlets are produced from the tips. Can be grown in a container but best in a shady situation in the ground. Fronds are brittle and easily damaged.

Diplazium squamigerum — see **Allantodia squamigera**

Diplazium subserratum
Malaysia, Indonesia
30–70 cm (12–28 in): entire Trop.–S.Trop.: Terr.

A delicate fern found in shady rainforests. Should become popular because of its slender, thick-textured dark green fronds carried in a neat rosette. Juvenile fronds are deeply lobed; mature fronds have slightly crenate margins. Requires warm, humid conditions and should not be overpotted.

Diplazium subsinuatum
Japan, China, Korea, North India
15–45 cm (6–18 in): entire S.Trop.–Temp.: Terr.
This is a delightful small fern which forms slowly spreading clumps of dark green fronds. Well suited to cultivation in a small pot or rockery, or as a terrarium plant. Likes a shady aspect and humus-rich soil. Similar to *D. tomitaroanum* but the fronds have entire margins.

Diplazium tomentosum
Malaysia, Thailand
30–70 cm (12–28 in): 1 pinnate Trop.–S.Trop.: Terr.
This fern grows in shady rainforests. It is considered to be ornamental because of its neat, attractively-lobed fronds which are dark green and quite thickly-textured. Old plants develop a short, erect trunk. Can be grown in a small container or a shady situation in the ground. Requires warm humid conditions.

Diplazium tomitaroanum
Japan, China
6–12 cm (2–5 in): entire-pinnate Temp.–S.Trop.: Terr.
A dwarf fern eminently suited for culture in a small container or in the pocket of a rockery. The growth is compact and the small fronds are produced close together to give a matted appearance. Plants may be slow growing but can be held in a container for a number of years. It is a prized fern in Japan where a number of unusual cultivars are grown.

'Giza Giza Hera Shida' — a form with attractively-lobed frond margins.

Diplazium wercklianum

Diplazium wercklianum
Central and South America
50–80 cm (20–32 in): 1 pinnate Trop.–S.Trop.: Terr.
An attractive fern with very dark green lustrous fronds which grow in an erect to spreading clump. The sheen of the fronds even shows up in the shady situations the species prefers to grow in. Makes an attractive garden plant and is also suitable for tubs and pots.

Lunathyrium japonicum Japanese Lady Fern
India, China, Japan, Malaysia, New Guinea, Australia, New Zealand
20–60 cm (8–24 in): 1 pinnate Trop.–Temp.: Terr.
A small growing fern found in a variety of habitats but frequent in and around the beds of streams. Adapts exceedingly well to cultivation and in fact may grow voluntarily in greenhouses, bush-houses and nurseries. Sporelings are fast growing and establish quickly. Plants appreciate the addition of lime to the potting mix. Fronds are brittle and easily damaged.

Lunathyrium thelypterioides (alt. **Athyrium thelypterioides**) Silver Glade Fern
North America, North India, China
60–120 cm (24–48 in): 1–2 pinnate Temp.–S.Trop.: Terr.
An easy fern to grow which is well suited to temperate regions, but which sheds its fronds with the onset of cold weather in the winter. Plants form a neat tussock and favour organically-rich, loamy soil in a shady situation. New growth in the spring is particularly decorative.

Pseudocystopteris atkinsonii (alt. **Athyrium atkinsonii**)
China, Japan, North India
60–90 cm (24–36 in): 2–3 pinnate S.Trop.–Temp.: Terr.
A fern of high altitudes which may be deciduous in very cold winters. Plants develop quite large, finely lacy fronds on a creeping rhizome. Suitable for a shady location.

Pseudocystopteris spinulosum (alt. **Athyrium spinulosum**)
China, Japan, USSR, North India
45–60 cm (18–24 in): 2–3 pinnate S.Trop.–Temp.: Terr.
An attractive fern with somewhat harshly-textured, dark green, broadly triangular fronds which arise at intervals from a creeping rhizome. Plants occur at fairly high altitudes and grow readily in a shady aspect in humus-rich soil.

33 Water ferns, hard ferns, rasp ferns and chain ferns

genera *Blechnum, Doodia, Woodwardia* and *Sadleria*

A group of related ferns which are generally easy to grow with some species being popular with fern enthusiasts the world over. A few are important commercial ferns.

Habitat

Most ferns of this group are terrestrials, although a few have a climbing growth habit. Many of them grow in moist to wet soils in shaded forests, commonly along the banks of streams, and in swamps. Some are colonizers, appearing on disturbed earth, road verges, embankments etc. Species of *Doodia* generally grow in dry situations, either in shade or exposed to filtered or partial sun. Some blechnums (such as *B. cartilagineum*) occupy similar habitats.

Cultivation

Uses

With few exceptions these ferns adapt well to cultivation and can be grown in gardens, ferneries and containers. Species with a spreading growth habit are ideal as a groundcover (*Blechnum occidentale, Doodia aspera*), some of the larger species provide shelter for smaller ferns (*Blechnum brasiliense*). Many of them blend in perfectly with landscaped areas where water is a feature, and in these settings should be planted thickly. Some species of *Blechnum* and *Doodia* produce colourful new fronds and are worth planting close to paths where this feature can be seen to effect.

Most species can also be grown in containers, although they generally make unsuitable indoor plants.

Soil Types

Ferns of this group are not fussy regarding soil type and will grow in almost any well-drained garden loam. Mostly they prefer acid soils and appreciate organic mulches on the soil surface. Some species of *Blechnum* thrive in wet soil (providing the water is not stagnant) and under such conditions will withstand considerable exposure to sun.

Potting Mix

An open mix based on a well-structured loam and fortified with peat moss, milled pine bark or tree-fern fibre is usually suitable. Many ferns of this group are strong growers and have a vigorous root system which quickly fills a pot. Such plants may need repotting or potting on once or twice a year.

Watering

These ferns like plenty of water but many of them suffer from the problem of sweating (see page 119) if their leaves are wet for long periods during wet or still weather. Affected fronds take on a watery appearance and eventually blacken; the plants are weakened and may even die. This is a very common problem with these ferns and the answer is to eliminate overhead watering when conditions are still, and also to place the plants where they will receive air movement.

Fertilizing

These ferns are gross feeders and respond to most types of fertilizers and manures. Applications should be restricted to spring or summer.

Situation

Most ferns in this group will grow in shady conditions and a few are easily damaged by sun (*Blechnum lanceolatum*). Some, however, prefer filtered sun or partial sun, e.g. *Doodia aspera, Blechnum orientale*. Because of the sweating problem in their fronds a position open to air movement is preferable to stagnant conditions. Some species from tropical regions have proved to be adaptable and are surprisingly tolerant of temperate conditions, including light frosts.

Pests

Pests are not a major problem to these ferns, but scale may be a persistent nuisance and young fronds are susceptible to aphids, caterpillars and slugs, particularly in the spring.

Blechnum brasiliense Photo D. L. Jones

Propagation

Ferns of this group differ considerably regarding ease of propagation from spores. Some species appear not to produce fertile spores every year, certainly not in quantity. In *Blechnum nudum*, for example, good crops appear to be produced only every 2–3 years. It can also be difficult to tell when the fronds are ready for collection, especially in those species with dimorphic fronds. Those fertile fronds in which the indusium is just beginning to deteriorate and the sporangia have a crystalline appearance are generally ideal. A sharp flick with the finger will often release a cloud of spores. Sporangia which present a fluffy appearance are over-mature. Checking with a hand lens is useful.

Some ferns of this group can also be propagated by division and a few of the Chain Ferns produce plantlets on their fronds.

A colony of *Blechnum capense* Photo D. L. Jones

SPECIES AND CULTIVARS

Blechnum alpinum — see **B. penna-marina** ssp. **alpinum**

Blechnum articulatum Rosy Water Fern
Australia
40–120 cm (16–48 in): 1 pinnate S.Trop.–Temp.: Terr.

The colourful new fronds of this species are very beautiful having a pink to bright red hue. Plants are very easy to grow in a shady situation in organically-rich, acid soil. They are slow but steady growers and appreciate added moisture and surface mulches.

Blechnum attenuatum Climbing Blechnum
Africa, Mascarene Islands, Polynesia
20–40 cm (8–16 in): 1 pinnate Trop.–S.Trop.: Climber

A vigorous climbing fern that scrambles over rocks and the trunks of tree ferns and trees. It occurs in shady, moist forests and may form large patches. Plants can be grown in baskets or as a ground cover or trained to climb up trees. This fern likes shady conditions and plenty of moisture.

Blechnum auriculatum — see under **B. australe**

Blechnum australe
Africa, South America, Madagascar
25–50 cm (10–20 in): 1 pinnate Temp.–S.Trop.: Terr.

An attractive fern forming clumps of dark green fronds which develop on the ends of slender rhizomes. Fronds are similar in general appearance to *B. orientale* and plants have a similar growth habit. In cultivation they like plenty of moisture and a semi-shady situation although they will tolerate exposure to a fair amount of sun. A useful ground cover fern.

The form *auriculatum* has sticky, glandular hairs on the fronds.

Blechnum brasiliense Brazilian Tree Fern
Brazil
60–150 cm (24–60 in): 1 pinnate Trop.–S.Trop.: Terr.

The common name of this fern is somewhat false for it is not a true tree fern, however, old plants do develop a prominent trunk and a crown of spreading fronds. It is commonly grown in gardens and tubs and likes a well lit situation in acid loamy soil. New fronds are reddish-bronze.

'Crispum' — the segments have prominently crisped margins.

'Cristatum' — the segments are crested; comes true from spore.

Blechnum capense Palm Leaf Fern
New Zealand, Lord Howe Island, Polynesia
50–300 cm (24–120 in): 1 pinnate Temp.–S.Trop.: Terr.

A widely distributed fern which is really a complex of many forms or even species. Some forms are huge and must be given sufficient space to develop. Generally these plants like moisture and thrive in moist to wet acid soils. They will grow from shady to quite sunny situations and once established are very hardy. See also *B. sylvaticum.*

Blechnum cartilagineum Gristle Fern
Australia, New Guinea
60–150 cm (24–60 in): 1 pinnate Temp.–Trop.: Terr.

A tough, very hardy fern which grows in a variety of habitats from open forest to rainforest. The rainforest form generally has darker green fronds and likes a protected situation in cultivation. Those from the open forest will tolerate considerable amounts of sun and dryness. New fronds are bronze-red.

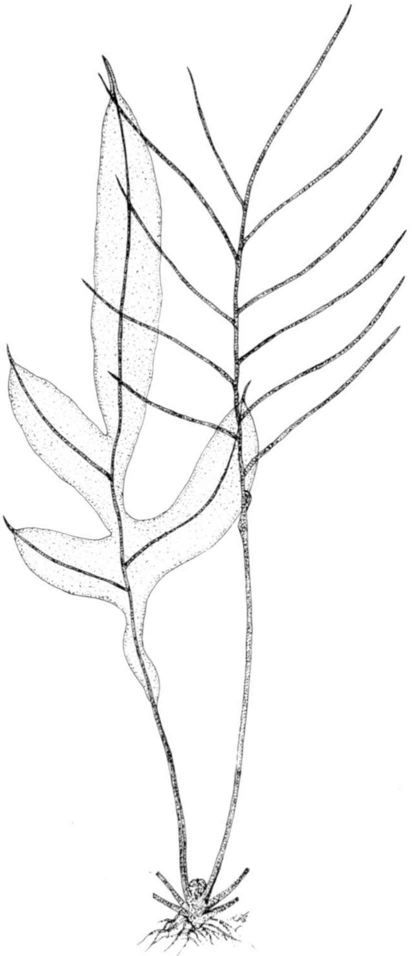

Blechnum colensoi

A new frond of *Blechnum cartilagineum*
Photo D. L. Jones

Blechnum chambersii — see under **B. lanceolatum**

Blechnum chilense
South America
30–90 cm (12–36 in): 1 pinnate Temp.–S.Trop.: Terr.

A hardy fern which succeeds well in cold climates. It is a robust species which in time can develop into a spreading colony. New fronds are decorative being covered with large scales. Plants like an abundance of water and will grow in shady or sunny situations. They can be readily propagated by division.

Blechnum colensoi
New Zealand
30–80 cm (12–32 in): entire-pinnatifid Temp.–S.Trop.: Terr.

A beautiful fern with thick, dark-green leathery fronds that appear almost black when wet. Plants always grow in wet, shady situations and in cultivation they need shade and an acid soil with plenty of moisture. A slow but steady grower. Similar to *B. patersonii* but with wider, much thicker-textured fronds.

Blechnum discolor Crown Fern
New Zealand
50–100 cm (20–40 in): 1 pinnate Temp.–S.Trop.: Terr.

A colony-forming fern which grows in moist to wet soils in shady situations. Plants have a distinctive, symmetrical rosette of light green fronds. They are very cold-hardy and will adapt well to a situation with wet soil (where in this case they will tolerate some sun).

Blechnum doodioides — see under **B. lanceolatum**

Blechnum filiforme
New Zealand
30–45 cm (12–18 in): 1 pinnate Temp.–S.Trop.: Climber

A climbing fern which in nature vigorously ascends

A colony of *Blechnum discolor* Photo D. L. Jones

trees, tree ferns and covers the ground between. Large plants form a mass of verdant green fronds. Juvenile fronds are quite different from mature fronds which are in turn dimorphic. Plants resent disturbance but sporelings establish readily. Requires shady conditions and an abundance of moisture.

Blechnum fluviatile Ray Water Fern
Australia, New Zealand
20–50 cm (8–20 in): 1 pinnate Temp.: Terr.

In nature, this fern forms spreading rosettes of a most appealing structure. The fronds are pale green with short, blunt segments that are spaced rather than crowded. Plants are ideal in a rockery and need shady conditions with plenty of moisture.

Blechnum fraxineum
Central and South America, West Indies
20–60 cm (8–24 in): 1 pinnate S.Trop.–Temp.: Terr.

A small to medium sized fern with a somewhat untidy appearance. The plants have a creeping growth habit and erect, dark green fronds and can be grown easily in a shady, moist situation. A useful ground cover fern or for a pocket in a rockery. The new fronds are pinkish.

An unrolling flush of new fronds in *Blechnum gibbum* Photo W. R. Elliot

Blechnum gibbum Photo D. L. Jones

Blechnum gibbum Dwarf Tree Fern
New Caledonia, New Hebrides, Fiji
30–70 cm (12–28 in): 1 pinnate Trop.–Temp.: Terr.

The common name of this fern has arisen because the old plants develop a short, stout trunk. This is a popular fern which has an appealing crown of finely divided fronds. New fronds are light green and contrast with the older ones. Plants are excellent for large containers but can also be grown in the ground in a moist, shady situation.

Blechnum glandulosum
Mexico, Central and South America
30–60 cm (12–24 in): 1 pinnate Trop.–S.Trop.: Terr.

A small fern very similar to *B. occidentale*, but with a covering of fine hairs on the rachis. An easily grown fern which is more shade tolerant than that species. Can spread to form a colony. Some authors regard this as a form of *B. occidentale*.

Blechnum indicum Swamp Water Fern
Australia, Malaysia, Polynesia, South America
60–100 cm (24–40 in): 1 pinnate Trop.–Temp.: Terr.

A colony-forming fern found in swamps and spreading by long, subterranean rhizomes. Fronds are an attractive bright green (pinkish when young) and are held stiffly erect. Plants have proved to be adaptable in cultivation and do not require swampy conditions although they appreciate plenty of moisture, and acid, peaty soils. This species is possibly not distinct from *B. serrulatum* of the New World.

Blechnum lanceolatum Lance Water Fern
Australia, New Zealand, Fiji, Samoa
30–45 cm (12–18 in): 1 pinnate Temp.–S.Trop.: Terr.

In nature, this species favours cool, sheltered situations, usually beside water and often in quite dense shade. Cultivated plants tend to be slow-growing and need shady, moist conditions. They look especially attractive when planted among rocks. In containers they are better underpotted rather than overpotted. There is much confusion about the correct name for this species, some authors referring to it as *B. chambersii* or *B. doodioides*.

Blechnum magellanicum
South America
60–90 cm (24–36 in): 1 pinnate Temp.–S.Trop.: Terr.

A hardy species which grows well in temperate regions tolerating very cold weather. In its native state it is found in mountainous districts. Plants have markedly dimorphic fronds, develop a large, stout rhizome and have filiform, hair-like scales. In cultivation they need plenty of water.

Blechnum minus
Australia, New Zealand
60–120 cm (24–48 in): 1 pinnate Temp.–S.Trop.: Terr.

A coarse fern which forms a very bushy clump and spreads freely by underground stolons. Plants thrive in wet soils and in this situation will tolerate full exposure to sun. A cold-hardy fern ideal for cold, temperate climates.

Young fronds of *Blechnum indicum* Photo D. L. Jones

Blechnum moorei
New Caledonia
50–80 cm (20–32 in): 1 pinnate Trop.–S.Trop.: Terr.

This fern is similar in many features to *B. gibbum* (and may be but a form of that species), but has much broader segments on the sterile fronds. Plants develop a thick black trunk to about 30 cm (12 in) tall. They are more cold sensitive than *B. gibbum* and like a warm moist position.

Blechnum glandulosum Photo D. L. Jones

Blechnum nudum Photo D. L. Jones

Blechnum patersonii Photo D. L. Jones

Blechnum nudum Fishbone Water Fern
Australia, Africa
60–100 cm (24–40 in): 1 pinnate Temp.–Trop.: Terr.

In nature, this fern commonly grows in and alongside streams, often in extensive colonies. It develops an upright rosette of verdant green fronds and is an excellent container fern. Can also be grown in the ground where it requires shady conditions and moist, acid soil. This species has green spores.

Blechnum occidentale Hammock Fern
South America, Mexico, West Indies
30–60 cm (12–24 in): 1 pinnate Trop.–S.Trop.: Terr.

This fern makes a very useful ground cover beneath trees, and it adapts well to general garden culture. It thrives best in a partially sunny situation and appreciates regular fertilizing and watering. New fronds are colourful pink to salmon shades.

Blechnum orientale
Asia, Malaysia, Polynesia, Australia
60–120 cm (24–48 in): 1 pinnate Trop.–S.Trop.: Terr.

This fern is a colonizer of tropical areas and is a familiar sight along road verges and embankments. Plants are rather cold sensitive but grow easily in warm, moist conditions where they can be quite fast growing. This species looks attractive when planted en masse on earth banks. It also makes a very useful tub plant.

Blechnum patersonii Strap Water Fern
Australia
30–80 cm (12–28 in): entire-pinnatifid Temp.–S.Trop.: Terr.

An attractive *Blechnum* which has entire or variously lobed fronds. Plants grow in shady situations near water with the fronds often hanging. Cultivated plants are slow growing and resent disturbance. They prefer a shady position and must be well supplied with water. New fronds are often pinkish-bronze. This species is similar to *B. colensoi* but with narrower, thinner-textured fronds.

Blechnum penna-marina Alpine Water Fern
Australia, New Zealand, South America
15–30 cm (6–12 in): 1 pinnate Temp.: Terr.

A delightful creeping fern ideal as a ground cover in a shady, moist situation or for planting among rocks. Likes friable humus-rich soil. Very fast growing in a suitable situation. Plants are quite cold-hardy and

Blechnum penna-marina

in moist situations will tolerate considerable exposure to sun.

The ssp. *alpina* has crowded pinnae and the fertile fronds are borne on short stipes.

Blechnum polypodioides
Central and South America, West Indies
20–70 cm (8–28 in): 1 pinnate Trop.–S.Trop.: Terr.

An uncommonly grown fern which can be rather tricky to maintain. Plants are fairly cold sensitive and also resent disturbance. This fern needs a fairly brightly-lit situation in well-drained soil with plenty of moisture. May be a colonizer in nature.

Blechnum serrulatum – see under **B. indicum**

Blechnum spicant Ladder Fern/Deer Fern
Europe, North-East Asia, North America (West)
15–70 cm (6–28 in): 1 pinnate Temp.–S.Trop.: Terr.

A hardy little fern with a neat, compact growth habit. It occurs naturally on rock ledges and in forests and grows easily in cultivation. Prefers a shady situation in acid soil and looks attractive among rocks. Very cold-hardy.

Blechnum spicant

Blechnum penna-marina Photo D. L. Jones

'Cristatum' – fronds are heavily crested on the tips.

Blechnum stoloniferum
Mexico, Guatemala
10–30 cm (4–12 in): pinnatifid S.Trop.–Trop.: Terr.

A small species with a spreading growth habit, forming colonies by the production of slender stolons. It occurs naturally in high altitude forest. It is a very useful ground cover fern requiring an abundance of water.

Blechnum sylvaticum
Africa
50–180 cm (20–72 in): 1 pinnate Temp.–S.Trop.: Terr.

This is a vigorous fern which forms colonies in wet to very wet shady forests. Until recently it has been known as *B. capense*. Plants adapt very well to cultivation and grow strongly in shady, moist conditions.

Blechnum tabulare
Africa, Madagascar, South America
50–150 cm (20–60 in): 1 pinnate Temp.–S.Trop.: Terr.

A large, coarse fern which develops a thick, dark trunk which may be upright or prostrate; it freely produces rhizomes which form colonies. The fronds arise in a spreading rosette with the fertile ones erect and with narrow segments. Plants like well-drained soils and plenty of moisture. In cultivation, this species has been confused with *B. chilense*.

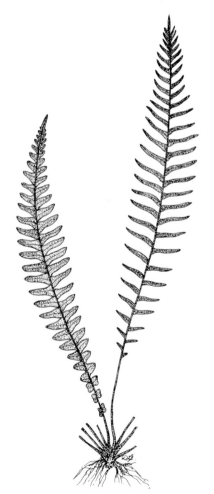

Blechnum unilaterale=**B. polypodioides**

A colony of *Doodia aspera* Photo D. L. Jones

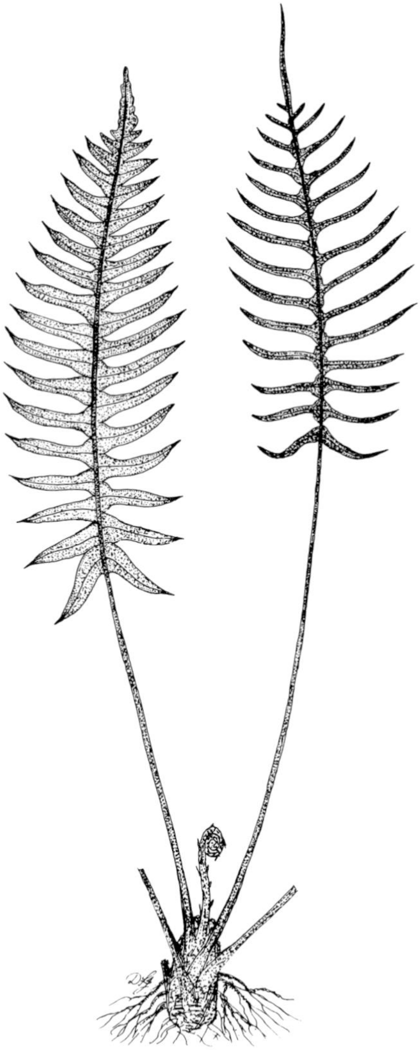

Blechnum vulcanicum

Blechnum vulcanicum Wedge Water Fern
Australia, New Zealand
40–80 cm (16–32 in): 1 pinnate Temp.: Terr.
A cold-hardy fern well suited to cultivation in temperate regions. Cultivated plants resent disturbance and are slow to re-establish. They require shade and plenty of moisture for successful growth.

Doodia aspera Prickly Rasp Fern
Australia, New Zealand, Norfolk Island
15–35 cm (6–14 in): pinnatifid Temp.–Trop.: Terr.
A tough but beautiful fern which grows in spreading colonies. The new fronds are bright pink to red. Very tolerant of dryness once established. Plants will grow in shade or sun and are not fussy as to soil type but demand good drainage.

Doodia caudata Small Rasp Fern
Australia, New Zealand, Norfolk Island
15–30 cm (6–12 in): 1 pinnate Temp.–Trop.: Terr.
This *Doodia* forms neat, rounded clumps rather than colonies, and is excellent for pot culture or in rockeries. It is variable in appearance with some forms having attractive verdant green fronds. Plants are hardy once established. Will grow in shade or partial sun in well-drained, acid soil.

Doodia media Common Rasp Fern
Australia, New Zealand, Norfolk Island
20–30 cm (8–12 in): pinnatifid Temp.–Trop.: Terr.
A neat fern with harsh-textured fronds. Grows in spreading clumps and is ideal as a ground cover or for rock pockets. Plants will tolerate considerable exposure to sun especially if kept well-watered. Easily propagated by division.

Doodia aspera

Sadleria cyatheoides
Hawaii
50–150 cm (20–60 in): 2 pinnate S.Trop.–Temp.: Terr.
In growth habit this very decorative fern looks like a miniature tree fern. Plants develop a small slender trunk and crown of neat, arching, light green fronds. It is a popular fern in cultivation and grows easily in shady conditions in organically rich soil.

Woodwardia angustifolia=W. areolata

Woodwardia areolata Dimorphic Chain Fern
North America
50–100 cm (20–40 in): 1 pinnate Temp.–S.Trop.: Terr.
This fern strongly resembles a species of *Blechnum* but its distinguishing feature is the interrupted sori. Plants form a spreading clump of glossy fronds. Grows easily in an acid soil but likes plenty of moisture and is tolerant of considerable sun.

Woodwardia chamissoi=W. fimbriata

Old plants of *Doodia caudata* Photo D. L. Jones

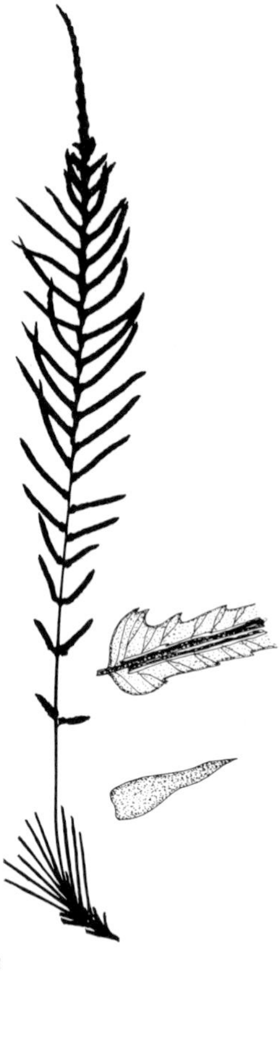

Doodia caudata

Doodia caudata

Doodia media

Woodwardia fimbriata Giant Chain Fern
North America, Mexico, Canada
100–200 cm (40–80 in): 2 pinnate S.Trop.–Temp.: Terr.

This fern bears a strong superficial resemblance to *Todea barbara*, but can be distinguished from that fern by its pattern of sori which resembles a chain. It makes a handsome clump of erect dark green fronds and grows readily in a shady, moist situation. Needs plenty of room to develop.

Woodwardia orientalis Oriental Chain Fern
Japan, China, Northern India
100–250 cm (40–100 in): 2 pinnate S.Trop.–Temp.: Terr.

A favourite garden fern prized for its long, wide leathery fronds which arch or sometimes lie flat on the ground. An added feature is the dozens of plantlets which sprout tiny pale-green fronds as the leaves age. These provide a ready means of propagation. The species grows easily in a moist position exposed to some sun.

Woodwardia radicans European Chain Fern
Europe, Asia
50–200 cm (20–80 in): 2 pinnate Temp.–S.Trop.: Terr.

A vigorous fern which has been cultivated for over 200 years. The large, arching, verdant green fronds produce a magnificent effect and provide a perfect backup in a fernery. Large bulbils are produced near the apex of each frond and make propagation easy. Plants are quite cold-hardy.

Woodwardia unigemmata
Japan, China, North India, Philippines
60–90 cm (24–36 in): 2 pinnate S.Trop.–Temp.: Terr.

A relatively hardy fern with broad, dark green, fairly thickly-textured fronds which arch in an attractive manner. A single plantlet may be formed near the end of each frond. Easily grown in a protected situation in acid, loamy soil.

Woodwardia virginica
North America
30–60 cm (12–24 in): 2 pinnate Temp.–S.Trop.: Terr.

A hardy fern very tolerant of wet soils (in nature it grows in bogs, often submerged). Plants have a creeping rhizome and spread steadily. New growth is bronze-green.

34 Lacy ground ferns

genera *Culcita, Dennstaedtia, Histiopteris, Hypolepis, Leptolepia, Microlepia, Paesia* and *Pteridium*

A loosely related group of ferns which are gathered together here because of similar growth features and cultural requirements. A few species may be grown by nurseries, but the majority have limited appeal and are mainly of interest to fern enthusiasts.

Habitat

Ferns of this group are mostly colony-formers, growing on shaded forest floors, along the banks of streams and on the margins of forests. A few species grow in quite open, sunny locations and some are colonizers of disturbed earth.

Cultivation

Uses

Because of their attractively divided fronds most of these ferns have ornamental appeal. Many, however, grow quite large and their spreading habit means that they need plenty of room to develop. Thus their use in home gardens may be limited, although the smaller growing species adapt well to such situations. All species have excellent prospects for large municipal gardens, botanic gardens etc. Once established, most are long-lived and require little maintenance. These ferns can be grown in containers but those species with spreading rhizomes soon must be planted out.

Soil Types

Ferns of this group like well-drained, organically-rich loams with an acid pH.

Potting Mix

An open mix based on a well-structured loam is suitable. Mixes containing peat moss or milled pine bark produce good growth. Most of these ferns have a strong root system and if they are grown in containers must be repotted regularly.

Watering

These ferns like plenty of water throughout the year, although those species which are deciduous should not be overwatered while dormant.

Fertilizing

Most ferns of this group are strong growers and respond to the use of manures and fertilizers. If, however, their spread is a problem then clumps are probably best left unfertilized. Slow-release fertilizers in the potting mix or liquid fertilizers applied at regular intervals are suitable for container-grown plants.

Situation

Exposure to morning sun or filtered sun is satisfactory for most species. Some like shady conditions and burn with exposure to hot sun (*Dennstaedtia davallioides*); others resent shade and need at least some sun (*Culcita dubia, Paesia scaberula*). Many of the tropical species are very sensitive to periods of cold, and especially frosts.

Pests

Caterpillars may completely strip the fronds and render whole clumps unsightly. Scale may be a problem on species of *Microlepia*.

Propagation

Ferns of this group are generally easy to raise from spores. Sporelings and young plants are very fast growing and quickly establish when planted out. Those species with creeping rhizomes can be easily propagated by division.

SPECIES AND CULTIVARS

Culcita dubia False Bracken
Australia
50–100 cm (20–40 in): 3–4 pinnate Temp.-Trop.: Terr.

This fern is useful for its hardiness and adaptability. It will grow happily in full sun and will tolerate the poorest soils providing that drainage is unimpeded. It is a colony-forming fern with soft, lacy fronds of a yellowish hue. Can be most attractive if given some care and attention.

Culcita straminea Photo W. R. Elliot

Culcita javanica
Indonesia, Borneo, Philippines
90–240 cm (30–96 in): 3–4 pinnate Trop.–S.Trop.: Terr.

An impressive fern with a prominent trunk and densely hairy, finely divided fronds. Young plants establish quickly and will tolerate situations from partial sun to shade.

Culcita straminea
New Caledonia, New Hebrides, Fiji, Polynesia
200–300 cm (80–120 in): 3–4 pinnate Trop.–S.Trop.: Terr.

A coarse, clumping fern with large, lacy fronds which are often yellow-green. Plants grow in brightly lit situations and are noticeable on cleared land. It is an easy species to grow and hardy once established.

Dennstaedtia bipinnata Couplet Fern
Central and South America, West Indies
200–300 cm (80–120 in): 1–2 pinnate Trop.–S.Trop.: Terr.

This fern is rather cold-tender but is an attractive addition to a large fernery or shady garden. It has a creeping growth habit and needs plenty of room to spread. Plants can also be grown in a large container. It grows naturally in rainforests.

Dennstaedtia cicutaria
Central and South America, West Indies
90–300 cm (36–120 in): 3–4 pinnate Trop.–S.Trop.: Terr.

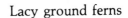

A ground fern found in rainforests. The long-creeping rhizomes spread and produce the large, lacy fronds at intervals. This is an attractive fern for a semi-shady or shady garden situation. Can also be grown effectively in a large pot.

Dennstaedtia davallioides Lacy Ground Fern
Australia
40–70 cm (16–28 in): 4–5 pinnate S.Trop.–Temp.: Terr.

This fern commonly forms scattered colonies in shady forests and quite often along stream banks. The long-creeping rhizome produces the dark green, lacy fronds at intervals. Plants can be easily grown in a large container or introduced into a shady, garden situation. In good conditions they spread freely. Fronds may be badly damaged by caterpillars.

Dennstaedtia dissecta
Central and South America, West Indies
150–360 cm (60–144 in): 3–4 pinnate Trop.–S.Trop.: Terr.

This species usually grows as a ground fern in

Dennstaedtia davalliodes

rainforest. The rhizomes produce closely-spaced fronds which are tall, finely divided and lacy. This is an attractive fern which can be grown in a shady location in loamy soil but needs plenty of room to spread.

Dennstaedtia punctiloba Hay-scented Fern
Canada, North America
15–45 cm (6–18 in): 2 pinnate Temp.–S.Trop.: Terr.

The most conspicuous feature of this fern is the erect to arching, delicately divided, yellow-green fronds which are produced in groups from the long-creeping underground rhizome. Plants can be readily established in a shady situation in loamy soil. The fronds are deciduous, dying off in the cool weather of winter. As this fern tends to be invasive it is best planted in large gardens where there is plenty of room to spread.

Dennstaedtia scandens
Indonesia, Polynesia, New Guinea, Philippines
90–900 cm (36–360 in): 3–4 pinnate Trop.–S.Trop.: Terr.

An unusual scrambling fern with long fronds almost capable of indefinite growth. The stipes and rachises bear a few small prickles. The species has limited appeal and plants would need considerable room to develop into clumps.

Histiopteris incisa Bat's-wing Fern
South Africa, Central and South America, South-East Asia, Malaysia, Australia, New Zealand
50–1500 cm (20–600 in): 2–4 pinnate Trop.–Temp.: Terr.

A most distinctive and easily-recognized fern that grows in a wide variety of habitats, from areas exposed to full sun (where the fronds are dwarfed and bleached), to shady situations where the fronds may thread their way through other vegetation. Fronds are divided in an attractive pattern. Plants are popularly grown in containers or in the ground. Adaptable to a variety of positions and may become weedy. Fronds are frequently damaged by grubs.

Hypolepis millefolium Dissected Ground Fern
New Zealand
30–90 cm (12–36 in): 3 pinnate Temp.–S.Trop.: Terr.

A fern valued for the fine division of its lacy fronds, which are a delicate green. They are deciduous and are replaced each year in the spring. The species adapts well to cultivation and can be grown in a container or shady situation in the ground. It is slower growing and not as weedy as many species in this genus.

Hypolepis punctata Downy Ground Fern
Asia, Japan, Malaysia, New Guinea, Australia, New Zealand
60–300 cm (24–120 in): 3–4 pinnate Temp.–Trop.: Terr.

A weedy species which grows in extensive colonies in sunny situations, usually in low-lying soils that may become inundated. It can be grown easily in a sunny situation in moist soil, but its spread may need to be contained. Can be a weed of greenhouses and bush-houses. The fronds are frequently disfigured by green caterpillars.

Histiopteris incisa Photo D. L. Jones

Hypolepis repens Bramble Fern
Florida, Central and South America, West Indies
90–300 cm (36–120 in): 3–4 pinnate Trop.–S.Trop.: Terr.

One of this fern's drawbacks is the spreading spines on the stipes and rachis of the fronds. It is a large growing species with wandering rhizomes and would seem to be best suited to larger public gardens under the shelter of trees, large shrubs or other plants.

Hypolepis rufobarbata
New Zealand
30–90 cm (12–36 in): 3 pinnate Temp.–S.Trop.: Terr.

The rhizomes, stipes and fronds of this fern are covered with soft, reddish-brown hairs. It forms colonies in moist situations often in fairly open positions. Easily grown as a garden fern.

Hypolepis rugosula Ruddy Ground Fern
Japan, Australia, New Zealand
60–120 cm (24–48 in): 3 pinnate Temp.–S.Trop.: Terr.

A colony-forming species with dark red stipes and coarse, triangular, hairy fronds. Quite cold-hardy and easily grown in a shady to semi-shady situation. In suitable conditions can spread rapidly and may need to be kept in check.

Hypolepis sparsisora Photo D. L. Jones

Hypolepis sparsisora

Hypolepis sparsisora
Africa, Malagasy
90–300 cm (36–120 in): 3–5 pinnate Temp.–S.Trop.: Terr.

A scrambling fern with finely divided, bright green fronds, widely spaced on slender, creeping rhizomes. In nature it forms large masses in wet situations in shady forests. An attractive fern which must be allowed plenty of space to develop.

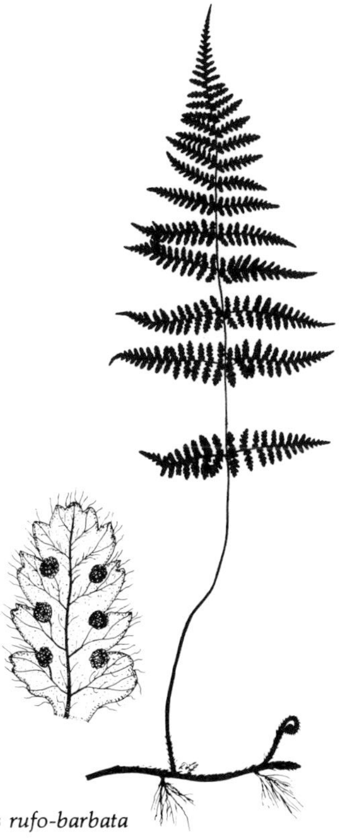

Hypolepis rufo-barbata

Hypolepis tenuifolia Soft Ground Fern
Australia, New Zealand, Philippines, Polynesia
60–210 cm (24–84 in): 3–4 pinnate Trop.–Temp.: Terr.

The delicate, soft appearance of this fern is somewhat misleading for it is a very strong grower and can quickly establish itself in a fernery or garden. The bright green hairy croziers are of delicate beauty as they unroll. Can be easily grown in a pot or sheltered garden position.

Leptolepia novae-zealandiae
New Zealand
15–45 cm (6–18 in): 3–4 pinnate Temp.–S.Trop.: Terr.

A delightful fern with finely cut, delicate, lacy fronds of a modest size. Plants are colony-formers with wiry rhizomes but tend to be fairly slow growing and are easily manageable. Can be grown in a pot or sheltered garden position and also makes a useful basket plant.

Leptolepia novae-zealandiae

Microlepia platyphylla Photo D. L. Jones

Microlepia firma
China
50–80 cm (20–32 in): 2–3 pinnate Trop.–S.Trop.: Terr.

An attractive fern with bright green erect, fine, lacy fronds. It grows easily in the garden and its upright growth habit also lends itself to pot culture. Likes a semi-shady or filtered sun situation in loamy soil.

Microlepia hirta
India, Sri Lanka
90–180 cm (36–72 in): 3 pinnate Trop.–S.Trop.: Terr.

A vigorous fern with large, lacy, very hairy fronds. Although it has a creeping rhizome the plants have a very bushy habit. Easily grown in a sheltered situation in loamy soil. Somewhat cold sensitive.

Microlepia marginata
North India, China, Japan
30–90 cm (24–36 in): 1 pinnate Temp.–S.Trop.: Terr.

An attractive fern with a long-creeping rhizome and erect fronds with narrow, falcate pinnae and hairy stipes and rachises. Plants grow readily in a shady position and like plenty of moisture.

Microlepia hirta

Microlepia platyphylla
India, Japan, Philippines, China
90–180 cm (36–72 in): 3–4 pinnate Trop.–S.Trop.: Terr.

At first glance this fern does not look like a *Microlepia*. Its tall fronds are divided into coarse segments which are bluish-green and quite shiny. They do, however, bear characteristic hairs and sori of the genus. It is a tall clumping fern which can be used to shelter smaller species. Likes shade in a well-drained, loamy soil.

Microlepia speluncae
Pantropical
50–150 cm (20–60 in): 3–4 pinnate Trop.–Temp.: Terr.

A very widespread fern which commonly grows in semi-exposed situations such as along forest margins, road banks etc. Fronds are impressively large, frequently with an arching habit. They are borne at close intervals from a creeping rhizome. This species can be grown easily as a garden plant but must be given room to achieve its potential. Can provide protection for smaller ferns.

Microlepia speluncae

Microlepia speluncae Photo D. L. Jones

Microlepia strigosa
India, Malaysia, Japan, Sri Lanka, Polynesia, China
30–80 cm (12–32 in): 2–3 pinnate Trop.–Temp.: Terr.

A vigorous but graceful fern which grows in semi-protected situations. Plants form slowly-spreading clumps with erect or arching lacy fronds. Can be grown in a moist, sheltered position in the ground, or as a pot plant. Also looks good in a basket.

'Cristata' — a choice greenhouse form with soft arching pale green fronds which are tasseled on the segment tips. Very cold sensitive. Plants are frequently sterile. Also called 'Pyramidata' and 'Corymbifera'.

Paesia scaberula Scented Fern
New Zealand
20–60 cm (8–24 in): 3 pinnate Temp.–S.Trop.: Terr.

In its native country this species grows in spreading, thick colonies, mostly in quite sunny situations. It is a very cold-hardy fern and can be grown in a pot or in a semi-exposed garden situation. Established plants resent disturbance but the young sections can be easily propagated.

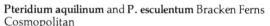

Microlepia strigosa

A colony of *Paesia scaberula* Photo D. L. Jones

The Bracken Fern, *Pteridium esculentum*
Photo D. L. Jones

Pteridium aquilinum and **P. esculentum** Bracken Ferns
Cosmopolitan
90–360 cm (36–144 in): 3 pinnate Trop.–Temp.: Terr.

Bracken is so common and widespread and invasive that its horticultural qualities are often overlooked. And yet it is a rugged and appealing fern and blends in well with large, open landscapes. The odd thing about brackens is that they are difficult to transplant and establish: in most cases the rhizomes simply rot. The best technique is to seek the young actively-growing tips and to pot a section that is at least 30 cm (24 in) long. After it begins new root growth it can be planted out. Bracken detests bad drainage, but otherwise is not fussy as to soil type. There are many species and/or varieties of bracken depending on one's interpretation of the genus. Some of the tropical types which are hairy are quite attractive (e.g. *P. semi-hastatum*). Occasionally forms with lobed or crested fronds are decorative.

35 Cloak ferns, lip ferns, hand ferns and their hardy relatives

genera *Bommeria, Cheilanthes, Doryopteris, Gymnopteris, Hemionitis, Notholaena, Paraceterach, Pellaea, Pleurosorus, Quercifilix*

As a group these ferns grow in relatively drier situations than most other ferns. Many attractive species are included here but they are usually regarded as difficult to grow because they have specialized requirements and will not mix with a general fern collection, however, under suitable conditions they are quite hardy and rewarding. These ferns are ideal for regions with a warm climate where the atmosphere tends to be dry. They can be grown in other conditions, providing attention is given to their specific requirements.

Habitat

Ferns of this group grow in a great diversity of habitats. Some species occur in high rainfall climates but are restricted to specialized niches such as rainshadow areas, in exposed situations on skeletal soils, in crevices or on rock faces or in the thin layer of soil which covers a boulder. Most species are found in low rainfall regions and have adapted their growth cycle to match the rigours of the climate. Many of these are Resurrection Ferns (see page 6).

Cultivation

Uses

As a general rule the ferns grouped here do not revel when given the usual fern requirements of shade, moisture and humidity. Their needs are for bright light, careful watering and low humidity. Some species grow well in pots but others are difficult to maintain and are better planted out in a suitable garden position. Most species blend in well with rocks. Ferns of this type may also grow well in a terrarium that is kept on the dry side or even left open (see page 184).

Soil Types

Ferns of this group will not tolerate wet conditions and free, unimpeded drainage is essential. Most species also prefer soils that are chemically poor rather than rich loams. Gravelly or sandy loams are suitable. Many species like alkaline soils (pH 7.5–8.5) and the addition of ground limestone, dolomite and limestone chips may be necessary. As a general rule most of the ferns included here appreciate annual dressings of lime. Mulches can be beneficial but they should not be applied too thickly or be of a heavy, clogging material.

Potting Mix

A very open, well-drained mix which is poor nutritionally provides the best chance of success. For many species the mix must be neutral to alkaline. Plants of this group must not be overpotted and most will grow happily in a small pot for a number of seasons. Most species are sensitive to disturbance and repotting should be carried out with care.

Watering

This can be a tricky aspect of the maintenance of these ferns and the species are quite variable in their requirements. In the main, ferns of this type are best kept on the dry side as overwatering can have rapid, fatal consequences. Most species can handle dryness and a little frond curling or shrivelling in between waterings will not be detrimental. In temperate regions they should be kept as dry as possible over winter.

Fertilizing

Ferns of this group are generally adapted to nutritionally-poor soils and supplementary fertilizing should be sparing and careful. Heavy applications of fertilizers or manures are usually fatal. A very light dressing annually is usually adequate. Surface applications of well-rotted animal manures are ideal.

Situation

As a group these ferns resent stagnant conditions and heavy shade. All need bright light and though some species are happy if exposed to considerable sun, others prefer limited exposure. All like adequate air movement. In temperate regions a useful aspect can often be found against a wall exposed to the winter sun. In tropical and subtropical regions a lightly shaded but dry situation is suitable. In inland regions these ferns may need protection from excessive sunshine and require more supplementary watering but generally, they adapt well to the drier prevailing atmospheres.

Pests

Sporadic attacks by slugs, snails and caterpillars. Very sensitive to root-rotting fungi.

Propagation

Many ferns of this group are surprisingly easy to raise from spores. Most like a coarse sowing mixture with a neutral to alkaline pH (7–8.5). Mixes containing a preponderance of scoria or fly ash are particularly suitable.

Spore collection can present a problem with some of these ferns especially those which have the sporangia masked by hairs, scales or waxy coatings. Many of these ferns have dark brown or black sporangia which have a crystalline or sugary appearance when mature. Those with a fluffy appearance are overmature. Checking with a hand lens can avoid frustration.

Large clumps can be divided with care but most species are very sensitive to disturbance and suffer a setback.

SPECIES AND CULTIVARS

Aleuritopteris dalhousiae – see **Cheilanthes dalhousiae**

Aleuritopteris farinosa – see **Cheilanthes farinosa**

Aleuritopteris kuhnii – see **Cheilanthes kuhnii**

Aspidotis californica – see **Cheilanthes californica**

Bommeria hispida
North America
10–25 cm (4–10 in): palmate Temp.–S.Trop.: Terr.

A small fern of rocky situations. Plants form a neat clump of broad fronds of a similar shape to *Doryopteris concolor*. Plants require well-drained soil and a sunny situation open to air movement. They must be watered sparingly.

Cheilanthes alabamensis
North America, Mexico, West Indies
20–50 cm (8–20 in): 3 pinnate Temp.–S.Trop.: Terr.

A clumping species with erect, fairly slender, dark green fronds. Plants need a neutral to alkaline freely-draining soil and a sunny to partially-sunny aspect.

Cheilanthes argentea Silver Cloak Fern
Northern India, Japan, China, Siberia
10–20 cm (4–8 in): 2 pinnate Temp.–S.Trop.: Terr.

A decorative dwarf fern with attractively-shaped fronds which are dark green on the surface and silvery on the underside from a covering of waxy powder. It is an easily grown species that requires plenty of

Cheilanthes brownii is a sun-loving small fern
Photo D. L. Jones

light, looks attractive among rocks and can also be grown in a small pot of acid, humus-rich mixture.

Cheilanthes austrotenuifolia Rock Fern
Australia, New Zealand
10–50 cm (4–20 in): 2–3 pinnate Temp.: Terr.

A recently described species which was previously confused with *C. tenuifolia*. This is a dwarf fern which develops into compact clumps of bright green, finely divided fronds. It usually occurs in rocky situations and plants look particularly appealing in a rockery, especially when situated against dark rocks. Plants require well-drained, acid, humus-rich soils in a sunny situation.

Cheilanthes brownii Silver Cloak Fern
Australia
10–25 cm (4–10 in): 2 pinnate Trop.–S.Trop.: Terr.

This is a fern of arid and semi-arid climates usually growing among rocks. The fronds are covered on both surfaces with a dense mat of woolly hairs. Plants are attractive when planted among dark rocks in a sunny rockery.

Cheilanthes californica California Lace Fern
North America (California), Mexico
5–15 cm (2–6 in): 3 pinnate Temp.–S.Trop.: Terr.

This species has lacy fronds of an attractive fresh green and occurs naturally on shaded, rocky sites. In cultivation it has proved tricky to maintain requiring a very porous, acid mixture, bright light but not sun, and ample air movement. Plants are susceptible to overwatering. This species is included by some authors in the genus *Aspidotis*.

A clump of *Cheilanthes distans* Photo D. L. Jones

Cheilanthes concolor – see **Doryopteris concolor**

Cheilanthes covillei Bead Fern
North America (California, Nevada, Utah, Arizona)
5–15 cm (2–6 in): 3 pinnate Temp.: Terr.
A desert-inhabiting fern found naturally in mountainous areas. It forms small clumps of pleasantly divided fronds which are bright green on the surface and covered with white or brown scales on the underside. Plants need very good drainage, bright light and plenty of air movement. Watering must be done carefully so as to keep the fronds dry.

Cheilanthes dalhousiae
China, North India
20–30 cm (8–12 in): 2 pinnate Temp.–S.Trop.: Terr.
A delightful fern which forms clumps of erect, narrow-deltoid fronds, the segments coarsely toothed. It occurs at high altitudes and is apparently cold-hardy. It is included by some authors in the genus *Aleuritopteris*.

Cheilanthes distans Bristly Cloak Fern
Australia, New Zealand, Lord Howe Island, New Caledonia
10–15 cm (4–6 in): 2 pinnate Temp.–S.Trop.: Terr.
A fairly easily grown species which forms clumps of slender fronds that are covered with bristly scales. Attractive in a pot or rock garden. Needs acid, humus-rich soil in a partial-sun situation.

Cheilanthes covillei

Cheilanthes argentea Photo D. L. Jones

Cheilanthes farinosa Floury Cloak Fern
Mexico, Central America, Asia, Fiji
10–30 cm (4–12 in): 2–3 pinnate Trop.–S.Trop.: Terr.
The common name of this fern alludes to the undersurface of the fronds which appear as if they have been liberally dusted with flour. This is a neat-clumping fern with finely divided fronds. Cultivation needs are for a brightly lit (partial-sun) situation in well-drained neutral to alkaline soils. This species is included in the genus *Aleuritopteris* by some authors.

Cheilanthes hastata – see **Pellaea hastata**

Cheilanthes kuhnii
China
20–30 cm (8–12 in): 2 pinnate Temp.–S.Trop.: Terr.
A small fern forming erect clumps. New fronds are attractively scaly and mature fronds are covered with silvery powder on the underside. Plants extend to high altitudes and are probably hardy in a temperate climate. This species is included in the genus *Aleuritopteris* by some authors.

Cheilanthes lasiophylla Woolly Cloak Fern
Australia
10–20 cm (4–8 in): 1–2 pinnate Temp.–S.Trop.: Terr.
This is a very hardy fern which adapts well to a dry climate, the fronds curling quickly in dry times and resurrecting within a few hours of rain. The narrow fronds are dark green above and have masses of brown hairs and scales on the underside. An attractive plant for a sunny rockery.

Cheilanthes lanosa Hairy Lip-fern
North America
20–40 cm (8–16 in): 2 pinnate Temp.–S.Trop.: Terr.
A neat fern with clumps of bright green fronds which are densely woolly on the underside. Likes dry conditions in a sunny situation. Soil requirements are acid to neutral with excellent drainage. Must not be overwatered.

Cheilanthes marantae – see **Gymnopteris marantae**

Cheilanthes multifida
Africa, St. Helena
20–50 cm (8–20 in): 3–4 pinnate Temp.–S.Trop.: Terr.
A variable species which is fairly widespread and grows in a variety of situations including shady positions in forests. It is a tufting species with broad-deltoid, finely lacy fronds which vary from soft to leathery in texture. Requires well-drained, loamy soils and should be kept on the dry side.

Cheilanthes sieberi Mulga Fern
Australia, New Zealand, New Caledonia
10–50 cm (4–20 in): 2–3 pinnate Temp.–Trop.: Terr.
This species is similar in many respects to *C. tenuifolia* but has much narrower fronds. It too is a decorative species when planted in an ideal situation, i.e. among rocks in a sunny situation, in acid humus-rich loam.

Cheilanthes lasiophylla Photo D. L. Jones

Cheilanthes sinuata – see **Notholaena sinuata**

Cheilanthes standleyi – see **Notholaena standleyi**

Cheilanthes tenuifolia
North India, Sri Lanka, South-East Asia, Polynesia, Australia
20–40 cm (8–16 in): 2–3 pinnate Trop.–S.Trop.: Terr.
A widely distributed species which grows actively during the monsoonal wet season and becomes dormant in the dry. The fronds are finely divided, with a lacy appearance and the new fronds are a fresh bright green. A difficult subject to grow away from the tropics. Best tried in a partially protected situation outside. See also *C. austrotenuifolia*.

Cheilanthes tomentosa
North America, Mexico
20–60 cm (8–24 in): 2 pinnate Temp.–S.Trop.: Terr.
An attractive species with brown woolly hairs on the stipes and grey to white woolly hairs on the fronds. These are especially noticeable on the undersurface. Can be tricky to grow needing very well-drained neutral to alkaline soils, sun and plenty of air movement.

Cheilanthes vellea = **C. brownii**

Cheilanthes vestita = **C. lanosa**

Cheilanthes viridis – see **Pellaea viridis**

Doryopteris concolor Photo D. L. Jones

Doryopteris pedata var. *palmata* Photo D. L. Jones

Doryopteris concolor (alt. **Cheilanthes concolor**)
Central and South America, West Indies, Africa, Asia, Polynesia, Australia
10–30 cm (4–12 in): palmate Trop.–S.Trop.: Terr.

A very widely distributed fern with dark green, hand-shaped fronds. Forms a pleasant little clump and blends well with rocks. Needs warm, dry, airy conditions in well-drained, acid to neutral soil. Some authors include this species in the genus *Cheilanthes*.

Doryopteris elegans – see **Hemionitis elegans**

Doryopteris ludens
India, Malaysia, Philippines, Indonesia, Australia
10–25 cm (4–10 in): palmate Trop.–S.Trop.: Terr.

An interesting species with a creeping rhizome and spaced fronds, the fertile ones of which are taller and more deeply-lobed. Fronds are dark green and leathery and are carried on wiry, black stems. Plants like warm, dry, airy conditions and a well-drained, alkaline soil mix.

Doryopteris pedata Hand Fern
Central and South America, West Indies
10–40 cm (4–16 in): palmate Trop.–S.Trop.: Terr.

A neat fern, popular for its appealing fronds which resemble the outline of a hand. Each is dark green and is carried on a long, slender, wiry, black stem. This is a tough fern which resents coddling and prefers warm, airy conditions in bright light. Drainage must be excellent and the addition of lime may be beneficial.

The var. *palmata* is a larger growing form with broad sterile fronds and taller, more deeply-lobed, fertile fronds.

Gymnogramma reynoldsii = Paraceterach reynoldsii

Gymnopteris marantae (alt. **Cheilanthes marantae**)
Africa, Southern Europe, Syria, Northern India, Canary Islands
10–25 cm (4–10 in): 2 pinnate Temp.–S.Trop.: Terr.

A widely distributed and very drought-tolerant little fern. The undersides of the fronds are covered in rusty red scales which add to its ornamental appeal. Best grown in a rock pocket exposed to partial or filtered sun. Likes air movement and must not be overwatered. Included by some authors in the genera *Cheilanthes* or *Notholaena*.

Doryopteris concolor

Gymnopteris muelleri – see **Paraceterach muelleri**

Gymnopteris quercifolia = **Quercifilix zeylanica**

Gymnopteris vestita Mouse-ear Fern
North India, China
5–15 cm (2–6 in): 1 pinnate Temp.-S.Trop.: Terr.

An interesting dwarf fern which forms a small tussock of narrow, wiry fronds which have rounded to ovate pinnae, dark green above and covered with rusty to silvery hairs beneath. Plants may be somewhat tricky to grow. They require excellent drainage and good light.

Hemionitis arifolia
India, Sri Lanka, Thailand, Malaysia, Philippines
10–15 cm (4–6 in): entire Trop.-S.Trop.: Terr.

A neat little fern which is very sensitive to overpotting and is best maintained in a small pot for as long as possible. Plants prefer an open, humus-rich neutral to alkaline soil mix, warm conditions and strong light. Small plantlets arise on the main veins of the leaf near the base.

Hemionitis elegans (alt **Doryopteris elegans**)
Mexico
10–25 cm (4–10 in): palmate Trop.-S.Trop.: Terr.

A very beautiful species with large, shallowly-lobed fronds of a pleasing shape. New fronds are light green and contrast with the darker green, mature fronds. Plants like warm, dry, airy conditions in a well-drained acid to neutral soil mix. This species is included in the genus *Doryopteris* by some authors.

Gymnopteris marantae

Hemionitis arifolia Photo D. L. Jones

The elegant fronds of *Hemionitis elegans*
Photo D. L. Jones

Hemionitis palmata Strawberry Fern
Central and South America, West Indies
10–30 cm (4–12 in): palmate Trop.-S.Trop.: Terr.

An attractive little fern with leaves of a similar shape to those of a strawberry. The sterile fronds have short stalks and are clustered below the much taller fertile fronds. Small plantlets arise on the main veins of the leaf near the base. Plants are popular in cultivation and like warm, airy conditions in a small pot.

Notholaena marantae – see **Gymnopteris marantae**

Notholaena sinuata (alt. **Cheilanthes sinuata**) Wavy Cloak Fern
North America (Texas, Arizona), Mexico, Central and South America
20–70 cm (8–28 in): 1 pinnate Temp.-S.Trop.: Terr.

A hardy fern usually growing in gravelly soils in sunny or shady situations. Fronds are slender with attractively lobed segments and are densely scaly.

Paraceterach reynoldsii is a very drought tolerant fern
Photo D. L. Jones

Plants are tricky to grow requiring excellent drainage, bright light and adequate air movement. Water with care.

Notholaena standleyi (alt. **Cheilanthes standleyi**) Star Cloak Fern
North America (south-west), Mexico
10–30 cm (4–12 in): 2–3 pinnate Temp.–S.Trop.: Terr.
An attractive fern with broad, dull green fronds with the undersurface covered with yellow or white waxy powder. In dry periods the fronds curl inwards to form a ball. Plants are clumping and look attractive among rocks. They need bright light, well-drained gravelly soils of a neutral to alkaline pH and plenty of air movement.

Paraceterach muelleri (alt. **Gymnopteris muelleri**) Scaly Resurrection Fern
Australia
10–30 cm (4–12 in): 1 pinnate Trop.–S.Trop.: Terr.
Expanded, fresh fronds of this fern are an attractive bright green, with the pinnae bearing numerous light brown papery scales. When dry, the fronds curl and become brown and brittle. Grows on rocky outcrops and is somewhat difficult to cultivate. Needs warm, dry, airy conditions, bright light, and a well-drained, humus-rich mixture.

Paraceterach reynoldsii
Australia
10–20 cm (4–8 in): 1 pinnate Temp.–S.Trop.: Terr.
This is a neat, Resurrection Fern which forms spreading colonies in the protection of acidic rocks. Fresh fronds are bright green with conspicuous brown scales on the upper surface. Plants grow fairly easily in a loamy, acid soil, in a situation exposed to some sun and with plenty of air movement. Also can be grown in a small pot.

Pellaea adiantoides = **P. viridis** var. **macrophylla**

Pellaea andromedifolia Coffee Fern
North America (California)
15–45 cm (6–18 in): 2 pinnate Temp.–S.Trop.: Terr.
The main rachis of the fronds of this fern is often zig-zagged. The segments are blunt, oblong in shape and dark green. Plants need an open, well-drained mixture of neutral to acid reaction, good light and air movement.

Pellaea atropurpurea Purple Rock Brake
North and Central America
15–50 cm (6–20 in): 2 pinnate Temp.–S.Trop.: Terr.
A hardy fern with leathery, greyish to blue-green fronds. Plants require a neutral to alkaline soil and warm, airy conditions in strong light (tolerant of some sun). They are hardy to mild frosts and may become deciduous in very cold conditions. Easily raised from spores.

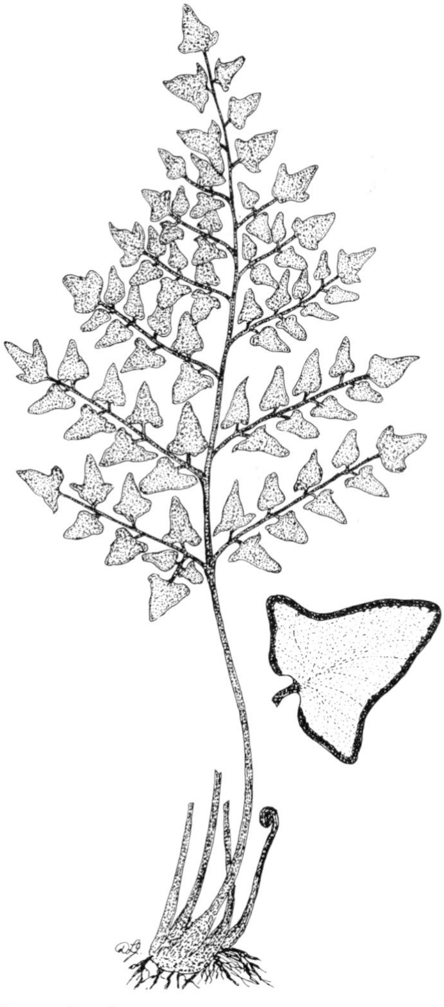

Pellaea calomelanos

Pellaea calomelanos Hard Fern
Africa, Madagascar, Mascarene Islands, Spain, Northern India
15–30 cm (6–12 in): 2–3 pinnate Temp.–S.Trop.: Terr.
A tough but attractive fern with rigid, blue-green triangular segments that have almost a leathery texture. These segments are carried on slender, shiny black stalks. Interestingly, the segments shed from old fronds and leave the network of wiry stems attached to the plant. Plants have similar cultural requirements to *P. viridis*.

Pellaea cordata = P. cordifolia

Pellaea cordifolia
Texas, Mexico
20–80 cm (8–32 in): 2 pinnate Trop.–S.Trop.: Terr.
This species is sometimes included as a variety of *P. sagittata*. It can be readily distinguished by the short, rounded to heart-shaped, light green segments. It is a delicate-looking fern with similar cultural requirements to *P. sagittata*.

Pellaea falcata Sickle Fern
Australia, New Zealand, India
10–60 cm (4–24 in): 1 pinnate Temp.–S.Trop.: Terr.
An interesting fern which grows in spreading colonies. Can be cultivated in shady or partial-sun situations in well-drained, loamy soil. Plants like plenty of water and can also be grown in pots. This is a variable species with some forms having large, coarse fronds of dull green; others are much more compact and shiny green.

Pellaea hastata (alt. **Cheilanthes hastata**)
Africa
15–25 cm (6–10 in): 1 pinnate Temp.–S.Trop.: Terr.
An interesting fern of semi-arid areas usually found growing among rocks. The form in cultivation has pinnate fronds, however, bipinnate forms are known in the wild. Segments are at right angles to the rachis, dark green and deltoid to triangular. Plants need an acid, loamy soil, bright light and adequate air movement. The species is regarded by some authors as belonging to the genus *Cheilanthes*.

Pellaea ovata
Texas, Central and South America
20–120 cm (8–48 in): 2–3 pinnate Trop.–S.Trop.: Terr.
A large-growing species with a creeping, wiry rhizome, strongly zig-zagged fronds and oval to heart-shaped leathery, dark green segments. Best grown in the ground in a partial-sun situation. Needs well-drained neutral to alkaline soil.

Pellaea paradoxa
Australia
10–60 cm (4–24 in): 1 pinnate Trop.–Temp.: Terr.
A creeping species which forms colonies in semi-shady situations, usually among rocks. The normal fronds are tall with leathery pinnae but the plants also frequently produce small, juvenile fronds which have a simple, rounded to heart-shaped lamina. This is an easily grown species although plants may be slow to settle down after disturbance. Needs acid, humus-rich soil and partial or filtered sun.

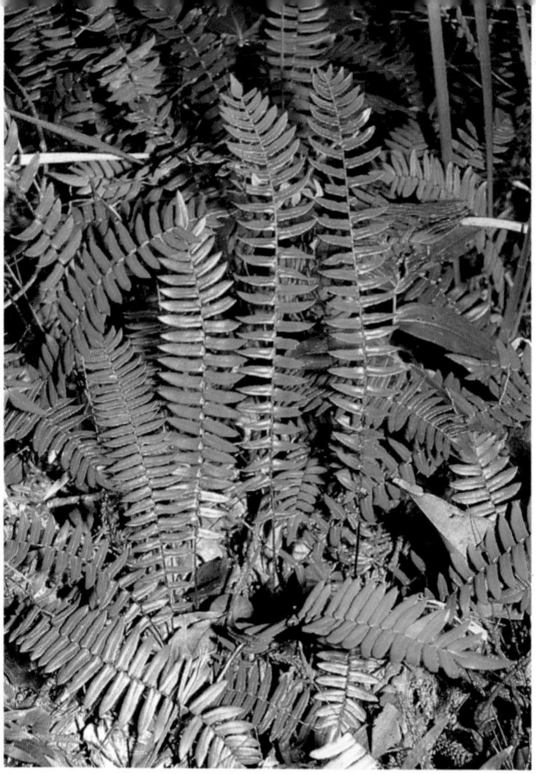

Pellaea falcata Photo D. L. Jones

Pellaea rotundifolia Button Fern
New Zealand
5–20 cm (2–8 in): 1 pinnate Temp.–S.Trop.: Terr.
A very popular fern both with enthusiasts and

Pleurosorus rutifolius

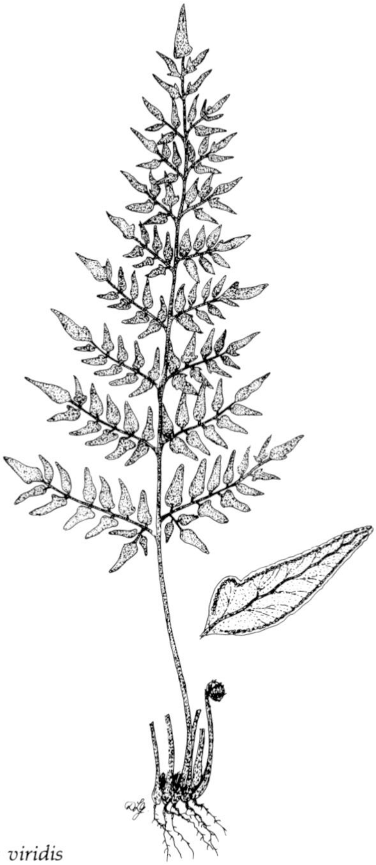

Pellaea viridis

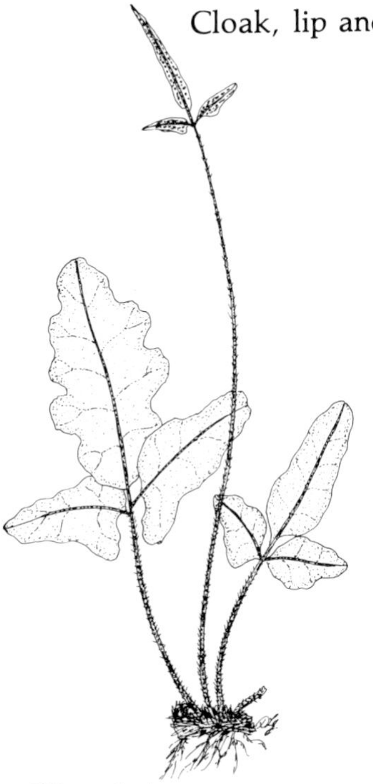

Quercifilix zeylanica

commercial growers, that is prized for its rosette of neat, dark green fronds with blunt to rounded segments. Excellent in a pot or among rocks in a shaded rockery. Likes an acid, humus-rich soil and bright light. Popular in some countries as an indoor plant.

Pellaea sagittata
Texas, Central and South America
20–80 cm (8–32 in): 1–2 pinnate Trop.–S.Trop.: Terr.
An interesting fern with light green, leathery fronds which have segments shaped like arrowheads. Plants need neutral to alkaline soils of free drainage and warm, airy conditions.

Pellaea ternifolia
North, Central and South America, Hawaii
30–60 cm (12–24 in): 1–2 pinnate Temp.–Trop.: Terr.
An attractive species with tall, slender, leathery fronds each with a few narrow leaflets which are grey-green and leathery. New fronds are glaucous. Plants need bright light, warmth and acid to neutral, freely-draining soil.

Pellaea viridis (alt. **Cheilanthes viridis**) Green Cliff Brake
Africa, Mauritius, Réunion
15–30 cm (6–12 in): 1–3 pinnate Trop.–Temp.: Terr.

A delightful fern which forms a clump of bright green fronds. Plants look attractive in a pot or sheltered rockery. They need soil of excellent drainage, warmth and strong light. Susceptible to slug damage. The addition of lime to the soil is frequently beneficial for this fern. This is a variable species.

var. *glauca* – erect 3-pinnate fronds with smaller, often blue-green segments.

var. *macrophylla* (*P. adiantoides*) – fronds 2 pinnate with large, coarse dark green segments.

All forms are included by some authors in the genus *Cheilanthes*.

Pleurosorus rutifolius Blanket Fern
Australia, New Zealand
10–15 cm (4–6 in): 1 pinnate Temp.–S.Trop.: Terr.
A hardy fern which grows in open situations with its roots in the shelter of rocks, in crevices etc. It is an appealing little fern usually found in colonies. Plants can be grown in a small pot but must not be overwatered and resent stale, humid conditions. Best in a sheltered situation among rocks.

Quercifilix zeylanica
China, Taiwan, Malaysia, Sri Lanka, Mauritius
5–15 cm (2–6 in): palmate Trop.–S.Trop.: Terr.
A tiny fern with hairy, dimorphic fronds. Can be grown in a small pot of well-drained loamy mixture or in a rockery in a lightly shaded situation. Has also been grown in a terrarium, however, the fronds may rot in a very humid atmosphere.

36 Primitive ferns and fern oddities

genera *Angiopteris, Botrychium, Christensenia, Danaea, Helminthostachys, Marattia, Ophioglossum, Osmunda* and *Todea*

These are a loosely related group of ferns which have primitive features. Some lack a typical fern appearance and are not recognizable as ferns to the non-specialist. Some have dimorphic fronds or specialized fertile blades attached to sterile blades of vastly different appearance. In size they range from tiny plants with fronds a few centimetres long to giants with fronds several metres in length. With the possible exception of species of *Osmunda*, few ferns in this group are commonly grown and lack commercial appeal.

Habitat

These ferns mostly occur in moist conditions, particularly in situations where the soils are moist to wet. Species of *Angiopteris, Marattia* and *Danaea* generally seek sheltered, shady situations while most of the others dealt with here grow in more open conditions. Species of *Botrychium, Helminthostachys* and the terrestrial *Ophioglossum* are deciduous and die back to a perennial root system each year. Some species of *Osmunda* may also be deciduous though the others are evergreen.

Cultivation

Uses

Ferns of this group are mainly grown by collectors for their interest value. Large plants of *Angiopteris* are impressive and can be the focal point of a planting. Species of *Osmunda* are very decorative and lend themselves well to landscaping where water is a feature. *Todea barbara* is an impressive fern which makes a very durable tub plant. *Ophioglossum pendulum* is unsurpassed as a basket plant. Species of *Botrychium* can be difficult to maintain and may succeed best in a garden situation.

Soil Types

Most ferns of this group will tolerate quite moist to wet soils, preferably with the water moving and not stagnant. Species of *Botrychium* and *Ophioglossum* like moist but not overwet soils.

Potting Mix

An open potting mix based on a well-structured loam is usually suitable. Despite their tolerance of moist soils a well-drained potting mix is necessary. Most species included here seem to need soils of an acid pH.

Watering

Ferns of this group like plenty of water and may suffer severe setbacks if allowed to dry out. Plants of *Helminthostachys* and the terrestrial species of *Ophioglossum* appreciate having the base of the pot submerged in a container of water while they are in active growth.

Fertilizing

Species of *Botrychium, Helminthostachys* and *Ophioglossum* require little in the way of nutrients and occasional applications of old manure or weak liquid fertilizers are adequate for their requirements. The other ferns included here will respond to applications of manures or fertilizers but are generally not heavy feeders.

Situation

Species of *Angiopteris, Christensenia, Danaea* and *Marattia* prefer shady conditions and have their best appearance when provided with such protection. The rest of this group needs bright light and will happily grow in the sun if the soils are moist to wet. Many of the tropical species are sensitive to cold, especially frosts.

Pests

Slugs and snails may be very damaging to the fleshy fronds and rhizomes of many of the ferns included here. For plants of *Botrychium* and *Ophioglossum* continual protection may be necessary.

Propagation

With the exception of species of *Osmunda* and *Todea* most of the ferns included here are very difficult

Angiopteris evecta Photo D. L. Jones

Angiopteris evecta

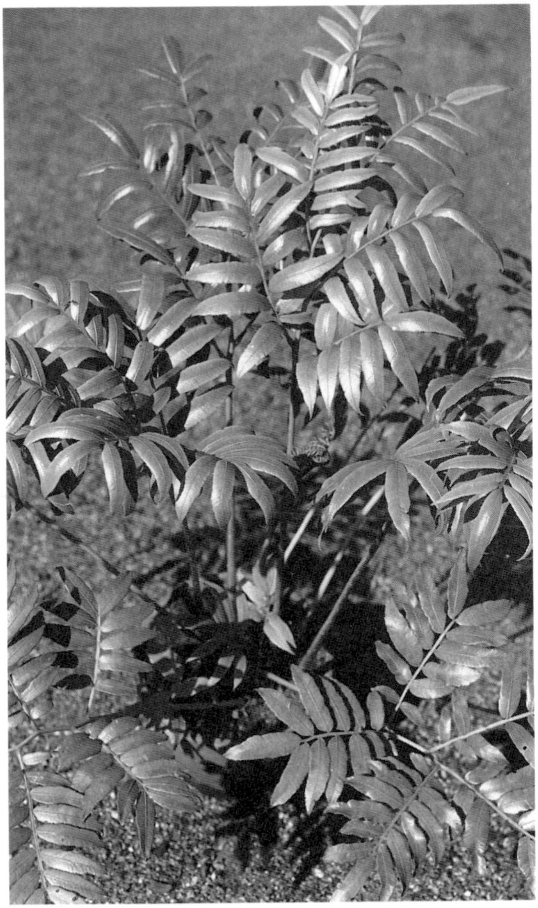

to propagate from spore. Many will only germinate in the dark and may also have a mycorrhizal relationship. Species of *Angiopteris* and *Marattia* can be successfully raised using a symbiotic technique such as the towelling technique outlined on page 156. Species of *Osmunda* and *Todea* have green spores which have a limited life and for certainty these should be sown within a few hours of collection.

Vegetatively large multi-crowned plants of *Osmunda* and *Todea* can be successfully divided and some species of *Ophioglossum* reproduce by small buds formed on the roots. Species of *Angiopteris* and *Marattia* can be propagated from auricles.

SPECIES AND CULTIVARS

Angiopteris evecta Giant Fern (Fig. p.60)
Malaysia, Polynesia, New Guinea, Australia
300–600 cm (120–240 in): 2 pinnate Trop.–Temp.: Terr.

A massive fern with huge, heavy arching fronds and a rounded, fleshy trunk. It usually grows in moist, shady forests close to streams. Plants can be easily grown in tubs or pots and are surprisingly adaptable in cultivation. Because of their ultimate size they must be given ample room to spread. Shade, moisture and well-drained acidic soils summarize its requirements.

Botrychium australe Southern Moonwort
South America, Asia, New Zealand, Australia
15–45 cm (6–18 in): 1 pinnate Temp.–S.Trop.: Terr.

A strange fern of interest chiefly to enthusiasts. Plants are above ground for only part of the year and consist of one or two fronds (sterile and fertile). Likes a loamy soil rich in humus. Susceptible to damage by slugs and snails.

Botrychium virginianum Rattlesnake Fern
North America
30–60 cm (12–24 in): 2 pinnate Temp.–S.Trop.: Terr.

A large species with similar features to the above. It apparently adapts well to garden culture in humus-rich loam. Likes a partial sun situation and must be protected from slugs and snails.

Christensenia aesculifolia
Northern India, Malaysia, New Guinea
30–90 cm (12–36 in): 1 pinnate Trop.: Terr.

An interesting fern with fronds that have a strong resemblance to a chestnut leaf. The stipes and rhizomes are quite fleshy. Can be easy to grow in a shady, protected situation and needs plenty of moisture. Plants are very cold sensitive.

Danaea elliptica
Central and South America, West Indies
30–90 cm (12–36 in): 1 pinnate Trop.: Terr.

Old plants of this species develop a slender, dark, fibrous trunk and have a sparse crown of spreading, dark green fronds. Could make an interesting container specimen. Can be grown in a shady position in acid, humus-rich soil and likes plenty of moisture.

Danaea moritziana
Central and South America, West Indies
15–45 cm (6–18 in): 1 pinnate Trop.: Terr.
This fern forms a spreading crown of dark green, leathery fronds, which tops a small trunk about 30 cm (12 in) tall. The fronds are winged along the rachis and develop a stout plantlet at the tip. Plants are easily grown in shady, moist conditions.

Helminthostachys zeylanica (Fig. p. 58)
India, Sri Lanka, Malaysia, Taiwan, Indonesia, New Guinea, Australia
20–40 cm (8–16 in): palmate Trop.–S.Trop.: Terr.
An interesting fern found in wet situations in seasonally dry climates. Plants grow with the onset of rains in summer and die back to a dormant root system over the dry season. Can be grown as a novelty in a pot of acid, humus-rich mixture. Must be kept wet while in active growth and much drier while dormant.

Marattia excavata
Mexico, Central and South America
200–500 cm (80–200 in): 3 pinnate Trop.: Terr.
A massive fern with heavy, arching, dark green fronds divided into segments 2–3 cm (1–1.25 in) long, with shallowly toothed margins. An easily grown fern requiring a shady, protected situation and plenty of moisture.

Marattia salicina Potato Fern
Australia, New Zealand
200–400 cm (80–160 in): 2–3 pinnate Trop.–S.Trop.: Terr.
A large, fleshy fern of shady, moist forests. Old plants develop a rounded fleshy trunk. Fronds are an attractive verdant green with a pleasant, arching habit. Plants are easily grown in a sheltered position and like plenty of moisture.

var. *howeana* from Lord Howe Island has fronds finely divided and compact.

Marattia smithii
New Hebrides, Fiji, Samoa
100–300 cm (40–120 in): 2 pinnate Trop.: Terr.
A large fern with arching, attractively-divided fronds which are dark green. The segments are 12–15 cm (5–6 in) long, toothed near the apex and are then drawn into a tail. The trunk is rounded and fleshy. Plants grow easily in a moist, sheltered situation.

Ophioglossum palmatum
Florida, Central and South America, West Indies
10–70 cm (4–28 in): palmate Trop.: Epi.
An intriguing epiphytic fern with attractively lobed, vivid green hanging fronds. Unfortunately plants resent disturbance and have proved to be impossible to grow.

A clump of *Ophioglossum pendulum* Photo D. L. Jones

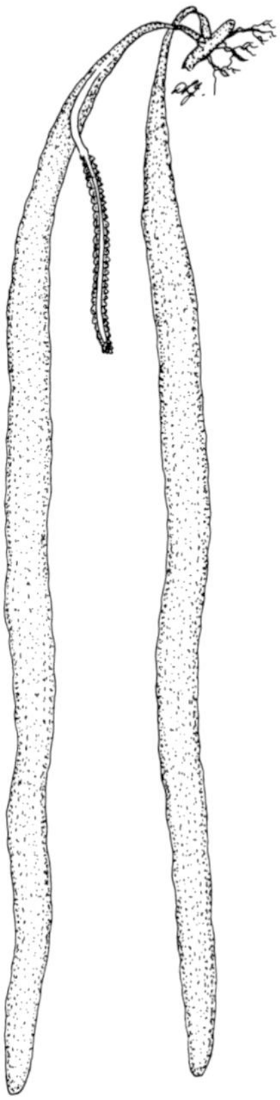
Ophioglossum pendulum

Ophioglossum pendulum Ribbon Fern
Madagascar, Asia, Polynesia, New Guinea, Australia
20–120 cm (8–48 in): entire Trop.–S.Trop.: Epi.

This species commonly grows in the fibrous root system of other large epiphytes with the bright green slender fronds hanging vertically. Plants resent disturbance but will continue growing if the host and ribbon fern is transferred to a basket. Grows best in *Platycerium* peat. Well grown specimens are extremely decorative.

Ophioglossum petiolatum Adder's-tongue Fern (Fig. p.58)
Asia, Africa, Central and South America, West Indies, Polynesia
5–20 cm (2–8 in): entire Temp.–Trop.: Terr.

A novelty fern which adapts well to cultivation and increases steadily. Best grown in a pot of soil-based mixture containing leaf mould. Plants like to be kept continually moist while in active growth and should be watered sparingly while dormant. In greenhouses this species may become weedy.

Ophioglossum reticulatum Adder's-tongue Fern
Central and South America, Africa, Asia, Polynesia
10–40 cm (4–16 in): entire Trop.–S.Trop.: Terr.

Similar in many respects to *O. petiolatum* but the leaf blades are much rounder. Often grows in clumps of several fronds arising from a tuberous root. Can be grown in loamy soil fortified with leaf mould.

Osmunda banksiifolia
China, Japan
30–90 cm (12–36 in): 1 pinnate Temp.–S.Trop.: Terr.

This fern has light green, fairly thinly-textured fronds which have slender segments with prominently lobed margins. Plants are easy to grow in a shady position and require humus-rich, acid soil and plenty of water.

Osmunda cinnamomea Cinnamon Fern (Fig. p.62)
North, Central and South America, West Indies, Asia (east)
60–150 cm (24–60 in): 1–2 pinnate Temp.–Trop.: Terr.

The sterile fronds of this fern tend to grow outwards from the crown, whereas the fertile segments are held erect. When mature, the fronds are bluish-green but as they age they change to a cinnamon brown, thus giving rise to the common name. Developing croziers are very decorative being densely covered with white to rusty hairs. Plants require acid, humus-rich soils and plenty of moisture. Spores are green and are best sown fresh.

Osmunda claytoniana The Interrupted Fern
North America, India
30–150 cm (12–60 in): 1–2 pinnate Temp.–S.Trop.: Terr.

The unusual common name for this fern arises because on the fertile fronds the fertile segments are carried in between sets of normal barren segments,

A large clump of *Osmunda regalis* in the spring
Photo W. R. Elliot

Osmunda regalis Photo W. R. Elliot

giving the appearance of a gap in the frond. Young fronds are covered with woolly, pinkish hairs. This is a strong growing fern which likes acid, organically-rich soils and plenty of moisture. Spores are green and have a limited life.

Osmunda japonica
China, Korea, Japan, Philippines, North India
30–90 cm (12–36 in): 2 pinnate Temp.–S.Trop.: Terr.
This species is very similar in general appearance to *O. regalis*, but is generally of smaller stature. It grows readily in a shady position in well-drained, humus-rich, acid soil.

Osmunda javanica
India, Malaysia, Indonesia
30–200 cm (12–80 in): 1 pinnate Trop.–S.Trop.: Terr.
A large fern with coarse, leathery fronds which have long narrow segments with entire or undulate margins. Young fronds are covered with sticky secretions. Plants grow readily in a partially sunny situation in moist to wet, acidic soils. Spores are green and are best sown fresh.

Osmunda lancea
Japan
60–90 cm (24–36 in): 2 pinnate Temp.–S.Trop.: Terr.
An attractive, clumping species with narrow segments imparting a lacy appearance to the fronds. Grows readily in a shady position in well-drained, loamy, acid soil.

Osmunda regalis Royal Fern
Europe, Asia, North and South America, Africa
30–300 cm (12–120 in): 2 pinnate Temp.–Trop.: Terr.
A majestic fern which grows in wet soils usually on the margins of permanent water. Plants form a dense clump of fresh green fronds and are an ideal subject for landscaping especially in conjunction with water features. In very cold climates they may become deciduous in winter. Plants have proved to be adaptable to a variety of soil types and situations. Spores are green and are best sown fresh.

'Crispa' — the segments have crisped margins. Fertile.

'Cristata' — the frond apex and individual segments are heavily crested. Fertile.

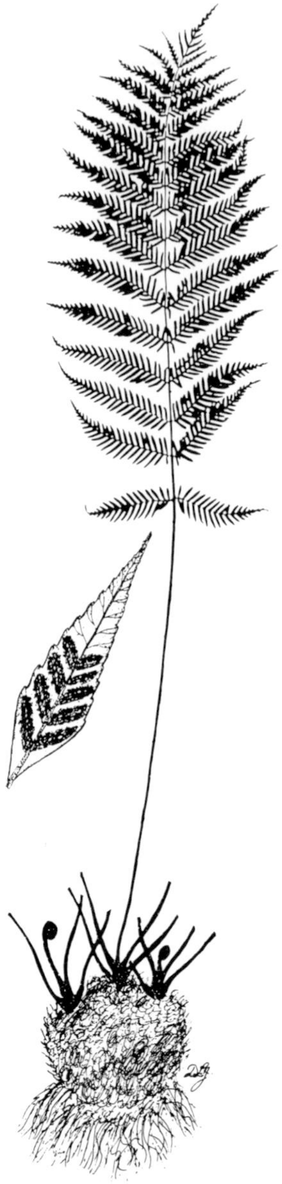

Todea barbara

Todea barbara Austral King Fern
Australia, New Zealand, South Africa
50–150 cm (20–60 in): 2 pinnate Temp.–Trop.: Terr.
A large fern which can develop massive trunks which bear multiple crowns and are covered with black, wiry, fibrous roots. Each crown bears a number of erect, leathery, bright green fronds so that a large specimen is quite an impressive sight. Plants are very adaptable and are easily grown in a variety of situations and soils. Spores are green and are best sown fresh.

Todea barbara grown as a basket fern
Photo D. L. Jones

37 Scrambling ferns, umbrella ferns, coral ferns and pouch ferns

genera *Dicranopteris*, *Diplopterygium*, *Gleichenia* and *Sticherus*

These are a familiar and interesting group of ferns especially in the tropics. Most species grow in clumps or spreading thickets and have a unique growth habit which results in successive tiers of fronds. As a group they are rarely encountered in cultivation, partly because of the final size many species achieve, but mostly because they resent disturbance and can be difficult to establish.

Habitat

Most ferns of this group are colonizers and are found along roadsides, embankments and forest margins. Some species can only survive in a sunny situation and die when shaded out by forest growth. Many grow extremely well on exposed clay; others favour acid podsols of very low fertility. A few species of *Sticherus* grow readily in shady situations.

Cultivation

Uses

The perfect frond symmetry, the tiers of fronds and the clumping growth habit are all attractive, ornamental features of this group. They can be grown in tubs for decoration and though some species are suitable for the garden, others have special requirements and are better suited to planting around ponds, dams and soaks. The fronds of most species in this group are stiff and lend themselves well to cutting or drying and painting for decoration.

Soil Types

Most ferns of this group, except some species of *Sticherus*, prefer clays or clay-loams or infertile sandy soils. Many will grow in wet to boggy soils providing the water is not stagnant. *Sticherus* species, such as *S. flabellatus* and *S. lobatus*, grow very well in loamy soils rich in organic matter.

Potting Mix

An open mix containing peat moss and based on a sandy loam is usually suitable for this group of ferns. Some species such as *Gleichenia microphylla* and *G. dicarpa* are sensitive to the presence of lime, and others may have a similar aversion. Most species have a strong root system and quickly fill a pot with roots. Vigorous plants will need potting on to the next size container annually.

Watering

Ferns of this group are remarkably sensitive to drying of the root system and such a lapse is invariably fatal. In nature, these ferns are able to survive periods of dry weather, however, dryness of the roots is disastrous for a container grown plant. This indicates the importance of not allowing container grown plants to get potbound. Plants grown in the ground have an enhanced ability to survive dryness but to be on the safe side should be watered during dry periods. Certainly this applies in the first few years until the plants are established. Plants grown in soils that are naturally moist to wet will not need extra watering.

Fertilizing

Plants of this group seem to be able to get by with very little supplementary nutrition. In fact highly fertile soils or potting mixes may cause their death. Light applications of slow-release fertilizers or half strength liquid fertilizers can be of benefit to potted plants.

Situation

Most of this group are sun ferns and need exposure to sun for at least part of the day. A few species of *Sticherus* will grow quite successfully in the shade, but these are an exception. In wet soils such as soaks or around the margins of permanent water, ferns of this group will tolerate full sun all day. Many of these ferns, even some tropical ones, are surprisingly cold-hardy and will even tolerate frosts.

Pests

This group of ferns can suffer sporadic attacks by slugs and snails on young fronds.

Dicranopteris linearis Photo D. L. Jones

A large colony of *Dicranopteris linearis* in forest, New Caledonia Photo W. R. Elliot

Propagation

Ferns of this group seem to be quite difficult to raise from spores, although this is not commonly tried. It is hard to tell when the sporangia are ripe and ready for collection, and this problem may account for some of the difficulty encountered with spore raising.

Transplanting an established specimen invariably results in its quick demise since these ferns resent any major disturbance of their roots. The best method is to transplant small plants and sporelings into a pot of suitable mixture. After these are established they can be potted into a bigger container or planted in the ground. Suitable small plants can often be found on embankments adjacent to established clumps. Once a plant is established in the garden it should not be disturbed and no attempt should be made to divide it. Potted plants can be successfully divided provided the root system receives a minimum of disturbance.

SPECIES AND CULTIVARS

Dicranopteris curranii
Malaysia, Indonesia
100–300 cm (40–120 in): tiered Trop.–S.Trop.: Terr.

A clump-forming but non-climbing fern which commonly grows in thickets along forest edges, embankments etc. Very young plants can be shifted and grown in a pot or in a sunny garden situation.

Dicranopteris linearis Scrambling Fern
Africa, Asia, Malaysia, New Guinea, Australia, Polynesia
100–400 cm (40–160 in): tiered Trop.–Temp.: Terr.

An extremely widespread and variable fern which has no less than 13 separate varieties. Some of these are tall scrambling ferns which grow on forest edges (even climbing trees) and embankments; others are low growing in spreading clumps. Some forms are very decorative in a pot and the smaller types can be grown in a garden. Requires a sunny to semi-protected situation and extra water during dry periods.

Diplopterygium longissimum Giant Scrambling Fern
China, South-East Asia, Malaysia, New Guinea, Australia
100–500 cm (40–200 in): tiered Trop.–S.Trop.: Terr.

A massive fern which forms thickets on forest margins, embankments etc. and can even climb into trees. Small plants can be successfully grown in pots where they make a very decorative specimen. They can also be planted in a sunny garden situation but need plenty of room to develop.

Gleichenia alpina Alpine Coral Fern
Australia, New Zealand
20–40 cm (8–16 in): tiered Temp.: Terr.

A low-growing species which forms spreading colonies in sub-alpine areas. It grows in infertile soils in situations exposed to full sun. This is one of the best of the genus to cultivate, as the plants do not grow tall. Needs a sunny situation in acid soil and shoul be kept continually moist.

Gleichenia circinnata = Gleichenia dicarpa

Gleichenia cunninghamii = Sticherus cunninghamii

Gleichenia dicarpa Pouched Coral Fern
New Guinea, Philippines, Australia, New Caledoni
100–300 cm (40–120 in): tiered Trop.–Temp.: Ter

This species forms tangled thickets in situatior where the roots are wet but the fronds are expose to full sun. Usually grows in infertile, acid podsoli soils and is often noticeable on embankments. Plant can be grown in large containers but are best plante in moist to wet acid soil in a sunny position.

Gleichenia dichotoma = Dicranopteris linearis

Gleichenia flabellata = Sticherus flabellatus

Gleichenia linearis = Dicranopteris linearis

Gleichenia dicarpa Photo D. L. Jones

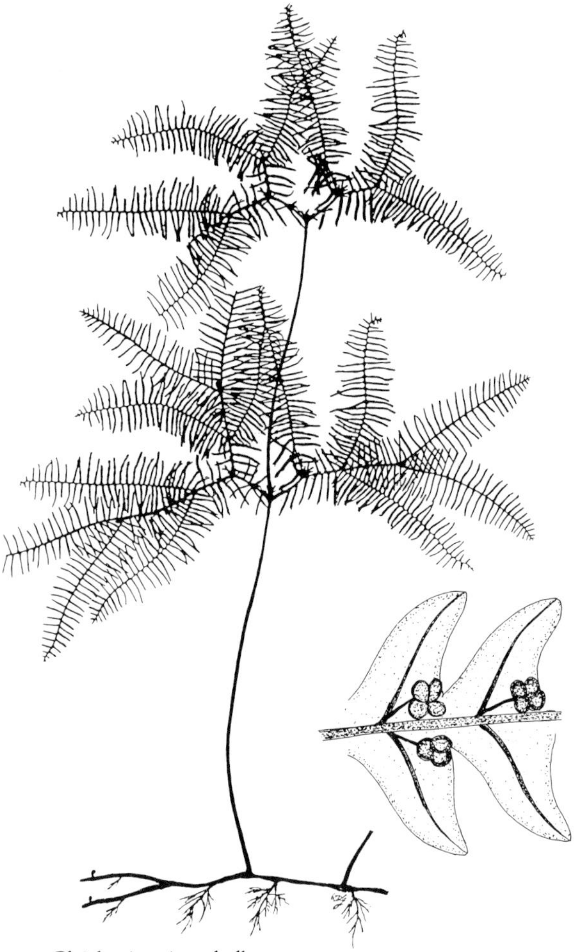

Gleichenia microphylla

Gleichenia microphylla

The attractive fronds of *Sticherus flabellatus*
Photo D. L. Jones

Sticherus cunninghamii

Gleichenia microphylla Umbrella Fern/Coral Fern
India, Malaysia, New Guinea, Australia, New Zealand, New Caledonia
100–300 cm (40–120 in): tiered Trop.-Temp.: Terr.

A widespread scrambling fern that forms thickets in exposed situations and always on soil that is wet or subject to periods of inundation. Can be grown easily around the margins of soaks or ponds or in artificially created bog gardens. Must have a sunny aspect. Fronds are useful for indoor decoration.

Gleichenia rupestris
Australia
100–200 cm (40–80 in): tiered Temp.-S.Trop.: Terr.

A scrambling fern usually found in seepage areas among rocks (often sandstone). Some plants are markedly glaucous on the underside of the fronds. Requires moist, acid soil in an open situation.

Gleichenia vulcanica
Malaysia, New Guinea
50–150 cm (20–60 in): tiered Trop.-S.Trop.: Terr.

A low growing species which colonizes open areas usually in mountainous regions. The undersurface of the fronds is prominently glaucous. Generally plants resent disturbance but small ones can be started in a pot and grown on.

Sticherus bifidus
Mexico, Central and South America, West Indies
100–200 cm (40–80 in): tiered Trop.-S.Trop.: Terr.

A thicket forming fern with attractive symmetrical fronds. It colonizes road embankments, disturbed earth, and forest margins in sunny places. Plants can be grown easily in a pot or in a partial sun situation in the garden.

Sticherus cunninghamii Umbrella Fern
New Zealand
60–100 cm (24–40 in): tiered Temp.-S.Trop.: Terr.

A most attractive fern with its symmetrically divided fronds which are greyish-white on the underside. Established specimens are impossible to transplant but small sporelings can be established in pots or in a semi-shady garden position. Plants like moisture in dry periods and mulching with organic litter.

Sticherus flabellatus Shiny Fan Fern
New Guinea, Australia, New Zealand, New Caledonia
50–150 cm (20–60 in): tiered Trop.-Temp.: Terr.

A delightful fern which forms clumps of tiered, symmetrically-lobed fronds of a verdant green. Frequently grows in large colonies on the banks of streams. Can be readily established as a garden plant in a semi-sun or shady situation. Very decorative when grown among rocks and can be used to help hold embankments, rock walls etc. Established plants do not tolerate disturbance.

Sticherus lobatus

Sticherus lobatus Spreading Fan Fern
Australia
50–200 cm (20–80 in): tiered Temp.–S.Trop.: Terr.

An ornamental fern which grows in colonies along forest margins, stream banks and in rocky areas. Large plants resent disturbance but small ones can be grown in a pot and eventually planted out. Plants will grow in a variety of situations from shade to sun but in a sunny situation must have plenty of water.

38 The filmy ferns and the crepe ferns

genera *Hymenophyllum*, *Trichomanes* and *Leptopteris*

The Filmy Ferns are an interesting group found in very moist, shady, sheltered conditions. In size they range from tiny plants with fronds less than 1 cm (0.5 in) long to giants nearly 2 m (80 in) long. The common name arises from the membranous thinly-textured fronds of most species, which vary from one to a few cells thick.

The Crepe Ferns belong to the genus *Leptopteris*. They too grow in moist, sheltered conditions and have membranous fronds. They are not related to Filmy Ferns but as they have similar cultural requirements they are included with them.

Filmy Ferns are rarely cultivated except by ardent enthusiasts or in botanical collections. Their specialized demands for high humidity, nearly constant moisture, shade and shelter from sun and wind, mean that they are not suitable for growing in a mixed fern collection, but must be enclosed in a structure which provides their requirements.

Habitat

Filmy Ferns are commonest in protected environments that are almost continually wet, although hardier types will grow in situations where dry periods occur. Their fronds may curl, but they can absorb water directly through the frond surface and can be readily refreshened by light showers, mist or even heavy dew. Filmy Ferns grow on mossy trunks, branches and twigs of trees, on dripping rock faces, ledges and boulders and as terrestrials in wet earth. Crepe Ferns are invariably terrestrials in moist, sheltered situations.

Cultivation

Uses

Filmy Ferns are extremely attractive ferns, but have limited use horticulturally because of their very specialized requirements. Some of the compact species are excellent for terrariums or bottle culture and can be grown indoors. The hardier species can be grown in pots in greenhouses or ferneries. To grow a large range however, specialized containers must be used or special structures built.

Special Containers

These are mostly closed structures which retain humidity but which are constructed of glass or plastic to allow light transmission. They include terrariums, large bottles, aquariums, Wardian cases and glass shades. Bell jars are also quite suitable but are becoming a rare item these days.

A special Filmy Fern case can be constructed along the lines shown in the accompanying drawing. This is a completely sealed unit made from glass and has a sliding front partition. The base is a shallow water reservoir which maintains humidity. A thin piece of absorbent material such as a section of tree fern is placed vertically on the glass at the back with its base in the water. The Filmy Ferns are pinned onto the moist fibre and allowed to develop with the unit closed. Mosses and weedy ferns may be a problem and must be controlled or else they may swamp the Filmy Ferns. This problem can be lessened by pre-sterilizing the whole unit with boiling water.

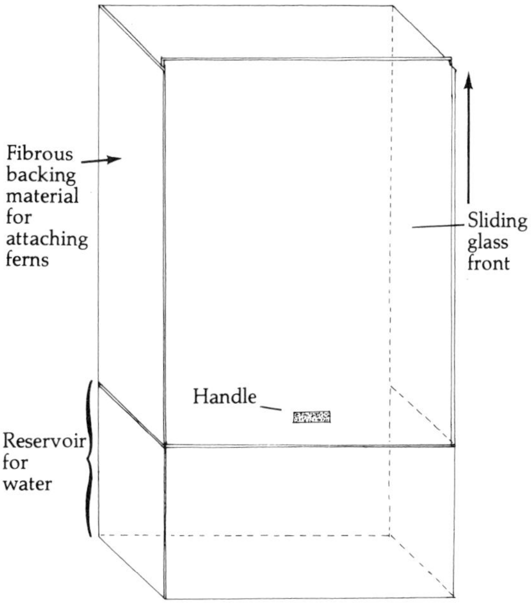

Special glass case for filmy fern culture

Special Structures

A Filmy Fern house is a specialized, well-sealed structure which retains humidity, and provides the correct amount of light for growth. A well-sealed greenhouse fitted with misting sprays can be suitable providing that it does not heat up too much in summer. High brick walls in a greenhouse can reduce temperature fluctuations, especially if they are of absorbent bricks (such as cinder bricks). Lining the walls with split tree-fern trunks or having the structure underground so that the earth banks act as walls, can also be successful ploys for their culture.

Potting Mix

Terrestrial Filmy Ferns should be potted into a freely draining but organically rich mix. A useful mix is equal parts tree-fern fibre, peat moss and sandy loam. This is also successful for species of *Leptopteris*. Some growers find peat moss and leaf mould to be successful.

Epiphytes can be grown on slabs of tree-fern fibre or potted into tree fern or osmunda fibre with or without peat moss and/or leaf mould.

Watering

Filmy Ferns and Crepe Ferns need plenty of water and humidity. Mist from special mist nozzles as used in cutting propagation is eminently suitable for them. If they are grown in sealed containers then there is little chance for them to dry out and watering is not so critical. Occasional mistings of the foliage are beneficial however.

Fertilizing

Filmy Ferns and Crepe Ferns benefit from an occasional spray with reduced strength liquid fertilizer but they are not gross feeders.

Situation

Many species of Filmy Fern will grow in quite heavy shade whereas others need a fair amount of light but not direct sun. The provision of a small fan to lightly stir the air in a Filmy Fern house is beneficial.

Pests

Filmy Ferns and Crepe Ferns suffer badly from the depredations of slugs, snails, earwigs and slaters.

Propagation

Filmy Ferns and Crepe Ferns have green spores which have a very short life. In general they are not difficult to raise from spores but may have preferences for certain media (e.g. *Trichomanes venosum* germinates well on *Dicksonia* fibre but not so well on *Cyathea* fibre). The spores of both of these groups of ferns must be sown fresh. In some species of Filmy Fern the spores germinate in the sorus before they are splashed free.

Trichomanes baueriana, Lord Howe Island
Photo D. L. Jones

Those Filmy Ferns with a creeping growth habit can be successfully divided but the pieces should not be too small or the division will not be successful.

SPECIES AND CULTIVARS

Callistopteris baueriana — see **Trichomanes baueriana**

Cardiomanes reniforme — see **Trichomanes reniforme**

Crepidomanes bipunctatum — see **Trichomanes bipunctatum**

Davalliopsis elegans — see **Trichomanes elegans**

Gonocormus minutus — see **Trichomanes minutum**

Gonocormus prolifer = Trichomanes minutum

Gonocormus saxifragoides — see **Trichomanes saxifragoides**

Hymenophyllum australe (alt. **Mecodium australe**)
Australia
5–15 cm (2–6 in): 3 pinnate Temp.: Epi.

An easily grown species which forms spreading clumps of dark green membranous fronds. Each has a prominently crinkled wing on the stipe. Will grow in a pot of fern fibre or on a tree-fern slab. Needs moisture and constant humidity.

Hymenophyllum bivalve (alt. **Meringium bivalve**)
Australia, New Zealand
10–25 cm (4–10 in): 3 pinnate Temp.–S.Trop.: Terr.

An elegant filmy fern which has broadly triangular light green fronds, crowded on a creeping rhizome. Looks attractive in a pot of fern fibre. Needs moisture and constant humidity.

Hymenophyllum dilatatum

Hymenophyllum demissum (alt. **Mecodium demissum**)
New Zealand
20–50 cm (8–20 in): 3 pinnate Temp.–S.Trop.: Epi.
Long lacy hanging fronds on a wiry, creeping rhizome. Fronds are a delicate green and translucent when wet. Grows well in fibrous or peaty mix or on a tree-fern slab.

Hymenophyllum dilatatum (alt. **Mecodium dilatatum**)
New Zealand
20–70 cm (8–28 in): 3–4 pinnate Temp.: Epi.
A large filmy fern with graceful hanging fronds carried at intervals on a wiry rhizome. Slow to establish but grows steadily. Grows well in fibrous mixture or on a tree-fern slab.

Hymenophyllum flabellatum (alt. **Mecodium flabellatum**)
Australia, New Zealand, Polynesia
10–30 cm (4–12 in): 2–4 pinnate Temp.–Trop.: Epi.
A filmy fern with arching to hanging attractively divided fronds of a light, yellowish green. Plants have a creeping rhizome. Can be grown in a pot of fibre or on a tree-fern slab in conditions of constant humidity.

Hymenophyllum javanicum (alt. **Mecodium javanicum**)
Australia, New Guinea, Indonesia, Polynesia, Malaysia
5–15 cm (2–6 in): 2 pinnate
A distinctive species with stiffly erect, deep green to almost blackish fronds which have prominently crinkled margins and a winged stipe. Creeps on rocks and trees. Can be grown in a pot of fibrous mixture in conditions of constant humidity.

Hymenophyllum peltatum Alpine Filmy Fern
Europe, Canary Islands, Australia, New Zealand, South Africa, South America
3–10 cm (1–4 in): 2 pinnate Temp.: Epi.
A widely distributed, filmy fern that forms mats of foliage on rocks, often at high altitudes. It adapts well to culture in an aquarium, bottle garden or terrarium. Prefers an acid, fibrous mix.

Hymenophyllum polyanthos (alt. **Mecodium polyanthos**)
Australia, New Guinea, Indonesia, Polynesia, Malaysia, South America
5–20 cm (2–8 in): 2 pinnate Trop.: Epi.
A distinctive species with slender, hanging fronds of a light, translucent green and a wiry, creeping rhizome. Plants can be grown on a tree-fern slab in conditions of constant humidity.

Hymenophyllum sanguinolentum (alt. **Mecodium sanguinolentum**)
New Zealand
10–20 cm (4–8 in): 3 pinnate Temp.: Epi.–Terr.
A neat small filmy fern with lacy, olive-green fronds

Hymenophyllum flabellatum

closely spaced on a wiry rhizome. Fairly easily grown in a pot of fibrous mixture or on a tree-fern slab.

Hymenophyllum tunbridgense
Europe, Africa, West Indies, South America
3–10 cm (1–4 in): 2 pinnate Temp.–S.Trop.: Epi.–Terr.

A widely distributed little filmy fern which colonizes rocks and trees in shady wet places. Easily grown in a shallow pot of fibrous mixture in an environment of constantly high humidity. An ideal subject for a bottle garden or terrarium.

Hymenophyllum wilsonii
Europe, Africa, South America
3–12 cm (1–5 in): 2 pinnate Temp.–S.Trop.: Epi.

This little filmy fern forms mats of olive-green fronds on wet rocks and trees. Easily grown in a fibrous mixture (also pure leaf mould) in constant humidity.

Leptopteris fraseri Australian Crepe Fern
Australia
50–140 cm (20–56 in): 3 pinnate

A fern with filmy, membranous bright green fronds which are carried in an arching crown atop a small trunk. Always grows in shady, wet places, frequently near waterfalls. Can be easily grown in a pot but requires protected, shady conditions and constant high humidity.

Leptopteris hymenophylloides Crepe Fern
New Zealand
40–90 cm (16–36 in): 3 pinnate Temp.: Terr.

The fronds of this fern are deep green and delicately divided. They are almost membranous and are semi-transparent when wet. They are carried in an arching crown from a rootstock which becomes a small trunk in old plants. Requires similar conditions to *L. superba*.

Leptopteris superba Prince of Wales Feather/Crepe Fern
New Zealand
60–150 cm (24–60 in): 3 pinnate Temp.: Terr.

Regarded as one of the most beautiful ferns in the world, this species is renowned for its rosette of delicately lacy, shimmering, lustrous green fronds. Old plants form a trunk up to 1 m tall. Thrives only in cool, moist forests. Plants require a constantly moist atmosphere and protection from sun and wind. Humus-rich acid soils are favoured. Plants are slow growing but long-lived.

Macroglena caudata – see **Trichomanes caudatum**

Macroglena meifolia – see **Trichomanes meifolium**

Mecodium australe – see **Hymenophyllum australe**

Mecodium demissum – see **Hymenophyllum demissum**

Leptopteris hymenophylloides

Mecodium dilatatum – see **Hymenophyllum dilatatum**

Mecodium flabellatum – see **Hymenophyllum flabellatum**

Mecodium javanicum – see **Hymenophyllum javanicum**

Mecodium polyanthos – see **Hymenophyllum polyanthos**

Mecodium sanguinolentum – see **Hymenophyllum sanguinolentum**

Meringium bivalve – see **Hymenophyllum bivalve**

Polyphlebium venosum – see **Trichomanes venosum**

Reediella humilis – see **Trichomanes humile**

Selenodesmium obscurum – see **Trichomanes obscurum**

Trichomanes baueriana (alt. **Callistopteris baueriana**)
Lord Howe Island, Norfolk Island
10–25 cm (4–10 in): 3 pinnate S.Trop.–Temp.: Terr.

Plants of this species form a compact clump of dark green, heavily dissected fronds. This is a very beautiful little fern which can be grown in a pot of acid, well-drained fibrous mix in conditions of constantly high humidity.

Trichomanes bipunctatum (alt. **Crepidomanes bipunctatum**) (Fig. p. 66)
Madagascar, Malaysia, Polynesia, Indonesia, New Guinea, Australia
2.5–7.5 cm (1–3 in): 1 pinnate Trop.–S.Trop.: Epi.

A small filmy fern that forms spreading mats on rocks and tree trunks. The fronds frequently curl in dry periods and refreshen and regreen within a few hours of rain. In the dry state the mats look black and when fresh, bright green. Easily grown in a pot or terrarium of fibrous mixture. Requires constant high humidity.

Trichomanes caudatum (alt. **Macroglena caudata**)
Jungle Bristle Fern
Australia, Polynesia
10–40 cm (4–16 in): 3 pinnate Trop.–Temp.: Epi.

This filmy fern has finely divided dark green fronds and a wiry, creeping rhizome. Fronds are closely spaced and the plants form attractive clumps. Can be grown in a fibrous mixture or on a tree-fern slab in constant humidity.

Trichomanes elegans (alt. **Davalliopsis elegans**)
Central and South America, West Indies
40–70 cm (16–28 in): 3–4 pinnate Trop.: Terr.

A tufted filmy fern with remarkably dimorphic fronds. The sterile fronds are dark green, leathery in texture, and with broad but deeply-lacerated segments. They have a lax or hanging habit. By contrast, the fertile fronds are erect and undivided with the sporangia borne around the margin. Requires a fibrous mixture with shady, moist conditions.

Trichomanes humile (alt. **Reediella humilis**) (Fig. p.66)
Malaysia, Polynesia, Indonesia, Australia
2.5–5 cm (1–2 in): pinnatifid Trop.–S.Trop.: Epi.

A tiny filmy fern that grows in small spreading patches on trees and rocks in dark, moist situations. It can be easily grown in a pot or terrarium in a fibrous, acid mixture. Requires constant high humidity.

Trichomanes reniforme

Trichomanes johnstonense
Australia
10–25 cm (4–10 in): 3 pinnate Trop.–S.Trop.: Terr.
A relatively tall species which grows on clay banks and small rocks in dark, moist situations (often in stream beds). It is a handsome filmy fern with a creeping rhizome and tufts of dark green, finely divided fronds. Can be established in a bottle garden or terrarium in a coarse, humus-rich mixture. Likes constant high humidity and a relatively dark situation.

Trichomanes meifolium (alt. **Macroglena meifolia**)
Malaysia, Polynesia, New Caledonia, Madagascar
10–30 cm (4–12 in): 3 pinnate Trop.: Terr.
A widely distributed, beautiful fern found in moist, shady situations, often on rocks. Plants form a neat rosette of finely dissected, dark green fronds. They resent disturbance and are somewhat slow growing. To grow well plants require fibrous mixture and constant humidity.

Trichomanes minutum (alt. **Gonocormus minutus**)
India, Sri Lanka, Malaysia, Polynesia, Australia
3–5 cm (1–2 in): palmate Trop.–S.Trop.: Epi.
A mat-forming species which grows on rocks and less commonly, trees in dark, moist situations. The dark green fronds can form plantlets on the upper part, resulting in 2–4 tiers of plants. Easily grown in a pot, bottle or terrarium. Requires constant high humidity.

Trichomanes obscurum (alt. **Selenodesmium obscurum**)
Southern India, Sri Lanka, Malaysia, New Guinea, Australia
10–20 cm (4–8 in): 3 pinnate Trop.–S.Trop.: Terr.
A widely distributed species found near streams in rainforest. Plants form a small rosette of dark green, lacy fronds. Roots are very stout and stilt-like. Generally very slow to recover from disturbance. Requires fibrous mix in constantly high humidity.

Trichomanes radicans (alt. **Vandenboschia radicans**)
Europe (West), Africa, Asia, Central and South America, Malaysia
20–50 cm (8–20 in): 3–4 pinnate Trop.–S.Trop.: Terr.–Epi.
A widely distributed and beautiful fern with a creeping rhizome and light green, lacy fronds. Plants resent disturbance and are slow to re-establish. Needs a fibrous mixture, plenty of moisture and constant humidity.

Trichomanes reniforme (alt. **Cardiomanes reniforme**)
Kidney Fern
New Zealand
10–25 cm (4–10 in): entire Temp.: Epi.–Terr.
A famous fern renowned for its large, rounded or kidney-shaped translucent green fronds. It is a strong growing species that colonizes trees, rocks and banks in moist, shady areas. Plants adapt to a pot of fibrous mixture or a tree-fern slab and need shady, moist conditions with constant humidity.

Trichomanes saxifragoides (alt. **Gonocormus saxifragoides**) (Fig. p.66)
India, Sri Lanka, Malaysia, Japan, Polynesia, Australia
1–2.5 cm (0.5–1 in): palmate Trop.–S.Trop.: Epi.
A tiny, mat-forming species which grows on rocks and trees. It is quite resilient for a filmy fern, the fronds often curling and drying between periods of rain, but refreshing within a few hours of soaking showers. Easily grown in a pot, bottle or terrarium in humid, fairly dark conditions.

Trichomanes venosum (alt. **Polyphlebium venosum**)
Veined Bristle Fern
Australia, New Zealand
3–10 cm (1–4 in): 1 pinnate Temp.–S.Trop.: Epi.
A hardy little filmy fern which forms mats of translucent foliage on *Dicksonia* trunks. It can be grown easily in a fibrous mix or on a tree-fern slab in conditions of constant humidity.

Vandenboschia radicans – see **Trichomanes radicans**

39 Aquatic ferns

genera *Azolla, Ceratopteris, Marsilea, Pilularia, Regnellidium* and *Salvinia*

Truly aquatic ferns are not particularly common or popular with fern enthusiasts. Within their ranks, however, are some very interesting ferns which have appeal for those growers prepared to try to meet their specialized cultural requirements.

Habitat

Aquatic ferns grow in shallow fresh water which is either still or moving slowly. They may either be free floating on the surface or rooting in the mud in which case they may have either submerged, floating or emergent leaves. Those which root in the mud can only grow in water to about 80 cm (32 in) deep. Aquatic ferns are also frequently found in low lying areas which are periodically flooded and here they may grow as annuals.

Cultivation

Uses

Some aquatic ferns have ornamental appeal and can be grown in aquaria, ponds and dams. They can also provide shelter and food for fish and sites for egg laying.

Soil Types

In aquaria the rhizomes can be planted in coarse sand or in small pots containing a soil-based potting mixture covered with a layer of fine sand. In dams or ponds the rhizomes can be planted directly into the mud at the bottom.

Many aquatics can also be grown in a pot of sphagnum moss or of soil-based mixture with the base of the pot permanently submerged in 8–10 cm (3–4 in) depth of water. The fronds will then grow emergent.

Fertilizing

Aquatic ferns respond to fertilizers and manures but their uses are hardly necessary.

Situation

Aquatic ferns like bright light and most grow best in full sun. Species from tropical regions are generally very sensitive to cold, especially frosts, and may need the protection of a heated greenhouse or a well lit tropical aquarium.

Pests

Caterpillars and water snails may eat the leaves but are rarely a problem. Transient attacks by aphis on emergent fronds may be a nuisance since sprays cannot be used near fish.

Propagation

Most aquatic ferns can be propagated readily by division of the long-creeping rhizomes. Free floating ferns such as *Azolla* and *Salvinia* propagate themselves freely by division. *Ceratopteris, Marsilea* and *Pilularia* can be propagated by sowing spores (or sporocarps) on mud but this is rarely necessary. Abrading the sporocarps of *Marsilea* prior to sowing improves germination.

SPECIES AND CULTIVARS

Azolla caroliniana Carolinian Azolla
North America
Trop.–S.Trop.: Aquatic
A free floating aquatic fern which forms colonies on still water. Plants turn from green to bright red in the summer and autumn. Easily grown in ponds etc. but very cold-sensitive.

Azolla filiculoides Ferny Azolla
North America, Central and South America, Asia, Australia
Trop.–Temp.: Aquatic
A free floating aquatic fern which forms colonies on still water such as lakes, ponds, dams, swamps etc. Plants propagate freely by vegetative techniques and soon cover the surface of the water. Can be used as an ornamental on the surface of man-made ponds and dams or fish tanks.

Azolla nilotica African Azolla
Africa
Trop.–S.Trop.: Aquatic
A very large species which may develop stems to 30 cm (12 in) long. Individuals branch freely and may form sizeable clumps before the lateral growths break away as separate plants. Forms colonies on still water and on wet mud. Useful as an ornamental on small ponds or aquaria.

Azolla pinnata Pacific Azolla (Fig. p.70)
Africa, Asia, Malaysia, Australia
Trop.–Temp.: Aquatic
This fern forms a mass of floating material which propagates itself freely by vegetative means. Commonly grows on still water. Plants in sunny situations may be bright red; those in the shade remain green. An interesting ornamental for the surface of ponds, dams, fish tanks etc.

Ceratopteris cornuta
Africa, India, Burma, Vietnam
15–30 cm (6–12 in): 1–2 pinnate Trop.–S.Trop.: Aquatic
This species may develop while floating, or more usually, takes root in marshes, swamps etc. It differs from *C. thalictroides* by having fewer dissected fronds with much broader segments. Plants adapt very well to tropical fish aquaria and are quite decorative.

Ceratopteris pteridoides
Central and South America, West Indies
15–45 cm (6–18 in): 1–2 pinnate Trop.–S.Trop.: Aquatic
In nature this species forms floating colonies in still water and favours fairly shady situations. It apparently grows well in a tropical fish aquarium.

Ceratopteris thalictroides Water Fern
Pantropical
15–45 cm (6–18 in): 1–2 pinnate Trop.–S.Trop.: Aquatic
This fern is a favourite of tropical fish fanciers for it thrives in the brightly-lit warm environment of a tropical fish tank. Plantlets are produced freely on the leaves and these float until they are able to take root. Its true emergent form shows when it grows rooted in mud in shallow water. Then the bright green tufts of finely divided fronds emerge from above the water and are most distinctive.

Marsilea coromandelina
Africa, India
variable length: quadrifoliar Trop.–S.Trop.: Aquatic
A small species with a threadlike rhizome and fairly narrow, wedge-shaped leaflets. It commonly grows in flooded depressions. Can be grown in a pot of soil permanently immersed in water.

Marsilea drummondii Photo D. L. Jones

Marsilea drummondii Nardoo
Australia
variable length: quadrifoliar Temp.–S.Trop.: Aquatic
A variable species, with the frond shape and degree of hairiness varying with factors such as the depth of water and the prevailing temperature. Plants commonly grow in temporary pools with the fronds floating when there is sufficient depth of water and becoming stiffly erect when in shallow water or mud. In the latter stage the fronds may be covered with silvery hairs and look very attractive. An easily grown species either in ponds or in a pot of soil permanently immersed in water.

Marsilea macrocarpa
Africa
variable length: quadrifoliar Temp.–S.Trop.: Aquatic
A robust species found in temporary depressions and also permanent water sometimes growing in streams. Fronds may be up to 8 cm (3 in) across and can be entire or crenate. A rewarding species that can be grown in ponds or in a pot of soil with the base permanently immersed in water.

Marsilea mutica (Fig. p.69)
Australia, New Caledonia
variable length: quadrifoliar Trop.–Temp.: Aquatic
A vigorous aquatic which spreads by long-creeping rhizomes which root in the mud. The large, four-lobed leaves have distinctive brown bands and float on the surface of the water creating an attractive effect. This is an excellent ornamental aquatic for fish ponds and containers. Propagates readily from pieces of the rhizomes.

Marsilea polycarpa Water Clover
Central and South America, West Indies
variable length: quadrifoliar Trop.–S.Trop.: Aquatic

An aquatic fern which grows in permanent water, forming colonies by its spreading rhizomes. Unusually in this species the floating leaves are sterile, but the emergent leaves bear fruiting bodies. Plants can be readily grown as aquatics in fish ponds and containers.

Marsilea quadrifolia Water Clover/Water Shamrock
Europe, North America, China, Japan, Korea
variable length: quadrifoliar Temp.–S.Trop.: Aquatic

This species grows around the margins of swamps and lakes and in wet depressions. It forms colonies by virtue of its creeping rhizomes and the bright green, four-lobed leaves may float or grow in clumps like clover. Plants can be grown readily in a pond or in a pot with the base permanently submerged in water.

Pilularia americana American Pillwort
North America
5–7.5 cm (2–3 in): entire Temp.–S.Trop.: Terr.

A small species which grows in mud at the edges of ponds etc. Plants have a sparsely branched thread-like rhizome, and filiform fronds in tufts. Cultural requirements as for *P. globulifera*.

Pilularia globulifera European Pillwort (Fig. p.69)
Europe
5–10 cm (2–4 in): entire Trop.–Temp.: Aquatic

This fern may grow as a submerged aquatic in shallow water or occasionally it is free floating. It is most un-fernlike with the fronds reduced to filiform structures and the plants more resembling a sedge. Plants appeal mainly to enthusiasts, however, they can be easily grown in a pot of soil-based mix, with the base of the pot permanently immersed in water. Can also be grown in a bog garden and terrarium.

Salvinia molesta Photo W. R. Elliot

Pilularia novae-hollandiae Australian Pillwort
Australia
5–7.5 cm (2–3 in): entire Temp.–S.Trop.: Terr.

A small species from ponds and low lying areas subject to periodic inundation, often growing in drying mud. Plants have a much branched, thread-like rhizome, and filiform fronds in tufts. Cultural requirements as for *P. globulifera*. Colonies may decline after a few years and benefit from restarting with a small division in a fresh mix.

Regnellidium diphyllum Latex Fern (Fig. p.69)
Brazil, Argentina
variable length: bifoliar Trop.: Aquatic

An interesting aquatic fern which grows in permanent water among other vegetation. The leaf-stems exude a white latex if broken, hence the common name. Plants have a long-creeping stem which roots in mud and long leaf stems which bear a pair of leaflets at the apex. These leaves either float on the water or are emergent from shallow water. Plants can be grown readily in a heated aquarium or a pot of sphagnum moss with the base permanently immersed in water. The species is very sensitive to cold and resents alkaline water.

Salvinia auriculata
South America
Trop.–S.Trop.: Aquatic

This species is similar in general appearance to *S. molesta*. It also forms colonies and may be used in ornamental ponds or in aquaria.

Salvinia hastata
Africa, Mascarene Islands
Trop.–S.Trop.: Aquatic

A floating species, similar in general appearance to *S. molesta*, but fertile, with simple hairs on the undersurface of the leaves rather than divided hairs. It is invasive but can be used as an ornamental in small ponds, aquaria etc.

Salvinia molesta Water Spangles/Kariba Weed (Fig. p.70)
Brazil
Trop.–Temp.: Aquatic

A free floating fern which is sterile and is believed to be of hybrid origin. Its effective system of vegetative reproduction is evidenced by the fact that it is now a weed in the tropical parts of many countries. It is widely used in dams, ponds and fish tanks as an ornamental aquatic and refuge for fish.

Salvinia natans Salvinia
Europe, Japan, India
Trop.–S.Trop.: Aquatic

This fern forms a mass of floating material which propagates itself freely by vegetative means. Frequently used in dams and ponds as an ornamental aquatic and also in tropical fish tanks.

40 Tassel ferns and clubmosses

genus *Lycopodium*

These are fern allies which have direct links via fossils to the Carboniferous Period. They are commonly known as Clubmosses (a name shared with Selaginellas) because of the shape of their fruiting body. One group, the Tassel Ferns, is commonly grown in the tropics and in greenhouses and conservatories of temperate regions, however the majority of species are neglected culturally except by ardent enthusiasts.

Habitat

The genus comprises terrestrial species and a unique group of epiphytes that are generally known as Tassel Ferns. The terrestrials grow in a variety of situations. Many species grow in moist infertile soils around the margins of swamps and in depressions. Some form scrambling colonies on earthen banks. A number grow in alpine and sub-alpine regions (some interesting species from South America are bright red).

The epiphytic species grow on trees, rocks, or less commonly, earthen banks. They are found mostly in rainforest or in moist situations in other forests. Many occur at high altitudes on trees covered with mosses and other epiphytes.

Cultivation

Uses

The terrestrial species of *Lycopodium* generally resent disturbance and are slow growing. Many have proved to be difficult to maintain in cultivation.

The Tassel Ferns are, by comparison, easy to grow but have fairly stringent requirements. They make extremely decorative basket plants and are ideal for greenhouses and conservatories. The hardier species can be grown in tropical gardens, on trees or even among large rocks.

Soil Types

The terrestrial species are variable in their requirements. Those from swampy and acidic podsolic soils prefer a sandy loam while the montane types will grow in heavier, but well-drained loams. Most species seem to prefer an acid pH.

Tassel Ferns will not survive in soil but must be grown in an epiphytic potting mix.

Potting Mix

Terrestrial species from swampy or acidic podsolic soils prefer a mixture of sandy loam and peat moss (3–4 parts sandy loam : 1 part peat). Those from montane regions may adapt to a mix based on well-structured loam, peat moss and coarse sand.

Tassel Ferns can be grown in a wide range of materials but the mixture must be free of soil and coarse. Suitable mixtures are well-drained, providing plenty of aeration around the roots and yet retaining moisture for growth. Materials such as tree-fern or osmunda fibre, chunks of pine bark, and charcoal are suitable. Some growers use large *Platycerium* pads as support for the Tassel Ferns or line wire or wooden baskets with pieces of pads before filling with a mixture of other materials. Growers sometimes report damage to Tassel Fern stems from the galvanizing of new wire baskets. If this could be a problem the wire should be allowed to age before use or else, for complete safety, covered to protect the stems.

Watering

The terrestrial species like to be kept continually moist, especially those from swampy ground. Some growers immerse the base of the pot in a shallow container of water.

Tassel Ferns like plenty of water and in the tropics should be watered daily. In temperate regions they must be grown in greenhouses and can receive plenty of water over summer but must be kept on the dry side during winter. Some growers maintain that Tassel Ferns should only be watered in the morning and this practice reduces the incidence of stem and leaf rot. Plants grown in *Platycerium* peat must be watered carefully as this material retains a lot of water (especially large clumps). It also may breakdown after a few years becoming very soggy and making it necessary to report.

Fertilizing

The terrestrial species prefer to grow in a low nutrient medium and do not seem to respond to fertilizers although old, rotted, cow manure may be of some benefit.

Lycopodium carinatum growing in a blister cut from a eucalypt Photo D. L. Jones

Lycopodium cernuum Photo D. L. Jones

Tassel Ferns appreciate applications of weak liquid fertilizer at regular intervals during the summer. Old cow manure placed on the surface of the potting mixture is also beneficial. Some growers use fish emulsion or seaweed extracts with good results.

Situation

Terrestrial species of *Lycopodium* prefer a semi-shady to sunny situation. Tassel Ferns on the other hand must have good light for growth but must be protected from scorching sun. Air movement and humidity are also vital factors for their successful culture. Specialist growers hang those species which like plenty of air movement near the roof of the greenhouse and those which like humidity closer to the floor.

Pests

Terrestrial species may be damaged by slugs, snails, earwigs and sporadic attacks by scale. Tassel Ferns are very subject to persistent attacks by scale particularly fern scale. This pest causes yellowing of the tissue around where it is feeding. Severe attacks may kill individual stems or whole plants (see page 110 for control). Slugs and snails eat the tips out of young shoots.

Propagation

Terrestrial *Lycopodiums* can be divided, but they are generally sensitive to disturbance and once a plant is successfully grown it is best left alone. Some creeping species, (such as *L. cernuum*) can be propagated by layering the tips of the creeping stems.

Tassel Ferns can be propagated by a variety of methods including division, from stem cuttings, or by tip layering (see pages 133 and 138). Tissue culture has also been successfully employed for a couple of species.

SPECIES AND CULTIVARS

Lycopodium billardieri
New Zealand
30–120 cm (12–48 in): Temp.–S.Trop.: Epi.–Terr.

This is possibly best described as a wiry tassel fern that forms open, pendulous clumps which may be slender or quite large. It is an attractive species suitable for basket culture. Likes good light, humidity and air movement.

Lycopodium carinatum Keeled Tassel Fern
India, Malaysia, Polynesia, New Guinea, Australia
30–60 cm (12–24 in) Trop.–S.Trop.: Epi.

A neat tassel fern with leathery, somewhat glaucous leaves. Plants form an open, hanging clump. They are best underpotted in a small container and hung where they receive warmth, humidity and air movement.

Lycopodium cernuum Nodding Clubmoss
Pantropical
creeping Trop.-S.Trop.: Terr.

A colonizing species which forms spreading patches on road verges and embankments in sunny situations. The tips of arching stems commonly take root and give rise to new erect stems. Plants are almost impossible to transplant but the small rooted tips can be established in a pot and then planted out. Needs warm sunny conditions in friable soil.

Lycopodium clavatum Running Pine (Fig. p.50)
North and South America, Asia, Polynesia
creeping Trop.-Temp.: Terr.

A long-creeping clubmoss with wiry, leafy stems that form a tangled, untidy mass. Cones are borne in groups of 2–3 on long, naked stems. Plants can be established from small pieces in pots or infertile soils in a semi-shady situation.

Lycopodium complanatum
North and South America
creeping Trop.-Temp.: Terr.

A clubmoss with long-creeping, leafy stems which root at intervals or even scramble through vegetation. Long, naked stems bear 2–3 fertile cones at the end. Plants resent disturbance and are rather difficult to establish. They need infertile soil in a semi-shady position.

Lycopodium nummularifolium

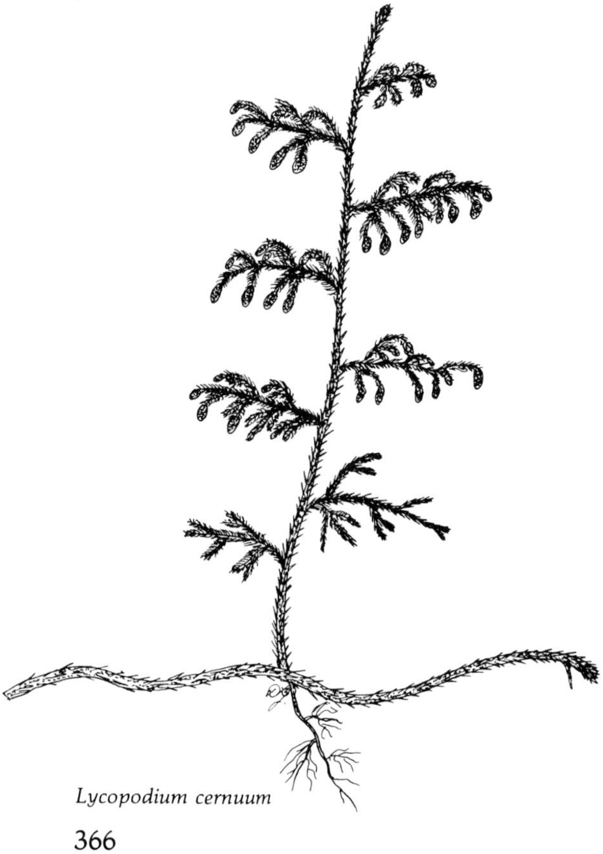

Lycopodium cernuum

Lycopodium dalhousianum Blue Tassel Fern
Australia, New Guinea
30–200 cm (12–80 in) Trop.: Epi.

A long slender tassel fern renowned for its broad, smoky-blue leafy stems which hang vertically. Plants do not branch freely and a large clump is usually quite slender. This is a tricky species to grow and is very tropical in its requirements.

Lycopodium fastigiatum Mountain Clubmoss
Australia, New Zealand
30–120 cm (12–48 in) Temp.: Terr.

A terrestrial clubmoss with subterranean stems and erect, much-branched, aerial growths which are dark green and leafy. Commonly grows in montane regions. Plants resent disturbance and are very slow to re-establish in cultivation. Can be grown in pots of acid, organically-rich soil.

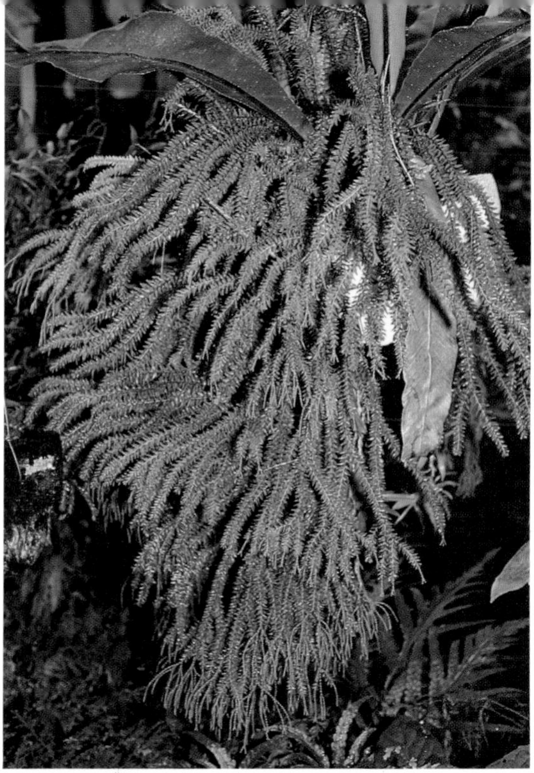

A specimen plant of *Lycopodium phlegmaria*
Photo D. L. Jones

Lycopodium magnificum
Fiji
30–130 cm (12–52 in) Trop.: Epi.
A rare tassel fern which is much like *L. squarrosum* but larger in all its parts. It also is a very beautiful species. Needs warmth, light, humidity and air movement.

Lycopodium myrtifolium (alt. **L. varium**)
Australia, New Zealand
10–30 cm (4–12 in) S.Trop.–Temp.: Epi.
A fairly small or compact tassel fern which has erect or arching fronds. Leaves are a pleasant dark green and a clump is quite decorative. Grows easily in a small pot or basket and needs shade, humidity and air movement.

Lycopodium nummularifolium
Malaysia, Polynesia, New Guinea
30–120 cm (12–48 in) Trop.: Epi.
A widely distributed and fairly common tassel fern with a very distinctive appearance due to its flat, rounded leaves appressed to the stem. Plants have a stiff branching pendulous habit and are most decorative with the long tassels on the ends. Easily grown in a basket in warm, humid, airy conditions.

Lycopodium phlegmaria Common Tassel Fern (Fig. p.50)
Asia, Malaysia, Polynesia, Indonesia, New Guinea, Australia
30–120 cm (12–48 in) Trop.–S.Trop.: Epi.
A very widely distributed and common tassel fern that is frequently grown by fern collectors. It exists in a range of forms. Plants can grow large and bushy and are most decorative. Best grown in hanging pots or baskets. Likes warmth, humidity and air movement.

Lycopodium phlegmarioides Layered Tassel Fern
New Guinea, Australia, New Caledonia
30–120 cm (12–48 in) Trop.–S.Trop.: Epi.
A well grown plant of this tassel fern is most distinctive for the bright green leaves have a shiny appearance as if lacquered. Another decorative feature are the yellowish stems which are prominently visible through the leaves. This is an easily grown species which looks most appealing in a hanging pot or basket.

Lycopodium phyllanthum
Malaysia, Polynesia
20–60 cm (8–24 in) Trop.: Epi.
A robust tassel fern which forms slender, sparsely branched clumps. The stems are very thick and the basal leaves are large, leathery and spreading. Very sensitive to cold. Needs warmth, humidity and air movement.

Lycopodium polytrichoides Rat's-tail Tassel Fern
Australia
30–120 cm (12–48 in) Trop.–S.Trop.: Epi.
A freely branching, tassel fern which forms large, intricate hanging clumps of slender, dark green stems. Plants occur in highland rainforests and adapt well to cultivation in a pot or basket, needing humidity and air movement.

Lycopodium proliferum Square Tassel Fern
Australia, New Guinea
20–60 cm (8–24 in) Trop.–S.Trop.: Epi.
A slender tassel fern of highland rainforests where it grows on mossy trees. Lateral growths take root on contact with the moss and the plants build up in colonies. An easily grown species which needs to be underpotted and held in shady, airy, humid conditions.

Lycopodium selago Fir Clubmoss
North America, New Zealand, Indonesia
10–20 cm (4–8 in) Temp.: Terr.
A stout terrestrial clubmoss of montane regions where it forms small clumps of erect stems each of which resembles a miniature pine tree. Plants resent disturbance and are very slow to re-establish in cultivation. They need shady, humid conditions and acid organically-rich soil.

Lycopodium serpentinum Bog Clubmoss
Australia, New Zealand, New Guinea, Malaysia, Africa, North and South America
creeping Trop.–Temp.: Terr.
A widely distributed species which grows in boggy soils of low fertility. Stems creep, rooting as they grow

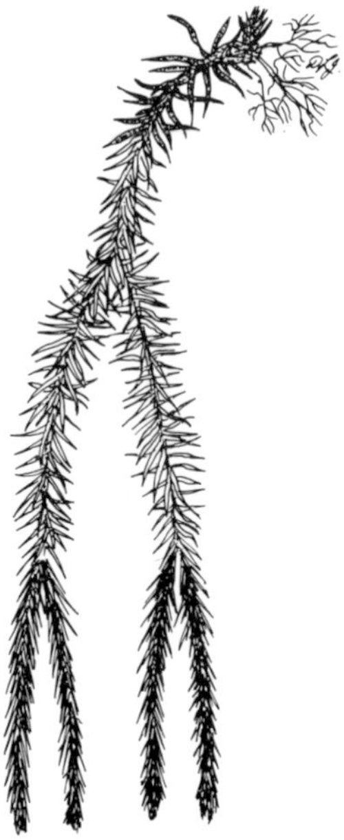

Lycopodium squarrosum

Lycopodium proliferum Photo D. L. Jones

Lycopodium subulatum

and produce small, erect cones. Plants can be grown in a pot of acid, peaty mix but are generally very slow growing. Needs humidity and constant moisture.

Lycopodium squarrosum Rock Tassel Fern
Asia, Polynesia, New Guinea, Australia
30–120 cm (12–48 in) Trop.–S.Trop.: Epi.

This is one of the most beautiful and commonly grown of all tassel ferns. Large specimens are fairly common in conservatories of municipal gardens and are prized for their finely-leaved, pale to yellowish-green, strongly weeping stems. They are easy to grow if given plenty of warmth, light, humidity and air movement.

Lycopodium subulatum
South America
30–100 cm (12–40 in) Trop.: Terr.

A strongly pendant tassel fern which forms large, extensively branched clumps that hang from the trees in rainforest. The basal leaves are large and spreading and they taper in size down the stems. The tassels are long and prominent. Can be grown in a pot or basket and needs warmth, air movement and humidity.

Lycopodium taxifolium
Central and South America, West Indies
20–70 cm (8–28 in) Trop.: Epi.

The leaves on individuals of this tassel fern are variable from 2 cm long to 0.5 cm (1–0.25 in) and may be spreading or closely embrace the stem. The stems are arching or pendulous. Plants can be grown in a pot or basket and need warmth, good light, humidity and air movement.

Lycopodium varium — see **L. myrtifolium**

41 Selaginellas (clubmosses or spikemosses)

genus *Selaginella*

The plants in this genus are fern allies like species of *Lycopodium*, and are not true ferns. They have many primitive characteristics and have links via fossils to the Carboniferous Period. A number of species share the common name of Clubmoss with the genus *Lycopodium*, because of their club-shaped fruiting bodies. Many Selaginellas are very popular with fern enthusiasts and are propagated for sale by nurseries in various countries of the world. Most Selaginellas are easy plants to grow.

Habitat

Selaginellas grow in a wide diversity of climates, soil types and conditions. The majority of species are terrestrials, but a few interesting ones are epiphytes. Selaginellas are mainly found in moist shaded forests usually near water. This is especially true of the group with the creeping growth habit. Those with subterranean stolons and erect, much branched stems are usually prominent in tropical rainforests, e.g. *S. flabellata*. A few interesting species may be climbers in rainforests or moist sites, e.g. *S. wildenovii*. Some hardy Selaginellas grow around the margins of swamps and in acid, podsolic soils or heathland, e.g. *S. uliginosa*. A few occur in sub-alpine conditions. A unique group grows in rocky deserts and survives dry periods by drying and curling their fronds in the manner of true resurrection plants (see also page 6). Some of these curl into balls and are sold as novelty resurrection plants, e.g. *S. lepidophylla*.

Cultivation

Uses

Selaginellas are generally an easy group of plants to grow with the possible exception of some species which are from specialized habitats. These can be difficult to grow. Those creeping species from rainforests and wet, shaded areas adapt very well to cultivation and can be used in pots, terrariums or even hanging baskets. They can also be readily grown under the benches of greenhouses or shadehouses or in shady moist situations in a garden. Some provide an attractive ground cover between ferns or other plants. Many of the tropical species may run rampant in tropical gardens and yet are never a nuisance. Selaginellas blend perfectly into settings using water and rocks. Some species are suitable for indoor decoration.

Soil Types

Selaginellas generally prefer well-drained soils although some can be grown in quite boggy situations. Many of the tropical species definitely prefer organically-rich soils and appreciate mulches on the soil surface. Most species seem to prefer an acid pH.

Potting Mix

Selaginellas are not generally fussy as to their potting mix, however, it must be well-drained and should have a fairly high organic component. An open mix based on a well-structured loam to which has been added peat moss, aged pine bark or fern fibre should provide excellent growth. A very fibrous, non-soil mix as used for epiphytic orchids can also be suitable.

Watering

Selaginellas like plenty of water and humidity. This applies especially to the creeping types. Those with underground stolons tend to be more tolerant of dry periods and they also respond to regular watering.

Fertilizing

Selaginellas respond to the application of fertilizers. Slow-release or liquid fertilizers are beneficial for plants in pots and for those in the ground manures and liquid fertilizers can be used. For Selaginellas light applications at regular intervals are far better than heavy doses. Fertilizers are best applied during the warm, growing months.

Situation

As a general rule, species of Selaginella are adapted to a shady situation but will also tolerate short periods of direct sun or filtered sun, particularly in moist soil. A few tropical species such as *S. uncinata* and *S. wildenovii* take on their best apperance if grown in a

A colourful array of potted Selaginellas in a commercial nursery Photo D. L. Jones

sunny situation. Air movement and humidity are very important for Selaginellas. In wet, still periods where dense mats of foliage may remain wet for several days at a time rotting can occur. This can be common in tropical regions during the wet season and in temperate areas during autumn and winter.

Pests

Selaginellas are not subject to many pests but can be damaged by slugs, snails and earwigs.

Propagation

Selaginellas are very easily propagated by division of the clumps, even small pieces often grow satisfactorily. This is particulary true of the creeping species which form mats and also applies to some of the rosetting types. In *S. pallescens*, for example, small pieces may break off the branches and these take root and grow into separate plants. Division of some of the species that spread by means of an underground stolon is more difficult and must be carried out with care. For some species large sections of the rhizome may be necessary before they will take. Selaginellas can be readily raised from spore, however, most plants are propagated vegetatively.

SPECIES AND CULTIVARS

Selaginella australiensis
Australia
creeping Trop.-Temp.: Terr.

A creeping species which forms a sparse mat of dark green. Stems branch freely and root as they grow. Can be easily established in a moist shady position or grown in containers. Propagates readily from stem pieces.

var. *leptostachya* — a superior variety with prominent long, slender cones that are held erect.

Selaginella braunii
China
15–30 cm (6–12 in) Trop.-Temp.: Terr.

This is a clumping species with erect, branched, somewhat frond-like stems. The leaves are dark green and leathery in texture. Plants are easily grown in a pot or sheltered position in the ground.

Selaginella canaliculata
North India, China, Malaysia, Philippines
50–120 cm (20–48 in) Trop.: Terr.

A tall-growing species which has erect much-branched, frond-like aerial stems and spreads by long-scrambling or creeping stems. The fronds are bright green and attractive. Useful as a pot plant.

Selaginella kraussiana 'Aurea' Photo D. L. Jones

Selaginella cuspidata = S. pallescens

Selaginella emmeliana Sweat Plant
South America
5–12 cm (2–5 in) Trop.–S.Trop.: Terr.
A commonly grown species which forms an upright to spreading rosette. Plants grow readily from small pieces which break off and the species tends to become weedy in suitable conditions. Likes moist soils and bright conditions.

Selaginella flabellata
Central and South America
30–80 cm (12–32 in) Trop.: Terr.
A *Selaginella* of exotic, tropical appearance. Spreads by subterranean stems and bears erect to arching aerial stems that are relatively quite broad, delicately-lobed and a verdant green. The fertile fronds have long, tassel-like clubs on the margins. Makes an attractive pot plant or ground cover for a shady moist position in tropical gardens.

Selaginella helvetica
Europe, China, Japan
creeping Temp.–S.Trop.: Terr.
The trailing stems of this species branch freely and in suitable situations plants quickly form a mat of dark green foliage. It is a useful ground-cover among ferns, under greenhouse benches etc.

Selaginella horizontalis
Mexico, Central America
creeping Trop.–S.Trop.: Terr.
A creeping species with horizontal, freely branching stems which root as they grow. Leaves are bright green and plants form a decorative mat of foliage. Likes moist, shady conditions.

Selaginella involvens
Japan, China, Korea
10–30 cm (4–12 in) S.Trop.–Temp.: Terr.
This species forms erect clumps of flattened, fan-like stems, which have dark green leaves (of two types) arranged in a spiral. Plants look appealing in a pot or when planted in a shady position among rocks. Leaves may curl inwards in dry times.

Selaginella kraussiana Spreading Clubmoss (Fig. p.52)
Africa
creeping Temp.–Trop.: Terr.
This is probably the most commonly grown *Selaginella* in the world and it is valued for its hardiness, adaptability and the dense mat of verdant green foliage that it forms. Plants like moist shady conditions and grow very rapidly even tending to become weedy. A useful ground cover under benches in a fernery or greenhouse. Can also be grown in a pot or basket and is quite useful for indoor decoration. Propagates easily from pieces. A few interesting forms are cultivated.

'Aurea' — a delightful form with golden new growth and yellow-green mature leaves. Makes an excellent contrast to the green form.

'Brownii' (Emerald Isle) — compact much-branched growth habit resulting in dense cushiony mounds of verdant green. Slow spreading and excellent for terrariums.

Selaginella lepidophylla Rose of Jericho/Resurrection Plant
USA (south west), Mexico, El Salvador
8–12 cm (3–5 in) Trop.–S.Trop.: Terr.
A truly remarkable fern-ally which grows in low rainfall areas on dry ledges and around boulders always on the north side. For most of the year plants are a curled ball of brown stems and leaves which are so dry they can be crushed in the hand. After rain however, the stems and leaves open and the leaves re-green so that the plants are transformed to verdant green rosettes. Plants are collected in large numbers and sold as a novelty, useful for forecasting changes in atmospheric moisture. They are very slow growing and should be potted in a well-drained mixture of neutral to alkaline pH.

Selaginella longipinna
Australia, New Guinea
20–50 cm (8–20 in) Trop.–S.Trop.: Terr.
This species forms large colonies in rainforest and frequently colonizes shady earth banks. It spreads by underground stems which bear much-branched aerial stems at intervals. Plants are slow to recover from disturbance but once established grow steadily. A useful ground cover for tropical gardens.

Selaginella martensii
Mexico, Central America
5–15 cm (2–6 in) S.Trop.–Temp.: Terr.

A pleasant species with glossy, verdant green leaves and a neat, clumping growth habit. Widely grown and popular in cultivation. Can be grown in the ground or as a decorative pot subject. Likes shady moist conditions. Several forms are grown.

'Divaricata' — slender form with short leaves.

'Variegata' — odd leaves and patches on the fronds are white.

'Watsoniana' — an upright form with deep green leaves and curled frond tips.

Selaginella martensii 'Variegata' Photo D. L. Jones

Selaginella mollis
Mexico, Central America
10–20 cm (4–8 in) Trop.–S.Trop.: Terr.

A delightful semi-creeping species which has bicoloured leaves which are dark green on the surface and silvery on the underside. They also often have a narrow white marginal band and a wrinkled surface. Stems are prostrate or partially erect and form roots at the base. Plants grow easily in moist, shady conditions.

Selaginella oaxacana
Mexico, Central America
30–90 cm (12–36 in) Trop.–S.Trop.: Terr.

A fairly large species which forms an upright to spreading clump. Leaves are dark green and contrast with the straw-coloured stems. Plants grow easily in a semi-shady situation and like plenty of moisture.

Selaginella pallescens Photo W. R. Elliot

Selaginella pallescens
Mexico, Central and South America
10–25 cm (4–10 in) Trop.–S.Trop.: Terr.

A rosette-forming species with leaves which are a colourful light yellow-green on the surface and silvery on the underside. Stems curl inwards when the plants are dry. A very easily grown species which naturalizes readily from small pieces. Attractive in a small pot or rockery.

Selaginella pilifera
USA (south west), Mexico
8–12 cm (3–5 in) Trop.–S.Trop.: Terr.

This *Selaginella* has similar hygroscopic qualities to the remarkable *S. lepidophylla*. When dry the fronds lose colour and curl inwards until the whole plant is a tight ball. When wet the fronds expand and re-green. Plants are collected from the wild and sold as a novelty item. They are frequently held in saucers of water. Plants are slow growing and should be potted in a mixture of neutral to alkaline reaction.

Selaginella plana
North India, Burma
10–30 cm (4–12 in) Trop.–S.Trop.: Terr.

A largy bushy species with wiry, freely branched

Selaginella willdenovii is a climbing species
Photo D. L. Jones

Selaginella uncinata Photo D. L. Jones

stems. Forms attractive spreading clumps of a greyish green with long, prominent clubs. Grows easily in moist, shady conditions.

Selaginella plumosa
North India, Sri Lanka, Burma, China
creeping S.Trop.–Temp.: Terr.

A creeping species which forms very dense mats of verdant green. Stems branch freely and root as they grow. Cones are held erect and are squat and square in cross-section. Plants are very easily grown in moist, shady conditions, and are readily propagated by division.

Selaginella serpens
West Indies
creeping Trop.: Terr.

A creeping species with long slender stems which root as they grow. Forms a verdant green mat. Easily grown in containers or a shady, moist situation.

Selaginella umbrosa (Fig. p.52)
Mexico, Central and South America
20–40 cm (8–16 in) Trop.: Terr.

A delightful subject with spreading underground stems at intervals. Stems are dark reddish and contrast with the light green leaves. Plants are slow to recover from disturbance but once established grow easily. They like warm, moist conditions and can be grown as a ground cover.

Selaginella uncinata Blue Selaginella/Rainbow Moss
China
mat plant Trop.–S.Trop.: Terr.

This species is valued for its compact mat of attractive bluish foliage. It is a spreading plant that likes moist, warm conditions and develops its best colour in fairly bright light. It can be used as a ground cover among ferns or under the benches in a greenhouse. In suitable conditions plants can be very fast growing.

Selaginella wallacei
North America (north-western states)
10–30 cm (4–12 in) Temp.–S.Trop.: Terr.

This species forms a sprawling clump of slender stems which are densely covered with narrow, pointed leaves. The leaves on the clubs are broader than the sterile leaves on the stems making the clubs quite distinctive. Plants are easily grown in a pot or sheltered position.

Selaginella wallichii
North India, Malaysia, Philippines, New Guinea
30–90 cm (12–36 in) Trop.: Terr.

This species forms colonies in rainforest spreading by long, underground stems. Tall, much-branched aerial stems are borne at intervals and these are frond-like, thick-textured and dark shiny-green. The long, drooping clubs present a tasseled appearance. A beautiful species of exotic appearance. Likes warm, moist, shady conditions.

Selaginella willdenovii Electric Fern
North India, Vietnam, Malaysia
climber Trop.–S.Trop.: Terr.

A spectacular species prized for its spreading fronds which are of a shimmering electric blue colour. It is a climbing or scrambling plant with wiry stems and likes to have its roots in cool, moist soils and its fronds in the sun. In suitable conditions it is an adaptable garden plant.

42 Miscellaneous ferns

Acrostichum aureum
Pantropical
100–400 cm (40–160 in): 1 pinnate Trop.–S.Trop. Terr.

A coarse fern which forms large clumps in wet soils. It is usually familiar in coastal districts and often grows in brackish water behind the mangroves. Large plants generally resent disturbance; small specimens adapt to cultivation readily. They all require bright light and plenty of moisture.

Acrostichum danaeifolium Giant Leather Fern
Florida, Central and South America, West Indies
100–350 cm (40–140 in): 1 pinnate Trop.–S.Trop.: Terr.

This species occurs around the margins of fresh and brackish swamps and springs. It is a very large, coarse fern which is sensitive to cold. Needs bright light and moist to wet conditions.

Acrostichum speciosum Mangrove Fern
India, Malaysia, Philippines, Indonesia, New Guinea, Australia
50–200 cm (20–80 in): 1 pinnate Trop.–S.Trop.: Terr.

A coarse fern which forms clumps in soils inundated by salt water in coastal districts, often growing with mangroves. Plants lack general appeal but are of interest to enthusiasts. They can be grown in a pot with the base immersed in water or in a well-watered garden position.

Actiniopteris semiflabella
Africa, Madagascar, Mauritius, North India
5–20 cm (2–8 in): palmate Trop.–S.Trop.: Terr.

An unusual fern with spreading, segmented fronds which resemble the sterile leaves of *Schizaea dichotoma*. It is a clumping species which grows in rock crevices in dry to arid climates. It is somewhat tricky to grow requiring a coarse open mixture and a fairly small pot. Plants should be watered profusely while they are in growth and sparingly when they are dormant. It is reported to succeed well in conditions similar to those in a terrarium.

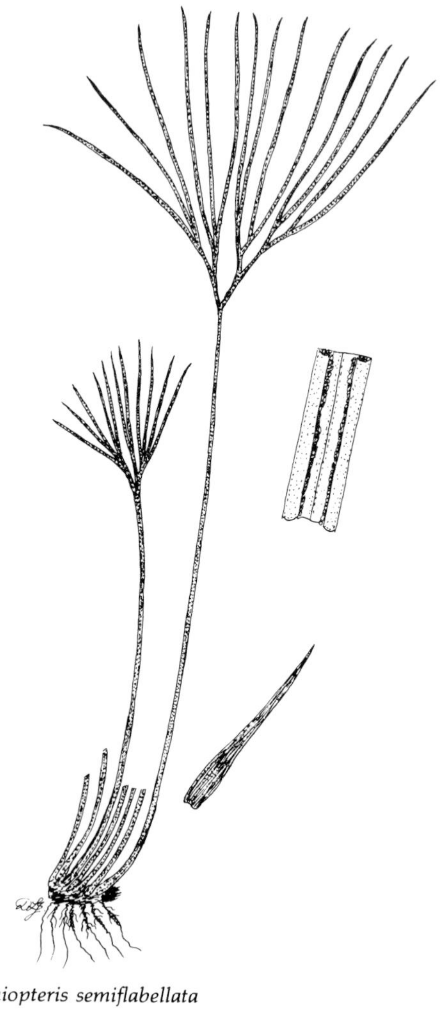

Actiniopteris semiflabellata

Anemia adiantifolia Pine Fern
Florida, Central and South America, West Indies
30–80 cm (12–32 in): 2 pinnate Trop.–S.Trop.: Terr.

In its native state this fern grows in rocky situations frequently in pine forests and sometimes in calcareous soils. The sterile fronds are attractively lobed and resemble those of some maidenhairs. Plants need a freely draining soil of slightly acid to neutral reaction.

A colony of *Acrostichum speciosum* Photo D. L. Jones

Anemia mexicana Flowering Fern
Mexico, Central and South America
30–70 cm (12–28 in): 2 pinnate Trop.–S.Trop.: Terr.
An interesting fern which adapts well to cultivation succeeding in a well-drained potting mix or in the ground in sandy soil. Spores are carried in a panicle-like cluster of sporangia which gives rise to the unusual common name. The sterile segments are attractively divided into broad, shiny segments.

Anemia phyllitidis (Fig. p.64)
Central and South America, West Indies
30–90 cm (12–36 in): 1 pinnate Trop.–S.Trop.: Terr.
This species can be readily recognized by its strongly anastomosing network of veins. The sterile segments have a dully papery texture and a resemblance to the Japanese Holly Fern (*Cyrtomium falcatum*); the fertile segments are very slender. Plants are cold-tender but can be grown in a pot or suitable garden position.

Anissorus hirsutus = Lonchitis hirsuta

Anogramma chaerophylla
Central and South America, West Indies
10–40 cm (4–16 in): 2 pinnate Temp.–S.Trop.: Terr.
A dainty fern with finely divided, light green, fragile fronds. Plants have only a superficial rhizome and consist of 3 or 4 fronds. They grow easily in a small pot needing moist, shady conditions. This species is very easy to raise from spore and sporelings can be quite fast growing. It can be a weed in greenhouses.

Anogramma leptophylla Annual Fern
India, Central and South America, Europe, Africa, Australia, New Zealand
2–20 cm (1–8 in): 2–4 pinnate Temp.–S.Trop.: Terr.
An unusual fern which produces annual fronds and then dies back to a tuberous gametophyte which is perennial. It is a tiny fern often producing fertile fronds only 2–4 cm (1–2 in) long and the whole plant may consist of 3 or 4 fronds. Plants can be grown in a small pot of loamy soil. They should be watered regularly while the fronds are green and more sparingly while the plants are dormant.

Anopteris hexagona
Puerto Rico, West Indies
10–30 cm (4–12 in): 3–4 pinnate Trop.–S.Trop.: Terr.
A profuse little fern which forms clumps on limestone cliffs and rocks and in sink holes. It is a variable species of two subspecies, one with coarse fronds and the other much more finely divided. In cultivation, plants like warm, humid conditions and a coarse, open mixture of neutral to alkaline reaction.

Blotiella lindeniana Tomato Fern
Central and South America, West Indies
30–90 cm (12–36 in): 3 pinnate Trop.–S.Trop.: Terr.
In nature, this fern grows in wet situations. It is a hairy, somewhat fleshy fern with a creeping rhizome. Plants develop readily into clumps and adapt well to cultivation requiring shady conditions, moisture and loamy soil.

Blotiella natalensis
Africa, Comoros Island
50–150 cm (20–60 in): 2–3 pinnate Temp.–S.Trop.: Terr.
This is a large fern with somewhat fleshy, distinctly hairy fronds which are very broad (up to 1 m). Plants grow easily in a shady situation protected from strong winds. They like organically rich, acid soils and plenty of moisture.

Bolbitis cladorrhizans = Bolbitis portoricensis

Bolbitis heteroclita
Japan, India, Malaysia, New Guinea
25–100 cm (10–40 in): 1 pinnate Trop.–S.Trop.: Terr.
A widespread species which exists in a very large range of forms, including sterile juvenile types which may form colonies and perpetuate themselves by vegetative propagation. Some of these forms are

Blotiella lindeniana Photo D. L. Jones

excellent for terrarium culture forming a mat of dark green, moss-like growth. They are easily grown if given shade and plenty of moisture.

Bolbitis portoricensis
Central and South America, West Indies
50–200 cm (20–80 in) Trop.–S.Trop.: Terr.
A fern of wet shady places usually growing on rocks which are sometimes of limestone formation. Fronds have a somewhat spindly appearance with prominent venation. Plants can be grown in a pot or sheltered position and require plenty of moisture.

Bolbitis quoyana
Japan, Philippines, Indonesia, New Guinea, Australia, Polynesia
50–150 cm (20–60 in): 1 pinnate Trop.–S.Trop.: Terr.
A large growing fern with attractively lobed, light to dark green fronds which have a prominent venation. Plants are easily grown in a sheltered, shady location and like an abundance of moisture. Acid, humus-rich soils are particularly suitable.

Bolbitis taylori
Australia
30–90 cm (12–36 in): 1 pinnate Trop.–Temp.: Terr.
When wet the fronds of this fern take on an appealing translucent look. It is an excellent species for a fernery revelling in dark, moist surroundings and quickly developing into an attractive clump. Can be grown in a container or in humus-rich soil in the ground.

Christella dentata (alt. **Thelypteris nymphalis**)
Malaysia, Asia, Philippines, New Guinea, Polynesia, Australia, New Zealand
30–90 cm (12–36 in): 1 pinnate Trop.–Temp.: Terr.
Although a weedy fern, this species has some value because of its adaptability and hardiness. It forms an appealing rosette of graceful fronds which vary from yellowish to dark green. Grows easily in a wide variety of soils (from acid to alkaline) and situations (from shade to full sun). Likes plenty of water. Sporelings commonly appear in any suitable position.

Christella parasitica (alt. **Thelypteris parasitica**)
Africa (east), Asia, Polynesia, New Guinea, Australia
30–50 cm (12–20 in): 1 pinnate Trop.–Temp.: Terr.
Another weedy fern with similar comments as for *C. dentata* (q.v.). Its fronds are generally more erect than that species and are softer. Likes plenty of water.

Coniogramme fraxinea
Asia, Philippines, Fiji, Samoa
60–120 cm (24–48 in): 1–2 pinnate Trop.–S.Trop.: Terr.
A widely distributed species which develops a clump of erect fronds from a shortly creeping rhizome. The lower 2–4 pairs of pinnae are often themselves pinnate. A handsome species, suitable for a container or shady position.

Coniogramme intermedia Photo D. L. Jones

Coniogramme intermedia

Coniogramme japonica Photo D. L. Jones

Coniogramme intermedia
Japan, China, Korea, North India
50–100 cm (20–40 in): 1–2 pinnate Temp.–S.Trop.: Terr.

An attractive fern with dark green, leathery textured fronds which grow in a compact clump. It is an excellent garden fern for a moist, semi-shady to shady position, favouring acid, humus-rich loams. Can also be successful in a container.

Coniogramme japonica Bamboo Fern
Japan, China, South Korea, Taiwan
60–120 cm (24–48 in): 1 pinnate Temp.–S.Trop.: Terr.

A deservedly popular fern valued for its clumping habit and broadly-segmented pale green fronds. Plants can be grown in a pot or rockery. They are very slow growing and like well-drained, humus-rich soil and continual moisture. Plants are generally slow but steady growers and have a dormant period during late winter. A form with a yellow band down the centre of each pinna is also available.

A clump of *Cyclosorus interruptus* Photo D. L. Jones

The glossy fronds of *Didymochlaena truncatula*
Photo D. L. Jones

Cryptogramma crispa Parsley Fern
Europe, Asia Minor, Afghanistan
5–20 cm (2–8 in): 1 pinnate Temp.: Terr.

A lime-hating fern which will only grow in acid soils that have not been dressed with lime or dolomite. Likes fairly bright light and good drainage. A suitable potting mix can be made up of coarse sand, leaf mould and peat moss.

Ctenitis sloanei Florida Tree Fern
Florida, Central and South America, West Indies
100–200 cm (40–80 in): 3 pinnate Trop.–S.Trop.: Terr.

Although not a true tree fern, plants of this species form a short trunk about 5 cm across, the apex of which is clothed with tangled, woolly, reddish scales. The fronds are finely-dissected, thin-textured and usually have yellowish-green hues. Plants can be grown in a shady situation and like humus-rich soil. They are particularly sensitive to drying out, rarely recovering from such an occurrence.

Cyclosorus dentatus=Christella dentata

Cyclosorus interruptus
India, Sri Lanka, Indochina, Malaysia, New Guinea, Australia
60–120 cm (24–48 in): 1 pinnate Trop.–Temp.: Terr.

A widely distributed, rather coarse fern which grows in colonies in moist to wet soils. Plants lack wide appeal but they are generally hardy, easy to grow and can be useful for landscaping. They will grow in sunny situations and require plenty of moisture.

Cyclosorus nymphalis = Christella dentata

Cyclosorus parasiticus = Christella parasitica

Didymochlaena truncatula Tree Maidenhair Fern
South America, Africa, Madagascar, India, Malaysia, New Guinea, Fiji
60–120 cm (24–48 in): 2–3 pinnate Trop.–S.Trop.: Terr.

A widely distributed fern which is a firm favourite among fern growers. It is prized for its lustrous green fronds which have a graceful symmetry. When young they are often tinted bright rosy pink or red. Old plants develop a short, thick trunk. This fern makes an attractive container specimen and performs very well indoors. In the ground it likes a shady situation and appreciates regular watering, mulching and dressings of organic fertilizers or manures.

The beautiful symmetrical fronds of *Dipteris conjugata*
Photo D. L. Jones

Dipteris conjugata
Indochina, China, Malaysia, New Guinea, New Caledonia, Australia
100–200 cm (40–80 in): palmate Trop.–S.Trop.: Terr.

A widely distributed fern which colonizes clearings, embankments, road verges etc. It is a spectacular species with its large, symmetrically divided fronds of an unusual shape. Plants can be somewhat tricky to establish and once growing are best left undisturbed. They like fairly bright light in well-drained acid soil.

Elaphoglossum callifolium
Malaysia, Philippines, Indonesia, New Guinea, Australia
15–50 cm (6–20 in): entire Trop.–S.Trop.: Epi.

A coarse fern which grows on tree trunks and rocks in moist, shady rainforests. Plants are fairly easily grown in a pot of coarse, open mixture. They prefer to be underpotted and require shady, humid conditions.

Elaphoglossum crinitum Elephant Ear Fern
South America, West Indies
20–50 cm (8–20 in): entire Trop.: Epi.

An intriguing fern with broad, simple, scaly fronds. The scales are black and are particularly noticeable on the stipes and young, unrolling fronds. It is a difficult fern to grow being very sensitive to desiccation and requiring almost constantly high humidity. Some growers keep plants under intermittent mist.

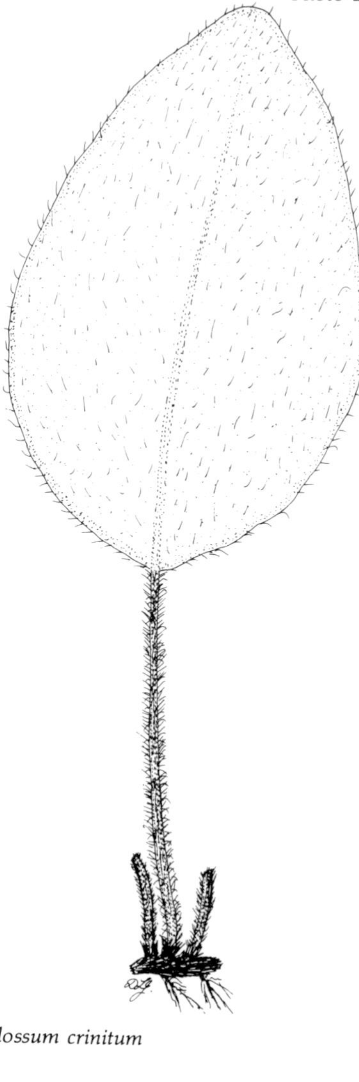

Elaphoglossum crinitum

Equisetum scirpoides Dwarf Scouring Rush
Europe, North America (northern states), Asia
creeping Temp.–S.Trop.: Terr.

A dwarf fern ally which forms a clump of twisted, tangled, dark green stems. Easily grown in wet soil in a sunny situation. Also makes an interesting pot subject.

Elaphoglossum callifolium Photo D. L. Jones

Fertile and sterile fronds of *Lygodium japonicum* Photo D. L. Jones

Gymnocarpium dryopteris Oak Fern
North America, Europe, India, China, Japan
20–50 cm (8–20 in): 3 pinnate Temp.–S.Trop.: Terr.
A useful fern for a shady aspect where it will form a clump, spreading by its slender, underground rhizomes. The fronds are fairly widely spaced but are broad, a delicate green and attractively divided. Plants thrive in an organically rich soil and must not be allowed to dry out. In very cold climates they may be deciduous.

'Plumosa' – a form with fuller, foliose fronds due to broader segments.

Gymnocarpium robertianum Limestone Oak Fern
Europe, North America (northern states)
20–45 cm (8–18 in): 3 pinnate Temp.: Terr.
An attractive fern with triangular fronds arising at intervals from a slender, creeping rhizome. Useful as a ground cover in shady situations. Plants need very well-drained soil and the addition of lime.

Gymnogramme japonicum = Coniogramme japonica

Gymnogramme javanica = Coniogramme fraxinea

Gymnogramme vestita = Gymnopteris vestita

Llavea cordifolia
Central America
30–50 cm (12–20 in): pinnate Temp.–S.Trop.: Terr.
A distinct fern of exposed rocky situations often on those of limestone origin. The fronds are an attractive lime-green and are frequently glaucous on the underside. The spores are borne on long, finger-like segments on the ends of mature fronds. Plants grow easily but have a winter dormant period when they should be kept on the dry side. An open mix of neutral to alkaline reaction is necessary.

Lonchitis hirsuta
Central and South America, West Indies
200–300 cm (80–120 in): 2 pinnate Trop.–S.Trop.: Terr.
A fleshy fern of wet forests, growing near streams and often where it is bathed by the spray of waterfalls. Plants are very cold-tender and sensitive to dryness. They need a sheltered, shady situation and must be kept moist especially during hot, dry weather.

Lygodium circinnatum
Northern India, Sri Lanka, China, Indochina, New Hebrides
climber: palmate Trop.–S.Trop.: Terr.
A strongly climbing fern which grows in wet soils and climbs to about 10 m (33 ft) tall. It is suitable for planting in a tropical garden requiring warmth and plenty of moisture. Can also be grown in a pot but is sensitive to drying of the roots.

Lygodium flexuosum
India, China, Sri Lanka, Malaysia, New Guinea, Australia
climber: 1 pinnate Trop.–S.Trop.: Terr.
A vigorous climbing fern which in nature may form thickets along the margins of forests and often in swampy areas. Plants can be grown easily but because of their vigour, should be planted in the ground and trained on trees, trellises etc.

Lygodium japonicum
India, China, Japan, Indochina, Malaysia, New Guinea, Australia
climber: 2 pinnate Trop.–S.Trop.: Terr.
A handsome climbing fern with quite large, attractively divided fronds. In nature it occurs in districts which are reasonably dry and the plants die back to a perennial root system. Can be grown in a pot or basket in a warm garden position.

Lygodium microphyllum Climbing Maidenhair (Fig. p.64)
Africa, India, Hong Kong, Malaysia, New Guinea, Australia
climber: 1 pinnate Trop.-Temp.: Terr.
A widely distributed climbing fern which frequently forms thickets in open, swampy situations. Plants adapt readily to cultivation and will succeed in pots, baskets or in a semi-shady garden position. Because of their rampant climbing habit they need regular trimming.

Lygodium palmatum Hartford Fern
North America (eastern and south-eastern states)
climber: palmate Temp.-S.Trop.: Terr.
The sterile leaves of this species are palmately lobed and spread from climbing stems in a most attractive manner. By contrast, the fertile fronds have greatly contracted segments. The species can be grown in a pot or even a basket but prefers a partially shady situation in the ground. It is a lime-hater and must be grown only in acid soil.

Lygodium scandens = L. microphyllum

Macrothelypteris polypodioides (alt. **Thelypteris polypodioides**)
South-East Asia, Malaysia, Philippines, New Guinea, Australia
90–150 cm (36–60 in): 3 pinnate Trop.-S.Trop.: Terr.
An attractive fern with finely divided, lacy, dark green, deltoid fronds which have crowded segments. Croziers are densely covered with a mixture of white scales and hairs. Easily grown in similar conditions to *M. torresiana* but much more cold-sensitive.

Macrothelypteris torresiana (alt. **Thelypteris torresiana**)
Asia, Malaysia, Polynesia, North America, Africa, Australia
60–120 cm (30–48 in): 3–4 pinnate Trop.-Temp.: Terr.
This is a fast growing fern with lacy, light green umbragenous fronds, useful for sheltering smaller ferns. Plants favour bright light, and in moist soil will tolerate full sun. Fronds are brittle and readily damaged by wind. May naturalize in suitable conditions.

Oeontrichia tripinnata
Australia
15–25 cm (6–10 in): 3 pinnate Trop.-Temp.: Terr.
A very beautiful fern which develops clumps of finely divided, dark green, lacy fronds. All parts are covered with soft, white hairs. In nature it grows on rocks in moist, shady gullies at high altitudes. Plants need cool, shady conditions in a small pot of organically-rich mix. Given these conditions they grow easily.

Macrothelypteris polypodioides Photo D. L. Jones

Oenotrichia tripinnata

The unusual Stilt Fern, *Oleandra neriiformis*
Photo D. L. Jones

Onoclea sensibilis used as a border for a path
Photo W. R. Elliot

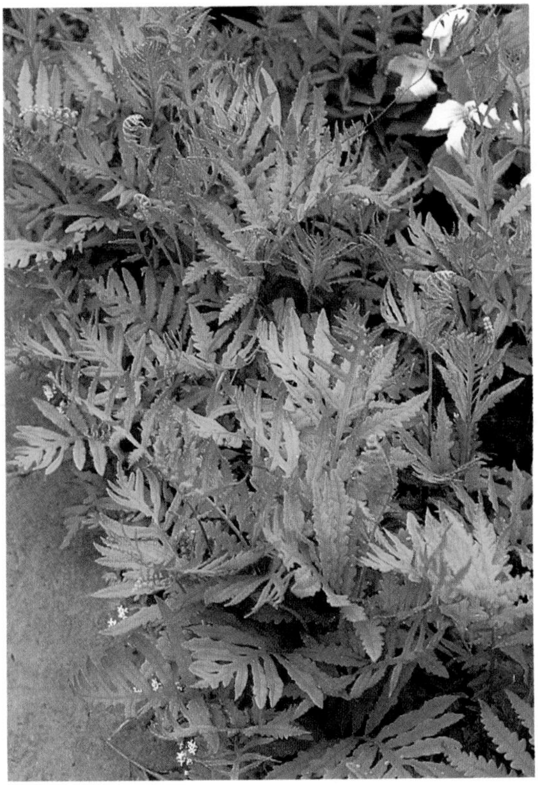

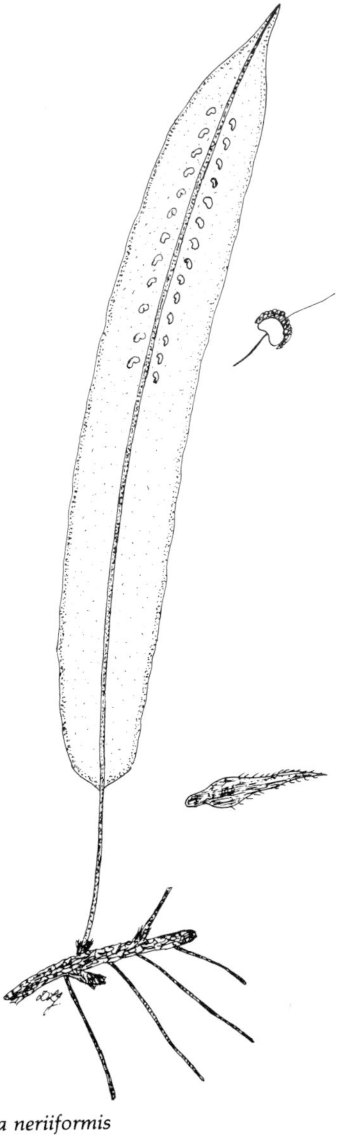

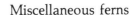

Oleandra neriiformis

Oleandra neriiformis Stilt Fern
Philippines, New Guinea, Australia
15–40 cm (6–16 in): entire Trop.–S.Trop.: Epi.

An unusual fern with exposed rhizomes supported by long, stilt-like roots and pale green, simple fronds. The rhizomes are covered by scales in an attractive pattern. Makes a very decorative basket plant and can also be grown on a tree-fern slab. Likes good light, warmth and humidity.

Onoclea sensibilis Sensitive Fern
North America, North Asia
30–60 cm (12–24 in): 1–2 pinnate Temp.–S.Trop.: Terr.

A coarse, weedy fern commonly found in wet soils

Onychium japonicum

where it may form spreading colonies. The fronds are markedly dimorphic with the fertile ones being reduced to small grape-like clusters of sporangia. Plants grow very easily in a pot or moist garden situation. In cold climates the fronds may be deciduous especially after frosts. In wet soils the plants will stand considerable exposure to sun. A form with prominent red stipes and rachises is in cultivation.

Onychium japonicum Carrot Fern
North India, Thailand, Japan, China
10–45 cm (4–18 in): 3 pinnate Temp.–S.Trop.: Terr.
A weedy fern of misleading, delicate appearance. It commonly naturalizes other pots and is remarkably fast growing. Although it grows easily, plants are often difficult to maintain in good condition. The fronds are finely divided, lacy and are usually dark green. Requires bright light and humidity.

Onychium strictum = Anopteris hexagona

Oreopteris limbosperma (alt. **Thelypteris limbosperma**) Mountain Fern
Europe, North America
30–120 cm (12–48 in): 1 pinnate Temp.–S.Trop.: Terr.
A vigorous fern which forms dense clumps of upright pale green to yellowish fronds. Plants are deciduous in cold climates. Requires acid loamy soils in a shady situation. A lime-hater.

Parathelypteris glanduligera (alt. **Thelypteris glanduligera**)
North India, China, Japan, Korea
30–60 cm (12–24 in): 1 pinnate Temp.–S.Trop.: Terr.
A fern of moist shady forests. Slender fronds arise at intervals from a long-creeping rhizome. Requires acid loamy soils in a shady situation.

Parathelypteris noveboracensis (alt. **Thelypteris noveboracensis**) New York Fern
North America
30–60 cm (12–24 in): 1 pinnate Temp.: Terr.
This species has erect lanceolate fronds which are produced at intervals from a long-creeping rhizome. It is an easily grown fern in a shady position in acid soil.

Phegopteris connectilis (alt. **Thelypteris phegopteris**) Beech Fern
Europe, North America (northern states), Asia
20–50 cm (8–20 in): 1–2 pinnate Temp.: Terr.
A fern of shady forests, forming clumps by its long-creeping, slender rhizomes. Fronds are pale green and thinly-textured. Plants are easily grown in humus-rich soil in a shady location.

Phegopteris hexagonoptera (alt. **Thelypteris hexagonoptera**) Southern Beech Fern
North America (northern states)
45–60 cm (18–24 in): 1–2 pinnate Temp.: Terr.
Similar to *P. connectilis*, but with broader fronds and the basal pair of pinnae spreading, not downcurved. Easily grown in humus-rich soil in a shady location.

Photinopteris speciosa
India, China, Indochina, Malaysia, Indonesia, Philippines
50–100 cm (20–40 in): 1 pinnate Trop.–S.Trop.: Terr.
A curious species which at first glance has little resemblance to a fern. Plants have a long-creeping rhizome which turns prominently white as it becomes older. The fronds are held erect and are leathery. Plants can be grown readily in warm conditions and need bright light.

Pityrogramma argentea Curly Gold Fern
Africa, Madagascar, Mascarene Island
15–25 cm (6–10 in): 2 pinnate Trop.–S.Trop.: Terr.
An attractive species of gold fern which has willowy fronds the segments of which tend to curl upwards at the edges. It looks very decorative when grown in a pot and may even be suitable for a basket. Needs good drainage and bright light.

Pityrogramma calomelanos Silver Fern
Florida, Central and South America, West Indies
15–45 cm (6–18 in): 2–3 pinnate Trop.–S.Trop.: Terr.
Although this is a highly ornamental fern, it exhibits a tremendous ability to naturalize suitable sites and

A clump of the Gold Fern *Pityrogramma calomelanos* var. *austroamericana* Photo D. L. Jones

Pneumatopteris sogerensis Photo D. L. Jones

become weedy. It has done this in many tropical countries and is now a familiar weed. It commonly colonizes harsh sites such as scree slopes and mine tailings but is also found in more favourable situations along embankments and in plantations. Plants can be cultivated readily but do not respond to coddling or excessively shady, moist conditions. A well-drained soil exposed to some sun is usually suitable. This is an extremely variable fern with three distinct varieties.

Pityrogramma chrysophylla

var. *calomelanos* — fronds usually have silvery-white powder on the underside, but this may be pale yellow or pink.

var. *austroamericana* — fronds with bright yellow to orange powder on the underside.

var. *ochracea* — fronds hairy on the underside, lacking any waxy powder.

Pityrogramma chrysophylla
Puerto Rico, West Indies
10–40 cm (4–16 in): 2 pinnate Trop.-S.Trop.: Terr.
An attractive fern which has become naturalized on Samoa. The underside of each frond is covered with a waxy powder which may be white, grey or pale yellow. Can be grown easily in a container or a sunny position in well-drained soil.

Pityrogramma triangularis Gold Back Fern
North America
15–45 cm (6–18 in): 2 pinnate Temp.-S.Trop.: Terr.
A distinctive species of gold back fern with triangular fronds borne on long stipes. The underside of the fronds is usually covered with gold powder but a silver variant is known (var. *pallida*). This species likes more shade then most other members of the genus. Drainage must be free and unimpeded.

Pneumatopteris sogerensis
New Guinea, Solomon Islands, Australia
60–150 cm (24–60 in): 1 pinnate Trop.-Temp.: Terr.
A graceful fern which forms clumps of arching light

green fronds. In nature plants always grow in wet soils usually in sheltered locations. In cultivation plants are adaptable to a protected position in well mulched soil.

Psilotum complanatum Flat Fork Fern
South America, Malaysia, Philippines, Indonesia, New Guinea, Australia
20–80 cm (8–32 in): forked Trop.–S.Trop.: Epi.
A delicate species with hanging, much branched flattened stems. It commonly grows in the clumps of *Platycerium* species with the stems spreading through the peat. It is unexcelled as a basket plant and with patience can be developed into a large specimen. Plants generally resent disturbance.

Psilotum nudum Fork Fern/Whisk Fern (Fig. p.45)
Cosmopolitan
20–80 cm (8–32 in): forked Trop.–Temp.: Epi.–Terr.
A very widely distributed species which commonly grows as an epiphyte but also favours crevices in rocks and may even grow as a terrestrial in sandy soil. Plants can be grown easily in a pot of fibrous mixture and can be an attractive basket specimen. Sporelings commonly volunteer in suitable situations.

Psilotum triquetrum = P. nudum

Stenochlaena palustris Climbing Swamp Fern
India, Malaysia, New Guinea, Australia, Polynesia
climber: 1 pinnate Trop.–S.Trop.: Terr.
A vigorous climber which in nature grows in swampy situations, frequently forming tangled thickets. Surprisingly, it has much to offer horticulture as it makes a very decorative basket plant and also succeeds well indoors. In tropical regions it can be grown as a ground cover with the rhizomes creeping over the ground and the fronds arching upwards. Plants like bright light and plenty of moisture.

Stenochlaena tenuifolia Vine Fern
Asia
climber: pinnate Trop.–S.Trop.: Terr.
A vigorous fern with slender green rhizomes and strongly dimorphic fronds to 90 cm (36 in) long. Plants can climb trees, covering them with a mass of foliage, or clamber over the ground in between. They can be used as a ground cover in tropical regions and also make an attractive basket plant.

Syngramme vestita = Gymnopteris vestita

Thelypteris dryopteris = Gymnocarpium dryopteris

Thelypteris glanduligera – see **Parathelypteris glanduligera**

Thelypteris hexagonoptera – see **Phegopteris hexagonoptera**

Thelypteris limbosperma – see **Oreopteris limbosperma**

A curtain of fronds of *Vittaria elongata*
Photo D. L. Jones

Thelypteris noveboracensis – see **Parathelypteris noveboracensis**

Thelypteris nymphalis – see **Christella dentata**

Thelypteris oreopteris = Oreopteris limbosperma

Thelypteris palustris Marsh Fern
Europe, North America
45–120 cm (18–48 in): 1–2 pinnate Temp.–S.Trop.: Terr.
A fern of wet situations, forming colonies by slender, much-branched, long-creeping rhizomes. Light green fronds are borne at intervals. Plants are easily grown in a lime-free soil with plenty of moisture. May be invasive.

Thelypteris parasitica – see **Christella parasitica**

Thelypteris phegopteris – see **Phegopteris connectilis**

Thelypteris polypodioides – see **Macrothelypteris polypodioides**

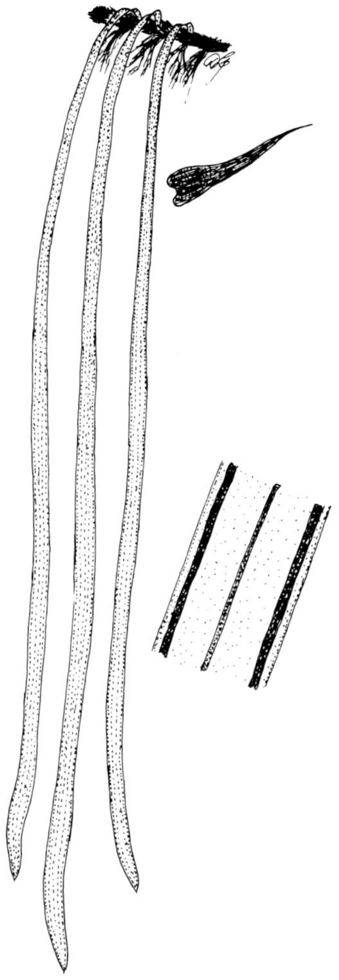

Vittaria scolopendrina

Thelypteris robertianum = Gymnocarpium robertianum

Thelypteris thelypteroides = Thelypteris palustris

Thelypteris torresiana – see **Macrothelypteris torresiana**

Vittaria elongata Ribbon Fern
Africa, India, Malaysia, Philippines, Indonesia, New Guinea, Polynesia, Australia
20–80 cm (8–32 in): entire Trop.–S.Trop.: Epi.

A widely distributed fern which commonly grows on trees and rocks in moist rainforests. It may grow into large clumps and looks attractive with its long, pendulous, simple green fronds. Can be grown in containers or baskets of fibrous mixture. Plants need shade, humidity and air movement.

Vittaria ensiformis
Africa, Malaysia, Philippines, Indonesia, New Guinea, Australia
15–40 cm (6–16 in): entire Trop.–S.Trop.: Epi.

A slender fern with fairly thickly-textured, almost wiry fronds which may be arching or hanging. Commonly grows on rocks or trees. Plants can be grown in a pot or on a slab of tree fern. They like shady, humid conditions with air movement.

Vittaria lineata Shoestring Fern
Florida, Central and South America, West Indies
20–100 cm (8–40 in): entire Trop.–S.Trop.: Epi.

A clumping fern with very narrow, deep green, hanging fronds. It grows as an epiphyte frequently on palm trunks, or on rocks. Can be grown in a pot or basket in warm, humid conditions. Plants resent disturbance.

Vittaria scolopendrina
Madagascar, Malaysia, Philippines, Polynesia
40–90 cm (16–36 in): entire Trop.: Epi.

A species of lowland jungles and swamps, often growing on trees in humid situations near water. It has dark green pendant fronds which are much broader than in most other species (to 2.5 cm [1 in] wide) and with a prominent mid vein. Can be grown in a pot or basket of fibrous mix.

Part Seven

Lists of Ferns for Various Purposes: Supplementary Information

Appendix 1

Ferns Suitable for Indoor Decoration

Species	*Region*	*Light Tolerance*	*Comments*
Adiantum capillus-veneris	Temp.–Trop.	bright	can be tricky
'Banksianum'	Temp.–Trop.	bright	excellent indoors
'Fimbriatum'	Temp.–Trop.	bright	deeply cut fronds
'Imbricatum'	Temp.–Trop.	bright	cascading fronds
'Scintilla'	Temp.–Trop.	bright	shallow pot
Adiantum raddianum	Temp.–Trop.	bright	an adaptable species
'Elegans'	Temp.–S.Trop.	bright	hardy
'Fragrantissimum'	Temp.–S.Trop.	bright	vigorous grower
'Fritz Luth'	Temp.–S.Trop.	bright	very popular
'Gracillimum'	Temp.–S.Trop.	bright	finely divided fronds
'Lawsonianum'	Temp.–Trop.	bright	hardy
'Pacific Maid'	S.Trop.–Trop.	bright	best in tropics
'Weigandii'	Temp.–S.Trop.	bright	hardy
Adiantum tenerum	Trop.	bright	good in tropics
'Fergusonii'	Trop.	bright	strong grower
'Gloriosum Roseum'	Trop.	bright	attractive fern
'Scutum Roseum'	Trop.	bright	pink new growth
Asplenium australasicum	Temp.–S.Trop.	bright	grows large, hardy
bulbiferum	Temp.–S.Trop.	dull–bright	very adaptable
cymbifolium	Trop.	bright	grows large
daucifolium	Temp.–Trop.	dull–bright	very adaptable
dimorphum	Temp.–Trop.	dull–bright	very adaptable
musifolium	Trop.	bright	grows large
nidus	Trop.	bright	grows large
oblongifolium	Temp.–S.Trop.	dull–bright	hardy
laserpitifolium	Trop.	bright	difficult subject
shuttleworthianum	Temp.–S.Trop.	dull–bright	very adaptable
simplicifrons	Temp.–Trop.	dull–bright	very adaptable
Blechnum articulatum	Temp.–S.Trop.	dull–bright	adaptable
brasiliense	S.Trop.–Trop.	bright	hardy and adaptable
gibbum	Temp.–Trop.	bright	very attractive
moorei	S.Trop.–Trop.	bright	seems hardy
occidentale	S.Trop.–Trop.	bright	colourful new growth
Cyrtomium caryotideum	Temp.–Trop.	bright	attractive
falcatum and cvs.	Temp.–Trop.	dull–bright	hardy and adaptable
macrophyllum	S.Trop.–Trop.	bright	adaptable
Davallia bullata	Temp.–S.Trop.	dull–bright	very hardy
fejeensis	S.Trop.–Trop.	bright	beautiful
mariesii	Temp.–S.Trop.	dull–bright	very hardy
solida	S.Trop.–Trop.	bright	adaptable
trichomanoides	Temp.–S.Trop.	dull–bright	very hardy
Dicksonia antarctica	Temp.–S.Trop.	dull–bright	very hardy
Didymochlaena truncatula	S.Trop.–Trop.	dull–bright	hardy and adaptable
Doryopteris pedata	Trop.–Temp.	bright	can be difficult
Drynaria quercifolia	Trop.–Temp.	bright	hardy

Species	*Region*	*Light Tolerance*	*Comments*
Dryopteris affinis	Temp.-S.Trop.	dull-bright	hardy
filix-mas	Temp.-S.Trop.	dull-bright	hardy
Goniophlebium persicifolium	Trop.-S.Trop.	bright	adaptable
subauriculatum	Trop.-Temp.	bright	hardy
verrucosum	Trop.-S.Trop.	bright	difficult
Humata griffithiana	S.Trop.-Temp.	bright	hardy, deciduous
tyermanii	S.Trop.-Temp.	bright	very attractive
Llavea cordifolia	Temp.-S.Trop.	dull-bright	hardy
Lycopodium phlegmaria	Trop.-S.Trop.	bright	difficult
phlegmaroides	Trop.-S.Trop.	bright	difficult
squarrosum	Trop.-S.Trop.	bright	difficult
Lygodium flexuosum	Trop.-S.Trop.	bright	hardy
japonicum	Trop.-S.Trop.	bright	hardy
microphyllum	Trop.-Temp.	bright	hardy
Macrothelypteris polypodioides	Trop.-S.Trop.	bright	attractive
Microlepia strigosa and cvs	Trop.-Temp.	dull-bright	attractive
Microsorum punctatum and cvs	Trop.-S.Trop.	bright	very hardy
Nephrolepis biserrata	Trop.-S.Trop.	dull-bright	grows large
cordifolia and cvs	Temp.-Trop.	dull-bright	very hardy and adaptable
exaltata and cvs	Trop.-Temp.	dull-bright	hardy
falcata 'Furcans'	Trop.-S.Trop.	bright	decorative
Onoclea sensibilis	Temp.-S.Trop.	bright	pale colour
Pellaea falcata	Temp.-S.Trop.	bright	hardy
rotundifolia	Temp.-S.Trop.	bright	very rewarding
viridis	Temp.-S.Trop.	bright	difficult
Phlebodium aureum and cvs	Trop.-Temp.	bright	hardy
Phymatosorus parksii	Trop.-Temp.	dull-bright	hardy
Polypodium australe and cvs	Temp.-S.Trop.	bright	hardy
formosanum	Temp.-S.Trop.	bright	popular
vulgare and cvs	Temp.-S.Trop.	bright	hardy
Polystichum lentum	Temp.-S.Trop.	bright	spreading habit
retroso-paleaceum	Temp.-S.Trop.	bright	shiny fronds
tsus-simense	Temp.-S.Trop.	bright	upright tussock
Pteris cretica and cvs	Temp.-S.Trop.	bright	colourful and interesting
ensiformis and cvs	Trop.-Temp.	bright	compact
tremula	Temp.-S.Trop.	bright	light green fronds
Pyrrosia confluens	S.Trop.-Temp.	dull-bright	hardy
longifolia	Trop.-S.Trop.	bright	cold sensitive
rupestris	S.Trop.-Temp.	dull-bright	hardy
serpens	Temp.-S.Trop.	dull-bright	hardy
Rumohra adiantiformis	Temp.-S.Trop.	dull-bright	very hardy
Sadleria cyatheoides	Trop.-Temp.	bright	very decorative
Scyphularia pentaphylla	Trop.-Temp.	dull-bright	coarse mix
pycnocarpa	Trop.-S.Trop.	dull-bright	coarse mix
Selaginella kraussiana	Temp.-S.Trop.	dull-bright	spreading
Stenochlaena palustris	Trop.-S.Trop.	dull-bright	adaptable
Tectaria heracleifolia	Trop.-S.Trop.	bright	interesting subject
Woodwardia orientalis	S.Trop.-Temp.	bright	large
radicans	S.Trop.-Temp.	bright	large

Appendix 2

Ferns Suitable for Terrariums

The following species are small enough for cultivation in terrariums. Those suitable only for larger terrariums are marked with an asterisk. The list includes creeping ferns as well as those with a clumping growth habit. Some ferns dislike excessive humidity but will succeed well in a drier terrarium. These are indicated under comments.

Species	*Region*	*Comments*
Actiniopteris semiflabella	Trop.–S.Trop.	excellent
*Adiantum capillus-veneris**	Trop.–Temp.	needs lime
diaphanum	Trop.–Temp.	excellent, spreading habit
*hispidulum**	Trop.–Temp.	performs well
*raddianum** and cvs	Trop.–Temp.	smaller growing cultivars
reniforme	Temp.–S.Trop.	likes dry atmosphere best
Anarthropteris lanceolata	Temp.–S.Trop.	spreading habit
Anogramma chaerophylla	Trop.–Temp.	fast growing, may naturalize
leptophylla	S.Trop.–Temp.	likes drier atmosphere
*Asplenium adiantum-nigrum**	Temp.–S.Trop.	performs well
alternans	Trop.–S.Trop.	drier atmosphere, alkaline mix
attenuatum	S.Trop.–Temp.	likes drier atmosphere
aureum	Temp.–S.Trop.	clumping
capillipes	S.Trop.–Temp.	small clump
cardiophyllum	S.Trop.–Temp.	tiny creeping species
ceterach	Temp.	drier atmosphere, alkaline mix
cheilosorum	S.Trop.–Temp.	creeping habit
flabellifolium	Temp.–S.Trop.	spreading habit
*formosum**	S.Trop.–Temp.	clumping
hookerianum	Temp.–S.Trop.	delicate fronds
normale	Trop.–Temp.	clumping
oligophlebium	S.Trop.–Temp.	clumping
pekinense	S.Trop.–Temp.	small clumps
prolongatum	S.Trop.–Temp.	tip rooting
rhizophyllum	Temp.–S.Trop.	needs lime, tip rooting
ruprechtii	Temp.–S.Trop.	tip rooting
ruta-muraria	Temp.	needs lime
septentrionale	Temp.	small clumps
trichomanes	Temp.–S.Trop.	needs lime
tripteropus	S.Trop.–Temp.	proliferous
varians	S.Trop.–Temp.	small clump
viride	Temp.	needs lime
*Blechnum chambersii**	Temp.	erect clump
*fluviatile**	Temp.	flat clump
membranaceum	Temp.	neat grower
penna-marina	Temp.	spreading habit
spicant and cvs	Temp.	small clumps
Bolbitis heteroclita form	S.Trop.–Temp.	spreading mossy carpet
Callistopteris bauerana	S.Trop.–Temp.	finely divided fronds
Cardiomanes reniforme	Temp.–S.Trop.	appealing fronds
Cheilanthes argentea	Temp.–S.Trop.	needs dry atmosphere
*austrotenuifolia**	Temp.–S.Trop.	spreading, adaptable
californica	Temp.–S.Trop.	needs dry atmosphere
covillei	Temp.	needs dry atmosphere
distans	Temp.–S.Trop.	spreading, adaptable
*sieberi**	Temp.–S.Trop.	spreading, adaptable

Species	*Region*	*Comments*
Cystopteris bulbifera	Temp.	may naturalize
fragilis	Temp.	delicate fronds
Diplazium subsinuatum	S.Trop.-Temp.	excellent, distinctive fronds
tomitaroanum	S.Trop.-Temp.	clumping
Doodia caudata	Temp.-S.Trop.	small clumps
Doryopteris concolor	Trop.-S.Trop.	likes drier atmosphere
ludens	Trop.-S.Trop.	dry, needs lime
palmata	Trop.-S.Trop.	dry, needs lime, difficult
Gymnopteris marantae	Temp.	dry, difficult
Hemionitis arifolia	S.Trop.-Temp.	dry, needs lime
palmata	S.Trop.-Temp.	dry
Hymenophyllum spp.	Trop.-Temp.	needs high humidity
Lemmaphyllum accedens	Trop.-Temp.	creeping habit
microphyllum	Trop.-S.Trop.	creeping habit
*Leptopteris fraseri**	S.Trop.-Temp.	needs high humidity
*hymenophylloides**	Temp.-S.Trop.	needs high humidity
*superba**	Temp.-S.Trop.	needs high humidity
Macroglena caudata	Trop.-Temp.	excellent, needs coarse mix
Nephrolepis exaltata 'Mini Ruffle'	Trop.-Temp.	small, ruffled clumps
*Notholaena sinuata**	Temp.-S.Trop.	dry
*standleyi**	Temp.-S.Trop.	dry, may need lime
*Oenotrichia tripinnata**	Temp.-S.Trop.	excellent
*Paraceterach muelleri**	S.Trop.-Temp.	dry
reynoldsii	S.Trop.-Temp.	dry
Pleurosorus rutifolius	Temp.-S.Trop.	dry
Pteris ensiformis and cvs	Trop.-Temp.	excellent
Pyrrosia rupestris	Temp.-S.Trop.	drier
serpens	Temp.-S.Trop.	drier
Quercifilix zeylanica	Temp.-S.Trop.	drier
Selaginella australiensis	Trop.-Temp.	spreading
brisbanensis	S.Trop.-Temp.	spreading
kraussiana	Temp.-S.Trop.	spreading
longipinna	Trop.-S.Trop.	clumping
martensii	S.Trop.-Temp.	clumping
mollis	S.Trop.-Temp.	spreading
serpens	Trop.-S.Trop.	spreading
umbrosa	S.Trop.-Temp.	clumping
Trichomanes spp.	Trop.-Temp.	needs high humidity

Appendix 3

Ferns for Hanging Baskets

The following ferns are suitable for cultivation in baskets and similar containers. Those with a creeping habit of growth are marked with an asterisk. See also Appendix 4 for a list of ferns with pendulous fronds.

Species	*Region*
*Adiantum diaphanum**	Trop.–Temp.
Aglaomorpha meyeniana	Trop.–Temp.
*Anarthropteris lanceolata**	Temp.–S.Trop.
Asplenium aethiopicum	Temp.–S.Trop.
alatum	Trop.–S.Trop.
attenuatum	S.Trop.–Temp.
auritum	Trop.–S.Trop.
belangeri	Trop.–S.Trop.
bulbiferum	Temp.–S.Trop.
cristatum	Trop.–S.Trop.
cuneatum	Trop.–S.Trop.
daucifolium	Temp.–S.Trop.
flabellifolium	Temp.–S.Trop.
lamprocaulon	Trop.–S.Trop.
normale	Trop.–S.Trop.
paleaceum	Trop.–S.Trop.
radicans	Trop.–S.Trop.
serra	Trop.–S.Trop.
serratum	Trop.–S.Trop.
simplicifrons	Trop.–Temp.
*Belvisia mucronata**	Trop.–Temp.
Blechnum fluviatile	Temp.–S.Trop.
occidentale	Trop.–S.Trop.
Campyloneurum latum	Trop.–S.Trop.
phyllitidis	Trop.–S.Trop.
radicans	Trop.–S.Trop.
*Colysis ampla**	Trop.–S.Trop.
*hemionitidea**	S.Trop.–Temp.
*sayeri**	Trop.–S.Trop.
Cyrtomium caryotideum	Temp.–S.Trop.
falcatum	Temp.–S.Trop.
macrophyllum	Temp.–S.Trop.
*Davallia bullata**	Temp.–S.Trop.
*canariensis**	Temp.–S.Trop.
*corniculata**	Trop.–S.Trop.
*denticulata**	Trop.–S.Trop.
*divaricata**	Trop.–S.Trop.
*embolostegia**	Trop.–S.Trop.
*epiphylla**	Trop.–S.Trop.
*fejeensis**	Trop.–S.Trop.
*mariesii**	Trop.–S.Trop.
*pyxidata**	Trop.–Temp.
*solida**	Trop.–S.Trop.
*tasmanii**	Temp.–S.Trop.
*trichomanoides**	Temp.–S.Trop.
*Davallodes hirsutum**	Trop.–S.Trop.
Dictymia brownii	Trop.–Temp.
Doodia aspera	Temp.–S.Trop.
caudata	Temp.–S.Trop.
media	Temp.–S.Trop.
Drynaria bonii	Trop.–S.Trop.
fortunei	Trop.–S.Trop.
mollis	Trop.–S.Trop.
propinqua	Trop.–S.Trop.
quercifolia	Trop.–S.Trop.
rigidula and cvs	Trop.–Temp.
sparsisora	Trop.–S.Trop.
Elaphoglossum callifolium	Trop.–S.Trop.
crinitum	Trop.–S.Trop.
*Humata griffithiana**	Trop.–Temp.
*heterophylla**	Trop.–S.Trop.
*pectinata**	Trop.–S.Trop.
*repens**	Trop.–S.Trop.
*tyermanii**	Trop.–S.Trop.
*Lecanopteris carnosa**	Trop.–S.Trop.
*Lemmaphyllum accedens**	Trop.–S.Trop.
*microphyllum**	Trop.–S.Trop.
Leptolepia novae-zealandiae	Temp.–S.Trop.
*Loxogramme involuta**	Trop.–S.Trop.
Lygodium flexuosum	Trop.–S.Trop.
microphyllum	Trop.–Temp.
Merinthosorus drynarioides	Trop.–S.Trop.
*Microgramma lycopodioides**	Trop.–S.Trop.
*nitida**	Trop.–S.Trop.
*piloselloides**	Trop.–S.Trop.
*vaccinifolia**	Trop.–S.Trop.
Microsorum linguiforme	Trop.–S.Trop.
musifolium	Trop.–S.Trop.
normale	Trop.–S.Trop.
punctatum and cvs	Trop.–S.Trop.
Niphidium crassifolium	Trop.–S.Trop.
Nephrolepis biserrata	Trop.–S.Trop.
cordifolia and cvs	Trop.–Temp.
exaltata and cvs	Trop.–Temp.
Neurodium lanceolatum	Trop.–S.Trop.
*Oleandra neriiformis**	Trop.–S.Trop.
Onychium japonicum	Trop.–Temp.
Phlebodium aureum and cvs	Trop.–Temp.
decumanum	Trop.–S.Trop.
*Phymatosorus diversifolius**	Temp.–S.Trop.
*scandens**	Trop.–Temp.
*scolopendria**	Trop.–S.Trop.
*sinuosa**	Trop.–S.Trop.
*Pleopeltis astrolepis**	Trop.–S.Trop.

Species	*Region*
*macrocarpa**	Trop.-S.Trop.
*percussa**	Trop.-S.Trop.
Polypodium australe and cvs*	Temp.-S.Trop.
*chnoodes**	Trop.-S.Trop.
*dissimile**	Trop.-S.Trop.
*formosanum**	S.Trop.-Temp.
*fraxinifolium**	Trop.-S.Trop.
*glaucophyllum**	Trop.-S.Trop.
*loriceum**	Trop.-S.Trop.
*pectinatum**	Trop.-S.Trop.
*plumula**	Trop.-S.Trop.
*polypodioides**	Temp.-S.Trop.
*sanctae-rosae**	Trop.-S.Trop.
*scouleri**	S.Trop.-Temp.
*thyssanolepis**	Trop.-S.Trop.
*triseriale**	Trop.-S.Trop.
vulgare and cvs	Temp.-S.Trop.
Polystichum lentum	Temp.-S.Trop.
Pseudodrynaria coronans	Trop.-S.Trop.
Psilotum nudum	Trop.-Temp.
Pteris ensiformis and cvs	Trop.-Temp.
multifida and cvs	Trop.-Temp.
*Pyrrosia confluens**	Trop.-Temp.
*hastata**	Trop.-S.Trop.
*lanceolata**	Trop.-S.Trop.
lingua and cvs	Trop.-Temp.
*longifolia**	Trop.-S.Trop.
*nummularifolia**	Trop.-S.Trop.
piloselloides	Trop.-S.Trop.
*polydactylis**	Trop.-S.Trop.
*rupestris**	Temp.-S.Trop.
*serpens**	Temp.-S.Trop.
*Rumohra adiantiformis**	Temp.-S.Trop.
Sadleria cyatheoides	Temp.-S.Trop.
*Scyphularia pentaphylla**	Trop.-Temp.
*triphylla**	Trop.-S.Trop.
*Selliguea feei**	S.Trop.-Temp.
*Stenochlaena palustris**	Trop.-S.Trop.
*tenuifolia**	Trop.-S.Trop.
Woodwardia orientalis	Temp.-S.Trop.

Appendix 4

Ferns with Pendulous Fronds or Weeping Growth Habit

These ferns make choice specimens for container or basket culture. They are presented as a separate group because growers often wish to select weeping ferns for this type of container. For other basket ferns see Appendix 3.

Species	*Region*
Adiantum caudatum	Trop.-S.Trop.
edgeworthii	Trop.-S.Trop.
malesianum	Trop.-S.Trop.
philippense	Trop.
zollingeri	Trop.-S.Trop.
Anetium citrifolium	Trop.
Asplenium affine	Trop.-S.Trop.
cuneatum	Trop.-S.Trop.
flaccidum	Temp.-S.Trop.
glaucophyllum	Trop.-S.Trop.
harpeoides	Trop.-S.Trop.
laserpitiifolium	Trop.-S.Trop.
mucronatum	Trop.-S.Trop.
pellucidum	Trop.-S.Trop.
polyodon	Trop.-Temp.
robustum	Trop.-S.Trop.
Campyloneurum angustifolium	S.Trop.-Temp.
Drynaria rigidula	Trop.-Temp.
'Vidgenii'	Trop.-S.Trop.
'Whitei'	Trop.-S.Trop.
Eriosorus hispidulus	Trop.-S.Trop.
Goniophlebium persicifolium	Trop.-S.Trop.
subauriculatum	Trop.-Temp.
'Knightiae'	Trop.-S.Trop.
verrucosum	Trop.-S.Trop.
Lycopodium aqualupianum	Trop.-S.Trop.
billardieri	Temp.-S.Trop.
carinatum	Trop.-S.Trop.
dalhousieanum	Trop.
dichotomum	Trop.-S.Trop.
linifolium	Trop.-S.Trop.
magnificum	Trop.
mexicanum	Trop.-S.Trop.
nummularifolium	Trop.
orizabae	Trop.-S.Trop.
polytrichoides	Trop.-S.Trop.
pringlei	Trop.-S.Trop.
proliferum	Trop.-S.Trop.
squarrosum	Trop.-S.Trop.
taxifolium	Trop.-S.Trop.
tenuicaule	Trop.-S.Trop.
verticillatum	Trop.-S.Trop.
Nephrolepis exaltata	
'Robusta'	Trop.-S.Trop.
falcata	Trop.-S.Trop.
occidentalis	Trop.-S.Trop.
pendula	Trop.-S.Trop.
rivularis	Trop.-S.Trop.

Species	*Region*
Ophioglossum pendulum	Trop.-S.Trop.
Pneumatopteris laevis	Trop.-S.Trop.
Psilotum complanatum	Trop.-S.Trop.
Vittaria dimorpha	Trop.-S.Trop.
elongata	Trop.-Temp.
ensiformis	Trop.-Temp.
graminifolia	Trop.-S.Trop.
lineata	Trop.-S.Trop.
scolopendrina	Trop.-S.Trop.

Appendix 5

Ground Cover Ferns

The following are either relatively small species with a spreading growth habit or are climbing ferns. All can act as a ground-cover and are useful for planting among shrubs or larger ferns. Those marked with an asterisk may die out in shady conditions. Those marked † have a strongly creeping habit.

Species	*Region*
Adiantum diaphanum	Temp.–Trop.
caudatum	Trop.–S.Trop.
edgeworthii	Trop.–S.Trop.
formosum	S.Trop.–Temp.
philippense	Trop.–S.Trop.
venustum	Temp.
Ampelopteris prolifera†	Trop.–S.Trop.
Asplenium oligophlebium	S.Trop.–Temp.
prolongatum	S.Trop.–Temp.
rhizophyllum	Temp.–S.Trop.
ruprechtii	Temp.–S.Trop.
tripteropus	S.Trop.–Temp.
Blechnum amabile	Trop.–S.Trop.
andinum	Trop.–S.Trop.
asperum	Trop.–S.Trop.
attenuatum†	S.Trop.–Temp.
asplenioides	Trop.–S.Trop.
penna-marina	Temp.
glandulosum	Trop.–S.Trop.
*occidentale**	Trop.–S.Trop.
oceanicum†	S.Trop.–Temp.
stoloniferum	Trop.–S.Trop.
Bolbitis heteroclita form	S.Trop.–Temp.
*Colysis hemionitidea**	Trop.–S.Trop.
*Cheilanthes austrotenuifolia**	Temp.–S.Trop.
*distans**	Temp.–S.Trop.
*Davallia bullata**	Temp.–S.Trop.
*tasmanii**	Temp.
*trichomanoides**	Temp.–S.Trop.
Doodia aspera	Trop.–Temp.
media	Trop.–Temp.
Gymnocarpium dryopteris	Temp.–S.Trop.
*Hypolepis sparsisora**	S.Trop.–Temp.
Lastreopsis munita	S.Trop.–Temp.
Microsorum diversifolium	Temp.–S.Trop.
*Pyrrosia confluens**	S.Trop.–Temp.
*hastata**	S.Trop.
*lingua**	Trop.–S.Trop.
*rupestris**	S.Trop.–Temp.
*serpens**	Temp.–S.Trop.
Selaginella australiensis	Trop.–S.Trop.
brisbanensis	S.Trop.–Temp.
emmelliana	Trop.–S.Trop.
flabellata	Trop.
helvetica	Temp.–S.Trop.
kraussiana and cvs	S.Trop.–Temp.
longipinna	Trop.–S.Trop.
martensii	S.Trop.–Temp.
mollis	S.Trop.–Temp.
nipponica	Temp.–S.Trop.
plumosa	Trop.
serpens	S.Trop.
sibirica	Temp.–S.Trop.
substipitata	S.Trop.
umbrosa	S.Trop.–Temp.
uncinata	Trop.–S.Trop.
Stenochlaena palustris†	Trop.–S.Trop.
tenuifolia†	Trop.–S.Trop.
Teratophyllum brightiae†	Trop.–S.Trop.

Appendix 6

Ferns Suitable for Outdoor Containers

Most of the species listed below need a protected semi-shady situation. Those marked with an asterisk can be tolerant of exposure to full sun.

Species	*Region*	*Comments*
Adiantum macrophyllum	Trop.–S.Trop.	fronds erect
peruvianum	Trop.–S.Trop.	arching fronds
polyphyllum	Trop.–S.Trop.	spreading
trapeziforme	Trop.–S.Trop.	spreading
Angiopteris evecta	Trop.–Temp.	needs plenty of water
Arachniodes aristata	Trop.–Temp.	very hardy
standishii	S.Trop.–Temp.	very attractive
*Asplenium australasicum**	Trop.–Temp.	excellent
bulbiferum	Temp.–S.Trop.	do not overpot, arching fronds
cymbifolium	Trop.–S.Trop.	sensitive to cold
daucifolium	Trop.–S.Trop.	fine and lacy
dimorphum	Trop.–S.Trop.	variable fronds
milnei	S.Trop.–Temp.	shiny fronds
musifolium	Trop.–S.Trop.	erect rosette
*nidus**	Trop.–S.Trop.	cold sensitive
*oblongifolium**	Temp.–S.Trop.	dense
*scleroprium**	Temp.–S.Trop.	dense, leathery
simplicifrons	S.Trop.–Temp.	rosette of narrow fronds
Athyrium filix-femina and cvs	Temp.–S.Trop.	may be deciduous
Blechnum brasiliense	Trop.–S.Trop.	attractive
capense	Temp.–S.Trop.	hardy
*cartilagineum**	Trop.–Temp.	hardy
gibbum	Trop.–S.Trop.	attractive
nudum	Temp.–Trop.	needs plenty of water
orientale	Trop.–S.Trop.	hardy
Cibotium glaucum	Trop.–S.Trop.	forms trunk
Coniogramme intermedia	S.Trop.–Temp.	dark fronds
*Culcita dubia**	Trop.–Temp.	very hardy
*Cyathea australis**	Temp.–S.Trop.	very hardy
*brownii**	Temp.–S.Trop.	fast
capensis	Temp.–S.Trop.	hardy
celebica	Trop.–Temp.	prickly
*contaminans**	Trop.–S.Trop.	fast
*cooperi**	Trop.–Temp.	fast
dealbata	Temp.–S.Trop.	excellent
dregei	Temp.–S.Trop.	hardy
*medullaris**	Temp.–S.Trop.	fast
rebeccae	Trop.–Temp.	excellent
robusta	Temp.–S.Trop.	decorative
woollsiana	Trop.–Temp.	excellent
*Dicksonia antarctica**	Temp.–S.Trop.	very hardy
fibrosa	Temp.–S.Trop.	very hardy
sellowiana	S.Trop.	slender
*squarrosa**	Temp.–S.Trop.	very hardy
youngiae	S.Trop.–Temp.	attractive
Didymochlaena truncatula	Trop.–S.Trop.	lovely fronds
Diplazium dilatatum	Trop.–Temp.	arching fronds

Species	*Region*	*Comments*
werckleanum	Trop.–S.Trop.	dark fronds
*Drynaria quercifolia**	Trop.–S.Trop.	very hardy
Dryopteris affinis	Temp.–S.Trop.	hardy
filix-mas	Temp.–S.Trop.	may be deciduous
Lastreopsis decomposita	S.Trop.–Temp.	hardy
marginans	S.Trop.–Temp.	shiny fronds
microsora	Trop.–Temp.	hardy
velutina	Temp.–S.Trop.	soft fronds
Leucostegia immersa	Trop.–S.Trop.	coarse mix
pallida	Trop.–S.Trop.	coarse mix
Marattia salicina	Trop.–Temp.	hardy
Microlepia firma	Trop.–S.Trop.	hardy
hirta	Trop.–S.Trop.	hardy
playtphylla	Trop.–S.Trop.	tall
speluncae	Trop.–S.Trop.	soft fronds
strigosa	Trop.–Temp.	graceful
Microsorum pappei	Trop.–Temp	slowly spreading
*punctatum** and cvs	Trop.–S.Trop.	hardy
Nephrolepis biserrata and cvs	Trop.–S.Trop.	needs plenty of water
*cordifolia** and cvs	Trop.–Temp.	hardy
*exaltata** (larger cvs)	Trop.–S.Trop.	hardy
*falcata** and cvs	Trop.–S.Trop.	hardy
*hirsutula**	Trop.–S.Trop.	hardy
*obliterata**	Trop.–S.Trop.	hardy
Niphidium crassifolium	Trop.–S.Trop.	coarse mix
Osmunda regalis	Temp.–S.Trop.	deciduous
Phlebodium aureum and cvs	Trop.–Temp.	coarse mix
Phymatosorus diversifolius	Temp.–S.Trop.	hardy
longissimus	Trop.–S.Trop.	coarse mix
nigrescens	Trop.–S.Trop.	coarse mix
*parksii**	Trop.–Temp.	bushy clump
scolopendria	Trop.–S.Trop.	coarse mix
*Pityrogramma calomelanos**	Trop.–S.Trop.	very hardy
Polystichum aculeatum	Temp.–S.Trop.	fronds harsh
proliferum	Temp.–S.Trop.	hardy
retroso-paleaceum	Temp.–S.Trop.	dark, glossy-green
setiferum	Temp.–S.Trop.	fronds spreading
vestitum	Temp.–S.Trop.	fronds harsh
*Pseudodrynaria coronans**	Trop.–S.Trop.	coarse mix
Pteris biaurita	Trop.–S.Trop.	hardy
hendersonii	S.Trop.–Temp.	attractive
microptera	Temp.–S.Trop.	hardy
pacifica	Trop.–S.Trop.	shiny fronds
quadriaurita	Trop.–S.Trop.	large
tripartita	Trop.–S.Trop.	large
umbrosa	Temp.–S.Trop.	bushy
wallichiana	Trop.–Temp.	large
*Rumohra adiantiformis** (Cape form)	Temp.–S.Trop.	large, very hardy
Woodwardia fimbriata	Temp.–S.Trop.	erect
orientalis	S.Trop.–Temp.	spreading fronds
radicans	S.Trop.–Temp.	hardy

Appendix 7

Ferns for Wet Soils

The following ferns will grow in wet soils but prefer situations where the water is not stagnant. Those marked with an asterisk are very tolerant of wet conditions.

Species	*Region*
Acrostichum aureum	Trop.-S.Trop.
danaeifolium	Trop.-S.Trop.
*speciosum**	Trop.-S.Trop.
Allantodia australis	Temp.-S.Trop.
*Ampelopteris prolifera**	Trop.-S.Trop.
Angiopteris evecta	Trop.-S.Trop.
Athyrium filix-femina	Temp.-S.Trop.
Blechnum articulatum	Trop.-Temp.
capense	Temp.-S.Trop.
*discolor**	Temp.-S.Trop.
fluviatile	Temp.
*indicum**	Trop.-Temp.
lanceolatum	Temp.-S.Trop.
*minus**	Temp.-S.Trop.
nudum	Temp.-S.Trop.
patersonii	Temp.-S.Trop.
*serrulatum**	Trop.-S.Trop.
*wattsii**	Temp.-S.Trop.
Blotiella lindeniana	S.Trop.-Temp.
*Cyathea australis**	Temp.-S.Trop.
*smithii**	Temp.-S.Trop.
*Cyclosorus interruptus**	Trop.-S.Trop.
*Dennstaedtia davallioides**	Temp.-S.Trop.
*Dicksonia antarctica**	Temp.-S.Trop.
*herbertii**	S.Trop.-Temp.
*Diplazium dietrichianum**	Trop.-S.Trop.
dilatatum	S.Trop.-Temp.
*esculentum**	Trop.-S.Trop.
riparium	Trop.-S.Trop.
*Equisetum myriochaetum**	Temp.-S.Trop.
*Helminthostachys zeylanica**	Trop.
*Histiopteris incisa**	Temp.-Trop.
*Hypolepis punctata**	Temp.-Trop.
rugosula	Temp.-S.Trop.
Lunathyrium japonicum	Temp.-S.Trop.
Lygodium circinnatum	Temp.-S.Trop.
flexuosum	Trop.-S.Trop.
*microphyllum**	Trop.-Temp.
Marattia salicina	Trop.-Temp.
Microlepia speluncae	Trop.-S.Trop.
*Nephrolepis biserrata**	Trop.-S.Trop.
*Onoclea sensibilis**	Temp.-S.Trop.
*Osmunda cinnamomea**	Temp.-S.Trop.
*regalis**	Temp.-S.Trop.
*Parathelypteris beddomei**	Trop.
Pilularia globifera	Temp.
Plagiogyria pectinata	S.Trop.
Pneumatopteris pennigera	Temp.-S.Trop.
sogerensis	Trop.-Temp.
Pseudophegopteris paludosa	Trop.-S.Trop.
*Pteris comans**	Temp.
*umbrosa**	Temp.-S.Trop.
Selaginella kraussiana	Temp.-S.Trop.
*Thelypteris confluens**	S.Trop.-Temp.
*Todea barbara**	Temp.-S.Trop.
Woodwardia virginica	Temp.-S.Trop.

Appendix 8

Cold-hardy Ferns

The following species will succeed very well in temperate regions. Those marked with an asterisk are very hardy to frosts or snow.

Species
Adiantum aethiopicum*
capillus-junonis
capillus-veneris*
diaphanum
formosum
hispidulum
pedatum*
raddianum
venustum*
Allantodia australis
squamigera
Arachniodes aristata
simplicior
standishii
Asplenium adiantum-nigrum*
australasicum
bulbiferum*
fissum*
flabellifolium
flaccidum
fontanum*
hookerianum*
marinum
oblongifolium
playtneuron
richardii
ruta-muraria
sarelii
scleroprium
scolopendrium and cvs
septentrionale*
trichomanes*
viride*
Athyrium asplenioides
brevifrons
deltoidofrons
distentifolium
filix-femina and cvs
flexile
frangulum
niponicum var pictum
otophorum
pycnocarpum
spinulosum
Blechnum capense
chilense
discolor*

Species
fluvialite*
lanceolatum
magellanicum
minus*
nudum*
patersonii
penna-marina*
procerum*
spicant*
tabulare*
vulcanicum*
Cheilanthes austrotenuifolia*
distans
gracillima
Coniogramme japonica
Cornopteris crenulatoserrulatum
Cryptogramma crispa*
Culcita dubia*
Cyathea australis*
brownii
colensoi*
cunninghamii
dealbata
medullaris
smithii*
woollsiana
Cyrtomium caryotideum
falcatum
fortunei
Cystopteris bulbifera*
fragilis*
Davallia canariensis
mariesii*
tasmanii
trichomanoides
Dennstaedtia davallioides
punctiloba*
Dicksonia antarctica*
fibrosa*
lanata*
squarrosa*
Diplazium assimile
sibiricum*
subsinuatum
tomitaroanum
Doodia aspera*
caudata

Species
media*
Dryopteris aemula
affinis and cvs
assimilis*
carthusiana*
clintoniana
cycadina
dilatata
erythrosora
filix-mas and cvs
goldiana
intermedia
marginalis
oreades
sieboldii
submontana
Gymnocarpium dryopteris*
robertianum
Histiopteris incisa*
Hypolepis australe
millefolium
punctata
rugosula
Lastreopsis acuminata*
decomposita
glabella
hispida
microsora
munita
velutina
Lemmaphyllum microphyllum
Leptolepia novae-zealandiae
Leptopteris hymenophylloides
superba
Lunathyrium japonicum
thelypterioides
Nephrolepis cordifolia
Onoclea sensibilis
Osmunda cinnamomea
claytoniana
regalis and cvs
Paesia scaberula
Pellaea atropurpurea
falcata
rotundifolia
viridis
Phegopteris connectilis

Species
hexagonoptera
Polypodium australe
formosanum
glycyrrhiza
polypodioides
scouleri
vulgare and cvs
*Polystichum acrostichoides**
*aculeatum** and cvs
andersonii
braunii
*cystostegia**
lonchitis
*munitum**
*polyblepharum**
*proliferum**
retroso-paleaceum
richardii
*setiferum**
tsus-simense
*vestitum**
Pseudocystopteris atkinsonii
spinulosum
Pteris comans
cretica and cvs
macilenta
multifida
tremula
umbrosa
vittata
Rumohra adiantiformis
Selaginella helvetica
*kraussiana**
wallacei
Thelypteris palustris
simulata
*Todea barbara**
*Woodsia alpina**
ilvensis
obtusa
Woodwardia areolata
*fimbriata**
orientalis
radicans
*virginica**

Appendix 9

Ferns found on Limestone or Basic Soils (Calciphiles)

The following fern species are recorded as growing on limestone, or in basic soils. They are presented here as an aid to understanding their cultivation requirements, as lime may be necessary for their successful growth. Some species only occur sporadically on limestone; others grow on it commonly and are marked*.

Species
Adenoderris glandulosa
sororia
Actiniopteris radiata
*braunii**
*Adiantum capillus-veneris**
caudatum
fragile
incisum
*malesianum**
melanoleucum
philippense
*reniforme**
resiliens
*soboliferum**
*stenochlamys**
*tenerum**
tricholepis
*wilesianum**
*zollingeri**
*Adiantopsis paupercula**
*pedata**
*Anemia adiantifolia**
cicutaria
mexicana
speciosa
wrightii
Anopteris hexagona
Arcypteris irregularis
*Asplenium adiantoides**
adiantum-nigrum
*ceterach**
cristatum
dentatum
ebenoides
fissum
fontanum
heterochroum
hoffmannii
lepidum
macrophyllum
majoricum
milnei
myriophyllum
olivaceum
palmeri
pellucidum
phyllitidis

Species
pumilum
resiliens
*rhizophyllum**
*ruta-muraria**
salignum
scolopendrium
seelosii
*squamulatum**
tenerum
trichomanes
*trichomanes-dentatum**
unilaterale
viride
Athyrium pinnatum
prescottianum
Blechnum finlaysonianum
*Bolbitis aliena**
*portoricensis**
*Bommeria hispida**
*pedata**
Ceterach cordatum
*Cheilanthes alabamensis**
candida
eastonii
*farinosa**
feei
horridula
induta
*leucopoda**
marlothii
*microphylla**
pteridioides
rufa
*scariosa**
villosa
Christella dentata
parasitica
Crypsinus enervis
Cryptogramma stelleri
*Ctenitis hirta**
sloanei
Cyclopeltis crenata
semicordata
Cyrtomium auriculatum
*falcatum**
juglandifolium
Cystopteris bulbifera

Species
fragilis
Davallia denticulata
solida
Diplazium cordifolium
esculentum
montanum
*Doryopteris allenae**
concolor
*ludens**
*papuana**
*Drynaria bonii**
quercifolia
rigidula
sparsisora
Dryopteris ludoviciana
submontana
villari
*Gymnocarpium robertianum**
*Hemionitis arifolia**
*Heterogonium alderwereltii**
*pinnatum**
Humata heterophylla
pectinata
Hypodematium crenatum
fauriei
Lemmaphyllum accedens
Lepisorus longifolius
Leptochilus decurrens
Llavea cordifolia
Loxogramme avenia
scolopendrina
*Lygodium polystachyum**
Matteuccia struthiopteris
Microgramma heterophyllum
Microlepia speluncae
Microsorum musifolium
punctatum
Neocheiropteris palmatopedata
Nephelea fulgens
woodwardioides
Nephrolepis biserrata
*dicksonioides**
falcata
hirsutula
radicans
*Notholaena aschenborniana**
*candida**

Species
dealbata
formosa*
grayi*
greggii*
limitanea
neglecta*
parvifolia*
rigida*
sinuata*
standleyi
Odontosoria clavata
Oleandra undulata
Ophioglossum englemanii
Pellaea atropurpurea*
breweri
dolomiticola*
glabella
intermedia
ovata*
pringlei
sagittata*
ternifolia*
Photinopteris speciosa
Phymatosorus nigrescens
scolopendria
Pityrogramma calomelanos
Pneumatopteris pennigera (some forms)
Polypodium australe
dispersum
papillosum
plumula
ptilodon
vulgare
Polystichum aculeatum
echinatum*
christianae*
harrisae*
lindsaeifolium*
triangulum
Pterideum aquilinum
(vars caudatum and feei)
esculentum
Pteridrys syrmatica*
Pteris bahamensis*
cretica*
ensiformis
longifolia
longipinnula*
mertensioides
multifida
scabripes
tripartita
vittata*
Pyrrosia floccigera
lanceolata
penangiana*
stigmosa*
varia
Selaginella lepidophylla*
pilifera*
Sphenomeris clavata
Taenitis blechnoides

Species
Tectaria × amesiana
amplifolia*
barberi
devexa*
griffithii
heracleifolia*
incisa
lobata*
macrodonta
pedata*
variolosa
Thelypteris augescens
blanda
guadalupensis*
immersa
leptoclada*
ovata
pilosa
reptans*
resiliens
toganetra
tuerckheimii
Vittaria angustifolia
elongata
Woodsia fragilis
glabella

Appendix 10

Lime-hating Ferns (Calcifluges)

The following ferns resent lime and may die (or suffer badly bleached foliage) if it is included in their potting mix or added to the soil around their roots. Those marked with an asterisk are particularly sensitive.

Species
Adiantum bradleyi
Asplenium forisiacum
montanum
pinnatifidum
septentrionale
trichomanes ssp. *trichomanes*
Blechnum spicant
*Cryptogramma brunnoniana**
*crispa**
Dryopteris celsa
Gleichenia alpina
dicarpa
microphylla
*Lygodium palmatum**
Oreopteris limbosperma
Phegopteris connectilis
Thelypteris palustris
simulata

Appendix 11

Ferns and Fern Allies with Green Spores

The following fern genera and species have green spores. They are included as a separate list because, as a general rule, green spores are short-lived and for successful propagation should be sown fresh. Note, however, that some species of *Osmunda* (e.g. *O. regalis*) have spores which may retain their viability for 4–6 months.

Species
Blechnum nudum
Calymmodon spp.
Christiopteris spp.
Ctenopteris spp.
Equisetum spp.
Grammitis spp.
Hymenophyllum spp.
Leptopteris spp.
Loxogramme spp.
Marginariopsis wiesbaurii
Matteuccia spp.
Onoclea sensibilis
Onocleopsis hintonii
Plagiogyria spp.
Platycerium wallichii
Pleurosoriopsis spp.
Scleroglossum spp.
Stenochlaena sorbifolia
Trichomanes spp.

Appendix 12

Common and Trade Names of Pesticides Mentioned in this Book

Common Name	*Trade Name Examples*	*Formulation*	*Useage*
Bacillus thuringiensis	Dipel, Biotrol, Thuricide, Agritol, Larvatrol	wettable powder	insecticide (caterpillars only
benomyl	Benlate	wettable powder	fungicide
captan	Captan, Orthocide	wettable powder	fungicide
carbaryl	Septene, Sevin, Bugmaster	wettable powder	insecticide
clensel	Clensel	dispersible oil	insecticide
copper oxychloride	Cuprox, Cupravit	wettable powder	fungicide
cupric hydroxide	Kocide	wettable powder	fungicide
derris dust	Derris dust	dusting powder	insecticide
dichloran	Allisan, Botran	wettable powder	fungicide
difocol	Kelthane, Difocol	liquid or wettable powder	miticide
dimethoate	Rogor, Cygon	liquid	insecticide
dinocarp	Karathane, Mildex	wettable powder	fungicide/miticide
fosetyl	Aliette	wettable powder	fungicide
iprodione	Rovral	wettable powder	fungicide
maldison	Malathion, Cythion	wettable powder	insecticide
oxycarboxin	Plantvax	wettable powder	fungicide
permethrin	Ambush	liquid	insecticide
propamacarb	Previcure	wettable powder	fungicide
pyrethrum	Pyrethrum	liquid	insecticide
sulphur	Cosan, Wettable sulphur	wettable powder	fungicide
tetradifon	Tedion	liquid	miticide
thiram	Thiram, Arasan, Thiotox, Thylate	wettable powder	fungicide
white oil	White oil	dispersible oil	insecticide

Glossary

The following glossary is comprehensive as to fern terminology. Some of the interpretations of words have been deliberately slanted towards ferns and their allies. Only some of the terms included in the glossary have been used in the text of this book. The comprehensive glossary has been provided to aid in the interpretation and understanding of language used in botanical texts such as scientific papers, floras etc.

abaxial The surface or side of an organ directed away from the axis
abbreviated Shortened
aberrant Unusual or atypical, differing from the normal form
abortive Barren or imperfectly developed, as is common in the spores of hybrid ferns
abrupt Changing suddenly rather than gradually
abscise To shed or throw off
abscission The shedding of plant parts either naturally from old age or prematurely from stress
acaulescent Without a trunk
accessory buds Lateral buds developed in frond axils on a rhizome. Usually they develop only if the main bud is damaged
acicular Needle-shaped, very narrow, stiff, pointed
acrophore Apical stalk
acrophyll A mature or adult frond of a climbing fern, cf. *bathyphyll*
acroscopic Directed towards the apex of a frond: the first lateral vein or leaflet on a pinna branching off in an upwards direction
acrostichoid A condition describing sori densely covering the undersurface of a frond and lacking distinct areas between sporangia, e.g. *Acrostichum*
actinostelic Said of a vascular strand with radiating ribs
aculeate Armed with prickles
acuminate Tapering to a long, drawn out point
acute Tapering to a short, sharp point
adaxial The surface or side of an organ facing towards the apex, or next to the axis
adnate Grown together or fused with another part
adpressed See *appressed*
adventitious Arising in an irregular position, e.g. adventitious roots, adventitious buds
adventive Introduced since colonization by man and becoming naturalized
aerial Borne above the surface of the ground
aerial roots Adventitious roots arising on a rootstock and growing in the air, e.g. on the trunks of tree ferns
aerophore Specialized pore on stipes or rachises associated with aeration
aff. affinity A botanical reference used to denote an undescribed species closely related to an already described species
alpine Occurring on very high and cold mountains
alternate Borne at different levels in a straight line or spiral: not opposite
amphibious Growing equally well on land or in water
amphiphytic Growing in mud, either seasonally wet or permanently wet
anadromous When the first branch of a frond or vein of a primary pinna is produced on the side facing towards the frond apex cf. *catadromous*
anastomosing Forming a network, as when the veins branch and run together
angulate With sharp corners or angles
annual A plant completing its life cycle within 12 months
annulate Having an annulus
annulus A specialized partial or complete ring of cells on the sporangium involved in spore release
anomalous An abnormal or freak form
anterior On the frond side of an organ away from the axis
antheridium (a) The male organ in ferns which produces the male gametes (antherozoids or spermatozoids)
antherozoid A male gamete or sperm
antrorse Directed towards the apex
apex The tip or distal end of an organ
aphlebiae A term for the reduced, skeletonized basal pinnae of the fronds of some species of tree-ferns, e.g. *Cyathea baileyana*
apical At the apex
apical dominance The dominance of the apical growing bud which produces hormones and prevents lateral buds developing while it is still growing actively
apiculate Ending abruptly in a short, sharp point
apogamy Development of sporophytes directly from the prothallus without the occurrence of fertilization
apospory The formation of prothalli directly on sporophyte tissue without the production of spores
appressed Pressed flat against something
approximate Close together but not united
aquatic A plant growing wholly or partially submerged in water
arachnoid Entangled and hairy, like a cobweb
arborescent With a tree-like growth habit
arched Curved or bowed
archegone A term for the egg cell produced in the archegonium
archegonium The female organ in ferns which produces the egg
archesporial cell The mother cell that divides to produce all of the spores in a sporangium
arcuate Curved or arched
areole (areolae) A space between the veins in reticulate venation
aristate Tipped with a small bristle or awn
armed Bearing spines or prickles

Glossary

articulate Jointed, separated easily at certain points
ascending Rising obliquely or curving upward
asexual reproduction Reproduction by vegetative means without the fusion of sex cells, e.g. bulbils in some ferns
athyrioid In the form of *Athyrium*, usually a reference to the arrangement of sori
attenuate Tapering and drawn out
auricle An ear shaped appendage
auriculate Bearing auricles: also refers to the presence of prominent basal lobes on pinnae or pinnules: also reduced, basal rounded pinnae on pinnate fronds
austral Southern
auxin A growth regulating compound controlling many growth processes such as frond production and root development
axil The angle formed by a leaf or leaflet with the rhizome or rachis
axillary Borne within the axil
axis The main stem of a plant or part of a plant

basifixed Attached to the base
basipetalous Maturing in succession from apex to base
basiscopic Directed towards the base of a frond: the first lateral vein or leaflet on a pinna branching off in a downwards direction
bathyphyll The juvenile or basal fronds of a climbing fern
bicolorous Having two colours
bicrenate Crenate with the lobes themselves crenate
bifid Deeply notched for more than half its length
biflagellate Having two flagella
bifoliar Bearing two leaflets arising at the same point, e.g. *Regnellidium diphyllum*
bifurcate Forked into two parts
bilateral Having two sides; also another term for monolete spores
bilobed Two-lobed
binomial The scientific name of a plant comprising the generic name and the species name
bipinnate Twice pinnately divided
bipinnatifid Twice pinnatifid
biserrate With the teeth of a serrate margin themselves bearing teeth
bisexual Both male and female sexes present
bivalvate Having two valves, as in the indusium of *Hymenophyllum*
blade The expanded leafy part of a frond
bloom A waxy, powdery secretion on the surface of an organ, e.g. the fronds of *Pityrogramma* spp.
boreal Northern
bottom heat A propagation term used to denote the application of artificial heat in the basal region of cuttings or sporelings
branch A division or subdivision of an axis
bristle A stiff hair expanded at the base where it is multicellular, e.g. *Taenitis* spp.
brittle Breaking readily with a smooth fracture
bud An undeveloped shoot; in ferns often used as an alternative to bulbil
bulbil A small bulb or bud borne on a frond at the junction of main veins and developing into a plantlet
bullate Bubble-like, puckered or blistered

caducous Short-lived or falling off early
caespitose Growing in a tuft or tussock
calcareous An excess of lime (*Calcium carbonate*), as in soil derived from limestone
calciphile A lime-loving plant, e.g. *Adiantum capillus-veneris*
calciphluge A lime-hating plant, e.g. *Cryptogramma crispa*
capillary Hair-like
capitate Enlarged and head-like; like a pinhead; having an enlarged apex; in a dense round cluster
carinate Bearing a keel on the lower surface
cartilaginous Hard and tough, but flexible (like gristle)
castaneous Deep reddish brown or chestnut coloured
catadromous When the first branch of a frond or vein of a primary pinna is produced on the side facing towards the base of a frond cf. *anadromous*
caudate With a tail-like appendage
caudex The trunk of a tree fern
ceraceous Waxy
ceriferous Wax-producing
chaff A term sometimes used for masses of thin, dry scales
chamaephyte A shallowly rooting plant of sprawling habit, e.g. some *Selaginella* species
channelled Deeply grooved longitudinally
chartaceous Having the texture of paper and often a brownish green colouration
chasmophyte A plant rooting in soil pockets or crevices of rocks, cliff-faces, gorges etc
ciliate With a fringe of fine hairs
circinate Coiled from the apex downwards, as in young fern fronds
circinate vernation The inrolling of young fronds
circumaustral Distributed around the southern hemisphere particularly the colder southern regions
circumboreal Distributed around the northern hemisphere particularly the colder northern regions
clathrate With the cell walls thickened in the form of a lattice
clavate Club-shaped
cleft Deeply cut
clone A group of vegetatively propagated plants with a common ancestry, e.g. *Pteris* 'Childsii'
coalescent Separate organs united by growth
coensorus An extended sorus or a combination of sori which have united so as to appear as one
commisural face The face of a spore in contact with an adjacent spore
commisure A joint or seam
compound Said of a frond with two or more separate leaflets
compressed Somewhat flattened
conceptacle Reproductive cavity or fruit case of a sporocarp, e.g. in *Marsilea*
concolorous Uniformly coloured, as on both sides of a frond
conduplicate Folded together lengthwise with the upper surface inwards
cone A popular term for a strobilus
confluent Blending or merging together
conform Same or similar in shape or outline, e.g. pinnate fronds with the apical pinnae similar to the lateral pinnae
congeneric Belonging to one and the same genus
congested Crowded closely together
connate Fused or joined
connivent Converging
conspecific Belonging to one and the same species
contiguous Adjoining or in contact but not united

continuous Without interruption
contorted Twisted
contracted Narrowed and/or shortened
convex With an arched or rounded surface
convolute Rolled together longitudinally
cordate Heart-shaped
coriaceous Leathery in texture
cosmopolitan World-wide in distribution
costa The midrib of a simple frond or pinna
costal Near the costa
costate Ribbed
costule Midrib of a pinnule or lobe
creeping Running along the ground and rooting at intervals
crenate Margins with rounded, scalloped, shallow teeth
crenulate Finely crenate
crested With an elevated ridge or crest
crisped The margins finely wavy, curled or crumpled
cristate With an appendage resembling a crest
crown The foliage canopy of a fern
crozier The coiled young frond of a fern, the fiddlehead
cruciate In the shape of a cross
cryptic Hidden
cryptogam Plants which are flowerless and reproduce by spores not seeds
cucullate Hood-shaped
cultigen A plant known only in cultivation and apparently originating under domestication
cultivar A horticultural variety of a plant which may breed true or else be propagated vegetatively
cultrate Knife-shaped
cuneate Wedge-shaped
cuspidate Tipped with a sharp, firm point
cyathiform Shaped like a drinking cup
cylindrical Elongate with a circular cross section
cymbiform Boat-shaped
cytotaxonomy A classification system based on the structure of cells

damping-off A condition in which young sporelings are attacked and killed by soil borne fungi
deciduous Falling off after maturity or at the end of the growing season, e.g. the fronds of *Athyrium filix-femina*
decompound Divided several times
decrescent Gradually reduced in size, as the basal pinnae of some thelypteroid ferns
decumbent Lying along the ground with the tip ascending
decurrent Running downward beyond the point of junction
decurved Curved downwards
decussate In opposite pairs, making four rows
deflexed Bent downwards towards the base
defoliate Shedding of leaves
dehisce To split open
dehiscence The process of opening by valves or splits
delicate Finely made
deltate A flat plate with the outline of a triangle
deltoid A solid-three dimensional object with its surfaces in the outline of a triangle
dentate With sharp teeth perpendicular to the margin
denticulate Finely toothed
depauperate Weak, reduced in size, starved and impoverished
determinate With a definite cessation of growth in the main axis

dichotomous Forking regularly into two equal branches or parts
dictyostele A complex stele with large, overlapping leaf gaps, in section composed of many meristeles
didymous Twinned, (or in pairs) the two parts similar and attached by a short portion of the inner surface, e.g. *Dipteris* fronds
difform Dissimilar
diffuse Spreading or of open or straggling form
digitate A compound frond with the parts spreading from the centre like the fingers of a hand
dilated Widened
dimidiate Said of a pinna or pinnule with the blade much reduced or lacking on the basiscopic side
dimorphic Existing in two easily recognizable forms
dioecious Unisexual with the male and female organs on separate plants or on separate prothalli
diplazoid In the form of *Diplazium*, usually a comparison with the paired elongate sori of that genus
diploid With a complement of two sets of chromosomes
disarticulate To separate readily at a joint
discolorous Of different colours, e.g. the upper and lower surfaces of a frond
discontinuous Interrupted or lacking sequence
discrete Clearly separate and not united
dissected Deeply divided or cut into many segments
distal Away from the point of attachment towards the free end of an organ
distant Not closely attached, not crowded
distelic With two steles
distichous Arranged in two, opposite rows
distinct Separate, clear
divaricate Spreading at a very wide angle
divergent Spreading apart at a wide angle
divided Separated to the base
dorsal Attached to the back of an organ
dorsiventral With a distinct upper and lower surface or structure: as in a creeping rhizome which bears roots on the lower surface and fronds on the upper surface
dune A mound formed from wind blown sand

echinate Bearing prickles or spines, as in some fern spores
ecology Study of the interaction of plants and animals within their natural environment
ecostate Lacking a costa or midrib
ecotype A form of a taxon arising under different ecological conditions
edaphic Pertaining to the soil
effuse Very open and spreading loosely
eglandular Lacking glands
elater One of the four filamentous appendages of the spores of *Equisetum*: a spirally thickened cell associated with spores and aiding in their dispersal
ellipsoid A solid object with a three-dimensional elliptical shape
elliptical Oval and flat, narrowed to each end which is rounded
elongate Drawn out in length
emarginate Having a notch at the apex
embryo The developing zygote in the fertilized archegonium
endemic Restricted to a particular country, region or area
endospore The innermost layer of a fern spore adjacent to the cytoplasm and consisting of a relatively thin layer of cellulose

ensiform Sword-shaped
entire With a continuous margin, not toothed or lobed in any way
ephemeral A plant with a very short life cycle
epilithic Growing on rocks
epipetric Growing on rocks
epiphyllous Borne on or growing on the leaves
epiphyte A plant growing on another plant but not attached parasitically
epispore Another name for a perispore
erect Upright
erose With an irregular cut or notched margin as if chewed
estuarine Pertaining to estuaries or river mouths, usually brackish conditions
eusporangiate With a sporangial wall more than one cell in thickness, originating from several cells (cf. *leptosporangiate*)
evanescent Short-lived, shrinking, fading
evergreen Remaining green throughout the year
excrescence Outgrowth from the surface
excurrent Proceeding outwards and away from the axis or vein: also a vein extending beyond the margin as a sharp point
exindusiate Without an indusium
exine The outer coat of a pollen grain or spore
exospore The intermediate layer of a fern spore; it consists of several layers and may be pitted or bear canals
exserted Protruding beyond the surrounding parts
extrorse Directed outward
exudate A liquid, resinous or gelatinous substance secreted by a plant organ

facultative Not essential, able to exist without
falcate Sickle-shaped
false indusium A covering over the sorus formed by a reflexed leaf margin, e.g. *Adiantum* spp.
false veins Elongated lines of epidermal cells which appear as veins but lack any vascular tissue; they are relics left from the union of adjacent leaf tissues, e.g. *Davallia*
family A taxonomic group of related genera
farina A mealy or flour-like covering, as on the fronds of *Cheilanthes farinosa*
farinose Covered with farina
fascicled Arranged in bundles or clusters, as the stipes of some ferns
fern allies Plants similar to ferns, reproducing by spores but having small leaves (microphylls)
ferruginous Rust-coloured
fertile Producing seeds or spores
fertilization The act of union of the antherozoids and the egg cell in the archegonium
feuillettes Plates of material which make up layers of the exospore
fibrillose With thread-like fibres or scales
fibrose Composed of, or resembling fibres
fiddlehead A popular term for a fern crozier
filamentose Hair-like
filiform Thread-like
fimbria The fine hair-like fringes of a scale
fimbriate Fringed with fine hairs
flabellate Fan-shaped
flaccid Soft, limp, lax
flagelliform Long and whip-like
flagellum A whip-like motile hair
flexible Easily bent but recovering the original form
flexuose Wavy or zig-zag
floccose With tufts of soft, woolly hair
flora The plant population of a given region: also a book detailing the plant species of an area
flush A period of rapid vegetative growth
foetid With a stinking, offensive odour
foliaceous Leafy
foliar Pertaining to the leaves
forked Divided into two equal branches arising at a common point on an axis
form A minor botanical division below the level of variety
fractiflex In intermittent zig-zag lines
free Not joined to any other part
friable A term for soil which is moist, open and loose
frond The leaf of a fern or palm, including the stipe
fruit dot A popular term for sorus
fugacious Falling or perishing early
fulvous Tawny-yellow or dull yellow
fungicide A chemical used to control fungus diseases
furcate Forked
furfuraceous With soft, scurfy scales
furrowed With longitudinal grooves or furrows
fuscous Dusky, blackish
fused Joined and growing together
fusiform Spindle-shaped, swollen in the middle and tapering to both ends

gamete The male and female sex cells that unite at fertilization to form the zygote
gametophyte The sexual stage in the life cycle of cryptogams producing the eggs and the sperm; it contains half the number of chromosomes of the sporophyte
gelatinous Jelly-like, of a slimy, clear sticky nature
geminate Arranged in pairs, like twins
gemma A vegetative bud, by which a plant propagates and disperses itself
gemmiparous Bearing vegetative buds
gene A hereditary factor located in linear order on a chromosome
geniculate Bent like a knee
genus A taxonomic group of closely related species
geophyte A plant well anchored in the soil cf. *hemicryptophyte*
gibbous Humped or swollen on one side
glabrescent Becoming glabrous, or nearly glabrous
glabrous Without hairs or scales, smooth
gland A fluid secreting organ
glandular Bearing glands
glaucescent Slightly glaucous or becoming glaucous
glaucous With a distinct, waxy bloom which gives a bluish appearance
globose Globe-like, nearly spherical
glochidium A small barbed hair or spine, e.g. in *Azolla*
glomerule A very dense cluster
glossy Smooth and shining
glutinose Covered with a sticky exudate
gradate Said of sorus with the younger sporangia at the apex and the older ones lower down
granular Appearing as if covered with small grains
grooved Channelled or furrowed

habit The general appearance of a plant
habitat The environment in which a plant grows

hair A slender epidermal appendage either unicellular or consisting of a single row of cells
halophyte A plant which grows in saline soils
haploid Having a single set of chromosomes
haptotype A specimen designated where doubt exists if the author actually handled the specimen mentioned in the description
hastate Shaped like an arrow-head and with spreading basal lobes
heliophilic Sun and light loving
heliophobic Shade loving
helophyte A plant growing in permanent or seasonal mud
hemicryptophyte A plant rooting shallowly and poorly in soil; not well anchored; cf. *geophyte*
herbaceous A perennial plant which dies down after maturity and reshoots when conditions are suitable; also referring to soft thinly-textured tissue, e.g. fronds
herbarium A collection of dried pressed plants permanently preserved
heteromorphic Existing in two or more easily distinguishable forms
heterophilous Bearing fronds of more than one kind
heterosporous Bearing spores of distinctly different types, e.g. *Selaginella* spp.
hirsute Covered with long, spreading coarse hairs
hispid Covered with stiff bristles or hairs
hispidulous Minutely hispid
hoary Covered with short, white hairs giving the surface a greyish appearance
holotype The one specimen designated by the author to which its name is permanently attached
homogenous Uniform or relatively so
homonym The same name
homosporous Producing only one type of spore
hormone A chemical substance produced in one part of a plant and inducing a growth response when transferred to another part
humus-collecting fronds Specialized overlapping or erect fronds which trap litter
hyaline Transparent or translucent
hybrid The progeny resulting from the cross-fertilization of parents
hydathode A water secreting gland on the surface or margin of a leaf: usually situated at the end of a vein and often surrounded by a concretion of white salts; similar to a stoma but with functionless guard cells; popularly termed lime-dot
hydrophyte A free-floating plant growing in water
hygromorphic A plant adapted to wet conditions
hygrophilous Preferring a wet climate
hygroscopic Expanding or contracting by absorbing or losing water and thus changing shape

idioblasts Specialized epidermal cells producing slime or gum
illegitimate Applied to a plant name not published in agreement with international rules of botanical nomenclature
imbricate Overlapping like fish scales
immersed Sunken in the surrounding tissue
imparipinnate Pinnate with the rachis terminated by a single leaflet
incised With the margin cut sharply and deeply
included Enclosed
inconspicuous Not easily seen, not prominent
incrassate Thickened
incurved Curved upwards
indefinite Of apparent unlimited growth
indehiscent Not splitting at maturity
indigenous Native to a country, region or area
indumentum Any covering on a plant surface such as hairs or scales
indurated Hardened and toughened
indusium Protective outgrowth of leaf tissue covering or partially covering the sorus, at least when young
inferior Situated below another organ
inflated Swollen, distended
inflexed Turning sharply inwards
infraspecific Describing taxonomic divisions of a rank lower than species
insecticide A chemical used to control insect pests
internode The portion of a stem between two adjacent nodes
interrupted Broken or discontinuous; an annulus not forming a complete circle
intramarginal Within the margin and near the edge
introduced Not native to an area where it now occurs; also adventive
involucre A skin under the sorus
involute With the edges rolled inwards
isomorphic Of the same form or appearance
isosporous Producing one type of spore
isotype A duplicate of the holotype from the same collection

jointed Bearing joints or nodes
juvenile The young stage of growth before a plant is capable of flowering or spore production

keel A ridge, usually on the back

labium A lip
labiate Having lips
lacerate With an irregular, ragged margin as though torn
laciniate Deeply and irregularly cut into narrow, pointed segments
lacuna A gap enclosed by, but free from, veins
laesurae Scars on spores caused by the process of shedding
lamina The expanded green part of a fern frond
lanate Woolly
lanceolate Lance-shaped: several times longer than wide, tapering slowly to the apex and rapidly to the base
lanuginose Cottony or woolly
lateral Arising at the side of an axis
latex A milky exudate, drying like rubber, e.g. the sap of *Regnellidium diphyllum*
lax Loosely arranged, open, scattered
leaf-gap A break in the vascular cylinder of the stem where the leaf-trace arises
leaflet The basic segment of a compound leaf
leaf-trace The vascular bundle that runs from the stele to the petiole
lectotype A holotype selected by a later author from the multiple types on which a name was based
lenticular Shaped like a biconvex lens
lepidote With small, scurfy scales
leptosporangiate With a sporangial wall one cell in thickness originating from a single cell
ligulate Strap-shaped
ligule A small, scale-like membranous appendage borne near the base of leaves in *Selaginella* and *Isoetes*

lime-dots A popular term for the outlet point of a hydathode where white salts accumulate
linear Long and narrow with parallel sides
lithophyte A plant that grows on rocks, cliff faces etc
littoral Growing in communities near the seashore
lobe A rounded segment of a leaf or a leaflet
lobule A small lobe
locule A compartment of an organ
longitudinal Running lengthwise
lunate Half moon or crescent-shaped
lustrous Shining, or with a sheen

macrospore Another term for megaspore
mangrove A specialized plant growing in brackish or sea water
marginal Attached to the edge
marginate With a margin of distinct character; a term for a stipe or rachis that is minutely keeled not winged
marine Pertaining to the sea or salt water
maritime Belonging to the sea, coastal
marsh A swamp
massula Rounded mass of hardened, cytoplasmic foam containing one or more spores (Salviniaceae)
matted Closely tangled together
mealy Covered with coarse, flour-like powder
medial Attached near the middle, especially between the midrib and the margin
megagametophyte The gametophyte developing vegetatively from the megaspore of a heterosporous plant, e.g. *Selaginella* spp.
megaphyll A large complex leaf, e.g. a fern frond
megasporangium The sporangium in heterosporous plants where the megaspores develop
megaspore The spore of heterosporous plants producing the female gametes; larger when compared with the microspore
megasporophyll Specialized leaf in heterosporous plants bearing or subtending the megasporangia
meiosis A reduction division whereby half the complement of chromosomes of a cell go into each of two daughter cells
membranous Thinly-textured
meristem A growing point, or an area of active cell division
mesoclinal Growing on the side of a slope where most rain falls cf. *xeroclinal*
mesomorphic Adapted to a moist climate, cf. *xeromorphic*
mesophyte A plant which favours a moist climate
mesophytic A moist habitat, neither too wet nor too dry
microgametophyte The gametophyte developing vegetatively from the microspore of a heterosporous plant, e.g. *Selaginella* spp.
micron A unit of length for microscopial measurements, equal to 1/25,000 of an inch or 1/1000 of a millimetre
microphyll The sterile leaves of fern allies; a small leaf
microsporangium The sporangium in heterosporous plants where the microspores develop
microspore The spore of heterosporous plants producing the male gametes: smaller when compared with the megaspore
microsporophyll Specialized leaf in heterosporous plants bearing or subtending the microsporangia
midrib The principal vein of a leaf that runs the full length
mixed sporangia A term used when sporangia of all ages are borne at all levels in a sorus
moniliform Constricted at intervals and appearing like a string of beads, e.g. the fertile segments of *Merinthosorus drynarioides*
monoecious Bisexual with both the male and female organs on the prothalli
monolete Describing a spore with a single linear scar, generally bean-shaped: also called bilateral because the spore has two nearly flat sides
monomorphic Having fronds of one type only
monotypic Having only one representative, e.g. a genus or a family with a single species
montane In the mountains
morphology The form and structure of a plant
motile Actively moving by its own propulsion
mucilaginous Covered in mucilage, a vegetable jelly of slimy consistency
mucro A short, sharp tip
mucronate With a short sharp tip or mucro
multicipital With many heads, a term sometimes used for the knobby branches on some fern rhizomes
multifarious In many rows or ranks
multifid Divided into many parts
multiseriate Arranged in many rows
muricate Roughened with hard tubercles
mycorrhizal A beneficial relationship between the roots of a plant (or a prothallus) and fungi or bacteria resulting in a nutrient exchange system
myrmecophilous Plants inhabited by ants and offering specialized shelters and/or food for them, e.g. *Lecanopteris* spp.

n The abbreviation used for the number of chromosomes in a cell (n=haploid, 2n=diploid, 3n=triploid etc.)
naked Lacking any covering or pubescence
naturalized An exotic plant growing and reproducing itself as though a native
neotropics The tropical areas of the New World, central America and the northern part of South America; the tropics of the western hemisphere
neotype A new holotype designated by a later author when the original type has been lost or destroyed
nerve A fine vein
nest-leaves Specialized sterile leaves modified for catching litter and debris, e.g. *Platycerium* spp.
net-veined Another term for reticulate
neuropteridian A venation pattern that resembles the venation in insect wings of the order Neuroptera
New World The area of central America and northern South America
node A point on a stem where leaves, bracts or branches arise
nomenclature The study of the application of the names of taxa
nomen nudum A plant name published without an accompanying description and therefore illegal
non-circinate vernation A characteristic where the young fronds are hooked rather than coiled
nutrient An element important in plant growth and supplied from the soil or by manures and fertilizers

obcordate Cordate with the broadest part above the middle
oblanceolate Lanceolate with the broadest part above the middle
obligate Essential, unable to exist without cf. facultative

oblique With the sides unequal or slanting
oblong Longer than broad, with parallel sides and rounded ends
obovate Ovate with the broadest part above the middle
obtuse Blunt or rounded at the apex
offset A growth arising at the base of a plant, or on a trunk
Old World The area of Europe, Africa, South-East Asia, and the Western Pacific
olivaceous Dark olive-green
opposite Arising on opposite sides but at the same level
orbicular Circular in outline
order A taxonomic grouping of similar families
oval Rounded but longer than wide
ovate A flat plane with the outline of an egg
ovoid A solid object with the outline of an egg

palaearctic A term for plants of the northern temperate regions
palea A scale
paleaceous Furnished with scales or chaff-like in texture
paleotropics The tropical areas of the Old World (Africa, South-East Asia and the Western Pacific); the tropics of the eastern hemisphere
palmate Divided like a hand, the divisions radiating from a single point
palmatifid Lobed like a hand, the divisions extending about half way
palmatisect Lobed like a hand, the divisions extending nearly to the base
palynology The science of the structure of spores
panicle A much branched racemose inflorescence: in ferns a loosely arranged cluster of sporangia as in *Botrychium* spp.
pantropic Found throughout the tropics
papillate With wart or nipple-like glands
papyraceous With a texture like parchment
paraphysate Bearing paraphyses
paraphysis (es) A sterile filament or hair borne among sporangia: may be simple or branched, pointed or clubbed
partite Divided nearly to the base into lobes or divisions
patent Spreading
pectinate Comb-like: deeply divided with the segments narrow and close
pedate Palmately divided but with the basal lobes again divided, e.g. fronds of *Doryopteris palmata* var. *pedata*
pedicel In ferns the stalk of a sporangium or a conceptacle
peduncle In ferns the stalk supporting a sporocarp
pellucid Transparent
peltate Of organs attached in from the margin, e.g. some indusia
pendant Hanging downwards
pendulous Hanging, drooping
penninerved The veins branching pinnately
perennate Maintain a dormant state through the non-growing season
perennial Living for more than two years
perispore A wrinkled or folded outer envelope covering some spores
persistent Remaining attached
pesticide A chemical used to control pests
petiole The stalk of a leaf: in ferns a stipe
petiolule The stalk of a leaflet
petrophilous Rock-loving, growing on rocks

pH The measure of acidity or alkalinity of a material
phloem Part of the vascular system of plants concerned with the transport of nutrients, organic compounds and hormones
photoperiod The length of the daylight hours suitable for photosynthesis
photosynthesis The conversion of carbon dioxide and water to sugars within green parts of the plant, using chlorophyll and energy from the sun's rays
photosynthetic spores Green spores containing chlorophyll and which can therefore photosynthesize
phyllopodium An outgrowth of the rhizome of some ferns to which the frond is joined
phytoxicity Damage symptoms induced in a plant by a toxin
pilose With scattered, long, simple hairs
pinna The leaflet of a pinnate leaf or the primary division of a compound leaf
pinnate Once divided with the divisions extending to the rachis
pinnate-pinnatifid An embracing term used to describe the divisions between pinnate and pinnatifid (pinnatisect etc.); a frond that is not quite bipinnate
pinnatifid Once divided with the divisions extending about one quarter to half way to the rachis
pinnatipartite Once divided with the divisions extending half to two thirds of the way to the rachis
pinnatisect Once divided with the divisions reaching nearly to the rachis (more than three quarters of the way)
pinnule A secondary pinna: the ultimate segment of a frond divided two or more times
pinnulet A term for segments of a tripinnate (or higher order frond); another term for pinnule
pitted With numerous small depressions on the surface
plagiotropic Growing laterally or obliquely, as in most fern rhizomes
plicate Folded lengthwise into pleats
plumose Feather-like
pluricostate With more than one midrib or main vein
pneumathodes Bands of pores of aerating tissue, especially prominent along the stipes of ferns
poikilohydrous Said of a plant with leaves which can inroll or shrivel when dry, but which can unfold and reopen when wet
polymorphic Existing in several forms
polyploid A plant with more than two sets of the basic chromosome number
polystichous Arranged in many rows
potbound Said of a potted fern when the roots are strongly intertwined and matted
proliferous Producing buds and new plants by vegetative means
propagule A body with the capacity to give rise to a new plant, e.g. spore, gemma, bulbil
prostrate Lying flat on the ground
prothallium (ia) See *prothallus*
prothallus (i) A thinly-textured flat growth resulting from the germination of a spore and bearing archegonia and antheridia
protostelic A stem with a single solid vascular strand
protruberance A swelling or lump on the surface
proximal Towards the base or attached end of an organ
pseudodichotomous Appearing as if dichotomous, but really two equal lateral branches with a dormant, terminal bud between, e.g. *Gleichenia* fronds

pseudoserrate Falsely toothed, a term used for the apparently toothed margins of some rhizome scales
pteridologist A student of ferns
pteridology The study of ferns
pteridophyte The general name for ferns and fern allies
puberulent Minutely pubescent, the hairs scarcely visible
puberulous Slightly hairy
pubescent Covered with short, soft hairs
punctate With dots or small spots
punctiform Reduced to a mere dot or point, e.g. the sori of *Microsorum punctatum*
punctulate Minutely dotted
pup A popular term for a bulbil, plantlet or offset as in *Platycerium*
pustule A low projection like a blister or pimple

quadrifoliar Bearing four leaflets arising at the same point, e.g. *Marsilea* leaves
quadripinnate Four times pinnate

rachides A term used for rachises
rachis (es) The main axis of a compound leaf
radial A rhizome bearing roots and leaves on all surfaces
radical Arranged in a basal rosette
radicant Rooting, a term applied to stems, fronds when they root at the tips, or proliferous buds
rainforest A complex vegetation dominated by trees in which the canopies intermingle
raphe The ridge that connects the sporocarp and stem in *Marsilea*
receptacle An axis or outgrowth of tissue bearing sporangia
recurved Curved downwards
reflexed Bent sharply backwards
renascent Springing up afresh each year
reniform Kidney-shaped
reticulate Branching and rejoining to form a network
reticulum A network of veins formed by branching and rejoining
retrorse Directed downwards or backwards
retuse The apex rounded and notched
revolute With the margins rolled backwards
rhachis See *rachis*
rheophyte A flood resistant plant living between the high and low water levels of rivers
rhizoid A filamentous, root-like structure as on a prothallus or on the sporophytes of some filmy-ferns
rhizome A modified underground stem from which the fronds are produced
rhizophore A specialized leafless stem which bears roots: purported to exist in some species of *Selaginella*
rhomboid Diamond-shaped
root hair A unicellular protruberance arising from the surface cells of a root
rootstock Another term for a rhizome
rosette A group of overlapping leaves radiating from the centre
rostrate With a beak
rudimentary Fragmentary, imperfectly developed
rugose Wrinkled
rugulose Finely wrinkled
runner A slender prostrate stem that terminates in a bud which produces leaves and roots (cf. *stolon*)
rupestral Growing on rocks, cliffs, walls etc.

saccate With a pouch or sac
sagenoid Anastomosing venation with regular areoles with included veinlets (simple or branched) protruding in all directions, e.g. *Tectaria* spp.
sagittate Shaped like an arrow head, with the basal lobes pointing downwards
saline Salty, brackish
sarmentose Producing long, flexuose runners or stolons
saxicolous Growing on or among rocks
scabrous Rough to the touch, due to minute projections
scale A dry, flattened, papery structure two or more cells wide found on ferns: a vestigial leaf
scandent Climbing
scarious Thin, dry and membranous
sciophilous Said of a plant which favours shady conditions
scurf A fine, scaly covering
scutelliform Shaped like a small shield
section A taxonomic subgroup of a genus containing closely related species
segment Each free part of a divided frond
semi-xeric Able to grow in semi-arid conditions
septate Divided by partitions
seriate In whorls or apparent whorls
serrate With sharp teeth oblique to the margin
serrulate Finely serrate
sessile Without a stalk
seta A stiff hair or bristle
setaceous With the character of a bristle
setiferous Bristle bearing
setose Bristly
setulose Covered with small bristly hairs
sheath A tubular envelope that clasps the stem, e.g. *Equisetum* spp.
shield fronds Sterile fronds which envelop the root system of *Platycerium* spp.
silky With a covering of very fine, lustrous hairs
simple Undivided, of one piece
sinuate With the margin strongly wavy
sinus The cleft or gap between lobes or teeth on a margin
sinus membrane A flap of membranous tissue occurring in the sinus of some ferns
siphonostele A stem with an interrupted pipe-like vascular strand
slender Long and thin
solitary Singly, not in groups
soriferous Bearing sori
sorophore Specialized outgrowth of a frond margin or segment margin bearing sporangia, e.g. *Lygodium* spp.
sorus (i) A group or arrangement of sporangia in ferns
spathulate Spoon-shaped
species A taxonomic group of related plants, all possessing a common set of characters which sets them apart from another species
spermatozoid A motile, male gamete
spicular Spiky
spike An undivided floral axis bearing sessile sporangia, e.g. *Ophioglossum* spp.
spinescent Ending in a spine
spinose Armed with spines
spinulose Having small spines
spiral Borne at different levels along the axis: coiling
sporangiophore The stalk of a sporangium; a peltate organ bearing sporangia in *Equisetum*
sporangium (a) A spore case

spore A vegetative reproductive unit that does not contain an embryo, found in cryptogams
sporeling A very young fern plant developing from the prothallus after fertilization
spore mother cells The 16 cells in a sporangium which undergo meiosis to produce the spores; each mother cell produces four spores
sporiferous Bearing spores
sporocarp A thick-walled organ containing sporangia in heterosporous aquatic ferns e.g. *Marsilea* spp.
sporogenous Spore-forming tissue
sporophyll A leaf-like structure which bears or subtends sporangia
sporophyte The diploid fern plant which produces spores
sporulation The formation of spores
squamose Scaly
squamulose Covered with small, papery scales
squarrose With spreading scales
stele The arrangement of vascular tissue in a stem
stellate Star-shaped, as in some hairs with several arms, e.g. *Pyrrosia* spp.
sterile Barren, not producing viable spores
stipe The petiole of a fern or palm frond: a stalk
stipitate Having a stipe or stalk
stipules Bract-like appendages borne in pairs at the base of a petiole
stolon Horizontal elongated stem rooting at the nodes
stoloniferous Spreading by stolons
stomata Pores in the epidermis of a leaf
stomium The opening of the annulus in a sporangium where dehiscence occurs
stramineous Straw-coloured
strand plant A plant growing by the sea
strobilus A cone formed by the aggregation of micro and/or mega sporophylls, e.g. *Selaginella* spp.
striate Marked with fine lines or ridges
subarborescent A term used for ferns which develop small trunks
suberose Corky
subfamily A taxonomic group of closely related genera within a family
subspecies A taxonomic grouping within a species used to describe geographically isolated variants
substrate The surface or medium to which a plant is anchored
subtend To occur immediately below
subulate Awl-shaped
succulent Juicy or fleshy
sucker A shoot arising from the roots or trunk below ground level
sulcate Furrowed
superior Situated above another organ
surcurrent With wings extending from the base of a pinna or segment up the rachis, costa or costule (opposite of decurrent)
symbiosis A beneficial association of different organisms
symptomology The symtoms of a pest, disease or some other malady
synaptospory The shedding of spores in small groups or in whole sporangia rather than separately
synganium A fertile body formed by the fusion of two or more sporangia, divided internally into locules and bearing spores
synonym Another name for the same taxon; may be an alternate name under a different classification system, or an old name now superseded
syntype One or more of the original collection of specimens when none is designated as the holotype. Usually one of these is later selected as the lectotype

tapetum The nutritional fluid which surrounds spores in their developmental stage
taxon A group of plants of the same type, e.g. family, genus, species
taxonomy The study of the division of life forms into categories
temperate Cooler areas of the world
terete Slender and cylindrical
ternate Growing in threes, in whorls of three
terrestrial Growing on the ground
tetrad A group of four
tetrahedral Made up of four sides; also describing a trilete spore
thallus A plant body not differentiated into leaves and stem
tomentose Densely covered with matted woolly hairs
tomentum A dense woolly or matted covering
topotype A specimen collected at the type locality but at a later date
tortuous Twisted
translucent Nearly transparent
transpiration The loss of water vapour to the atmosphere through the openings in the fronds
trapezoid Trapezium-shaped
tribe A taxonomic grouping of similar genera within a family or subfamily
trichome An unbranched, hair-like outgrowth of the epidermis, often glandular tipped
trifid Divided into three, more or less equal parts
trilete Describing a spore with a three-armed scar; also tetrahedral
tripartite Divided into three more or less equal parts, nearly to the base
tripinnate Three times pinnate
triplinerved With three main veins
triquetrous With three prominent, acutely angled ridges
tropical Warmer or equatorial areas of the world
truncate Ending abruptly as if cut off
trunk The erect, unbranched portion of a tree-like plant
tuber A swollen, underground organ
tuberculate Bearing knobby projections
tubular Hollow and elongate
tufted Growing in small clumps
turgid Swollen
type The specimen to which the name of a taxon is always attached

umbrophile A plant which favours shady conditions
unarmed Without spines or prickles
undulate Wavy
united Fused or growing together

variegated Where the basic colour is broken by areas of another colour
variety Recognizable entities within a species that are not genetically isolated from each other
vascular Of tissue containing the veins or main conducting elements
vascular bundle The internal conduction system of plants

vegetation The whole plant communities of an area
vegetative Asexual development or propagation
vein The conducting tissue of leaves
veinlet A small or slender vein
velum A membranous veil: a covering over the sporangia of *Isoetes*
velutinous Covered with fine, soft, spreading hairs; velvety
venation The pattern formed by veins
ventral The undersurface
vernation The arrangement of unexpanded leaves or fronds in a bud
verrucose Warty
verticillate Whorled
vestigial Rudimentary, of a relic nature
viable Alive and able to germinate
villous Covered in long, soft hairs
vining Climbing by twining of the stems
viscid Sticky or gluey
viviparous Sprouting from a bud while still attached to the parent plant

whorl Three or more leaves at a node
wig A popular term for the reduced and skeletonized basal pinnae of the fronds of some tree ferns (aphlebiae)
wing A membranous flattened border to an axis
woolly Bearing long, soft, matted hairs

xeric Drought-resistant, able to grow in arid and semi-arid conditions, cf. *mesic*
xeroclinal Growing on the dry side of slopes, cf. *mesoclinal*
xeromorphic Adapted to dry climatic conditions, cf. *mesomorphic*
xerophyte A drought resistant plant growing in arid climatic conditions
xylem Vascular tissue concerned with water transport from the roots to the leaves

zygote The fertilized egg

Bibliography

Allan, H. H. (1961), *Flora of New Zealand*, Vol 1, Government Printer, Wellington, New Zealand

Alston, A. H. G. (1959), *The Ferns and Fern Allies of West Tropical Africa*, Supplement to the Flora, Crown Agents, Millbank, London, England.

Alston, A. H. G., & E. A. C. L. E. Schelpe. (1952), 'An Annotated Checklist of the Pteridophyta of Southern Africa', *Journal of South African Botany*, 18:153–176.

Aston, H. I. (1973), *Aquatic Plants of Australia*, Melbourne University Press, Victoria, Australia.

Backer, C. A., & O. Posthumus. (1939), *Varenflora voor Java*, Vitgave Lands Plantentuin, Buitenzorg Java.

Badre, F., & T. Cadet. (1978), 'The Pteridophytes of Réunion Island', *Fern Gazette II*: 349–365.

Bailey, F. M. (1874), *Handbook to the Ferns of Queensland*, Thorne & Greenwell, Brisbane, Australia.

Bailey, F. M. (1881), *The Fern World of Australia*, Gordon & Gotch, Brisbane, Australia.

Baishya, A. K., & R. R. Rao. (1982), *Ferns and Fern Allies of Meghalaya State*, India, Scientific Publishers, Jodhpur, India.

Baker, J. G. (1887), *Handbook to the Fern Allies*, George Bell & Sons, London, England.

Baker, J. G. (1892), *A Summary of the New Ferns which have been Discovered or Described since 1874*, Clarendon Press, Oxford, England.

Barrington, D. S. (1978), 'A Revision of *Trichipteris* (Cyatheaceae)', *Contributions from Gray Herbarium* 208:3–93.

Beddome, R. H. (1865–70), *The Ferns of British India*, Gantz Bros, Madras, India.

Beddome, R. H. (1863), *The Ferns of Southern India*, Gantz Bros, Madras, India.

Beddome, R. H. (1892), *Handbook to the Ferns of British India*, Thacker, Spink & Co, Calcutta, India.

Billington, C. (1952), *Ferns of Michigan*, Cranbrook Press, Michigan, USA.

Birkenhead, J. (no date), *Ferns and Fern Culture*, H. B. May and Sons, London, England.

Blasdell, R. F. (1963), 'A Monographic Study of the Fern Genus *Cystopteris*', *Memoirs Torrey Botanical Club*, 21:1–102.

Blatter, E., & J. F. d'Almeida. (1922), *The Ferns of Bombay*, D. B. Taraporevala & Sons, Bombay, India.

Bocher, W., Kjeld Holmen, and K. Jakobsen. (1968), *The Flora of Greenland*, P. Haase & Sons, Copenhagen, Denmark.

Bower, F. O. (1923), *The Ferns*, Cambridge University Press, Vol I 1923, Vol II 1926, Vol III 1928.

Bower, F. O. (1935), *Primitive Land Plants*, Macmillan & Co., London, England.

Brooks, M. G., & A. S. Margolin. (1938), 'The Pteridophytes of West Virginia', *West Virginia University Bulletin* 39 (2).

Brown, D. F. M. (1964), 'A Monographic Study of the Fern Genus *Woodsia*', *Beihefte Nova Hedwigia*, 16:1–154.

Brown, E. D., & F. B. H. Brown. (1931), 'Flora of Southeastern Polynesia' 2 Pteridophytes, *Bulletin Bernice Bishop Museum* no. 89, 1–123.

Brownlie, G. (1969), *Flore de la Nouvelle-Caledonie et Dependances*, 3 Pteridophytes, Museum National D'Histoire Naturelle, Paris, France.

Brownlie, G. (1977), *The Pteridophyte Flora of Fiji*, J. Cramer, Germany.

Ching, R. C. (1940), 'On a Natural Classification of the Family Polypodiaceae', *Sunyatensia*, 6:201–270.

Ching, R. C. (1963), 'A Reclassification of the family Thelypteridaceae from the Mainland of Asia', *Acta Phytotaxica Sinica*, 8:289–335.

Ching, R. C. (1964), 'On Some Confused Genera of the Family Athyriaceae', *Acta Phytoxica Sinica*, 9:41–48.

Chinnock, R. J., & E. Heath. (1981), *Common Ferns & Fern Allies*, Mobil New Zealand Nature Series, A. H. & A. W. Reed Ltd, Christchurch, New Zealand.

Christensen, C. (1906–1934), *Index Filicum & supplements*, by R. E. G. Pichi-Sermolli (1934–1960), International Bureau of Plant Taxonomy, Utrecht, Netherlands.

Christensen, C. (1925), 'Revised List of Hawaiian Pteridophyta', *Bulletin Bernice Bishop Museum* no. 25:1–30.

Christensen, C. (1932), *The Pteridophyta of Madagascar*, *Dansk Botanic Archives* 7:1–253.

Christensen, C. (1943), 'A Revision of the Pteridophyta of Samoa', *Bulletin Bernice Bishop Museum* no. 177:1–138.

Clarke, C. B. (1880), *Ferns of Northern India, A Review*, Taylor & Francis, London, England.

Clausen, R. T. (1938), 'A Monograph of the Ophioglossaceae', *Memoirs Torrey Botanical Club*, 19:1–177.

Clifford, H. T., & J. Constantine. (1980), *Ferns, Fern Allies and Conifers of Australia, A Laboratory Manual*, University of Queensland Press, St. Lucia, Qld, Australia.

Cody, W. J. (1956), *Ferns of the Ottawa District*, Canada Department of Agriculture, Ottowa, Ontario, Canada.

Conant, D. S. (1983), 'A Revision of the genus *Alsophila* in the Americas', *Journal Arnold Arboretum*, 64:333–379.

Copeland, E. B. (1929), 'Ferns of Fiji', *Bulletin Bernice Bishop Museum* no. 59:1–105.

Bibliography

Copeland, E. B. (1932), 'Pteridophytes of the Society Islands', *Bulletin Bernice Bishop Museum* no. 93:1–86.

Copeland, E. B., & T. G. Collado. (1936), 'Crop Ferns', *Philippine Journal Agriculture* 7:367–377.

Copeland, E. B. (1936), 'Solomon Island Ferns', *Philippine Journal Science*, 60:99–117.

Copeland, E. B. (1938), 'Genera Hymenophyllacearum', *Philippine Journal Science*, 67:1–110.

Copeland, E. B. (1942), 'Edible Ferns', *American Fern Journal*, 32:121–126.

Copeland, E. B. (1947), *Genera Filicum*, Chronica Botanica Coy, New Delhi, India.

Copeland, E. B. (1953–60), *Fern Flora of the Philippines*, Vol 1–3, National Institute of Science and Technology, Manila, Philippines.

Correll, D. S. (1956), *Ferns and Fern Allies of Texas*, Texas Research Foundation, Renner, Texas, USA.

Crabbe, J. A., A. C. Jermy, & J. T. Mickel. (1975), 'A New Generic Sequence for the Pteridophyte Herbarium', *Fern Gazette*, 11:141–162.

Cranfill, R. (1980), *Ferns and Fern Allies of Kentucky*, Kentucky Nature Preserves Commission, Kentucky, USA.

Crittenden, M. (1978), *The Fern Book*, Celestial Arts, Millbrae, California, USA.

Crookes, M. (1963), *New Zealand Ferns*, 6th ed., Whitcombe & Tombs, Christchurch, New Zealand.

Dhir, K. K. (1980), *Ferns of North-western Himalayas*, J. Cramer, Germany.

Dobbie, H. B., & M. Crookes, (1951), *New Zealand Ferns*, Whitcombe & Tombs Ltd, Auckland, New Zealand.

Domin, K. (1929), *The Pteridophyta of the Island of Dominica*, Praha, Czechoslovakia.

Druery, C. T. (1910), *British Ferns and their Varieties*, G. Routledge & Sons, London, England.

Dunk, G. (1982), *Ferns for the Home and Garden*, Angus & Robertson, Melbourne, Australia.

Edie, H. H. (1978), *Ferns of Hong Kong*, Libra Press, Hong Kong.

Foster, F. G. (1976), *Ferns to Know and Grow*, Hawthorn Books, New York, USA.

Foster, R. C. (1958), 'A Catalogue of the Ferns and Flowering Plants of Bolivia', *Contributions from Gray Herbarium*, 184:1–223.

Francis, G. W. (1855), *An Analysis of the British Ferns and their Allies*, Simpkin Marshall & Coy, London, England.

Franks, W. (1969), *Platycerium Fern Facts*, private printing, Los Angeles, California.

Graf, A. B. (1976), *Exotica series 3*, 9th Edition, E. Rutherford, New Jersey, USA.

Gastony, G. J. (1973), 'A Revision of the Fern Genus *Nephelea*', *Contributions from Gray Herbarium*, 203:81–148.

Goudey, C. J. (1985) *'Maidenhair Ferns in Cultivation'*. Lothian Publishing Co., Melbourne Australia.

Grounds, R. (1974), *Ferns*, Pelham Books, London, England.

Guilcher, J. M., & R. H. Noailles. (1973), *A Fern is Born*, Sterling Publishing Coy, New York, USA.

Hancock, F. D. & A. Lucas. (1973), *Ferns of the Witwatersrand*, University Press, Johannesburg, South Africa.

Hara, H. (1966), *The Flora of Eastern Himalayas*, University of Tokyo Press, Japan.

Harris, W. F. (1955), *A Manual of the Spores of the New Zealand Pteridophyta*, DSIR, Wellington, New Zealand.

Hauke, R. L. (1978), 'A Taxonomic Monograph of *Equisetum* subgenus *Equisetum*', *Nova Hedwigia*, 30:385–455.

Heath, E., & R. J. Chinnock. (1974), *Ferns and Fern Allies of New Zealand*, A. H. & A. W. Reed Pty Ltd, Wellington, New Zealand.

Hennipman, E. (1977), 'A Monograph of the Fern Genus *Bolbitis*', University Press, Leiden, The Netherlands.

Herter, W. G. (1949), 'Flora del Uruguay I Pteridophyta', *Review Sudam Botany*, 9:1–28.

Hevly, R. H. (1964), 'Adaptations of Cheilanthoid Ferns to Desert Environments', *Journal Arizona Academy Science* 2:164–175.

Hibberd, S. (1879), *The Fern Garden*, Groombridge & Sons, London, England.

Hodge, W. H. (1973), 'Fern Foods of Japan and the Problem of Toxicity', *American Fern Journal* 63:77–80.

Holttum, R. E. (1947), 'A Revised Classification of Leptosporangiate Ferns', *Journal Linnaen Society, Botany* 53:123–158.

Holttum, R. E. (1949), 'The Classification of Ferns', *Biological Review*, 24:267–296.

Holttum, R. E. (1957), 'Morphology, Growth Habit and Classification in the family Gleicheniaceae', *Phytomorphology*, 7:168–184.

Holttum, R. E. (1957), 'The Scales of Cyatheaceae', *Kew Bulletin*, 41–45.

Holttum, R. E. (1959), 'Gleicheniaceae', in *Flora Malesiana*, series II, 1(1) 1–61.

Holttum, R. E. & U. Sen. (1961), 'Morphology and Classification of the Tree Ferns', *Phytomorphology*, 11:406–20.

Holttum, R. E. (1963), 'Cyatheaceae', in *Flora Malesiana*, series II, 1 (2) 65–176.

Holttum, R. E. (1968), *Flora of Malaya*, Vol. II, *Ferns of Malaya*, Government Printing Office, Singapore.

Holttum, R. E. (1982), 'Thelypteridaceae', in *Flora Malesiana*, series II, 1 (5) 331–560.

Holttum, R. E. & E. Hennipman, (1978), '*Lomariopsis* Group', in *Flora Malesiana*, series II, 1 (4) 255–330.

Hooker, Sir. W. J. (1846), *Species Filicum*, Vol 1 – 1856, II – 1858, III – 1860, IV – 1862, V – 1864, William Pamplin, London, England.

Hooker, Sir, W. J. (1854), *A Century of Ferns*, W. Pamplin, London, England.

Hooker, Sir, W. J. (1859), *Exotic Ferns*, Lovell Reeve, London, England.

Hooker, Sir, W. J. (1861), *A Second Century of Ferns*, William Pamplin, London, England.

Hooker, Sir, W. J., & J. G. Baker. (1868), *Synopsis Filicum*, Robert Hardwicke, London, England.

Hooker, Sir, W. J. (1862), *Garden Ferns*, Lovell Reeve & Co, London, England.

Hooker, Sir, W. J., & F. Bauer. (1888), *The Genera of Ferns*, Henry G. Bohn, London, England.

Hoshizaki, B. J. (1972), 'Morphology and Phylogeny of *Platycerium* species', *Biotropica*, 4:93–117.

Hoshizaki, B. J. (1970), 'The Genus *Adiantum* in Cultivation', *Baileya*, 17:97–191.

Hoshizaki, B. J. (1979), *Fern Growers Manual*, Alfred A. Knopf, New York, USA.

Hoshizaki, B. J. (1981), 'The Fern Genus *Davallia* in Cultivation (Davalliaceae)', *Baileya*, 21:1–42.

Hoshizaki, B. J. (1981), 'The Genus *Pyrrosia* in Cultivation', *Baileya*, 21:43–50.

Hoshizaki, B. J. (1982), 'The Genus *Polypodium* in Cultivation', *Baileya*, 22(1):1–98.

Hyde, H. A. & A. E. Wade. (1978), *Welsh Ferns, Clubmosses, Quillworts and Horsetails*, National Museum, Cardiff, Wales.

Jacobsen, W. B. G. (1983), *The Ferns and Fern Allies of Southern Africa*, Butterworth, Durban, South Africa.

Jermy, A. C., J. A. Crabbe, & B. A. Thomas. (1973), *The Phylogeny and Classification of the Ferns*, Academic Press, London, England.

Joe, B. (1964), 'A Review of the Species of *Platycerium* (Polypodiaceae)', *Baileya*, 12:70–128.

Johns, R. J., & A. Bellamy, (1979), *The Ferns and Fern Allies of Papua New Guinea*, Parts 1–5, Forestry College, Bulolo, Papua New Guinea.

Johns, R. J., & A. Bellamy. (1981), *The Ferns and Fern Allies of Papua New Guinea*, Parts 6–12, University of Technology, Lae, Papua New Guinea.

Johnson, A. (1957), *A Student's Guide to the Ferns of Singapore Island*, Malayan Nature Society, Kuala Lumpur, Malaysia.

Jones, D. L., & S. C. Clemesha. (1981), *Australian Ferns and Fern Allies*, A. H. & A. W. Reed Pty Ltd, Sydney, Australia.

Jones, D. L., & C. J. Goudey. (1981), *Exotic Ferns in Australia*, A. H. & A. W. Reed Pty Ltd, Sydney, Australia.

Jones, D. L., & C. J. Goudey. (1984), *Ferns in Australia*, A. H. & A. W. Reed Pty Ltd, Sydney, Australia.

Kaye, R. (1968), *Hardy Ferns*, Faber & Faber Ltd, London, England.

Kaye, R. (1980), 'Ferns', *Wisley Handbook*, 32, Royal Horticultural Society, London, England.

Kepler, A. K. (1975), *Common Ferns of Luquillo Forest*, Puerto Rico, Inter American University Press, Puerto Rico.

Knobloch, I. W., & D. S. Correll. (1962), *Ferns and Fern Allies of Chihuahua*, Mexico, Texas Research Foundation, Texas, USA.

Kramer, K. U. (1962), 'Pteridophyta', in *Flora of the Netherland Antilles*, ed. A. L. Stoffers, Utrecht, Holland.

Kramer, K. U. (1971), '*Lindsaea* Group', in *Flora Malesiana*, series II, 1 (3) 177–254.

Kramer, K. U. (1978), *The Pteridophytes of Suriname*, Utrecht, Holland.

Kunkel, G. (1965), 'Catalogue of the Pteridophytes of the Juan Fernandez Islands', *Nova Hedwigia*, 9:249–50.

Lakela, O., & R. W. Long. (1976), *Ferns of Florida*, Banyan Books, Florida, USA.

Lloyd, R. M. (1974), 'Systematics of the genus *Ceratopteris* II, Taxonomy', *Brittonia*, 26:139–160.

Looser, G. (1955), 'The Ferns of Southern Chile', *American Fern Journal*, 38:33–44, 71–87.

Lovis, J. D. (1968), 'Fern Hybridists and Fern Hybridizing II, Fern Hybridizing at the University of Leeds', *British Fern Gazette*, 10:13–20.

Lowe, E. J., & A. M. Jones. (1889), 'Abnormal Ferns, Hybrids and their Parents', *Annals of Botany*, 3:27–30.

Lumpkin, T. A., & D. L. Plunknett. (1980), '*Azolla*: Botany, physiology and use as a green manure', *Economic Botany*, 34:111–153.

Macself, A. J. (1952), *Ferns for Garden and Greenhouse*, W. H. & L. Collingridge Ltd, London, England.

May, L. W. (1978), 'The Economic Uses and Associated Folklore of Ferns and Fern Allies', *Botanical Review*, 44:491–528.

Mickel, J. T. (1979), *How to Know the Ferns and Fern Allies*, W. C. Brown & Co, Iowa, USA.

Moore, T. (1855), *A Popular History of the British Ferns*, George Routledge, London, England.

Moore, T. (1857), *Index Filicum*, William Pamplin, London, England.

Nayar, B. K., & S. Kaur. (1974), *Companion to R. H. Beddomes Handbook to the Ferns of British India*, Chronica Botanica, New Delhi, India.

Olson, W. W. (1977), *The Fern Dictionary*, Los Angeles Fern Society, Los Angeles, USA.

Page, C. N. (1977), 'An Ecological Survey of the Ferns of the Canary Island', *Fern Gazette*, II:19–77.

Parham, J. W. (1972), *Plants of the Fiji Islands*, Government Printer, Suva, Fiji.

Petrick-Ott, A. J. (1979), *The Pteridophytes of Kansas, Nebraska, South Dakota and North Dakota, USA*, J. Cramer, Germany.

Pfeiffer, N. E. (1922), 'Monograph of the Isoetaceae', *Annals Missouri Botanical Gardens*, 9:79–232.

Piggot, A. (1979), *Common Epiphytic Ferns of Malaysia & Singapore*, Heinemann Educational Books, Singapore.

Posthumus, O. (1943), 'The Ferns of the Lesser Sunda Islands', *Annals Jardine Botanique*, 35–113.

Proctor, George R. (1977), *Flora of the Lesser Antilles, Leeward and Windward Islands*, Vol 2, Pteridophyta, Arnold Arboretum, Massachusetts, USA.

Roux, J. P. (1979), *Cape Peninsula Ferns*, National Botanic Gardens, Kirstenbosch, South Africa.

Rush, R. (1984), *A Guide to Hardy Ferns*, British Pteridological Society, London.

Schelpe, E.A.C.L.E. (1969), 'Reviews of Tropical African Pteridophyta 1', *Bolus Herbarium*, South Africa.

Schelpe, E.A.C.L.E. (1970), 'Pteridophyta', in *Flora Zambesiaca*, University Press, Glasgow, United Kingdom.

Shaver, J. M. (1954), *Ferns of the Eastern Central States*, Dover Publications, New York, USA.

Shieh, W. (1980), 'Pteridophyta', in *Flora of Taiwan*, Vol 1, Epoch Publishing Coy, China.

Sim, T. R. (1915), *The Ferns of South Africa*, Cambridge, England.

Small, J. K. (1918), *Ferns of Tropical Florida*, Published by Author, New York, USA.

Small, J. K. (1975), *Ferns of the Vicinity of New York*, Dover Publications, New York, USA.

Smith, J. (1875), *Historia Filicum*, Macmillan & Co, London, England.

Smith, J. (1879), *Ferns British and Foreign*, David Bogue, London, England.

Smith, A. R. (1981), 'Pteridophytes', in *Flora of Chiapas*, p 2, ed. D. E. Breedlove, Jr., Academy of Sciences, California, USA.

Sporne, K. R. (1975), *The Morphology of the Pteridophytes*, Hutchison, London, England.

Step, E. (1908), *Wayside and Woodland Ferns*, Frederick Warne & Co., London, England.

Stolze, R. G. (1974), 'A Taxonomic Revision of the genus *Cnemidaria*', *Fieldiana*, 37:1–98.

Stolze, R. G. (1976), 'Ferns and Fern Allies of Guatemala', Part I, *Fieldiana Botany*, 39:1–130.

Stolze, R. G. (1981), 'Ferns and Fern Allies of Guatemala', Part II, *Fieldiana Botany*, n.s. 6:1–522.

Stone, B. C. (1970), 'Psilophyta, Lepidophyta and Pteridophyta in "The Flora of Guam" ', *Micronesica*, 6:48–64.

Taylor, T. M. C. (1970), *Pacific Northwest Ferns and their Allies*, University Press, Toronto, Canada.

Thieret, J. W. (1980), *Louisiana Ferns and Fern Allies*, Lafayette Natural History Museum, Louisiana, USA.

Tindale, M. D. (1965), 'A Monograph of the genus *Lastreopsis*', Ching, Contributions NSW National, *Herbarium* 3:249–339.

Tryon, A. F. (1957), 'A Revision of the genus *Pellaea*, section *Pellaea*', *Annals Missouri Botanic Garden*, 44:125–193.

Tryon, R. M. (1941), 'A Revision of the genus *Pteridium*', *Rhodora*, 43:1–31:37–67.

Tryon, R. M. (1956), 'A Revision of the American species of *Notholaena*', *Contributions from Gray Herbarium*, 179:1–106.

Tryon, R. M. (1964), 'The Ferns of Peru', *Contributions from Gray Herbarium*, 194:135–180.

Tryon, R. M. (1970), 'The Classification of the Cyatheaceae', Contributions from Gray, *Herbarium*, 200:3–53.

Tryon, R. M., & D. S. Conant. (1975), 'The Ferns of Brazilian Amazonia', *Acta Amazonica*, 5:23–34.

Tryon, R. M., & A. F. Tryon. (1982), *Ferns and Allied Plants with Special Reference to Tropical America*, Springer-Verlag, New York, USA.

Valletin, E. F., & E. M. Cotton. (1921), *Illustrations of Flowering Plants and Ferns of the Falkland Islands*, L. Reeve & Coy, London, England.

Vareschi, V. (1968), 'Aspleniaceae – Salviniaceae', in *Flora de Venezuela*, Vol I, part II, ed. T. Lasser, Caracas, Venezuela.

Vereschi, V. (1969), 'Lycopodiaceae – Aspidiaceae', in *Flora de Venezuela*, Vol 1, part I, ed. T. Lasser, Caracas, Venezuela.

Verdoon, Fr. (1938), *Manual of Pteridology*, Martinus Nijhoff, The Hague, Netherlands.

Wagner, W. H. Jr., & D. F. Grether. (1948), 'Pteridophytes of Guam', *Bulletin Bernice Bishop Museum* no 8.

Wagner, W. H., & D. F. Grether. (1948), 'The Pteridophytes of the Admiralty Islands', University California Publications, *Botany*, 23:17–110.

Wagner, W. H. (1974), 'Pteridology 1947–1972', *Annals Missouri Botanic Garden*, 61:86–111.

Wagner, D. (1979), 'Systematics of *Polystichum* in West North America, north of Mexico', *Pteridologia*, 1:1–64.

Wherry, E. T. (1964), *The Southern Fern Guide*, American Fern Society, New York, USA.

Wiley, F. A. (1973), *Ferns of the Northeastern United States*, Dover Publications Inc., New York, USA.

Willis, J. C. (1973), *A Dictionary of Flowering Plants and Ferns* (8th ed.), revised by H. K. Airy Shaw, Cambridge University Press, England.

Fern Societies and Study Groups

Australia
The Fern Society of Victoria,
P.O. Box 45, Heidelberg, Victoria 3081.

Fern Society of Western Australia,
C/o Mrs. G. E. J. Bromley, 73 Point Walter Road, Bicton, Western Australia 6157.

Fern Society of South Australia,
P.O. Box 711, G.P.O., Adelaide,
South Australia 5001.

Tasmanian Fern Society,
C/o Julie Haas, 72 Bush Creek Road, Lenah Valley, Tasmania 7008.

Fern Study Group of the Society for Growing Australian Plants,
Mr John Lee, 76 The Bulwark, Castlecrag, N.S.W. 2068.

Japan
Japanese Pteridological Society,
C/o Prof. K. Iwatsuki, Department of Botany, Faculty of Science, Kyoto University, Kyoto, Japan.

Nippon Fernist Club,
C/o Institute of Forest Botany, Faculty of Agriculture, University of Tokyo, Yayoi-cho, Bunkyo-ku, Tokyo, Japan.

New Zealand
Nelson Fern Society, C/o Mrs. J. Bonnington, 9 Bay View Road, Atawhai, Nelson.

Philippine Islands
Fern Society of the Philippines,
National Museum,
P. Burgos Street, Manilla.

Switzerland
Schweizerische Vereiningung der Farnfreunde,
C/o Dr. J. J. Schneller, Obere Heslibachstrasse 16, CH 8700 Kusnacht.

United Kingdom
British Pteridological Society,
C/o Mr. A. R. Busby, 42 Lewisham Road, Smethwick, Warley, West Midlands. B66 2BS.

United States of America
American Fern Society,
C/o Mr. Michael I. Cousens, Faculty of Biology, University of West Florida, Pensacola, Florida 32504.

Birmingham Fern Society
C/o Mrs. R. E. Smith, 4736 7th Avenue South, Birmingham, Alabama 35222.

Corpus Christi Fern Society,
C/o P. Coleman, 438 Claremont Street, Corpus Christi, Texas 78412.

Delaware Valley Fern Society,
C/o Mrs. M. B. Peterson, 22 West Southampton Avenue, Philadelphia, Pennsylvania 19118.

Fern Study Group of the Northwest Horticultural Society,
C/o Mr. N. Hall, 1230 North East 88th Street, Seattle, Washington 98115.

International Tropical Fern Society,
C/o 8720 South West 34th Street, Miami, Florida 33165.

Los Angeles International Fern Society,
C/o 14895 Gardenhill Drive, La Mirada, California 90638.

Louisiana Fern Society,
Los Angeles International Fern Society,
P.O. Box 90943, Pasadena, CA 91109-0943

Memphis Fern Society,
C/o Ms. B. Feuerstein, 2357 Thornwood Lane, Memphis, Tennessee 38138.

Southwestern Fern Society,
C/o Mrs. M. Duncan, 3014 San Paula, Dallas, Texas 75228.

West Florida Fern Society,
C/o Dr. M. Cousens, Department of Biology, University of West Florida, Pensacola, Florida 32504.

Index

Figures marked in bold represent the major entry.

Index

Encyclopaedia

of Ferns